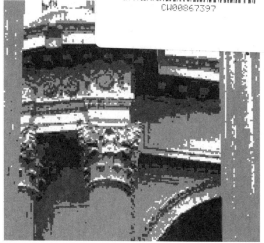

Windows 2000 Programming from the Ground Up

About the Author ...

Herbert Schildt is the world's leading programming author. He is an authority on the C and C++ languages, a master Windows programmer, and an expert on Java. His programming books have sold more than 2.5 million copies worldwide and have been translated into all major foreign languages. He is the author of numerous bestsellers, including *Windows 98 Programming from the Ground Up, MFC Programming from the Ground Up, C: The Complete Reference, C++: The Complete Reference*, and co-author of *Java 2: The Complete Reference*. Schildt is president of Universal Computing Laboratories, Inc., a software consulting firm in Mahomet, Illinois. He holds a master's degree in computer science from the University of Illinois. He can be reached at his consulting office at (217) 586-4683.

Windows 2000 Programming
from the Ground Up

Herbert Schildt

Osborne/**McGraw-Hill**

Berkeley New York St. Louis San Francisco
Auckland Bogotá Hamburg London Madrid
Mexico City Milan Montreal New Delhi
Panama City Paris São Paulo Singapore
Sydney Tokyo Toronto

Osborne/**McGraw-Hill**
2600 Tenth Street
Berkeley, California 94710
U.S.A.

For information on translations or book distributors outside the U.S.A., or to arrange bulk purchase discounts for sales promotions, premiums, or fund-raisers, please contact Osborne/**McGraw-Hill** at the above address.

Windows 2000 Programming from the Ground Up

1234567890 AGM AGM 019876543210

ISBN 0-07-212189-0

Publisher	**Copy Editor**
Brandon A. Nordin	Carl Wikander
Associate Publisher and Editor-in-Chief	**Proofreader**
Scott Rogers	Carroll Proffitt
Acquisitions Editor	**Indexer**
Wendy Rinaldi	Sheryl Schildt
Associate Acquisitions Editor	**Computer Designers**
Ann Sellers	Elizabeth Jang
	Jani Beckwith
Project Editor	**Illustrator**
Jody McKenzie	Beth Young
Acquisitions Coordinator	**Series Design**
Monika Faltiss	Peter Hancik
Technical Editor	**Cover Design**
Greg Guntle	John Nedwidek

This book was composed with Corel VENTURA™ Publisher.

Contents

Contents

vii

Preface

Windows 2000 is the operating system that Microsoft has designed to run computers well into the 21st century. It defines the standard for high-end, 32-bit computing and is a force to be regarded seriously. It is also one of the most challenging programming environments you are likely to encounter. Of course, the rewards of meeting this challenge are significant.

Windows 2000 is a finely tuned, carefully thought out piece of software. It is flexible yet powerful, and its ease of use masks sophisticated internals. Its stability and built-in security features make it the operating system favored by corporate users. Of course, many software developers use it for the same reasons.

This book teaches you how to write programs for Windows 2000. It starts with the basics, covers all of the essentials, and includes many advanced topics. If you have never written a Windows program before, then you will want to read this book in order, starting at Chapter 1. Resist the temptation to skip ahead, because each new chapter builds upon material presented earlier. If you have experience programming another version of Windows, such as Windows 95, then you will be able to advance more quickly. However, you should still skim through the introductory chapters because, in some areas, Windows 2000 differs significantly from other versions of Windows.

What Programming Background is Required

To use this book effectively, you must be an experienced C/C++ programmer. C and C++ are *the* languages of Windows 2000. If you feel that your C/C++ skills are a little weak, then take some time to fortify them. Programming for Windows 2000 relies heavily on such things as structures, unions, and pointers. If you are not comfortable with these items, you will have trouble learning to write Windows 2000 programs.

What Software is Needed

To compile the code in this book you will need a C++ compiler capable of producing programs for Windows 2000. The compiler used to test the code in this book is Microsoft's Visual C++ 6.

The examples in this book are written in standard C++ and you should use the .CPP file extension. However, for the most part, only the C-like features of C++ were used, so whether you are ultimately going to be writing your application in C or C++, the code in this book is compatible.

When compiling the programs in this book, use the default compiler settings suggested for compiling Windows-based code. Also, do not select any class library support, such as MFC. Specifically, when using Microsoft Visual C++, select Win32 Application when creating a new project.

Watch for the In Depth Boxes

Scattered throughout this book you will find special "In Depth" boxes. In Depth boxes delve deeper into specific programming topics. Often they explain options, enhancements, or alternative methods that can be applied to an example described in the book. They also serve as pointers to areas of programming that you will want to explore further on your own.

Source Code Free on the Web

The source code contained in this book is available free on-line at **www.osborne.com**.

For Further Study

Windows 2000 Programming From the Ground Up is just one of the many programming books written by Herbert Schildt. Here are some others that you will find of interest.

To learn more about Windows programming, we recommend the following:

Windows 98 Programming From the Ground Up

Windows NT 4 Programming From the Ground Up

Schildt's Windows 95 Programming in C and C++

Schildt's Advanced Windows 95 Programming in C and C++

The Windows Programming Annotated Archives

If you want to learn more about the C language, then the following titles will be of interest:

C: The Complete Reference

Teach Yourself C

To learn more about C++, you will find these books especially helpful:

C++: The Complete Reference

Teach Yourself C++

C++ From the Ground Up

Expert C++

The C/C++ Programming Annotated Archives

If you are interested in Java, then you will want to read

Java: The Complete Reference

co-authored by Herbert Schildt.

When you need solid answers, fast, turn to Herbert Schildt, the recognized authority on programming.

CHAPTER 1

Windows 2000 Overview

Windows 2000 is the latest version of Microsoft's high-end 32-bit operating system. This book teaches you how to write programs for it.

As a practical, "how-to" guide, this book does not spend much time on the theoretical aspects of Windows 2000 except as they relate directly to the creation of programs. Instead, it provides a hands-on approach that will have you writing Windows 2000 applications as soon as possible. That said, the first step in learning to program for Windows 2000 is understanding several of its key features.

Keep in mind that Windows 2000 is a very large and sophisticated operating system. It cannot be fully described in any single volume. This book describes those aspects of Windows 2000 that are common to all programs, that are used frequently, or that are important innovations. That is, it covers those things that all Windows 2000 programmers must know. It also gives you a firm foundation on which to launch your further study of this important operating environment.

What Is Windows 2000?

Windows 2000 is the next evolutionary step in Microsoft's professional 32-bit Windows platform, which was begun by Windows NT. Although built upon the NT technology, Windows 2000 represents a major rewrite and redesign effort. It is more powerful and more flexible than its predecessor. For example, it includes improved security, better network integration, and enhanced hardware support. In short, Windows 2000 is the OS designed to take Windows into the 21st century.

There are four flavors of Windows 2000:

◆   Windows 2000 Professional
◆   Windows 2000 Server
◆   Windows 2000 Advanced Server
◆   Windows 2000 Datacenter Server

The material in this book applies to all environments, since the general programming techniques for each is the same. Of course, most readers will be using Windows 2000 Professional to write and test their programs, because it is the end-user version of Windows 2000. Windows 2000 Professional is the direct upgrade from Windows NT 4 Workstation.

Windows 2000 is a full 32-bit operating system. This means that it does not use the 16-bit/32-bit hybrid code that is found in Windows 95, for example.

By providing a clean, 32-bit system, Windows 2000 does not have the quirks and problems that have plagued older systems.

1

In addition to code written explicitly for it, Windows 2000 is also able to run most Windows 95/98/NT programs. Further, Windows 2000 provides compatibility with older, 16-bit code, including DOS programs. Windows 2000 automatically creates the right environment for the type of program you run. For example, when you execute a DOS program, Windows 2000 automatically creates a 16-bit DOS virtual machine and windowed command prompt for running the program.

Windows 2000 provides a secure environment that meets the DoD C2 security classification. This level of security provides for password-protected log-ons, resource access control and ownership, and activity logs that provide an audit tail of certain activities. Also, memory is cleared before reuse. Further, memory used by one program is protected from memory used by another. It is not possible for one program to "corrupt" another or to interrogate the contents of the other program's variables.

The Application Programming Interface

The API defines the programming interface to Windows 2000.

From the programmer's point of view, Windows 2000 is defined by the way that a program interacts with it. All application programs communicate with Windows 2000 through a *call-based interface*. The Windows 2000 call-based interface is an extensive set of system-defined functions that provide access to operating system features. Collectively, these functions are termed the *Application Programming Interface*, or *API* for short. The API contains several hundred functions that your application program uses to perform all necessary operating system-related activities, such as allocating memory, outputting to the screen, creating windows, and the like. There is a subset to the API called the GDI (Graphics Device Interface) that is the part of Windows that provides device-independent graphics support.

Win16 is the 16-bit API used by Windows 3.1.

Win32 is the 32-bit API used by Windows 2000.

There are two basic flavors of the API in common use: Win16 and Win32. Win16 is the older, 16-bit version of the API. Win32 is the modern, 32-bit version. Win16 is used by Windows 3.1. Windows 2000 programs use Win32. In general, Win32 is a superset of Win16. Indeed, for the most part the functions are called by the same name and are used in the same way. However, even though similar in spirit and purpose, the two APIs differ in two fundamental ways. First, Win32 supports 32-bit, flat addressing, while Win16 supports only the 16-bit, segmented memory model. This difference means that Win32 often uses 32-bit arguments and return values in places where Win16 uses 16-bit values. Second, Win32 includes API functions that support thread-based multitasking, security, and the other enhanced features that are not available in Win16. If you are new to Windows programming in general, then these changes will not affect you significantly. However, if you will be porting 16-bit code to Windows 2000, then you will need to carefully examine the arguments you pass to each API function.

NOTE: The Win16 API is still available for use by Windows 3.1 applications running in a DOS environment. However, Windows 2000 programs must use the Win32 API.

Dynamic Link Libraries (DLLs)

The Windows 2000 API is implemented in DLLs.

The Win32 API functions are contained in *Dynamic Link Libraries*, or *DLLs* for short, which each program has access to when it is executed. The API functions are stored in a relocatable format within a DLL. During the compilation phase, when your program calls an API function, the linker does not add the code for that function to the executable version of your program. Instead, it adds loading instructions for that function, such as what DLL it resides in and its name. When your program is executed, the necessary API routines are also loaded by the Windows 2000 loader. In this way, each application program does not need to contain the actual API code while stored on disk. The code is added only when the program is loaded into memory for execution.

Dynamic linking has some very important benefits. First, since virtually all programs will use the API functions, DLLs prevent disk space from being wasted by the significant amount of duplicated object code that would be created if the API functions were actually added to each program's executable file on disk. Second, updates and enhancements to Windows 2000 can be accomplished by changing the dynamic link library routines. Existing application programs do not need to be recompiled. Third, using the dynamic link approach makes the emulation of other operating systems an easier task.

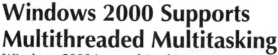

Windows 2000 Supports Multithreaded Multitasking

Windows 2000 is a multitasking operating system. As such, it can run two or more programs concurrently. Of course, on systems with only one processor, the programs share the CPU and do not, technically, run simultaneously. However, Windows 2000 can be run on computers than have two or more CPUs. When this is the case, programs may, indeed, actually execute simultaneously. Since you can't always know what type of computer your program will be executed on, it is best to assume that true, concurrent execution is always occurring.

A process is essentially a program that is executing.

Windows 2000 supports two forms of multitasking: process based and thread based. A *process* is a program that is executing. Because Windows 2000 can multitask processes, it can run more than one program at a time. Thus, Windows 2000 supports the traditional process-based multitasking with which you are probably familiar.

A thread is an individual unit of executable code within a process.

Windows 2000's second form of multitasking is thread based. A *thread* is a dispatchable unit of executable code. The name comes from the concept of a "thread of execution." All processes have at least one thread. However, a Windows 2000 process may have several.

Since Windows 2000 multitasks threads and since each process can have more than one thread, it is possible for one process to have two or more pieces of itself executing simultaneously. Therefore, when working with Windows 2000, it is possible to multitask both programs and pieces of a single program. You can take advantage of this to write very efficient programs.

Multiple File Systems

One other thing to know about Windows 2000 is that it supports several file systems, including the following:

◆ FAT (File Allocation Table)

◆ FAT32 (enhanced, 32-bit version of FAT)

◆ NTFS (NT File System)

FAT stands for File Allocation Table

NTFS stands for the NT File System.

The FAT file system is the approach initially designed for DOS. It has been around a long time and continues to be widely used. However, the FAT system is inherently limited because of its need to maintain compatibility with DOS. Some of the limitations of FAT are alleviated by FAT32, which can support larger drives. The NTFS was designed specifically for Windows NT and has been improved for 2000. There are many advantages to using NTFS, including its security features. For the purposes of this book, it doesn't matter what file system your computer uses.

Challenging but Rewarding

Now that the stage has been set, we are ready to begin writing programs. If you have never written any type of Windows program before, then the next few chapters will contain many unfamiliar concepts and require the use of several new programming techniques. Just be patient. Although a bit overwhelming at first, before long, writing programs for Windows 2000 will be second nature. Windows 2000 is a challenging environment, but it is also a rewarding one. Once mastered, you will possess some of the most highly demanded skills in the programming profession.

CHAPTER 2

Windows 2000 Programming Fundamentals

This chapter introduces Windows 2000 programming. It has two purposes. First, it discusses how a program must interact with Windows 2000 and what rules must be followed by every Windows 2000 application. Second, it develops an application skeleton that will be used as a basis for the other Windows 2000 programs developed in this book. As you will see, all Windows 2000 programs share several traits. It is these shared attributes that will be contained in the application skeleton.

We will begin by explaining the two ways that you can write Windows 2000 programs.

Two Ways to Program for Windows

There are two ways you can write programs for Windows 2000. The first is to use the API functions defined by Win32. In this approach, your programs directly utilize the API and explicitly handle all of the details associated with a Windows 2000 program. This is the method used in this book.

The second way to program for Windows 2000 uses a C++ class library, which encapsulates the API. By far the most popular Windows programming class library is MFC (Microsoft Foundation Classes). MFC, and other Windows class libraries, are powerful development tools that offer significant advantages in many situations. But they are best employed after you have gained a firm foundation in Windows programming using the API. The reasons for this are easy to understand.

First, there is a fundamental architecture that all Windows programs share. MFC masks many elements of this architecture. Knowledge of the Windows architecture is crucial to long-term programming success. For example, it makes debugging a Windows application easier. Second, using the API gives you detailed and complete control over how your program executes. Third, all Windows 2000 programming environments support API-based programming. It is a portable skill. Finally, if you can program for Windows 2000 using the API, you can more easily learn to use MFC or any other class library. Simply put: You cannot be a top-notch, professional Windows programmer unless you know how to program using the API.

NOTE: If you are interested in MFC programming, I suggest my book *MFC Programming From the Ground Up* (Osborne/McGraw-Hill, Berkeley, CA, 1998). It contains a detailed description of MFC programming.

Windows 2000 Programming Perspective

At its most fundamental level, the goal of Windows 2000 (and Windows in general) is to enable a person who has basic familiarity with the system to sit down and run virtually any application without prior training. Towards this end, Windows provides a consistent interface to the user. In theory, if you can run one Windows-based program, you can run them all. Of course, in actuality, most useful programs will still require some sort of training in order to be used effectively, but at least this instruction can be restricted to *what* the program *does*, not *how* the user must *interact* with it. In fact, much of the code in a Windows application is there just to support the user interface.

It is important to understand that not every program that runs under Windows 2000 will automatically present the user with a Windows-style interface. Windows defines an environment that encourages consistency, but does not enforce it. For example, it is possible to write Windows programs that do not take advantage of the standard Windows interface elements. To create a Windows-style program, you must purposely do so using the techniques described in this book. Only those programs written to take advantage of Windows will look and feel like Windows programs. While you can override the basic Windows design philosophy, you should have a good reason to do so, because your program will be violating the most fundamental goal of Windows: a consistent user interface. In general, if you are writing application programs for Windows 2000, they should conform to the standard Windows style guidelines and design practices.

Let's look at some the essential elements that define the Windows 2000 application environment.

The Desktop Model

With few exceptions, the point of a window-based user interface is to provide the equivalent of a desktop on the screen. On a desk there may be several different pieces of paper, one on top of another, often with fragments of different pages visible beneath the top page. The equivalent of the desktop in Windows 2000 is the screen. The equivalents of pieces of paper are the windows on the screen. On a desk you may move pieces of paper about, maybe switching which piece of paper is on top or changing how much of another is exposed to view. Windows 2000 allows the same type of operations on its windows. By selecting a window you can make it current, which means putting it on top of all other windows. You can enlarge or shrink a window, or move it about on the screen. In short, Windows lets you control the surface of the screen the way you control the surface of your desk. All conforming programs must allow these types of user interactions.

The Mouse

As in all preceding versions of Windows, Windows 2000 uses the mouse for almost all control, selection, and drawing operations. Of course, the keyboard may also be used, but Windows is optimized for the mouse. Thus, your programs must support the mouse as an input device wherever possible. Fortunately, most of the common tasks, such as those involving menu selection, scroll bars, and the like, automatically utilize the mouse.

Icons, Bitmaps, and Graphics

Icons and bitmaps are graphical images.

Windows 2000 encourages the use of icons, bitmaps, and other types of graphics. The rationale behind the use of these items is found in the old adage, "A picture is worth a thousand words." An *icon* is a small symbol that is used to represent some operation, resource, or program. A *bitmap* is a rectangular graphics image often used to simply convey information quickly to the user. However, bitmaps can also be used as menu elements. Windows 2000 supports a full range of graphics capabilities, including the ability to draw lines, rectangles, and circles. The proper use of these graphical elements is an important part of successful Windows programming.

Menus, Controls, and Dialog Boxes

A menu is a list from which the user may select an option.

Windows provides several standard items that allow user input. These include the menu, various types of controls, and the dialog box. Briefly, a *menu* displays options from which the user makes a selection. Since menus are standard elements in Windows programming, built-in menu-selection functions are provided in the API. Therefore, your program does not need to handle all of the clerical overhead associated with menus.

A control allows a specific type of user interaction.

A *control* is a special type of window that allows a specific type of user interaction. Examples are pushbuttons, scroll bars, edit windows, and check boxes. As with menus, the controls defined by Windows are nearly completely automated. Your program can use one without having to handle the details.

A dialog box is used when non-menu input is required.

A *dialog box* is a special window that enables more complex interaction with the application than that allowed by a menu. For example, your application might use a dialog box to input a filename. Dialog boxes are typically used to house controls. With few exceptions, non-menu input is accomplished via a dialog box.

The Components of a Window

Before moving on to specific aspects of Windows 2000 programming, a few important terms need to be defined. Figure 2-1 shows a standard window with each of its elements pointed out.

All windows have a border that defines the limits of the window and is used to resize the window. At the top of the window are several items. On the far left is the system menu icon (also called the title bar icon). Clicking on this box causes the system menu to be displayed. To the right of the system menu box is the window's title. At the far right are the minimize, maximize, and close boxes. The client area is the part of the window in which your program activity takes place. Most windows also have horizontal and vertical scroll bars that are used to move text through the window.

2

How Windows and Your Program Interact

In the traditional operating system/program structure, it is your program that initiates interaction with the operating system. For example, in a DOS

The elements
of a standard
window

Figure 2-1.

program, it is the program that requests such things as input and output. Put differently, programs written in the "traditional way" call the operating system. The operating system does not call your program. However, in a large measure, Windows works in the opposite way. It is Windows that calls your program. The process works like this: a program waits until it is sent a *message* by Windows. The message is passed to your program through a special function that is called by Windows. Once a message is received, your program is expected to take an appropriate action. While your program may call one or more API functions when responding to a message, it is still Windows that initiates the activity. More than anything else, it is the message-based interaction with Windows, including Windows 2000, that dictates the general form of all Windows programs.

Windows communicates with your program by sending it messages.

There are many different types of messages that Windows 2000 may send your program. For example, each time the mouse is clicked on a window belonging to your program, a mouse-clicked message will be sent to your program. Another type of message is sent each time a window belonging to your program must be redrawn. Still another message is sent each time the user presses a key when your program is the focus of input. Keep one fact firmly in mind: as far as your program is concerned, messages arrive randomly. This is why Windows programs resemble interrupt-driven programs. You can't know what message will be next.

Some Windows 2000 Application Basics

Before developing the Windows 2000 application skeleton, some basic concepts common to all Windows 2000 programs need to be discussed.

WinMain( )

All Windows 2000 programs begin execution with a call to **WinMain( )**. (Windows programs do not have a **main( )** function.) **WinMain( )** has some special properties that differentiate it from other functions in your application. First, it must be compiled using the **WINAPI** calling convention. By default, functions in your C/C++ programs use the C calling convention, but it is possible to compile a function so that it uses a different calling convention. For example, a common alternative is to use the **PASCAL** calling convention. For various technical reasons, the calling convention Windows 2000 uses to call **WinMain( )** is WINAPI. The return type of **WinMain( )** must be **int**.

WinMain( ) is where a Windows program begins execution.

HISTORICAL PERSPECTIVE: For older 16-bit Windows programs, the calling convention used for **WinMain( )** was **PASCAL**. However, this should be changed to **WINAPI** when porting existing applications to Windows 2000.

The Window Procedure

A window procedure is a function called by Windows, not by your program.

All Windows programs must contain a special function that is *not* called by your program, but is called by Windows. This function is generally called the *window procedure* or *window function*. It is through this function that Windows 2000 communicates with your program. The window function is called by Windows 2000 when it needs to pass a message to your program. The window function receives the message in its parameters. All window functions must be declared as returning type **LRESULT CALLBACK**. The type **LRESULT** is a 32-bit integer. The **CALLBACK** calling convention is used with those functions that will be called by Windows. In Windows terminology, any function that is called by Windows is referred to as a *callback* function.

HISTORICAL PERSPECTIVE: Older 16-bit Windows code specifies a window function as **LONG FAR PASCAL**. You should change this to **LRESULT CALLBACK** when porting to Windows 2000.

In addition to receiving the messages sent by Windows 2000, the window function must initiate any actions indicated by a message. Typically, a window function's body consists of a **switch** statement that links a specific response to each message that the program will respond to. Your program need not respond to every message that it is sent. For messages that your program doesn't care about, you can let Windows 2000 provide default processing. Since there are hundreds of different messages that Windows can generate, it is common for most messages to simply be processed by Windows and not by your program.

All messages are 32-bit integer values. Further, all messages are accompanied by any additional information that the message requires.

Window Classes

A window class defines the style of a window.

When your Windows 2000 program first begins execution, it will need to define and register a *window class*. (Here, the word *class* is not being used in its C++ sense. Rather, it means *style* or *type*.) When you register a window class, you are telling Windows about the form and function of the window. However, registering the window class does not cause a window to come into existence. To actually create a window requires additional steps.

The Message Loop

The message loop retrieves messages from your application's message queue.

As explained earlier, Windows 2000 communicates with your program by sending it messages. All Windows applications must establish a *message loop* inside the **WinMain( )** function. This loop reads any pending message from the application's message queue and then dispatches that message back to Windows, which then calls your program's window function with that message as a parameter. This may seem to be an overly complex way of passing messages, but it is, nevertheless, the way that all Windows programs must function. (Part of the reason for this method is to return control to Windows so that the scheduler can allocate CPU time as it sees fit rather than waiting for your application's time slice to end.)

Windows Data Types

As you will soon see, the Windows API functions do not make extensive use of standard C/C++ data types, such as **int** or **char ***. Instead, many data types used by Windows have been **typdef**ed within the WINDOWS.H file and/or its related files. This file is supplied by Microsoft (and any other company that makes a Windows C++ compiler) and must be included in all Windows programs. Some of the most common types are **HANDLE, HWND, UINT, BYTE, WORD, DWORD, LONG, BOOL**, **LPSTR**, and **LPCSTR**. **HANDLE** is a 32-bit integer that is used as a handle. There are a number of handle types, but they all are the same size as **HANDLE**. A *handle* is simply a value that identifies some resource. For example, **HWND** is a 32-bit integer that is used as a window handle. Also, all handle types begin with an *H*. **BYTE** is an 8-bit unsigned character. **WORD** is a 16-bit unsigned short integer. **DWORD** is an unsigned 32-bit integer. **UINT** is an unsigned 32-bit integer. **LONG** is a signed 32-bit integer. **BOOL** is an integer and is used to indicate values that are either true or false, but it differs from the standard C++ **bool** type in that **BOOL** can store any integer value. **LPSTR** is a pointer to a string, and **LPCSTR** is a **const** pointer to a string.

2

In addition to the basic types described above, Windows 2000 defines several structures. The two that are needed by the skeleton program are **MSG** and **WNDCLASSEX.** The **MSG** structure holds a Windows 2000 message and **WNDCLASSEX** is a structure that defines a window class. These structures will be discussed later in this chapter.

HISTORICAL PERSPECTIVE: **UINT** is a 32-bit unsigned integer when compiling Windows 2000 programs. It is a 16-bit unsigned integer if you compile your code for 16-bit Windows. This change can affect older applications ported to Windows 2000.

A Windows 2000 Skeleton

Now that the necessary background information has been covered, it is time to develop a minimal Windows 2000 application. As stated, all Windows 2000 programs have certain things in common. In this section a Windows 2000 skeleton is developed that provides these necessary features. In the world of Windows programming, application skeletons are commonly used because there is a substantial "price of admission" when creating a Windows program. Unlike DOS programs, for example, in which a minimal program is about 5 lines long, a minimal Windows program is approximately 50 lines long. Therefore, application skeletons are commonly used when developing for Windows.

A minimal Windows 2000 program contains two functions: **WinMain( )** and the window function. The **WinMain( )** function must perform the following general steps:

1. Define a window class
2. Register that class with Windows 2000
3. Create a window of that class
4. Display the window
5. Begin running the message loop

The window function must respond to all relevant messages. Since the skeleton program does nothing but display its window, the only message that it must respond to is the one that tells the application that the user has terminated the program.

Before considering the specifics, examine the following program, which is a minimal Windows 2000 skeleton. It creates a standard window that includes a title, a system menu, and the standard minimize, maximize, and close boxes. The window is, therefore, capable of being minimized, maximized, moved, resized, and closed.

```
// A minimal Windows 2000 skeleton.

#include <windows.h>

LRESULT CALLBACK WindowFunc(HWND, UINT, WPARAM, LPARAM);

char szWinName[] = "MyWin"; // name of window class

int WINAPI WinMain(HINSTANCE hThisInst, HINSTANCE hPrevInst,
                   LPSTR lpszArgs, int nWinMode)
{
  HWND hwnd;
  MSG msg;
  WNDCLASSEX wcl;

  // Define a window class.
  wcl.cbSize = sizeof(WNDCLASSEX);

  wcl.hInstance = hThisInst;       // handle to this instance
  wcl.lpszClassName = szWinName;   // window class name
  wcl.lpfnWndProc = WindowFunc;    // window function
  wcl.style = 0;                   // default style

  wcl.hIcon = LoadIcon(NULL, IDI_APPLICATION); // large icon
  wcl.hIconSm = NULL; // use small version of large icon
  wcl.hCursor = LoadCursor(NULL, IDC_ARROW);   // cursor style

  wcl.lpszMenuName = NULL; // no class menu
  wcl.cbClsExtra = 0;       // no extra memory needed
  wcl.cbWndExtra = 0;

  // Make the window background white.
  wcl.hbrBackground = (HBRUSH) GetStockObject(WHITE_BRUSH);

  // Register the window class.
  if(!RegisterClassEx(&wcl)) return 0;

  /* Now that a window class has been registered, a window
     can be created. */
```

```
   hwnd = CreateWindow(
     szWinName, // name of window class
     "Windows 2000 Skeleton", // title
     WS_OVERLAPPEDWINDOW, // window style - normal
     CW_USEDEFAULT, // X coordinate - let Windows decide
     CW_USEDEFAULT, // Y coordinate - let Windows decide
     CW_USEDEFAULT, // width - let Windows decide
     CW_USEDEFAULT, // height - let Windows decide
     NULL,          // no parent window
     NULL,          // no menu
     hThisInst,     // instance handle
     NULL           // no additional arguments
   );

   // Display the window.
   ShowWindow(hwnd, nWinMode);
   UpdateWindow(hwnd);

   // Create the message loop.
   while(GetMessage(&msg, NULL, 0, 0))
   {
     TranslateMessage(&msg); // translate keyboard messages
     DispatchMessage(&msg);  // return control to Windows 2000
   }
   return msg.wParam;
}

/* This function is called by Windows 2000 and is passed
   messages from the message queue.
*/
LRESULT CALLBACK WindowFunc(HWND hwnd, UINT message,
                            WPARAM wParam, LPARAM lParam)
{
  switch(message) {
    case WM_DESTROY: // terminate the program
      PostQuitMessage(0);
      break;
    default:
      /* Let Windows 2000 process any messages not specified in
         the preceding switch statement. */
      return DefWindowProc(hwnd, message, wParam, lParam);
  }
  return 0;
}
```

Let's go through this program step by step.

First, all Windows 2000 programs must include the header file WINDOWS.H. As stated, this file (along with its support files) contains the API function prototypes and various types, macros, and definitions used by Windows 2000. For example, the data types **HWND** and **WNDCLASSEX** are defined in WINDOWS.H (or its subordinate files).

The window function used by the program is called **WindowFunc( )**. It is declared as a callback function because this is the function that Windows 2000 calls to communicate with the program.

As stated, program execution begins with **WinMain( )**. **WinMain( )** is passed four parameters. **hThisInst** and **hPrevInst** are handles. **hThisInst** refers to the current instance of the program. Remember, Windows 2000 is a multitasking system, so it is possible that more than one instance of your program may be running at the same time. For Windows 2000, **hPrevInst** will always be **NULL**. The **lpszArgs** parameter is a pointer to a string that holds any command line arguments specified when the application was begun. In Windows 2000, the string contains the entire command line, including the name of the program. The **nWinMode** parameter contains a value that determines how the window will be displayed when your program begins execution.

Inside the function, three variables are created. The **hwnd** variable will hold the handle to the program's window. The **msg** structure variable will hold window messages, and the **wcl** structure variable will be used to define the window class.

 HISTORICAL PERSPECTIVE: As mentioned, the **hPrevInst** parameter will always be **NULL** in a Windows 2000 program. In a 16-bit Windows program, **hPrevInst** would be nonzero if there were other instances of the program currently executing. This reflects a fundamental difference between 16-bit Windows and Windows 2000. In the 16-bit environment, multiple instances of a program share window classes and various other bits of data. Therefore, it was important for an application to know if another version of itself was running in the system. However, in Windows 2000 each process is isolated from the next and there is no automatic sharing of window classes and the like. The only reason that the **hPrevInst** exists in Windows 2000 is for the sake of compatibility.

Defining the Window Class

The first two actions that **WinMain( )** takes is to define a window class and then register it. A window class is defined by filling in the fields defined by the **WNDCLASSEX** structure. Its fields are shown here:

2

```
UINT cbSize;              // size of the WNDCLASSEX structure
UINT style;               // type of window
WNDPROC lpfnWndProc;      // address to window func
int cbClsExtra;           // extra class memory
int cbWndExtra;           // extra window memory
HINSTANCE hInstance;      // handle of this instance
HICON hIcon;              // handle of large icon
HICON hIconSm;            // handle of small icon
HCURSOR hCursor;          // handle of mouse cursor
HBRUSH hbrBackground;     // background color
LPCSTR lpszMenuName;      // name of main menu
LPCSTR lpszClassName;     // name of window class
```

As you can see by looking at the program, **cbSize** is assigned the size of the **WNDCLASSEX** structure. The **hInstance** member is assigned the current instance handle as specified by **hThisInst**. The name of the window class is pointed to by **lpszClassName**, which is the string "MyWin," in this case. The address of the window function is assigned to **lpfnWndProc**. In the program, no default style is specified, no extra information is needed, and no main menu is specified. While most programs will contain a main menu, none is required by the skeleton.

All Windows applications need to define a default shape for the mouse cursor and for the application's icons. An application can define its own custom version of these resources or it may use one of the built-in styles, as the skeleton does. In either case, handles to these resources must be assigned to the appropriate members of the **WNDCLASSEX** structure. To see how this is done, let's begin with icons.

A Windows 2000 application has two icons associated with it: one large and one small. The small icon is used when the application is minimized, and it is also the icon that is used for the system menu. The large icon is displayed when you move or copy an application to the desktop. Typically, large icons are 32-by-32 bitmaps and small icons are 16-by-16 bitmaps. The large icon is loaded by the API function **LoadIcon( )**, whose prototype is shown here:

HICON LoadIcon(HINSTANCE *hInst*, LPCSTR *lpszName*);

This function returns a handle to an icon, or **NULL** on failure. Here, *hInst* specifies the handle of the module that contains the icon, and its name is specified in *lpszName*. However, to use one of the built-in icons, you must use **NULL** for the first parameter and specify one of the following macros for the second.

Icon Macro	Shape
IDI_APPLICATION	Default icon
IDI_ERROR	Error symbol
IDI_INFORMATION	Information
IDI_QUESTION	Question mark
IDI_WARNING	Exclamation point
IDI_WINLOGO	Windows logo

Here are two important points about loading icons. First, if your application does not specify a small icon, the large icon's resource file is examined. If it contains a small icon, then that icon is used. Otherwise, the large icon is simply shrunk when the small icon is needed. If you don't want to specify a small icon, assign **hIconSm** the value **NULL**, as the skeleton does. Second, in general, **LoadIcon( )** can only be used to load the large icon. You can use **LoadImage( )** to load icons of differing sizes. For most of the examples in this book, we will simply be using the built-in icons, and Windows 2000 will provide the large and small icons for us.

To load the mouse cursor, use the API **LoadCursor( )** function. This function has the following prototype:

    HCURSOR LoadCursor(HINSTANCE *hInst*, LPCSTR *lpszName*);

This function returns a handle to a cursor resource, or **NULL** on failure. Here, *hInst* specifies the handle of the module that contains the mouse cursor, and its name is specified in *lpszName*. However, to use one of the built-in cursors, you must use **NULL** for the first parameter and specify one of the built-in cursors using its macro for the second parameter. Here are a few of the built-in cursors.

Cursor Macro	Shape
IDC_ARROW	Default arrow pointer
IDC_CROSS	Cross hairs
IDC_HAND	Hand (New for Windows 2000)
IDC_IBEAM	Vertical I-beam
IDC_WAIT	Hourglass

The background color of the window created by the skeleton is specified as white, and a handle to this brush is obtained using the API function **GetStockObject( ).** A *brush* is a resource that paints the screen using a predetermined size, color, and pattern. The function **GetStockObject( )** is used to obtain a handle to a number of standard display objects, including brushes, pens (which draw lines), and character fonts. It has this prototype:

HGDIOBJ GetStockObject(int *object*);

The function returns a handle to the object specified by *object*. **NULL** is returned on failure. (The type **HGDIOBJ** is a GDI handle.) Here are some of the built-in brushes available to your program.

Macro Name	Background Type
BLACK_BRUSH	Black
DKGRAY_BRUSH	Dark gray
HOLLOW_BRUSH	See-through window
LTGRAY_BRUSH	Light gray
WHITE_BRUSH	White

You may use these macros as parameters to **GetStockObject( )** to obtain a brush.

Once the window class has been fully specified, it is registered with Windows 2000 using the API function **RegisterClassEx( )**, whose prototype is shown here:

```
ATOM RegisterClassEx(CONST WNDCLASSEX *lpWClass);
```

The function returns a value that identifies the window class. **ATOM** is a **typedef** that means **WORD**. Each window class is given a unique value. *lpWClass* must be the address of a **WNDCLASSEX** structure.

Creating a Window

Once a window class has been defined and registered, your application can actually create a window of that class using the API function **CreateWindow( )**, whose prototype is shown here:

```
HWND CreateWindow(
                LPCSTR lpClassName,   // name of window class
                LPCSTR lpWinName,     // title of window
                DWORD dwStyle,        // type of window
                int X, int Y,         // upper-left coordinates
                int Width, int Height, // dimensions of window
                HWND hParent,         // handle of parent window
                HMENU hMenu,          // handle of main menu
                HINSTANCE hThisInst,  // handle of creator
                LPVOID lpszAdditional // pointer to additional info
);
```

As you can see by looking at the skeleton program, many of the parameters to **CreateWindow( )** may be defaulted or specified as **NULL**. In fact, most often the *X, Y, Width*, and *Height* parameters will simply use the macro **CW_USEDEFAULT**, which tells Windows 2000 to select an appropriate size and location for the window. If the window has no parent, which is the case in the skeleton, then *hParent* can be specified as **NULL**. (You can also use **HWND_DESKTOP** for this parameter.) If the window does not contain a main menu or uses the main menu defined by the window class, then *hMenu* must be **NULL**. (The *hMenu* parameter has other uses, too.) Also, if no additional information is required, as is most often the case, then *lpszAdditional* is **NULL.** (The type **LPVOID** is **typedef**ed as **void ***. Historically, **LPVOID** stands for long pointer to **void**.)

The remaining four parameters must be explicitly set by your program. First, *lpszClassName* must point to the name of the window class. (This is the name you gave it when it was registered.) The title of the window is a string pointed to by *lpszWinName*. This can be a null string, but usually a window will be given a title. The style (or type) of window actually created is determined by the value of *dwStyle*. The macro **WS_OVERLAPPEDWINDOW** specifies a standard window that has a system menu, a border, and minimize, maximize, and close boxes. While this style of window is the most common, you can construct one to your own specifications. To accomplish this, simply OR together the various style macros that you want. Some other common styles are shown here:

Style Macros	Window Feature
WS_OVERLAPPED	Overlapped window with border
WS_MAXIMIZEBOX	Maximize box
WS_MINIMIZEBOX	Minimize box
WS_SYSMENU	System menu
WS_HSCROLL	Horizontal scroll bar
WS_VSCROLL	Vertical scroll bar

The *hThisInst* parameter is ignored by Windows 2000, but for Windows 95/98 it must contain the current instance handle of the application. Thus, to ensure portability to those environments—and to prevent future problems—*hThisInst* should be assigned the current instance handle, as the skeleton does. All of the programs in this book will follow this approach.

The **CreateWindow( )** function returns the handle of the window it creates, or **NULL** if the window cannot be created.

Once the window has been created, it is still not displayed on the screen. To cause the window to be displayed, call the **ShowWindow( )** API function. This function has the following prototype:

    BOOL ShowWindow(HWND *hwnd*, int *nHow*);

The handle of the window to display is specified in *hwnd*. The display mode is specified in *nHow*. The first time the window is displayed, you will want to pass **nWinMode** (in **WinMain**) as the *nHow* parameter. Remember, the value of **nWinMode** determines how the window will be displayed when the program begins execution. Subsequent calls can display (or remove) the window as necessary. Some common values for *nHow* are shown here:

Display Macros	Effect
SW_HIDE	Removes the window.
SW_MINIMIZE	Minimizes the window into an icon.
SW_MAXIMIZE	Maximizes the window.
SW_RESTORE	Returns a window to normal size.

The **ShowWindow( )** function returns the previous display status of the window. If the window had been displayed, then nonzero is returned. If the window had not been displayed, zero is returned.

Although not technically necessary for the skeleton, a call to **UpdateWindow( )** is included because it is needed by virtually every Windows 2000 application that you will create. It essentially tells Windows 2000 to send a message to your application that the main window needs to be updated. (This message will be discussed in the next chapter.)

The Message Loop

The final part of the skeletal **WinMain( )** is the *message loop*. The message loop is a part of all Windows applications. Its purpose is to receive and process messages sent by Windows 2000. When an application is running, it is continually being sent messages. These messages are stored in the application's message queue until they can be read and processed. Each time your application is ready to read another message, it must call the API function **GetMessage( )**, which has this prototype:

BOOL GetMessage(LPMSG *msg*, HWND *hwnd*, UINT *min*, UINT *max*);

The message will be received by the structure pointed to by *msg.* All Window messages are of structure type **MSG**, shown here:

```
// Message structure
typedef struct tagMSG
{
  HWND hwnd;      // window that message is for
  UINT message;   // message
  WPARAM wParam;  // message-dependent info
  LPARAM lParam;  // more message-dependent info
  DWORD time;     // time message posted
```

```
   POINT pt;        // X,Y location of mouse
} MSG;
```

In **MSG**, the handle of the window for which the message is intended is contained in **hwnd**. All Windows 2000 messages are 32-bit integers, and the message is contained in **message**. Additional information relating to each message is passed in **wParam** and **lParam.** The types **WPARAM** and **LPARAM** are both 32-bit quantities.

2

HISTORICAL PERSPECTIVE: The **message** field of **MSG** is 16 bits long in 16-bit Windows. It is 32 bits in Windows 2000. Also, the **wparam** field, which is 16 bits in 16-bit Windows, is 32 bits in Windows 2000.

The time the message was sent (posted) is specified in milliseconds in the **time** field.

The **pt** member will contain the coordinates of the mouse when the message was sent. The coordinates are held in a **POINT** structure, which is defined here:

```
typedef struct tagPOINT {
  LONG x, y;
} POINT;
```

If there are no messages in the application's message queue, then a call to **GetMessage( )** will pass control back to Windows 2000.

The *hwnd* parameter to **GetMessage( )** specifies for which window messages will be obtained. It is possible (even likely) that an application will contain several windows and that you only want to receive messages for a specific window. If you want to receive all messages directed at your application, this parameter must be **NULL**.

The remaining two parameters to **GetMessage( )** specify a range of messages that will be received. Generally, you want your application to receive all messages. To accomplish this, specify both *min* and *max* as 0, as the skeleton does.

GetMessage( ) returns zero when the user terminates the program, causing the message loop to terminate. Otherwise it returns nonzero. It will return −1 if an error occurs. Errors can only occur under unusual circumstances that do not apply to the programs in this book.

Inside the message loop two functions are called. The first is the API function **TranslateMessage( )**. This function translates virtual key codes generated by Windows 2000 into character messages. (Virtual keys are discussed later in this book.) Although it is not necessary for all applications, most call **TranslateMessage( )** because it is needed to allow full integration of the keyboard into your application program.

Once the message has been read and translated, it is dispatched back to Windows 2000 using the **DispatchMessage( )** API function. Windows 2000 then holds this message until it can pass it to the program's window function.

Once the message loop terminates, the **WinMain( )** function ends by returning the value of **msg.wParam** to Windows 2000. This value contains the return code generated when your program terminates.

The Window Function

The second function in the application skeleton is its window function. In this case the function is called **WindowFunc( )**, but it could have any name you like. The window function is passed messages by Windows 2000. The first four members of the **MSG** structure are its parameters. For the skeleton, the only parameter that is used is the message itself. In the next chapter you will learn more about the parameters to this function.

The skeleton's window function responds to only one message explicitly: **WM_DESTROY**. This message is sent when the user terminates the program. When this message is received, your program must execute a call to the API function **PostQuitMessage( )**. The argument to this function is an exit code that is returned in **msg.wParam** inside **WinMain( ).** Calling **PostQuitMessage( )** causes a **WM_QUIT** message to be sent to your application, which causes **GetMessage( )** to return false, thus stopping your program.

Any other messages received by **WindowFunc( )** are passed along to Windows 2000, via a call to **DefWindowProc( )**, for default processing. This step is necessary because all messages must be dealt with in one fashion or another.

Each message specifies the value that must be returned by the window function after the message has been processed. Most of the commonly handled messages require that you return zero. But a few require a different return value.

2

Positioning a Window

Although it is common for an application to allow Windows 2000 to choose a position and size for its window when the program begins execution, it is possible to explicitly specify these attributes. To do so, simply pass the coordinates of the window's upper-left corner and its width and height to **CreateWindow( ).** For example, if you substitute the following call to **CreateWindow( )** into the skeleton, the window will be displayed in the upper-left corner of the screen and will be 300 units wide and 100 units tall.

```
hwnd = CreateWindow(
  szWinName,                // name of window class
  "Windows 2000 Skeleton", // title
  WS_OVERLAPPEDWINDOW,      // window style - normal
  0,     // X coordinate
  0,     // Y coordinate
  300,   // width
  100,   // height
  NULL, // no parent window
  NULL, // no menu
  hThisInst, // handle of this instance of the program
  NULL       // no additional arguments
);
```

When determining the location and dimensions of a window, keep in mind that these are specified in *device units,* which are the physical units used by the device (in this case, pixels). This means that the coordinates and dimensions are relative to the screen. The coordinates of the upper-left corner are 0,0. As you will see later in this book, output to a window is generally specified in terms of *logical units*, which are mapped to a window according to the current mapping mode. However, since the position of a window is relative to the entire screen, it makes sense that **CreateWindow( )** would require physical units rather than logical ones.

Definition File No Longer Needed

If you are familiar with 16-bit Windows programming, then you have used *definition files*. For 16-bit versions of Windows, all programs need to have a definition file associated with them. A definition file is simply a text file that specifies certain information and settings needed by the 16-bit environment. Because of the 32-bit architecture of Windows 2000 (and other improvements), definition files are not usually needed for Windows 2000 programs. If you are new to Windows programming and don't know what a definition file is, the following discussion will give you a brief overview.

Definition files are not usually needed by Windows 2000 programs.

All definition files use the extension .DEF. For example, the definition file for the skeleton program could be called SKEL.DEF. Here is a definition file that you can use to provide downward compatibility to Windows 3.1.

```
DESCRIPTION 'Skeleton Program'
EXETYPE WINDOWS
CODE PRELOAD MOVEABLE DISCARDABLE
DATA PRELOAD MOVEABLE MULTIPLE
HEAPSIZE 8192
STACKSIZE 8192
EXPORTS WindowFunc
```

This file specifies the name of the program and its description, both of which are optional. It also states that the executable file will be compatible with Windows (rather than DOS, for example). The **CODE** statement tells Windows 2000 to load all of the program at startup (PRELOAD), that the code may be moved in memory (MOVEABLE), and that the code may be removed from memory and reloaded if (and when) necessary (DISCARDABLE). The file also states that your program's data must be loaded upon execution and may be moved about in memory. It also specifies that each instance of the program has its own data (MULTIPLE). Next, the size of the heap and stack allocated to the program are specified. Finally, the name of the window function is exported. Exporting allows Windows 3.1 to call the function.

REMEMBER: Definition files are seldom used when programming for Windows 2000.

Naming Conventions

Before this chapter concludes, a short comment on naming functions and variables needs to be made. If you are new to Windows programming, several of the variable and parameter names in the skeleton program and its description probably seem rather unusual. The reason for this is that they follow a set of naming conventions that was invented by Microsoft for Windows programming. For functions, the name consists of a verb followed by a noun. The first character of the verb and noun are capitalized. For the most part, this book will use this convention for function names.

For variable names, Microsoft chooses to use a rather complex system of embedding the data type into a variable's name. To accomplish this, a lowercase data type prefix is added to the start of the variable's name. The name, itself, is begun with a capital letter. The data type prefixes are shown in Table 2-1. Frankly, the use of type prefixes is controversial and is not universally accepted. Many Windows programmers use this method, many others do not. This method will be used by the programs in this book when it seems reasonable to do so. However, you are free to use any naming convention you like.

2

Prefix	Data Type
b	Boolean (one byte)
c	character (one byte)
dw	long unsigned integer
f	16-bit bitfield (flags)
fn	function
h	handle
l	long integer
lp	long pointer
n	short integer
p	pointer
pt	long integer holding screen coordinates
w	short unsigned integer
sz	pointer to null-terminated string
lpsz	long pointer to null-terminated string
rgb	long integer holding RGB color values

Variable
Type Prefix
Characters
Table 2-1.

CHAPTER 3

Application Essentials: Messages and Basic I/O

Although the skeleton developed in Chapter 2 forms the framework for a Windows 2000 program, by itself it is useless. To be useful, a program must be capable of performing two fundamental operations. First, it must be able to respond to a variety of messages. The processing of messages is at the core of all Windows 2000 applications. Second, a program must provide some means of outputting information to the user (that is, it must be able to display information on the screen). Unlike programs that you may have written for other operating systems, outputting information to the user is a nontrivial task in Windows. In fact, managing output forms a large part of any Windows application. Without the ability to process messages and display information, no useful Windows program can be written. These two important areas, message processing and the basic I/O operations, are the subjects of this chapter. We will begin by examining a simple way to output a string.

Message Boxes

A message box is a predefined window that displays simple output.

The easiest way to output information to the screen is to use a *message box*. As you will see, many of the examples in this book make use of message boxes. A message box is a window that displays a message to the user and waits for an acknowledgement. Unlike other types of windows that you must create, a message box is a system-defined window. In general, the purpose of a message box is to inform the user that some event has taken place. However, it is possible to construct a message box that allows the user to select between a few basic alternatives in response to the message. For example, one common form of message box allows a user to select either OK or Cancel.

NOTE: In the term *message box*, the word *message* refers to human-readable text that is displayed on the screen. It does not refer to Windows 2000 messages, which are sent to your program's window function. Although there is a certain overlap in terminology, *message boxes* and *messages* are two entirely separate concepts.

To create a message box, use the **MessageBox( )** API function. Its prototype is shown here:

int MessageBox(HWND *hwnd*, LPCSTR *lpText*, LPCSTR *lpCaption*,
UINT *MBType*);

Here, *hwnd* is the handle to the parent window. The *lpText* parameter is
a pointer to a string that will appear inside the message box. The string
pointed to by *lpCaption* is used as the title for the box. The value of *MBType*
determines the exact nature of the message box, including what type of
buttons and icons will be present; some of its most common values are
shown in Table 3-1. These macros are defined by including WINDOWS.H
and you can OR together two or more of these macros so long as they are
not mutually exclusive.

3

Value	Effect
MB_ABORTRETRYIGNORE	Displays Abort, Retry, and Ignore push buttons.
MB_CANCELTRYCONTINUE	Displays Cancel, Try Again, and Continue push buttons (new for Windows 2000).
MB_ICONEXCLAMATION	Displays Exclamation-point icon.
MB_ICONERROR	Displays a stop sign icon.
MB_ICONINFORMATION	Displays an information icon.
MB_ICONQUESTION	Displays a question mark icon.
MB_ICONSTOP	Same as MB_ICONERROR.
MB_OK	Displays OK button.
MB_OKCANCEL	Displays OK and Cancel push buttons.
MB_RETRYCANCEL	Displays Retry and Cancel push buttons.
MB_YESNO	Displays Yes and No push buttons.
MB_YESNOCANCEL	Displays Yes, No, and Cancel push buttons.

Some
Common
Values for
MBType
Table 3-1.

MessageBox( ) returns the user's response to the box. The possible return values are shown here:

Button Pressed	Return Value
Abort	IDABORT
Retry	IDRETRY
Ignore	IDIGNORE
Cancel	IDCANCEL
Continue	IDCONTINUE (New for Windows 2000)
No	IDNO
Yes	IDYES
OK	IDOK
Try Again	IDTRYAGAIN (New for Windows 2000)

Remember that, depending upon the value of *MBType*, only certain buttons will be present. Quite often message boxes are used to simply display an item of information and the only response offered to the user is the OK button. In these cases, the return value of a message box is usually ignored by the program.

To display a message box, just call the **MessageBox( )** function. Windows 2000 will display it at its first opportunity. **MessageBox( )** automatically creates a window and displays your message in it. You need do nothing else. For example, this call to **MessageBox( )**

```
i = MessageBox(hwnd, "This is Caption", "This is Title", MB_OKCANCEL);
```

produces the following message box:

Depending upon which button the user presses, **i** will either contain **IDOK** or **IDCANCEL**.

Message boxes are typically used to notify the user that some event has occurred, such as an error. In addition, because message boxes are so easy to use, they make excellent debugging tools when you need a simple way to output something to the screen. As you will see, many examples in this book use a message box as an expedient means of displaying information.

Now that we have a means of outputting information, we can move on to processing messages.

3

NEW FOR 2000:   The **MessageBox( )** style macro **MB_ CANCELTRYCONTINUE**, and the **IDTRYAGAIN** and **IDCONTINUE** return values are new for Windows 2000. Depending upon your compiler, you may need to define the macro **WINVER** as 0x500 in order to use these options.

Understanding Windows 2000 Messages

As it relates to Windows 2000, a message is a unique 32-bit integer value. Windows 2000 communicates with your program by sending it messages. Each message corresponds to some event. For example, there are messages to indicate that the user has pressed a key, that the mouse has moved, or that a window has been resized.

Although you could, in theory, refer to each message by its numeric value, in practice this is seldom done. Instead, there are macro names defined for all Windows 2000 messages. Typically, you will use the macro name, not the actual integer value, when referring to a message. The standard names for the messages are defined by including WINDOWS.H in your program. Here are some common Windows 2000 message macros:

WM_CHAR	WM_PAINT	WM_MOVE
WM_CLOSE	WM_LBUTTONUP	WM_LBUTTONDOWN
WM_COMMAND	WM_HSCROLL	WM_SIZE

Two other values accompany each message and contain information related to each message. One of these values is of type **WPARAM**, the other is of type **LPARAM**. For Windows 2000, both of these types translate into 32-bit integers. These values are commonly called **wParam** and **lParam**, respectively. The content of **wParam** and **lParam** is determined by which message is received. They typically hold things like mouse coordinates or the value of a keypress. As each message is discussed, the meaning of the values contained in **wParam** and **lParam** will be described.

HISTORICAL PERSPECTIVE: In 16-bit Windows, *wParam* is a 16-bit value. It is a 32-bit value in Windows 2000. As a result, some messages differ between the 16- and 32-bit environments. This difference can cause problems when moving 16-bit code to Windows 2000.

As mentioned in Chapter 2, the function that actually processes messages is your program's window function. As you should recall, this function is passed four parameters: the handle of the window that the message is for, the message itself, and the parameters **wParam** and **lParam**.

Sometimes two pieces of information are encoded into the two words that comprise the **wParam** or **lParam** parameters. To provide easy access to each value Windows defines two macros called **LOWORD** and **HIWORD**. They return the low-order and high-order words of a long integer, respectively. They are used like this:

```
x = LOWORD(lParam);
x = HIWORD(lParam);
```

You will soon see these macros in use.

Windows 2000 defines a large number of messages. Although it is not possible to examine every message, this chapter discusses some of the most common. Other messages are described throughout the remainder of this book as the need arises.

Responding to a Keypress

One of the most common Windows 2000 messages is generated when a key is pressed. This message is called **WM_CHAR**. It is important to understand that your application never receives keystrokes directly from the keyboard. Instead, each time a key is pressed, a message is sent to the active window (that is, the one that currently has input focus). To see how this process works, this section extends the skeletal application developed in Chapter 2 so that it processes keystroke messages.

Each time **WM_CHAR** is sent, **wParam** contains the ASCII value of the key pressed. **LOWORD(lParam)** contains the number of times the key has been repeated as a result of the key being held down. The bits of **HIWORD(lParam)** are encoded as shown in Table 3-2.

3

Bit	Meaning
15	Set if the key is being released; cleared if the key is being pressed.
14	Set if the key was pressed before the message was sent; cleared if it was not pressed.
13	Set if the ALT key is also being pressed; cleared if ALT is not pressed.
12	Used by Windows 2000
11	Used by Windows 2000
10	Used by Windows 2000
9	Used by Windows 2000
8	Set if the key pressed is an extended key provided by an enhanced keyboard; cleared otherwise.
7 - 0	Manufacturer-dependent key code (that is, the scan code)

How **HIWORD (lParam)** Is Encoded for Keyboard Data

Table 3-2.

For our purposes, the only value that is important at this time is **wParam**, since it holds the key that was pressed. Notice, however, how detailed the information is that Windows 2000 supplies about the state of the system. Of course, you are free to use as much or as little of this information as you like.

To process a **WM_CHAR** message, you must add it to the **switch** statement inside your program's window function. For example, here is a program that processes a keystroke by displaying the character on the screen using a message box.

```
// Processing WM_CHAR messages.

#include <windows.h>
#include <cstring>
#include <cstdio>

LRESULT CALLBACK WindowFunc(HWND, UINT, WPARAM, LPARAM);

char szWinName[] = "MyWin"; // name of window class

char str[255] = ""; // holds output string

int WINAPI WinMain(HINSTANCE hThisInst, HINSTANCE hPrevInst,
                   LPSTR lpszArgs, int nWinMode)
{
  HWND hwnd;
  MSG msg;
  WNDCLASSEX wcl;

  // Define a window class.
  wcl.cbSize = sizeof(WNDCLASSEX);

  wcl.hInstance = hThisInst;      // handle to this instance
  wcl.lpszClassName = szWinName;  // window class name
  wcl.lpfnWndProc = WindowFunc;   // window function
  wcl.style = 0;                  // default style

  wcl.hIcon = LoadIcon(NULL, IDI_APPLICATION); // large icon
  wcl.hIconSm = NULL; // use small version of large icon
  wcl.hCursor = LoadCursor(NULL, IDC_ARROW);   // cursor style

  wcl.lpszMenuName = NULL; // no class menu
```

```
      wcl.cbClsExtra = 0;        // no extra memory needed
      wcl.cbWndExtra = 0;

      // Make the window background white.
      wcl.hbrBackground = (HBRUSH) GetStockObject(WHITE_BRUSH);

      // Register the window class.
      if(!RegisterClassEx(&wcl)) return 0;

      /* Now that a window class has been registered, a window
         can be created. */
      hwnd = CreateWindow(
        szWinName, // name of window class
        "Processing WM_CHAR Messages", // title
        WS_OVERLAPPEDWINDOW, // window style - normal
        CW_USEDEFAULT, // X coordinate - let Windows decide
        CW_USEDEFAULT, // Y coordinate - let Windows decide
        CW_USEDEFAULT, // width - let Windows decide
        CW_USEDEFAULT, // height - let Windows decide
        NULL,          // no parent window
        NULL,          // no menu
        hThisInst,     // instance handle
        NULL           // no additional arguments
      );

      // Display the window.
      ShowWindow(hwnd, nWinMode);
      UpdateWindow(hwnd);

      // Create the message loop.
      while(GetMessage(&msg, NULL, 0, 0))
      {
        TranslateMessage(&msg); // translate keyboard messages
        DispatchMessage(&msg);  // return control to Windows 2000
      }

      return msg.wParam;
    }

    /* This function is called by Windows 2000 and is passed
       messages from the message queue.
    */
    LRESULT CALLBACK WindowFunc(HWND hwnd, UINT message,
```

```
                              WPARAM wParam, LPARAM lParam)
{
  switch(message) {
    case WM_CHAR: // process keystroke
      sprintf(str, "Character is %c", (char) wParam);
      MessageBox(hwnd, str, "WM_CHAR Received", MB_OK);
      break;
    case WM_DESTROY: // terminate the program
      PostQuitMessage(0);
      break;
    default:
      /* Let Windows 2000 process any messages not specified in
         the preceding switch statement. */
      return DefWindowProc(hwnd, message, wParam, lParam);
  }

  return 0;
}
```

Sample output produced by this program is shown in Figure 3-1. In the program, look carefully at these lines of code from **WindowFunc( )**.

```
case WM_CHAR: // process keystroke
  sprintf(str, "Character is %c", (char) wParam);
  MessageBox(hwnd, str, "WM_CHAR Received", MB_OK);
  break;
```

Sample output
from the
WM_CHAR
program
Figure 3-1.

As you can see, the **WM_CHAR** message has been added to the **case** statement. When you run the program, each time you press a key, a **WM_CHAR** message is generated and sent to **WindowFunc( )**. Inside the **WM_CHAR** case, the character received in **wParam** is converted into a string using **sprintf( )** and then displayed using a message box.

A Closer Look at Keyboard Messages   3

While **WM_CHAR** is probably the most commonly handled keyboard message, it is not the only one. In fact, **WM_CHAR** is actually a synthetic message that is constructed by the **TranslateMessage( )** function inside your program's message loop. At the lowest level, Windows 2000 generates two messages each time you press a key. When a key is pressed, a **WM_KEYDOWN** message is sent. When the key is released, a **WM_KEYUP** message is posted. If possible, a **WM_KEYDOWN/WM_KEYUP** message combination is translated into a **WM_CHAR** message by **TranslateMessage( )**. Thus, unless you include **TranslateMessage( )** in your message loop, your program will not receive **WM_CHAR** messages. To prove this to yourself, try commenting out the call to **TranslateMessage( )** in the preceding program. After doing so, it will no longer respond to your keypresses.

The reason that you will seldom use **WM_KEYDOWN** or **WM_KEYUP** for character input is that the information they contain is in a raw format. For example, the value in **wParam** contains the *virtual key code*, not the key's ASCII value. Part of what **TranslateMessage( )** does is transform the virtual key codes into ASCII characters, taking into account such things as the state of the shift key. **TranslateMessage( )** also automatically handles auto-repeat.

Virtual keys are device-independent key mappings.

A virtual key is a device-independent key code. As you may know, there are keys on nearly all computer keyboards that do not correspond to the ASCII character set. (The arrow keys and the function keys are examples.) Each key that can be generated has been assigned a value, which is its virtual key code. All of the virtual key codes are defined as macros in the header file WINUSER.H (which is automatically included in your program when you include WINDOWS.H). The codes begin with **VK_**. Here are some examples:

Virtual Key Code	Corresponding Key
VK_DOWN	Down arrow
VK_LEFT	Left arrow
VK_RIGHT	Right Arrow
VK_UP	Up arrow
VK_SHIFT	SHIFT
VK_CONTROL	CONTROL
VK_ESCAPE	ESCAPE
VK_F1 through VK_F24	Function keys
VK_HOME	HOME
VK_END	END
VK_INSERT	INSERT
VK_DELETE	DELETE
VK_PRIOR	PAGE UP
VK_NEXT	PAGE DOWN
VK_A through VK_Z	The letters of the alphabet
VK_0 through VK_9	The digits 0 through 9

For keys that have ASCII equivalents, **TranslateMessage( )** converts the virtual key code into its ASCII code and sends it in a **WM_CHAR** message. Of course, the non-ASCII keys are not converted. Thus, if your program wants to handle non-ASCII keypresses it must use **WM_KEYDOWN** or **WM_KEYUP** (or both).

Here is an enhanced version of the preceding program that handles both **WM_KEYDOWN** and **WM_CHAR** messages. The handler for **WM_KEYDOWN** reports if the key is an arrow, shift, or control key. Sample output is shown in Figure 3-2.

Sample output from the **WM_ KEYDOWN** program
Figure 3-2.

3

```cpp
// Processing WM_KEYDOWN and WM_CHAR messages.

#include <windows.h>
#include <cstring>
#include <cstdio>

LRESULT CALLBACK WindowFunc(HWND, UINT, WPARAM, LPARAM);

char szWinName[] = "MyWin"; // name of window class

char str[255] = ""; // holds output string

int WINAPI WinMain(HINSTANCE hThisInst, HINSTANCE hPrevInst,
                   LPSTR lpszArgs, int nWinMode)
{
  HWND hwnd;
  MSG msg;
  WNDCLASSEX wcl;

  // Define a window class.
  wcl.cbSize = sizeof(WNDCLASSEX);

  wcl.hInstance = hThisInst;      // handle to this instance
  wcl.lpszClassName = szWinName; // window class name
  wcl.lpfnWndProc = WindowFunc;  // window function
  wcl.style = 0;                  // default style

  wcl.hIcon = LoadIcon(NULL, IDI_APPLICATION); // large icon
  wcl.hIconSm = NULL; // use small version of large icon
  wcl.hCursor = LoadCursor(NULL, IDC_ARROW);  // cursor style
```

```
wcl.lpszMenuName = NULL; // no class menu
wcl.cbClsExtra = 0;       // no extra memory needed
wcl.cbWndExtra = 0;

// Make the window background white.
wcl.hbrBackground = (HBRUSH) GetStockObject(WHITE_BRUSH);

// Register the window class.
if(!RegisterClassEx(&wcl)) return 0;

/* Now that a window class has been registered, a window
   can be created. */
hwnd = CreateWindow(
  szWinName, // name of window class
  "Processing WM_CHAR and WM_KEYDOWN Messages",
  WS_OVERLAPPEDWINDOW, // window style - normal
  CW_USEDEFAULT, // X coordinate - let Windows decide
  CW_USEDEFAULT, // Y coordinate - let Windows decide
  CW_USEDEFAULT, // width - let Windows decide
  CW_USEDEFAULT, // height - let Windows decide
  NULL,          // no parent window
  NULL,          // no menu
  hThisInst,     // instance handle
  NULL           // no additional arguments
);

// Display the window.
ShowWindow(hwnd, nWinMode);
UpdateWindow(hwnd);

// Create the message loop.
while(GetMessage(&msg, NULL, 0, 0))
{
  TranslateMessage(&msg); // translate keyboard messages
  DispatchMessage(&msg);  // return control to Windows 2000
}

  return msg.wParam;
}

/* This function is called by Windows 2000 and is passed
   messages from the message queue.
*/
LRESULT CALLBACK WindowFunc(HWND hwnd, UINT message,
                            WPARAM wParam, LPARAM lParam)
{
  switch(message) {
    case WM_CHAR: // process character
```

```
        sprintf(str, "Character is %c", (char) wParam);
        MessageBox(hwnd, str, "WM_CHAR Received", MB_OK);
        break;
      case WM_KEYDOWN: // process raw keystroke
        switch((char)wParam) {
          case VK_UP:
            strcpy(str, "Up Arrow");
            break;
          case VK_DOWN:
            strcpy(str, "Down Arrow");
            break;
          case VK_LEFT:
            strcpy(str, "Left Arrow");
            break;
          case VK_RIGHT:
            strcpy(str, "Right Arrow");
            break;
          case VK_SHIFT:
            strcpy(str, "Shift");
            break;
          case VK_CONTROL:
            strcpy(str, "Control");
            break;
          default:
            strcpy(str, "Other Key");
        }
        MessageBox(hwnd, str, "WM_KEYDOWN Received", MB_OK);
        break;
      case WM_DESTROY: // terminate the program
        PostQuitMessage(0);
        break;
      default:
        /* Let Windows 2000 process any messages not specified in
           the preceding switch statement. */
        return DefWindowProc(hwnd, message, wParam, lParam);
  }

  return 0;
}
```

Notice one important point: when you press a standard ASCII key, such as X, the program will receive two messages: one will be **WM_CHAR** and the other will be **WM_KEYDOWN**. The reason for this is easy to understand. Each time you press a key, a **WM_KEYDOWN** message is generated (that is, all keystrokes generate a key-down message). If the key is an ASCII key, it is transformed into a **WM_CHAR** message by **TranslateMessage( )**.

More Keyboard Messages

In addition to **WM_KEYDOWN** and **WM_KEYUP**, there are other keyboard messages, which are shown here:

WM_SYSKEYDOWN	Raw keyboard message when a system key is pressed. **wParam** contains virtual key code.
WM_SYSKEYUP	Raw keyboard message when a system key is released. **wParam** contains virtual key code.
WM_DEADCHAR	Message generated by **TranslateMessage( )** when a key has no translation into the current environment. **wParam** contains character code.
WM_SYSCHAR	Message generated by **TranslateMessage( )** when a system key is pressed. **wParam** contains character code.
WM_SYSDEADCHAR	Message generated by **TranslateMessage( )** when a system key has no translation into the current environment. **wParam** contains character code.

A system key is generated by holding down both the key and the ALT key (for example, ALT-F). For all keyboard messages, the value of **lParam** is similar to that described for **WM_CHAR**.

For most applications, you will include **TranslateMessage( )** in your message loop and process messages for **WM_CHAR**. The other messages are available for those few programs that have specialized keyboard needs. Although the low-level control of keyboard input may have been essential in other programming environments in which you have worked, it is seldom necessary in Windows. This is because Windows defines several controls, such as edit boxes and list controls, that automate the handling of keyboard input.

Outputting Text to a Window

Although the message box is the easiest means of displaying information, it is obviously not suitable for all situations. Although it is a little more complicated than using a message box, there is another way for your program to output information: it can write directly to the client area of its window. Windows 2000 supports both text and graphics output. In this section, you will learn the basics of text output. Graphics output is reserved for later in this book.

The first thing to understand about outputting text to a window is that you cannot use the standard C or C++ I/O system. The reason for this is easy to understand: the standard C/C++ I/O functions and operators direct their output to standard output. However, in a Windows program, output is directed to a window. To see how text can be written to a window, let's begin with an example that outputs each character that you type to the program's window, instead of using a message box. Here is a version of **WindowFunc( )** that does this.

```
LRESULT CALLBACK WindowFunc(HWND hwnd, UINT message,
                            WPARAM wParam, LPARAM lParam)
{
  HDC hdc;
  static unsigned j=0;

  switch(message) {
    case WM_CHAR: // process keystroke
      hdc = GetDC(hwnd); // get device context
      sprintf(str, "%c", (char) wParam); // stringize character
      TextOut(hdc, j*10, 0, str, strlen(str)); // output char
      j++; // try commenting-out this line
      ReleaseDC(hwnd, hdc); // release device context
      break;
    case WM_DESTROY: // terminate the program
      PostQuitMessage(0);
      break;
    default:
      /* Let Windows 2000 process any messages not specified in
         the preceding switch statement. */
      return DefWindowProc(hwnd, message, wParam, lParam);
  }

  return 0;
}
```

Look carefully at the code inside the **WM_CHAR** case. It simply echoes each character that you type to the program's window. Compared to using the standard C/C++ I/O functions or operators, this code probably seems overly complex. The reason for this is that Windows must establish a link between your program and the screen. This is called a *device context* (DC for short), and it is acquired by calling **GetDC( )**. For now, don't worry about the precise definition of a device context. It will be discussed in the next section. However, once you obtain a device context, you may write to the window. At the end of the process, the device context is released using **ReleaseDC( )**. Your program *must* release the device context when it is done with it. Although the number of device contexts is limited only by the size of free memory, that number is still finite. If your program doesn't release the DC, eventually, the available DCs will be exhausted and a subsequent call to **GetDC( )** will fail. Also, failure to release the DC will result in a *memory leak*.

Both **GetDC( )** and **ReleaseDC( )** are API functions. Their prototypes are shown here:

A memory leak occurs when a program fails to free resources that it has allocated.

    HDC GetDC(HWND *hwnd*);
    int ReleaseDC(HWND *hwnd*, HDC *hdc*);

GetDC( ) returns a device context associated with the window whose handle is specified by *hwnd*. The type **HDC** specifies a handle to a device context. If a device context cannot be obtained, the function returns **NULL**.

ReleaseDC( ) returns true if the device context was released, false otherwise. The *hwnd* parameter is the handle of the window for which the device context is released. The *hdc* parameter is the handle of the device context obtained through the call to **GetDC( )**.

HISTORICAL PERSPECTIVE: In 16-bit Windows, there are only five device contexts available. In Windows 2000, the number is limited only by the amount of free memory.

The function that actually outputs the character is the API function **TextOut( )**. Its prototype is shown here.

    BOOL TextOut(HDC *DC*, int *x*, int *y*, LPCSTR *lpstr*, int *nlength*);

The **TextOut( )** function outputs the string pointed to by *lpstr* at the window coordinates specified by *x, y*. (By default, these coordinates are measured in pixels.) The length of the string is specified in *nlength*. The **TextOut( )** function returns non-zero if successful, zero otherwise.

In the **WindowFunc( )**, each time a **WM_CHAR** message is received, the character that is typed by the user is converted, using **sprintf( )**, into a string that is one character long and then displayed, using **TextOut( ),** in the window. The first character is displayed at location 0, 0. Remember, in a window, the upper-left corner of the client area is location 0, 0. Window coordinates are always relative to the window, not the screen. Therefore, the first character is displayed in the upper-left corner no matter where the window is physically located on the screen. The variable **j** allows each character to be displayed to the right of the preceding character. That is, the second character is displayed at 10,0, the third at 20,0, and so on. Windows does not support any concept of a text cursor that is automatically advanced. Instead, you must explicitly specify where each **TextOut( )** string will be written. Also, **TextOut( )** does not advance to the next line when a newline character is encountered, nor does it expand tabs. You must perform all these activities yourself.

Before moving on, you might want to try one simple experiment: comment out the line of code that increments **j.** Doing this will cause all characters to be displayed at location 0, 0. Next, run the program and try typing several characters. Specifically, try typing a **W** followed by an **i.** Because Windows is a graphics-based system, characters are typically of different sizes, and the overwriting of one character by another does not necessarily cause all of the previous character to be erased. For example, when you typed a **W** followed by an **i**, part of the **W** will still be displayed. The fact that characters are not proportional also explains why, in the preceding example, the spacing between characters that you type is not even.

Bear in mind that the method used in this example to output text to a window is quite crude. In fact, no real Windows 2000 application would use this approach. Later in this book, you will learn how to manage text output in a more sophisticated, and more pleasing, fashion.

No Windows 2000 API function will allow output beyond the borders of a window. Output will automatically be clipped to prevent the boundaries from being crossed. To confirm this for yourself, try typing characters past the border of the window. As you will see, once the right edge of the window has been reached, no further characters are displayed.

At first you might think that using **TextOut( )** to output a single character is an inefficient application of the function. The fact is that Windows 2000 (and Windows, in general) does not contain a function that simply outputs a character. Instead, Windows 2000 performs much of its user interaction through dialog boxes, menus, toolbars, and the like; it contains only a few functions that output text to the client area. Further, you will generally construct output in advance and then use **TextOut( )** to simply move that output to the screen.

Here is the entire program that echoes keystrokes to the window. Figure 3-3 shows sample output.

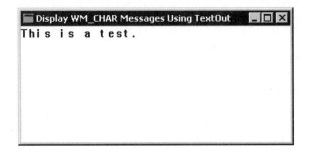

Sample
window
produced
using
TextOut( )
Figure 3-3.

```
// Displaying text using TextOut().

#include <windows.h>
#include <cstring>
#include <cstdio>

LRESULT CALLBACK WindowFunc(HWND, UINT, WPARAM, LPARAM);

char szWinName[] = "MyWin"; // name of window class

char str[255] = ""; // holds output string

int WINAPI WinMain(HINSTANCE hThisInst, HINSTANCE hPrevInst,
                    LPSTR lpszArgs, int nWinMode)
{
  HWND hwnd;
  MSG msg;
  WNDCLASSEX wcl;

  // Define a window class.
  wcl.cbSize = sizeof(WNDCLASSEX);

  wcl.hInstance = hThisInst;     // handle to this instance
  wcl.lpszClassName = szWinName; // window class name
  wcl.lpfnWndProc = WindowFunc;  // window function
  wcl.style = 0;                 // default style

  wcl.hIcon = LoadIcon(NULL, IDI_APPLICATION); // large icon
  wcl.hIconSm = NULL; // use small version of large icon
  wcl.hCursor = LoadCursor(NULL, IDC_ARROW);   // cursor style

  wcl.lpszMenuName = NULL; // no class menu
```

```
    wcl.cbClsExtra = 0;        // no extra memory needed
    wcl.cbWndExtra = 0;

    // Make the window background white.
    wcl.hbrBackground = (HBRUSH) GetStockObject(WHITE_BRUSH);

    // Register the window class.
    if(!RegisterClassEx(&wcl)) return 0;

    /* Now that a window class has been registered, a window
       can be created. */
    hwnd = CreateWindow(
      szWinName, // name of window class
      "Display WM_CHAR Messages Using TextOut", // title
      WS_OVERLAPPEDWINDOW, // window style - normal
      CW_USEDEFAULT, // X coordinate - let Windows decide
      CW_USEDEFAULT, // Y coordinate - let Windows decide
      CW_USEDEFAULT, // width - let Windows decide
      CW_USEDEFAULT, // height - let Windows decide
      NULL,           // no parent window
      NULL,           // no menu
      hThisInst,      // instance handle
      NULL            // no additional arguments
    );

    // Display the window.
    ShowWindow(hwnd, nWinMode);
    UpdateWindow(hwnd);

    // Create the message loop.
    while(GetMessage(&msg, NULL, 0, 0))
    {
      TranslateMessage(&msg); // translate keyboard messages
      DispatchMessage(&msg);  // return control to Windows 2000
    }

    return msg.wParam;
}

/* This function is called by Windows 2000 and is passed
   messages from the message queue.
*/
LRESULT CALLBACK WindowFunc(HWND hwnd, UINT message,
                            WPARAM wParam, LPARAM lParam)
{
  HDC hdc;
```

```
      static unsigned j=0;

      switch(message) {
        case WM_CHAR: // process keystroke
          hdc = GetDC(hwnd); // get device context
          sprintf(str, "%c", (char) wParam); // stringize character
          TextOut(hdc, j*10, 0, str, strlen(str)); // output char
          j++; // try commenting-out this line
          ReleaseDC(hwnd, hdc); // release device context
          break;
        case WM_DESTROY: // terminate the program
          PostQuitMessage(0);
          break;
        default:
          /* Let Windows 2000 process any messages not specified in
             the preceding switch statement. */
          return DefWindowProc(hwnd, message, wParam, lParam);
      }

      return 0;
    }
```

Device Contexts

The program in the previous section had to obtain a device context prior to outputting to the window. Also, that device context had to be released prior to the termination of that function. It is now time to understand what a device context is. A device context is a structure that describes the display environment of a window, including its device driver and various display parameters, such as the current type font. As you will see later in this book, you have substantial control over the display environment of a window.

A device context is a structure that describes a window's output environment.

Before your application can output information to the client area of the window, a device context must be obtained. Until this is done, there is no linkage between your program and the window relative to output. Since **TextOut( )**, and other output functions, require a handle to a device context, this is a self-enforcing rule.

Processing the WM_PAINT Message

One of the most important messages that your program will receive is **WM_PAINT**. This message is sent when your program needs to restore the contents of its window. To understand why this is important, run the program from the previous section and enter a few characters. Next, minimize and then restore the window. As you will see, the characters that you typed are not displayed after the window is restored. Also, if the window is overwritten by another window and then uncovered, the characters will not be redisplayed. The reason for this is simple: in general, Windows does not keep a record of what a window contains. Instead, it is your program's job to maintain the contents of a window. To help your program accomplish this, each time the contents of a window must be redisplayed, your program will be sent a **WM_PAINT** message. (This message will also be sent when your window is first created.) Each time your program receives this message it must redisplay the contents of the window.

Before explaining how to respond to a **WM_PAINT** message it might be useful to explain why Windows does not automatically rewrite your window. The answer is short and to the point. In many situations, it is easier for your program, which has intimate knowledge of the contents of the window, to rewrite it than it would be for Windows to do so. While the merits of this approach have been much debated by programmers, you should simply accept it, because it is unlikely to change.

The first step to processing a **WM_PAINT** message is to add it to the **switch** statement inside the window function. For example, here is one way to add a **WM_PAINT** case to the previous program.

```
case WM_PAINT: // process a repaint request
  hdc = BeginPaint(hwnd, &paintstruct); // get DC
  TextOut(hdc, 0, 0, str, strlen(str));
  EndPaint(hwnd, &paintstruct); // release DC
  break;
```

Let's look at this closely. First, notice that a device context is obtained using a call to **BeginPaint( )** instead of **GetDC( )**. For various reasons, when you process a **WM_PAINT** message, you must obtain a device context using **BeginPaint( )**, which has this prototype:

HDC BeginPaint(HWND *hwnd*, PAINTSTRUCT **lpPS*);

BeginPaint( ) returns a device context if successful or **NULL** on failure. Here, *hwnd* is the handle of the window for which the device context is being obtained. The second parameter is a pointer to a structure of type **PAINTSTRUCT**. On return, the structure pointed to by *lpPS* will contain information that your program can use to repaint the window. **PAINTSTRUCT** is defined like this:

```
typedef struct tagPAINTSTRUCT {
  HDC hdc;                  // handle to device context
  BOOL fErase;              // true if background must be erased
  RECT rcPaint;             // coordinates of region to redraw
  BOOL fRestore;            // reserved
  BOOL fIncUpdate;          // reserved
  BYTE rgbReserved[32];     // reserved
} PAINTSTRUCT;
```

Here, **hdc** will contain the device context of the window that needs to be repainted. This DC is also returned by the call to **BeginPaint( )**. **fErase** will be nonzero if the background of the window needs to be erased. However, as long as you specified a background brush when you created the window, you can ignore the **fErase** member. Windows 2000 will erase the window for you.

The type **RECT** is a structure that specifies the upper-left and lower-right coordinates of a rectangular region. This structure is shown here:

```
typedef tagRECT {
  LONG left, top;     // upper left
  LONG right, bottom; // lower right
} RECT;
```

In **PAINTSTRUCT**, the **rcPaint** element contains the coordinates of the region of the window that needs to be repainted. For now, you will not need to use the contents of **rcPaint** because you can assume that the entire window must be repainted. However, real programs that you write will probably need to utilize this information.

Once the device context has been obtained, output can be written to the window. After the window has been repainted, you must release the device context using a call to **EndPaint( )**, which has this prototype:

BOOL EndPaint(HWND *hwnd*, CONST PAINTSTRUCT **lpPS*);

EndPaint( ) returns nonzero (it cannot fail). Here, *hwnd* is the handle of the window that was repainted. The second parameter is a pointer to the **PAINTSTRUCT** structure used in the call to **BeginPaint( )**.

It is critical to understand that a device context obtained using **BeginPaint( )** must be released only through a call to **EndPaint( )**. Further, **BeginPaint( )** must only be used when a **WM_PAINT** message is being processed.

Here is the full program that now processes **WM_PAINT** messages.

```cpp
// Process WM_PAINT messages.

#include <windows.h>
#include <cstring>
#include <cstdio>

LRESULT CALLBACK WindowFunc(HWND, UINT, WPARAM, LPARAM);

char szWinName[] = "MyWin"; // name of window class

char str[255] = "Sample Output"; // holds output string

int WINAPI WinMain(HINSTANCE hThisInst, HINSTANCE hPrevInst,
                   LPSTR lpszArgs, int nWinMode)
{
  HWND hwnd;
  MSG msg;
  WNDCLASSEX wcl;

  // Define a window class.
  wcl.cbSize = sizeof(WNDCLASSEX);

  wcl.hInstance = hThisInst;      // handle to this instance
  wcl.lpszClassName = szWinName; // window class name
  wcl.lpfnWndProc = WindowFunc;  // window function
  wcl.style = 0;                 // default style

  wcl.hIcon = LoadIcon(NULL, IDI_APPLICATION); // large icon
  wcl.hIconSm = NULL; // use small version of large icon
  wcl.hCursor = LoadCursor(NULL, IDC_ARROW);   // cursor style

  wcl.lpszMenuName = NULL; // no class menu
  wcl.cbClsExtra = 0;      // no extra memory needed
  wcl.cbWndExtra = 0;

  // Make the window background white.
  wcl.hbrBackground = (HBRUSH) GetStockObject(WHITE_BRUSH);

  // Register the window class.
  if(!RegisterClassEx(&wcl)) return 0;

  /* Now that a window class has been registered, a window
     can be created. */
  hwnd = CreateWindow(
    szWinName, // name of window class
```

```
            "Process WM_PAINT Messages", // title
            WS_OVERLAPPEDWINDOW, // window style - normal
            CW_USEDEFAULT, // X coordinate - let Windows decide
            CW_USEDEFAULT, // Y coordinate - let Windows decide
            CW_USEDEFAULT, // width - let Windows decide
            CW_USEDEFAULT, // height - let Windows decide
            NULL,          // no parent window
            NULL,          // no menu
            hThisInst,     // instance handle
            NULL           // no additional arguments
        );

        // Display the window.
        ShowWindow(hwnd, nWinMode);
        UpdateWindow(hwnd);

        // Create the message loop.
        while(GetMessage(&msg, NULL, 0, 0))
        {
            TranslateMessage(&msg); // translate keyboard messages
            DispatchMessage(&msg);  // return control to Windows 2000
        }

        return msg.wParam;
    }

/* This function is called by Windows 2000 and is passed
   messages from the message queue.
*/
LRESULT CALLBACK WindowFunc(HWND hwnd, UINT message,
                            WPARAM wParam, LPARAM lParam)
{
    HDC hdc;
    static unsigned j=0;
    PAINTSTRUCT paintstruct;

    switch(message) {
        case WM_CHAR: // process keystroke
            hdc = GetDC(hwnd); // get device context
            sprintf(str, "%c", (char) wParam); // stringize character
            TextOut(hdc, j*10, 0, str, strlen(str)); // output char
            j++; // try commenting-out this line
            ReleaseDC(hwnd, hdc); // release device context
            break;
```

```
      case WM_PAINT: // process a repaint request
        hdc = BeginPaint(hwnd, &paintstruct); // get DC
        TextOut(hdc, 0, 0, str, strlen(str));
        EndPaint(hwnd, &paintstruct); // release DC
        break;
      case WM_DESTROY: // terminate the program
        PostQuitMessage(0);
        break;
      default:
        /* Let Windows 2000 process any messages not specified in
           the preceding switch statement. */
        return DefWindowProc(hwnd, message, wParam, lParam);
  }

  return 0;
}
```

Before continuing, enter, compile, and run this program. Try typing a few characters and then minimizing and restoring the window. As you will see, each time the window is redisplayed, the last character you typed is automatically redrawn. The reason that only the last character is redisplayed is that **str** contains only the last character that you typed. You might find it fun to alter the program so that it adds each character to a string and then redisplays that string each time a **WM_PAINT** message is received. (You will see one way to do this in the next example.) Notice that the global array **str** is initialized to **Sample Output** and that this is displayed when the program begins execution. This happens because a **WM_PAINT** message is automatically generated when a window is created.

While the handling of the **WM_PAINT** message in this program is quite simple, it must be emphasized that most real-world applications will be more complex because most windows contain considerably more output. Since it is your program's responsibility to restore the window if it is resized or overwritten, you must always provide some mechanism to accomplish this. In real-world programs, this is usually accomplished in one of three ways. First, your program can regenerate the output by computational means. This choice is most feasible when no user input is used. Second, in some instances, you can keep a record of events and replay the events when the window needs to be redrawn. Finally, your program can maintain a virtual window that you copy to the actual window each time it must be redrawn. This is the most general method. (The implementation of this approach is described later in this book.) Which approach is best depends completely upon the application. Most of the examples in this book won't bother to redraw the window because doing so typically involves substantial additional code which often just muddies the point of an example. However, your programs will need to restore their windows in order to be conforming Windows 2000 applications.

Generating a WM_PAINT Message

It is possible for your program to cause a **WM_PAINT** message to be generated. At first, you might wonder why your program would need to generate a **WM_PAINT** message since it seems that it can repaint its window whenever it wants. However, this is a false assumption. Remember, updating a window is a costly process in terms of time. Because Windows is a multitasking system that might be running other programs that are also demanding CPU time, sometimes it is better if your program simply tells Windows that it wants to output information, but lets Windows decide when it is best to actually perform that output. This method allows Windows to efficiently allocate CPU time to all the tasks in the system. Using this approach, your program simply holds all output until a **WM_PAINT** message is received.

In the previous example, the **WM_PAINT** message was received only when the window was resized or uncovered. However, if all output is held until a **WM_PAINT** message is received, then to achieve interactive I/O, there must be some way to tell Windows that it needs to send a **WM_PAINT** message to your window whenever output is pending. As expected, Windows 2000 includes such a feature. Thus, when your program has information to output, it simply requests that a **WM_PAINT** message be sent when Windows is ready to do so.

To cause Windows to send a **WM_PAINT** message, your program will call the **InvalidateRect( )** API function. Its prototype is shown here:

BOOL InvalidateRect(HWND *hwnd*, CONST RECT **lpRect*, BOOL *bErase*);

Here, *hwnd* is the handle of the window to which you want to send the **WM_PAINT** message. The **RECT** structure pointed to by *lpRect* specifies the coordinates within the window that must be redrawn. If this value is **NULL**, then the entire window will be specified. If *bErase* is true, then the background will be erased. If it is 0, then the background is left unchanged. The function returns nonzero if successful and zero otherwise. (In general, this function will always succeed.)

When **InvalidateRect( )** is called, it tells Windows that the window is invalid and must be redrawn. This, in turn, causes Windows to send a **WM_PAINT** message to the program's window function.

Here is a reworked version of the previous program that routes all output through the **WM_PAINT** message. The code that responds to a **WM_CHAR** message simply stores each character and then calls **InvalidateRect( ).** In

IN DEPTH

Generating a Message

As you know, **InvalidateRect( )** is used to generate a **WM_PAINT** message. However, this raises a larger question: How, in general, does a program generate a message? The answer is quite easy: it uses the **SendMessage( )** API function. **SendMessage( )** enables you to send a message to any window you want. Its prototype is shown here:

LRESULT SendMessage(HWND *hwnd*, UINT *message*,
                    WPARAM *wParam*, LPARAM *lParam*);

Here, *hwnd* is the handle of the window to which the message will be sent. The message to send is specified in *message*. Any additional information associated with the message is passed in *wParam* and *lParam*. **SendMessage( )** returns a response related to the message.

SendMessage( ) is used frequently when working with Windows 2000's control elements—especially its common controls. You will see examples of this usage later in this book. However, it can be used any time you want to send a message to a window. For example, the following version of **WindowFunc( )** uses **SendMessage( )** to generate a stream of **WM_CHAR** messages whenever the user presses CTRL-A.

```
LRESULT CALLBACK WindowFunc(HWND hwnd, UINT message,
                             WPARAM wParam, LPARAM lParam)
{
  HDC hdc;
  unsigned i;
  static unsigned j=0;
  char s[] = "Hello There";
```

```
switch(message) {
  case WM_CHAR: // process keystroke
    hdc = GetDC(hwnd); // get device context

    // print Hello There if user presses Ctrl-A
    if((char)wParam == (char) 1) for(i=0; s[i]; i++)
      SendMessage(hwnd, WM_CHAR, (WPARAM) s[i], (LPARAM) 0);
    else {
      sprintf(str, "%c", (char) wParam); // stringize
      TextOut(hdc, j*10, 0, str, strlen(str)); // output char
      j++;
    }

    ReleaseDC(hwnd, hdc); // release device context
    break;
  case WM_DESTROY: // terminate the program
    PostQuitMessage(0);
    break;
  default:
    /* Let Windows 2000 process any messages not specified in
       the preceding switch statement. */
    return DefWindowProc(hwnd, message, wParam, lParam);
  }
  return 0;
}
```

If you substitute this version of **WindowFunc( )** into one of the
preceding programs, then each time you press CTRL-A, the string "Hello
There" will be sent as a series of **WM_CHAR** messages to your program.
You could use this basic concept to provide a keyboard macro capability
in programs that you write.

One other point: Since the information contained in **lParam** is not used
by the program when a **WM_CHAR** message is processed, this parameter
was simply specified as zero inside the call to **SendMessage( ).** However,
in other contexts you may need to generate the appropriate values for
this information.

this version of the program, notice that inside the **WM_CHAR** case, each character you type is added to the string **str.** Thus, each time the window is repainted, the entire string containing all the characters you typed is output, not just the last character as was the case with the preceding program.

```cpp
/* A Windows skeleton that routes output through
   the WM_PAINT message. */

#include <windows.h>
#include <cstring>
#include <cstdio>

LRESULT CALLBACK WindowFunc(HWND, UINT, WPARAM, LPARAM);

char szWinName[] = "MyWin"; // name of window class

char str[255] = ""; // holds output string

int WINAPI WinMain(HINSTANCE hThisInst, HINSTANCE hPrevInst,
                   LPSTR lpszArgs, int nWinMode)
{
  HWND hwnd;
  MSG msg;
  WNDCLASSEX wcl;

  // Define a window class.
  wcl.cbSize = sizeof(WNDCLASSEX);

  wcl.hInstance = hThisInst;       // handle to this instance
  wcl.lpszClassName = szWinName;   // window class name
  wcl.lpfnWndProc = WindowFunc;    // window function
  wcl.style = 0;                   // default style

  wcl.hIcon = LoadIcon(NULL, IDI_APPLICATION); // large icon
  wcl.hIconSm = NULL; // use small version of large icon
  wcl.hCursor = LoadCursor(NULL, IDC_ARROW);   // cursor style

  wcl.lpszMenuName = NULL; // no class menu
  wcl.cbClsExtra = 0;        // no extra memory needed
  wcl.cbWndExtra = 0;

  // Make the window background white.
  wcl.hbrBackground = (HBRUSH) GetStockObject(WHITE_BRUSH);
```

```
// Register the window class.
if(!RegisterClassEx(&wcl)) return 0;

/* Now that a window class has been registered, a window
   can be created. */
hwnd = CreateWindow(
  szWinName, // name of window class
  "Routing Output Through WM_PAINT", // title
  WS_OVERLAPPEDWINDOW, // window style - normal
  CW_USEDEFAULT, // X coordinate - let Windows decide
  CW_USEDEFAULT, // Y coordinate - let Windows decide
  CW_USEDEFAULT, // width - let Windows decide
  CW_USEDEFAULT, // height - let Windows decide
  NULL,          // no parent window
  NULL,          // no menu
  hThisInst,     // instance handle
  NULL           // no additional arguments
);

// Display the window.
ShowWindow(hwnd, nWinMode);
UpdateWindow(hwnd);

// Create the message loop.
while(GetMessage(&msg, NULL, 0, 0))
{
  TranslateMessage(&msg); // translate keyboard messages
  DispatchMessage(&msg);  // return control to Windows 2000
}

return msg.wParam;
}

/* This function is called by Windows 2000 and is passed
   messages from the message queue.
*/
LRESULT CALLBACK WindowFunc(HWND hwnd, UINT message, WPARAM wParam,
                LPARAM lParam)
{
  HDC hdc;
  PAINTSTRUCT paintstruct;
  char temp[2];

  switch(message) {
    case WM_CHAR: // process keystroke
      hdc = GetDC(hwnd); // get device context
      sprintf(temp, "%c", (char) wParam); // stringize character
```

```
    strcat(str, temp); // add character to string
    InvalidateRect(hwnd, NULL, 1); // paint the screen
    break;
  case WM_PAINT: // process a repaint request
    hdc = BeginPaint(hwnd, &paintstruct); // get DC

    TextOut(hdc, 0, 0, str, strlen(str)); // output char

    EndPaint(hwnd, &paintstruct); // release DC
    break;
  case WM_DESTROY: // terminate the program
    PostQuitMessage(0);
    break;
  default:
      /* Let Windows 2000 process any messages not specified in
         the preceding switch statement. */
      return DefWindowProc(hwnd, message, wParam, lParam);
  }

  return 0;
}
```

Many Windows applications route all (or most) output to the client area through **WM_PAINT**, for the reasons already stated. However, there is nothing technically wrong with outputting text or graphics as needed. Which method you should use will depend upon the precise demands of your program.

Responding to Mouse Messages

Since Windows is, to a great extent, a mouse-based operating system, all Windows 2000 programs should respond to mouse input. Because the mouse is so important, there are several different types of mouse messages. The ones discussed in this chapter are:

WM_LBUTTONDOWN	WM_LBUTTONUP	WM_LBUTTONDBLCLK
WM_RBUTTONDOWN	WM_RBUTTONUP	WM_RBUTTONDBLCLK

While most computers use a two-button mouse, Windows 2000 is capable of handling a mouse with up to three buttons. These buttons are called the left, middle, and right. Also, Windows 2000 supports special X buttons which are used for application-based commands, but we won't be examining these here. For the rest of this chapter we will be concerned only with the left and right buttons.

Let's begin with the two most common mouse messages, **WM_ LBUTTONDOWN** and **WM_RBUTTONDOWN**. They are generated when the left button and right buttons are pressed, respectively.

When either a **WM_LBUTTONDOWN** or **WM_RBUTTONDOWN** message is received, the mouse's current X, Y location is specified in the low-order and high-order words of **lParam**, respectively. The value of **wParam** contains various pieces of status information, which are described in the next section.

There are two ways to retrieve the X and Y coordinates from **lParam** when a mouse message is received. One way is to use **HIWORD( )** and **LOWORD( )**. This is the traditional approach, and it is the method used by this book. Alternatively, you can use the **GET_X_LPARAM( )** and **GET_Y_LPARAM( )** macros, which are essentially just different names for **HIWORD( )** and **LOWORD( )**, but might be easier to remember. They are shown here:

```
int GET_X_LPARAM(LPARAM lParam);
int GET_Y_LPARAM(LPARAM lParam);
```

To use **GET_X_LPARAM( )** and **GET_Y_LPARAM( )**, you will need to include WINDOWSX.H in your program. Again, the examples in this book will use **HIWORD( )** and **LOWORD( )** to decode the coordinates in a mouse message.

The following program responds to mouse messages. Each time you press a mouse button when the program's window contains the mouse cursor, a message will be displayed at the current location of the mouse pointer.

```
// Process mouse messages.

#include <windows.h>
#include <cstring>
#include <cstdio>

LRESULT CALLBACK WindowFunc(HWND, UINT, WPARAM, LPARAM);

char szWinName[] = "MyWin"; // name of window class

char str[255] = ""; // holds output string

int WINAPI WinMain(HINSTANCE hThisInst, HINSTANCE hPrevInst,
                    LPSTR lpszArgs, int nWinMode)
{
  HWND hwnd;
  MSG msg;
  WNDCLASSEX wcl;
```

```
// Define a window class.
wcl.cbSize = sizeof(WNDCLASSEX);

wcl.hInstance = hThisInst;      // handle to this instance
wcl.lpszClassName = szWinName; // window class name
wcl.lpfnWndProc = WindowFunc;   // window function
wcl.style = 0;                  // default style

wcl.hIcon = LoadIcon(NULL, IDI_APPLICATION); // large icon
wcl.hIconSm = NULL; // use small version of large icon
wcl.hCursor = LoadCursor(NULL, IDC_ARROW);   // cursor style

wcl.lpszMenuName = NULL; // no class menu
wcl.cbClsExtra = 0;         // no extra memory needed
wcl.cbWndExtra = 0;

// Make the window background white.
wcl.hbrBackground = (HBRUSH) GetStockObject(WHITE_BRUSH);

// Register the window class.
if(!RegisterClassEx(&wcl)) return 0;

/* Now that a window class has been registered, a window
   can be created. */
hwnd = CreateWindow(
  szWinName, // name of window class
  "Processing Mouse Messages", // title
  WS_OVERLAPPEDWINDOW, // window style - normal
  CW_USEDEFAULT, // X coordinate - let Windows decide
  CW_USEDEFAULT, // Y coordinate - let Windows decide
  CW_USEDEFAULT, // width - let Windows decide
  CW_USEDEFAULT, // height - let Windows decide
  NULL,          // no parent window
  NULL,          // no menu
  hThisInst,     // instance handle
  NULL           // no additional arguments
);

// Display the window.
ShowWindow(hwnd, nWinMode);
UpdateWindow(hwnd);

// Create the message loop.
while(GetMessage(&msg, NULL, 0, 0))
{
  TranslateMessage(&msg); // translate keyboard messages
```

3

```
      DispatchMessage(&msg);  // return control to Windows 2000
  }

  return msg.wParam;
}


/* This function is called by Windows 2000 and is passed
   messages from the message queue.
*/
LRESULT CALLBACK WindowFunc(HWND hwnd, UINT message,
                           WPARAM wParam, LPARAM lParam)
{
  HDC hdc;

  switch(message) {
    case WM_RBUTTONDOWN: // process right button
      hdc = GetDC(hwnd); // get DC
      sprintf(str, "Right button is down at %d, %d",
              LOWORD(lParam), HIWORD(lParam));
      TextOut(hdc, LOWORD(lParam), HIWORD(lParam),
              str, strlen(str));
      ReleaseDC(hwnd, hdc); // Release DC
      break;
    case WM_LBUTTONDOWN: // process left button
      hdc = GetDC(hwnd); // get DC
      sprintf(str, "Left button is down at %d, %d",
              LOWORD(lParam), HIWORD(lParam));
      TextOut(hdc, LOWORD(lParam), HIWORD(lParam),
              str, strlen(str));
      ReleaseDC(hwnd, hdc); // Release DC
      break;
    case WM_DESTROY: // terminate the program
      PostQuitMessage(0);
      break;
    default:
      /* Let Windows 2000 process any messages not specified in
         the preceding switch statement. */
      return DefWindowProc(hwnd, message, wParam, lParam);
  }

  return 0;
}
```

Figure 3-4 shows sample output from this program.

Sample output
from the
Mouse
Messages
program

Figure 3-4.

A Closer Look at Mouse Messages

For all of the mouse messages described in this chapter, the meaning of
lParam and **wParam** is the same. As described earlier, the value of **lParam**
contains the coordinates of the mouse when the message was generated. The
value of **wParam** supplies information about the state of the mouse and
keyboard. It may contain any combination of the following values:

MK_CONTROL
MK_SHIFT
MK_MBUTTON
MK_RBUTTON
MK_LBUTTON
MK_XBUTTON1
MK_XBUTTON2

If the CTRL key is pressed when a mouse button is pressed, then **wParam**
will contain **MK_CONTROL.** If the SHIFT key is pressed when a mouse
button is pressed, then **WParam** will contain **MK_SHIFT.** If the right
button is down when the left button is pressed, then **wParam** will contain
MK_RBUTTON. If the left button is down when the right button is pressed,
then **wParam** will contain **MK_LBUTTON.** If the middle button (if it

exists) is down when one of the other buttons is pressed, then **wParam** will contain **MK_MBUTTON**. If one of the X buttons is pressed, then either **MK_XBUTTON1** or **MK_XBUTTON2** will be present. Before moving on, you might want to try experimenting with these messages.

NEW FOR 2000:   The **MK_XBUTTON1** and **MK_XBUTTON2** values are new for Windows 2000.

Using Button-Up Messages

When a mouse button is clicked, your program actually receives two messages. The first is a button-down message, such as **WM_LBUTTONDOWN**, when the button is pressed. The second is a button-up message, when the button is released. The button-up messages for the left and right buttons are called **WM_LBUTTONUP** and **WM_RBUTTONUP**. For some applications, such as selecting an item, it is better to process button-up, rather than button-down messages. This gives the user a chance to change his or her mind after the mouse button has been pressed.

Responding to a Double Click

While it is easy to respond to a single-click, handling double-clicks requires a bit more work. First, you must enable your program to receive double-click messages. By default, double-click messages are not sent to your program. Second, you will need to add message response code for the double-click message to which you want to respond.

To allow your program to receive double-click messages, you will need to specify **CS_DBLCLKS** in the **style** member of the **WNDCLASSEX** structure prior to registering the window class. That is, you must use a line of code like that shown here.

```
wcl.style = CS_DBLCLKS; // allow double-clicks
```

After you have enabled double-clicks, your program can receive double-click messages, including **WM_LBUTTONDBLCLK** and **WM_RBUTTONDBLCLK**. The contents of the **lParam** and **wParam** parameters are the same as they are for the other mouse messages.

As you know, a double-click is two presses of a mouse button in quick succession. You can obtain and/or set the time interval in which two presses of a mouse button must occur in order for a double-click message to be generated. To obtain the double-click interval, use the API function **GetDoubleClickTime( ),** whose prototype is shown here:

    UINT GetDoubleClickTime(void);

3

This function returns the interval of time (specified in milliseconds) within which a double-click must occur. To set the double-click interval, use **SetDoubleClickTime( ).** Its prototype is shown here:

    BOOL SetDoubleClickTime(UINT *interval*);

Here, *interval* specifies the number of milliseconds within which two presses of a mouse button must occur in order for a double-click to be generated. If you specify zero, then the default double-click time is used. (The default interval is approximately half a second.) The function returns nonzero if successful or zero on failure.

The following program responds to double-click messages. It also demonstrates the use of **GetDoubleClickTime( )** and **SetDoubleClickTime( )**. Each time you press the up arrow key, the double-click interval is increased. Each time you press the down arrow, the interval is decreased. Each time you double-click either the right or left mouse button, a message box that reports the current double-click interval is displayed. Since the double-click interval is a system wide setting, changes to it will affect all other programs in the system. For this reason, when the program begins, it saves the current double-click interval. When the program ends, the original interval is restored. In general, if your program changes a system-wide setting, it should be restored before the program ends. Sample output is shown in Figure 3-5.

Sample output
from the
Double-Click
program
Figure 3-5.

```cpp
// Respond to double clicks and control the double-click interval.

#include <windows.h>
#include <cstring>
#include <cstdio>

LRESULT CALLBACK WindowFunc(HWND, UINT, WPARAM, LPARAM);

char szWinName[] = "MyWin"; // name of window class

char str[255] = ""; // holds output string

UINT OrgDblClkTime; // holds original double-click interval

int WINAPI WinMain(HINSTANCE hThisInst, HINSTANCE hPrevInst,
                   LPSTR lpszArgs, int nWinMode)
{
  HWND hwnd;
  MSG msg;
  WNDCLASSEX wcl;

  // Define a window class.
  wcl.cbSize = sizeof(WNDCLASSEX);

  wcl.hInstance = hThisInst;       // handle to this instance
  wcl.lpszClassName = szWinName; // window class name
  wcl.lpfnWndProc = WindowFunc;  // window function
  wcl.style = CS_DBLCLKS;        // allow double-clicks

  wcl.hIcon = LoadIcon(NULL, IDI_APPLICATION); // large icon
  wcl.hIconSm = NULL; // use small version of large icon
  wcl.hCursor = LoadCursor(NULL, IDC_ARROW);   // cursor style

  wcl.lpszMenuName = NULL; // no class menu
  wcl.cbClsExtra = 0;        // no extra memory needed
  wcl.cbWndExtra = 0;

  // Make the window background white.
  wcl.hbrBackground = (HBRUSH) GetStockObject(WHITE_BRUSH);

  // Register the window class.
  if(!RegisterClassEx(&wcl)) return 0;

  /* Now that a window class has been registered, a window
     can be created. */
```

```
        hwnd = CreateWindow(
          szWinName, // name of window class
          "Processing Double-Clicks", // title
          WS_OVERLAPPEDWINDOW, // window style - normal
          CW_USEDEFAULT, // X coordinate - let Windows decide
          CW_USEDEFAULT, // Y coordinate - let Windows decide
          CW_USEDEFAULT, // width - let Windows decide
          CW_USEDEFAULT, // height - let Windows decide
          NULL,          // no parent window
          NULL,          // no menu
          hThisInst,     // instance handle
          NULL           // no additional arguments
        );

        // save original double-click time interval
        OrgDblClkTime = GetDoubleClickTime();

        // Display the window.
        ShowWindow(hwnd, nWinMode);
        UpdateWindow(hwnd);

        // Create the message loop.
        while(GetMessage(&msg, NULL, 0, 0))
        {
          TranslateMessage(&msg); // translate keyboard messages
          DispatchMessage(&msg);  // return control to Windows 2000
        }

        return msg.wParam;
      }

      LRESULT CALLBACK WindowFunc(HWND hwnd, UINT message,
                                  WPARAM wParam, LPARAM lParam)
      {
        HDC hdc;
        UINT interval;

        switch(message) {
          case WM_KEYDOWN:
            if((char)wParam == VK_UP) { // increase interval
              interval = GetDoubleClickTime();
              interval += 100;
              SetDoubleClickTime(interval);
            }
```

```
      if((char)wParam == VK_DOWN) { // decrease interval
        interval = GetDoubleClickTime();
        interval -= 100;
        if(interval < 0) interval = 0;
        SetDoubleClickTime(interval);
      }
      sprintf(str, "New interval is %u milliseconds",
              interval);
      MessageBox(hwnd, str, "Setting Double-Click Interval",
                MB_OK);
      break;
    case WM_RBUTTONDOWN: // process right button
      hdc = GetDC(hwnd); // get DC
      sprintf(str, "Right button is down at %d, %d",
              LOWORD(lParam), HIWORD(lParam));
      TextOut(hdc, LOWORD(lParam), HIWORD(lParam),
            str, strlen(str));
      ReleaseDC(hwnd, hdc); // Release DC
      break;
    case WM_LBUTTONDOWN: // process left button
      hdc = GetDC(hwnd); // get DC
      sprintf(str, "Left button is down at %d, %d",
              LOWORD(lParam), HIWORD(lParam));
      TextOut(hdc, LOWORD(lParam), HIWORD(lParam),
              str, strlen(str));
      ReleaseDC(hwnd, hdc); // Release DC
      break;
    case WM_LBUTTONDBLCLK: // process left button double-click
      interval = GetDoubleClickTime();
      sprintf(str, "Left Button\nInterval is %u milliseconds",
              interval);
      MessageBox(hwnd, str, "Double Click", MB_OK);
      break;
    case WM_RBUTTONDBLCLK: // process right button double-click
      interval = GetDoubleClickTime();
      sprintf(str, "Right Button\nInterval is %u milliseconds",
              interval);
      MessageBox(hwnd, str, "Double Click", MB_OK);
      break;
    case WM_DESTROY: // terminate the program
      SetDoubleClickTime(OrgDblClkTime); // restore interval
      PostQuitMessage(0);
      break;
```

```
        default:
          /* Let Windows 2000 process any messages not specified in
             the preceding switch statement. */
          return DefWindowProc(hwnd, message, wParam, lParam);
    }

    return 0;
}
```

3

More Messages

As mentioned at the start, Windows 2000 generates many more messages than the ones described in this chapter. Others are described, as needed, throughout the rest of this book. Even so, you will still want to study the Windows 2000 messages on your own. The Windows 2000 message environment is both rich and varied.

CHAPTER 4

Introducing Menus

This chapter begins our exploration of Windows 2000's user interface. If you are learning to program Windows for the first time, it is important to understand that your application will most often communicate with the user through one or more predefined interface components. There are several different types of these supported by Windows. This chapter introduces the most fundamental: the *menu*. Virtually any program you write will use one. As you will see, the basic style of the menu is predefined. You need only supply the specific information that relates to your application. Because of their importance, Windows 2000 provides extensive support for menus. The topic is a large one, and this chapter describes the fundamentals. Later, the advanced features are covered.

This chapter also introduces the *resource*. A resource is, essentially, an object defined outside your program but used by your program. Icons, cursors, bitmaps, and menus themselves are common resources. Resources are a crucial part of nearly all Windows applications.

Menu Basics

The most common element of control within a Windows program is the menu. Windows 2000 supports three general types:

The menu bar is an application's top-most menu.

1. The menu bar (or main menu)
2. Pop-up submenus
3. Floating, stand-alone pop-up menus

In a Windows application, the menu bar is displayed across the top of the window. This is frequently called the main menu. The menu bar is your application's top-level menu. Submenus descend from the menu bar and are displayed as pop-up menus. (You should be accustomed to this approach because virtually all Windows programs use it.) Floating pop-up menus are free-standing menus that are typically activated by pressing the right mouse button. In this chapter, we will explore the first two types: the menu bar and pop-up submenus. Floating menus are described in a later chapter.

A pop-up submenu drops down from the main menu.

It is actually quite easy to add a menu bar to your program's main window. To do so involves just these three steps:

A floating pop-up menu is a free-standing menu.

1. Define the form of the menu in a resource file.
2. Load the menu when your program creates its main window.
3. Process menu selections.

In the remainder of this chapter, you will see how to implement these steps.

Resources

A resource is an object used by your program, but defined outside of it. A menu is one type of resource.

Windows defines several common types of objects as *resources*. As was previously mentioned, resources are essentially objects that are used by your program but are defined outside your program. A menu is one type of resource. A resource is created separately from your program, but is added to the EXE file when your program is linked. Resources are contained in *resource files*, which have the extension RC. For small projects, the name of the resource file is often the same as that of your program's EXE file. For example, if your program is called PROG.EXE, then its resource file will typically be called PROG.RC. Of course, you can call a resource file by any name you like as long as it has the RC extension.

4

Some resources are text files that you create using a standard text editor. Text resources are typically defined within the resource file. Others, such as icons, are most easily generated using a resource editor, but they still must be referred to in the RC file that is associated with your application. The resource files in this chapter are text files because menus are text-based resources.

Resources are contained within a resource file, which uses the RC extension.

Resource files do not contain C/C++ statements. Instead, resource files consist of special resource statements. In the course of this chapter, the resource commands needed to support menus are discussed. Others are described as needed throughout this book.

Compiling RC Files

Resource files are not used directly by your program. Instead, they must be converted into a linkable format. Once you have created an RC file, you compile it into a RES file using a *resource compiler*. (Often, the resource compiler is called RC.EXE, but this varies.) Exactly how you compile a resource file will depend upon what compiler you are using. Also, most integrated development environments handle this phase for you. For example, Microsoft's Visual C++ compiles and incorporates resource files automatically. In any event, the output of the resource compiler will be an RES file, and it is this file that is linked with your program to build the complete Windows 2000 application.

Creating a Simple Menu

Menus are defined within a resource file by using the **MENU** resource statement. All menu definitions have this general form:

```
MenuName MENU [options]
{
   menu items
}
```

Here, *MenuName* is the name of the menu. (It may also be an integer value
identifying the menu, but all examples in this book will use the name when
referring to the menu.) The keyword **MENU** tells the resource compiler that a
menu is being created. There are only a few options that apply to Windows
2000 programs. They are shown here:

Option	Meaning
CHARACTERISTICS *info*	Application-specific information, which is specified as a DWORD value in *info*.
LANGUAGE *lang, sub-lang*	The language used by the resource is specified by *lang* and *sub-lang*. This is used by internationalized menus.
VERSION *ver*	Application-defined version number is specified in the DWORD *ver*.

Most simple applications do not require the use of any options and use the
default settings.

HISTORICAL PERSPECTIVE: 16-bit Windows 3.1 defines several
additional options that may be applied to a **MENU** statement, such as
PRELOAD. But they have no effect for Windows 2000 programs. When
porting code, you can eliminate these obsolete options.

There are two types of items that can be used to define a menu: **MENUITEM**s
and **POPUP**s. A **MENUITEM** specifies a final selection. A **POPUP** specifies a
pop-up submenu, which may contain other **MENUITEM**s or **POPUP**s. The
general form of these two statements is shown here:

MENUITEM *"ItemName"*, *MenuID* [, *Options*]

POPUP *"PopupName"* [, *Options*]

Here, *ItemName* is the name of the menu selection, such as "Help" or "File."
MenuID is a unique integer associated with a menu item that will be sent to

your application when a selection is made. Typically, these values are defined as macros inside a header file that is included in both your application code and in its resource file. *PopupName* is the name of the pop-up menu. For both cases, the values for *Options* (defined by including WINDOWS.H) are shown in Table 4-1.

Here is a simple menu that will be used by subsequent example programs. Call the file MENU.RC.

```
// Sample menu resource file.
#include "menu.h"

MyMenu MENU
{
  POPUP "&File"
  {
    MENUITEM "&Open", IDM_OPEN
    MENUITEM "&Close", IDM_CLOSE
    MENUITEM "E&xit", IDM_EXIT
  }
  POPUP "&Options"
  {
    MENUITEM "&Colors", IDM_COLORS
    POPUP "&Priority"
    {
      MENUITEM "&Low", IDM_LOW
      MENUITEM "&High", IDM_HIGH
    }
    MENUITEM "&Fonts", IDM_FONT
    MENUITEM "&Resolution", IDM_RESOLUTION
  }
  MENUITEM "&Help", IDM_HELP
}
```

4

This menu, called **MyMenu**, contains three top-level, menu bar options: File, Options, and Help. The File and Options entries contain pop-up submenus. The Priority option activates a pop-up submenu of its own. Notice that the options that activate submenus do not have menu ID values associated with them. Only actual menu items have ID numbers. In this menu, all menu ID values are specified as macros beginning with **IDM**. (These macros are defined in the header file MENU.H.) The names you give these values are arbitrary.

An **&** in an item's name causes the key that it precedes to become the shortcut key associated with that option. That is, once that menu is active, pressing that key causes that menu item to be selected. It doesn't have to be the first key in the name, but usually it should be unless a conflict with

Option	Meaning
CHECKED	A check mark is displayed next to the name. (Not applicable to top-level menus.)
GRAYED	The name is shown in gray and cannot be selected.
HELP	May be associated with a help selection.
INACTIVE	The option cannot be selected.
MENUBARBREAK	For menu bar, causes the item to be put on a new line. For pop-up menus, causes the item to be put in a different column. In this case, the item is separated using a bar.
MENUBREAK	Same as MENUBARBREAK, except that no separator bar is used.
SEPARATOR	Creates an empty menu item that acts as a separator. Applies to MENUITEMs only.

The
MENUITEM
and **POPUP**
Options
Table 4-1.

another name exists, or, as is the case with Exit, a different letter is most naturally associated with the option.

As MENU.RC shows, you can embed comments into a resource file on a line-by-line basis using C/C++ style comments.

The MENU.H header file, which is included in MENU.RC, contains the macro definitions of the menu ID values. It is shown here:

```
#define IDM_OPEN         100
#define IDM_CLOSE        101
#define IDM_EXIT         102
#define IDM_COLORS       103
#define IDM_LOW          104
#define IDM_HIGH         105
#define IDM_FONT         106
#define IDM_RESOLUTION   107
#define IDM_HELP         108
```

This file defines the menu ID values that will be returned when the various menu items are selected. This file will also be included in the program that uses the menu. Remember, the actual names and values you give the menu items are arbitrary, but each value must be unique. Also, the valid range for ID values is 1 through 65,565.

Including a Menu in Your Program

Once you have created a menu, the easiest way to include that menu in a program is by specifying its name when you create the window's class. Specifically, you assign **lpszMenuName** a pointer to a string that contains the name of the menu. For example, to use **MyMenu**, you would write this line when defining the window's class:

```
wcl.lpszMenuName = "MyMenu"; // main menu
```

Now, **MyMenu** is the default main menu for all windows of its class. This means that all windows of this type will have the menu defined by **MyMenu**. (As you will see, you can override this class menu, if you like.)

4

Responding to Menu Selections

Each time the user makes a menu selection, your program's window function is sent a **WM_COMMAND** command message. When that message is received, the value of **LOWORD(wParam)** contains the menu item's ID value. That is, **LOWORD(wParam)** contains the value you associated with the item when you defined the menu in its RC file. Since **WM_COMMAND** is sent whenever a menu item is selected and the value associated with that item is contained in **LOWORD(wParam)**, you will need to use a nested **switch** statement to determine which item was selected. For example, this fragment responds to a selection made from **MyMenu**.

```
switch(message) {
  case WM_COMMAND:
    switch(LOWORD(wParam)) {
      case IDM_OPEN:
        MessageBox(hwnd, "Open File", "Open", MB_OK);
        break;
      case IDM_CLOSE:
        MessageBox(hwnd, "Close File", "Close", MB_OK);
        break;
      case IDM_EXIT:
        response = MessageBox(hwnd, "Quit the Program?",
                             "Exit", MB_YESNO);
        if(response == IDYES) PostQuitMessage(0);
        break;
      case IDM_COLORS:
        MessageBox(hwnd, "Set Colors", "Colors", MB_OK);
        break;
      case IDM_LOW:
```

```
      MessageBox(hwnd, "Low", "Priority", MB_OK);
      break;
    case IDM_HIGH:
      MessageBox(hwnd, "High", "Priority", MB_OK);
      break;
    case IDM_RESOLUTION:
       MessageBox(hwnd, "Resolution Options",
                         "Resolution", MB_OK);
      break;
    case IDM_FONT:
      MessageBox(hwnd, "Font Options","Fonts", MB_OK);
      break;
    case IDM_HELP:
      MessageBox(hwnd, "No Help", "Help", MB_OK);
      break;
  }
  break;
```

For the sake of illustration, the response to each selection simply displays an acknowledgment of that selection on the screen. Of course, real applications will perform the specified operations.

A Sample Menu Program

Here is a program that demonstrates the previously defined menu. Sample output from the program is shown in Figure 4-1.

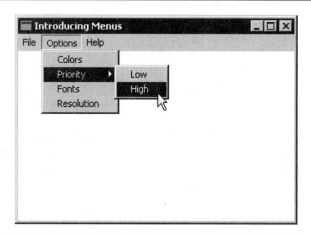

Sample output from the menu example

Figure 4-1.

```cpp
// Demonstrate menus.

#include <windows.h>
#include <cstring>
#include <cstdio>
#include "menu.h"

LRESULT CALLBACK WindowFunc(HWND, UINT, WPARAM, LPARAM);

char szWinName[] = "MyWin"; // name of window class

int WINAPI WinMain(HINSTANCE hThisInst, HINSTANCE hPrevInst,
                   LPSTR lpszArgs, int nWinMode)
{
  HWND hwnd;
  MSG msg;
  WNDCLASSEX wcl;

  // Define a window class.
  wcl.cbSize = sizeof(WNDCLASSEX);

  wcl.hInstance = hThisInst;      // handle to this instance
  wcl.lpszClassName = szWinName; // window class name
  wcl.lpfnWndProc = WindowFunc;   // window function
  wcl.style = 0;                  // default style

  wcl.hIcon = LoadIcon(NULL, IDI_APPLICATION); // large icon
  wcl.hIconSm = NULL; // use small version of large icon
  wcl.hCursor = LoadCursor(NULL, IDC_ARROW);  // cursor style

  // Specify name of menu resource.
  wcl.lpszMenuName = "MyMenu";

  wcl.cbClsExtra = 0; // no extra memory needed
  wcl.cbWndExtra = 0;

  // Make the window background white.
  wcl.hbrBackground = (HBRUSH) GetStockObject(WHITE_BRUSH);

  // Register the window class.
  if(!RegisterClassEx(&wcl)) return 0;

  // Create the window.
  hwnd = CreateWindow(
    szWinName, // name of window class
```

```
            "Introducing Menus", // title
            WS_OVERLAPPEDWINDOW, // window style - normal
            CW_USEDEFAULT, // X coordinate - let Windows decide
            CW_USEDEFAULT, // Y coordinate - let Windows decide
            CW_USEDEFAULT, // width - let Windows decide
            CW_USEDEFAULT, // height - let Windows decide
            NULL,          // no parent window
            NULL,          // no menu
            hThisInst,     // instance handle
            NULL           // no additional arguments
  );

  // Display the window.
  ShowWindow(hwnd, nWinMode);
  UpdateWindow(hwnd);

  // Create the message loop.
  while(GetMessage(&msg, NULL, 0, 0))
  {
    TranslateMessage(&msg); // translate keyboard messages
    DispatchMessage(&msg);  // return control to Windows 2000
  }

  return msg.wParam;
}

/* This function is called by Windows 2000 and is passed
   messages from the message queue.
*/
LRESULT CALLBACK WindowFunc(HWND hwnd, UINT message,
                            WPARAM wParam, LPARAM lParam)
{
  int response;

  switch(message) {
    case WM_COMMAND:
      switch(LOWORD(wParam)) {
        case IDM_OPEN:
          MessageBox(hwnd, "Open File", "Open", MB_OK);
          break;
        case IDM_CLOSE:
```

```
               MessageBox(hwnd, "Close File", "Close", MB_OK);
               break;
            case IDM_EXIT:
               response = MessageBox(hwnd, "Quit the Program?",
                                     "Exit", MB_YESNO);
               if(response == IDYES) PostQuitMessage(0);
               break;
            case IDM_COLORS:
               MessageBox(hwnd, "Set Colors", "Colors", MB_OK);
               break;
            case IDM_LOW:
               MessageBox(hwnd, "Low", "Priority", MB_OK);
               break;
            case IDM_HIGH:
               MessageBox(hwnd, "High", "Priority", MB_OK);
               break;
            case IDM_RESOLUTION:
                MessageBox(hwnd, "Resolution Options",
                                 "Resolution", MB_OK);
               break;
            case IDM_FONT:
               MessageBox(hwnd, "Font Options","Fonts", MB_OK);
               break;
            case IDM_HELP:
               MessageBox(hwnd, "No Help", "Help", MB_OK);
               break;
        }
        break;
      case WM_DESTROY: // terminate the program
        PostQuitMessage(0);
        break;
      default:
        /* Let Windows 2000 process any messages not specified in
           the preceding switch statement. */
        return DefWindowProc(hwnd, message, wParam, lParam);
  }

  return 0;
}
```

4

IN DEPTH

Using MessageBox( ) Responses

In the example menu program, when the user selects Exit, the following
code sequence is executed:

```
case IDM_EXIT:
  response = MessageBox(hwnd, "Quit the Program?",
                        "Exit", MB_YESNO);
  if(response == IDYES) PostQuitMessage(0);
  break;
```

The message box displayed by this fragment is shown here:

As you can see, it contains two buttons: Yes and No. As discussed in
Chapter 3, a message box will return the user's response. In this case,
MessageBox( ) will return either **IDYES** or **IDNO.** If the user's response
is **IDYES,** then the program terminates. Otherwise, it continues
execution.

This is an example of a situation in which a message box is used to allow
the user to select between two courses of action. As you begin to write
your own Windows 2000 programs, keep in mind that the message box
is useful in any situation in which the user must choose from among a
small number of choices.

Adding Menu Accelerator Keys

There is a feature of Windows that is commonly used in conjunction with a
menu. This feature is the accelerator key. *Accelerator keys* are special
keystrokes you define that, when pressed, automatically select a menu option

even though the menu in which that option resides is not displayed. Put differently, you can select an item directly by pressing an accelerator key, bypassing the menu entirely. The term *accelerator key* is an accurate description because pressing one is a faster way to select a menu item than first activating a menu and then selecting the item.

To define accelerator keys relative to a menu, you must add an accelerator key table to your resource file. An accelerator table has this general form:

```
TableName ACCELERATORS [accel-options]
{
  Key1, MenuID1 [, type] [options]
  Key2, MenuID2 [, type] [options]
  Key3, MenuID3 [, type] [options]
      .
      .
      .
  KeyN, MenuIDN [, type] [options]
}
```

4

Here, *TableName* is the name of the accelerator table. An **ACCELERATORS** statement can have the same options as those described for **MENU**. If needed, they are specified by *accel-options*. However, most applications simply use the default settings.

An accelerator key allows you to select a menu item using the keyboard, bypassing the menu itself.

Inside the accelerator table, *Key* is the keystroke that selects the item and *MenuID* is the ID value associated with the desired item. The *type* specifies whether the key is a standard key (the default) or a virtual key. The *options* may be one of the following macros: **NOINVERT, ALT, SHIFT,** and **CONTROL. NOINVERT** prevents the selected menu item from being highlighted when its accelerator key is pressed. **ALT** specifies an ALT key. **SHIFT** specifies a SHIFT key. **CONTROL** specifies a CTRL key.

The value of *Key* will be either a quoted character, an ASCII integer value corresponding to a key, or a virtual key code. If a quoted character is used, then it is assumed to be an ASCII character. If it is an integer value, then you must tell the resource compiler explicitly that this is an ASCII character by specifying *type* as **ASCII**. If it is a virtual key, then *type* must be **VIRTKEY**.

If the key is an uppercase quoted character then its corresponding menu item will be selected if it is pressed while holding down the SHIFT key. If it is a lowercase character, then its menu item will be selected if the key is pressed by itself. If the key is specified as a lowercase character and **ALT** is specified as an option, then pressing ALT and the character will select the item. (If the

key is uppercase and **ALT** is specified, then you must press SHIFT and ALT to
select the item.) Finally, if you want the user to press CTRL and the character
to select an item, precede the key with a ^.

As explained in Chapter 3, a virtual key is a system-independent code for a
key. To use a virtual key as an accelerator, specify its macro for the *Key* and
specify **VIRTKEY** for its *type*. You may also specify **ALT, SHIFT,** or
CONTROL to achieve the desired key combination.

Here are some examples:

```
"A", IDM_x           // select by pressing Shift+A
"a", IDM_x           // select by pressing a
"^a", IDM_x          // select by pressing Ctrl+a
"a", IDM_x, ALT      // select by pressing Alt+a
VK_F2, IDM_x         // select by pressing F2
VK_F2, IDM_x, SHIFT  // select by pressing Shift+F2
```

Here is the MENU.RC resource file that also contains accelerator key
definitions for **MyMenu**.

```
// Sample menu resource file and accelerators.
#include <windows.h>
#include "menu.h"

MyMenu MENU
{
  POPUP "&File"
  {
    MENUITEM "&Open\tF2", IDM_OPEN
    MENUITEM "&Close\tF3", IDM_CLOSE
    MENUITEM "E&xit\tCtrl+X", IDM_EXIT
  }
  POPUP "&Options"
  {
    MENUITEM "&Colors\tCtrl+C", IDM_COLORS
    POPUP "&Priority"
    {
      MENUITEM "&Low\tF4", IDM_LOW
      MENUITEM "&High\tF5", IDM_HIGH
    }
    MENUITEM "&Fonts\tCtrl+F", IDM_FONT
    MENUITEM "&Resolution\tCtrl+R", IDM_RESOLUTION
  }
```

```
   MENUITEM "&Help", IDM_HELP
}

// Define menu accelerators
MyMenu ACCELERATORS
{
  VK_F2, IDM_OPEN, VIRTKEY
  VK_F3, IDM_CLOSE, VIRTKEY
  "^X", IDM_EXIT
  "^C", IDM_COLORS
  VK_F4, IDM_LOW, VIRTKEY
  VK_F5, IDM_HIGH, VIRTKEY
  "^F", IDM_FONT
  "^R", IDM_RESOLUTION
  VK_F1, IDM_HELP, VIRTKEY
}
```

4

Notice that the menu definition has been enhanced to display which accelerator key selects which option. Each item is separated from its accelerator key using a tab. The header file WINDOWS.H is included because it defines the virtual key macros.

Loading the Accelerator Table

Even though the accelerators are contained in the same resource file as the menu, they must be loaded separately using another API function called **LoadAccelerators( )**, whose prototype is

HACCEL LoadAccelerators(HINSTANCE *ThisInst*, LPCSTR *Name*);

where *ThisInst* is the instance handle of the application and *Name* is the name of the accelerator table. The function returns a handle to the accelerator table or **NULL** if the table cannot be loaded.

You must call **LoadAccelerators( )** soon after the window is created. For example, the following shows how to load the **MyMenu** accelerator table:

```
HACCEL hAccel;

hAccel = LoadAccelerators(hThisInst, "MyMenu");
```

The value of **hAccel** will be used later to help process accelerator keys.

Translating Accelerator Keys

Although the **LoadAccelerators( )** function loads the accelerator table, your program still cannot process accelerator keys unless you add another API function to the message loop. This function is called **TranslateAccelerator( ),** and its prototype is shown here:

int TranslateAccelerator(HWND *hwnd*, HACCEL *hAccel*, LPMSG *lpMess*);

Here, *hwnd* is the handle of the window for which accelerator keys will be translated. *hAccel* is the handle to the accelerator table that will be used. This is the handle returned by **LoadAccelerator( )**. Finally, *lpMess* is a pointer to the message. The **TranslateAccelerator( )** function returns true if an accelerator key was pressed and false otherwise.

TranslateAccelerator( ) translates an accelerator keystroke into its corresponding **WM_COMMAND** message and sends that message to the window. In this message, the value of **LOWORD(wParam)** will contain the ID associated with the accelerator key. Thus, to your program, the **WM_COMMAND** message will appear to have been generated by a menu selection.

Since **TranslateAccelerator( )** sends a **WM_COMMAND** message whenever an accelerator key is pressed, your program must not execute **TranslateMessage( )** or **DispatchMessage( )** when such a translation takes place. When using **TranslateAccelerator( )**, your message loop should look like this:

```
while(GetMessage(&msg, NULL, 0, 0))
{
  if(!TranslateAccelerator(hwnd, hAccel, &msg)) {
    TranslateMessage(&msg); // translate keyboard messages
    DispatchMessage(&msg);  // return control to Windows 2000
  }
}
```

Trying Accelerator Keys

To try using accelerators, substitute the following version of **WinMain( )** into the preceding application and add the accelerator table to your resource file.

```cpp
// Process accelerator keys.

#include <windows.h>
#include <cstring>
#include <cstdio>
#include "menu.h"

LRESULT CALLBACK WindowFunc(HWND, UINT, WPARAM, LPARAM);

char szWinName[] = "MyWin"; // name of window class

int WINAPI WinMain(HINSTANCE hThisInst, HINSTANCE hPrevInst,
                   LPSTR lpszArgs, int nWinMode)
{
  HWND hwnd;
  MSG msg;
  WNDCLASSEX wcl;
  HACCEL hAccel;

  // Define a window class.
  wcl.cbSize = sizeof(WNDCLASSEX);

  wcl.hInstance = hThisInst;     // handle to this instance
  wcl.lpszClassName = szWinName; // window class name
  wcl.lpfnWndProc = WindowFunc;  // window function
  wcl.style = 0;                 // default style

  wcl.hIcon = LoadIcon(NULL, IDI_APPLICATION); // large icon
  wcl.hIconSm = NULL; // use small version of large icon
  wcl.hCursor = LoadCursor(NULL, IDC_ARROW);   // cursor style

  // Specify name of menu resource.
  wcl.lpszMenuName = "MyMenu";

  wcl.cbClsExtra = 0; // no extra memory needed
  wcl.cbWndExtra = 0;

  // Make the window background white.
  wcl.hbrBackground = (HBRUSH) GetStockObject(WHITE_BRUSH);

  // Register the window class.
  if(!RegisterClassEx(&wcl)) return 0;

  // Create the window.
  hwnd = CreateWindow(
```

```
      szWinName, // name of window class
      "Adding Accelerator Keys", // title
      WS_OVERLAPPEDWINDOW, // window style - normal
      CW_USEDEFAULT, // X coordinate - let Windows decide
      CW_USEDEFAULT, // Y coordinate - let Windows decide
      CW_USEDEFAULT, // width - let Windows decide
      CW_USEDEFAULT, // height - let Windows decide
      NULL,          // no parent window
      NULL,          // no menu
      hThisInst,     // instance handle
      NULL           // no additional arguments
    );

    // Load the keyboard accelerators.
    hAccel = LoadAccelerators(hThisInst, "MyMenu");

    // Display the window.
    ShowWindow(hwnd, nWinMode);
    UpdateWindow(hwnd);

    // Create the message loop.
    while(GetMessage(&msg, NULL, 0, 0))
    {
      if(!TranslateAccelerator(hwnd, hAccel, &msg)) {
        TranslateMessage(&msg); // translate keyboard messages
        DispatchMessage(&msg);  // return control to Windows 2000
      }
    }

    return msg.wParam;
}
```

Non-Menu Accelerator Keys

Although keyboard accelerators are most commonly used to provide a fast means of selecting menu items, they are not limited to this role. For example, you can define an accelerator key for which there is no corresponding menu item. You might use such a key to activate a keyboard macro or to initiate some frequently used option. To define a non-menu accelerator key, simply add it to the accelerator table, assigning it a unique ID value.

As an example, let's add a non-menu accelerator key to the menu program. The key will be CTRL-T, and each time that it is pressed, the current time and

A Closer Look at WM_COMMAND

As you know, each time you make a menu selection or press an accelerator key, a **WM_COMMAND** message is sent and the value in **LOWORD(wParam)** contains the ID of the menu item selected or the accelerator key pressed. However, using only the value in **LOWORD(wParam)** it is not possible to determine which event occurred. In most situations, it doesn't matter whether the user actually made a menu selection or just pressed an acclerator key. But in those situations in which it does, you can find out because Windows provides this information in the high-order word of **wParam**. If the value in **HIWORD(wParam)** is 0, then the user has made a menu selection. If this value is 1, then the user pressed an accelerator key. For example, try substituting the following fragment into the menu program. It reports whether the Open option was selected using the menu or by pressing an accelerator key.

```
case IDM_OPEN:
  if(HIWORD(wParam))
    MessageBox(hwnd, "Open File via Accelerator", "Open",
              MB_OK);
  else
    MessageBox(hwnd, "Open File via Menu Selection", "Open",
              MB_OK);
  break;
```

The value of **lParam** for **WM_COMMAND** messages generated by menu selections or accelerator keys is unused and always contains **NULL**.

As you will see in the next chapter, a **WM_COMMAND** is also generated when the user interacts with various types of controls. In this case, the meaning of **lParam** and **wParam** are somewhat different. For example, the value of **lParam** will contain the handle of the control.

4

date will be displayed in a message box. The standard C/C++ time and date functions are used to obtain the current time and date. To begin, change the key table so that it looks like this:

```
MyMenu ACCELERATORS
{
  VK_F2, IDM_OPEN, VIRTKEY
  VK_F3, IDM_CLOSE, VIRTKEY
  "^X", IDM_EXIT
  "^C", IDM_COLORS
  VK_F4, IDM_LOW, VIRTKEY
  VK_F5, IDM_HIGH, VIRTKEY
  "^R", IDM_RESOLUTION
  "^F", IDM_FONT
  VK_F1, IDM_HELP, VIRTKEY
  "^T", IDM_TIME
}
```

Next, add this line to MENU.H:

```
#define IDM_TIME  500
```

Finally, substitute this version of **WindowFunc( )** into the menu program. You will also need to include the **<ctime>** header file.

```
LRESULT CALLBACK WindowFunc(HWND hwnd, UINT message,
                            WPARAM wParam, LPARAM lParam)
{
  int response;
  struct tm *tod;
  time_t t;
  char str[80];

  switch(message) {
    case WM_COMMAND:
      switch(LOWORD(wParam)) {
        case IDM_OPEN:
          MessageBox(hwnd, "Open File", "Open", MB_OK);
          break;
        case IDM_CLOSE:
          MessageBox(hwnd, "Close File", "Close", MB_OK);
          break;
        case IDM_EXIT:
```

```
          response = MessageBox(hwnd, "Quit the Program?",
                                "Exit", MB_YESNO);
          if(response == IDYES) PostQuitMessage(0);
          break;
        case IDM_COLORS:
          MessageBox(hwnd, "Set Colors", "Colors", MB_OK);
          break;
        case IDM_LOW:
          MessageBox(hwnd, "Low", "Priority", MB_OK);
          break;
        case IDM_HIGH:
          MessageBox(hwnd, "High", "Priority", MB_OK);
          break;
        case IDM_RESOLUTION:
           MessageBox(hwnd, "Resolution Options",
                            "Resolution", MB_OK);
          break;
        case IDM_FONT:
          MessageBox(hwnd, "Font Options","Fonts", MB_OK);
          break;
        case IDM_TIME: // show time
          t = time(NULL);
          tod = localtime(&t);
          strcpy(str, asctime(tod));
          str[strlen(str)-1] = '\0'; // remove /r/n
          MessageBox(hwnd, str, "Time and Date", MB_OK);
          break;
        case IDM_HELP:
          MessageBox(hwnd, "No Help", "Help", MB_OK);
          break;
      }
      break;
    case WM_DESTROY: // terminate the program
      PostQuitMessage(0);
      break;
    default:
      /* Let Windows 2000 process any messages not specified in
         the preceding switch statement. */
      return DefWindowProc(hwnd, message, wParam, lParam);
  }

  return 0;
}
```

When you run this program, each time you press CTRL-T, you will see a
message box similar to the following:

Overriding the Class Menu

In the preceding programs the main menu has been specified in the
lpszMenuName member of the **WNDCLASSEX** structure. This specifies
a class menu that will be used by all windows that are created of its class
and is the way that most main menus are specified for simple applications.
However, there is another way to specify a main menu that uses the
CreateWindow( ) function. As you may recall from Chapter 2,
CreateWindow( ) is defined like this:

```
HWND CreateWindow(
          LPCSTR lpClassName,   // name of window class
          LPCSTR lpWinName,     // title of window
          DWORD dwStyle,        // type of window
          int X, int Y,         // upper-left coordinates
          int Width, int Height,   // dimensions of window
          HWND hParent,         // handle of parent window
          HMENU hMenu,          // handle of main menu
          HINSTANCE hThisInst,  // handle of creator
          LPVOID lpszAdditional // pointer to additional info
);
```

Notice the *hMenu* parameter. It can be used to specify a main menu for the
window being created. In the preceding programs, this parameter has been
specified as **NULL**. When *hMenu* is **NULL**, the class menu is used. However, if
it contains the handle to a menu, then that menu will be used as the main
menu for the window. In this case, the menu specified by *hMenu* overrides
the class menu. Although simple applications, such as those shown in this
book, do not need to override the class menu, there can be times when doing
so is beneficial. For example, you might want to define a generic window
class that your application will tailor to specific needs.

To specify a main menu using **CreateWindow( )**, you need a handle to the menu. The easiest way to obtain one is by calling the **LoadMenu( )** API function, shown here.

HMENU LoadMenu(HINSTANCE *hInst*, LPCSTR *lpName*);

Here, *hInst* is the instance handle of your application. A pointer to the name of the menu is passed in *lpName*. **LoadMenu( )** returns a handle to the menu if successful or **NULL** on failure. Once you have obtained a handle to a menu, it can be used as the *hMenu* parameter to **CreateWindow( )**.

When you load a menu using **LoadMenu( )** you are creating an object that allocates memory. This memory must be released before your program ends. If the menu is linked to a window, then this is done automatically when your program terminates. However, when it is not, then you must free it explicitly. This is accomplished using the **DestroyMenu( )** API function. Its prototype is shown here:

4

BOOL DestroyMenu(HMENU *hMenu*);

Here, *hMenu* is the handle of the menu being destroyed. The function returns nonzero if successful or zero on failure. As stated, you will not need to use **DestroyMenu( )** if the menu you load is linked to a window.

An Example that Overrides the Class Menu

To illustrate how the class menu can be overridden, let's modify the preceding menu program. To do so, add a second menu, called **PlaceHolder**, to the MENU.RC file, as shown here:

```
// Define two menus.
#include <windows.h>
#include "menu.h"

// Placeholder class menu.
PlaceHolder MENU
{
  POPUP "&File"
  {
    MENUITEM "&Exit\tCtrl+X", IDM_EXIT
  }
  MENUITEM "&Help", IDM_HELP
}
```

```
// Menu used by CreateWindow.
MyMenu MENU
{
  POPUP "&File"
  {
    MENUITEM "&Open\tF2", IDM_OPEN
    MENUITEM "&Close\tF3", IDM_CLOSE
    MENUITEM "E&xit\tCtrl+X", IDM_EXIT
  }
  POPUP "&Options"
  {
    MENUITEM "&Colors\tCtrl+C", IDM_COLORS
    POPUP "&Priority"
    {
      MENUITEM "&Low\tF4", IDM_LOW
      MENUITEM "&High\tF5", IDM_HIGH
    }
    MENUITEM "&Font\tCtrl+F", IDM_FONT
    MENUITEM "&Resolution\tCtrl+R", IDM_RESOLUTION
  }
  MENUITEM "&Help", IDM_HELP
}

// Define menu accelerators
MyMenu ACCELERATORS
{
  VK_F2, IDM_OPEN, VIRTKEY
  VK_F3, IDM_CLOSE, VIRTKEY
  "^X", IDM_EXIT
  "^C", IDM_COLORS
  VK_F4, IDM_LOW, VIRTKEY
  VK_F5, IDM_HIGH, VIRTKEY
  "^F", IDM_FONT
  "^R", IDM_RESOLUTION
  VK_F1, IDM_HELP, VIRTKEY
  "^T", IDM_TIME
}
```

The **PlaceHolder** menu will be used as the class menu. That is, it will be assigned to the **lpszMenuName** member of **WNDCLASSEX**. **MyMenu** will be loaded separately and its handle will be used in the *hMenu* parameter of **CreateWindow( )**. Thus, **MyMenu** will override **PlaceHolder**.

The contents of MENU.H are shown here. They are unchanged from the original version except for the addition of **IDM_TIME**, from the previous section.

```
#define IDM_OPEN          100
#define IDM_CLOSE         101
#define IDM_EXIT          102
#define IDM_COLORS        103
#define IDM_LOW           104
#define IDM_HIGH          105
#define IDM_FONT          106
#define IDM_RESOLUTION    107
#define IDM_HELP          108
#define IDM_TIME          500
```

Here is the complete program that overrides the class menu. This program incorporates all of the features discussed in this chapter. Since we have made so many changes to the menu program throughout the course of this chapter, the entire program is shown here for your convenience.

```
// Overriding the class menu.

#include <windows.h>
#include <cstring>
#include <cstdio>
#include <ctime>
#include "menu.h"

LRESULT CALLBACK WindowFunc(HWND, UINT, WPARAM, LPARAM);

char szWinName[] = "MyWin"; // name of window class

int WINAPI WinMain(HINSTANCE hThisInst, HINSTANCE hPrevInst,
                   LPSTR lpszArgs, int nWinMode)
{
  HWND hwnd;
  MSG msg;
  WNDCLASSEX wcl;
  HACCEL hAccel;
  HMENU hMenu;

  // Define a window class.
  wcl.cbSize = sizeof(WNDCLASSEX);
```

4

```
wcl.hInstance = hThisInst;      // handle to this instance
wcl.lpszClassName = szWinName; // window class name
wcl.lpfnWndProc = WindowFunc;   // window function
wcl.style = 0;                  // default style

wcl.hIcon = LoadIcon(NULL, IDI_APPLICATION); // large icon
wcl.hIconSm = NULL; // use small version of large icon
wcl.hCursor = LoadCursor(NULL, IDC_ARROW);   // cursor style

// Specify name of menu resource -- this will be overridden.
wcl.lpszMenuName = "PlaceHolder";

wcl.cbClsExtra = 0; // no extra memory needed
wcl.cbWndExtra = 0;

// Make the window background white.
wcl.hbrBackground = (HBRUSH) GetStockObject(WHITE_BRUSH);

// Register the window class.
if(!RegisterClassEx(&wcl)) return 0;

// Load main menu manually.
hMenu = LoadMenu(hThisInst, "MyMenu");

// Create the window.
hwnd = CreateWindow(
  szWinName, // name of window class
  "Using an Alternative Menu", // title
  WS_OVERLAPPEDWINDOW, // window style - normal
  CW_USEDEFAULT, // X coordinate - let Windows decide
  CW_USEDEFAULT, // Y coordinate - let Windows decide
  CW_USEDEFAULT, // width - let Windows decide
  CW_USEDEFAULT, // height - let Windows decide
  NULL,          // no parent window
  hMenu,         // specify alternate main menu
  hThisInst,     // instance handle
  NULL           // no additional arguments
);

// Load the keyboard accelerators.
hAccel = LoadAccelerators(hThisInst, "MyMenu");

// Display the window.
ShowWindow(hwnd, nWinMode);
UpdateWindow(hwnd);
```

```
  // Create the message loop.
  while(GetMessage(&msg, NULL, 0, 0))
  {
    if(!TranslateAccelerator(hwnd, hAccel, &msg)) {
      TranslateMessage(&msg); // translate keyboard messages
      DispatchMessage(&msg);  // return control to Windows 2000
    }
  }

  return msg.wParam;
}

/* This function is called by Windows 2000 and is passed
   messages from the message queue.
*/
LRESULT CALLBACK WindowFunc(HWND hwnd, UINT message,
                            WPARAM wParam, LPARAM lParam)
{
  int response;
  struct tm *tod;
  time_t t;
  char str[80];

  switch(message) {
    case WM_COMMAND:
      switch(LOWORD(wParam)) {
        case IDM_OPEN:
          MessageBox(hwnd, "Open File", "Open", MB_OK);
          break;
        case IDM_CLOSE:
          MessageBox(hwnd, "Close File", "Close", MB_OK);
          break;
        case IDM_EXIT:
          response = MessageBox(hwnd, "Quit the Program?",
                               "Exit", MB_YESNO);
          if(response == IDYES) PostQuitMessage(0);
          break;
        case IDM_COLORS:
          MessageBox(hwnd, "Set Colors", "Colors", MB_OK);
          break;
        case IDM_LOW:
          MessageBox(hwnd, "Low", "Priority", MB_OK);
          break;
        case IDM_HIGH:
```

4

```
          MessageBox(hwnd, "High", "Priority", MB_OK);
          break;
       case IDM_RESOLUTION:
         MessageBox(hwnd, "Resolution Options",
                          "Resolution", MB_OK);
          break;
       case IDM_FONT:
          MessageBox(hwnd, "Font Options","Fonts", MB_OK);
          break;
       case IDM_TIME: // show time
          t = time(NULL);
          tod = localtime(&t);
          strcpy(str, asctime(tod));
          str[strlen(str)-1] = '\0'; // remove /r/n
          MessageBox(hwnd, str, "Time and Date", MB_OK);
          break;
       case IDM_HELP:
          MessageBox(hwnd, "No Help", "Help", MB_OK);
          break;
     }
     break;
   case WM_DESTROY: // terminate the program
     PostQuitMessage(0);
     break;
   default:
     /* Let Windows 2000 process any messages not specified in
        the preceding switch statement. */
     return DefWindowProc(hwnd, message, wParam, lParam);
  }

  return 0;
}
```

Pay special attention to the code inside **WinMain( )**. It creates a window class that specifies **PlaceHolder** as its class menu. However, before a window is actually created, **MyMenu** is loaded and its handle is used in the call to **CreateWindow( )**, causing the class menu to be overridden and **MyMenu** to be displayed. You might want to experiment with this program a little. For example, since the class menu is being overridden, there is no reason to specify one at all. To prove this, assign **lpszMenuName** the value **NULL**. The operation of the program is unaffected.

In this example, both **MyMenu** and **PlaceHolder** contain menus that can be processed by the same window function. That is, they both use the same set of menu IDs. (Of course, **PlaceHolder** contains only two selections.) This feature allows either menu to work in the preceding program. Although you are not restricted in the form or structure of an overriding menu, you must always make sure that whatever menu you use, your window function contains the proper code to respond to it.

Remember, it is usually easier to specify the main menu using **WNDCLASSEX** rather than **CreateWindow( )**. This is the approach used by the rest of the programs in this book.

One last point: since **MyMenu** is linked to the window created by **CreateWindow( )**, it is destroyed automatically when the program terminates. There is no need to call **DestroyMenu( )**.

4

More Menus to Come

The menus discussed in this chapter form the backbone of the Windows 2000 menu system. However, once you have learned more about Windows 2000 programming in general, we will return to the topic of menus. As you will see, there are several exciting features supported by these foundational input components.

CHAPTER 5

Dialog Boxes

Although menus are an important part of nearly every Windows 2000 application, they cannot be used to handle all types of user responses. For example, it would be difficult to use a menu to input the time or date. To handle this and other types of input, Windows supplies the *dialog box*. A dialog box is a special window that provides a flexible means by which the user can interact with your application. In general, dialog boxes allow the user to select or enter information that would be difficult or impossible to enter using a menu. In this chapter, you will learn how to create and manage a dialog box.

Within a dialog box, interaction with the user is performed through a control. In a sense, a dialog box is simply a container that holds various control elements. Three of Windows' standard controls will be discussed in this chapter.

As a means of illustrating the dialog box and several controls, a very simple database application will be developed. The database contains the titles of several books along with the names of their authors, publishers, and copyright dates. The dialog box created in this chapter will allow you to select a title and obtain information about it. While the database example is, necessarily, quite simple, it will give you the flavor of how a real application can effectively use a dialog box.

Dialog Boxes Use Controls

A control is a special window that provides for input or output.

By itself, a dialog box does nothing. Technically, the dialog box is simply a management device. It is the controls within the dialog box that interact with the user. Formally stated, a *control* is a special type of input or output window. A control is owned by its parent window, which, for the examples presented in this chapter, is the dialog box. Windows 2000 supports several standard controls, including push buttons, check boxes, radio buttons, list boxes, edit boxes, combo boxes, scroll bars, and static controls. (Windows 2000 also supports several enhanced controls, called *common controls,* which are discussed later in this book.) The examples in this chapter illustrate three of the standard controls: the push button, the list box, and the edit box. In the next chapter, other controls will be examined.

A *push button* is a control that the user "pushes on" to activate some response. You have already been using push buttons in message boxes. For example, the OK button that we have been using in most message boxes is a push button.

A *list box* displays a list of items from which the user selects one (or more). List boxes are commonly used to display things such as filenames.

An *edit box* allows the user to enter a string. Edit boxes provide all necessary text editing features. Therefore, to input a string, your program simply displays an edit box and waits until the user has finished typing in the string.

It is important to understand that controls both generate messages (when accessed by the user) and receive messages (from your application). A message generated by a control indicates what type of interaction the user has had with it. A message sent to the control is essentially an instruction to which the control must respond.

Modal vs. Modeless Dialog Boxes

A modal dialog box must be closed before its owner window can be reactivated.

There are two types of dialog boxes: *modal* and *modeless*. The most common dialog boxes are modal. A modal dialog box demands a response from the user before the program will continue. When a modal dialog box is active, the user cannot refocus input to another part of the application without first closing the dialog box. More precisely, the *owner window* of a modal dialog box is deactivated until the dialog box is closed. (The owner window is usually the one that activates the dialog box.)

5

A modeless dialog box allows its owner window to remain active.

A modeless dialog box does not prevent other parts of the program from being used. That is, it does not need to be closed before input can be refocused to another part of the program. The owner window of a modeless dialog box remains active. In essence, modeless dialog boxes are more independent than modal ones.

We will examine modal dialog boxes first, since they are the most common. A modeless dialog box example concludes this chapter.

Receiving Dialog Box Messages

A dialog box is a type of window. Events that occur within it are sent to your program using the same message passing mechanism that the main window uses. However, dialog box messages are not sent to your program's main window function. Instead, each dialog box that you define will need its own window function, which is generally called a *dialog function or dialog procedure*. This function must have the following prototype (of course, the name of the function may be anything that you like):

```
BOOL CALLBACK DFunc(HWND hdwnd, UINT message, WPARAM wParam,
                    LPARAM lParam);
```

Dialog box
messages are
handled by a
dialog
procedure.

As you can see, a dialog function receives the same parameters as your program's main window function. However, it differs from the main window function in that it returns a true or false result. As with your program's main window function, the dialog box window function will receive many messages. If it processes a message, then it must return true. If it does not respond to a message, it must return false.

Each control within a dialog box will be given its own resource ID. Each time that control is accessed by the user, a **WM_COMMAND** message will be sent to the dialog function, indicating the ID of the control and the type of action the user has taken. That function will then decode the message and take appropriate actions. This process parallels the way messages are decoded by your program's main window function.

Activating a Dialog Box

To activate a modal dialog box (that is, to cause it to be displayed) you must call the **DialogBox( )** API function, whose prototype is shown here:

```
int DialogBox(HINSTANCE hThisInst, LPCSTR lpName, HWND hwnd,
              DLGPROC lpDFunc);
```

Here, *hThisInst* is a handle to the current application that is passed to your program in the instance parameter to **WinMain( )**. The name of the dialog box as defined in the resource file is pointed to by *lpName*. The handle to the window that owns the dialog box is passed in *hwnd*. (This is typically the handle of the window that calls **DialogBox( )**.) The *lpDFunc* parameter contains a pointer to the dialog function described in the preceding section. If **DialogBox( )** fails, then it returns −1. Otherwise, the return value is that specified by **EndDialog( ),** discussed next.

HISTORICAL PERSPECTIVE: In 16-bit Windows, the *lpDFunc* parameter to **DialogBox**( ) is a pointer to a *procedure-instance*, which is a short piece of code that links the dialog function with the data segment that the program is currently using. A procedure-instance is obtained using the **MakeProcInstance( )** API function. However, this does not apply to Windows 2000. The *lpDFunc* parameter is a pointer to the dialog function itself. You should remove calls to **MakeProcInstance( )** if you are converting older, Win16 code.

Deactivating a Dialog Box

To deactivate (that is, destroy and remove from the screen) a modal dialog box, use **EndDialog( ).** It has this prototype:

> BOOL EndDialog(HWND *hdwnd*, int *nStatus*);

Here, *hdwnd* is the handle to the dialog box, and *nStatus* is a status code returned by the **DialogBox( )** function. (The value of *nStatus* may be ignored if it is not relevant to your program.) This function returns nonzero if successful and zero otherwise. (In normal situations, the function is successful.).

Creating a Simple Dialog Box

5

To illustrate the basic dialog box concepts, we will begin with a simple dialog box. This dialog box will contain four push buttons, called *Author*, *Publisher*, *Copyright*, and *Cancel*. When either the Author, Publisher, or Copyright button is pressed, it will activate a message box indicating the choice selected. (Later these push buttons will be used to obtain information from the database; for now, the message boxes are simply placeholders.) The dialog box will be removed from the screen when the Cancel button is pressed.

The Dialog Box Resource File

A dialog box is another resource that is contained in your program's resource file. Before developing a program that uses a dialog box, you will need a resource file that specifies one. Although it is possible to specify the contents of a dialog box using a text editor, entering its specifications as you do when creating a menu, this procedure is seldom followed. Instead, most programmers use a dialog editor because dialog box definitions involve the positioning of the various controls inside the dialog box, a task that is best done interactively. However, since the complete RC files for the examples in this chapter are supplied in their text form, you should simply enter them as text. Just remember that when creating your own dialog boxes, you will usually want to use a dialog editor.

Since, in practice, most dialog boxes are created using a dialog editor, only a brief explanation of the dialog box definition in the resource file is given for the examples in this chapter.

Dialog boxes are defined within your program's resource file using either the **DIALOG** or the **DIALOGEX** statement. **DIALOG** is now considered obsolete, but is still accepted. **DIALOGEX** supports several valuable extensions, some of which we will use in a later chapter. Since **DIALOGEX** is currently the recommended statement, we will be using it throughout this book. The form of **DIALOGEX** used in this chapter is shown here:

Dialog-name DIALOGEX *X, Y, Width, Height*
Features
{
Dialog-items
}

The *Dialog-name* is the name of the dialog box. The box's upper-left corner will be at *X,Y*, and the box will have the dimensions specified by *Width* and *Height*. One or more optional features of the dialog box may be specified. As you will see, two of these are the caption and the style of the box. The *Dialog-items* are the controls that comprise the dialog box.

The following resource file defines the dialog box required by the first example program. It includes a menu that is used to activate the dialog box, the menu accelerator keys, and then the dialog box, itself. You should enter it into your computer at this time, calling it DIALOG.RC.

```
// Sample dialog box and menu resource file.
#include <windows.h>
#include "dialog.h"

MyMenu MENU
{
  POPUP "&Dialog"
  {
    MENUITEM "&Dialog\tF2", IDM_DIALOG
    MENUITEM "E&xit\tCtrl+X", IDM_EXIT
  }
  MENUITEM "&Help", IDM_HELP
}

MyMenu ACCELERATORS
{
  VK_F2, IDM_DIALOG, VIRTKEY
```

```
    "^X", IDM_EXIT
    VK_F1, IDM_HELP, VIRTKEY
}


MyDB DIALOGEX 10, 10, 210, 110
CAPTION "Books Dialog Box"
STYLE DS_MODALFRAME | WS_POPUP | WS_CAPTION | WS_SYSMENU
{
    DEFPUSHBUTTON "Author", IDD_AUTHOR, 11, 10, 36, 14
    PUSHBUTTON "Publisher", IDD_PUBLISHER, 11, 34, 36, 14
    PUSHBUTTON "Copyright", IDD_COPYRIGHT, 11, 58, 36, 14
    PUSHBUTTON "Cancel", IDCANCEL, 11, 82, 36, 16
}
```

5

This defines a dialog box called **MyDB** that has its upper-left corner at
location 10, 10. Its width is 210, and its height is 110. The string after
CAPTION becomes the title of the dialog box. The **STYLE** statement
determines what type of dialog box is created. Some common style values,
including those used in this chapter, are shown in Table 5-1. You can OR
together the values that are appropriate for the style of dialog box that you
desire. These style values may also be used by other controls.

Value	Meaning
DS_MODALFRAME	Dialog box has a modal frame.
WS_BORDER	Include a border. This style can be used with modeless dialog boxes.
WS_CAPTION	Include title bar.
WS_CHILD	Create as child window.
WS_POPUP	Create as a pop-up window.
WS_SYSMENU	Include system menu.
WS_TABSTOP	Control can be tabbed to.
WS_VISIBLE	Box is visible when activated.

Some
Common
Dialog Box
Style Options
Table 5-1.

Within the **MyDB** definition are defined four push buttons. The first is the
default push button. This button is automatically highlighted when the
dialog box is first displayed. The general form of a push button declaration
is shown here:

   PUSHBUTTON *"string"*, *PBID*, *X*, *Y*, *Width*, *Height* [, *Style*]

Here, *string* is the text that will be shown inside the push button. *PBID* is the
value associated with the push button. It is this value that is returned to your
program when this button is pushed. The button's upper-left corner will be at
X,Y, and the button will have the dimensions specified by *Width* and *Height*.
Style determines the exact nature of the push button. If no style parameters
are included, then the style defaults to **WS_TABSTOP** and the button is
visible. To specify a default push button use the **DEFPUSHBUTTON**
statement. It has same parameters as the regular push buttons.

The header file DIALOG.H, which is also used by the example program, is
shown here:

```
#define IDM_DIALOG    100
#define IDM_EXIT      101
#define IDM_HELP      102

#define IDD_AUTHOR    200
#define IDD_PUBLISHER 201
#define IDD_COPYRIGHT 202
```

Enter this file now.

The Dialog Box Window Function

As stated earlier, events that occur with a dialog box are passed to the
window function associated with that dialog box and not to your program's
main window function. The following dialog box window function responds
to the events that occur within the **MyDB** dialog box.

```
// A simple dialog function.
BOOL CALLBACK DialogFunc(HWND hdwnd, UINT message,
                         WPARAM wParam, LPARAM lParam)
{
```

```
switch(message) {
  case WM_COMMAND:
    switch(LOWORD(wParam)) {
      case IDCANCEL:
        EndDialog(hdwnd, 0);
        return 1;
      case IDD_COPYRIGHT:
        MessageBox(hdwnd, "Copyright", "Copyright", MB_OK);
        return 1;
      case IDD_AUTHOR:
        MessageBox(hdwnd, "Author", "Author", MB_OK);
        return 1;
      case IDD_PUBLISHER:
        MessageBox(hdwnd, "Publisher", "Publisher", MB_OK);
        return 1;
    }
}

return 0;
}
```

Each time a control within the dialog box is accessed, a **WM_COMMAND** message is sent to **DialogFunc( )**, and **LOWORD(wParam)** contains the ID of the control affected. The handle of the control is passed in **lParam**.

DialogFunc( ) processes the four messages that can be generated by the box. If the user presses **Cancel**, then **IDCANCEL** is sent, causing the dialog box to be closed using a call to the API function **EndDialog( )**. (**IDCANCEL** is a standard ID defined by including WINDOWS.H.) Pressing any of the other three buttons causes a message box to be displayed that confirms the selection. As mentioned, these buttons will be used by later examples to display information from the database.

A First Dialog Box Sample Program

Here is the entire dialog box example. When the program begins execution, only the top-level menu is displayed on the menu bar. By selecting **Dialog**, the user causes the dialog box to be displayed. Once the dialog box is displayed, selecting a push button causes the appropriate response. A sample screen is shown in Figure 5-1. Notice that the **books** database is included in this program, but is not used. It is needed by subsequent examples.

5

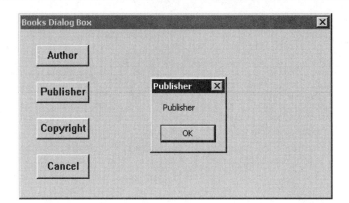

```
// Demonstrate a modal dialog box.

#include <windows.h>
#include <cstring>
#include <cstdio>
#include "dialog.h"

#define NUMBOOKS 7

LRESULT CALLBACK WindowFunc(HWND, UINT, WPARAM, LPARAM);
BOOL CALLBACK DialogFunc(HWND, UINT, WPARAM, LPARAM);

char szWinName[] = "MyWin"; // name of window class

HINSTANCE hInst;

// books database
struct booksTag {
  char title[40];
  unsigned copyright;
  char author[40];
  char publisher[40];
} books[NUMBOOKS] = {
  { "C++: The Complete Reference", 1998,
    "Herbert Schildt", "Osborne/McGraw-Hill" },
  { "MFC Programming from the Ground Up", 1998,
    "Herbert Schildt", "Osborne/McGraw-Hill" },
  { "Java: The Complete Reference", 1999,
    "Naughton and Schildt", "Osborne/McGraw-Hill" },
```

```
  { "The C++ Programming Language", 1997,
    "Bjarne Stroustrup", "Addison-Wesley" },
  { "Inside OLE", 1995,
    "Kraig Brockschmidt", "Microsoft Press" },
  { "HTML Sourcebook", 1996,
    "Ian S. Graham", "John Wiley & Sons" },
  { "Standard C++ Library", 1995,
    "P. J. Plauger", "Prentice-Hall" }
};

int WINAPI WinMain(HINSTANCE hThisInst, HINSTANCE hPrevInst,
                   LPSTR lpszArgs, int nWinMode)
{
  HWND hwnd;
  MSG msg;
  WNDCLASSEX wcl;
  HACCEL hAccel;

  // Define a window class.
  wcl.cbSize = sizeof(WNDCLASSEX);

  wcl.hInstance = hThisInst;      // handle to this instance
  wcl.lpszClassName = szWinName;  // window class name
  wcl.lpfnWndProc = WindowFunc;   // window function
  wcl.style = 0;                  // default style

  wcl.hIcon = LoadIcon(NULL, IDI_APPLICATION); // large icon
  wcl.hIconSm = NULL; // use small version of large icon
  wcl.hCursor = LoadCursor(NULL, IDC_ARROW);  // cursor style

  // Specify name of menu resource.
  wcl.lpszMenuName = "MyMenu";

  wcl.cbClsExtra = 0;        // no extra memory needed
  wcl.cbWndExtra = 0;

  // Make the window background white.
  wcl.hbrBackground = (HBRUSH) GetStockObject(WHITE_BRUSH);

  // Register the window class.
  if(!RegisterClassEx(&wcl)) return 0;

  /* Now that a window class has been registered, a window
     can be created. */
  hwnd = CreateWindow(
    szWinName, // name of window class
```

```
        "Demonstrate Dialog Boxes", // title
        WS_OVERLAPPEDWINDOW, // window style - normal
        CW_USEDEFAULT, // X coordinate - let Windows decide
        CW_USEDEFAULT, // Y coordinate - let Windows decide
        CW_USEDEFAULT, // width - let Windows decide
        CW_USEDEFAULT, // height - let Windows decide
        NULL,          // no parent window
        NULL,          // no override of class menu
        hThisInst,     // instance handle
        NULL           // no additional arguments
    );

    hInst = hThisInst; // save the current instance handle

    // Load accelerators.
    hAccel = LoadAccelerators(hThisInst, "MyMenu");

    // Display the window.
    ShowWindow(hwnd, nWinMode);
    UpdateWindow(hwnd);

    // Create the message loop.
    while(GetMessage(&msg, NULL, 0, 0))
    {
      if(!TranslateAccelerator(hwnd, hAccel, &msg)) {
        TranslateMessage(&msg); // translate keyboard messages
        DispatchMessage(&msg);  // return control to Windows 2000
      }
    }

    return msg.wParam;
}

/* This function is called by Windows 2000 and is passed
   messages from the message queue.
*/
LRESULT CALLBACK WindowFunc(HWND hwnd, UINT message,
                            WPARAM wParam, LPARAM lParam)
{
  int response;

  switch(message) {
    case WM_COMMAND:
      switch(LOWORD(wParam)) {
        case IDM_DIALOG:
          DialogBox(hInst, "MyDB", hwnd, (DLGPROC) DialogFunc);
          break;
```

```
          case IDM_EXIT:
            response = MessageBox(hwnd, "Quit the Program?",
                                  "Exit", MB_YESNO);
            if(response == IDYES) PostQuitMessage(0);
            break;
          case IDM_HELP:
            MessageBox(hwnd, "No Help", "Help", MB_OK);
            break;
        }
        break;
      case WM_DESTROY: // terminate the program
        PostQuitMessage(0);
        break;
      default:
        /* Let Windows 2000 process any messages not specified in
           the preceding switch statement. */
        return DefWindowProc(hwnd, message, wParam, lParam);
  }

  return 0;
}

// A simple dialog function.
BOOL CALLBACK DialogFunc(HWND hdwnd, UINT message,
                         WPARAM wParam, LPARAM lParam)
{
  switch(message) {
    case WM_COMMAND:
      switch(LOWORD(wParam)) {
        case IDCANCEL:
          EndDialog(hdwnd, 0);
          return 1;
        case IDD_COPYRIGHT:
          MessageBox(hdwnd, "Copyright", "Copyright", MB_OK);
          return 1;
        case IDD_AUTHOR:
          MessageBox(hdwnd, "Author", "Author", MB_OK);
          return 1;
        case IDD_PUBLISHER:
          MessageBox(hdwnd, "Publisher", "Publisher", MB_OK);
          return 1;
      }
  }

  return 0;
}
```

Notice the global variable **hInst**. This variable is assigned a copy of the current instance handle passed to **WinMain( )**. This variable is required because the dialog box needs access to the current instance handle. However, the dialog box is not created in **WinMain( )**. Instead, it is created in **WindowFunc( )**. Therefore, a copy of the instance parameter must be made so that it can be accessible outside of **WinMain( )**.

Adding a List Box

To continue exploring dialog boxes, let's add another control to the dialog box defined in the previous program. One of the most frequently used controls after the push button is the list box. We will use the list box to display a list of the titles in the database and allow the user to select the one he/she is interested in. The **LISTBOX** statement has this general form:

LISTBOX *LBID*, *X*, *Y*, *Width*, *Height* [, *Style*]

Here, *LBID* is the value that identifies the list box. The box's upper-left corner will be at *X,Y*, and the box will have the dimensions specified by *Width* and *Height*. *Style* determines the exact nature of the list box. In addition to the standard style values, the list box defines several of its own. Some commonly used ones are shown here:

LBS_NOTIFY	Notify parent when user double-clicks on an item.
LBS_SORT	The list is sorted.
LBS_MULTICOLUMN	List box has multiple columns.
LBS_EXTENDEDSEL	Two or more items can be selected. Normally, only one item can be selected at any one time.

If you don't specify a style, then **LBS_NOTIFY** and **WS_BORDER** are used by default and the list box is visible.

To add a list box you must change the dialog box definition in DIALOG.RC. First, add this list box description to the dialog box definition.

```
LISTBOX IDD_LB1, 60, 5, 140, 33, LBS_NOTIFY |
       WS_BORDER | WS_VSCROLL | WS_TABSTOP
```

Second, add this push button to the dialog box definition.

```
PUSHBUTTON "Select Book", IDD_SELECT, 103, 41, 54, 14
```

After these changes, your dialog box definition should now look like this:

```
MyDB DIALOGEX 10, 10, 210, 110
CAPTION "Books Dialog Box"
STYLE DS_MODALFRAME | WS_POPUP | WS_CAPTION | WS_SYSMENU
{
  DEFPUSHBUTTON "Author", IDD_AUTHOR, 11, 10, 36, 14
  PUSHBUTTON "Publisher", IDD_PUBLISHER, 11, 34, 36, 14
  PUSHBUTTON "Copyright", IDD_COPYRIGHT, 11, 58, 36, 14
  PUSHBUTTON "Cancel", IDCANCEL, 11, 82, 36, 16
  LISTBOX IDD_LB1, 60, 5, 140, 33, LBS_NOTIFY |
            WS_BORDER | WS_VSCROLL | WS_TABSTOP
  PUSHBUTTON "Select Book", IDD_SELECT, 103, 41, 54, 14
}
```

5

You will also need to add these macros to DIALOG.H:

```
#define IDD_LB1     203
#define IDD_SELECT  204
```

IDD_LB1 identifies the list box specified in the dialog box definition in the resource file. **IDD_SELECT** is the ID value of the Select Book push button.

List Box Basics

When using a list box, you must perform two operations. First, you must initialize the list box when the dialog box is first displayed. This task consists of sending the list box the list that it will display. (By default, the list box will be empty.) Second, once the list box has been initialized, you will need to respond to the user selecting an item from the list.

A notification message describes a control event.

List boxes generate various types of *notification messages*. A notification message describes what type of control event has occurred. (Several of the standard controls generate notification messages.) For the list box used in the following example, the only notification message we will use is **LBN_DBLCLK**. This message is sent when the user has double-clicked on an entry in the list. This message is contained in **HIWORD(wParam)** each time a **WM_COMMAND** is generated for the list box. (The list box must have the **LBS_NOTIFY** style flag included in its definition in order to generate **LBN_DBLCLK** messages.) Once a selection has been made, you will need to query the list box to find out which item has been selected.

To receive double-click messages, a list box must include the LBS_NOTIFY style.

Unlike a push button, a list box is a control that receives messages as well as generates them. You can send a list box several different messages.

To send a message to the list box (or any other control) use the **SendDlgItemMessage( )** API function. Its prototype is shown here:

LONG SendDlgItemMessage(HWND *hdwnd*, int *ID*, UINT *IDMsg*,
                        WPARAM *wParam*, LPARAM *lParam*);

SendDlgItemMessage( ) sends to the control (within the dialog box) whose ID is specified by *ID* the message specified by *IDMsg*. The handle of the dialog box is specified in *hdwnd*. Any additional information required by the message is specified in *wParam* and *lParam*. The additional information, if any, varies from message to message. If there is no additional information to pass to a control, the *wParam* and the *lParam* arguments should be 0. The value returned by **SendDlgItemMessage( )** contains the information requested by *IDMsg*.

Here are a few of the many messages that you can send to a list box.

Macro	Purpose
LB_ADDSTRING	Adds a string (selection) to the list box.
LB_GETCURSEL	Requests the index of the selected item.
LB_SETCURSEL	Selects an item.
LB_FINDSTRING	Finds a matching entry.
LB_SELECTSTRING	Finds a matching entry and selects it.
LB_GETTEXT	Obtains the text associated with an item.

Let's take a closer look at these messages, now.

LB_ADDSTRING adds a string to the list box. That is, the specified string becomes another selection within the box. The string must be pointed to by *lParam*. (*wParam* is unused by this message.) The value returned by the list box is the index of the string in the list. If an error occurs, **LB_ERR** is returned.

The **LB_GETCURSEL** message causes the list box to return the index of the currently selected item. All list box indexes begin with 0. Both *lParam* and *wParam* are unused. If an error occurs, **LB_ERR** is returned. If no item is currently selected, then an error results.

You can set the current selection inside a list box using the **LB_SETCURSEL** command. For this message, *wParam* specifies the index of the item to select. *lParam* is not used. On error, **LB_ERR** is returned.

You can find an item in the list that matches a specified prefix using **LB_FINDSTRING**. That is, **LB_FINDSTRING** attempts to match a partial string with an entry in the list box. *wParam* specifies the index at which point the search begins, and *lParam* points to the string that will be matched. If a match is found, the index of the matching item is returned. Otherwise, **LB_ERR** is returned. **LB_FINDSTRING** does not select the item within the list box.

If you want to find a matching item and select it, use **LB_SELECTSTRING**. It takes the same parameters as **LB_FINDSTRING** but also selects the matching item.

You can obtain the text associated with an item in a list box using **LB_GETTEXT**. In this case, *wParam* specifies the index of the item, and *lParam* points to the character array that will receive the null terminated string associated with that index. The length of the string is returned if successful. **LB_ERR** is returned on failure.

Initializing the List Box

As mentioned, when a list box is created, it is empty. This means that you will need to initialize it each time the dialog box is displayed. This is easy to accomplish because each time a dialog box is activated, its window function is sent a **WM_INITDIALOG** message. Therefore, you will need to add this case to the outer **switch** statement in **DialogFunc( )**.

```
case WM_INITDIALOG: // initialize list box
  for(i=0; i<NUMBOOKS; i++)
    SendDlgItemMessage(hdwnd, IDD_LB1,
              LB_ADDSTRING, 0, (LPARAM)books[i].title);
  // select first item
  SendDlgItemMessage(hdwnd, IDD_LB1, LB_SETCURSEL, 0, 0);

  return 1;
```

This code loads the list box with the titles of books as defined in the **books** array. Each string is added to the list box by calling **SendDlgItemMessage( )** with the **LB_ADDSTRING** message. The string to add is pointed to by the *lParam* parameter. (The type cast to **LPARAM** is necessary in this case to convert a pointer into an unsigned integer.) In this example, each string is added to the list box in the order it is sent. (However, if the list box includes the **LBS_SORT** style, the items will be stored in alphabetical order.) If the number of items you send to a list box is more than can be displayed in its window, vertical scroll bars will be added automatically.

This code also selects the first item in the list box. When a list box is first created, no item is selected. While this might be desirable under certain circumstances, it is not in this case. Most often, you will want to automatically select the first item in a list box as a convenience to the user.

REMEMBER: **WM_INITDIALOG** is sent to a dialog box each time it is activated. You should perform all initializations required by the dialog box when this message is received.

Processing a Selection

After the list box has been initialized, it is ready for use. There are essentially two ways a user makes a selection from a list box. First, the user can double-click on an item in the list box. Doing this causes a **WM_COMMAND** message to be passed to the dialog box's window function. In this case, **LOWORD(wParam)** contains the ID associated with the list box, and **HIWORD(wParam)** contains the **LBN_DBLCLK** notification message. Double-clicking causes your program to be immediately aware of the user's selection. The other way to use a list box is to simply highlight a selection (either by single-clicking or by using the arrow keys to move the highlight). The list box remembers the selection and waits until your program requests it. Both methods are demonstrated in the example program.

Once an item has been selected in a list box, you determine which item was chosen by sending the **LB_GETCURSEL** message to the list box. The list box then returns the index of the selected item. If this message is sent before an item has been selected, the list box returns **LB_ERR**. This is one reason why it is a good idea to select an item when the list box is initialized.

To demonstrate how to process a list box selection, add the following cases to the inner switch inside **DialogFunc( )**. You will also need to declare a long integer called **i** and character array called **str** inside **DialogFunc( )**. Your dialog box will now look like that shown in Figure 5-2. Each time a selection is made because of a double-click or when the user presses the "Select Book" push button, the currently selected book has its information displayed.

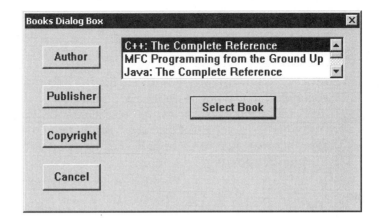

A dialog box
that contains a
list box

Figure 5-2.

5

```
case IDD_LB1: // process a list box LBN_DBLCLK
  // see  if user made a selection
  if(HIWORD(wParam)==LBN_DBLCLK) {
    i = SendDlgItemMessage(hdwnd, IDD_LB1,
            LB_GETCURSEL, 0, 0);  // get index
    sprintf(str, "%s\n%s\n%s, %u",
            books[i].title, books[i].author,
            books[i].publisher, books[i].copyright);

    MessageBox(hdwnd, str, "Selection Made", MB_OK);

    // get string associated with that index
    SendDlgItemMessage(hdwnd, IDD_LB1, LB_GETTEXT,
        i, (LPARAM) str);
  }
  return 1;
case IDD_SELECT: // Select Book button has been pressed
  i = SendDlgItemMessage(hdwnd, IDD_LB1,
          LB_GETCURSEL, 0, 0);  // get index
  sprintf(str, "%s\n%s\n%s, %u",
          books[i].title, books[i].author,
          books[i].publisher, books[i].copyright);

  MessageBox(hdwnd, str, "Selection Made", MB_OK);

  // get string associated with that index
```

```
SendDlgItemMessage(hdwnd, IDD_LB1, LB_GETTEXT,
    i, (LPARAM) str);

return 1;
```

Notice the code under the **IDD_LB1** case. Since the list box can generate several different types of notification messages, it is necessary to examine the high-order word of **wParam** to determine if the user double-clicked on an item. That is, just the fact that the control generates a notification message does not mean that it is a double-click message. (You will want to explore the other list box notification messages on your own.)

Adding an Edit Box

In this section we will add an edit control to the dialog box. Edit boxes are particularly useful because they allow users to enter a string of their own choosing. The edit box in this example will be used to allow the user to enter the title (or part of a title) of a book. If the title is in the list, then it will be selected and information about the book can be obtained. Although the addition of an edit box enhances our simple database application, it also serves another purpose. It will illustrate how two controls can work together.

Before you can use an edit box, you must define one in your resource file. For this example, change **MyDB** so that it looks like this:

```
MyDB DIALOGEX 10, 10, 210, 110
CAPTION "Books Dialog Box"
STYLE DS_MODALFRAME | WS_POPUP | WS_CAPTION | WS_SYSMENU
{
  DEFPUSHBUTTON "Author", IDD_AUTHOR, 11, 10, 36, 14
  PUSHBUTTON "Publisher", IDD_PUBLISHER, 11, 34, 36, 14
  PUSHBUTTON "Copyright", IDD_COPYRIGHT, 11, 58, 36, 14
  PUSHBUTTON "Cancel", IDCANCEL, 11, 82, 36, 16
  LISTBOX IDD_LB1, 60, 5, 140, 33, LBS_NOTIFY |
            WS_BORDER | WS_VSCROLL | WS_TABSTOP
  PUSHBUTTON "Select Book", IDD_SELECT, 103, 41, 54, 14
  EDITTEXT IDD_EB1, 65, 73, 130, 12, ES_LEFT |
            WS_BORDER | ES_AUTOHSCROLL | WS_TABSTOP
  PUSHBUTTON "Title Search", IDD_DONE, 107, 91, 46, 14
}
```

This version adds a push button called Title Search that will be used to tell the program that you entered the title of a book into the edit box. It also adds the edit box itself. The ID for the edit box is **IDD_EB1**. This definition causes a standard edit box to be created.

The **EDITTEXT** statement has this general form:

EDITTEXT *EDID, X, Y, Width, Height* [,*Style*]

Here, *EDID* is the value that identifies the edit box. The box's upper-left corner will be at *X,Y*, and its dimensions are specified by *Width* and *Height*. *Style* determines the exact nature of the listbox. In addition to the style values described in Table 5-1, **EDITTEXT** supports several of its own. Perhaps the most important is **ES_AUTOHSCROLL**, which automatically scrolls text, right to left, within the edit box.

Next, add these macro definitions to DIALOG.H:

```
#define IDD_EB1     205
#define IDD_DONE    206
```

Edit boxes recognize many messages and generate several of their own. However, for the purposes of this example, there is no need for the program to respond to any messages. As you will see, edit boxes perform the editing function on their own, independently. No program interaction is required. Your program simply decides when it wants to obtain the current contents of the edit box.

To obtain the current contents of the edit box, use the API function **GetDlgItemText( )**. It has this prototype:

UINT GetDlgItemText(HWND *hdwnd*, int *nID*, LPSTR *lpstr*, int *nMax*);

This function causes the edit box to copy the contents of the box to the string pointed to by *lpstr*. The handle of the dialog box is specified by *hdwnd*. The ID of the edit box is specified by *nID*. The maximum number of characters to copy is specified by *nMax*. The function returns the length of the string.

Although not required by all applications, it is possible to initialize the contents of an edit box using the **SetDlgItemText( )** function. Its prototype is shown here:

BOOL SetDlgItemText(HWND *hdwnd*, int *nID*, LPSTR *lpstr*);

This function sets the contents of the edit box to the string pointed to by *lpstr*. The handle of the dialog box is specified by *hdwnd*. The ID of the edit box is specified by *nID*. The function returns nonzero if successful or zero on failure.

To add an edit box to the sample program, add this case statement to the inner **switch** of the **DialogFunc( )** function. Each time the Title Search button is pressed, the list box is searched for a title that matches the string that is currently in the edit box. If a match is found, then that title is selected in the list box. Remember that you need to enter only the first few characters of the title. The list box will automatically attempt to match them with a title.

```
case IDD_DONE: // Title Search button pressed
  // get current contents of edit box
  GetDlgItemText(hdwnd, IDD_EB1, str, 80);

  // find a matching string in the list box
  i = SendDlgItemMessage(hdwnd, IDD_LB1, LB_FINDSTRING,
          0, (LPARAM) str);

  if(i != LB_ERR) { // if match is found
    // select the matching title in list box
    SendDlgItemMessage(hdwnd, IDD_LB1, LB_SETCURSEL, i, 0);

    // get string associated with that index
    SendDlgItemMessage(hdwnd, IDD_LB1, LB_GETTEXT,
        i, (LPARAM) str);

    // update text in edit box
    SetDlgItemText(hdwnd, IDD_EB1, str);
  }
  else
    MessageBox(hdwnd, str, "No Title Matching", MB_OK);
  return 1;
```

This code obtains the current contents of the edit box and looks for a match with the strings inside the list box. If it finds one, it selects the matching item in the list box and then copies the string from the list box back into the edit box. In this way, the two controls work together, complementing each other. As you become a more experienced Windows 2000 programmer, you will find that there are often instances in which two or more controls can work together.

You will also need to add this line of code to the **INITDIALOG** case—it causes the edit box to be initialized each time the dialog box is activated:

```
// initialize the edit box
SetDlgItemText(hdwnd, IDD_EB1, books[0].title);
```

In addition to these changes, the code that processes the list box will be enhanced so that it automatically copies the name of the book selected in the list box into the edit box. These changes are reflected in the full program listing given in the next section. You should have no trouble understanding them.

The Entire Modal Dialog Box Program

5

The entire modal dialog box sample program, which includes push buttons, a list box, and an edit box, is shown here. Notice that the code associated with the push buttons now displays information about the title currently selected in the list box.

```
// A complete modal dialog box example.
#include <windows.h>
#include <cstring>
#include <cstdio>
#include "dialog.h"

#define NUMBOOKS 7

LRESULT CALLBACK WindowFunc(HWND, UINT, WPARAM, LPARAM);
BOOL CALLBACK DialogFunc(HWND, UINT, WPARAM, LPARAM);

char szWinName[] = "MyWin"; // name of window class

HINSTANCE hInst;

// books database
struct booksTag {
  char title[40];
  unsigned copyright;
  char author[40];
  char publisher[40];
} books[NUMBOOKS] = {
  { "C++: The Complete Reference", 1998,
```

```
      "Herbert Schildt", "Osborne/McGraw-Hill" },
    { "MFC Programming from the Ground Up", 1998,
      "Herbert Schildt", "Osborne/McGraw-Hill" },
    { "Java: The Complete Reference", 1999,
      "Naughton and Schildt", "Osborne/McGraw-Hill" },
    { "The C++ Programming Language", 1997,
      "Bjarne Stroustrup", "Addison-Wesley" },
    { "Inside OLE", 1995,
      "Kraig Brockschmidt", "Microsoft Press" },
    { "HTML Sourcebook", 1996,
      "Ian S. Graham", "John Wiley & Sons" },
    { "Standard C++ Library", 1995,
      "P. J. Plauger", "Prentice-Hall" }
};

int WINAPI WinMain(HINSTANCE hThisInst, HINSTANCE hPrevInst,
                LPSTR lpszArgs, int nWinMode)
{
  HWND hwnd;
  MSG msg;
  WNDCLASSEX wcl;
  HACCEL hAccel;

  // Define a window class.
  wcl.cbSize = sizeof(WNDCLASSEX);

  wcl.hInstance = hThisInst;      // handle to this instance
  wcl.lpszClassName = szWinName; // window class name
  wcl.lpfnWndProc = WindowFunc;   // window function
  wcl.style = 0;                  // default style

  wcl.hIcon = LoadIcon(NULL, IDI_APPLICATION); // large icon
  wcl.hIconSm = NULL; // use small version of large icon
  wcl.hCursor = LoadCursor(NULL, IDC_ARROW);   // cursor style

  // Specify name of menu resource.
  wcl.lpszMenuName = "MyMenu";

  wcl.cbClsExtra = 0;      // no extra memory needed
  wcl.cbWndExtra = 0;

  // Make the window background white.
  wcl.hbrBackground = (HBRUSH) GetStockObject(WHITE_BRUSH);

  // Register the window class.
  if(!RegisterClassEx(&wcl)) return 0;
```

```c
   /* Now that a window class has been registered, a window
      can be created. */
   hwnd = CreateWindow(
     szWinName, // name of window class
     "Demonstrate Dialog Boxes", // title
     WS_OVERLAPPEDWINDOW, // window style - normal
     CW_USEDEFAULT, // X coordinate - let Windows decide
     CW_USEDEFAULT, // Y coordinate - let Windows decide
     CW_USEDEFAULT, // width - let Windows decide
     CW_USEDEFAULT, // height - let Windows decide
     NULL,          // no parent window
     NULL,          // no override of class menu
     hThisInst,     // instance handle
     NULL           // no additional arguments
   );

   hInst = hThisInst; // save the current instance handle

   // Load accelerators.
   hAccel = LoadAccelerators(hThisInst, "MyMenu");

   // Display the window.
   ShowWindow(hwnd, nWinMode);
   UpdateWindow(hwnd);

   // Create the message loop.
   while(GetMessage(&msg, NULL, 0, 0))
   {
     if(!TranslateAccelerator(hwnd, hAccel, &msg)) {
       TranslateMessage(&msg); // translate keyboard messages
       DispatchMessage(&msg);  // return control to Windows 2000
     }
   }

   return msg.wParam;
}

/* This function is called by Windows 2000 and is passed
   messages from the message queue.
*/
LRESULT CALLBACK WindowFunc(HWND hwnd, UINT message,
                            WPARAM wParam, LPARAM lParam)
{
  int response;

  switch(message) {
```

```
    case WM_COMMAND:
      switch(LOWORD(wParam)) {
        case IDM_DIALOG:
          DialogBox(hInst, "MyDB", hwnd, (DLGPROC) DialogFunc);
          break;
        case IDM_EXIT:
          response = MessageBox(hwnd, "Quit the Program?",
                                "Exit", MB_YESNO);
          if(response == IDYES) PostQuitMessage(0);
          break;
        case IDM_HELP:
          MessageBox(hwnd, "No Help", "Help", MB_OK);
          break;
      }
      break;
    case WM_DESTROY: // terminate the program
      PostQuitMessage(0);
      break;
    default:
      /* Let Windows 2000 process any messages not specified in
         the preceding switch statement. */
      return DefWindowProc(hwnd, message, wParam, lParam);
  }

  return 0;
}

// A simple dialog function.
BOOL CALLBACK DialogFunc(HWND hdwnd, UINT message,
                         WPARAM wParam, LPARAM lParam)
{
  long i;
  char str[255];

  switch(message) {
    case WM_COMMAND:
      switch(LOWORD(wParam)) {
        case IDCANCEL:
          EndDialog(hdwnd, 0);
          return 1;
        case IDD_COPYRIGHT:
          i = SendDlgItemMessage(hdwnd, IDD_LB1,
                  LB_GETCURSEL, 0, 0);  // get index
          sprintf(str, "%u", books[i].copyright);
          MessageBox(hdwnd, str, "Copyright", MB_OK);
          return 1;
```

```
case IDD_AUTHOR:
  i = SendDlgItemMessage(hdwnd, IDD_LB1,
         LB_GETCURSEL, 0, 0);  // get index
  sprintf(str, "%s", books[i].author);
  MessageBox(hdwnd, str, "Author", MB_OK);
  return 1;
case IDD_PUBLISHER:
  i = SendDlgItemMessage(hdwnd, IDD_LB1,
         LB_GETCURSEL, 0, 0);  // get index
  sprintf(str, "%s", books[i].publisher);
  MessageBox(hdwnd, str, "Publisher", MB_OK);
  return 1;
case IDD_DONE: // Title Search button pressed
  // get current contents of edit box
  GetDlgItemText(hdwnd, IDD_EB1, str, 80);

  // find a matching string in the list box
  i = SendDlgItemMessage(hdwnd, IDD_LB1, LB_FINDSTRING,
         0, (LPARAM) str);

  if(i != LB_ERR) { // if match is found
    // select the matching title in list box
    SendDlgItemMessage(hdwnd, IDD_LB1, LB_SETCURSEL, i, 0);

    // get string associated with that index
    SendDlgItemMessage(hdwnd, IDD_LB1, LB_GETTEXT,
        i, (LPARAM) str);

    // update text in edit box
    SetDlgItemText(hdwnd, IDD_EB1, str);
  }
  else
    MessageBox(hdwnd, str, "No Title Matching", MB_OK);
  return 1;
case IDD_LB1: // process a list box LBN_DBLCLK
  // see  if user made a selection
  if(HIWORD(wParam)==LBN_DBLCLK) {
    i = SendDlgItemMessage(hdwnd, IDD_LB1,
           LB_GETCURSEL, 0, 0); // get index
    sprintf(str, "%s\n%s\n%s, %u",
           books[i].title, books[i].author,
           books[i].publisher, books[i].copyright);

    MessageBox(hdwnd, str, "Selection Made", MB_OK);

    // get string associated with that index
    SendDlgItemMessage(hdwnd, IDD_LB1, LB_GETTEXT,
```

```
                      i, (LPARAM) str);

             // update edit box
              SetDlgItemText(hdwnd, IDD_EB1, str);
          }
          return 1;
        case IDD_SELECT: // Select Book button has been pressed
          i = SendDlgItemMessage(hdwnd, IDD_LB1,
                  LB_GETCURSEL, 0, 0); // get index
          sprintf(str, "%s\n%s\n%s, %u",
                  books[i].title, books[i].author,
                  books[i].publisher, books[i].copyright);

          MessageBox(hdwnd, str, "Selection Made", MB_OK);

          // get string associated with that index
          SendDlgItemMessage(hdwnd, IDD_LB1, LB_GETTEXT,
              i, (LPARAM) str);

          // update edit box
          SetDlgItemText(hdwnd, IDD_EB1, str);
          return 1;
      }
      break;
    case WM_INITDIALOG: // initialize list box
      for(i=0; i<NUMBOOKS; i++)
        SendDlgItemMessage(hdwnd, IDD_LB1,
                LB_ADDSTRING, 0, (LPARAM)books[i].title);

      // select first item
      SendDlgItemMessage(hdwnd, IDD_LB1, LB_SETCURSEL, 0, 0);

      // initialize the edit box
      SetDlgItemText(hdwnd, IDD_EB1, books[0].title);

      return 1;
  }

  return 0;
}
```

Figure 5-3 shows sample output created by the complete modal dialog box program.

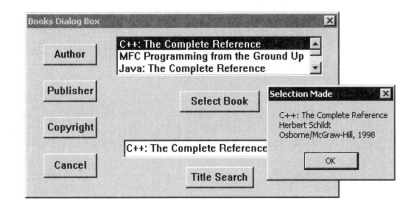

Sample output
produced by
the complete
modal dialog
box program

Figure 5-3.

5

Using a Modeless Dialog Box

To conclude this chapter, the modal dialog box used by the preceding program will be converted into a modeless dialog box. As you will see, using a modeless dialog box requires a little more work. The main reason for this is that a modeless dialog box is more independent than a modal dialog box.

Specifically, the rest of your program is still active when a modeless dialog box is displayed. Both it and your application's window function continue to receive messages. Thus, some additional overhead is required in your application's message loop to accommodate the modeless dialog box.

To create a modeless dialog box, you do not use **DialogBox( )**. Instead, you must use the **CreateDialog( )** API function. Its prototype is shown here:

HWND CreateDialog(HINSTANCE *hThisInst*, LPCSTR *lpName*,
                              HWND *hwnd*, DLGPROC *lpDFunc*);

Here, *hThisInst* is a handle to the current application that is passed to your program in the instance parameter to **WinMain( )**. The name of the dialog box as defined in the resource file is pointed to by *lpName*. The handle to the owner of the dialog box is passed in *hwnd*. (This is typically the handle to the window that calls **CreateDialog( )**.) The *lpDFunc* parameter contains a pointer to the dialog function. The dialog function is of the same type as that used for a modal dialog box. **CreateDialog( )** returns a handle to the dialog box. If the dialog box cannot be created, **NULL** is returned.

Disabling a Control

Sometimes you will have a control that is not applicable to all situations. When this is the case, it can be (and should be) disabled. A control that is disabled is displayed in gray and can not be selected. To disable a control, use the **EnableWindow( )** API function, shown here:

    BOOL EnableWindow(HWND *hCntl*, BOOL *How*);

Here, *hCntl* specifies the handle of the window to be affected. (Remember, controls are specialized windows.) If *How* is nonzero, then the control is enabled—that is, it is activated. If *How* is zero, the control is disabled. The function returns nonzero if the control was already disabled. It returns zero if the control was previously enabled.

To obtain the handle of a control, use the **GetDlgItem( )** API function. It is shown here:

    HWND GetDlgItem(HWND *hDwnd*, int *ID*);

Here, *hDwnd* is the handle of the dialog box that owns the control. The control ID is passed in *ID*. This is the value that you associate with the control in its resource file. The function returns the handle of the specified control, or **NULL** on failure.

To see how you can use these functions to disable a control, the following fragment disables the Author push button. In this example **hwpb** is a handle of type **HWND**.

```
hwpb = GetDlgItem(hdwnd, IDD_AUTHOR); // get handle of button
EnableWindow(hwpb, 0); // disable it
```

On your own, you might want to try disabling and enabling the other controls used by the examples in this and later chapters.

Unlike a modal dialog box, a modeless dialog box is not automatically visible, so you may need to call **ShowWindow( )** to cause it to be displayed after it has been created. However, if you add **WS_VISIBLE** to the dialog box's definition in its resource file, then it will automatically be visible.

To close a modeless dialog box your program must call **DestroyWindow( )**, rather than **EndDialog( )**. The prototype for **DestroyWindow( )** is shown here:

BOOL DestroyWindow(HWND *hwnd*);

Here, *hwnd* is the handle to the window (in this case, dialog box) being closed. The function returns nonzero if successful and zero on failure.

Since your application's window function will continue receiving messages while a modeless dialog box is active, you must make a change to your program's message loop by adding a call to **IsDialogMessage( )**. This function routes dialog box messages to your modeless dialog box. It has this prototype:

BOOL IsDialogMessage(HWND *hdwnd*, LPMSG *msg*);

Here, *hdwnd* is the handle of the modeless dialog box, and **msg** is the message obtained from **GetMessage( )** within your program's message loop. The function returns nonzero if the message is for the dialog box. It returns false otherwise. If the message is for the dialog box, then it is automatically passed to the dialog box function. Therefore, assuming that **hDlg** is the handle to a dialog box, to process modeless dialog box messages, your program's message loop must look something like this:

```
while(GetMessage(&msg, NULL, 0, 0))
  {
    if(!hDlg || !IsDialogMessage(hDlg, &msg)) {
      // not dialog box message
      if(!TranslateAccelerator(hwnd, hAccel, &msg)) {
        TranslateMessage(&msg); // translate keyboard message
        DispatchMessage(&msg);  // return control to Windows 2000
      }
    }
  }
```

As you can see, the message is processed by the rest of the message loop only if **hDlg** is not null and the message is not a dialog box message. The test on **hDlg** prevents **IsDialogMessage( )** from being called with an invalid handle.

Creating a Modeless Dialog Box

To convert the modal dialog box shown in the preceding example into a modeless one, surprisingly few changes are needed. The first change is to the dialog box definition in the DIALOG.RC resource file. Since a modeless dialog box is not automatically visible, add **WS_VISIBLE** to the dialog box definition. Also, remove the **DS_MODALFRAME** style and subsitute **WS_BORDER**. Since we have made several changes to DIALOG.RC since the start of the chapter, its final form is shown here after making these adjustments.

```
// Sample dialog box and menu resource file.
#include <windows.h>
#include "dialog.h"

MyMenu MENU
{
  POPUP "&Dialog"
  {
    MENUITEM "&Dialog\tF2", IDM_DIALOG
    MENUITEM "E&xit\tCtrl+X", IDM_EXIT
  }
  MENUITEM "&Help", IDM_HELP
}

MyMenu ACCELERATORS
{
  VK_F2, IDM_DIALOG, VIRTKEY
  "^X", IDM_EXIT
  VK_F1, IDM_HELP, VIRTKEY
}

MyDB DIALOGEX 10, 10, 210, 110
CAPTION "Books Dialog Box"
STYLE WS_POPUP | WS_CAPTION | WS_SYSMENU | WS_VISIBLE | WS_BORDER
{
  DEFPUSHBUTTON "Author", IDD_AUTHOR, 11, 10, 36, 14
  PUSHBUTTON "Publisher", IDD_PUBLISHER, 11, 34, 36, 14
  PUSHBUTTON "Copyright", IDD_COPYRIGHT, 11, 58, 36, 14
  PUSHBUTTON "Cancel", IDCANCEL, 11, 82, 36, 16
  LISTBOX IDD_LB1, 60, 5, 140, 33, LBS_NOTIFY |
          WS_BORDER | WS_VSCROLL | WS_TABSTOP
  PUSHBUTTON "Select Book", IDD_SELECT, 103, 41, 54, 14
  EDITTEXT IDD_EB1, 65, 73, 130, 12, ES_LEFT |
```

```
                    WS_BORDER | ES_AUTOHSCROLL | WS_TABSTOP
       PUSHBUTTON "Title Search", IDD_DONE, 107, 91, 46, 14
}
```

Next, you must make the following changes to the program:

1. Create a global handle called **hDlg**, initializing it to null.
2. Add **IsDialogMessage( )** to the message loop.
3. Create the dialog box using **CreateDialog( )** rather than **DialogBox( )**.
4. Close the dialog box using **DestroyWindow( )** instead of **EndDialog( )**.

The entire listing (which incorporates these changes) for the modeless dialog box example is shown here. Pay special attention to the handle **hDlg**. It is initialized to null. When the dialog box is created, **hDlg** is assigned the handle to that box. When the dialog box terminates, **hDlg** is reset to null. Thus, **hDlg** is non-null only when the dialog box is active. Since **hDlg** is tested within the message loop, **IsDialogMessage( )** is never called with an invalid handle.

Sample output from this program is shown in Figure 5-4. (You should try this program on your own to fully understand the difference between modal and modeless dialog boxes.)

5

Sample output using the modeless dialog box

Figure 5-4.

```cpp
// A modeless dialog box example.

#include <windows.h>
#include <cstring>
#include <cstdio>
#include "dialog.h"

#define NUMBOOKS 7

LRESULT CALLBACK WindowFunc(HWND, UINT, WPARAM, LPARAM);
BOOL CALLBACK DialogFunc(HWND, UINT, WPARAM, LPARAM);

char szWinName[] = "MyWin"; // name of window class

HINSTANCE hInst;

HWND hDlg = 0; // dialog box handle

// books database
struct booksTag {
  char title[40];
  unsigned copyright;
  char author[40];
  char publisher[40];
} books[NUMBOOKS] = {
  { "C++: The Complete Reference", 1998,
    "Herbert Schildt", "Osborne/McGraw-Hill" },
  { "MFC Programming from the Ground Up", 1998,
    "Herbert Schildt", "Osborne/McGraw-Hill" },
  { "Java: The Complete Reference", 1999,
    "Naughton and Schildt", "Osborne/McGraw-Hill" },
  { "The C++ Programming Language", 1997,
    "Bjarne Stroustrup", "Addison-Wesley" }
  { "Inside OLE", 1995,
    "Kraig Brockschmidt", "Microsoft Press" },
  { "HTML Sourcebook", 1996,
    "Ian S. Graham", "John Wiley & Sons" },
  { "Standard C++ Library", 1995,
    "P. J. Plauger", "Prentice-Hall" }
};

int WINAPI WinMain(HINSTANCE hThisInst, HINSTANCE hPrevInst,
                   LPSTR lpszArgs, int nWinMode)
{
  HWND hwnd;
  MSG msg;
```

```
WNDCLASSEX wcl;
HACCEL hAccel;

// Define a window class.
wcl.cbSize = sizeof(WNDCLASSEX);

wcl.hInstance = hThisInst;      // handle to this instance
wcl.lpszClassName = szWinName;  // window class name
wcl.lpfnWndProc = WindowFunc;   // window function
wcl.style = 0;                  // default style

wcl.hIcon = LoadIcon(NULL, IDI_APPLICATION); // large icon
wcl.hIconSm = NULL; // use small version of large icon
wcl.hCursor = LoadCursor(NULL, IDC_ARROW);  // cursor style

// Specify name of menu resource.
wcl.lpszMenuName = "MyMenu";

wcl.cbClsExtra = 0;        // no extra memory needed
wcl.cbWndExtra = 0;

// Make the window background white.
wcl.hbrBackground = (HBRUSH) GetStockObject(WHITE_BRUSH);

// Register the window class.
if(!RegisterClassEx(&wcl)) return 0;

/* Now that a window class has been registered, a window
   can be created. */
hwnd = CreateWindow(
  szWinName, // name of window class
  "Demonstrate a Modeless Dialog Box", // title
  WS_OVERLAPPEDWINDOW, // window style - normal
  CW_USEDEFAULT, // X coordinate - let Windows decide
  CW_USEDEFAULT, // Y coordinate - let Windows decide
  CW_USEDEFAULT, // width - let Windows decide
  CW_USEDEFAULT, // height - let Windows decide
  NULL,          // no parent window
  NULL,          // no override of class menu
  hThisInst,     // instance handle
  NULL           // no additional arguments
);

hInst = hThisInst; // save the current instance handle

// Load accelerators.
```

```
    hAccel = LoadAccelerators(hThisInst, "MyMenu");

    // Display the window.
    ShowWindow(hwnd, nWinMode);
    UpdateWindow(hwnd);

    // Create the message loop.
    while(GetMessage(&msg, NULL, 0, 0))
    {
      if(!hDlg || !IsDialogMessage(hDlg, &msg)) {
        // is not a dialog message
        if(!TranslateAccelerator(hwnd, hAccel, &msg)) {
          TranslateMessage(&msg); // translate keyboard messages
          DispatchMessage(&msg);  // return control to Windows 2000
        }
      }
    }

  return msg.wParam;
}

/* This function is called by Windows 2000 and is passed
   messages from the message queue.
*/
LRESULT CALLBACK WindowFunc(HWND hwnd, UINT message,
                            WPARAM wParam, LPARAM lParam)
{
  int response;

  switch(message) {
    case WM_COMMAND:
      switch(LOWORD(wParam)) {
        case IDM_DIALOG:
          hDlg = CreateDialog(hInst, "MyDB", hwnd,
                     (DLGPROC) DialogFunc);
          break;
        case IDM_EXIT:
          response = MessageBox(hwnd, "Quit the Program?",
                                "Exit", MB_YESNO);
          if(response == IDYES) PostQuitMessage(0);
          break;
        case IDM_HELP:
          MessageBox(hwnd, "No Help", "Help", MB_OK);
          break;
      }
```

```
        break;
    case WM_DESTROY: // terminate the program
      PostQuitMessage(0);
      break;
    default:
      /* Let Windows 2000 process any messages not specified in
         the preceding switch statement. */
      return DefWindowProc(hwnd, message, wParam, lParam);
  }

  return 0;
}

// A simple modeless dialog function.
BOOL CALLBACK DialogFunc(HWND hdwnd, UINT message,
                         WPARAM wParam, LPARAM lParam)
{
  long i;
  char str[255];

  switch(message) {
    case WM_COMMAND:
      switch(LOWORD(wParam)) {
        case IDCANCEL:
          DestroyWindow(hdwnd);
          hDlg = 0; // invalidate the handle
          return 1;
        case IDD_COPYRIGHT:
          i = SendDlgItemMessage(hdwnd, IDD_LB1,
                 LB_GETCURSEL, 0, 0); // get index
          sprintf(str, "%u", books[i].copyright);
          MessageBox(hdwnd, str, "Copyright", MB_OK);
          return 1;
        case IDD_AUTHOR:
          i = SendDlgItemMessage(hdwnd, IDD_LB1,
                 LB_GETCURSEL, 0, 0); // get index
          sprintf(str, "%s", books[i].author);
          MessageBox(hdwnd, str, "Author", MB_OK);
          return 1;
        case IDD_PUBLISHER:
          i = SendDlgItemMessage(hdwnd, IDD_LB1,
                 LB_GETCURSEL, 0, 0); // get index
          sprintf(str, "%s", books[i].publisher);
          MessageBox(hdwnd, str, "Publisher", MB_OK);
          return 1;
```

5

```
case IDD_DONE: // Title Search button pressed
  // get current contents of edit box
  GetDlgItemText(hdwnd, IDD_EB1, str, 80);

  // find a matching string in the list box
  i = SendDlgItemMessage(hdwnd, IDD_LB1, LB_FINDSTRING,
          0, (LPARAM) str);

  if(i != LB_ERR) { // if match is found
    // select the matching title in list box
    SendDlgItemMessage(hdwnd, IDD_LB1, LB_SETCURSEL, i, 0);

    // get string associated with that index
    SendDlgItemMessage(hdwnd, IDD_LB1, LB_GETTEXT,
        i, (LPARAM) str);

    // update text in edit box
    SetDlgItemText(hdwnd, IDD_EB1, str);
  }
  else
    MessageBox(hdwnd, str, "No Title Matching", MB_OK);
  return 1;
case IDD_LB1: // process a list box LBN_DBLCLK
  // see  if user made a selection
  if(HIWORD(wParam)==LBN_DBLCLK) {
    i = SendDlgItemMessage(hdwnd, IDD_LB1,
          LB_GETCURSEL, 0, 0); // get index
    sprintf(str, "%s\n%s\n%s, %u",
          books[i].title, books[i].author,
          books[i].publisher, books[i].copyright);

    MessageBox(hdwnd, str, "Selection Made", MB_OK);

    // get string associated with that index
    SendDlgItemMessage(hdwnd, IDD_LB1, LB_GETTEXT,
        i, (LPARAM) str);

    // update edit box
    SetDlgItemText(hdwnd, IDD_EB1, str);
  }
  return 1;
case IDD_SELECT: // Select Book button has been pressed
  i = SendDlgItemMessage(hdwnd, IDD_LB1,
        LB_GETCURSEL, 0, 0); // get index
  sprintf(str, "%s\n%s\n%s, %u",
```

```
                    books[i].title, books[i].author,
                    books[i].publisher, books[i].copyright);

            MessageBox(hdwnd, str, "Selection Made", MB_OK);

            // get string associated with that index
            SendDlgItemMessage(hdwnd, IDD_LB1, LB_GETTEXT,
                i, (LPARAM) str);

            // update edit box
            SetDlgItemText(hdwnd, IDD_EB1, str);
            return 1;
        }
        break;
    case WM_INITDIALOG: // initialize list box
        for(i=0; i<NUMBOOKS; i++)
            SendDlgItemMessage(hdwnd, IDD_LB1,
                    LB_ADDSTRING, 0, (LPARAM)books[i].title);

        // select first item
        SendDlgItemMessage(hdwnd, IDD_LB1, LB_SETCURSEL, 0, 0);

        // initialize the edit box
        SetDlgItemText(hdwnd, IDD_EB1, books[0].title);

        return 1;
    }

    return 0;
}
```

5

CHAPTER 6

More Controls

This chapter continues our examination of controls by examining three more of Windows 2000's standard controls: scroll bars, check boxes, and radio buttons. As you will see, many of the techniques that you learned when using controls in Chapter 5 will apply to the controls discussed here.

This chapter begins with a discussion of the scroll bar and illustrates its use in a short example program. Although scroll bars offer a bit more of a programming challenge than do the other standard controls, they are still quite easy to use. Next, check boxes and radio buttons are discussed. To illustrate the practical use of scroll bars, check boxes, and radio buttons, a simple countdown timer application is developed. You could use such a program as, for example, a dark room timer. In the process of developing the countdown timer, timer interrupts and the **WM_TIMER** message are explored. The chapter concludes with a look at Windows' static controls.

Scroll Bars

Standard scroll bars are attached to a window.

The scroll bar is one of Windows most important controls. Scroll bars have two forms. The first type of scroll bar is an integral part of a normal window or dialog box. This is the *standard scroll bar*. The other type of scroll bar exists separately as a control and is called a *scroll bar control*. Both types of scroll bars are managed in much the same way.

A scroll bar control is a free-standing scroll bar.

Activating the Standard Scroll Bars

To add standard scroll bars to a window, specify the WS_VSCROLL and/or WS_HSCROLL styles.

For a window to include standard scroll bars, you must explicitly request it. For windows created using **CreateWindow( )**, such as your application's main window, you do this by including the styles **WS_VSCROLL** and/or **WS_HSCROLL** in the style parameter. In the case of a dialog box, you include the **WS_VSCROLL** and/or **WS_HSCROLL** styles in the dialog box's definition inside its resource file. As expected, the **WS_VSCROLL** causes a standard vertical scroll bar to be included and **WS_HSCROLL** activates a horizontal scroll bar. After you have added these styles, the window will automatically display the standard vertical and horizontal scroll bars.

Receiving Scroll Bar Messages

Unlike other controls, a scroll bar control does not generate a **WM_COMMAND** message. Instead, scroll bars send a **WM_VSCROLL** or a **WM_HSCROLL** message when a vertical or horizontal scroll bar is accessed, respectively. The value of the low-order word of **wParam** contains a code that describes the activity. For the standard window scroll bars, **lParam** is 0. However, if a scroll bar control generates the message, then **lParam** contains its handle.

As mentioned, the value in **LOWORD(wParam)** specifies what type of scroll bar action has taken place. Here are some common scroll bar values.

SB_LINEUP	SB_LINERIGHT
SB_LINEDOWN	SB_PAGELEFT
SB_PAGEUP	SB_PAGERIGHT
SB_PAGEDOWN	SB_THUMBPOSITION
SB_LINELEFT	SB_THUMBTRACK

For vertical scroll bars, each time the user moves the scroll bar up one position, **SB_LINEUP** is sent. Each time the scroll bar is moved down one position, **SB_LINEDOWN** is sent. **SB_PAGEUP** and **SB_PAGEDOWN** are sent when the scroll bar is moved up or down one page.

For horizontal scroll bars, each time the user moves the scroll bar left one position, **SB_LINELEFT** is sent. Each time the scroll bar is moved right one position, **SB_LINERIGHT** is sent. **SB_PAGELEFT** and **SB_PAGERIGHT** are sent when the scroll bar is moved left or right one page.

For both types of scroll bars, the **SB_THUMBPOSITION** value is sent after the slider box (thumb) of the scroll bar has been dragged to a new position. The **SB_THUMBTRACK** message is also sent when the thumb is dragged to a new position. The difference is that **SB_THUMBTRACK** is sent each time the thumb passes over a new position. This allows you to "track" the movement of the thumb before it is released. When **SB_THUMBPOSITION** or **SB_THUMBTRACK** is received, the high-order word of **wParam** contains the current slider box position.

HISTORICAL PERSPECTIVE: In 16-bit Windows, the organization of **lParam** and **wParam** differs from the organization of their equivalents in Windows 2000. Specifically, the handle of the scroll bar is in the high-order word of **lParam**. The position of the slider box is in the low-order word of **lParam**. The nature of the scroll bar action is in **wParam**. Because of these differences, you must rewrite all scroll bar message-handling code when porting from 16-bit Windows to Windows 2000.

6

SetScrollInfo( ) and GetScrollInfo( )

Scroll bars are, for the most part, manually managed controls. This means that in addition to responding to scroll bar messages, your program will also need to update various attributes associated with a scroll bar. For example, your program must update the position of the slider box manually. Windows 2000 supplies two functions that help you manage scroll bars. The first is **SetScrollInfo( )**, which is used to set various attributes associated with a scroll bar. Its prototype is shown here:

    int SetScrollInfo(HWND *hwnd*, int *which*, LPSCROLLINFO *lpSI*,
                      BOOL *repaint*);

Here, *hwnd* is the handle that identifies the scroll bar. For window scroll bars, this is the handle of the window that owns the scroll bar. For scroll bar controls, this is the handle of the scroll bar itself. The value of *which* determines which scroll bar is affected. If you are setting the attributes of the vertical window scroll bar, then this parameter must be **SB_VERT**. If you are setting the attributes of the horizontal window scroll bar, this value must be **SB_HORZ**. However, to set a scroll bar control, this value must be **SB_CTL**, and *hwnd* must be the handle of the control. The attributes are set according to the information pointed to by *lpSI* (discussed shortly). If *repaint* is true, then the scroll bar is redrawn. If false, the bar is not redisplayed. The function returns the position of the slider box.

To obtain the attributes associated with a scroll bar, use **GetScrollInfo( )**, shown here:

    BOOL GetScrollInfo(HWND *hwnd*, int *which*, LPSCROLLINFO *lpSI*);

The *hwnd* and *which* parameters are the same as those just described for **SetScrollInfo( )**. The information obtained by **GetScrollInfo( )** is put into the structure pointed to by *lpSI*. The function returns nonzero if successful and zero on failure.

The *lpSI* parameter of both functions points to a structure of type **SCROLLINFO**, which is defined like this:

```
typedef struct tagSCROLLINFO
{
  UINT cbSize;    // size of SCROLLINFO
  UINT fMask;     // Operation performed
  int nMin;       // minimum range
  int nMax;       // maximum range
  UINT nPage;     // Page value
```

```
    int nPos;      // slider box position
    int nTrackPos; // current tracking position
} SCROLLINFO;
```

Here, **cbSize** must contain the size of the **SCROLLINFO** structure. The value
or values contained in **fMask** determine which of the remaining members
are meaningful. When used in a call to **SetScrollInfo( )**, the value in
fMask specifies which scroll bar values will be updated. When used with
GetScrollInfo( ), the value in **fMask** determines which settings will be
obtained. **fMask** must be one or more of these values. (To combine values,
simply OR them together.)

SIF_ALL	Same as SIF_PAGE	SIF_POS	SIF_RANGE	SIF_TRACKPOS.
SIF_DISABLENOSCROLL	Scroll bar is disabled rather than removed if its range is set to zero.
SIF_PAGE	**nPage** contains valid information.
SIF_POS	**nPos** contains valid information.
SIF_RANGE	**nMin** and **nMax** contain valid information.
SIF_TRACKPOS	**nTrackPos** contains valid information.

nPage contains the current page setting for proportional scroll bars. **nPos**
contains the position of the slider box. **nMin** and **nMax** contain the
minimum and maximum range of the scroll bar. **nTrackPos** contains the
current tracking position. The tracking position is the current position of the
slider box while it is being dragged by the user. This value cannot be set.

HISTORICAL PERSPECTIVE: Win16 programs use the API
functions **SetScrollRange( )** and **SetScrollPos( )** to manage scroll bars.
Although these functions are still supported under Win32, their use is not
recommended and you should upgrade them to calls to **SetScrollInfo( )**
when porting older programs.

Working with Scroll Bars

As previously stated, scroll bars are manually managed controls. This means
that your program will need to update the position of the slider box within
the scroll bar each time it is moved. To do this, you will need to assign **nPos**

the value of the new position, assign **fMask** the value **SIF_POS,** and then call **SetScrollInfo( ).** For example, to update the slider box for the vertical scroll bar, your program will need to execute a sequence like the following:

```
SCROLLINFO si;
// ...
si.cbSize = sizeof(SCROLLINFO);
si.fMask = SIF_POS;
si.nPos = newposition;
SetScrollInfo(hwnd, SB_VERT, &si, 1);
```

The range of the scroll bar determines how many positions there are between one end and the other. By default, window scroll bars have a range of 0 to 100. However, you can set their range to meet the needs of your program. Control scroll bars have a default range of 0 to 0, which means that the range needs to be set before the scroll bar control can be used. (A scroll bar that has a zero range is inactive.) Setting the range can make it easier for your application to maintain the position of the slider box.

A Sample Scroll Bar Program

The following program demonstrates both vertical and horizontal standard scroll bars. The scroll bar program requires this resource file.

```
// Demonstrate scroll bars.
#include "scroll.h"
#include <windows.h>

MyMenu MENU
{
  POPUP "&Dialog"
  {
    MENUITEM "&Scroll Bars\tF2", IDM_DIALOG
    MENUITEM "E&xit\tCtrl+X", IDM_EXIT
  }
  MENUITEM "&Help", IDM_HELP
}

MyMenu ACCELERATORS
{
```

```
  VK_F2, IDM_DIALOG, VIRTKEY
  "^X", IDM_EXIT
  VK_F1, IDM_HELP, VIRTKEY
}

MyDB DIALOGEX 18, 18, 142, 92
CAPTION "Using Scroll Bars"
STYLE DS_MODALFRAME | WS_POPUP | WS_CAPTION | WS_SYSMENU
      | WS_VSCROLL | WS_HSCROLL
{
}
```

As you can see, the dialog box definition is empty. The scroll bars are added automatically because of the **WS_VSCROLL** and **WS_HSCROLL** style specifications.

You will also need to create this header file, called SCROLL.H.

```
#define IDM_DIALOG   100
#define IDM_EXIT     101
#define IDM_HELP     102
```

6

The entire scroll bar demonstration program is shown next. The vertical scroll bar responds to the **SB_LINEUP**, **SB_LINEDOWN**, **SB_PAGEUP**, **SB_PAGEDOWN**, **SB_THUMBPOSITION**, and **SB_THUMBTRACK** messages by moving the slider box appropriately. It also displays the current position of the thumb. The position will change as you move the slider. The horizontal scroll bar responds only to **SB_LINELEFT** and **SB_LINERIGHT.** Its thumb position is also displayed. (On your own, you might try adding the necessary code to make the horizontal scroll bar respond to other messages.) Notice that the range of both the horizontal and vertical scroll bar is set when the dialog box receives a **WM_INITDIALOG** message. You might want to try changing the range of the scroll bars and observing the results.

One other point: notice that the thumb position of each scroll bar is displayed by outputting text into the client area of the dialog box using **TextOut( )**. Although a dialog box performs a special purpose, it is still a window with the same basic characteristics as the main window. Sample output from the program is shown in Figure 6-1.

Sample output
from the
standard
scroll bar
demonstration
program
Figure 6-1.

```
// Demonstrate Standard Scroll Bars

#include <windows.h>
#include <cstring>
#include <cstdio>
#include "scroll.h"

#define VERTRANGEMAX 200
#define HORZRANGEMAX  50

LRESULT CALLBACK WindowFunc(HWND, UINT, WPARAM, LPARAM);
BOOL CALLBACK DialogFunc(HWND, UINT, WPARAM, LPARAM);

char szWinName[] = "MyWin"; // name of window class

HINSTANCE hInst;

int WINAPI WinMain(HINSTANCE hThisInst, HINSTANCE hPrevInst,
                   LPSTR lpszArgs, int nWinMode)
{
  HWND hwnd;
  MSG msg;
  WNDCLASSEX wcl;
  HACCEL hAccel;

  // Define a window class.
  wcl.cbSize = sizeof(WNDCLASSEX);
```

6

```
wcl.hInstance = hThisInst;     // handle to this instance
wcl.lpszClassName = szWinName; // window class name
wcl.lpfnWndProc = WindowFunc;  // window function
wcl.style = 0;                 // default style

wcl.hIcon = LoadIcon(NULL, IDI_APPLICATION); // large icon
wcl.hIconSm = NULL; // use small version of large icon
wcl.hCursor = LoadCursor(NULL, IDC_ARROW);   // cursor style

// Specify name of menu resource.
wcl.lpszMenuName = "MyMenu";

wcl.cbClsExtra = 0;       // no extra memory needed
wcl.cbWndExtra = 0;

// Make the window background white.
wcl.hbrBackground = (HBRUSH) GetStockObject(WHITE_BRUSH);

// Register the window class.
if(!RegisterClassEx(&wcl)) return 0;

/* Now that a window class has been registered, a window
   can be created. */
hwnd = CreateWindow(
  szWinName, // name of window class
  "Managing Scroll Bars", // title
  WS_OVERLAPPEDWINDOW, // window style - normal
  CW_USEDEFAULT, // X coordinate - let Windows decide
  CW_USEDEFAULT, // Y coordinate - let Windows decide
  CW_USEDEFAULT, // width - let Windows decide
  CW_USEDEFAULT, // height - let Windows decide
  NULL,          // no parent window
  NULL,          // no override of class menu
  hThisInst,     // instance handle
  NULL           // no additional arguments
);

hInst = hThisInst; // save the current instance handle

// Load accelerators.
hAccel = LoadAccelerators(hThisInst, "MyMenu");

// Display the window.
ShowWindow(hwnd, nWinMode);
UpdateWindow(hwnd);
```

```
    // Create the message loop.
    while(GetMessage(&msg, NULL, 0, 0))
    {
      if(!TranslateAccelerator(hwnd, hAccel, &msg)) {
        TranslateMessage(&msg); // translate keyboard messages
        DispatchMessage(&msg);  // return control to Windows 2000
      }
    }

    return msg.wParam;
}

/* This function is called by Windows 2000 and is passed
   messages from the message queue.
*/
LRESULT CALLBACK WindowFunc(HWND hwnd, UINT message,
                            WPARAM wParam, LPARAM lParam)
{
  int response;

  switch(message) {
    case WM_COMMAND:
      switch(LOWORD(wParam)) {
        case IDM_DIALOG:
          DialogBox(hInst, "MyDB", hwnd, (DLGPROC) DialogFunc);
          break;
        case IDM_EXIT:
          response = MessageBox(hwnd, "Quit the Program?",
                                "Exit", MB_YESNO);
          if(response == IDYES) PostQuitMessage(0);
          break;
        case IDM_HELP:
          MessageBox(hwnd, "Try the Scroll Bar", "Help", MB_OK);
          break;
      }
      break;
    case WM_DESTROY: // terminate the program
      PostQuitMessage(0);
      break;
    default:
      /* Let Windows 2000 process any messages not specified in
         the preceding switch statement. */
      return DefWindowProc(hwnd, message, wParam, lParam);
  }
```

```
      return 0;
}

// Dialog function
BOOL CALLBACK DialogFunc(HWND hdwnd, UINT message,
                         WPARAM wParam, LPARAM lParam)
{
  char str[80];
  static int vpos = 0;  // vertical slider box position
  static int hpos = 0;  // horizontal slider box position
  static SCROLLINFO si; // scroll bar info structure

  HDC hdc;
  PAINTSTRUCT paintstruct;

  switch(message) {
    case WM_COMMAND:
      switch(LOWORD(wParam)) {
        case IDCANCEL:
          EndDialog(hdwnd, 0);
          return 1;
      }
      break;
    case WM_INITDIALOG:
      si.cbSize = sizeof(SCROLLINFO);
      si.fMask = SIF_RANGE;
      si.nMin = 0; si.nMax = VERTRANGEMAX;
      SetScrollInfo(hdwnd, SB_VERT, &si, 1);
      si.nMax = HORZRANGEMAX;
      SetScrollInfo(hdwnd, SB_HORZ, &si, 1);
      vpos = hpos = 0;
      return 1;
    case WM_PAINT:
      hdc = BeginPaint(hdwnd, &paintstruct);
      sprintf(str, "Vertical: %d", vpos);
      TextOut(hdc, 1, 1, str, strlen(str));
      sprintf(str, "Horizontal: %d", hpos);
      TextOut(hdc, 1, 30, str, strlen(str));
      EndPaint(hdwnd, &paintstruct);
      return 1;
    case WM_VSCROLL:
      switch(LOWORD(wParam)) {
        case SB_LINEDOWN:
          vpos++;
          if(vpos>VERTRANGEMAX) vpos = VERTRANGEMAX;
```

```
      break;
    case SB_LINEUP:
      vpos--;
      if(vpos<0) vpos = 0;
      break;
    case SB_THUMBPOSITION:
      vpos = HIWORD(wParam); // get current position
      break;
    case SB_THUMBTRACK:
      vpos = HIWORD(wParam); // get current position
      break;
    case SB_PAGEDOWN:
      vpos += 5;
      if(vpos>VERTRANGEMAX) vpos = VERTRANGEMAX;
      break;
    case SB_PAGEUP:
      vpos -= 5;
      if(vpos<0) vpos = 0;
  }
  // update vertical bar position
  si.fMask = SIF_POS;
  si.nPos = vpos;
  SetScrollInfo(hdwnd, SB_VERT, &si, 1);
  hdc = GetDC(hdwnd);
  sprintf(str, "Vertical: %d   ", vpos);
  TextOut(hdc, 1, 1, str, strlen(str));
  ReleaseDC(hdwnd, hdc);
  return 1;
case WM_HSCROLL:
  switch(LOWORD(wParam)) {
    /* Try adding the other event handling code
       for the horizontal scroll bar, here. */
    case SB_LINERIGHT:
      hpos++;
      if(hpos>HORZRANGEMAX) hpos = HORZRANGEMAX;
      break;
    case SB_LINELEFT:
      hpos--;
      if(hpos<0) hpos = 0;
  }
  // update horizontal bar position
  si.fMask = SIF_POS;
  si.nPos = hpos;
  SetScrollInfo(hdwnd, SB_HORZ, &si, 1);
  hdc = GetDC(hdwnd);
```

```
        sprintf(str, "Horizontal: %d   ", hpos);
        TextOut(hdc, 1, 30, str, strlen(str));
        ReleaseDC(hdwnd, hdc);
        return 1;
    }

    return 0;
}
```

Using a Scroll Bar Control

A scroll bar control is a stand alone scroll bar; it is not attached to a window. Scroll bar controls are handled much like standard scroll bars, but two important differences do exist.

First, the range of a scroll bar control must be set because it has a default range of zero. Thus, it is initially inactive. This differs from standard scroll bars, whose default range is 0 through 100.

6

The second difference has to do with the meaning of **lParam** when a scroll bar message is received. Recall that all scroll bars—standard or control—generate a **WM_HSCROLL** or a **WM_VSCROLL** message, depending upon whether the scroll bar is horizontal or vertical. When these messages are generated by a standard scroll bar, **lParam** is always zero. However, when they are generated by a scroll bar control, the handle of the control is passed in **lParam**. In windows that contain both standard and control scroll bars, you will need to make use of this distinction to determine which scroll bar generated the message.

When a control scroll bar generates a message, its handle is passed in **lParam**.

Creating a Scroll Bar Control

To create a scroll bar control in a dialog box, use the **SCROLLBAR** statement, which has this general form:

SCROLLBAR *SBID*, *X*, *Y*, *Width*, *Height* [, *Style*]

Here, *SBID* is the value associated with the scrollbar. The scroll bar's upper-left corner will be at *X,Y*, and the scroll bar will have the dimensions specified by *Width* and *Height*. *Style* determines the exact nature of the scroll bar. Its default style is **SBS_HORZ**, which creates a horizontal scroll bar. For a vertical scroll bar, specify the **SBS_VERT** style. If you want the scroll bar to be able to receive keyboard focus, include the **WS_TABSTOP** style.

Demonstrating a Scroll Bar Control

To demonstrate a control scroll bar, one will be added to the preceding program. First, change the dialog box definition as shown here. This version adds a vertical scroll bar control.

```
MyDB DIALOGEX 18, 18, 142, 92
CAPTION "Adding a Control Scroll Bar"
STYLE DS_MODALFRAME | WS_POPUP | WS_CAPTION | WS_SYSMENU
     | WS_VSCROLL | WS_HSCROLL
{
  SCROLLBAR ID_SB1, 110, 10, 10, 70, SBS_VERT | WS_TABSTOP
}
```

Then, add this line to SCROLL.H:

```
#define ID_SB1 200
```

Next, you will need to add the code that handles the control scroll bar. This code will need to distinguish between the standard scroll bars and the scroll bar control, since both generate **WM_VSCROLL** messages. To do this, just remember that a scroll bar control passes its handle in **lParam**. For standard scroll bars, **lParam** is zero. For example, here is the **SB_LINEDOWN** case that distinguishes between the standard scroll bar and the control scroll bar.

```
case SB_LINEDOWN:
  if((HWND)lParam==GetDlgItem(hdwnd, ID_SB1)) {
    // is control scroll bar
    cntlpos++;
    if(cntlpos>VERTRANGEMAX) cntlpos = VERTRANGEMAX;
  }
  else {
    // is window scroll bar
    vpos++;
    if(vpos>VERTRANGEMAX) vpos = VERTRANGEMAX;
  }
  break;
```

Here, the handle in **lParam** is compared to the handle of the scroll bar control, as obtained using **GetDlgItem( )**. If the handles are the same, then the message was generated by the scroll bar control. If not, then the message came from the standard scroll bar.

As explained in Chapter 5, the **GetDlgItem( )** API obtains the handle of a control. Recall that its prototype is:

HWND GetDlgItem(HWND *hDwnd*, int *ID*);

Here, *hDwnd* is the handle of the dialog box that owns the control. The control ID is passed in *ID*. This is the value that you associate with the control in its resource file. The function returns the handle of the specified control, or **NULL** on failure.

Here is the entire program that includes the vertical scroll bar control. It is the same as the preceding program except for the following additions. First, **DialogFunc( )** defines the static variable **cntlpos**, which holds the position of the control scroll bar. Second, the control scroll bar is initialized inside **WM_INITDIALOG**. Third, the handlers that process **WM_VSCROLL** messages determine whether the message came from the standard scroll bar or the control scroll bar. Finally, code has been added to display the current position of the control scroll bar.

Sample output is shown in Figure 6-2. On your own, try adding a horizontal control scroll bar.

6

Sample output from the control scroll bar program

Figure 6-2.

```
// Demonstrate a Control Scroll Bar

#include <windows.h>
#include <cstring>
#include <cstdio>
#include "scroll.h"

#define VERTRANGEMAX 200
#define HORZRANGEMAX  50

LRESULT CALLBACK WindowFunc(HWND, UINT, WPARAM, LPARAM);
BOOL CALLBACK DialogFunc(HWND, UINT, WPARAM, LPARAM);

char szWinName[] = "MyWin"; // name of window class

HINSTANCE hInst;

int WINAPI WinMain(HINSTANCE hThisInst, HINSTANCE hPrevInst,
                   LPSTR lpszArgs, int nWinMode)
{
  HWND hwnd;
  MSG msg;
  WNDCLASSEX wcl;
  HACCEL hAccel;

  // Define a window class.
  wcl.cbSize = sizeof(WNDCLASSEX);

  wcl.hInstance = hThisInst;      // handle to this instance
  wcl.lpszClassName = szWinName;  // window class name
  wcl.lpfnWndProc = WindowFunc;   // window function
  wcl.style = 0;                  // default style

  wcl.hIcon = LoadIcon(NULL, IDI_APPLICATION); // large icon
  wcl.hIconSm = NULL; // use small version of large icon
  wcl.hCursor = LoadCursor(NULL, IDC_ARROW);   // cursor style

  // Specify name of menu resource.
  wcl.lpszMenuName = "MyMenu";

  wcl.cbClsExtra = 0;       // no extra memory needed
  wcl.cbWndExtra = 0;

  // Make the window background white.
  wcl.hbrBackground = (HBRUSH) GetStockObject(WHITE_BRUSH);
```

```
    // Register the window class.
    if(!RegisterClassEx(&wcl)) return 0;

    /* Now that a window class has been registered, a window
       can be created. */
    hwnd = CreateWindow(
      szWinName, // name of window class
      "Managing Scroll Bars", // title
      WS_OVERLAPPEDWINDOW, // window style - normal
      CW_USEDEFAULT, // X coordinate - let Windows decide
      CW_USEDEFAULT, // Y coordinate - let Windows decide
      CW_USEDEFAULT, // width - let Windows decide
      CW_USEDEFAULT, // height - let Windows decide
      NULL,          // no parent window
      NULL,          // no override of class menu
      hThisInst,     // instance handle
      NULL           // no additional arguments
    );

    hInst = hThisInst; // save the current instance handle

    // Load accelerators.
    hAccel = LoadAccelerators(hThisInst, "MyMenu");

    // Display the window.
    ShowWindow(hwnd, nWinMode);
    UpdateWindow(hwnd);

    // Create the message loop.
    while(GetMessage(&msg, NULL, 0, 0))
    {
      if(!TranslateAccelerator(hwnd, hAccel, &msg)) {
        TranslateMessage(&msg); // translate keyboard messages
        DispatchMessage(&msg);  // return control to Windows 2000
      }
    }

    return msg.wParam;
}

/* This function is called by Windows 2000 and is passed
   messages from the message queue.
*/
LRESULT CALLBACK WindowFunc(HWND hwnd, UINT message,
                              WPARAM wParam, LPARAM lParam)
```

```
{
  int response;

  switch(message) {
    case WM_COMMAND:
      switch(LOWORD(wParam)) {
        case IDM_DIALOG:
          DialogBox(hInst, "MyDB", hwnd, (DLGPROC) DialogFunc);
          break;
        case IDM_EXIT:
          response = MessageBox(hwnd, "Quit the Program?",
                                       "Exit", MB_YESNO);
          if(response == IDYES) PostQuitMessage(0);
          break;
        case IDM_HELP:
          MessageBox(hwnd, "Try the Scroll Bar", "Help", MB_OK);
          break;
      }
      break;
    case WM_DESTROY: // terminate the program
      PostQuitMessage(0);
      break;
    default:
      /* Let Windows 2000 process any messages not specified in
         the preceding switch statement. */
      return DefWindowProc(hwnd, message, wParam, lParam);
  }

  return 0;
}

// Dialog function
BOOL CALLBACK DialogFunc(HWND hdwnd, UINT message,
                         WPARAM wParam, LPARAM lParam)
{
  char str[80];
  static int vpos = 0;     // vertical slider box position
  static int hpos = 0;     // horizontal slider box position
  static int cntlpos = 0;  // control slider box position
  static SCROLLINFO si;    // scroll bar info structure

  HDC hdc;
  PAINTSTRUCT paintstruct;

  switch(message) {
```

```
         case WM_COMMAND:
           switch(LOWORD(wParam)) {
             case IDCANCEL:
               EndDialog(hdwnd, 0);
               return 1;
           }
           break;
         case WM_INITDIALOG:
           si.cbSize = sizeof(SCROLLINFO);
           si.fMask = SIF_RANGE;
           si.nMin = 0; si.nMax = VERTRANGEMAX;

           // set range of standard vertical scroll bar
           SetScrollInfo(hdwnd, SB_VERT, &si, 1);

           // set range of scroll bar control
           SetScrollInfo(GetDlgItem(hdwnd, ID_SB1), SB_CTL, &si, 1);

           si.nMax = HORZRANGEMAX;
           // set range of standard horizontal scroll bar
           SetScrollInfo(hdwnd, SB_HORZ, &si, 1);

           vpos = hpos = cntlpos = 0;
           return 1;
         case WM_PAINT:
           hdc = BeginPaint(hdwnd, &paintstruct);
           sprintf(str, "Vertical: %d", vpos);
           TextOut(hdc, 1, 1, str, strlen(str));
           sprintf(str, "Horizontal: %d", hpos);
           TextOut(hdc, 1, 30, str, strlen(str));
           sprintf(str, "Scroll Bar Control: %d   ", cntlpos);
           TextOut(hdc, 1, 60, str, strlen(str));
           EndPaint(hdwnd, &paintstruct);
           return 1;
         case WM_VSCROLL:
           /* Now we must now determine whether the control
              scroll bar or the standard scroll bar generated
              the message. */
           switch(LOWORD(wParam)) {
             case SB_LINEDOWN:
               if((HWND)lParam==GetDlgItem(hdwnd, ID_SB1)) {
                 // is control scroll bar
                 cntlpos++;
                 if(cntlpos>VERTRANGEMAX) cntlpos = VERTRANGEMAX;
               }
```

6

```
        else {
          // is window scroll bar
          vpos++;
          if(vpos>VERTRANGEMAX) vpos = VERTRANGEMAX;
        }
        break;
      case SB_LINEUP:
        if((HWND)lParam==GetDlgItem(hdwnd, ID_SB1)) {
          // is control scroll bar
          cntlpos--;
          if(cntlpos<0) cntlpos = 0;
        }
        else {
          /* is window scroll bar */
          vpos--;
          if(vpos<0) vpos = 0;
        }
        break;
      case SB_THUMBPOSITION:
        if((HWND)lParam==GetDlgItem(hdwnd, ID_SB1)) {
          // is control scroll bar
          cntlpos = HIWORD(wParam); // get current position
        }
        else {
          // is window scroll bar
          vpos = HIWORD(wParam); // get current position
        }
        break;
      case SB_THUMBTRACK:
        if((HWND)lParam==GetDlgItem(hdwnd, ID_SB1)) {
          // is control scroll bar
          cntlpos = HIWORD(wParam); // get current position
        }
        else {
          // is window scroll bar
          vpos = HIWORD(wParam); // get current position
        }
        break;
      case SB_PAGEDOWN:
        if((HWND)lParam==GetDlgItem(hdwnd, ID_SB1)) {
          // is control scroll bar
          cntlpos += 5;
          if(cntlpos>VERTRANGEMAX) cntlpos = VERTRANGEMAX;
        }
        else {
```

```
          // is window scroll bar
          vpos += 5;
          if(vpos>VERTRANGEMAX) vpos = VERTRANGEMAX;
        }
        break;
      case SB_PAGEUP:
        if((HWND)lParam==GetDlgItem(hdwnd, ID_SB1)) {
          // is control scroll bar
          cntlpos -= 5;
          if(cntlpos<0) cntlpos = 0;
        }
        else {
          // is window scroll bar
          vpos -= 5;
          if(vpos<0) vpos = 0;
        }
        break;
    }

    if((HWND)lParam==GetDlgItem(hdwnd, ID_SB1)) {
      // update control scroll bar position
      si.fMask = SIF_POS;
      si.nPos = cntlpos;
      SetScrollInfo((HWND)lParam, SB_CTL, &si, 1);
      hdc = GetDC(hdwnd);
      sprintf(str, "Scroll Bar Control: %d   ", cntlpos);
      TextOut(hdc, 1, 60, str, strlen(str));
      ReleaseDC(hdwnd, hdc);
    }
    else {
      // update standard scroll bar position
      si.fMask = SIF_POS;
      si.nPos = vpos;
      SetScrollInfo(hdwnd, SB_VERT, &si, 1);
      hdc = GetDC(hdwnd);
      sprintf(str, "Vertical: %d   ", vpos);
      TextOut(hdc, 1, 1, str, strlen(str));
      ReleaseDC(hdwnd, hdc);
    }
    return 1;
  case WM_HSCROLL:
    switch(LOWORD(wParam)) {
      /* Try adding the other event handling code
         for the horizontal scroll bar, here. */
      case SB_LINERIGHT:
```

6

```
        hpos++;
        if(hpos>HORZRANGEMAX) hpos = HORZRANGEMAX;
        break;
      case SB_LINELEFT:
        hpos--;
        if(hpos<0) hpos = 0;
    }
    // update horizontal scroll bar position
    si.fMask = SIF_POS;
    si.nPos = hpos;
    SetScrollInfo(hdwnd, SB_HORZ, &si, 1);
    hdc = GetDC(hdwnd);
    sprintf(str, "Horizontal: %d    ", hpos);
    TextOut(hdc, 1, 30, str, strlen(str));
    ReleaseDC(hdwnd, hdc);
    return 1;
  }

  return 0;
}
```

Check Boxes

A *check box* is a control that is used to turn on or off an option. It consists of a small rectangle, which can either contain a check mark, or not. A check box has associated with it a label that describes what option the box represents. If the box contains a check mark, the box is said to be *checked* and the option is selected. If the box is empty, the option will be deselected.

A check box is a control that is typically part of a dialog box and is generally defined within the dialog box's definition in your program's resource file. To add a check box to a dialog box definition, use either the **CHECKBOX** or **AUTOCHECKBOX** command, which have these general forms:

CHECKBOX "*string*", *CBID, X, Y, Width, Height* [, *Style*]

AUTOCHECKBOX "*string*", *CBID, X, Y, Width, Height* [, *Style*]

Here, *string* is the text that will be shown alongside the check box. *CBID* is the value associated with the check box. The box's upper-left corner will be at *X,Y*, and the box plus its associated text will have the dimensions specified by *Width* and *Height*. *Style* determines the exact nature of the check box. If no explicit style is specified, then the check box defaults to displaying the string on the right and allowing the box to be tabbed to. When a check box is first created, it is unchecked.

As you know from using Windows 2000, check boxes are toggles. Each time you select a check box, its state changes from checked to unchecked, and vice versa. However, this is not necessarily automatically accomplished. When you use the **CHECKBOX** resource command, you are creating a *manual check box*, which your program must manage by checking and unchecking the box each time it is selected. (That is, a manual check box must be manually toggled by your program.) You can have Windows 2000 perform this housekeeping function for you by creating an *automatic check box* using **AUTOCHECKBOX**. With an automatic check box, Windows automatically toggles its state (between checked and not checked) each time it is selected. Since most applications do not need to manually manage a check box, we will be using only **AUTOCHECKBOX** in the examples that follow.

Obtaining the State of a Check Box

A check box is either checked or unchecked. You can determine the status of a check box by sending it the message **BM_GETCHECK** using the **SendDlgItemMessage( )** API function. **SendDlgItemMessage( )** was described in Chapter 5; its prototype is shown again here for convenience:

6

LONG SendDlgItemMessage(HWND *hdwnd*, int *ID*, UINT *IDMsg*,
                    WPARAM *wParam*, LPARAM *lParam*);

The control (within the dialog box) is specified by *ID*, and the message is specified by *IDMsg*. The handle of the dialog box is passed in *hdwnd*. When sending **BM_GETCHECK**, both *wParam* and *lParam* are zero. The check box returns **BST_CHECKED** if the box is checked and **BST_UNCHECKED** otherwise.

Checking a Check Box

A check box can be checked by your program. To do this, send the check box a **BM_SETCHECK** message using the **SendDlgItemMessage( )** API function. In this case, *wParam* determines whether the check box will be checked or cleared. If *wParam* is **BST_CHECKED**, the check box is checked. If it is **BST_UNCHECKED**, the box is cleared. In both cases, *lParam* is zero.

As mentioned, manual check boxes will need to be manually checked or cleared by your program each time they are toggled by the user. However, when using an automatic check box your program will need to explicitly check or clear a check box during program initialization only. When you use an automatic check box, the state of the box will be changed automatically each time it is selected.

Check boxes are cleared (that is, unchecked) when they are created. Thus, they are cleared when the dialog box in which they are contained is created.

If you want the check boxes to reflect their previous state, then you must initialize them each time the dialog box is activated. The easiest way to do this is to send them the appropriate **BM_SETCHECK** messages when the dialog box receives a **WM_INITDIALOG** message.

Check Box Messages

Each time the user clicks on the check box or selects the check box and then presses the space bar, a **WM_COMMAND** message is sent to the dialog function. The low-order word of **wParam** contains the identifier associated with that check box, and the high-order word of **wParam** contains the **BN_CLICKED** notification code. If you are using a manual check box, then you will want to respond to this command by changing the state of the box.

IN DEPTH

The 3-State Check Box

Windows 2000 provides an interesting variation of the check box called the *3-state box*. This check box has three possible states: checked, cleared, or grayed. (When the control is grayed, it is disabled.) Like its relative, the 3-state check box can be implemented as either an automatic or a manually managed control, using the **AUTO3STATE** and **STATE3** resource commands, respectively. The general forms are shown here:

STATE3 "*string*", *ID*, *X*, *Y*, *Width*, *Height* [, *Style*]
AUTO3STATE "*string*", *ID*, *X*, *Y*, *Width*, *Height* [, *Style*]

Here, *string* is the text that will be shown alongside the check box. *ID* is the value associated with the check box. The box's upper left-corner will be at *X,Y*, and the box plus its associated text will have the dimensions specified by *Width* and *Height*. *Style* determines the exact nature of the check box. If no explicit style is specified, then the check box defaults to displaying the string on the right and allowing the box to be tabbed to. When a 3-state check box is first created, it is unchecked.

In response to a **BM_GETCHECK** message, 3-state check boxes return **BST_UNCHECKED** if unchecked, **BST_CHECKED** if checked, and **BST_INDETERMINATE** if grayed. Correspondingly, when setting a 3-state check box using **BM_SETCHECK**, use **BST_UNCHECKED** to clear it, **BST_CHECKED** to check it, and **BST_INDETERMINATE** to gray it.

Radio Buttons

The next control that we will examine is the *radio button*. Radio buttons are used to present mutually exclusive options. A radio button consists of a label and a small circular button. If the button is empty, then the option is not selected. If the button is filled, then the option is selected. Windows 2000 supports two types of radio buttons: manual and automatic. The manual radio button (like the manual check box) requires that you perform all management functions. The automatic radio button performs the management functions for you. Because automatic radio buttons are used almost exclusively, they are the only ones examined here.

Like other controls, automatic radio buttons are defined in your program's resource file, within a dialog definition. To create an automatic radio button, use **AUTORADIOBUTTON**, which has this general form:

> AUTORADIOBUTTON *"string"*, *RBID*, *X*, *Y*, *Width*, *Height* [, *Style*]

6

Here, *string* is the text that will be shown alongside the button. *RBID* is the value associated with the radio button. The button's upper-left corner will be at *X,Y*, and the button plus its associated text will have the dimensions specified by *Width* and *Height*. *Style* determines the exact nature of the radio button. If no explicit style is specified, then the button defaults to displaying the string on the right and allowing the button to be tabbed to. By default, a radio button is unchecked.

As stated, radio buttons are generally used to create groups of mutually exclusive options. When you use automatic radio buttons to create such a group, then Windows automatically manages the buttons in a mutually exclusive manner. That is, each time the user selects one button, the previously selected button is turned off. Also, it is not possible for the user to select more than one button at any one time.

A radio button (even an automatic one) may be set to a known state by your program by sending it the **BM_SETCHECK** message using the **SendDlgItemMessage( )** function. The value of *wParam* determines whether the button will be checked or cleared. If *wParam* is **BST_CHECKED**, then the button will be checked. If it is **BST_UNCHECKED**, the box will be cleared. By default, all buttons are cleared.

NOTE: It is possible to manually set more than one button or to clear all buttons using **SendDlgItemMessage( )**. However, normal Windows style dictates that radio buttons be used in a mutually exclusive fashion, with one (and only one) option selected. It is strongly suggested that you do not violate this rule.

You can obtain the status of a radio button by sending it the
BM_GETCHECK message. The button returns **BST_CHECKED** if the button
is selected and **BST_UNCHECKED** if it is not.

When a radio button is accessed by the user, a **WM_COMMAND** message is
sent. Usually your program need not respond to that message unless you are
using manual radio buttons.

Demonstrating Check Boxes, Radio Buttons, and Scroll Bars

In this section a simple but useful program is developed that demonstrates
check boxes, radio buttons, and scroll bars. The program implements a
countdown timer. Using the timer, you can set the number of seconds that
you want to delay. The program will then wait that number of seconds and
notify you when the time is up. The countdown timer uses a scroll bar
to set the delay. It uses check boxes and radio buttons to set various options,
such as whether the program will beep when the end of the time has been
reached. However, before we can develop the program, you will need to learn
about another feature of Windows 2000: *timers*. The countdown program
will use one of Windows' built-in timers to monitor the passage of time. As
you will see, using a timer is straightforward. Also, as you begin to write your
own applications, you will find that timers are useful in a variety of
programming situations.

Generating Timer Messages

Windows 2000
provides
timers that
your program
can use.

With Windows, it is possible to establish a timer that will interrupt your
program at periodic intervals. At the end of each period, Windows 2000
sends a **WM_TIMER** message to your program. Using a timer is a good way
to "wake up your program" every so often. This is particularly useful when
your program is running as a background task.

To start a timer, use the **SetTimer( )** API function, whose prototype is
shown here:

    UINT SetTimer(HWND *hwnd*, UINT *nID*, UINT *wLength*,
            TIMERPROC *lpTFunc*);

Here, *hwnd* is the handle of the window that uses the timer. Generally, this
window will be either your program's main window or a dialog box window.
The value of *nID* specifies a value that will be associated with this timer.
(More than one timer can be active.) The value of *wLength* specifies the
length of the period, in milliseconds. That is, *wLength* specifies how long

there is between interrupts. The function pointed to by *lpTFunc* is the timer function that will be called when the timer goes off. However, if the value of *lpTFunc* is **NULL**, then the window function associated with the window specified by *hwnd* will be called and there is no need to specify a separate timer function. In this case, when the timer goes off, a **WM_TIMER** message is put into the message queue for your program and processed like any other message. This is the approach used by the example that follows. The **SetTimer( )** function returns *nID* if successful. If the timer cannot be allocated, zero is returned.

If you wish to define a separate timer function, it must be a callback function that has the following prototype (of course, the name of the function may be different):

> VOID CALLBACK TFunc(HWND *hwnd*, UINT *msg*, UINT *TimerID*,
> DWORD *SysTime*);

Here, *hwnd* will contain the handle of the timer window, *msg* will contain the message **WM_TIMER**, *TimerID* will contain the ID of the timer that went off, and *SysTime* will contain the current system time.

6

Once a timer has been started, it continues to interrupt your program until either you terminate the application or your program executes a call to the **KillTimer( )** API function, whose prototype is shown here:

> BOOL KillTimer(HWND *hwnd*, UINT *nID*);

Here, *hwnd* is the window that contains the timer, and *nID* is the value that identifies that particular timer. The function returns nonzero if successful and zero on failure.

Each time a **WM_TIMER** message is generated, the value of **wParam** contains the ID of the timer, and **lParam** contains the address of the timer callback function (if it is specified). For the countdown timer example that follows, **lParam** will be **NULL**.

The Countdown Timer Resource and Header Files

The countdown timer uses the following resource file.

```
// Demonstrate scroll bars, check boxes, and radio buttons.
#include <windows.h>
#include "cd.h"

MyMenu MENU
```

```
{
  POPUP "&Dialog"
  {
    MENUITEM "&Timer\tF2", IDM_DIALOG
    MENUITEM "&Exit\tF3", IDM_EXIT
  }
  MENUITEM "&Help", IDM_HELP
}

MyMenu ACCELERATORS
{
  VK_F2, IDM_DIALOG, VIRTKEY
  VK_F3, IDM_EXIT, VIRTKEY
  VK_F1, IDM_HELP, VIRTKEY
}

MyDB DIALOGEX 18, 18, 152, 92
CAPTION "A Countdown Timer"
STYLE DS_MODALFRAME | WS_POPUP | WS_CAPTION | WS_SYSMENU
      | WS_VSCROLL
{
  PUSHBUTTON "Start", IDD_START, 10, 60, 30, 14
  PUSHBUTTON "Cancel", IDCANCEL, 60, 60, 30, 14
  AUTOCHECKBOX "Show Countdown", IDD_CB1, 1, 20, 70, 10
  AUTOCHECKBOX "Beep At End", IDD_CB2, 1, 30, 50, 10
  AUTORADIOBUTTON "Minimize", IDD_RB1, 80, 20, 50, 10
  AUTORADIOBUTTON "Maximize", IDD_RB2, 80, 30, 50, 10
  AUTORADIOBUTTON "As-Is", IDD_RB3, 80, 40, 50, 10
}
```

The header file required by the timer program is shown here. Call this file CD.H.

```
#define IDM_DIALOG   100
#define IDM_EXIT     101
#define IDM_HELP     102

#define IDD_START    300
#define IDD_TIMER    301

#define IDD_CB1      400
#define IDD_CB2      401
#define IDD_RB1      402
#define IDD_RB2      403
#define IDD_RB3      404
```

The Countdown Timer Program

The entire countdown timer program is shown here.

```cpp
// A Countdown Timer

#include <windows.h>
#include <cstring>
#include <cstdio>
#include "cd.h"

#define VERTRANGEMAX 200

LRESULT CALLBACK WindowFunc(HWND, UINT, WPARAM, LPARAM);
BOOL CALLBACK DialogFunc(HWND, UINT, WPARAM, LPARAM);

char szWinName[] = "MyWin"; // name of window class

HINSTANCE hInst;

HWND hwnd;

int WINAPI WinMain(HINSTANCE hThisInst, HINSTANCE hPrevInst,
                   LPSTR lpszArgs, int nWinMode)
{
  MSG msg;
  WNDCLASSEX wcl;
  HACCEL hAccel;

  // Define a window class.
  wcl.cbSize = sizeof(WNDCLASSEX);

  wcl.hInstance = hThisInst;     // handle to this instance
  wcl.lpszClassName = szWinName; // window class name
  wcl.lpfnWndProc = WindowFunc;  // window function
  wcl.style = 0;                 // default style

  wcl.hIcon = LoadIcon(NULL, IDI_APPLICATION); // large icon
  wcl.hIconSm = NULL; // use small version of large icon
  wcl.hCursor = LoadCursor(NULL, IDC_ARROW);   // cursor style

  // Specify name of menu resource.
  wcl.lpszMenuName = "MyMenu";

  wcl.cbClsExtra = 0;        // no extra memory needed
```

6

```
      wcl.cbWndExtra = 0;

      // Make the window background white.
      wcl.hbrBackground = (HBRUSH) GetStockObject(WHITE_BRUSH);

      // Register the window class.
      if(!RegisterClassEx(&wcl)) return 0;

      /* Now that a window class has been registered, a window
         can be created. */
      hwnd = CreateWindow(
        szWinName, // name of window class
        "Demonstrating Controls", // title
        WS_OVERLAPPEDWINDOW, // window style - normal
        CW_USEDEFAULT, // X coordinate - let Windows decide
        CW_USEDEFAULT, // Y coordinate - let Windows decide
        CW_USEDEFAULT, // width - let Windows decide
        CW_USEDEFAULT, // height - let Windows decide
        NULL,          // no parent window
        NULL,          // no override of class menu
        hThisInst,     // instance handle
        NULL           // no additional arguments
      );

      hInst = hThisInst; // save the current instance handle

      // Load accelerators.
      hAccel = LoadAccelerators(hThisInst, "MyMenu");

      // Display the window.
      ShowWindow(hwnd, nWinMode);
      UpdateWindow(hwnd);

      // Create the message loop.
      while(GetMessage(&msg, NULL, 0, 0))
      {
        if(!TranslateAccelerator(hwnd, hAccel, &msg)) {
          TranslateMessage(&msg); // translate keyboard messages
          DispatchMessage(&msg);  // return control to Windows 2000
        }
      }

      return msg.wParam;
    }
```

```
/* This function is called by Windows 2000 and is passed
   messages from the message queue.
*/
LRESULT CALLBACK WindowFunc(HWND hwnd, UINT message,
                              WPARAM wParam, LPARAM lParam)
{
  int response;

  switch(message) {
    case WM_COMMAND:
      switch(LOWORD(wParam)) {
        case IDM_DIALOG:
          DialogBox(hInst, "MyDB", hwnd, (DLGPROC) DialogFunc);
          break;
        case IDM_EXIT:
          response = MessageBox(hwnd, "Quit the Program?",
                                "Exit", MB_YESNO);
          if(response == IDYES) PostQuitMessage(0);
          break;
        case IDM_HELP:
          MessageBox(hwnd, "Try the Timer", "Help", MB_OK);
          break;
      }
      break;
    case WM_DESTROY: // terminate the program
      PostQuitMessage(0);
      break;
    default:
      /* Let Windows 2000 process any messages not specified in
         the preceding switch statement. */
      return DefWindowProc(hwnd, message, wParam, lParam);
  }
  return 0;
}

// Dialog function
BOOL CALLBACK DialogFunc(HWND hdwnd, UINT message,
                         WPARAM wParam, LPARAM lParam)
{
  char str[80];
  static int vpos = 0;  // vertical slider box position
  static SCROLLINFO si; // scroll bar info structure

  HDC hdc;
  PAINTSTRUCT paintstruct;
```

6

```
static int t;

switch(message) {
  case WM_COMMAND:
    switch(LOWORD(wParam)) {
      case IDCANCEL:
        EndDialog(hdwnd, 0);
        return 1;
      case IDD_START: // start the timer
        SetTimer(hdwnd, IDD_TIMER, 1000, NULL);
        t = vpos;
        if(SendDlgItemMessage(hdwnd,
              IDD_RB1, BM_GETCHECK, 0, 0) == BST_CHECKED)
          ShowWindow(hwnd, SW_MINIMIZE);
        else
        if(SendDlgItemMessage(hdwnd,
              IDD_RB2, BM_GETCHECK, 0, 0) == BST_CHECKED)
          ShowWindow(hwnd, SW_MAXIMIZE);
        return 1;
    }
    break;
  case WM_TIMER: // timer went off
    if(t==0) {
      KillTimer(hdwnd, IDD_TIMER);
      if(SendDlgItemMessage(hdwnd,
            IDD_CB2, BM_GETCHECK, 0, 0) == BST_CHECKED)
        MessageBeep(MB_OK);
      else MessageBox(hdwnd, "Timer Went Off", "Timer", MB_OK);
      ShowWindow(hwnd, SW_RESTORE);
      return 1;
    }
    t--;

    // see if count down is to be displayed
    if(SendDlgItemMessage(hdwnd,
          IDD_CB1, BM_GETCHECK, 0, 0) == BST_CHECKED) {
      hdc = GetDC(hdwnd);
      sprintf(str, "Counting: %d   ", t);
      TextOut(hdc, 1, 1, str, strlen(str));
      ReleaseDC(hdwnd, hdc);
    }
    return 1;
  case WM_INITDIALOG:
    si.cbSize = sizeof(SCROLLINFO);
    si.fMask = SIF_RANGE;
```

```
        si.nMin = 0; si.nMax = VERTRANGEMAX;
        SetScrollInfo(hdwnd, SB_VERT, &si, 1);

        // check the As-Is radio button
        SendDlgItemMessage(hdwnd, IDD_RB3, BM_SETCHECK, BST_CHECKED, 0);
        return 1;
    case WM_PAINT:
      hdc = BeginPaint(hdwnd, &paintstruct);
      sprintf(str, "Interval: %d", vpos);
      TextOut(hdc, 1, 1, str, strlen(str));
      EndPaint(hdwnd, &paintstruct);
      return 1;
    case WM_VSCROLL:
      switch(LOWORD(wParam)) {
        case SB_LINEDOWN:
          vpos++;
          if(vpos>VERTRANGEMAX) vpos = VERTRANGEMAX;
          break;
        case SB_LINEUP:
          vpos--;
          if(vpos<0) vpos = 0;
          break;
        case SB_THUMBPOSITION:
          vpos = HIWORD(wParam); // get current position
          break;
        case SB_THUMBTRACK:
          vpos = HIWORD(wParam); // get current position
          break;
        case SB_PAGEDOWN:
          vpos += 5;
          if(vpos>VERTRANGEMAX) vpos = VERTRANGEMAX;
          break;
        case SB_PAGEUP:
          vpos -= 5;
          if(vpos<0) vpos = 0;
      }
      si.fMask = SIF_POS;
      si.nPos = vpos;
      SetScrollInfo(hdwnd, SB_VERT, &si, 1);
      hdc = GetDC(hdwnd);
      sprintf(str, "Interval: %d   ", vpos);
      TextOut(hdc, 1, 1, str, strlen(str));
      ReleaseDC(hdwnd, hdc);
      return 1;
```

```
    }

    return 0;
}
```

Sample output from this program is shown in Figure 6-3.

A Closer Look at the Countdown Program

To better understand how each control in the countdown program operates, let's take a closer look at it now. As you can see, the vertical scroll bar is used to set the delay. It uses much of the same code that was described earlier in this chapter when scroll bars were examined, so no further explanation is needed. However, the code that manages the check boxes and radio buttons deserves detailed attention.

As mentioned, by default no radio buttons are checked when they are first created. Thus, the program must manually select one each time the dialog box is activated. In this example, each time a **WM_INITDIALOG** message is received, the As-Is radio button (**IDD_RB3**) is checked using this statement:

```
SendDlgItemMessage(hwnd, IDD_RB3, BM_SETCHECK, BST_CHECKED, 0);
```

Sample output
from the
countdown
timer program

Figure 6-3.

To start the timer, the user presses the Start button. Doing this causes the following code to execute:

```
case IDD_START: // start the timer
  SetTimer(hdwnd, IDD_TIMER, 1000, NULL);
  t = vpos;
  if(SendDlgItemMessage(hdwnd,
        IDD_RB1, BM_GETCHECK, 0, 0) == BST_CHECKED)
    ShowWindow(hwnd, SW_MINIMIZE);
  else
  if(SendDlgItemMessage(hdwnd,
        IDD_RB2, BM_GETCHECK, 0, 0) == BST_CHECKED)
    ShowWindow(hwnd, SW_MAXIMIZE);
  return 1;
```

Here, the timer is set to go off once every second (1,000 milliseconds). The value of the counter variable **t** is set to the value determined by the position of the vertical scroll bar. If the Minimize radio button is checked, the program windows are minimized. If the Maximize button is checked, the program windows are maximized. Otherwise, the program windows are left unchanged. Notice that the main window handle, **hwnd**, not the dialog box handle, **hdwnd**, is used in the call to **ShowWindow( ).** To minimize or maximize the program, the main window handle must be used—not the handle of the dialog box. Also, notice that **hwnd** is a global variable in this program. This allows it to be used inside **DialogFunc( ).**

Each time a **WM_TIMER** message is received, the following code executes:

```
case WM_TIMER: // timer went off
  if(t==0) {
    KillTimer(hdwnd, IDD_TIMER);
    if(SendDlgItemMessage(hdwnd,
          IDD_CB2, BM_GETCHECK, 0, 0) == BST_CHECKED)
      MessageBeep(MB_OK);
    else MessageBox(hdwnd, "Timer Went Off", "Timer", MB_OK);
    ShowWindow(hwnd, SW_RESTORE);
    return 1;
  }
  t--;

  // see if count down is to be displayed
  if(SendDlgItemMessage(hdwnd,
```

```
        IDD_CB1, BM_GETCHECK, 0, 0) == BST_CHECKED) {
    hdc = GetDC(hdwnd);
    sprintf(str, "Counting: %d   ", t);
    TextOut(hdc, 1, 1, str, strlen(str));
    ReleaseDC(hdwnd, hdc);
  }
  return 1;
```

If the countdown has reached zero, the timer is killed and the window is
restored to its former size, if necessary. If the Beep at End button is checked,
then the computer's speaker is beeped using a call to the API function
MessageBeep( ). Otherwise, a message box is displayed. If there is still time
remaining, then the counter variable **t** is decremented. If the Show Countdown
button is checked, then the time remaining in the countdown is displayed.

MessageBeep( ) is a function you will probably find useful in other
programs that you write. Its prototype is shown here:

BOOL MessageBeep(UINT *sound*);

Here, *sound* specifies the type of sound that you want to make. It can be −1,
which produces a standard beep, or one of these built-in values.

MB_ICONASTERISK	MB_ICONEXCLAMATION	MB_ICONHAND
MB_ICONQUESTION	MB_OK	

MB_OK also produces a standard beep. **MessageBeep( )** returns nonzero if
successful or zero on failure.

As you can see by looking at the program, since automatic check boxes and
radio buttons are mostly managed by Windows 2000, there is surprisingly
little code within the countdown program that actually deals with these two
controls. In fact, the ease of use of check boxes and radio buttons helps make
them two of the most commonly used control elements.

Static Controls

Although none of the standard controls are difficult to use, there is no
question that the static controls are the easiest. The reason for this is simple:
a static control is one that neither receives nor generates any messages. In
short, the term *static control* is just a formal way of describing something that

Static controls
do not generate
or receive
messages.

is displayed in a dialog box. Static controls include **CTEXT**, **RTEXT**, and **LTEXT**, which are static text controls, and **GROUPBOX**, which is used to visually group other controls.

The **CTEXT** control outputs a string that is centered within a predefined area. **LTEXT** displays the string left-justified. **RTEXT** outputs the string right-justified. The general forms for these controls are shown here:

CTEXT "*text*", *ID, X, Y, Width, Height* [, *Style*]
RTEXT "*text*", *ID, X, Y, Width, Height* [, *Style*]
LTEXT "*text*", *ID, X, Y, Width, Height* [, *Style*]

Here, *text* is the text that will be displayed. *ID* is the value associated with the text. The text will be shown in a box whose upper-left corner will be at *X,Y*, and dimensions are specified by *Width* and *Height*. *Style* determines the exact nature of the control. Usually, the default style is sufficient. Understand that the box itself is *not* displayed. The box simply defines the space that the text is allowed to occupy.

6

The static text controls provide a convenient means of outputting text to a dialog box. Frequently, static text is used to label other dialog box controls or to provide simple directions to the user. You will want to experiment with the static text controls on your own.

A group box is simply a box the surrounds other dialog elements and is used to visually group other items. The box may contain a title. The general form for **GROUPBOX** is shown here:

GROUPBOX "*title*", *ID, X, Y, Width, Height* [, *Style*]

Here, *title* is the title to the box. *ID* is the value associated with the box. The upper-left corner will be at *X,Y*, and its dimensions are specified by *Width* and *Height*. *Style* determines the exact nature of the group box. Generally, the default setting is sufficient.

To see the effect of a group box, add the following definition to the resource file you created for the countdown program.

```
GROUPBOX "Display As", 1, 72, 10, 60, 46
```

After you have added the group box, the dialog box will now look like that shown in Figure 6-4. Remember that although a group box changes the appearance of the dialog box, its function has not been changed.

The count-
down dialog
box that
includes a
group box
static control

Figure 6-4.

IN DEPTH

Stand Alone Controls

Although controls are most often used within a dialog box, they
may also be free-standing within the client area of the main window.
To create a free-standing control, simply use the **CreateWindow( )**
function, specifying the name of the control class and the style
of control that you desire. The standard control class names are
shown here:

    BUTTON
    COMBOBOX
    EDIT
    LISTBOX
    SCROLLBAR
    STATIC

Each of these classes has several style macros associated with it that can
be used to customize the control. A list of these style macros can be
found by examining WINDOWS.H (and its support files) or by referring
to an API reference guide.

The following code creates a free-standing scroll bar and push button.

```
hsbwnd = CreateWindow(
  "SCROLLBAR", // name of scroll bar class
  "",          // no title
  SBS_HORZ | WS_CHILD | WS_VISIBLE, // horizontal scroll bar
  10, 10,      // position
  120, 20,     // dimensions
  hwnd,        // parent window
  NULL,        // no control ID needed for scroll bar
  hThisInst,   // handle of this instance of the program
  NULL         // no additional arguments
);

hpbwnd = CreateWindow(
  "BUTTON",       // name of pushbutton class
  "Push Button", // text inside button
  BS_PUSHBUTTON | WS_CHILD | WS_VISIBLE, // pushbutton
  10, 60,        // position
  90, 30,        // dimensions
  hwnd,          // parent window
  (HMENU) 500,   // control ID
  hThisInst,     // handle of this instance of the program
  NULL           // no additional arguments
);
```

As the push button shows, the ID associated with a free-standing control (when required) is specified in the ninth parameter to **CreateWindow( )**. As you recall, this is the parameter that we used to specify the handle of a menu that overrides the class menu. However, when creating a control, you use this parameter to specify the control's ID. It must be cast to **HMENU**.

When a free-standing control generates a message, it is sent to the parent window. You will need to add code to handle these messages within the parent's window function.

6

CHAPTER 7

Working with Bitmaps and Solving the Repaint Problem

185

A *bitmap* is a display object that contains a graphical image. The term comes from the fact that a bitmap contains a set of bits that define the image. Since Windows is a graphics-based operating system, it makes sense that you can include graphical images as resources in your applications. However, bitmaps have a broader application than simply providing support for graphical resources. As you will see, bitmaps underlie many of the features that comprise the Windows user interface. They can also help solve one of the most fundamental programming problems facing the Windows programmer: repainting a Window. Once you gain mastery over the bitmap you are well on your way to taking charge of many other aspects of Windows.

Windows has two special types of bitmaps: the icon and the cursor. As you know, an icon represents some resource or object. The cursor indicates the current mouse position. So far, we have only been using built-in icons and cursors. Here you will learn to create your own custom versions.

Two Types of Bitmaps

A device-dependent bitmap (DDB) is tied to a specific device.

There are two general types of bitmaps supported by Windows 2000: device-independent and device-dependent. Device-dependent bitmaps (DDB) are designed for use with a specific device. Device independent-bitmaps (DIB) are not tied to a specific device. Device-dependent bitmaps were initially the only type available in Windows. However, all versions of Windows since 3.0 have included device-independent bitmaps, too.

A device-independent bitmap (DIB) works with different types of devices.

DIBs are most valuable when you are creating a bitmap that will be used in environments other than the one in which it was created. For example, if you want to distribute a bitmap, the best way to do this is with a device-independent bitmap. However, DDBs are still commonly used when a program needs to create a bitmap for its own, internal use, and this accounts for the fact that DDBs remain widely used. Win32 provides various functions that allow you to convert between DDBs and DIBs, should you need to.

The organization of a DDB differs from that of a DIB. However, for the purposes of this chapter, the differences are not important. In fact, the binary format of a bitmap is seldom significant from the application's perspective because Windows provides high-level API functions that manage bitmaps—you will seldom need to "get your hands dirty" with their internals.

For the purposes of this chapter, we will be using device-dependent bitmaps because we will be focusing on bitmaps used by the program that creates them.

Two Ways to Obtain a Bitmap

A bitmap can be obtained in two different ways: it may be specified as a resource, or it may be created dynamically by your program. A bitmap resource is a graphical image that is defined outside your program, but specified in the program's resource file. A dynamic bitmap is created by your program during its execution. Each type is discussed in this chapter, beginning with the bitmap resource.

Using a Bitmap Resource

In general, to use a bitmap resource you must follow these three steps:

1. The bitmap must be specified within your program's resource file.
2. The bitmap must be loaded by your program.
3. The bitmap must be selected into a device context.

The next section describes the procedures necessary to accomplish these steps.

Creating a Bitmap Resource

Bitmap resources are not like the resources, such as menus, dialog boxes, and controls, described in the preceding chapters. Those resources are defined using textual statements in a resource file. Bitmaps are graphical images that must reside in special, bitmap files. However, the bitmap file must still be referred to in your program's resource file.

7

A bitmap resource is typically created using an *image editor*. An image editor will usually be supplied with your compiler. It displays an enlarged view of your bitmap. This enables you to easily construct or alter the image. For example, a custom bitmap displayed inside the Microsoft Visual C++ image editor is shown in Figure 7-1.

Except for specialized bitmaps, such as icons and cursors, the size of a bitmap is arbitrary and under your control. Within reason, you can create bitmaps as large or as small as you like. For the example that follows, your bitmap must be 256 x 128 pixels. Call your bitmap file BP.BMP. If you want your program to produce the results shown in the figures in this chapter, then make your bitmap look like the one shown in Figure 7-1. After you have defined your bitmap, create a resource file called BP.RC that contains this line:

```
MyBP BITMAP BP.BMP
```

As you can guess, the BITMAP statement defines a bitmap resource called **MyBP** that is contained in the file BP.BMP. The general form of the BITMAP statement is

BitmapName BITMAP *Filename*

An image
editor

Figure 7-1.

Here, *BitmapName* is the name that identifies the bitmap. This name is used by your program to refer to the bitmap. *Filename* is the name of the file that contains the bitmap.

Displaying a Bitmap

Once you have created a bitmap and included it in your application's resource file you can display it whenever you want in the client area of a window. However, to do so requires a little work on your part. The following discussion explains the proper procedure.

Before you can use your bitmap, you must load it and store its handle. This can be done inside **WinMain( )** or when your application's main window receives a **WM_CREATE** message. A **WM_CREATE** message is sent to a window when it is first created, but before it is visible. **WM_CREATE** is a good place to perform any initializations that relate to (and are subordinate to) a window. Since the bitmap resource will be displayed within the client area of the main window, it makes sense to load the bitmap when the window receives the **WM_CREATE** message. This is the approach that will be used in this chapter.

The easiest way to load the bitmap is to use the **LoadBitmap( )** API function, whose prototype is shown here:

HBITMAP LoadBitmap(HINSTANCE *hThisInst*, LPCSTR *lpszName*);

The current instance is specified in *hThisInst*, and a pointer to the name of the bitmap as specified in the resource file is passed in *lpszName*. The function returns the handle to the bitmap, or **NULL** if an error occurs. For example:

```
HBITMAP hbit; // handle of bitmap
// ...
hbit = LoadBitmap(hInst, "MyBP"); // load bitmap
```

This fragment loads a bitmap called **MyBP** and stores a handle to it in **hbit**.

When it comes time to display the bitmap, your program must follow these four steps:

1. Obtain the device context so that your program can output to the window.
2. Obtain an equivalent memory device context that will hold the bitmap until it is displayed. (A bitmap is held in memory until it is copied to your window.)
3. Select the bitmap into the memory device context.
4. Copy the bitmap from the memory device context to the window device context. Doing this causes the bitmap to be displayed.

To see how the preceding four steps can be implemented, consider the following fragment. It causes a bitmap to be displayed at two different locations each time a **WM_PAINT** message is received.

```
HDC hdc, memdc;
PAINTSTRUCT ps;

// ...

case WM_PAINT:
  hdc = BeginPaint(hwnd, &ps); // get device context

  memdc = CreateCompatibleDC(hdc); // create compatible DC
  SelectObject(memdc, hbit); // select bitmap

  BitBlt(hdc, 10, 10, 256, 128,
```

```
          memdc, 0, 0, SRCCOPY); // display image
BitBlt(hdc, 300, 100, 256, 128,
          memdc, 0, 0, SRCCOPY); // display image

EndPaint(hwnd, &ps); // release DC
DeleteDC(memdc); // free the memory context
break;
```

Let's examine this code, step by step.

First, two device context handles are declared. **hdc** will hold the current window device context as obtained by **BeginPaint( )**. The other, called **memdc**, will hold the device context of the memory that stores the bitmap until it is drawn in the window.

Within the **WM_PAINT** case, the window device context is obtained. This is necessary because the bitmap will be displayed in the client area of the window and no output can occur until your program is granted a device context. Next, a memory context is created that will hold the bitmap. This memory device context must be compatible with the window device context. The compatible memory device context is created using the **CreateCompatibleDC( )** API function. Its prototype is shown here:

HDC CreateCompatibleDC(HDC *hdc*);

This function returns a handle to a memory device context that is compatible with the device context of the window, specified by *hdc*. This memory will be used to construct an image before it is actually displayed. The function returns **NULL** if an error occurs.

Next, the bitmap must be selected into the memory device context using the **SelectObject( )** API function. Its prototype is shown here:

HGDIOBJ SelectObject(HDC *hdc*, HGDIOBJ *hObject*);

A bitmap must be selected into a memory device context before it can be displayed.

Here, *hdc* specifies the device context and *hObject* is the handle of the object being selected into that context. The function returns the handle of the previously selected object (if one exists), allowing it to be reselected later, if desired.

To actually display the bitmap, use the **BitBlt( )** API function. This function copies a bitmap from one device context to another. Its prototype is shown here:

BOOL BitBlt(HDC *hDest*, int *X*, int *Y*, int *Width*, int *Height*, HDC *hSource*, int *SourceX*, int *SourceY*, DWORD *dwHow*);

Here, *hDest* is the handle of the target device context, and *X* and *Y* are the upper-left coordinates at which point the bitmap will be drawn. The width and height of the destination region are specified in *Width* and *Height*. The *hSource* parameter contains the handle of the source device context, which in this case will be the memory context obtained using **CreateCompatibleDC( ).** The *SourceX* and *SourceY* parameters specify the upper-left coordinates within the bitmap at which the copy operation will begin. To begin copying at the upper-left corner of the bitmap, these values must be zero. The value of *dwHow* determines how the bit-by-bit contents of the bitmap will be drawn on the screen. Some of the most common values are shown here:

Macro	Effect
DSTINVERT	Inverts the bits in the destination bitmap.
SRCAND	ANDs bitmap with current destination.
SRCCOPY	Copies bitmap as is, overwriting any preexisting output.
SRCPAINT	ORs bitmap with current destination.
SRCINVERT	XORs bitmap with current destination.

7

BitBlt( ) returns nonzero if successful and zero on failure.

In the example, each call to **BitBlt( )** displays the entire bitmap by copying it to the client area of the window.

After the bitmap is displayed, both device contexts are released. In this case, **EndPaint( )** is called to release the device context obtained by calling **BeginPaint( ).** To release the memory device context obtained using **CreateCompatibleDC( )**, you must use **DeleteDC( )**, which takes as its parameter the handle of the device context to release. You cannot use **ReleaseDC( )** for this purpose. (Only a device context obtained through a call to **GetDC( )** can be released using a call to **ReleaseDC( ).**)

Deleting a Bitmap

A bitmap is a resource that must be removed before your application ends. To do this, your program must call **DeleteObject( )** when the bitmap is no longer needed or when a **WM_DESTROY** message is received. **DeleteObject( )** has this prototype:

    BOOL DeleteObject(HGDIOBJ *hObj*);

Here, *hObj* is the handle to the object being deleted. The function returns nonzero if successful and zero on failure.

The Complete Bitmap Example Program

Here is the complete bitmap program. Sample output is shown in Figure 7-2.

```cpp
// Display a bitmap.

#include <windows.h>
#include <cstring>
#include <cstdio>

LRESULT CALLBACK WindowFunc(HWND, UINT, WPARAM, LPARAM);

char szWinName[] = "MyWin"; // name of window class

HBITMAP hbit;      // handle of bitmap
HINSTANCE hInst;   // handle to this instance

int WINAPI WinMain(HINSTANCE hThisInst, HINSTANCE hPrevInst,
                   LPSTR lpszArgs, int nWinMode)
{
  HWND hwnd;
  MSG msg;
  WNDCLASSEX wcl;

  // Define a window class.
  wcl.cbSize = sizeof(WNDCLASSEX);

  wcl.hInstance = hThisInst;      // handle to this instance
  wcl.lpszClassName = szWinName;  // window class name
  wcl.lpfnWndProc = WindowFunc;   // window function
  wcl.style = 0;                  // default style

  wcl.hIcon = LoadIcon(NULL, IDI_APPLICATION); // large icon
  wcl.hIconSm = NULL; // use small version of large icon
  wcl.hCursor = LoadCursor(NULL, IDC_ARROW);  // cursor style

  wcl.lpszMenuName = NULL; // no class menu
  wcl.cbClsExtra = 0;      // no extra memory needed
  wcl.cbWndExtra = 0;

  // Make the window background white.
  wcl.hbrBackground = (HBRUSH) GetStockObject(WHITE_BRUSH);

  // Register the window class.
  if(!RegisterClassEx(&wcl)) return 0;

  hInst = hThisInst; // save the current instance handle
```

```
/* Now that a window class has been registered, a window
   can be created. */
hwnd = CreateWindow(
  szWinName, // name of window class
  "Displaying a Bitmap", // title
  WS_OVERLAPPEDWINDOW, // window style - normal
  CW_USEDEFAULT, // X coordinate - let Windows decide
  CW_USEDEFAULT, // Y coordinate - let Windows decide
  CW_USEDEFAULT, // width - let Windows decide
  CW_USEDEFAULT, // height - let Windows decide
  NULL,          // no parent window
  NULL,          // no menu
  hThisInst,     // instance handle
  NULL           // no additional arguments
);

// Display the window.
ShowWindow(hwnd, nWinMode);
UpdateWindow(hwnd);

// Create the message loop.
while(GetMessage(&msg, NULL, 0, 0))
{
  TranslateMessage(&msg); // translate keyboard messages
  DispatchMessage(&msg);  // return control to Windows 2000
}

  return msg.wParam;
}

/* This function is called by Windows 2000 and is passed
   messages from the message queue.
*/
LRESULT CALLBACK WindowFunc(HWND hwnd, UINT message,
                            WPARAM wParam, LPARAM lParam)
{
  HDC hdc, memdc;
  PAINTSTRUCT ps;

  switch(message) {
    case WM_CREATE:
      // load the bitmap
      hbit = LoadBitmap(hInst, "MyBP"); // load bitmap
      break;
    case WM_PAINT:
      hdc = BeginPaint(hwnd, &ps); // get device context
```

7

```
    memdc = CreateCompatibleDC(hdc); // create compatible DC
    SelectObject(memdc, hbit); // select bitmap

    BitBlt(hdc, 10, 10, 256, 128,
           memdc, 0, 0, SRCCOPY); // display image
    BitBlt(hdc, 300, 100, 256, 128,
           memdc, 0, 0, SRCCOPY); // display image

    EndPaint(hwnd, &ps); // release DC
    DeleteDC(memdc); // free the memory context
    break;
  case WM_DESTROY: // terminate the program
    DeleteObject(hbit); // remove the bitmap
    PostQuitMessage(0);
    break;
  default:
    /* Let Windows 2000 process any messages not specified in
       the preceding switch statement. */
    return DefWindowProc(hwnd, message, wParam, lParam);
  }

  return 0;
}
```

You might want to experiment with the bitmap program before continuing.
For example, try using different copy options with **BitBlt( ).** Also, try
different size bitmaps.

Sample output
using the
custom bitmap

Figure 7-2.

XORing an Image to a Window

As explained, **BltBlt( )** can copy the bitmap contained in one device context into another device context in a number of different ways. For example, if you specify **SRCPAINT**, the image is ORed with the destination. Using **SRCAND** causes the bitmap to be ANDed with the destination. Perhaps the most interesting way to copy the contents of one DC to another uses **SRCINVERT**. This method XORs the source with the destination. There are two reasons this is particularly valuable.

First, XORing an image onto a window guarantees that the image will be visible. It doesn't matter what color or colors the source image or the destination use, an XORed image is always visible. Second, XORing an image to the same destination twice removes the image and restores the destination to its original condition. As you might guess, XORing is an efficient way to temporarily display and then remove an image from a window without disturbing its original contents.

To see the effects of XORing an image to a window, insert the following cases into **WindowFunc( )** in the first bitmap program.

```
case WM_LBUTTONDOWN:
  hdc = GetDC(hwnd);

  memdc = CreateCompatibleDC(hdc); // create compatible DC
  SelectObject(memdc, hbit); // select bitmap

  // XOR image onto the window
  BitBlt(hdc, LOWORD(lParam), HIWORD(lParam), 256, 128,
         memdc, 0, 0, SRCINVERT);
  ReleaseDC(hwnd, hdc);
  DeleteDC(memdc);
  break;
case WM_LBUTTONUP:
  hdc = GetDC(hwnd);

  memdc = CreateCompatibleDC(hdc); // create compatible DC
  SelectObject(memdc, hbit); // select bitmap

  // XOR image onto the window a second time
```

7

```
BitBlt(hdc, LOWORD(lParam), HIWORD(lParam), 256, 128,
     memdc, 0, 0, SRCINVERT);

ReleaseDC(hwnd, hdc);
DeleteDC(memdc);
break;
```

The code works like this. Each time the left mouse button is pressed, the bitmap is XORed to the window starting at the location of the mouse pointer, causing an inverted image of the bitmap to be displayed. When the left mouse pointer is released, the image is XORed a second time, causing the bitmap to be removed and the previous contents to be restored. Be careful not to move the mouse while you are holding down the left button. If you do, then the second XOR copy will not take place directly over the top of the first, and the original contents of the window will not be restored.

Creating a Bitmap Dynamically

In addition to using bitmap resources, your program can create bitmaps dynamically. As you know, the size and content of a bitmap resource is predefined; this is not the case for bitmaps created during the execution of your program. The easiest way to create a bitmap is to call the **CreateCompatibleBitmap( )** API function. It creates a device-dependent bitmap that is compatible with a specified device context. The function's prototype is shown here:

HBITMAP CreateCompatibleBitmap(HDC *hdc*, int *width*, int *height*);

Here, *hdc* is the handle for the device with which the bitmap will be compatible. The dimensions of the bitmap are specified in *width* and *height*. These values are in pixels. The function returns a handle to the compatible bitmap or **NULL** on failure. The bitmap will initially be empty.

Using a Dynamically Created Bitmap

The ability to create bitmaps as needed allows you to perform several types of useful operations. For example, you can use a dynamically created bitmap to construct some type of image during runtime. Or, you can use a dynamically created bitmap to temporarily store an image (or part of an image) that is contained in a larger bitmap. One of the most interesting uses of a dynamically constructed bitmap is for copying information from the client area of a window into a bitmap, giving you an easy way to save the contents of a window.

To demonstrate the use of a dynamically created bitmap, a short program is developed next that allows you to copy a region of the screen from one part of a window to another. The program works like this. Each time you press the left mouse button, a 100 by 100 region of the window that has its upper-left corner at the current mouse position is copied into a bitmap. Each time you press the right mouse button, the bitmap is copied to the window at the current location of the mouse. Thus, you can copy pieces of the main window within the client area.

The entire dynamic bitmap program is shown here. Sample output is shown in Figure 7-3.

```
/* This program creates a bitmap dynamically and uses it
   to copy portions of the client area of its main window. */

#include <windows.h>
#include <cstring>
#include <cstdio>

LRESULT CALLBACK WindowFunc(HWND, UINT, WPARAM, LPARAM);

char szWinName[] = "MyWin"; // name of window class

HINSTANCE hInst; // handle to this instance
HBITMAP hdynbit; // handle to dynamically created bitmap

int WINAPI WinMain(HINSTANCE hThisInst, HINSTANCE hPrevInst,
                   LPSTR lpszArgs, int nWinMode)
{
  HWND hwnd;
  MSG msg;
  WNDCLASSEX wcl;

  // Define a window class.
  wcl.cbSize = sizeof(WNDCLASSEX);

  wcl.hInstance = hThisInst;     // handle to this instance
  wcl.lpszClassName = szWinName; // window class name
  wcl.lpfnWndProc = WindowFunc;  // window function
  wcl.style = 0;                 // default style
```

7

```
  wcl.hIcon = LoadIcon(NULL, IDI_APPLICATION); // large icon
  wcl.hIconSm = NULL; // use small version of large icon
  wcl.hCursor = LoadCursor(NULL, IDC_ARROW);  // cursor style

  wcl.lpszMenuName = NULL; // no class menu
  wcl.cbClsExtra = 0;        // no extra memory needed
  wcl.cbWndExtra = 0;

  // Make the window background white.
  wcl.hbrBackground = (HBRUSH) GetStockObject(WHITE_BRUSH);

  // Register the window class.
  if(!RegisterClassEx(&wcl)) return 0;

  hInst = hThisInst; // save instance handle

  /* Now that a window class has been registered, a window
     can be created. */
  hwnd = CreateWindow(
    szWinName, // name of window class
    "Using Dynamic Bitmaps", // title
    WS_OVERLAPPEDWINDOW, // window style - normal
    CW_USEDEFAULT, // X coordinate - let Windows decide
    CW_USEDEFAULT, // Y coordinate - let Windows decide
    CW_USEDEFAULT, // width - let Windows decide
    CW_USEDEFAULT, // height - let Windows decide
    NULL,          // no parent window
    NULL,          // no menu
    hThisInst,     // instance handle
    NULL           // no additional arguments
  );

  // Display the window.
  ShowWindow(hwnd, nWinMode);
  UpdateWindow(hwnd);

  // Create the message loop.
  while(GetMessage(&msg, NULL, 0, 0))
  {
    TranslateMessage(&msg); // translate keyboard messages
    DispatchMessage(&msg);  // return control to Windows 2000
  }

  return msg.wParam;
}

/* This function is called by Windows 2000 and is passed
```

```
         messages from the message queue.
*/
LRESULT CALLBACK WindowFunc(HWND hwnd, UINT message,
                            WPARAM wParam, LPARAM lParam)
{
  HDC hdc, memdc;
  PAINTSTRUCT ps;
  int i;
  char str[80] = "Using a dynamic bitmap.";
  char instructions[] =  "Click left button at source, "
                         "right button at destination.";

  switch(message) {
    case WM_CREATE:
      // dynamically create a bitmap
      hdc = GetDC(hwnd);
      hdynbit = CreateCompatibleBitmap(hdc, 100, 100);
      ReleaseDC(hwnd, hdc);
      break;
    case WM_LBUTTONDOWN: // copy region of window to bitmap
      hdc = GetDC(hwnd);

      memdc = CreateCompatibleDC(hdc); // create compatible DC

      // select dynamic bitmap into memory DC
      SelectObject(memdc, hdynbit);

      // copy region into dynamic bitmap
      BitBlt(memdc, 0, 0, 100, 100,
             hdc, LOWORD(lParam), HIWORD(lParam), SRCCOPY);

      ReleaseDC(hwnd, hdc);
      DeleteDC(memdc);
      break;
    case WM_RBUTTONDOWN: // copy bitmap to window
      hdc = GetDC(hwnd);

      memdc = CreateCompatibleDC(hdc); // create compatible DC

      // select dynamic bitmap into memory DC
      SelectObject(memdc, hdynbit);

      // copy dynamic bitmap to window
      BitBlt(hdc, LOWORD(lParam), HIWORD(lParam), 100, 100,
             memdc, 0, 0, SRCCOPY);
```

```
          ReleaseDC(hwnd, hdc);
          DeleteDC(memdc);
          break;
      case WM_PAINT:
        hdc = BeginPaint(hwnd, &ps); // get device context

        TextOut(hdc, 1, 0, instructions, strlen(instructions));

        for(i=1; i<10; i++)
          TextOut(hdc, 1, i*20, str, strlen(str));

        EndPaint(hwnd, &ps); // release DC
        break;
      case WM_DESTROY: // terminate the program
        DeleteObject(hdynbit); // remove the bitmap
        PostQuitMessage(0);
        break;
      default:
        /* Let Windows 2000 process any messages not specified in
           the preceding switch statement. */
        return DefWindowProc(hwnd, message, wParam, lParam);
  }

  return 0;
}
```

When the program first begins execution, the main window receives a
WM_CREATE message and a bitmap is created that is compatible with the
device context used by the main window. The handle to this bitmap is saved

Sample output
from the
dynamic
bitmap
program

Figure 7-3.

in **hdynbit**, which is a global variable. Each time the left mouse button is pressed, a compatible memory DC is created, the bitmap is selected into that device context, and a 100 by 100 rectangular region of the window is copied into the bitmap. Each time the right mouse button is pressed, a similar sequence occurs, but the source and targets are reversed. This sequence causes the current contents of the bitmap to be copied to the window.

As you can undoubtedly imagine, the ability to create bitmaps dynamically has several important uses. Perhaps the most important is described in the following section.

Solving the Repaint Problem

Now that you know the basic operations involved with using bitmaps, you can use that knowledge to solve one of the most fundamental problems encountered when writing a Windows 2000 program: restoring the contents of a window when a **WM_PAINT** message is received. As you know, in Windows 2000 (and all versions of Windows) it is the application's responsibility to redraw the contents of the client area of a window each time a **WM_PAINT** message is received. In general, a window needs to be redrawn each time it is uncovered. That is, when you run a program, display something in the client area of a window, and then overlay the window with another, your output is lost. Thus, when the window is uncovered, its contents will need to be repainted. The same techniques that were used to display a bitmap also form the basis by which you can solve the repaint problem.

7

Let's start by reviewing the three basic methods that you can use to repaint a window. First, you can regenerate the output if that output is created by some computational method. Second, you can store a record of display events and "replay" those events. Third, you can maintain a virtual window and simply copy the contents of the virtual window to the physical window each time a **WM_PAINT** message is received. The most general of these is, of course, the third, and this is the method that we will develop here.

A virtual window is a memory device context combined with a bitmap that is compatible with the physical device context used by your program.

Here is how output will be accomplished using a virtual window. First, a memory device context and bitmap (that is, the virtual window) are created that are compatible with the physical device context used by your application. Thus, a virtual window is simply a compatible bitmap that has the same characteristics as your program's actual window. Once you have created a virtual window, all output intended for the client area of the main window must also be written to the virtual window. Doing this causes the virtual window to contain a complete and current copy of whatever you output to the physical window. Each time a **WM_PAINT** message is received, the contents of the virtual window are copied into the actual window, restoring its contents. Therefore, a window that has been covered and then uncovered will automatically be redrawn when it receives the **WM_PAINT** message.

Some Additional API Functions

The implementation of a virtual window requires the use of several API functions. Five have been discussed already. These are **CreateCompatibleBitmap( )**, **CreateCompatibleDC( )**, **SelectObject( )**, **GetStockObject( )**, and **BitBlt( )**. We will also be using **PatBlt( )** and **GetSystemMetrics( )**, which are described here.

PatBlt( )

The **PatBlt( )** function fills a rectangle with the color and pattern of the currently selected *brush*. A brush is an object that specifies how a window (or region) will be filled. Filling an area using a brush is also commonly referred to as *painting* the region. **PatBlt( )** has this prototype:

BOOL PatBlt(HDC *hdc*, int *X*, int *Y*, int *width*, int *height*, DWORD *dwHow*);

Here, *hdc* is the handle of the device to fill. The coordinates *X* and *Y* specify the upper-left corner of the region to be filled. The width and height of the region are specified in *width* and *height*. The value passed in *dwHow* determines how the brush will be applied; it must be one of these macros:

Macro	Meaning
BLACKNESS	Region is black (brush is ignored).
WHITENESS	Region is white (brush is ignored).
PATCOPY	Brush is copied to region.
PATINVERT	Brush is ORed to region.
DSTINVERT	Region is inverted (brush is ignored).

Therefore, if you wish to apply the current brush unaltered, you would select **PATCOPY** for the value of *dwHow*. The function returns nonzero if successful, zero otherwise.

Obtaining the System Metrics

To create a virtual window requires that we know how big to make the bitmap that will be used as the virtual window. One way to do this is to obtain the size, in pixels, of the screen and use its dimensions for the bitmap. To obtain the size of the screen, and other information, use the **GetSystemMetrics( )** API function, whose prototype is shown here:

    int GetSystemMetrics(int *what*);

Here, *what* will be a value that specifies the value that you want to obtain. **GetSystemMetrics( )** can obtain many different values. Here are the macros for some common values:

Value	Metric Obtained
SM_CXFULLSCREEN	Width of maximized client area
SM_CYFULLSCREEN	Height of maximized client area
SM_CXICON	Width of standard icon
SM_CYICON	Height of standard icon
SM_CXSMICON	Width of small icon
SM_CYSMICON	Height of small icon
SM_CXSCREEN	Width of entire screen
SM_CYSCREEN	Height of entire screen

We will be using the values associated with **SM_CXSCREEN** and **SM_CYSCREEN** as the dimensions of the virtual window. These values are returned in pixel units.

Creating and Using a Virtual Window

Let's begin by restating the procedure that will be implemented. To create an easy and convenient means of restoring a window after a **WM_PAINT** message has been received, a virtual window will be maintained. All output intended for the client area will be written to the virtual window as well as to the physical window. This means that the virtual window will always contain a complete copy of whatever has been output to the physical window. Each time a repaint request is received, the contents of the virtual window are copied into the window that is physically on the screen. Doing this causes the contents of the physical window to be restored. Now, let's implement this approach.

The first step you must follow to create a virtual window is to obtain a memory device context that is compatible with the current physical device context. This will be done only once, when the window is first created. This compatible device context will stay in existence the entire time the program is executing. Here is the code that performs this function:

```
case WM_CREATE:
  // get screen coordinates
  maxX = GetSystemMetrics(SM_CXSCREEN);
  maxY = GetSystemMetrics(SM_CYSCREEN);

  // make a compatible memory image
  hdc = GetDC(hwnd);
  memdc = CreateCompatibleDC(hdc);
  hbit = CreateCompatibleBitmap(hdc, maxX, maxY);
  SelectObject(memdc, hbit);
  hbrush = GetStockObject(WHITE_BRUSH);
  SelectObject(memdc, hbrush);
  PatBlt(memdc, 0, 0, maxX, maxY, PATCOPY);
  ReleaseDC(hwnd, hdc);
  break;
```

Let's examine this code closely. First, the dimensions of the screen are obtained. They will be used to create a compatible bitmap. Then, the current device context is obtained. Next, a compatible device context is created in memory, using **CreateCompatibleDC( )**; the handle to this device context is stored in **memdc**, which is a global variable. Then, a compatible bitmap is created. This establishes a one-to-one mapping between the virtual window and the physical window. The dimensions of the bitmap are those of the maximum screen size, ensuring that the bitmap will always be large enough to fully restore the window no matter how large the physical window is. (Actually, slightly smaller values could be used, since the borders aren't repainted, but this minor improvement is left to you, as an exercise.) The handle to the bitmap is stored in the global variable **hbit**. It is also selected into the memory device context. Next, a stock white brush is obtained and its handle is stored in the global variable **hbrush**. This brush is selected into the memory device context, and then **PatBlt( )** paints the entire virtual window using the brush. Thus, the virtual window will have a white background, which matches the background of the physical window in the example program that follows. (Remember, the colors you use are under your control. The colors used here are arbitrary.) Finally, the physical device context is released. However, the memory device context stays in existence until the program ends.

Once the virtual window has been created, you must make sure that a complete copy of all output is also written to the virtual window. Each time a **WM_PAINT** message is received, you will use the contents of the virtual window to restore the contents of the physical window. You will do this in much the same way that you copied a bitmapped image to the window in the preceding section: by using the **BitBlt( )** function.

The Entire Virtual Window Demonstration Program

Here is the complete program that demonstrates using a virtual window to solve the repaint problem. The program responds to **WM_CHAR** messages by outputting each character to both the virtual window and the physical window. (That is, it echoes the characters you type to both the physical window and the virtual window.) When a **WM_PAINT** message is received, the contents of the virtual window are used to restore the physical window.

```
// Repaint using a virtual window.

#include <windows.h>
#include <cstring>
#include <cstdio>

LRESULT CALLBACK WindowFunc(HWND, UINT, WPARAM, LPARAM);

char szWinName[] = "MyWin"; // name of window class

char str[255]; // holds output strings

int X=0, Y=0;   // current output location
int maxX, maxY; // screen dimensions

HDC memdc;      // store the virtual device handle
HBITMAP hbit;   // store the virtual bitmap
HBRUSH hbrush;  // store the brush handle

int WINAPI WinMain(HINSTANCE hThisInst, HINSTANCE hPrevInst,
                   LPSTR lpszArgs, int nWinMode)
{
  HWND hwnd;
  MSG msg;
  WNDCLASSEX wcl;
```

7

```
// Define a window class.
wcl.cbSize = sizeof(WNDCLASSEX);

wcl.hInstance = hThisInst;      // handle to this instance
wcl.lpszClassName = szWinName; // window class name
wcl.lpfnWndProc = WindowFunc;   // window function
wcl.style = 0;                  // default style

wcl.hIcon = LoadIcon(NULL, IDI_APPLICATION); // large icon
wcl.hIconSm = NULL; // use small version of large icon
wcl.hCursor = LoadCursor(NULL, IDC_ARROW);  // cursor style

wcl.lpszMenuName = NULL; // no class menu
wcl.cbClsExtra = 0;         // no extra memory needed
wcl.cbWndExtra = 0;

// Make the window background white.
wcl.hbrBackground = (HBRUSH) GetStockObject(WHITE_BRUSH);

// Register the window class.
if(!RegisterClassEx(&wcl)) return 0;

/* Now that a window class has been registered, a window
   can be created. */
hwnd = CreateWindow(
  szWinName, // name of window class
  "Using a Virtual Window", // title
  WS_OVERLAPPEDWINDOW, // window style - normal
  CW_USEDEFAULT, // X coordinate - let Windows decide
  CW_USEDEFAULT, // Y coordinate - let Windows decide
  CW_USEDEFAULT, // width - let Windows decide
  CW_USEDEFAULT, // height - let Windows decide
  NULL,          // no parent window
  NULL,          // no menu
  hThisInst,     // instance handle
  NULL           // no additional arguments
);

// Display the window.
ShowWindow(hwnd, nWinMode);
UpdateWindow(hwnd);

// Create the message loop.
while(GetMessage(&msg, NULL, 0, 0))
{
  TranslateMessage(&msg); // translate keyboard messages
```

```
          DispatchMessage(&msg);  // return control to Windows 2000
   }

   return msg.wParam;
}


/* This function is called by Windows 2000 and is passed
   messages from the message queue.
*/
LRESULT CALLBACK WindowFunc(HWND hwnd, UINT message,
                            WPARAM wParam, LPARAM lParam)
{
   HDC hdc;
   PAINTSTRUCT ps;

   switch(message) {
     case WM_CREATE:
       // get screen coordinates
       maxX = GetSystemMetrics(SM_CXSCREEN);
       maxY = GetSystemMetrics(SM_CYSCREEN);

       // make a compatible memory image
       hdc = GetDC(hwnd);
       memdc = CreateCompatibleDC(hdc);
       hbit = CreateCompatibleBitmap(hdc, maxX, maxY);
       SelectObject(memdc, hbit);
       hbrush = (HBRUSH) GetStockObject(WHITE_BRUSH);
       SelectObject(memdc, hbrush);
       PatBlt(memdc, 0, 0, maxX, maxY, PATCOPY);
       ReleaseDC(hwnd, hdc);
       break;
     case WM_CHAR:
       hdc = GetDC(hwnd);
       sprintf(str, "%c", (char) wParam); // stringize character

       // a "primitive" carriage return, linefeed sequence
       if((char)wParam == '\r') {
         Y += 14; // advance to next line
         X = 0;   // reset to start of line
       }
       else {
         TextOut(memdc, X, Y, str,
                 strlen(str)); // output to memory
         TextOut(hdc, X, Y, str,
                 strlen(str)); // output to window
         X += 10;
```

7

```
        }
        ReleaseDC(hwnd, hdc);
        break;
      case WM_PAINT: // process a repaint request
        hdc = BeginPaint(hwnd, &ps); // get DC

        // copy memory image onto screen
        BitBlt(hdc, 0, 0, maxX, maxY, memdc, 0, 0, SRCCOPY);
        EndPaint(hwnd, &ps); // release DC
        break;
      case WM_DESTROY: // terminate the program
        DeleteDC(memdc); // delete the memory device
        DeleteObject(hbit); // remove the bitmap
        PostQuitMessage(0);
        break;
      default:
        /* Let Windows 2000 process any messages not specified in
           the preceding switch statement. */
        return DefWindowProc(hwnd, message, wParam, lParam);
  }

  return 0;
}
```

Sample output is shown in Figure 7-4. Let's look at this program in detail. First, examine the code associated with the **WM_CHAR** message. It is shown here for your convenience.

```
case WM_CHAR:
  hdc = GetDC(hwnd);
  sprintf(str, "%c", (char) wParam); // stringize character

  // a "primitive" carriage return, linefeed sequence
  if((char)wParam == '\r') {
    Y += 14; // advance to next line
    X = 0;   // reset to start of line
  }
  else {
    TextOut(memdc, X, Y, str,
            strlen(str)); // output to memory
    TextOut(hdc, X, Y, str,
            strlen(str)); // output to window
    X += 10;
  }
  ReleaseDC(hwnd, hdc);
  break;
```

Sample output
from the
virtual window
program

Figure 7-4.

The variables **X** and **Y** are two global integers that are used to maintain the coordinates at which the next character will be displayed. They are initially zero. Each time a character is typed, it is "stringized" and output to both the physical window and the virtual window. Thus, a complete copy of each keystroke is maintained in the virtual window.

As you can see, **X** is advanced by 10 for each character typed and **Y** is increased by 14 to advance to the next line each time ENTER is pressed. This method of determining the proper X,Y location is a crude, temporary measure. In the next chapter, you will learn the proper way to manage text output.

Each time a **WM_PAINT** message is received, the contents of the virtual window are copied into the physical window, restoring its contents. This is accomplished by the following code:

```
case WM_PAINT: // process a repaint request
  hdc = BeginPaint(hwnd, &ps); // get DC

  // copy memory image onto screen
  BitBlt(hdc, 0, 0, maxX, maxY, memdc, 0, 0, SRCCOPY);
  EndPaint(hwnd, &ps); // release DC
  break;
```

The **BitBlt( )** function copies the image from **memdc** into **hdc**. Remember, the parameter **SRCCOPY** simply means that the image is to be copied without alteration directly from the source to the target. Because all output has been stored in **memdc**, this statement causes the window to be restored. You should experiment by entering some characters and then covering and

7

uncovering the window. As you will see, the characters that you typed are redisplayed.

There is a variation on the virtual window mechanism that you might find useful in some situations. Instead of outputting information twice, once to the physical window and once to the virtual window, your program can simply write all information to the virtual window and then call **InvalidateRect( )** to cause the information to be displayed. (Remember from the discussion in Chapter 3 that **InvalidateRect( )** generates a **WM_PAINT** message.) If you try this approach in the example program, you will find that the window seems to "flash" each time you press a key because the entire window is being updated with each keypress, which makes this method inappropriate for this example. However, for programs that do infrequent output, such an approach may make sense.

Improving Repaint Efficiency

The method just described shows the general technique for using a virtual window to handle repaint requests. However, it is possible to make a rather significant improvement to the preceding program. As the program is written, it suffers from two inefficiencies. First, the entire virtual window is copied to the physical window no matter how large (or small) the physical window actually is. Since the virtual window is the size of the entire screen, this approach is clearly inefficient. Although no harm is caused by this approach (because output is automatically clipped), it does waste CPU time.

The second problem is that no matter how much of the physical window actually needs to be repainted, the entire window is repainted each time a **WM_PAINT** message arrives. This is the way most beginning Windows programmers handle a repaint request. It is, of course, not the best way. The trouble is that often only a corner of a window actually needs to be restored. It is important to understand that restoring a window is expensive in terms of time. The larger the window, the longer it takes to restore it. Repainting parts of a window that don't need it wastes time and can make your application sluggish.

Both of these inefficiencies are rooted in the fact that the preceding program paints more of the window that it needs to. The solution is to change the program so that it repaints only those portions of the window that actually need to be restored. Using this approach, repaints take less time and your application has a much snappier feel. Frankly, optimizing window repainting is one of the most important performance improvements that you can make to your program.

Fortunately, Windows 2000 automatically provides the information that we need to implement a more efficient repaint handler. This information is supplied by **BeginPaint( )**. Our first step will be to review this information.

A Closer Look at BeginPaint( )

As you learned in Chapter 3, when a **WM_PAINT** message is processed, you must call **BeginPaint( )** to obtain a device context. In addition to acquiring a device context, **BeginPaint( )** also obtains information about the display state of the window. We will use this information to optimize repainting.

Recall that the prototype for **BeginPaint( )** is the following:

HDC BeginPaint(HWND *hwnd*, PAINTSTRUCT **lpPS*);

BeginPaint( ) returns a device context if successful or **NULL** on failure. Here, *hwnd* is the handle of the window for which the device context is being obtained. The second parameter is a pointer to a structure of type **PAINTSTRUCT**. The structure pointed to by *lpPS* will contain information that your program can use to repaint the window. **PAINTSTRUCT** is defined like this:

```
typedef struct tagPAINTSTRUCT {
  HDC hdc;                  // handle to device context
  BOOL fErase;             // true if background must be erased
  RECT rcPaint;            // coordinates of region to redraw
  BOOL fRestore;           // reserved
  BOOL fIncUpdate;         // reserved
  BYTE rgbReserved[32];    // reserved
} PAINTSTRUCT;
```

The field that is of particular interest to us is **rcPaint**. This element contains the coordinates of the region of the window that needs to be repainted. We can take advantage of this information to reduce the time needed to restore a window.

Reducing Virtual Window Repaint Time

The key to decreasing the time it takes to restore a window when a **WM_PAINT** message is received is to restore only the portion of the window defined by **rcPaint.** This goal is easy to accomplish when using a virtual window. Simply copy the same region from the virtual window to the physical window. Since the two device contexts are identical, so are their coordinate systems. The coordinates that are contained in **rcPaint** can be used for both the physical window and the virtual window. For example, here is one way to respond to **WM_PAINT**:

```
case WM_PAINT: // an improved response to a repaint request
  hdc = BeginPaint(hwnd, &ps); // get DC

  // copy a portion of the virtual window
  BitBlt(hdc, ps.rcPaint.left, ps.rcPaint.top,
         ps.rcPaint.right-ps.rcPaint.left, // width
         ps.rcPaint.bottom-ps.rcPaint.top, // height
         memdc,
         ps.rcPaint.left, ps.rcPaint.top,
         SRCCOPY);

  EndPaint(hwnd, &ps); // release DC
  break;
```

To see the effectiveness of this version, substitute it into the program from the preceding section. Because this version copies only the rectangle defined by **rcPaint**, no time is wasted copying information that has not been overwritten or that is outside the current boundaries of the window.

Notice how easy it is to optimize the repainting of a window when using the virtual window method. Almost no additional programming effort is required. The virtual window method of repainting is an elegant solution to many repaint-related operations.

As an experiment, you can see the coordinates associated with each **WM_PAINT** message by putting this code directly after the call to **BeginPaint( )**:

```
sprintf(str, "top, left: %d %d\nBotton, right: %d %d",
        ps.rcPaint.top, ps.rcPaint.left,
        ps.rcPaint.bottom, ps.rcPaint.right);
MessageBox(hwnd, str, "coordinates", MB_OK);
```

Here, **str** is a character array. When you run the program, try overlaying two or more different portions of its window. You will see a separate message for each portion that you uncover.

For most of the examples in this book, efficient repaints are not needed. In fact, most programs won't even bother repainting the client area because the extra code will simply obscure the point of the example. However, in real programs that you write, the efficient handling of **WM_PAINT** is a crucial performance issue.

Creating a Custom Icon and Cursor

To conclude this chapter we will examine the creation and use of custom icons and cursors. As you know, all Windows 2000 applications first create a window class, which defines the attributes of the window, including the shape of the application's icon and mouse cursor. The handles to the icons and the mouse cursor are stored in the **hIcon, hIconSm**, and **hCursor** fields of the **WNDCLASSEX** structure. So far, we have been using the built-in icons and cursors supplied by Windows 2000. However, it is possible to define your own.

Defining Icons and Cursors

To use a custom icon and mouse cursor, you must first define their images with an image editor. Remember, you will need to make a small icon and a large icon. The small icon is 16 by 16 and the large icon is 32 by 32. Both sizes of icons are defined within a single icon file. All cursors are the same size, 32 by 32.

7

HISTORICAL PERSPECTIVE: 16-bit versions of Windows define only the large icon.

For the examples that follow, you should call the file that holds your icons ICON.ICO. Be sure to create both the 32 by 32 and the 16 by 16 pixel icons. Remember that both of these icons must be defined within the same file.

Call the file that holds your cursor, CURSOR.CUR. Figure 7-5 shows the icons and cursor used by the example in this chapter.

Once you have defined the icon and cursor images, you will need to add both an **ICON** and a **CURSOR** statement to your program's resource file. These statements have these general forms:

Custom icons
and cursor

Figure 7-5.

Custom icons
and cursor
(continued)

Figure 7-5.

IconName ICON *filename*
CursorName CURSOR *filename*

Here, the *IconName* is the name that identifies the icon and *CursorName* is the name that identifies the cursor. These names are used by your program to refer to the icon and cursor. The *filename* specifies the file that holds the custom icon or cursor.

For the example program, you will need a resource file that contains the following statements:

```
MyCursor CURSOR CURSOR.CUR
MyIcon ICON ICON.ICO
```

Loading Your Icons and Cursor

To use your custom icons and cursor, you must load them and assign their handles to the appropriate fields in the **WNDCLASSEX** structure before the window class is registered. To accomplish this you must use the API functions **LoadIcon( )** and **LoadCursor( )**, which you learned about in Chapter 2. For example, the following loads the icons identified as **MyIcon** and the cursor called **MyCursor** and stores their handles in the appropriate fields of **WNDCLASSEX**.

```
wcl.hIcon = LoadIcon(hThisInst, "MyIcon"); // large icon
wcl.hIconSm = NULL; // use small icon contained in MyIcon
wcl.hCursor = LoadCursor(hThisInst, "MyCursor"); // cursor
```

Here, **hThisInst** is the handle of the current instance of the program. In the previous programs in this book, these functions have been used to load default icons and cursors. Here, they are used to load the custom icons and cursor.

Notice that **hIconSm** is assigned **NULL**. When **hIconSm** is **NULL**, the small icon defined in the file that holds the large icon is automatically loaded. In other words, when **hIconSm** is **NULL**, the small icon is the one associated with the large icon assigned to **hIcon**. Of course, you are free to specify a different icon resource for this icon, if you like. However, to do so you will need to use the **LoadImage( )** function, described at the end of the this chapter. For most applications, you will simply define the small icon in the same file that contains the large icon.

A Sample Program that Demonstrates a Custom Icon and Cursor

The following program uses the custom icons and cursor. The small icon is displayed in the main window's system menu box and in the program's entry in the task bar. The large icon is displayed when you move your program to the desktop. The cursor will be used when the mouse pointer is over the window. That is, the shape of the mouse cursor will automatically change to the one defined by your program when the mouse moves over the program's window. It will automatically revert to its default shape when it moves off the program's window.

Remember, before you try to compile this program, you must define the custom icons and cursor using an image editor and then add these resources to the resource file associated with the program.

```cpp
// Demonstrate custom icons and mouse cursor.

#include <windows.h>
#include <cstring>
#include <cstdio>

LRESULT CALLBACK WindowFunc(HWND, UINT, WPARAM, LPARAM);

char szWinName[] = "MyWin"; // name of window class

int WINAPI WinMain(HINSTANCE hThisInst, HINSTANCE hPrevInst,
                   LPSTR lpszArgs, int nWinMode)
{
  HWND hwnd;
  MSG msg;
  WNDCLASSEX wcl;

  // Define a window class.
  wcl.cbSize = sizeof(WNDCLASSEX);

  wcl.hInstance = hThisInst;       // handle to this instance
  wcl.lpszClassName = szWinName;   // window class name
  wcl.lpfnWndProc = WindowFunc;    // window function
  wcl.style = 0;                   // default style

  wcl.hIcon = LoadIcon(hThisInst, "MyIcon"); // large icon
  wcl.hIconSm = NULL; // use small version of large icon
  wcl.hCursor = LoadCursor(hThisInst, "MyCursor"); // cursor

  wcl.lpszMenuName = NULL; // no class menu
  wcl.cbClsExtra = 0;      // no extra memory needed
  wcl.cbWndExtra = 0;

  // Make the window background white.
  wcl.hbrBackground = (HBRUSH) GetStockObject(WHITE_BRUSH);

  // Register the window class.
  if(!RegisterClassEx(&wcl)) return 0;

  /* Now that a window class has been registered, a window
     can be created. */
  hwnd = CreateWindow(
    szWinName, // name of window class
    "Custom Icons and Cursor", // title
    WS_OVERLAPPEDWINDOW, // window style - normal
```

```
        CW_USEDEFAULT, // X coordinate - let Windows decide
        CW_USEDEFAULT, // Y coordinate - let Windows decide
        CW_USEDEFAULT, // width - let Windows decide
        CW_USEDEFAULT, // height - let Windows decide
        NULL,          // no parent window
        NULL,          // no menu
        hThisInst,     // instance handle
        NULL           // no additional arguments
    );

    // Display the window.
    ShowWindow(hwnd, nWinMode);
    UpdateWindow(hwnd);

    // Create the message loop.
    while(GetMessage(&msg, NULL, 0, 0))
    {
      TranslateMessage(&msg); // translate keyboard messages
      DispatchMessage(&msg);  // return control to Windows 2000
    }

    return msg.wParam;
}

/* This function is called by Windows 2000 and is passed
   messages from the message queue.
*/
LRESULT CALLBACK WindowFunc(HWND hwnd, UINT message,
                            WPARAM wParam, LPARAM lParam)
{
  switch(message) {
    case WM_DESTROY: // terminate the program
      PostQuitMessage(0);
      break;
    default:
      /* Let Windows 2000 process any messages not specified in
         the preceding switch statement. */
      return DefWindowProc(hwnd, message, wParam, lParam);
  }

  return 0;
}
```

The small custom icon is shown in action in Figure 7-6. (Of course, your custom icon will look different from this one.) The custom mouse cursor will

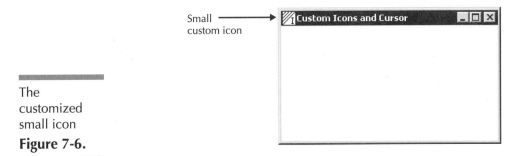

Small custom icon

The customized small icon

Figure 7-6.

appear when you move the mouse over the window. (Try doing this before continuing.)

One last point about custom icons: When you create custom icons for your application, you will usually want both sizes of icons to display the same general image, since it is this image that is associated with your program.

7

Using LoadImage( )

Throughout this book we have been using **LoadIcon( )** and **LoadCursor( )** to load the icons and cursors used by the application examples. As you have just seen, you can use **LoadBitmap( )** to load a bitmapped image. These are the functions that have been used to accomplish these tasks since Windows was first invented. They are still perfectly acceptable functions to use. However, Windows 2000 includes a function called **LoadImage( )** that provides a useful alternative. **LoadImage( )** is a more flexible function that can be used to load icons, cursors, and bitmaps of any size and provides more detailed control over how these items are loaded. For example, you can use it to load a small custom icon that is not part of the file specified by the large icon. While we won't need the fine-grained control that **LoadImage( )** offers for the examples in this book, it is a function that you may find useful for your programs, and for this reason it is examined here.

LoadImage( ) has the following prototype:

HANDLE LoadImage(HINSTANCE *hThisInst*, LPCSTR *lpszName*,
                 UINT *what*, int *width*, int *height*, UINT *how*);

The current instance handle is specified in *hThisInst*. A pointer to the name of the resource being loaded is passed in *lpszName*. The value of *what* determines what type of image is being loaded. It must be one of the following:

IMAGE_ICON	IMAGE_CURSOR	IMAGE_BITMAP

The width and the height of the image are passed in *width* and *height*. The *how* parameter determines how the image is loaded. Two commonly used values are

LR_DEFAULTSIZE	LR_LOADFROMFILE

If **LR_DEFAULTSIZE** is specified and if *width* and *height* are zero, the standard size of an icon or cursor is used for the width and height. If **LR_DEFAULTSIZE** is not specified and *width* and *height* are zero, then the actual size of the image determines its width and height. If **LR_LOADFROMFILE** is specified, then *lpszName* specifies the name of a file that contains the image rather than the name of the resource itself.

LoadImage( ) returns a handle to the image if successful, or **NULL** if an error occurs.

To try **LoadImage( )**, substitute the following line in the **WM_CREATE** handler of the first bitmap example.

```
hbit = (HBITMAP) LoadImage(hInst, "MyBP", IMAGE_BITMAP, 256, 128, 0);
```

As you will see, the program works the same as before. As an experiment, try changing the dimensions. For example, try using 128-by-64 and observe the results. As you will see, only part of the bitmaps are loaded.

As stated, while **LoadImage( )** gives you greater control over the way images are loaded by your program, the examples in this book will not make further use of it since they do not require this extended control.

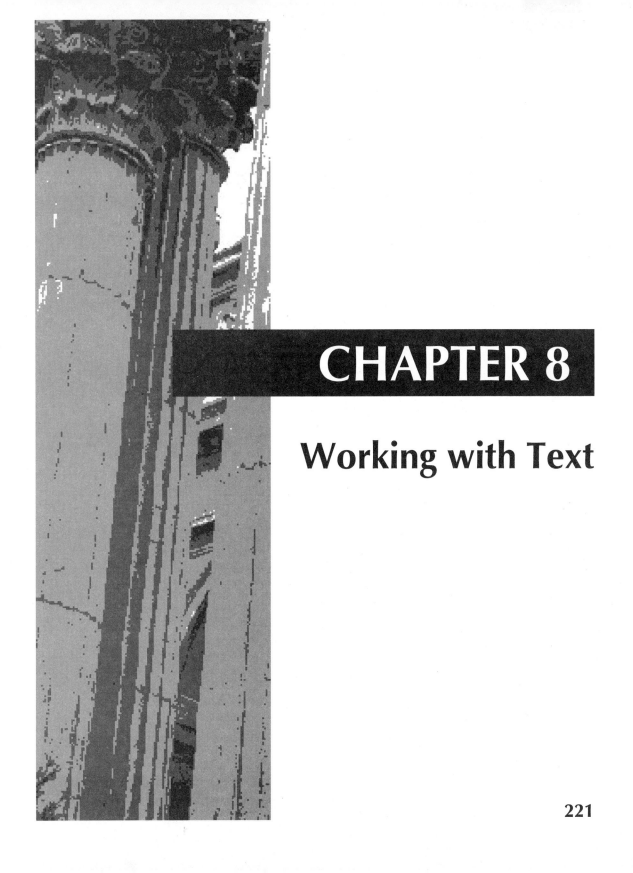

CHAPTER 8

Working with Text

Windows 2000 provides extensive, detailed, and sophisticated support for displaying text in the client area of a window. In the preceding chapters we have been performing only the most rudimentary text output. For example, we have been using an arbitrary and fixed spacing between lines and characters. Of course, this approach is inherently inadequate because Windows 2000 uses proportional character fonts and adjustable font sizes. In this chapter you will learn the correct way to manage text output.

As with most other aspects of the Windows 2000 environment, you, the programmer, have nearly unlimited control over the way that text is displayed, including its size, weight, and typeface. You can fine-tune a type font to your choosing and can change fonts whenever you desire. You can even change the orientation of a line of text so that it displays diagonally or vertically, rather than horizontally. Of course, this high level of control comes at a price: the management overhead incurred by your program is much greater than you might otherwise expect. But the results are definitely worth the added effort.

This chapter begins with a discussion of the window coordinate system and how text is mapped to it. Next, several text and window API functions that help you control and manage text output to the client area of a window are described. Then, a sample program is developed that illustrates how to apply these functions and how to properly manage the spacing of text within the client area. The chapter concludes by examining Windows support for text fonts.

Window Coordinates

Window coordinates are specified in logical units, which by default are equal to pixels.

As you know, **TextOut( )** is one of Windows' text output functions. It displays a string at the specified coordinates, which are always relative to the window. Therefore, where a window is positioned on the screen has no affect upon the coordinates passed to **TextOut( ).** By default, the upper-left corner of the client area of the window is location 0, 0. The X value increases to the right and the Y value increases downward.

So far, we have been using window coordinates for **TextOut( )** without any specific mention of what those coordinates actually refer to. Now is the time to clarify a few details. First, the coordinates that are specified in **TextOut( )** are *logical coordinates*. That is, the units used by **TextOut( )** (and other window display functions, including the graphics functions described in the next chapter) are *logical units*. Windows maps these logical units onto pixels when output is actually displayed. The reason that we haven't had to worry about this distinction is that, by default, logical units are the same as pixels. It is important to understand, however, that different mapping modes can be selected in which this convenient default will not be the case.

Setting the Text and Background Color

By default, when you output text to a window using **TextOut( )**, it is shown as black text against the current background. However, you can set both the color of the text and the background color using the API functions **SetTextColor( )** and **SetBkColor( )**, whose prototypes are shown here:

COLORREF SetTextColor(HDC *hdc*, COLORREF *color*);

COLORREF SetBkColor(HDC *hdc*, COLORREF *color*);

The **SetTextColor( )** function sets the current text color of the device associated with *hdc* to that specified by *color* (or the closest color that the display device is capable of displaying). The **SetBkColor( )** function sets the current text background color to that specified by *color* (or the closest possible). For both functions, the previous color setting is returned. If an error occurs, then the value **CLR_INVALID** is returned.

COLORREF
defines a color.

The color is specified as a value of type **COLORREF**, which is a 32-bit integer. Windows 2000 allows colors to be specified in three different ways. The first way, and by far most common, is as an RGB (red, green, blue) value. In an RGB value, the relative intensities of the three colors are combined to produce the actual color. The second way a color can be specified is as an index into a logical palette. The third way is as an RGB value relative to a palette. In this chapter, only the first way will be discussed.

8

A long integer value that holds an RGB color is passed to either **SetTextColor( )** or **SetBkColor( )** using the following encoding:

Byte	Color
byte 0 (low-order byte)	red
byte 1	green
byte 2	blue
byte 3 (high-order byte)	must be zero

Each color in an RGB value is in the range 0 through 255, with 0 being the lowest intensity and 255 being the brightest intensity.

Although you are free to manually construct a **COLORREF** value, Windows defines the macro **RGB( )** that does this for you. It has this general form:

COLORREF RGB(BYTE *red*, BYTE *green*, BYTE *blue*);

Here, *red, green,* and *blue* must be values in the range 0 through 255. Therefore, to create bright pink, use **RGB(255, 0, 255)**. To create white, use **RGB(255, 255, 255)**. To create the color black use **RGB(0, 0, 0)**. To create other colors, combine the three basic colors in varying intensities. For example, this creates a light aqua: **RGB(0, 100, 100)**. You can experiment to determine which colors are best for your application.

Setting the Background Display Mode

You can control the way that the background is affected when text is displayed on the screen by using the **SetBkMode( )** API function, whose prototype is shown here:

int SetBkMode(HDC *hdc*, int *mode*);

This function determines what happens to the current background color when text (or certain other types of output) is displayed. The handle of the device context is specified by *hdc*. The background mode is specified in *mode* and must be one of these two macros: **OPAQUE** or **TRANSPARENT**. The function returns the previous setting, or 0 if an error occurs.

If *mode* is **OPAQUE**, then each time text is output, the background is changed to that of the current background color. If *mode* is **TRANSPARENT**, then the background is not altered. In this case, any effects of a call to **SetBkColor( )** are effectively ignored. By default, the background mode is **OPAQUE**.

Obtaining the Text Metrics

As you know, characters are not all the same dimension—in Windows, most text fonts are proportional. Thus, the character "i" is not as wide as a character "w". Also, the height of each character and length of descenders vary between fonts. The amount of space between horizontal lines is also changeable. The variability of these (and other) attributes would not be of much consequence except for the fact that Windows demands that you, the programmer, manually manage virtually all text output.

Windows provides only a few functions that output text to the client area of a window. The main one is **TextOut( )**, which we have been using. As you know, this function does only one thing: it displays a string at a specified location. It will not, for example, format output or even automatically perform a carriage return/linefeed sequence. Instead, these operations are totally your job.

The fact that the size of each font may be different—and that fonts may be changed while your program is executing—implies that there must some way to determine the dimensions and various other attributes of the currently selected font. For example, in order to write one line of text after another implies that you have some way of knowing how tall the font is and how many pixels are between lines. The API function that obtains information about the current font is called **GetTextMetrics( )**, and it has this prototype:

BOOL GetTextMetrics(HDC *hdc*, LPTEXTMETRIC *lpTAttrib*);

Here, *hdc* is the handle of the output device, which is generally obtained using **GetDC( )** or **BeginPaint( ),** and *lpTAttrib* is a pointer to a structure of type **TEXTMETRIC,** which will, upon return, contain the text metrics for the currently selected font. The **TEXTMETRIC** structure is defined as shown here:

```
typedef struct tagTEXTMETRIC
{
  LONG tmHeight;            // total height of font
  LONG tmAscent;            // height above base line
  LONG tmDescent;           // length of descenders
  LONG tmInternalLeading;   // space above characters
  LONG tmExternalLeading;   // blank space between rows
  LONG tmAveCharWidth;      // average width
  LONG tmMaxCharWidth;      // maximum width
  LONG tmWeight;            // weight
  LONG tmOverhang;          // extra width added to special fonts
  LONG tmDigitizedAspectX;  // horizontal aspect
  LONG tmDigitizedAspectY;  // vertical aspect
  BYTE tmFirstChar;         // first character in font
  BYTE tmLastChar;          // last character in font
  BYTE tmDefaultChar;       // default character
  BYTE tmBreakChar;         // character used to break words
  BYTE tmItalic;            // non-zero if italic
  BYTE tmUnderlined;        // non-zero if underlined
  BYTE tmStruckOut;         // non-zero if struckout
  BYTE tmPitchAndFamily;    // pitch and family of font
  BYTE tmCharSet;           // character set identifier
} TEXTMERIC;
```

8

NEWTEXTMETRIC and NEWTEXTMETRICEX

There is an enhanced version of **TEXTMETRIC**, called **NEWTEXTMETRIC**. **NEWTEXTMETRIC** is the same as **TEXTMETRIC,** except that it adds four additional fields at the end. These fields provide support for TrueType fonts. (TrueType fonts provide superior scalability features.) The new fields in **NEWTEXTMETRIC** are shown here.

```
DWORD ntmFlags;      // indicates style of font
UINT ntmSizeEM;      // size of an em
UINT ntmCellHeight;  // font height
UINT ntmAvgWidth;    // average character width
```

There has recently been added to Win32 an extension to **NEWTEXTMETRIC**, called **NEWTEXTMETRICEX**. It is defined as shown here:

```
typedef struct tagNEWTEXTMETRICEX
{
  NEWTEXTMETRIC ntmTm;
  FONTSIGNATURE ntmFontSig; // font signature
} NEWTEXTMETRICEX;
```

As you can see, it includes all of **NEWTEXTMETRIC** and adds the structure **FONTSIGNATURE**, which contains information relating to Unicode and code pages.

For the purposes of this chapter, none of these fields added by **NEWTEXTMETRIC** or **NEWTEXTMETRICEX** are needed. However, they may be of value to applications that you create. You should consult an API reference manual for details.

While most of the values obtained by this function will not be used in this chapter, two are very important because they are needed to compute the vertical distance between lines of text. The distance between lines is required if you want to output more than one line of text to a window. Unlike a console-based application in which there is only one font and its size is fixed, there

The vertical
distance
between
lines of text is
tmHeight plus
**tmExternal-
Leading**.

may be several Windows fonts and they may vary in size. Specifically, each font defines the height of its characters and its row spacing. Therefore, it is not possible to know in advance the proper vertical (Y) distance between one line of text and the next. To determine where the next line of text will begin, you must call **GetTextMetrics( )** to acquire two values: **tmHeight** and **tmExternalLeading**. These contain the character height and the amount of blank space that should be left between lines. By adding together these two values, you obtain the total number of vertical units between the start of one line of text and the start of the next.

Remember: the value **tmExternalLeading** contains, in essence, the number of vertical units that should be left blank between lines of text. This value is separate from the height of the font. Thus, both values are needed to compute the total height of a line of text.

Computing the Length of a String

Windows does not automatically maintain a text cursor or keep track of your current output location. Therefore, if you wish to display one string after another on the same line, you will need to remember where the previous output left off. This implies that you must have some way of knowing the length of a string in logical units. Because characters in most fonts are not the same size, it is not possible to know the length of a string, in logical units, by simply knowing how many characters it contains. That is, the result returned by **strlen( )** is not meaningful to managing output to a window because characters are of differing widths. To solve this problem, Windows 2000 includes the API function **GetTextExtentPoint32( )**, whose prototype is shown here:

BOOL GetTextExtentPoint32(HDC *hdc*, LPCSTR *lpszString*, int *len*,
LPSIZE *lpSize*);

Here, *hdc* is the handle of the output device. The string whose length you want is pointed to by *lpszString*. The number of characters in the string is specified in *len*. The width and height of the string, in logical units, are returned in the **SIZE** structure pointed to by *lpSize*. The **SIZE** structure is defined as shown here:

```
typedef struct tagSIZE {
  LONG cx; // width
  LONG cy; // height
} SIZE;
```

8

Upon return from a call to **GetTextExtentPoint32( )**, the **cx** field will contain the length of the string. This value can be used to determine the location of the end point of the string when displayed. To display another string on the same line, continue on from where the previous output left off.

GetTextExtentPoint32( ) returns nonzero if successful, zero on failure.

HISTORICAL PERSPECTIVE: **GetTextExtentPoint32( )** replaces the older, Win16 function **GetTextExtent( )** used by Windows 3.1 programs.

A Short Text Demonstration

The following program demonstrates text output and the text-based functions just described. It displays several lines of text within the client area of the main window each time a **WM_PAINT** message is received.

```
// Managing Text Output

#include <windows.h>
#include <cstring>
#include <cstdio>

LRESULT CALLBACK WindowFunc(HWND, UINT, WPARAM, LPARAM);

char szWinName[] = "MyWin"; // name of window class

char str[255]; // holds output strings
int X=0, Y=0;  // current output location

int WINAPI WinMain(HINSTANCE hThisInst, HINSTANCE hPrevInst,
                   LPSTR lpszArgs, int nWinMode)
{
  HWND hwnd;
  MSG msg;
  WNDCLASSEX wcl;

  // Define a window class.
  wcl.cbSize = sizeof(WNDCLASSEX);
```

```
    wcl.hInstance = hThisInst;      // handle to this instance
    wcl.lpszClassName = szWinName;  // window class name
    wcl.lpfnWndProc = WindowFunc;   // window function
    wcl.style = 0;                  // default style

    wcl.hIcon = LoadIcon(NULL, IDI_APPLICATION); // large icon
    wcl.hIconSm = NULL; // use small version of large icon
    wcl.hCursor = LoadCursor(NULL, IDC_ARROW);   // cursor style

    wcl.lpszMenuName = NULL; // no class menu
    wcl.cbClsExtra = 0;       // no extra memory needed
    wcl.cbWndExtra = 0;

    // Make the window background white.
    wcl.hbrBackground = (HBRUSH) GetStockObject(WHITE_BRUSH);

    // Register the window class.
    if(!RegisterClassEx(&wcl)) return 0;

    /* Now that a window class has been registered, a window
       can be created. */
    hwnd = CreateWindow(
      szWinName, // name of window class
      "Managing Text Output", // title
      WS_OVERLAPPEDWINDOW, // window style - normal
      CW_USEDEFAULT, // X coordinate - let Windows decide
      CW_USEDEFAULT, // Y coordinate - let Windows decide
      CW_USEDEFAULT, // width - let Windows decide
      CW_USEDEFAULT, // height - let Windows decide
      NULL,          // no parent window
      NULL,          // no menu
      hThisInst,     // instance handle
      NULL           // no additional arguments
    );

    // Display the window.
    ShowWindow(hwnd, nWinMode);
    UpdateWindow(hwnd);

    // Create the message loop.
    while(GetMessage(&msg, NULL, 0, 0))
    {
      TranslateMessage(&msg); // translate keyboard messages
      DispatchMessage(&msg);  // return control to Windows 2000
    }
```

8

```
    return msg.wParam;
}

/* This function is called by Windows 2000 and is passed
   messages from the message queue.
*/
LRESULT CALLBACK WindowFunc(HWND hwnd, UINT message,
                            WPARAM wParam, LPARAM lParam)
{
  HDC hdc;
  TEXTMETRIC tm;
  SIZE size;
  PAINTSTRUCT paintstruct;

  switch(message) {
    case WM_PAINT:
      hdc = BeginPaint(hwnd, &paintstruct);

      // get text metrics
      GetTextMetrics(hdc, &tm);

      X = Y = 0;

      sprintf(str, "This is on the first line.");
      TextOut(hdc, X, Y, str, strlen(str));
      Y = Y + tm.tmHeight + tm.tmExternalLeading; // next line

      strcpy(str, "This is on the second line. ");
      TextOut(hdc, X, Y, str, strlen(str));
      Y = Y + tm.tmHeight + tm.tmExternalLeading; // next line

      strcpy(str, "This is on the third line. ");
      TextOut(hdc, X, Y, str, strlen(str));

      // compute length of a string
      GetTextExtentPoint32(hdc, str, strlen(str), &size);
      sprintf(str, "The preceding sentence is %ld units long",
              size.cx);
      X = size.cx; // advance to end of previous string
      TextOut(hdc, X, Y, str, strlen(str));
      Y = Y + tm.tmHeight + tm.tmExternalLeading; // next line
      X = 0; // return to start of line

      sprintf(str, "The space between lines is %ld pixels.",
```

```
                     tm.tmExternalLeading+tm.tmHeight);
         TextOut(hdc, X, Y, str, strlen(str));
         Y = Y + tm.tmHeight + tm.tmExternalLeading; // next line

         sprintf(str, "Average character width is %ld pixels",
                 tm.tmAveCharWidth);
         TextOut(hdc, X, Y, str, strlen(str));
         Y = Y + tm.tmHeight + tm.tmExternalLeading; // next line

         // set text color to red
         SetTextColor(hdc, RGB(255, 0, 0));
         // set background color to blue
         SetBkColor(hdc, RGB(0, 0, 255));

         sprintf(str, "This line is red on blue background.");
         TextOut(hdc, X, Y, str, strlen(str));
         Y = Y + tm.tmHeight + tm.tmExternalLeading; // next line

         // switch to transparent mode
         SetBkMode(hdc, TRANSPARENT);
         sprintf(str,
           "This line is red. The background is unchanged.");
         TextOut(hdc, X, Y, str, strlen(str));

         EndPaint(hwnd, &paintstruct);
         break;
      case WM_DESTROY: // terminate the program
        PostQuitMessage(0);
        break;
      default:
        /* Let Windows 2000 process any messages not specified in
           the preceding switch statement. */
        return DefWindowProc(hwnd, message, wParam, lParam);
  }

  return 0;
}
```

Sample output is shown in Figure 8-1. Let's take a closer look at this program. The program declares two global variables called **X** and **Y** and initializes both to 0. These variables contain the current window location at which text will be displayed. They are updated by the program after each output sequence.

The interesting part of this program is contained mostly within the
WM_PAINT message. Each time a **WM_PAINT** message is received, a device
context is obtained and the text metrics are acquired. Next, the first line of
text is output. Notice that it is constructed using **sprintf( )** and then actually
output using **TextOut( )**. As you know, **TextOut( )** does not perform text
formatting, so it is up to you, the programmer, to construct your output first.
After the string is displayed, the **Y** coordinate is advanced to the next line by
adding the font height to the distance between rows.

The program continues by next outputting the lines "This is on the second
line." and "This is on the third line."—each on its own line. Then, the length
of the third line is computed using a call to **GetTextExtentPoint32( )**. This
value is then used to advance the **X** coordinate to the end of the previous
line before the next line is printed. Notice that, here, the **Y** coordinate is
unchanged, thereby causing the next string to be displayed immediately after
the previous one, but still on the same line. Before continuing, the program
advances **Y** to the next line and resets **X** to 0, which is the leftmost coordinate.
Doing this causes subsequent output once again to be started at the beginning
of the next line.

Next, some information about the currently selected character font is
displayed. Then, the background color is set to blue, the text color is set to
red, and a line of text is displayed. Finally, the background mode is set to
transparent and a line of text is displayed. In this case, the blue background
color is ignored.

Working with Fonts

Windows in general and Windows 2000, specifically, gives you nearly complete control over the user interface. As such, it has a rich and varied set of text-based features that you can take advantage of. One such feature is its collection of various type fonts. By taking control of the type fonts used by your application, you can create a unique and distinct look that sets your program apart from the crowd. Using Windows 2000 you have several built-in type fonts to choose from. You can also create custom fonts. These features are discussed here. We will begin by defining a few terms.

Fonts, Families, Typefaces, and Styles

A font defines a complete set of characters in a particular size, style, and typeface.

In the most general sense, a *font* describes a set of characters and features common to those characters. As you probably know, there are many different kinds of type fonts in common use. For example, Courier and Times Roman are two of the most popular. A *font* defines four attributes: a character set, a typeface, a style, and a size. Let's look at each.

Windows 2000 supports various character sets. The one that we will be using is the standard Windows character set. This set is based upon the ANSI character set, and each character is 8 bits, making the Windows character set suitable for most Western languages. Other character sets supported by Windows are Unicode, OEM (Original Equipment Manufacturer), and symbol (a set of symbolic characters used for mathematical expressions). Custom character sets are also allowed.

8

A typeface specifies a particular design of type.

A *typeface* defines the precise shape and design of the characters within a font. Thus, the typeface determines the unique visual characteristics of a font.

In general, the *style* of a font determines whether a font is displayed normally, in bold, or in italics. In Windows, you have fine-grained control over the weight (that is, thickness) of a font, so there are actually several gradients of font thickness.

Type size is measured in *points*, which are 1/72 of an inch.

A serif is a small line found at the endpoints of characters.

Windows organizes fonts into five *families*, which share basic attributes. These families are Decorative, Modern, Roman, Script, and Swiss. Decorative fonts are specialty fonts. *Modern* fonts are nonproportional. The *Roman* family is proportional and includes serifs. (*Serifs* are short lines found at the endpoints of characters.) Members of the *Script* family appear somewhat like handwriting. The *Swiss* family is proportional and sans-serif (that is, without serifs).

The pitch of a font determines its character spacing.

In proportional fonts, the width of each character, or *pitch*, may differ. These are also called *variable-pitch* fonts. In nonproportional fonts, the width of each character is the same. These are called *fixed-pitch* or *monospaced* fonts.

Raster, Vector, and TrueType Fonts

A glyph is a character or symbol.

Windows 2000 supports four ways in which a font can be stored and displayed. These are called a *raster, vector, TrueType*, and *OpenType*. Raster fonts store bitmaps for each character, or *glyph*, in the font. This makes them easy to display, but they scale poorly. Raster fonts are most often used on display monitors and bitmapped printers. Vector fonts store the end points to the line segments that make up each glyph. These segments are then drawn to display each character. Vector fonts are best when used on plotters. TrueType fonts store information about the lines and arcs that make up each glyph, as well as instructions on how to draw the character. This approach gives TrueType fonts excellent scalability. They are also the most faithfully translated from screen to printer. For these reasons, TrueType fonts are quite popular for desktop publishing applications. OpenType fonts are essentially TrueType fonts that support PostScript-style glyph definitions.

Using Built-in Fonts

Windows 2000's built-in fonts are stock objects that are selected using **GetStockObject( )**. At the time of this writing, Windows 2000 supports seven built-in fonts. The macros associated with these fonts are shown here:

Font	Description
ANSI_FIXED_FONT	Fixed-pitch font
ANSI_VAR_FONT	Variable-pitch font
DEVICE_DEFAULT_FONT	Default device font
DEFAULT_GUI_FONT	Default GUI font
OEM_FIXED_FONT	OEM-defined font
SYSTEM_FONT	Font used by Windows 2000
SYSTEM_FIXED_FONT	Font used by older versions of Windows

The system fonts are those character fonts used by Windows for things like menus and dialog boxes. Older versions of Windows used a fixed-pitch system font, but beginning with Windows 3.0, a variable font has been used. Windows 2000 also uses the variable font.

Selecting and using a built-in font is easy. To do so, your program must first create a font handle, which is of type **HFONT**. Next, it must load the desired font, using **GetStockObject( )**, which returns a handle to the font. To switch to the font, select the font using **SelectObject( ),** with the new font as a parameter. **SelectObject( )** will return a handle to the old font, which you may want to save so that you can switch back to it after you are done using the other font.

The following program demonstrates changing fonts. It uses the virtual window technology developed in Chapter 7 to handle repainting.

```
// Demonstrate built-in fonts.

#include <windows.h>
#include <cstring>
#include <cstdio>
#include "text.h"

LRESULT CALLBACK WindowFunc(HWND, UINT, WPARAM, LPARAM);

char szWinName[] = "MyWin"; // name of window class

char str[255]; // holds output strings

int X=0, Y=0;    // current output location
int maxX, maxY; // screen dimensions

HDC memdc;          // store the virtual device handle
HBITMAP hbit;       // store the virtual bitmap
HBRUSH hbrush;      // store the brush handle
HFONT holdf, hnewf; // store the font handles

int WINAPI WinMain(HINSTANCE hThisInst, HINSTANCE hPrevInst,
                   LPSTR lpszArgs, int nWinMode)
{
  HWND hwnd;
  MSG msg;
  WNDCLASSEX wcl;
  HACCEL hAccel;

  // Define a window class.
```

8

```
wcl.cbSize = sizeof(WNDCLASSEX);

wcl.hInstance = hThisInst;      // handle to this instance
wcl.lpszClassName = szWinName; // window class name
wcl.lpfnWndProc = WindowFunc;   // window function
wcl.style = 0;                  // default style

wcl.hIcon = LoadIcon(NULL, IDI_APPLICATION); // large icon
wcl.hIconSm = NULL; // use small version of large icon
wcl.hCursor = LoadCursor(NULL, IDC_ARROW);   // cursor style

wcl.lpszMenuName = "FontMenu"; // main menu

wcl.cbClsExtra = 0;       // no extra memory needed
wcl.cbWndExtra = 0;

// Make the window background white.
wcl.hbrBackground = (HBRUSH) GetStockObject(WHITE_BRUSH);

// Register the window class.
if(!RegisterClassEx(&wcl)) return 0;

/* Now that a window class has been registered, a window
   can be created. */
hwnd = CreateWindow(
  szWinName, // name of window class
  "Using Built-in Fonts", // title
  WS_OVERLAPPEDWINDOW, // window style - normal
  CW_USEDEFAULT, // X coordinate - let Windows decide
  CW_USEDEFAULT, // Y coordinate - let Windows decide
  CW_USEDEFAULT, // width - let Windows decide
  CW_USEDEFAULT, // height - let Windows decide
  NULL,           // no parent window
  NULL,           // no menu
  hThisInst,      // instance handle
  NULL            // no additional arguments
);

// Load the keyboard accelerators.
hAccel = LoadAccelerators(hThisInst, "FontMenu");

// Display the window.
ShowWindow(hwnd, nWinMode);
UpdateWindow(hwnd);

// Create the message loop.
```

```
     while(GetMessage(&msg, NULL, 0, 0))
     {
       if(!TranslateAccelerator(hwnd, hAccel, &msg)) {
         TranslateMessage(&msg); // translate keyboard messages
         DispatchMessage(&msg); // return control to Windows 2000
       }
     }

     return msg.wParam;
}

/* This function is called by Windows 2000 and is passed
   messages from the message queue.
*/
LRESULT CALLBACK WindowFunc(HWND hwnd, UINT message,
                            WPARAM wParam, LPARAM lParam)
{
  HDC hdc;
  PAINTSTRUCT paintstruct;
  static TEXTMETRIC tm;
  SIZE size;
  static fontswitch = 0;
  int response;

  switch(message) {
    case WM_CREATE:
      // get screen coordinates
      maxX = GetSystemMetrics(SM_CXSCREEN);
      maxY = GetSystemMetrics(SM_CYSCREEN);

      // create a virtual window
      hdc = GetDC(hwnd);
      memdc = CreateCompatibleDC(hdc);
      hbit = CreateCompatibleBitmap(hdc, maxX, maxY);
      SelectObject(memdc, hbit);
      hbrush = (HBRUSH) GetStockObject(WHITE_BRUSH);
      SelectObject(memdc, hbrush);
      PatBlt(memdc, 0, 0, maxX, maxY, PATCOPY);

      // get new font
      hnewf = (HFONT) GetStockObject(ANSI_VAR_FONT);

      ReleaseDC(hwnd, hdc);
      break;
    case WM_COMMAND:
      switch(LOWORD(wParam)) {
```

8

```
case IDM_SHOW:
  // set text color to black and mode to transparent
  SetTextColor(memdc, RGB(0, 0, 0));
  SetBkMode(memdc, TRANSPARENT);

  // get text metrics
  GetTextMetrics(memdc, &tm);

  sprintf(str, "The font is %ld pixels high.",
          tm.tmHeight);
  TextOut(memdc, X, Y, str, strlen(str));
  Y = Y + tm.tmHeight + tm.tmExternalLeading; // next line

  strcpy(str, "This is on the next line. ");
  TextOut(memdc, X, Y, str, strlen(str));

  // compute length of a string
  GetTextExtentPoint32(memdc, str, strlen(str), &size);
  sprintf(str, "Previous string is %ld units long",
          size.cx);
  X = size.cx; // advance to end of previous string
  TextOut(memdc, X, Y, str, strlen(str));
  Y = Y + tm.tmHeight + tm.tmExternalLeading; // next line
  X = 0; // reset X

  sprintf(str, "Screen dimensions: %d %d", maxX, maxY);
  TextOut(memdc, X, Y, str, strlen(str));
  Y = Y + tm.tmHeight + tm.tmExternalLeading; // next line
  InvalidateRect(hwnd, NULL, 1);
  break;
case IDM_RESET:
  X = Y = 0;
  // erase by repainting background
  PatBlt(memdc, 0, 0, maxX, maxY, PATCOPY);

  InvalidateRect(hwnd, NULL, 1);
  break;
case IDM_FONT:
  if(!fontswitch) {  // switch to new font
    holdf = (HFONT) SelectObject(memdc, hnewf);
    fontswitch = 1;
  }
  else { // switch to old font
    SelectObject(memdc, holdf);
    fontswitch = 0;
  }
```

```
              break;
           case IDM_EXIT:
             response = MessageBox(hwnd, "Quit the Program?",
                                   "Exit", MB_YESNO);
             if(response == IDYES) PostQuitMessage(0);
             break;
           case IDM_HELP:
             MessageBox(hwnd,
                       "F2: Display\nF3: Change Font\nF4: Reset",
                       "Font Fun", MB_OK);
             break;
         }
         break;
       case WM_PAINT: // process a repaint request
         hdc = BeginPaint(hwnd, &paintstruct); // get DC

         // copy virtual window onto screen
         BitBlt(hdc, 0, 0, maxX, maxY, memdc, 0, 0, SRCCOPY);

         EndPaint(hwnd, &paintstruct); // release DC
         break;
       case WM_DESTROY: // terminate the program
         DeleteDC(memdc);
         PostQuitMessage(0);
         break;
       default:
         /* Let Windows 2000 process any messages not specified in
            the preceding switch statement. */
         return DefWindowProc(hwnd, message, wParam, lParam);
     }

     return 0;
   }
```

The resource file used by the program is shown here:

```
#include <windows.h>
#include "text.h"

FontMenu MENU
{
  POPUP "&Fonts" {
    MENUITEM "&Display\tF2", IDM_SHOW
    MENUITEM "Change &Font\tF3", IDM_FONT
    MENUITEM "&Reset\tF4", IDM_RESET
```

8

```
    MENUITEM "E&xit\tCtrl+X", IDM_EXIT
  }
  MENUITEM "&Help", IDM_HELP
}

FontMenu ACCELERATORS
{
  VK_F1, IDM_HELP, VIRTKEY
  VK_F2, IDM_SHOW, VIRTKEY
  VK_F3, IDM_FONT, VIRTKEY
  VK_F4, IDM_RESET, VIRTKEY
  "^X", IDM_EXIT
}
```

The TEXT.H header file is shown here:

```
#define IDM_SHOW    100
#define IDM_FONT    101
#define IDM_RESET   102
#define IDM_EXIT    103
#define IDM_HELP    104
```

Sample output produced by this program is shown in Figure 8-2.

Sample output
from the
built-in font
program

Figure 8-2.

The program works like this. Each time you select Display, text is output using the currently selected font. Each time you select Change Font, the currently selected font is toggled between the ANSI variable font and the default font. You can clear the window by selecting Reset. Notice that this option simply resets the X and Y coordinates to zero and then calls **PatBlt( )** using **PATCOPY** to overpaint the background of the virtual window.

IN DEPTH

Unicode

As you probably know, the character sets associated with Western languages, such as English or German, can be represented by the ANSI character set. ANSI uses an 8-bit character and is, therefore, capable of holding no more than 256 individual characters. (The ANSI character set is a superset of the 7-bit ASCII characters.) The trouble is that several Eastern languages, such as Chinese, require more than 256 characters. To handle these languages, the Unicode character set was created. Unicode characters are 16 bits long and can therefore represent very large character sets (up to 16,536 characters). To provide for compatibility, the first 256 characters in Unicode are the same as those defined by the ANSI character set.

Windows 2000 provides full support for Unicode to allow for the creation of international versions of Windows 2000 programs. There are a number of Win32 API functions that provide a means of translating into and out of Unicode. For example, **ToUnicode( )** converts a virtual key code into its Unicode equivalent. Also, Windows 2000 provides generic character data types that will automatically map to either Unicode or ASCII, depending upon how you compile your program.

While it is beyond the scope of this book to discuss the creation of international applications, it is something that you will probably need to look into if you will be creating code for the world market.

8

Creating Custom Fonts

Although it may sound complex, the creation of custom fonts is actually very easy. There are two major advantages to custom fonts. First, a custom font gives your application a unique look that will set it apart. Second, creating your own font lets you control precisely what occurs when text is output. Before you begin this process, it is important to understand that you will not be defining a new typeface. Instead, you will be tailoring an existing typeface so that it meets the specifications that you desire. Thus, you won't need to define the shape of each character in the font that you create.

To create your own font, use the **CreateFont( )** API function, whose prototype is shown here:

HFONT CreateFont(int *Height*, int *Width*, int *Escapement*,
int *Orientation*, int *Weight*,
DWORD *Ital*, DWORD *Underline*,
DWORD *StrikeThru*, DWORD *Charset*,
DWORD *Precision*, DWORD *ClipPrecision*,
DWORD *Quality*, DWORD *PitchFam*,
LPCSTR *TypefaceName*);

The height of the font is passed in *Height*. If *Height* is zero, then a default size is used. The width of the font is specified in *Width*. If *Width* is zero, then Windows chooses an appropriate value based upon the current aspect ratio. Both *Height* and *Width* are expressed in terms of logical units.

Escapement specifies the angle of a line of text. Orientation specifes the angle of a character itself.

Text can be output at any angle within the window. The angle at which it is displayed is determined by the *Escapement* parameter. For normal, horizontal text, this value should be 0. Otherwise, it specifies the number of 1/10 degree increments through which the text will be rotated in a counterclockwise direction. For example, a value of 900 causes the text to be rotated 90 degrees, causing output to be vertical.

The angle of each individual character can also be specified using the *Orientation* parameter. It too uses 1/10 degree increments to specify the angle of each character relative to horizontal in a counterclockwise direction.

NOTE: By default, both the *Escapement* and *Orientation* parameters of **CreateFont( )** must be the same. However, if you set the graphics mode to **GM_ADVANCED**, then these two parameters may differ. You will see how to set the graphics mode in Chapter 9.

Weight specifies the preferred weight of the font in the range of 0 to 1000. A value of 0 specifies the default weight. To specify a normal weight, use 400. For bold, use 700. You can also use any of these macros to specify the font weight.

```
FW_DONTCARE
FW_THIN
FW_EXTRALIGHT
FW_LIGHT
FW_NORMAL
FW_MEDIUM
FW_SEMIBOLD
FW_BOLD
FW_EXTRABOLD
FW_HEAVY
```

To create an italic font, specify *Ital* as nonzero; otherwise, this parameter should be zero. To create an underlined font, specify *Underline* as nonzero; otherwise, this parameter should be zero. To create a strike-through font, specify *StrikeThru* as nonzero; otherwise, this parameter should be zero.

Charset indicates which character set is desired. The example that follows uses **ANSI_CHARSET**. *Precision* specifies the preferred output precision, which determines just how closely the output must match the requested font's characteristics. The examples in this chapter use **OUT_DEFAULT_PRECIS**. *ClipPrecision* specifies the preferred clipping precision, which determines how each character that extends beyond the clipping region is to be "clipped." The value used by the example in this chapter is **CLIP_DEFAULT_PRECIS**. (For other valid values for *Charset, Precision,* and *ClipPrecision,* consult an API reference.)

8

Quality determines how closely the logical font will be matched with the actual physical fonts provided for the requested output device. Here are three commonly used values:

DEFAULT_QUALITY	DRAFT_QUALITY	PROOF_QUALITY

PitchFam specifies the pitch and family of the font. There are three pitch choices:

DEFAULT_PITCH	FIXED_PITCH	VARIABLE_PITCH

There are six possible font families:

FF_DECORATIVE	FF_DONTCARE	FF_MODERN
FF_ROMAN	FF_SCRIPT	FF_SWISS

The **FF_DONTCARE** family is used when you don't care what font family is used. The font family is meaningful only if the typeface you specify is not available on the system. To create the value for *PitchFam*, OR together one pitch value and one font family value.

A pointer to the name of the typeface is passed in *TypefaceName*. This name cannot be longer than 32 characters. The font you specify must be installed in your system. Alternatively, you can specify **NULL** for this parameter and Windows 2000 will automatically select a font that is compatible with the characteristics that you specify in the other parameters. (You will see how to obtain a list of available fonts later in this chapter.)

If successful, **CreateFont( )** returns a handle to the font. On failure, **NULL** is returned. Fonts created using **CreateFont( )** must be deleted before your program ends. To delete a font, call **DeleteObject( )**.

Here is a program that demonstrates two custom fonts. The first is based upon the Courier New font, the second upon Century Gothic. Each time you choose the Change Font menu item, a new font is selected and displayed. This program uses the same resource and header files as the program in the preceding section. Sample output is shown in Figure 8-3.

Sample output from the custom font program

Figure 8-3.

```
// Create a custom font.

#include <windows.h>
#include <cstring>
#include <cstdio>
#include "text.h"

LRESULT CALLBACK WindowFunc(HWND, UINT, WPARAM, LPARAM);

char szWinName[] = "MyWin"; // name of window class

char str[255]; // holds output strings
char fname[40] = "Default"; // name of font

int X=0, Y=0;   // current output location
int maxX, maxY; // screen dimensions

HDC memdc;      // store the virtual device handle
HBITMAP hbit;   // store the virtual bitmap
HBRUSH hbrush;  // store the brush handle
HFONT holdf, hnewf1, hnewf2; // store the font handles

int WINAPI WinMain(HINSTANCE hThisInst, HINSTANCE hPrevInst,
                   LPSTR lpszArgs, int nWinMode)
{
  HWND hwnd;
  MSG msg;
  WNDCLASSEX wcl;
  HACCEL hAccel;

  // Define a window class.
  wcl.cbSize = sizeof(WNDCLASSEX);

  wcl.hInstance = hThisInst;      // handle to this instance
  wcl.lpszClassName = szWinName;  // window class name
  wcl.lpfnWndProc = WindowFunc;   // window function
  wcl.style = 0;                  // default style

  wcl.hIcon = LoadIcon(NULL, IDI_APPLICATION); // large icon
  wcl.hIconSm = NULL; // use small version of large icon
  wcl.hCursor = LoadCursor(NULL, IDC_ARROW);   // cursor style

  wcl.lpszMenuName = "FontMenu"; // main menu

  wcl.cbClsExtra = 0;       // no extra memory needed
  wcl.cbWndExtra = 0;
```

8

```
  // Make the window background white.
  wcl.hbrBackground = (HBRUSH) GetStockObject(WHITE_BRUSH);

  // Register the window class.
  if(!RegisterClassEx(&wcl)) return 0;

  /* Now that a window class has been registered, a window
     can be created. */
  hwnd = CreateWindow(
    szWinName, // name of window class
    "Using Custom Fonts", // title
    WS_OVERLAPPEDWINDOW, // window style - normal
    CW_USEDEFAULT, // X coordinate - let Windows decide
    CW_USEDEFAULT, // Y coordinate - let Windows decide
    CW_USEDEFAULT, // width - let Windows decide
    CW_USEDEFAULT, // height - let Windows decide
    NULL,          // no parent window
    NULL,          // no menu
    hThisInst,     // instance handle
    NULL           // no additional arguments
  );

  // Load the keyboard accelerators.
  hAccel = LoadAccelerators(hThisInst, "FontMenu");

  // Display the window.
  ShowWindow(hwnd, nWinMode);
  UpdateWindow(hwnd);

  // Create the message loop.
  while(GetMessage(&msg, NULL, 0, 0))
  {
    if(!TranslateAccelerator(hwnd, hAccel, &msg)) {
      TranslateMessage(&msg); // translate keyboard messages
      DispatchMessage(&msg); // return control to Windows 2000
    }
  }

  return msg.wParam;
}

/* This function is called by Windows 2000 and is passed
   messages from the message queue.
*/
```

```
LRESULT CALLBACK WindowFunc(HWND hwnd, UINT message,
                            WPARAM wParam, LPARAM lParam)
{
  HDC hdc;
  PAINTSTRUCT paintstruct;
  static TEXTMETRIC tm;
  SIZE size;
  static fontswitch = 0;
  int response;

  switch(message) {
    case WM_CREATE:
      // get screen coordinates
      maxX = GetSystemMetrics(SM_CXSCREEN);
      maxY = GetSystemMetrics(SM_CYSCREEN);

      // create a virtual window
      hdc = GetDC(hwnd);
      memdc = CreateCompatibleDC(hdc);
      hbit = CreateCompatibleBitmap(hdc, maxX, maxY);
      SelectObject(memdc, hbit);
      hbrush = (HBRUSH) GetStockObject(WHITE_BRUSH);
      SelectObject(memdc, hbrush);
      PatBlt(memdc, 0, 0, maxX, maxY, PATCOPY);

      // create new fonts
      hnewf1 = CreateFont(14, 0, 0, 0, FW_NORMAL,
                          0, 0, 0, ANSI_CHARSET,
                          OUT_DEFAULT_PRECIS,
                          CLIP_DEFAULT_PRECIS,
                          DEFAULT_QUALITY,
                          DEFAULT_PITCH | FF_DONTCARE,
                          "Courier New");
      hnewf2 = CreateFont(20, 0, 0, 0, FW_SEMIBOLD,
                          0, 0, 0, ANSI_CHARSET,
                          OUT_DEFAULT_PRECIS,
                          CLIP_DEFAULT_PRECIS,
                          DEFAULT_QUALITY,
                          DEFAULT_PITCH | FF_DONTCARE,
                          "Century Gothic");
      ReleaseDC(hwnd, hdc);
      break;
    case WM_COMMAND:
      switch(LOWORD(wParam)) {
```

8

```
case IDM_SHOW:
  // set text to black and mode to transparent
  SetTextColor(memdc, RGB(0, 0, 0));
  SetBkMode(memdc, TRANSPARENT);

  // get text metrics
  GetTextMetrics(memdc, &tm);

  sprintf(str, "%s font is %ld pixels high.",
          fname, tm.tmHeight);
  TextOut(memdc, X, Y, str, strlen(str));
  Y = Y + tm.tmHeight + tm.tmExternalLeading; // next line

  strcpy(str, "This is on the next line. ");
  TextOut(memdc, X, Y, str, strlen(str));

  // compute length of a string
  GetTextExtentPoint32(memdc, str, strlen(str), &size);
  sprintf(str, "Previous string is %ld units long",
          size.cx);
  X = size.cx; // advance to end of previous string
  TextOut(memdc, X, Y, str, strlen(str));
  Y = Y + tm.tmHeight + tm.tmExternalLeading; // next line
  X = 0; // reset X

  sprintf(str, "Screen dimensions: %d %d", maxX, maxY);
  TextOut(memdc, X, Y, str, strlen(str));
  Y = Y + tm.tmHeight + tm.tmExternalLeading; // next line

  InvalidateRect(hwnd, NULL, 1);
  break;
case IDM_RESET:
  X = Y = 0;
  // erase by repainting background
  PatBlt(memdc, 0, 0, maxX, maxY, PATCOPY);
  InvalidateRect(hwnd, NULL, 1);
  break;
case IDM_FONT:
  switch(fontswitch) {
    case 0: // switch to new font1
      holdf = (HFONT) SelectObject(memdc, hnewf1);
      fontswitch = 1;
      strcpy(fname, "Courier New");
      break;
```

```
                        case 1: // switch to new font2
                          SelectObject(memdc, hnewf2);
                          fontswitch = 2;
                          strcpy(fname, "Century Gothic");
                          break;
                        default: // switch to old font
                          SelectObject(memdc, holdf);
                          fontswitch = 0;
                          strcpy(fname, "Default");
                   }
                   break;
                 case IDM_EXIT:
                   response = MessageBox(hwnd, "Quit the Program?",
                                         "Exit", MB_YESNO);
                   if(response == IDYES) PostQuitMessage(0);
                   break;
                 case IDM_HELP:
                   MessageBox(hwnd,
                             "F2: Display\nF3: Change Font\nF4: Reset",
                             "Custom Fonts", MB_OK);
                   break;
             }
             break;
           case WM_PAINT: // process a repaint request
             hdc = BeginPaint(hwnd, &paintstruct); // get DC

             // copy virtual window onto screen
             BitBlt(hdc, 0, 0, maxX, maxY, memdc, 0, 0, SRCCOPY);

             EndPaint(hwnd, &paintstruct); // release DC
             break;
           case WM_DESTROY: // terminate the program
             DeleteDC(memdc);
             DeleteObject(hnewf1);
             DeleteObject(hnewf2);
             PostQuitMessage(0);
             break;
           default:
             /* Let Windows 2000 process any messages not specified in
                the preceding switch statement. */
             return DefWindowProc(hwnd, message, wParam, lParam);
       }

       return 0;
    }
```

8

Using CreateFontIndirect( )

There is an alternative to **CreateFont( )** that you will find useful in some situations. It is called **CreateFontIndirect( ),** and it creates a font based upon the information contained in a **LOGFONT** structure. Its prototype is shown here:

HFONT CreateFontIndirect(CONST LOGFONT *lpFont);

The function returns a handle to the font that best matches the information supplied in the structure pointed to by *lpFont*. It returns **NULL** on failure. You must delete the font handle, using **DeleteObject( ),** before your program ends.

The **LOGFONT** structure encapsulates logical information about a font. It is defined as this:

```
typedef struct tagLOGFONT
{
  LONG lfHeight;            // height of font
  LONG lfWidth;            // width of font
  LONG lfEscapement;       // angle of text
  LONG lfOrientation;      // angle of character
  LONG lfWeight;           // darkness
  BYTE lfItalic;           // non-zero if ital
  BYTE lfUnderline;        // non-zero if underline
  BYTE lfStrikeOut;        // non-zero if strike-through
  BYTE lfCharSet;          // character set
  BYTE lfOutPrecision;     // output precision
  BYTE lfClipPrecision;    // clipping precision
  BYTE lfQuality;          // display quality
  BYTE lfPitchAndFamily;   // pitch and family
  CHAR lfFaceName[LF_FACESIZE]; // name
} LOGFONT;
```

The fields in **LOGFONT** have the same meaning and use the same values as the parameters to **CreateFont( )** described earlier. For example, here is the call to **CreateFontIndirect( )** that creates the same Century Gothic font that was created by calling **CreateFont( )** in the preceding program.

```
LOGFONT lf;

lf.lfHeight = 20;
lf.lfWidth = 0;
```

```
lf.lfEscapement = 0;
lf.lfOrientation = 0;
lf.lfWeight = FW_SEMIBOLD;
lf.lfItalic = 0;
lf.lfUnderline = 0;
lf.lfStrikeOut = 0;
lf.lfCharSet = ANSI_CHARSET;
lf.lfOutPrecision = OUT_DEFAULT_PRECIS;
lf.lfClipPrecision = CLIP_DEFAULT_PRECIS;
lf.lfQuality = DEFAULT_QUALITY;
lf.lfPitchAndFamily = DEFAULT_PITCH | FF_DONTCARE;
strcpy(lf.lfFaceName, "Century Gothic");
hnewf2 = CreateFontIndirect(&lf);
```

While there is no particular benefit in this situation to using
CreateFontIndirect( ) over **CreateFont( )**, there are times when there
will be. For example, when you obtain information about existing fonts,
each font's description is stored in a **LOGFONT** structure. The contents of
this structure can then be used in a call to **CreateFontIndirect( )** to create
the font.

Rotating Text

8

One of the most exciting features of Windows 2000's font system is that you
can easily rotate and orient text relative to the X axis. Doing this allows you
to display text in ways other than just horizontally on the screen. To change
the angle of text output, specify the desired angle in the *Escapement* and
Orientation parameters when creating a font using **CreateFont( )**. Recall
that these angles are specified in tenths of a degree from horizontal, with
counterclockwise being the positive direction. Escapement determines
the angle of a line of text, and orientation determines the angle of each
individual character. For our present purposes, both of these angles must
be the same. This is usually what you want anyway, because it aligns each
individual character with the rotated base line.

The following program modifies the Courier and Gothic fonts created by the
preceding program so that they print at 45 degree angles. The Courier text is
printed sloping up because it is given a positive escapement and orientation.
The Gothic text is displayed sloping downward because it is given a negative
escapement and orientation. Sample output is shown in Figure 8-4.

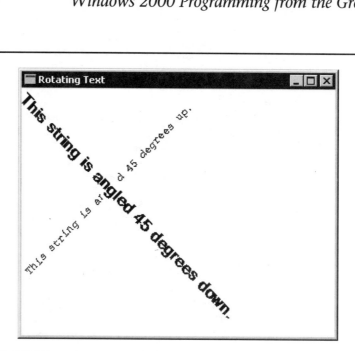

Rotating text

Figure 8-4.

```
// Rotating Text.

#include <windows.h>
#include <cstring>
#include <cstdio>

LRESULT CALLBACK WindowFunc(HWND, UINT, WPARAM, LPARAM);

char szWinName[] = "MyWin"; // name of window class

char str[255]; // holds output strings

HFONT hnewf1, hnewf2; // store the font handles

int WINAPI WinMain(HINSTANCE hThisInst, HINSTANCE hPrevInst,
                   LPSTR lpszArgs, int nWinMode)
{
  HWND hwnd;
  MSG msg;
  WNDCLASSEX wcl;

  // Define a window class.
```

```
wcl.cbSize = sizeof(WNDCLASSEX);

wcl.hInstance = hThisInst;      // handle to this instance
wcl.lpszClassName = szWinName; // window class name
wcl.lpfnWndProc = WindowFunc;  // window function
wcl.style = 0;                  // default style

wcl.hIcon = LoadIcon(NULL, IDI_APPLICATION); // large icon
wcl.hIconSm = NULL; // use small version of large icon
wcl.hCursor = LoadCursor(NULL, IDC_ARROW);  // cursor style

wcl.lpszMenuName = NULL; // no class menu
wcl.cbClsExtra = 0;       // no extra memory needed
wcl.cbWndExtra = 0;

// Make the window background white.
wcl.hbrBackground = (HBRUSH) GetStockObject(WHITE_BRUSH);

// Register the window class.
if(!RegisterClassEx(&wcl)) return 0;

/* Now that a window class has been registered, a window
   can be created. */
hwnd = CreateWindow(
  szWinName, // name of window class
  "Rotating Text", // title
  WS_OVERLAPPEDWINDOW, // window style - normal
  CW_USEDEFAULT, // X coordinate - let Windows decide
  CW_USEDEFAULT, // Y coordinate - let Windows decide
  CW_USEDEFAULT, // width - let Windows decide
  CW_USEDEFAULT, // height - let Windows decide
  NULL,          // no parent window
  NULL,          // no menu
  hThisInst,     // instance handle
  NULL           // no additional arguments
);

// Display the window.
ShowWindow(hwnd, nWinMode);
UpdateWindow(hwnd);

// Create the message loop.
while(GetMessage(&msg, NULL, 0, 0))
{
  TranslateMessage(&msg); // translate keyboard messages
```

8

```
      DispatchMessage(&msg);  // return control to Windows 2000
  }
  return msg.wParam;
}

/* This function is called by Windows 2000 and is passed
   messages from the message queue.
*/
LRESULT CALLBACK WindowFunc(HWND hwnd, UINT message,
                            WPARAM wParam, LPARAM lParam)
{
  HDC hdc;
  PAINTSTRUCT ps;

  switch(message) {
    case WM_CREATE:
      // This font is angled 45 degrees up
      hnewf1 = CreateFont(14, 0, 450, 450, FW_NORMAL,
                          0, 0, 0, ANSI_CHARSET,
                          OUT_DEFAULT_PRECIS,
                          CLIP_DEFAULT_PRECIS,
                          DEFAULT_QUALITY,
                          DEFAULT_PITCH | FF_DONTCARE,
                          "Courier New");

      // This font is angled 45 degrees down
      hnewf2 = CreateFont(20, 0, -450, -450, FW_SEMIBOLD,
                          0, 0, 0, ANSI_CHARSET,
                          OUT_DEFAULT_PRECIS,
                          CLIP_DEFAULT_PRECIS,
                          DEFAULT_QUALITY,
                          DEFAULT_PITCH | FF_DONTCARE,
                          "Century Gothic");
      break;
    case WM_PAINT: // process a repaint request
      hdc = BeginPaint(hwnd, &ps); // get DC

      SelectObject(hdc, hnewf1);

      strcpy(str, "This string is angled 45 degrees up.");
      TextOut(hdc, 0, 200, str, strlen(str));

      SelectObject(hdc, hnewf2);
      strcpy(str, "This string is angled 45 degrees down.");
      TextOut(hdc, 10, 0, str, strlen(str));
```

specify the name of that set in **lfCharSet**. To enumerate fonts with any type of character set, use **DEFAULT_CHARSET**. To enumerate all fonts of a particular typeface, specify the name of the typeface in **lfFaceName**. To enumerate a representative font for all typefaces, initialize this member using the null string. Finally, **lfPitchAndFamily** must be set to zero.

Each time Windows 2000 enumerates a font, it calls the function pointed to by *EnumFunc*. This function processes each enumerated font and then returns nonzero if it wishes to process another font, or zero to stop. This function must have this general form:

> int CALLBACK EnumFunc(ENUMLOGFONTEX *lpLFInfo,
> NEWTEXTMETRICEX *lpTMInfo,
> int *type*, LPARAM *lParam*);

Here, *lpLFInfo* is a pointer to an **ENUMLOGFONTEX** structure that contains logical information about the enumerated font. *lpTMInfo* is a pointer to a **NEWTEXTMETRICEX** structure that contains physical information about the font. Non-TrueType fonts receive a pointer to a **TEXTMETRIC** structure, instead. The value of *type* indicates the font type. It can be one of these:

RASTER_FONTTYPE	TRUETYPE_FONTTYPE	DEVICE_FONTTYPE.

lParam receives the value passed in *lParam* by **EnumFontFamiliesEx( )**.

HISTORICAL PERSPECTIVE: Windows 3.1 does not support **EnumFontFamiliesEx( )**. Windows 3.1 programs use either **EnumFonts( )** or **EnumFontFamilies( )**. You will want to upgrade these when porting to Windows 2000.

The **ENUMLOGFONTEX** structure is defined as shown here:

```
typedef struct tagENUMLOGFONTEX
{
  LOGFONT elfLogFont;
  BYTE elfFullName[LF_FULLFACESIZE];  // full name of font
  BYTE elfStyle[LF_FACESIZE];         // style of font
  BYTE elfScript[LF_FACESIZE];        // script used by font
} ENUMLOGFONTEX;
```

```
      EndPaint(hwnd, &ps); // release DC
      break;
    case WM_DESTROY: // terminate the program
      DeleteObject(hnewf1);
      DeleteObject(hnewf2);
      PostQuitMessage(0);
      break;
    default:
      /* Let Windows 2000 process any messages not s|
      the preceding switch statement. */
      return DefWindowProc(hwnd, message, wParam, 1P
  }
  return 0;
}
```

Enumerating Fonts

When creating fonts in the preceding programs, it was assu
desired fonts were available. However, it is usually not a go
anything when programming for Windows. For example, i
fonts to or to remove fonts from a system. Fortunately, the
easy way to determine what fonts are available for use.

To enumerate the available fonts, you will use the **EnumF**
API function, shown here.

int EnumFontFamiliesEx(HDC *hdc*, LPLOGFONT *lpFont*
FONTENUMPROC *EnumFunc*,
LPARAM *lParam*, DWORD *No*

Here, *hdc* is the device context from which the fonts are b
Different device contexts may support different fonts. Var
that define the type of fonts that you want enumerated a
LOGFONT structure pointed to by *lpFontInfo*. (**LOGFON**
earlier in this chapter.) *EnumFunc* is a pointer to a callbac
be called once for each font enumerated. You can use *lPa*
application-dependent information to the callback functi
EnumProc. *NotUsed* is unused and must be zero. The funct
value returned by *EnumProc*.

Before calling **EnumFontFamiliesEx( )**, you must initiali
the **LOGFONT** structure pointed by *lpFontInfo*: **lfCharSet**, l
and **lfFaceName**. To enumerate only fonts with a particul

elfLogFont is a **LOGFONT** structure that contains most of the logical font information. The information used in this structure could be used in a call to **CreateFont( )** or **CreateFontIndirect( )**. The full name of the font is contained in **elfFullName**. The style (that is, bold, italics, and so forth) is contained in **elfStyle**. This field is not valid for non-TrueType fonts. The name of the script is found in **elfScript**.

A Font Enumeration Program

The following program shows how to enumerate fonts two different ways. First, when you select Available Fonts from the Enumerate menu, you obtain representative fonts for all of the supported typefaces. By choosing Selected Typeface, you obtain all fonts for the typeface that you specify. Sample output is shown in Figure 8-5.

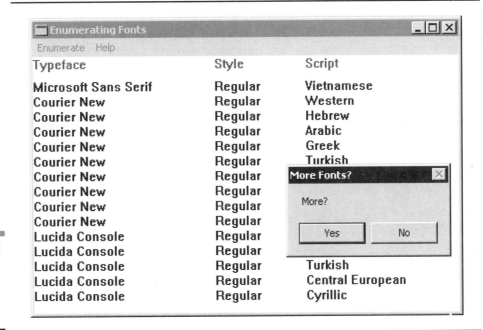

Sample output from the font enumeration program

Figure 8-5.

8

```cpp
// Enumerating Fonts

#include <windows.h>
#include <cstring>
#include <cstdio>
#include "font.h"

LRESULT CALLBACK WindowFunc(HWND, UINT, WPARAM, LPARAM);
int CALLBACK FontFunc(ENUMLOGFONTEX *lpLF,
                      NEWTEXTMETRICEX *lpTM,
                      int type, LPARAM lParam);
BOOL CALLBACK FontDialog(HWND hdwnd, UINT message,
                         WPARAM wParam, LPARAM lParam);

char szWinName[] = "MyWin"; // name of window class

char str[255];     // holds output strings
char fontstr[255]; // holds user-entered font name

int X=0, Y=0;   // current output location
int maxX, maxY; // screen dimensions

int linespacing; // spacing between lines

HDC memdc;     // store the virtual device handle
HBITMAP hbit;  // store the virtual bitmap
HBRUSH hbrush; // store the brush handle

HINSTANCE hInst;

int WINAPI WinMain(HINSTANCE hThisInst, HINSTANCE hPrevInst,
                   LPSTR lpszArgs, int nWinMode)
{
  HWND hwnd;
  MSG msg;
  WNDCLASSEX wcl;
  HACCEL hAccel;

  // Define a window class.
  wcl.cbSize = sizeof(WNDCLASSEX);

  wcl.hInstance = hThisInst;       // handle to this instance
  wcl.lpszClassName = szWinName; // window class name
  wcl.lpfnWndProc = WindowFunc;   // window function
  wcl.style = 0;                   // default style
```

```
wcl.hIcon = LoadIcon(NULL, IDI_APPLICATION); // large icon
wcl.hIconSm = NULL; // use small version of large icon
wcl.hCursor = LoadCursor(NULL, IDC_ARROW);   // cursor style

wcl.lpszMenuName = "FontEnumMenu"; // main menu

wcl.cbClsExtra = 0; // no extra memory needed
wcl.cbWndExtra = 0;

// Make the window background white.
wcl.hbrBackground = (HBRUSH) GetStockObject(WHITE_BRUSH);

// Register the window class.
if(!RegisterClassEx(&wcl)) return 0;

/* Now that a window class has been registered, a window
   can be created. */
hwnd = CreateWindow(
  szWinName, // name of window class
  "Enumerating Fonts", // title
  WS_OVERLAPPEDWINDOW, // window style - normal
  CW_USEDEFAULT, // X coordinate - let Windows decide
  CW_USEDEFAULT, // Y coordinate - let Windows decide
  CW_USEDEFAULT, // width - let Windows decide
  CW_USEDEFAULT, // height - let Windows decide
  NULL,          // no parent window
  NULL,          // no menu
  hThisInst,     // instance handle
  NULL           // no additional arguments
);

hInst = hThisInst; // save the current instance handle

// Load the keyboard accelerators.
hAccel = LoadAccelerators(hThisInst, "FontEnumMenu");

// Display the window.
ShowWindow(hwnd, nWinMode);
UpdateWindow(hwnd);

// Create the message loop.
while(GetMessage(&msg, NULL, 0, 0))
{
  if(!TranslateAccelerator(hwnd, hAccel, &msg)) {
    TranslateMessage(&msg); // translate keyboard messages
```

8

```
          DispatchMessage(&msg); // return control to Windows 2000
      }
    }

    return msg.wParam;
}

/* This function is called by Windows 2000 and is passed
   messages from the message queue.
*/
LRESULT CALLBACK WindowFunc(HWND hwnd, UINT message,
                            WPARAM wParam, LPARAM lParam)
{
    HDC hdc;
    static TEXTMETRIC tm;
    PAINTSTRUCT ps;
    LOGFONT lf;
    int result;
    int response;

    switch(message) {
      case WM_CREATE:
        // get screen coordinates
        maxX = GetSystemMetrics(SM_CXSCREEN);
        maxY = GetSystemMetrics(SM_CYSCREEN);

        // create a virtual window
        hdc = GetDC(hwnd);
        memdc = CreateCompatibleDC(hdc);
        hbit = CreateCompatibleBitmap(hdc, maxX, maxY);
        SelectObject(memdc, hbit);
        hbrush = (HBRUSH) GetStockObject(WHITE_BRUSH);
        SelectObject(memdc, hbrush);
        PatBlt(memdc, 0, 0, maxX, maxY, PATCOPY);

        // get text metrics
        GetTextMetrics(memdc, &tm);
        // compute linespacing
        linespacing = tm.tmHeight + tm.tmExternalLeading;

        // display header in bright red/orange
        SetTextColor(memdc, RGB(255, 100, 0));
        TextOut(memdc, X, 0, "Typeface", strlen("Typeface"));
        TextOut(memdc, X+200, 0, "Style", strlen("Style"));
        TextOut(memdc, X+300, 0, "Script", strlen("Script"));
```

```
            SetTextColor(memdc, RGB(0, 0, 0));

            ReleaseDC(hwnd, hdc);
            break;
        case WM_COMMAND:
            switch(LOWORD(wParam)) {
                case IDM_FONTS: // display fonts
                    Y = linespacing + linespacing/2;
                    PatBlt(memdc, 0, linespacing, maxX, maxY, PATCOPY);

                    lf.lfCharSet = DEFAULT_CHARSET;
                    strcpy(lf.lfFaceName, "");
                    lf.lfPitchAndFamily = 0;

                    // enumerate fonts
                    hdc = GetDC(hwnd);
                    EnumFontFamiliesEx(hdc, &lf,
                        (FONTENUMPROC) FontFunc, (LPARAM)hwnd, 0);
                    ReleaseDC(hwnd, hdc);

                    break;
                case IDM_TYPEFACE: // display selected typeface
                    // get name of font
                    result = DialogBox(hInst, "FontDB", hwnd,
                                        (DLGPROC) FontDialog);

                    if(!result) break; // user cancelled

                    Y = linespacing + linespacing/2;
                    PatBlt(memdc, 0, linespacing, maxX, maxY, PATCOPY);

                    lf.lfCharSet = DEFAULT_CHARSET;
                    strcpy(lf.lfFaceName, fontstr);
                    lf.lfPitchAndFamily = 0;

                    // enumerate all styles for given font
                    hdc = GetDC(hwnd);
                    EnumFontFamiliesEx(hdc, &lf,
                        (FONTENUMPROC) FontFunc, (LPARAM) hwnd, 0);
                    ReleaseDC(hwnd, hdc);

                    break;
                case IDM_EXIT:
                    response = MessageBox(hwnd, "Quit the Program?",
                                        "Exit", MB_YESNO);
```

8

```
          if(response == IDYES) PostQuitMessage(0);
          break;
        case IDM_HELP:
          MessageBox(hwnd,
                    "F2: Show Fonts\nF3: Show Typeface\n"
                    "F3: Exit", "Show Fonts", MB_OK);
          break;
      }
      break;
    case WM_PAINT: // process a repaint request
      hdc = BeginPaint(hwnd, &ps); // get DC

      // copy virtual window onto the screen
      BitBlt(hdc, 0, 0, maxX, maxY, memdc, 0, 0, SRCCOPY);
      EndPaint(hwnd, &ps); // release DC
      break;
    case WM_DESTROY: // terminate the program
      DeleteDC(memdc);
      PostQuitMessage(0);
      break;
    default:
      /* Let Windows 2000 process any messages not specified in
         the preceding switch statement. */
      return DefWindowProc(hwnd, message, wParam, lParam);
  }

  return 0;
}

// Enumerate fonts callback function.
int CALLBACK FontFunc(ENUMLOGFONTEX *lpLF,
                      NEWTEXTMETRICEX *lpTM,
                      int type, LPARAM lParam)
{
  int response;
  RECT rect;

  // display font info
  TextOut(memdc, X, Y, lpLF->elfLogFont.lfFaceName,
          strlen(lpLF->elfLogFont.lfFaceName)); // font name

  if(type == TRUETYPE_FONTTYPE)
    TextOut(memdc, X+200, Y, (char *)lpLF->elfStyle,
            strlen((char *)lpLF->elfStyle)); // style
  else
```

```
      TextOut(memdc, X+200, Y, "N/A", 3);

    TextOut(memdc, X+300, Y, (char *)lpLF->elfScript,
            strlen((char *)lpLF->elfScript)); // script style

    Y += linespacing;

    InvalidateRect((HWND)lParam, NULL, 0);

    // get current dimensions of the client area
    GetClientRect((HWND)lParam, &rect);

    // pause at bottom of window
    if( (Y + linespacing) >= rect.bottom) {
      Y = linespacing + linespacing/2; // reset to top
      response = MessageBox((HWND)lParam, "More?",
                            "More Fonts?", MB_YESNO);
      if(response == IDNO) return 0;
      PatBlt(memdc, 0, linespacing, maxX, maxY, PATCOPY);
    }

    return 1;
}

// Enumerate font dialog box.
BOOL CALLBACK FontDialog(HWND hdwnd, UINT message,
                            WPARAM wParam, LPARAM lParam)
{
  switch(message) {
    case WM_COMMAND:
      switch(LOWORD(wParam)) {
        case IDCANCEL:
          EndDialog(hdwnd, 0);
          return 1;
        case IDD_ENUM:
          // get typeface name
          GetDlgItemText(hdwnd, IDD_EB1, fontstr, 80);
          EndDialog(hdwnd, 1);
          return 1;
      }
      break;
  }

  return 0;
}
```

8

This program uses the following resource file.

```
#include <windows.h>
#include "font.h"

FontEnumMenu MENU
{
  POPUP "Enumerate" {
    MENUITEM "Available &Fonts\tF2", IDM_FONTS
    MENUITEM "Selected &Typeface\tF3", IDM_TYPEFACE
    MENUITEM "E&xit\tCtrl+X", IDM_EXIT
  }
  MENUITEM "&Help", IDM_HELP
}


FontEnumMenu ACCELERATORS
{
  VK_F1, IDM_HELP, VIRTKEY
  VK_F2, IDM_FONTS, VIRTKEY
  VK_F3, IDM_TYPEFACE, VIRTKEY
  "^X", IDM_EXIT
}

FontDB DIALOGEX 10, 10, 100, 60
CAPTION "Enumerate Typeface"
STYLE WS_POPUP | WS_CAPTION | WS_SYSMENU
{
  CTEXT "Enter Typeface", 300, 10, 10, 80, 12
  EDITTEXT IDD_EB1, 10, 20, 80, 12, ES_LEFT |
          WS_BORDER | ES_AUTOHSCROLL | WS_TABSTOP
  DEFPUSHBUTTON "Enumerate" IDD_ENUM, 30, 40, 40, 14
}
```

The FONT.H header file is shown here:

```
#define IDM_FONTS      100
#define IDM_TYPEFACE   101
#define IDM_EXIT       102
#define IDM_HELP       103

#define IDD_EB1        200
#define IDD_ENUM       201
```

Let's take a closer look at this program. When you select Available fonts, **EnumFontFamiliesEx( )** is called with **lf.lfFaceName** containing a null string. This causes a representative font from each typeface supported by the system to be returned. When you choose Selected Typeface, you activate a small dialog box in which you can enter the name of the desired typeface. This string is then used for the **lf.lfFaceName** field. Doing this causes all fonts of only that typeface to be enumerated.

The callback function **FontFunc( )** receives each enumerated font and displays it. For simplicity, the function displays a window full of fonts and then pops up a message box, asking if you want to see more. If you do, the next window's worth is shown. To determine the current size of the window, **FontFunc( )** calls **GetClientRect( )**. **GetClientRect( )** has this prototype:

BOOL GetClientRect(HWND *hwnd*, LPRECT *lpDim*);

Here, *hwnd* is the handle of the window in question and *lpDim* is a pointer to a **RECT** structure that will receive the current coordinates of the client area of the window. (The **RECT** structure was described in Chapter 3.) The function returns nonzero if successful and zero on failure. This function is useful whenever you need to know the current size of the client area of a window. In this program, the value in **rect.bottom** is used to determine if there is sufficient room to display another line of text within the current height of the window.

Here is a challenge that you might find interesting: Each time a font is enumerated, its logical settings are returned in a **LOGFONT** structure. Use this structure to create a font, using **CreateFontIndirect( )**, for each font that is enumerated, and then display a string in that font. Doing this provides an easy way to actually see what fonts are available for your use.

8

Remember, Windows 2000 support for fonts and text is quite rich. You will want to explore this area on your own. In the next chapter, we will continue exploring window output by working with graphics.

CHAPTER 9

Using Graphics

Windows 2000 supports a wide array of graphics-oriented API functions that allow you to draw in a window. This is not surprising, since Windows is a graphical operating system. Graphics are easy to handle because they are fully integrated into the overall landscape of the Windows environment.

While it is not possible to examine every graphics-related function supported by Windows 2000, this chapter describes the most important, including those used to draw a point, a line, a rectangle, and an ellipse. It also explains how to change the way graphics output is written to a window. The Windows 2000 graphics system is quite powerful, and you will want to explore it further on your own.

To demonstrate the graphics functions and techniques, a simple version of the standard Paint accessory is developed. As you will see, because of the power of the Windows 2000 graphics subsystem, surprisingly little code is required for this program.

The Graphics Coordinate System

The graphics coordinate system is the same as that used by the text-based functions. This means that, by default, the upper-left corner is location 0, 0 and that logical units are equivalent to pixels. However, the coordinate system and the mapping of logical units to pixels is under your control and can be changed.

Windows 2000 (and Windows in general) maintains a *current position* that is used and updated by certain graphics functions. When your program begins, the current location is set to 0, 0. Keep in mind that the location of the current position is completely invisible. That is, no graphics "cursor" is displayed. Instead, the current position is simply the next place in the window at which certain graphics functions will begin.

Pens and Brushes

The Windows graphics system is based upon two important objects: pens and brushes. By default, closed graphics shapes, such as rectangles and ellipses, are filled using the currently selected brush. Pens are resources that draw the lines and curves specified by the various graphics functions. The default pen is black and one pixel thick, but you can alter these attributes.

• Pens draw lines and brushes fill areas.

Until now, we have been working with only stock objects, such as the stock white brush that has been used to paint the client area of a window. In this chapter you will learn how to create custom brushes and pens.

Setting a Pixel

You can set the color of any specific pixel using the API function **SetPixel( )**, whose prototype is shown here:

COLORREF SetPixel(HDC *hdc*, int *X*, int *Y*, COLORREF *color*);

Here, *hdc* is the handle to the desired device context. The coordinates of the point to set are specified by *X*, *Y*, and the color is specified in *color*. (The **COLORREF** data type is described in Chapter 8.) The function returns the original color of the pixel, or −1 if an error occurs or if the location specified is outside the window.

Drawing a Line

To draw a line, use the **LineTo( )** function. This function draws a line using the currently selected pen. Its prototype is shown here:

BOOL LineTo(HDC *hdc*, int *X*, int *Y*);

The handle of the device context in which to draw the line is specified by *hdc*. The line is drawn from the current graphics position to the coordinates specified by *X*, *Y*. The current position is then changed to *X*, *Y*. The function returns nonzero if successful (that is, the line is drawn) and zero on failure.

Some programmers are surprised that **LineTo( )** uses the current position as its starting location and then sets the current position to the endpoint of the line that is drawn (instead of leaving it unchanged). However, there is a good reason for this. Many times, when displaying lines, one line will begin at the end of the previous line. When this is the case, **LineTo( )** operates very efficiently by avoiding the additional overhead caused by passing an extra set of coordinates. When this is not the case, you can set the current location to any position you like using the **MoveToEx( )** function (described next) prior to calling **LineTo( )**.

9

Setting the Current Location

To set the current position, use the **MoveToEx( )** function, whose prototype is shown here:

BOOL MoveToEx(HDC *hdc*, int *X*, int *Y*, LPPOINT *lpCoord*);

The handle to the device context is specified in *hdc*. The coordinates of the new current position are specified by *X*, *Y*. The previous current position is returned in the **POINT** structure pointed to by *lpCoord*. **POINT** is defined like this:

```
typedef struct tagPOINT {
  LONG x;
  LONG y;
} POINT;
```

However, if you use **NULL** for the *lpCoord* parameter, then **MoveToEx( )** does not return the previous position.

MoveToEx( ) returns nonzero if successful and zero on failure.

Drawing an Arc

You can draw an elliptical arc (a portion of an ellipse) in the current pen color using the **Arc( )** function. Its prototype is shown here:

BOOL Arc(HDC *hdc*, int *upX*, int *upY*, int *lowX*, int *lowY*,
　　　　int *startX*, int *startY*, int *endX*, int *endY*);

Here, *hdc* is the handle of the device context in which the arc will be drawn. The arc is defined by two objects. First, the arc is a portion of an ellipse that is bounded by the rectangle whose upper-left corner is at *upX*, *upY* and whose lower right corner is at *lowX*, *lowY*. The portion of the ellipse that is actually drawn (that is, the arc) starts at the intersection of a line from the center of the rectangle through the point specified by *startX*, *startY* and ends at the intersection of a line from the center of the rectangle through the point *endX*, *endY*. By default, the arc is drawn counterclockwise starting from *startX*, *startY*. You can set the drawing direction using the **SetArcDirection( )** API function. Figure 9-1 illustrates how **Arc( )** works.

Arc( ) returns nonzero if successful and zero on failure.

Displaying Rectangles

You can display a rectangle in the current pen color using the **Rectangle( )** function, whose prototype is shown here:

BOOL Rectangle(HDC *hdc*, int *upX*, int *upY*, int *lowX*, int *lowY*);

As usual, *hdc* is the handle of the device context. The upper-left corner of the rectangle is specified by *upX*, *upY* and the lower right corner is specified by

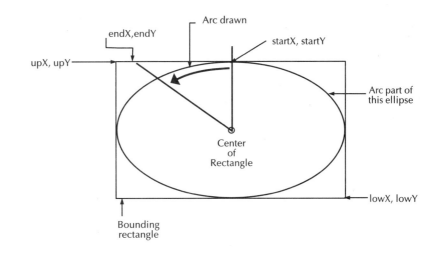

How the
Arc( ) function
operates
Figure 9-1.

lowX, lowY. The function returns nonzero if successful and zero if an error occurs. The rectangle is automatically filled using the current brush.

You can display a rounded rectangle using the **RoundRect( )** function. A rounded rectangle has its corners rounded slightly. The prototype for **RoundRect( )** is shown here:

9

BOOL RoundRect(HDC *hdc*, int *upX*, int *upY*, int *lowX*, int *lowY*,
      int *curveX*, int *curveY*);

The first five parameters are the same as for **Rectangle( )**. How the corners are curved is determined by the values of *curveX* and *curveY*, which define the width and the height of the ellipse that describes the curve. The function returns nonzero if successful and zero if a failure occurs. The rounded rectangle is automatically filled using the current brush.

Drawing Ellipses and Pie Slices

To draw an ellipse or a circle in the current pen color, use the **Ellipse( )** function, whose prototype is shown here:

BOOL Ellipse(HDC *hdc*, int *upX*, int *upY*, int *lowX*, int *lowY*);

Here, *hdc* is the handle of the device context in which the ellipse will be drawn. The ellipse is defined by specifying its bounding rectangle. The upper-left corner of the rectangle is specified by *upX, upY* and the lower-right corner is specified by *lowX, lowY*. To draw a circle, specify a square.

The function returns nonzero if successful and zero if a failure occurs. The ellipse is filled using the current brush.

Related to the ellipse is the pie slice. A pie slice is an object that includes an arc and lines from each end point of the arc to the center. To draw a pie slice use the **Pie( )** function, whose prototype is shown here:

```
BOOL Pie(HDC hdc, int upX, int upY, int lowX, int lowY,
            int startX, int startY, int endX, int endY);
```

Here, *hdc* is the handle of the device context in which the pie slice will be drawn. The arc of the slice is defined by two objects. First, the arc is a portion of an ellipse that is bounded by the rectangle whose upper-left corner is at *upX, upY* and whose lower right corner is at *lowX, lowY*. The portion of the ellipse that is actually drawn (that is, the arc of the slice) starts at the intersection of a line from the center of the rectangle through the point specified by *startX, startY* and ends at the intersection of a line from the center of the rectangle through the point *endX, endY*. By default, the arc is drawn in a counterclockwise direction.

The slice is drawn in the current pen color and filled using the current brush. The **Pie( )** function returns nonzero if successful and zero if an error occurs.

Working with Pens

Graphics objects are drawn using the currently selected pen. By default, this is a black pen that is one pixel wide. There are three stock pens: black, white, and null. A handle to each of these can be obtained using **GetStockObject( )**, discussed earlier in this book. The macros for these stock pens are **BLACK_PEN**, **WHITE_PEN**, and **NULL_PEN**. Pen handles are of type **HPEN**.

Frankly, the stock pens are quite limited, and usually you will want to define your own pens for your application. This is accomplished using the function **CreatePen( )**, whose prototype is shown here:

```
HPEN CreatePen(int style, int width, COLORREF color);
```

The *style* parameter determines what type of pen is created. It must be one of these values:

Macro	Pen style
PS_DASH	Dashed
PS_DASHDOT	Dash-dot
PS_DASHDOTDOT	Dash-dot-dot
PS_DOT	Dotted
PS_INSIDEFRAME	Solid pen that is within a bounded region
PS_NULL	None
PS_SOLID	Solid line

The dotted and/or dashed styles can be applied only to pens that are one unit thick. The **PS_INSIDEFRAME** pen is a solid pen that will be completely within the dimensions of any object that is drawn, even when that pen is more than one unit thick. For example, if a pen with **PS_INSIDEFRAME** style and width greater than 1 is used to draw a rectangle, then the outside of the line will be within the coordinates of the rectangle. (When a wide pen of a different style is used, the line may be partially outside the dimensions of the object.)

The thickness of a pen is specified by *width*, which is in logical units. The color of the pen is specified by *color*, which is a **COLORREF** value. **CreatePen( )** returns a handle to the pen if successful or **NULL** on failure.

9

Once a pen has been created, it is selected into a device context using **SelectObject( )**. For example, the following fragment creates a red pen and then selects it for use.

```
HPEN hRedpen;
hRedpen = CreatePen(PS_SOLID, 1, RGB(255,0,0));
SelectObject(dc, hRedpen);
```

You must delete any custom pens you create by calling **DeleteObject( )** before your program terminates.

Creating Custom Brushes

As is the case with the stock pens, the stock brushes provided by Windows 2000 are also quite limited. Often you will want to create your own brushes. Custom brushes are created in a way similar to custom pens. There are various styles of brushes. The most common custom brush is a *solid brush*. A solid brush is created using the **CreateSolidBrush( )** API function, whose prototype is shown here:

   HBRUSH CreateSolidBrush(COLORREF *color*);

The color of the brush is specified in *color,* and a handle to the brush is returned. **NULL** is returned on failure.

Once a custom brush has been created, it is selected into the device context using **SelectObject( )**. For example, the following fragment creates a green brush and then selects it for use.

```
HBRUSH hGreenbrush

hGreenbrush = CreateSolidBrush(RGB(0, 255 ,0));
SelectObject(dc, hGreenbrush);
```

In addition to solid brushes, there are two other types of brushes that you can create: a pattern brush and a hatch brush. A pattern brush fills areas with a bitmapped image. A hatch brush uses some form of hatchwork design. These brushes are created using **CreatePatternBrush( )** and **CreateHatchBrush( )**. The prototypes for these functions are shown here:

   HBRUSH CreatePatternBrush(HBITMAP *hBMap*);

   HBRUSH CreateHatchBrush(int *Style*, COLORREF *color*);

For **CreatePatternBrush( ),** *hBMap* is the handle of the bitmap whose pattern will be used as the brush. That is, the specified bitmap will be used to fill areas and paint backgrounds. The function returns a handle to the brush or **NULL** on error.

NOTE: To create a brush using a device-independent bitmap, use **CreateDIBPatternBrushPt( )**.

Brushes created using **CreateHatchBrush( )** have a hatched appearance. The exact nature of the hatching is determined by the value of *Style*, which must be one of those shown here.

Style	Hatching
HS_BDIAGONAL	Angled downward
HS_CROSS	Horizontal and vertical
HS_DIAGCROSS	Angled crosshatch
HS_FDIAGONAL	Angled upward
HS_HORIZONTAL	Horizontal
HS_VERTICAL	Vertical

The color of the brush is determined by the **COLORREF** value specified in *color*. It returns a handle to the brush or **NULL** on failure.

Deleting Custom Pens and Brushes

You must delete custom pens and brushes when they are no longer needed. You do this using the **DeleteObject( )** API function. Remember, you cannot (and must not) delete stock objects. Also, the object being deleted must not be currently selected into any device context.

Setting the Output Mode

Whenever your program outputs graphics to a window, how that output is actually copied to the window is determined by the output mode in effect at the time. By default, information is copied as-is to the window, overwriting any previous contents, but other output modes can be used. For example, output can be ANDed, ORed, or XORed with the current contents of the window. To specify the output mode, use the **SetROP2( )** function. Its prototype is shown here:

    int SetROP2(HDC *hdc*, int *Mode*);

Here, *hdc* is the handle of the device context being affected, and *Mode* specifies the new drawing mode. **SetROP2( )** returns the previous drawing mode or 0 on failure. *Mode* must be one of the values shown in Table 9-1.

9

Macro	Drawing Mode
R2_BLACK	Result is black.
R2_COPYPEN	Output is copied to the window, overwriting current contents.
R2_MASKPEN	Output is ANDed with the current screen color.
R2_MASKNOTPEN	Inverse of output is ANDed with the current screen color.
R2_MASKPENNOT	Output is ANDed with the inverse of the current screen color.
R2_MERGEPEN	Output is ORed with the current screen color.
R2_MERGENOTPEN	Inverse of output is ORed with the current screen color.
R2_MERGEPENNOT	Output is ORed with the inverse current screen color.
R2_NOP	No effect.
R2_NOT	Result is the inverse of the current screen color.
R2_NOTCOPYPEN	Inverse of the output color is copied to the window.
R2_NOTMASKPEN	Resulting color is the inverse of R2_MASKPEN.
R2_NOTMERGEPEN	Resulting color is the inverse of R2_MERGEPEN.
R2_NOTXORPEN	Resulting color is the inverse of R2_XORPEN.
R2_WHITE	Result is white.
R2_XORPEN	Output is exclusive-ORed with the current screen color.

The Available
Output Modes
Table 9-1.

R2_XORPEN is especially useful because it allows output to be temporarily written to the screen without losing the information that is already on the screen. This capability derives from a special property of the XOR operation. Consider the following: when one value, called A, is XORed with another, called B, it produces a result that, when XORed with B a second time, produces the original value, A. Thus, if you XOR output to the screen and then XOR the same output to the screen a second time, the original contents of the screen will be restored. This means that you can XOR output to the screen to display something temporarily and then simply XOR it to the screen again to restore the screen's original contents. This technique was briefly discussed in Chapter 7 as it related to the displaying of bitmaps; as you will see in the graphics demonstration program that follows, it can be applied to all types of output.

One final point: the ROP in the name of the function stands for Raster OPerations. This function applies only to raster devices, such as monitors.

A Graphics Demonstration

The following program demonstrates several of the graphics functions just discussed. It implements a simplified version of the standard Paint accessory. The program uses the virtual window technique developed in Chapter 7 to allow the window to be properly restored when a **WM_PAINT** message is received.

```
// A Simple Paint Program

#include <windows.h>
#include "graph.h"

LRESULT CALLBACK WindowFunc(HWND, UINT, WPARAM, LPARAM);

char szWinName[] = "MyWin"; // name of window class

int maxX, maxY; // screen dimensions

HDC memdc; // handle of memory DC
HBITMAP hbit; // handle of compatible bitmap
HBRUSH hCurrentbrush, hOldbrush; // handles of brushes
HBRUSH hRedbrush, hGreenbrush, hBluebrush, hNullbrush;

// create pens
HPEN hOldpen; // handle of old pen
HPEN hCurrentpen; // currently selected pen
HPEN hRedpen, hGreenpen, hBluepen, hBlackpen;

int X=0, Y=0;
int pendown = 0;
int endpoints = 0;
int StartX=0, StartY=0, EndX=0, EndY=0;
int Mode;

int WINAPI WinMain(HINSTANCE hThisInst, HINSTANCE hPrevInst,
```

9

```
                        LPSTR lpszArgs, int nWinMode)
{
  HWND hwnd;
  MSG msg;
  WNDCLASSEX wcl;
  HACCEL hAccel;

  // Define a window class.
  wcl.cbSize = sizeof(WNDCLASSEX);

  wcl.hInstance = hThisInst;      // handle to this instance
  wcl.lpszClassName = szWinName;  // window class name
  wcl.lpfnWndProc = WindowFunc;   // window function
  wcl.style = 0;                  // default style

  wcl.hIcon = LoadIcon(NULL, IDI_APPLICATION); // large icon
  wcl.hIconSm = NULL; // use small version of large icon
  wcl.hCursor = LoadCursor(NULL, IDC_ARROW);   // cursor style

  wcl.lpszMenuName = "GraphMenu"; // main menu

  wcl.cbClsExtra = 0; // no extra memory needed
  wcl.cbWndExtra = 0;

  // Make the window background white.
  wcl.hbrBackground = (HBRUSH) GetStockObject(WHITE_BRUSH);

  // Register the window class.
  if(!RegisterClassEx(&wcl)) return 0;

  /* Now that a window class has been registered, a window
     can be created. */
  hwnd = CreateWindow(
    szWinName, // name of window class
    "A Simple Paint Program", // title
    WS_OVERLAPPEDWINDOW, // window style - normal
    CW_USEDEFAULT, // X coordinate - let Windows decide
    CW_USEDEFAULT, // Y coordinate - let Windows decide
    CW_USEDEFAULT, // width - let Windows decide
    CW_USEDEFAULT, // height - let Windows decide
    NULL,          // no parent window
    NULL,          // no menu
    hThisInst,     // instance handle
    NULL           // no additional arguments
  );
```

```
       // Load the keyboard accelerators.
       hAccel = LoadAccelerators(hThisInst, "GraphMenu");

       // Display the window.
       ShowWindow(hwnd, nWinMode);
       UpdateWindow(hwnd);

       // Create the message loop.
       while(GetMessage(&msg, NULL, 0, 0))
       {
         if(!TranslateAccelerator(hwnd, hAccel, &msg)) {
           TranslateMessage(&msg); // translate keyboard messages
           DispatchMessage(&msg); // return control to Windows 2000
         }
       }

     return msg.wParam;
   }

   /* This function is called by Windows 2000 and is passed
      messages from the message queue.
   */
   LRESULT CALLBACK WindowFunc(HWND hwnd, UINT message,
                               WPARAM wParam, LPARAM lParam)
   {
     HDC hdc;
     PAINTSTRUCT paintstruct;
     int response;

     switch(message) {
       case WM_CREATE:
         // get screen coordinates
         maxX = GetSystemMetrics(SM_CXSCREEN);
         maxY = GetSystemMetrics(SM_CYSCREEN);

         // create virtual window
         hdc = GetDC(hwnd);
         memdc = CreateCompatibleDC(hdc);
         hbit = CreateCompatibleBitmap(hdc, maxX, maxY);
         SelectObject(memdc, hbit);
         hCurrentbrush = (HBRUSH) GetStockObject(WHITE_BRUSH);
         SelectObject(memdc, hCurrentbrush);
         PatBlt(memdc, 0, 0, maxX, maxY, PATCOPY);
```

9

```
    // create pens
    hRedpen = CreatePen(PS_SOLID, 1, RGB(255,0,0));
    hGreenpen = CreatePen(PS_SOLID, 1, RGB(0,255,0));
    hBluepen = CreatePen(PS_SOLID, 1, RGB(0,0,255));

    // create brushes
    hRedbrush = CreateSolidBrush(RGB(255,0,0));
    hGreenbrush = CreateSolidBrush(RGB(0,255,0));
    hBluebrush = CreateSolidBrush(RGB(0,0,255));
    hNullbrush = (HBRUSH) GetStockObject(HOLLOW_BRUSH);

    // save default pen
    hBlackpen = hOldpen = (HPEN) SelectObject(memdc, hRedpen);
    hCurrentpen = hOldpen;
    SelectObject(memdc, hOldpen);

    ReleaseDC(hwnd, hdc);
    break;
case WM_RBUTTONDOWN: // start defining a region
    endpoints = 1;
    X = StartX = LOWORD(lParam);
    Y = StartY = HIWORD(lParam);
    break;
case WM_RBUTTONUP: // stop defining a region
    endpoints = 0;
    EndX = LOWORD(lParam);
    EndY = HIWORD(lParam);
    break;
case WM_LBUTTONDOWN: // start drawing
    pendown = 1;
    X = LOWORD(lParam);
    Y = HIWORD(lParam);
    break;
case WM_LBUTTONUP: // stop drawing
    pendown = 0;
    break;
case WM_MOUSEMOVE:
    if(pendown) { // draw
      hdc = GetDC(hwnd);
      SelectObject(memdc, hCurrentpen);
      SelectObject(hdc, hCurrentpen);
      MoveToEx(memdc, X, Y, NULL);
      MoveToEx(hdc, X, Y, NULL);
      X = LOWORD(lParam);
      Y = HIWORD(lParam);
```

```
      LineTo(memdc, X, Y);
      LineTo(hdc, X, Y);
      ReleaseDC(hwnd, hdc);
    }
  if(endpoints) { // display region boundaries
    hdc = GetDC(hwnd);

    // select "shadow" pen
    hOldpen = (HPEN) SelectObject(hdc, hRedpen);

    // change display mode to XOR
    Mode = SetROP2(hdc, R2_XORPEN);

    // display, but don't fill
    hOldbrush =
        (HBRUSH) SelectObject(hdc, GetStockObject(HOLLOW_BRUSH));

    // erase old shadow rectangle
    Rectangle(hdc, StartX, StartY, X, Y);

    X = LOWORD(lParam);
    Y = HIWORD(lParam);

    // display new shadow rectangle
    Rectangle(hdc, StartX, StartY, X, Y);

    // restore default brush
    SelectObject(hdc, hOldbrush);
    SelectObject(hdc, hOldpen);
    SetROP2(hdc, Mode);
    ReleaseDC(hwnd, hdc);
  }
  break;
case WM_COMMAND:
  switch(LOWORD(wParam)) {
    case IDM_LINE:
      // select current pen
      SelectObject(memdc, hCurrentpen);

      // draw the line
      MoveToEx(memdc, StartX, StartY, NULL);
      LineTo(memdc, EndX, EndY);

      InvalidateRect(hwnd, NULL, 1);
      break;
```

9

```
case IDM_RECTANGLE:
  // select fill brush and pen
  SelectObject(memdc, hCurrentbrush);
  SelectObject(memdc, hCurrentpen);

  // draw rectangle
  Rectangle(memdc, StartX, StartY, EndX, EndY);

  InvalidateRect(hwnd, NULL, 1);
  break;
case IDM_ELLIPSE:
  // select fill brush and pen
  SelectObject(memdc, hCurrentbrush);
  SelectObject(memdc, hCurrentpen);

  // draw ellipse
  Ellipse(memdc,  StartX, StartY, EndX, EndY);

  InvalidateRect(hwnd, NULL, 1);
  break;
case IDM_RED:
  hCurrentpen = hRedpen;
  break;
case IDM_BLUE:
  hCurrentpen = hBluepen;
  break;
case IDM_GREEN:
  hCurrentpen = hGreenpen;
  break;
case IDM_BLACK:
  hCurrentpen = hBlackpen;
  break;
case IDM_REDFILL:
  hCurrentbrush = hRedbrush;
  break;
case IDM_BLUEFILL:
  hCurrentbrush = hBluebrush;
  break;
case IDM_GREENFILL:
  hCurrentbrush = hGreenbrush;
  break;
case IDM_WHITEFILL:
  hCurrentbrush = hOldbrush;
  break;
case IDM_NULLFILL:
```

```
        hCurrentbrush = hNullbrush;
        break;
      case IDM_RESET:
        // reset current position to 0,0
        MoveToEx(memdc, 0, 0, NULL);

        // erase by repainting background
        SelectObject(memdc, hOldbrush);
        PatBlt(memdc, 0, 0, maxX, maxY, PATCOPY);

        InvalidateRect(hwnd, NULL, 1);
        break;
      case IDM_EXIT:
        response = MessageBox(hwnd, "Quit the Program?",
                                "Exit", MB_YESNO);
        if(response == IDYES) PostQuitMessage(0);
        break;
      case IDM_HELP:
        MessageBox(hwnd, "F2: Line\nF3: Rectangle\n"
                    "F4: Ellipse\nF5: Reset",
                    "Paint Hot Keys", MB_OK);
        break;
    }
    break;
  case WM_PAINT: // process a repaint request
    hdc = BeginPaint(hwnd, &paintstruct); // get DC

    // copy virtual window onto screen
    BitBlt(hdc, 0, 0, maxX, maxY, memdc, 0, 0, SRCCOPY);

    EndPaint(hwnd, &paintstruct); // release DC
    break;
  case WM_DESTROY: // terminate the program
    DeleteObject(hRedpen); // delete pens
    DeleteObject(hGreenpen);
    DeleteObject(hBluepen);
    DeleteObject(hBlackpen);

    DeleteObject(hRedbrush); // delete brushes
    DeleteObject(hGreenbrush);
    DeleteObject(hBluebrush);

    DeleteDC(memdc);
    DeleteObject(hbit);
```

9

```
      PostQuitMessage(0);
      break;
    default:
      /* Let Windows 2000 process any messages not specified in
         the preceding switch statement. */
      return DefWindowProc(hwnd, message, wParam, lParam);
  }

  return 0;
}
```

This program requires the resource file shown here:

```
#include <windows.h>
#include "graph.h"

GraphMenu MENU
{
  POPUP "&Shapes"
  {
    MENUITEM "&Line\tF2", IDM_LINE
    MENUITEM "&Rectangle\tF3", IDM_RECTANGLE
    MENUITEM "&Ellipse\tF4", IDM_ELLIPSE
    MENUITEM "E&xit\tCtrl+X", IDM_EXIT
  }
  POPUP "&Options"
  {
    POPUP "&Pen Color"
    {
      MENUITEM "&Red", IDM_RED
      MENUITEM "&Blue", IDM_BLUE
      MENUITEM "&Green", IDM_GREEN
      MENUITEM "Bl&ack", IDM_BLACK
    }
    POPUP "&Fill Color"
    {
      MENUITEM "&Red", IDM_REDFILL
      MENUITEM "&Blue", IDM_BLUEFILL
      MENUITEM "&Green", IDM_GREENFILL
      MENUITEM "&White", IDM_WHITEFILL
      MENUITEM "&Null", IDM_NULLFILL
    }
    MENUITEM "&Reset\tF5", IDM_RESET
  }
  MENUITEM "&Help", IDM_HELP
```

```
     }

GraphMenu ACCELERATORS
{
  VK_F1,  IDM_HELP,  VIRTKEY
  VK_F2,  IDM_LINE,  VIRTKEY
  VK_F3,  IDM_RECTANGLE,  VIRTKEY
  VK_F4,  IDM_ELLIPSE,  VIRTKEY
  VK_F5,  IDM_RESET,  VIRTKEY
  "^X",  IDM_EXIT
}
```

It also requires the header file GRAPH.H, shown here:

```
#define IDM_LINE       100
#define IDM_RECTANGLE  101
#define IDM_ELLIPSE    102
#define IDM_RED        103
#define IDM_GREEN      104
#define IDM_BLUE       105
#define IDM_BLACK      106
#define IDM_REDFILL    107
#define IDM_GREENFILL  108
#define IDM_BLUEFILL   109
#define IDM_WHITEFILL  110
#define IDM_NULLFILL   111
#define IDM_RESET      112
#define IDM_HELP       113
#define IDM_EXIT       114
```

Sample output is shown in Figure 9-2.

The paint program works like this. Free-style lines can be drawn using the mouse. To draw, press and hold the left button. The right button is used to define a region. To do this, move the mouse pointer to the first corner, press and hold the right mouse button, and then move the mouse pointer to the opposite corner. Release the right button when you reach the desired location. When defining a region, a "shadow" rectangle will appear that outlines the region as you define it. Once a region has been defined, you can then draw a line, a rectangle, or an ellipse within that region. These options are selected from the Shapes menu. Using the Options menu, you can select a new pen color, a new brush color, or erase and reset the window. Most of the code in the paint program should be easy to understand. However, let's take a look at few of the more interesting sections.

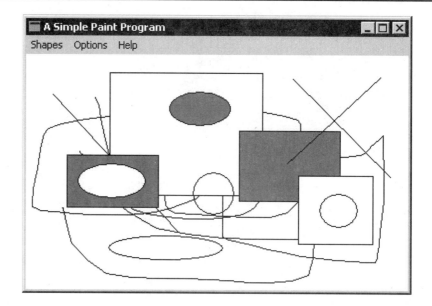

Figure 9-2.

A Closer Look at the Paint Program

When the paint program first begins execution, the following objects are
created: the virtual window bitmap and the pens and brushes needed by the
program. These are destroyed when the program terminates.

The variable **pendown** is set to 1 when the left mouse button is pressed.
Otherwise, it is 0. The variable **endpoints** is set to 1 when a region is being
defined (by pressing the right mouse button). Otherwise, it is zero. These
variables are used to determine the precise meaning of a **WM_MOUSEMOVE**
message.

Perhaps the most involved part of the program is contained within the
WM_MOUSEMOVE case. Let's go through it carefully. It is repeated here for
your convenience.

```
case WM_MOUSEMOVE:
  if(pendown) { // draw
    hdc = GetDC(hwnd);
    SelectObject(memdc, hCurrentpen);
    SelectObject(hdc, hCurrentpen);
    MoveToEx(memdc, X, Y, NULL);
    MoveToEx(hdc, X, Y, NULL);
    X = LOWORD(lParam);
```

```
      Y = HIWORD(lParam);
      LineTo(memdc, X, Y);
      LineTo(hdc, X, Y);
      ReleaseDC(hwnd, hdc);
    }
  if(endpoints) { // display region boundaries
    hdc = GetDC(hwnd);

    // select "shadow" pen
    hOldpen = (HPEN) SelectObject(hdc, hRedpen);

    // change display mode to XOR
    Mode = SetROP2(hdc, R2_XORPEN);

    // display, but don't fill
    hOldbrush =
        (HBRUSH) SelectObject(hdc, GetStockObject(HOLLOW_BRUSH));

    // erase old shadow rectangle
    Rectangle(hdc, StartX, StartY, X, Y);

    X = LOWORD(lParam);
    Y = HIWORD(lParam);

    // display new shadow rectangle
    Rectangle(hdc, StartX, StartY, X, Y);

    // restore default brush
    SelectObject(hdc, hOldbrush);
    SelectObject(hdc, hOldpen);
    SetROP2(hdc, Mode);
    ReleaseDC(hwnd, hdc);
  }
  break;
```

9

A **WM_MOUSEMOVE** message is sent each time the mouse is moved. The X coordinate of the mouse is passed in the low-order word of **lParam**, and the Y coordinate is passed in the high-order word of **lParam**.

If **pendown** is true, then the user is drawing a line. In this situation, each time the mouse is moved, the current pen is selected into both the window device context (**hdc**) and the virtual window device context (**memdc**). Next, a line is drawn (in both contexts) connecting the previous location of the mouse with the new location. This ensures that a smooth, unbroken line is displayed as you move the mouse. (As an experiment, try using **SetPixel( )**, rather than **LineTo( )**, and observe the results. As you will see, a

IN DEPTH

Drawing Irregular Polygons

In addition to the basic graphical elements, such as lines, ellipses, and rectangles, Windows 2000 allows you to define and draw irregular objects. One such object is the polygon. Relative to Windows 2000, a polygon consists of three or more sides that enclose an area. To draw a polygon, use the **Polygon( )** function, shown here:

BOOL Polygon(HDC *hdc*, CONST POINT **vertices*, int *num*);

Here, *hdc* identifies the device context. An array containing the coordinates of the endpoints of the polygon is pointed to by *vertices*, and the number of vertices is passed in *num*. The function returns nonzero if successful and zero on failure. The polygon is drawn using the currently selected pen and is filled using the currently selected brush. The **Polygon( )** function automatically draws a line from the last point to the first point in the *vertices* array, thus ensuring that the figure is enclosed. **Polygon( )** does not use or modify the current position.

To try **Polygon( )**, add this global declaration to the example paint program.

```
POINT polygon[5] = {
  10, 10,
  10, 40,
  40, 70,
  40, 90,
  10, 10};
```

Next, add this line to the **IDD_LINE** case.

```
Polygon(memdc, polygon, 5);
```

Now, each time you select the Line option, the five-sided polygon will also be displayed.

Here are some other API functions that draw complex objects that you might find of interest: **Polyline( )**, **PolylineTo( )**, **PolyPolyline( )**, **PolyPolygon( )**, **PolyBezier( )** and **PolyBezierTo( )**.

WM_MOUSEMOVE message is not generated for every pixel in the mouse's path, causing a disjointed line.) After each line is drawn, the current graphics location is updated to the current mouse position. Remember, **LineTo( )** advances the current location to the end of the line.

If **endpoints** is true, then the mouse is being used to define a rectangular region. The first endpoint is set when the **WM_RBUTTONDOWN** message is received. The second endpoint is set when the **WM_RBUTTONUP** message is received. These messages also contain the X, Y coordinates of the mouse in **LOWORD(lParam)** and **HIWORD(lParam),** respectively. As the mouse is moved, a "shadow" rectangle is displayed that shows the current extents of the region. This rectangle is XORed onto the window. The reason for this is that the outcome of two XORs is the original value. Thus, using the **X2_XORPEN** drawing mode, one call to **Rectangle( )** displays the shadow rectangle; a second call erases it. This makes it easy to display the shadow rectangle without disrupting the current contents of the window.

Before moving on, make sure that you understand all of the graphics operations contained in the paint program. The next section will be building upon it.

Using World Transforms

While all versions of Windows can perform the type of graphics operations found in the preceding paint program, Windows 2000 offers the programmer an exciting and powerful extension not supported by Windows 95/98: *world transforms*. World transforms make it possible to perform a number of transformations that change the way output is mapped to a window. These transformations include rotation, translation, scaling, shearing, and reflection. With Windows 2000, you can easily perform sophisticated graphical manipulations of the type found in a typical CAD (Computer-Aided Design) environment. For example, you can rotate or enlarge an image.

A world transform changes the way output is mapped to a window.

9

Windows 2000 handles world transformations by mapping one coordinate space onto another. Therefore, we will begin by describing Windows 2000's coordinate spaces.

Coordinate Spaces

Windows 2000 defines three coordinate spaces. The first is called the *world space*. This coordinate space is used to perform world transformations. The second is called *page space*. This is the logical coordinate space used by your program. The third is *device space*, which uses physical coordinates. Device space is mapped onto the physical device itself. Sometimes the physical device is referred to as the fourth coordinate space.

As you know, output coordinates are specified in logical units (which are pixels, by default, but may vary). These units are mapped to the physical device, one coordinate space at a time. When world transforms are not in effect, output is mapped beginning at page space. When using world transforms, output mapping begins at world space. At each coordinate space transition, the contents of the previous space are mapped onto the next space. For example, the mapping from page space to device space converts logical units into physical ones. When using world transforms, the mapping from world space to page space performs the transformation that you have specified.

SetWorldTransform( )

World transforms are specified by calling **SetWorldTransform( )**. Its prototype is shown here:

BOOL SetWorldTransform(HDC *hdc*, CONST XFORM **lpTransform*);

Here, *hdc* is the handle of the device context that you wish to transform. The specific transformation is specified in the structure pointed to by *lpTransform*. The function returns nonzero if successful and zero on failure. After **SetWorldTransform( )** has been called, the transformation that you specify will be in effect.

The type of transform is specified in a structure of type **XFORM**, which has this definition:

```
typedef struct    tagXFORM
{
  FLOAT eM11;
  FLOAT eM12;
  FLOAT eM21;
  FLOAT eM22;
  FLOAT eDx;
  FLOAT eDy;
} XFORM;
```

The exact transformation that takes place is determined by the values you place in the matrix defined by **XFORM**. Let's see how each type of transformation can be achieved.

To translate output (that is, to offset the origin) the X offset is specified in **eDx**, and the Y offset is specified in **eDy**. This is the simplest transformation that you can specify. It causes output to be shifted. It can also be combined with the other transforms.

To rotate output through an angle *theta*, the values of **eM11**, **eM12**, **eM21**, and **eM22** must be as shown here:

Field	Meaning
eM11	cosine of *theta*
eM12	sine of *theta*
eM21	−sine of *theta*
eM22	cosine of *theta*

To scale output, put the X scaling factor in **eM11** and the Y scaling factor in **eM22**. **eM12** and **eM21** are not used (and should be zero).

To shear output, put the X shear factor in **eM12** and the Y shear factor in **eM21**. **eM11** and **eM22** are not used (and should be zero).

To reflect output along the X axis, put −1 in **eM11** and 1 in **eM22**. To reflect output along the Y axis, put −1 in **eM22** and 1 in **eM11**. To reflect output along both axes, put −1 into both **eM11** and **eM22**. **eM12** and **eM21** are not used (and should be zero).

Although there is nothing difficult about initializing the **XFORM** structure to achieve a desired transformation, the various ways the fields in **XFORM** are used makes it seem more complicated than it is. The best way to understand the effects of each transformation is to try each one experimentally.

9

Setting the Graphics Mode

In order for **SetWorldTransform( )** to have effect, you must have first enabled Windows 2000's advanced graphics mode. To do this use the **SetGraphicsMode( )** function, shown here.

```
int SetGraphicsMode(HDC hdc, int GraphMode);
```

Here, *hdc* is the device context being affected, and *GraphMode* determines the graphics mode. It must be either **GM_COMPATIBLE** or **GM_ADVANCED**. The function returns the previous mode or zero on failure.

By default, the graphics mode is **GM_COMPATIBLE**. This is the mode used by Windows 95/98. To use **SetWorldTransform( )**, you must set the mode to **GM_ADVANCED**.

Adding Rotation to the Paint Program

To illustrate **SetWorldTransform( )**, the paint program has been enhanced so that you can rotate the images that you create. Each time you press the left arrow key, the image currently in view is rotated counterclockwise 30 degrees. Pressing the right arrow key rotates the image clockwise 30 degrees. In each case, the image is rotated about the center of the current client area. The program is shown next. Sample output is shown in Figure 9-3.

Sample output
that shows
rotation

Figure 9-3.

```
// Using SetWorldTransform() to rotate images.

#include <windows.h>
#include "graph.h"
#include <cmath>

LRESULT CALLBACK WindowFunc(HWND, UINT, WPARAM, LPARAM);

char szWinName[] = "MyWin"; // name of window class

int maxX, maxY; // screen dimensions

HDC memdc; // handle of memory DC
HBITMAP hbit; // handle of compatible bitmap
HBRUSH hCurrentbrush, hOldbrush; // handles of brushes
HBRUSH hRedbrush, hGreenbrush, hBluebrush, hNullbrush;

// create pens
HPEN hOldpen; // handle of old pen
HPEN hCurrentpen; // currently selected pen
HPEN hRedpen, hGreenpen, hBluepen, hBlackpen;

int X=0, Y=0;
int pendown = 0;
int endpoints = 0;
int StartX=0, StartY=0, EndX=0, EndY=0;
int Mode;

int theta = 0; // angle of rotation

int WINAPI WinMain(HINSTANCE hThisInst, HINSTANCE hPrevInst,
                    LPSTR lpszArgs, int nWinMode)
{
  HWND hwnd;
  MSG msg;
  WNDCLASSEX wcl;
  HACCEL hAccel;

  // Define a window class.
  wcl.cbSize = sizeof(WNDCLASSEX);

  wcl.hInstance = hThisInst;        // handle to this instance
  wcl.lpszClassName = szWinName;    // window class name
  wcl.lpfnWndProc = WindowFunc;     // window function
  wcl.style = 0;                    // default style
```

```
wcl.hIcon = LoadIcon(NULL, IDI_APPLICATION); // large icon
wcl.hIconSm = NULL; // use small version of large icon
wcl.hCursor = LoadCursor(NULL, IDC_ARROW);  // cursor style

wcl.lpszMenuName = "GraphMenu"; // main menu

wcl.cbClsExtra = 0; // no extra memory needed
wcl.cbWndExtra = 0;

// Make the window background white.
wcl.hbrBackground = (HBRUSH) GetStockObject(WHITE_BRUSH);

// Register the window class.
if(!RegisterClassEx(&wcl)) return 0;

/* Now that a window class has been registered, a window
   can be created. */
hwnd = CreateWindow(
  szWinName, // name of window class
  "Paint With Rotation", // title
  WS_OVERLAPPEDWINDOW, // window style - normal
  CW_USEDEFAULT, // X coordinate - let Windows decide
  CW_USEDEFAULT, // Y coordinate - let Windows decide
  CW_USEDEFAULT, // width - let Windows decide
  CW_USEDEFAULT, // height - let Windows decide
  NULL,          // no parent window
  NULL,          // no menu
  hThisInst,     // instance handle
  NULL           // no additional arguments
);

// Load the keyboard accelerators.
hAccel = LoadAccelerators(hThisInst, "GraphMenu");

// Display the window.
ShowWindow(hwnd, nWinMode);
UpdateWindow(hwnd);

// Create the message loop.
while(GetMessage(&msg, NULL, 0, 0))
{
  if(!TranslateAccelerator(hwnd, hAccel, &msg)) {
    TranslateMessage(&msg); // translate keyboard messages
```

```
        DispatchMessage(&msg); // return control to Windows 2000
    }
  }

  return msg.wParam;
}

/* This function is called by Windows 2000 and is passed
   messages from the message queue.
*/
LRESULT CALLBACK WindowFunc(HWND hwnd, UINT message,
                            WPARAM wParam, LPARAM lParam)
{
  HDC hdc;
  PAINTSTRUCT paintstruct;
  int response;
  RECT rect;
  XFORM tf; // transformation matrix

  switch(message) {
    case WM_CREATE:
      // get screen coordinates
      maxX = GetSystemMetrics(SM_CXSCREEN);
      maxY = GetSystemMetrics(SM_CYSCREEN);

      // create virtual window
      hdc = GetDC(hwnd);
      memdc = CreateCompatibleDC(hdc);
      hbit = CreateCompatibleBitmap(hdc, maxX, maxY);
      SelectObject(memdc, hbit);
      hCurrentbrush = (HBRUSH) GetStockObject(WHITE_BRUSH);
      SelectObject(memdc, hCurrentbrush);
      PatBlt(memdc, 0, 0, maxX, maxY, PATCOPY);

      // create pens
      hRedpen = CreatePen(PS_SOLID, 1, RGB(255,0,0));
      hGreenpen = CreatePen(PS_SOLID, 1, RGB(0,255,0));
      hBluepen = CreatePen(PS_SOLID, 1, RGB(0,0,255));

      // create brushes
      hRedbrush = CreateSolidBrush(RGB(255,0,0));
      hGreenbrush = CreateSolidBrush(RGB(0,255,0));
      hBluebrush = CreateSolidBrush(RGB(0,0,255));
      hNullbrush = (HBRUSH) GetStockObject(HOLLOW_BRUSH);
```

9

```
    // save default pen
    hBlackpen = hOldpen = (HPEN) SelectObject(memdc, hRedpen);
    hCurrentpen = hOldpen;
    SelectObject(memdc, hOldpen);

    ReleaseDC(hwnd, hdc);
    break;
case WM_KEYDOWN: // rotate image
    switch((char) wParam) {
      case VK_LEFT: // counterclockwise
        theta -= 30;
        InvalidateRect(hwnd, NULL, 1);
        break;
      case VK_RIGHT: // clockwise
        theta += 30;
        InvalidateRect(hwnd, NULL, 1);
        break;
    }
    break;
case WM_RBUTTONDOWN: // start defining a region
    if(theta) { // restore view
      theta = 0;
      InvalidateRect(hwnd, NULL, 1);
    }
    endpoints = 1;
    X = StartX = LOWORD(lParam);
    Y = StartY = HIWORD(lParam);
    break;
case WM_RBUTTONUP: // stop defining a region
    endpoints = 0;
    EndX = LOWORD(lParam);
    EndY = HIWORD(lParam);
    break;
case WM_LBUTTONDOWN: // start drawing
    if(theta) { // restore view
      theta = 0;
      InvalidateRect(hwnd, NULL, 1);
    }
    pendown = 1;
    X = LOWORD(lParam);
    Y = HIWORD(lParam);
    break;
```

```
case WM_LBUTTONUP: // stop drawing
  pendown = 0;
  break;
case WM_MOUSEMOVE:
  if(pendown) { // draw
    hdc = GetDC(hwnd);
    SelectObject(memdc, hCurrentpen);
    SelectObject(hdc, hCurrentpen);
    MoveToEx(memdc, X, Y, NULL);
    MoveToEx(hdc, X, Y, NULL);
    X = LOWORD(lParam);
    Y = HIWORD(lParam);
    LineTo(memdc, X, Y);
    LineTo(hdc, X, Y);
    ReleaseDC(hwnd, hdc);
  }
  if(endpoints) { // display region boundaries
    hdc = GetDC(hwnd);

    // select "shadow" pen
    hOldpen = (HPEN) SelectObject(hdc, hRedpen);

    // change display mode to XOR
    Mode = SetROP2(hdc, R2_XORPEN);

    // display, but don't fill
    hOldbrush =
        (HBRUSH) SelectObject(hdc, GetStockObject(HOLLOW_BRUSH));

    // erase old shadow rectangle
    Rectangle(hdc, StartX, StartY, X, Y);

    X = LOWORD(lParam);
    Y = HIWORD(lParam);

    // display new shadow rectangle
    Rectangle(hdc, StartX, StartY, X, Y);

    // restore default brush
    SelectObject(hdc, hOldbrush);
    SelectObject(hdc, hOldpen);
    SetROP2(hdc, Mode);
    ReleaseDC(hwnd, hdc);
  }
```

9

```
      break;
case WM_COMMAND:
  switch(LOWORD(wParam)) {
    case IDM_ROTATERESET:
      theta = 0;
      InvalidateRect(hwnd, NULL, 1);
      break;
    case IDM_LINE:
      // select current pen
      SelectObject(memdc, hCurrentpen);

      // draw the line
      MoveToEx(memdc, StartX, StartY, NULL);
      LineTo(memdc, EndX, EndY);

      InvalidateRect(hwnd, NULL, 1);
      break;
    case IDM_RECTANGLE:
      // select fill brush and pen
      SelectObject(memdc, hCurrentbrush);
      SelectObject(memdc, hCurrentpen);

      // draw rectangle
      Rectangle(memdc, StartX, StartY, EndX, EndY);

      InvalidateRect(hwnd, NULL, 1);
      break;
    case IDM_ELLIPSE:
      // select fill brush and pen
      SelectObject(memdc, hCurrentbrush);
      SelectObject(memdc, hCurrentpen);

      // draw ellipse
      Ellipse(memdc, StartX, StartY, EndX, EndY);

      InvalidateRect(hwnd, NULL, 1);
      break;
    case IDM_RED:
      hCurrentpen = hRedpen;
      break;
    case IDM_BLUE:
      hCurrentpen = hBluepen;
      break;
    case IDM_GREEN:
      hCurrentpen = hGreenpen;
```

```
          break;
        case IDM_BLACK:
          hCurrentpen = hBlackpen;
          break;
        case IDM_REDFILL:
          hCurrentbrush = hRedbrush;
          break;
        case IDM_BLUEFILL:
          hCurrentbrush = hBluebrush;
          break;
        case IDM_GREENFILL:
          hCurrentbrush = hGreenbrush;
          break;
        case IDM_WHITEFILL:
          hCurrentbrush = hOldbrush;
          break;
        case IDM_NULLFILL:
          hCurrentbrush = hNullbrush;
          break;
        case IDM_RESET:
          // reset current position to 0,0
          MoveToEx(memdc, 0, 0, NULL);

          // erase by repainting background
          SelectObject(memdc, hOldbrush);
          PatBlt(memdc, 0, 0, maxX, maxY, PATCOPY);

          theta = 0;

          InvalidateRect(hwnd, NULL, 1);
          break;
        case IDM_EXIT:
          response = MessageBox(hwnd, "Quit the Program?",
                            "Exit", MB_YESNO);
          if(response == IDYES) PostQuitMessage(0);
          break;
        case IDM_HELP:
          MessageBox(hwnd, "F2: Line\nF3: Rectangle\n"
                    "F4: Ellipse\nF5: Rotation Reset\n"
                    "F6: Reset\n",
                    "Paint and Rotate", MB_OK);
          break;
      }
      break;
    case WM_PAINT: // process a repaint request
```

```
      hdc = BeginPaint(hwnd, &paintstruct); // get DC

      // use Windows 2000's advanced graphics mode
      SetGraphicsMode(hdc, GM_ADVANCED);

      // get current dimensions of client area
      GetClientRect(hwnd, &rect);

      // rotate image
      tf.eM11 = (float) cos(theta * 3.1416/180);
      tf.eM12 = (float) sin(theta * 3.1416/180);
      tf.eM21 = (float) -sin(theta * 3.1416/180);
      tf.eM22 = (float) cos(theta * 3.1416/180);
      tf.eDx = (float) rect.right/2;
      tf.eDy = (float) rect.bottom/2;
      SetWorldTransform(hdc, &tf); // set transform

      // copy virtual window onto screen
      BitBlt(hdc, -rect.right/2, -rect.bottom/2,
             rect.right, rect.bottom, memdc, 0, 0, SRCCOPY);

      EndPaint(hwnd, &paintstruct); // release DC
      break;
    case WM_DESTROY: // terminate the program
      DeleteObject(hRedpen); // delete pens
      DeleteObject(hGreenpen);
      DeleteObject(hBluepen);
      DeleteObject(hBlackpen);

      DeleteObject(hRedbrush); // delete brushes
      DeleteObject(hGreenbrush);
      DeleteObject(hBluebrush);

      DeleteDC(memdc);
      DeleteObject(hbit);

      PostQuitMessage(0);
      break;
    default:
      /* Let Windows 2000 process any messages not specified in
         the preceding switch statement. */
      return DefWindowProc(hwnd, message, wParam, lParam);
  }

  return 0;
}
```

The program uses this resource file.

```
#include <windows.h>
#include "graph.h"

GraphMenu MENU
{
  POPUP "&Shapes"
  {
    MENUITEM "&Line\tF2", IDM_LINE
    MENUITEM "&Rectangle\tF3", IDM_RECTANGLE
    MENUITEM "&Ellipse\tF4", IDM_ELLIPSE
    MENUITEM "E&xit\tCtrl+X", IDM_EXIT
  }
  POPUP "&Options"
  {
    POPUP "&Pen Color"
    {
      MENUITEM "&Red", IDM_RED
      MENUITEM "&Blue", IDM_BLUE
      MENUITEM "&Green", IDM_GREEN
      MENUITEM "Bl&ack", IDM_BLACK
    }
    POPUP "&Fill Color"
    {
      MENUITEM "&Red", IDM_REDFILL
      MENUITEM "&Blue", IDM_BLUEFILL
      MENUITEM "&Green", IDM_GREENFILL
      MENUITEM "&White", IDM_WHITEFILL
      MENUITEM "&Null", IDM_NULLFILL
    }
    MENUITEM "Ro&tation Reset\tF5", IDM_ROTATERESET
    MENUITEM "&Reset\tF6", IDM_RESET
  }
    MENUITEM "&Help", IDM_HELP
}

GraphMenu ACCELERATORS
{
  VK_F1, IDM_HELP, VIRTKEY
  VK_F2, IDM_LINE, VIRTKEY
  VK_F3, IDM_RECTANGLE, VIRTKEY
  VK_F4, IDM_ELLIPSE, VIRTKEY
  VK_F5, IDM_ROTATERESET, VIRTKEY
  VK_F6, IDM_RESET, VIRTKEY
  "^X", IDM_EXIT
}
```

9

You must add this line to GRAPH.H:

```
#define IDM_ROTATERESET     200
```

A Closer Look at the Rotation Mechanism

To handle the rotation of images, the paint program adds the following items:

◆ The global variable **theta**, which holds the current angle of rotation, in degrees.

◆ The local variable **tf**, which holds the current transformation matrix.

◆ Handlers for the left and right arrow keys, which increase or decrease **theta** by 30 degrees each time one is pressed.

◆ The call to **SetWorldTransform( )** inside the handler for **WM_PAINT**.

◆ The Rotation Reset menu option.

Here is how they work. The value of **theta** determines the angle of rotation that will be applied to the image when it is copied from the virtual window device context (**memdc**) to the physical device context (**hdc**) inside **WM_PAINT**. The handlers for **VK_LEFT** and **VK_RIGHT** simply increase or decrease **theta** by 30 degrees each time one is pressed and then cause the window to be repainted.

The actual rotation of the image occurs inside the **WM_PAINT** handler, which is shown here. Let's go through it carefully.

```
case WM_PAINT: // process a repaint request
  hdc = BeginPaint(hwnd, &paintstruct); // get DC

  // use Windows 2000's advanced graphics mode
  SetGraphicsMode(hdc, GM_ADVANCED);

  // get current dimensions of client area
  GetClientRect(hwnd, &rect);

  // rotate image
  tf.eM11 = (float) cos(theta * 3.1416/180);
  tf.eM12 = (float) sin(theta * 3.1416/180);
  tf.eM21 = (float) -sin(theta * 3.1416/180);
  tf.eM22 = (float) cos(theta * 3.1416/180);
  tf.eDx = (float) rect.right/2;
  tf.eDy = (float) rect.bottom/2;
```

```
SetWorldTransform(hdc, &tf); // set transform

// copy virtual window onto screen
BitBlt(hdc, -rect.right/2, -rect.bottom/2,
       rect.right, rect.bottom, memdc, 0, 0, SRCCOPY);

EndPaint(hwnd, &paintstruct); // release DC
break;
```

Each time a **WM_PAINT** message is received, the device context is obtained and set to advanced graphics mode, the current dimensions of the client area are retrieved, and the transformation matrix is initialized for rotation through the angle contained in **theta**. As you may know, the standard C/C++ sine and cosine functions require that their arguments be in radians, so the expressions used as parameters to these functions simply convert the degrees in **theta** into their equivalent number of radians. When **theta** is zero (its initial value), then no rotation occurs.

Notice that the transformation matrix sets **eDx** and **eDy** to **rect.right/2** and **rect.bottom/2**, respectively. Remember, all transformations occur relative to the origin, which for a window is the upper-left corner by default. By translating the origin by one half of the length and width of the client area, we are effectively moving it to the center of the window. Doing this causes the rotation to occur around the center of the window.

After **SetWorldTransform( )** is called, the specified transformation is activated and subsequent output is modified accordingly. Thus, when **BitBlt( )** is called inside the **WM_PAINT** handler to copy the contents of the virtual window onto the physical window, the rotation is automatically applied. Look closely at the call to **BitBlt( )**. Notice that the upper-left corner starts at −**rect.right/2** and −**rect.bottom/2**—not at 0, 0. The reason for this is that the transformation moves the origin down and right by half the size of the window. We must compensate for this when copying the virtual window.

9

To return the image to its initial, unrotated perspective, select Rotation Reset from the Options menu. This option simply sets **theta** equal to zero and then repaints the window. This sequence is also executed when you press either the left or right mouse button.

Things to Try

On your own, try implementing the following enhancements to the paint program. Allow the user to select between standard rectangles and rounded rectangles. Allow the user to draw an arc. Add an option that lets the user erase a portion of the window. Allow the user to select different line thicknesses. Implement the various other transformations supported by **SetWorldTransform( )**. (An easy one to try first is scaling.) Finally, add an "Undo" option that undoes the previous drawing command.

Mapping Modes and Viewports

Before concluding, we will examine two more aspects of Windows 2000's graphics system: mapping modes and viewports. As you know, the text and graphics API functions operate on logical units. These logical units are then translated by Windows into physical units (that is, pixels) when an object is displayed. The ratio of logical units to physical units is determined by the current *mapping mode*. That is, the mapping mode determines how page space units are mapped to the device space. (The mapping mode has nothing directly to do with the various transformations described in the previous section.) The mapping mode also affects the position of the origin.

The mapping mode determines how logical units are converted into physical units.

In addition to changing the mapping mode, you can also set two other attributes that affect the translation of logical to physical units. First, you can define the length and width of a window in terms of logical units that you select. Second, for certain mapping modes you can set the physical extents of the viewport. The *viewport* is a rectangular region defined within the device space. The dimensions of the viewport help determine the ratio of logical units to physical units. Output is mapped so that it fits within the viewport's boundaries. For most mapping modes, the size of the viewport is predetermined and cannot be altered. But there are two mapping modes in which the size of the viewport is under your control. You can also set the origin of the viewport.

A viewport is a rectangular region defined in device space.

Setting the Mapping Mode

By default, logical units are the same as pixels. Thus, the default ratio of logical units to pixels is one to one. However, you can change this ratio by changing the mapping mode. To set the current mapping mode use **SetMapMode( )**. It has this prototype:

    int SetMapMode(HDC *hdc,* int *mode*);

The handle to the device context is specified by *hdc. mode* specifies the new mapping mode, which can be any one of the following constants:

Mapping Mode	Meaning
MM_ANISOTROPIC	Maps logical units to programmer-defined units with arbitrarily scaled axes.
MM_HIENGLISH	Maps each logical unit to 0.001 inch.
MM_HIMETRIC	Maps each logical unit to 0.01 millimeter.
MM_ISOTROPIC	Maps logical units to programmer-defined units with equally scaled axes. (This establishes a one-to-one aspect ratio.)
MM_LOMETRIC	Maps each logical unit to 0.1 millimeter.
MM_LOENGLISH	Maps each logical unit to 0.01 inch.
MM_TEXT	Maps each logical unit to one device pixel.
MM_TWIPS	Maps each logical unit to one twentieth of a printer's point, or approximately 1/1440 inch.

For **MM_TEXT,** positive X values move right and positive Y values move down. For **MM_ANISOTROPIC** and **MM_ISOTROPIC,** the positive direction of the X and Y coordinates are user definable. For the remaining modes, positive X values move right and positive Y values move up as in the normal Cartesian coordinate plane.

SetMapMode( ) returns the previous mapping mode or zero if an error occurs. The default mapping mode is **MM_TEXT**.

9

There are several reasons why you might want to change the current mapping mode. First, if you want your program's output to be displayed in physical units, then you can select one of the real-world modes, such as **MM_LOMETRIC**. Second, you might want to define units for your program that best fit the nature of what you are displaying. Third, you might want to change the scale of what is displayed. (That is, you might want to enlarge or shrink the size of what is output.) Finally, you may want to establish a one-to-one aspect ratio between the X and Y axes. When this is done, each X unit represents the same physical distance as each Y unit.

Defining Window Extents

If you select either the **MM_ISOTROPIC** or **MM ANISOTROPIC** mapping modes, then you must define the size of the window in terms of logical units. (Since **MM_ISOTROPIC** and **MM_ANISOTROPIC** operate on programmer-defined units, the limits are technically undefined until you

define them.) To define the X and Y extents of a window, use the
SetWindowExtEx( ) function, shown here.

> BOOL SetWindowExtEx(HDC *hdc,* int *Xextent,*
>   int *Yextent,* LPSIZE *lpOldSize*);

The handle of the device context is specified in *hdc. Xextent* and *Yextent*
specify the new horizontal and vertical extents measured in logical units.
The previous window extents are copied into the **SIZE** structure pointed to
by *lpOldSize.* However, if *lpOldSize* is **NULL**, then the previous extents are
ignored. The function returns nonzero if successful, and zero on failure.
SetWindowExtEx( ) only has effect when the mapping mode is
MM_ANISOTROPIC or **MM_ISOTROPIC**.

Keep in mind that when you change the logical dimensions of a window,
you are not changing the physical size of the window on the screen. You are
simply defining the size of the window in terms of logical units that you
choose. (Or, more precisely, you are defining the relationship between the
logical units used by the window and the physical units (pixels) used by the
device.) For example, the same window could be given logical dimensions of
100 x 100 or 50 x 75. The only difference is the ratio of logical units to pixels
when an image is displayed.

Defining a Viewport

As mentioned, a viewport is a region within the device space that helps
determines how logical units are mapped to the physical device. The
viewport dimensions define the physical part of the ratio used to convert
logical units into pixels. (The window extents define the logical part.) For
most mapping modes, the size of the viewport is fixed and cannot be altered
by your program. However, for **MM_ISOTROPIC** and **MM_ANISOTROPIC**
the size of the viewport can be defined; this means that in these mapping
modes, the ratio of logical units to pixels is under your control.

A viewport is defined using the **SetViewportExtEx()** function. Its
prototype is shown here:

> BOOL SetViewportExtEx(HDC *hdc,* int *Xextent,* int *Yextent,* LPSIZE *lpOldSize*);

The handle of the device context is specified in *hdc. Xextent* and *Yextent*
specify the new horizontal and vertical viewport extents, in pixels. The
function returns nonzero if successful and zero on failure. The previous
viewport extents are returned in the **SIZE** structure pointed to by *lpOldSize.*
However, if *lpOldSize* is **NULL**, then the previous extents are ignored.

REMEMBER: **SetViewportExtEx( )** only has effect when the mapping mode is **MM_ANISOTROPIC** or **MM_ISOTROPIC**.

A viewport can be any size you desire. That is, it can encompass the entire window, be larger than the window, or simply be a part of it.

Output is automatically mapped from page space (logical units) to the viewport (pixels) and scaled accordingly. Therefore, by changing the X and Y extents of the viewport, you are changing the ratio of logical units to pixels. Doing this, in effect, changes the size of anything displayed within it. Thus, if you make the viewport extents larger, the contents of the viewport will get larger. Conversely, if you make the extents smaller, the contents of the viewport will shrink. This feature can be used as a means of enlarging or shrinking an image.

Setting the Viewport Origin

By default, the origin of the viewport is at 0, 0 within the window. However, you can change this using **SetViewportOrgEx()**, shown here.

    BOOL SetViewportOrgEx(HDC *hdc*, int *X*, int *Y*, LPPOINT *lpOldOrg*);

The handle of the device context is passed in *hdc*. The new origin (specified in pixels) for the viewport is passed in *X*, *Y*. The previous origin is returned in the **POINT** structure pointed to by *lpOldOrg*. If this parameter is **NULL,** the previous origin is ignored. The function returns nonzero if successful and zero on failure.

Changing the origin of the viewport changes where images are drawn in the window.

A Viewport and Mapping Mode Demonstration Program

The following program demonstrates mapping modes and viewports. Its operation is quite simple. Inside the **WM_PAINT** handler, the mapping mode is set to **MM_ANISOTROPIC**, the window extents are set to 200 by 200, the viewport extents are set to the values contained in **Xext** and **Yext**, and the viewport origin is set to the location specified by **Xorg** and **Yorg**. Next, some graphical objects are drawn. Each time you press the left mouse

9

button, the origin is moved. Each time you press the right mouse button, the viewport's size is increased. Moving the origin translates the images within the window. Increasing the size of the viewport has the effect of enlarging the images. Sample output is shown in Figure 9-4. You may want to experiment with this program a little, just to make sure that you understand what is taking place.

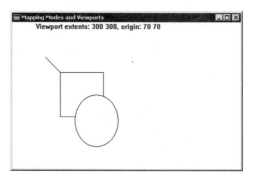

Sample output
from the
viewports
program

Figure 9-4.

```
// Demonstrate mapping modes and viewports.

#include <windows.h>
#include <cstring>
#include <cstdio>

LRESULT CALLBACK WindowFunc(HWND, UINT, WPARAM, LPARAM);

char szWinName[] = "MyWin"; // name of window class
// viewport extents and origin
int Xext=50, Yext=50;
int Xorg=0, Yorg=0;

int WINAPI WinMain(HINSTANCE hThisInst, HINSTANCE hPrevInst,
                   LPSTR lpszArgs, int nWinMode)
{
  HWND hwnd;
  MSG msg;
  WNDCLASSEX wcl;

  // Define a window class.
  wcl.cbSize = sizeof(WNDCLASSEX);

  wcl.hInstance = hThisInst;      // handle to this instance
  wcl.lpszClassName = szWinName; // window class name
  wcl.lpfnWndProc = WindowFunc;  // window function
  wcl.style = 0;                 // default style

  wcl.hIcon = LoadIcon(NULL, IDI_APPLICATION); // large icon
  wcl.hIconSm = NULL; // use small version of large icon
  wcl.hCursor = LoadCursor(NULL, IDC_ARROW);  // cursor style

  wcl.lpszMenuName = NULL; // no class menu
  wcl.cbClsExtra = 0;      // no extra memory needed
  wcl.cbWndExtra = 0;

  // Make the window background white.
  wcl.hbrBackground = (HBRUSH) GetStockObject(WHITE_BRUSH);

  // Register the window class.
  if(!RegisterClassEx(&wcl)) return 0;

  /* Now that a window class has been registered, a window
     can be created. */
  hwnd = CreateWindow(
    szWinName, // name of window class
```

```
              "Mapping Modes and Viewports", // title
              WS_OVERLAPPEDWINDOW, // window style - normal
              CW_USEDEFAULT, // X coordinate - let Windows decide
              CW_USEDEFAULT, // Y coordinate - let Windows decide
              CW_USEDEFAULT, // width - let Windows decide
              CW_USEDEFAULT, // height - let Windows decide
              NULL,          // no parent window
              NULL,          // no menu
              hThisInst,     // instance handle
              NULL           // no additional arguments
  );

  // Display the window.
  ShowWindow(hwnd, nWinMode);
  UpdateWindow(hwnd);

  // Create the message loop.
  while(GetMessage(&msg, NULL, 0, 0))
  {
    TranslateMessage(&msg); // translate keyboard messages
    DispatchMessage(&msg);  // return control to Windows 2000
  }

  return msg.wParam;
}

/* This function is called by Windows 2000 and is passed
   messages from the message queue.
*/
LRESULT CALLBACK WindowFunc(HWND hwnd, UINT message,
                            WPARAM wParam, LPARAM lParam)
{
  HDC hdc;
  PAINTSTRUCT paintstruct;
  char str[80];

  switch(message) {
    case WM_RBUTTONDOWN: // increase size of viewport
      Xext += 10;
      Yext += 10;
      InvalidateRect(hwnd, NULL, 1);
      break;
    case WM_LBUTTONDOWN: // move origin
      Xorg += 10;
      Yorg += 10;
      InvalidateRect(hwnd, NULL, 1);
```

```
      break;
    case WM_PAINT:
      hdc = BeginPaint(hwnd, &paintstruct); // get DC

      sprintf(str, "Viewport extents: %d %d, origin: %d %d",
              Xext, Yext, Xorg, Yorg);
      TextOut(hdc, 50, 0, str, strlen(str));

      // set mapping mode
      SetMapMode(hdc, MM_ANISOTROPIC);

      // set window and viewport extents
      SetWindowExtEx(hdc, 200, 200, NULL);
      SetViewportExtEx(hdc, Xext, Yext, NULL);

      // set viewport origin
      SetViewportOrgEx(hdc, Xorg, Yorg, NULL);

      // draw some objects
      LineTo(hdc, 50, 50);
      Rectangle(hdc, 20, 20, 80, 80);
      Ellipse(hdc, 40, 50, 100, 120);

      EndPaint(hwnd, &paintstruct); // release DC
      break;
    case WM_DESTROY: // terminate the program
      PostQuitMessage(0);
      break;
    default:
      /* Let Windows 2000 process any messages not specified
         in the preceding switch statement. */
      return DefWindowProc(hwnd, message, wParam, lParam);
  }

  return 0;
}
```

9

Experiment with the GDI

Some of the concepts in this chapter, such as coordinate spaces, world transforms, viewports, and mapping modes, are not intuitive. The best way to become comfortable with these features, and the GDI in general, is to write a number of short programs that exercise various options. An afternoon spent experimenting with viewports, world transforms, and the like is time well invested.

CHAPTER 10

Introducing Common Controls and Common Dialog Boxes

This chapter begins our look at some of the most exciting features of Windows 2000: common controls. In the preceding chapters you have learned about the standard controls, such as push buttons, scroll bars, and check boxes. In addition to these, Windows 2000 defines several sophisticated, high-powered components that expand the types of user interactions that your program may have. Without a doubt, the use of the common controls is the easiest way to give your application the modern look that users will expect. The common controls are so important to successful Windows 2000 programming that we will be spending several chapters on them.

This chapter also introduces two of Windows common dialog boxes. Common dialog boxes are simply predefined dialog boxes that your program is free to use. The advantage of using common dialog boxes is twofold. First, they provide a standard interface for frequently used input tasks. Second, they simplify some rather tedious input situations. In general, common dialog boxes are substantially easier to use than the common controls and there are fewer of them, so we won't be spending as much time on them.

This chapter begins with an overview of the common controls. It then discusses one of the most important: the toolbar. The common dialogs are described at the end.

The Common Controls

The common controls supported by Windows 2000 are the following:

Control	Description
Animation Control	Displays an AVI file.
ComboBoxEx Control	Combo box with extended capabilities.
Date and Time Picker Controls	Updates date and time.
Drag List Box	A list box that allows items to be dragged.
Flat Scroll Bars	Flat rather than three-dimensional scroll bars.
Header Control	A column heading.
Hot key Control	Supports user-created hot keys.
Image List	A list of graphical images.

Control	Description
IP Control	Supports user-entered Internet Protocol (IP) addresses.
List View Control	A list of icons and labels.
Month Calendar Control	A calendar-based control used for dates.
Pager Control	Scrollable control that contains other controls.
Progress Bar	A visual gauge used to indicate the degree to which a task is completed.
Property Sheet	A properties dialog box.
Rebar Control	A bar that contains other controls.
Rich Edit Control	A sophisticated edit box.
Status Window	A bar that displays information related to an application.
Tab Control	A tab-based menu. (This control looks like the tabs on file folders.)
Toolbar	A graphics-based menu.
Tooltip	Small pop-up text boxes. Typically used to describe toolbar buttons or other control elements.
Trackbar	A slider-based control. (Similar in concept to a scroll bar, but looks like a fader control on a stereo.)
Tree View Control	A tree-structured display.
Up-Down (Spin) Control	Up and down arrows. Called a *spin control* when linked with an edit box.

10

Common controls are sophisticated, predefined controls.

These controls are called *common controls* because they represent a set of predefined controls that can be used by any application. You have certainly encountered several (if not all) of these controls. While it won't be possible to discuss every common control in this book, we will look at several of the most important and representative.

Including and Initializing the Common Controls

Before you can use the common controls you must include the standard header file COMMCTRL.H in your program. You must also make sure that the common controls library is linked into your program. For Microsoft Visual C++, the common controls library is called COMCTL32.LIB. This library is not automatically included, so you will need to add it to your project's linker options. For other compilers, consult your user manual.

COMCTL32.LIB must be added to the link in order to compile code that uses a common control.

Applications that use one or more common controls must first call **InitCommonControlsEx( )**. **InitCommonControlsEx( )** ensures that the appropriate components found in the common controls dynamic link library (DLL) are loaded and that the common controls subsystem is initialized. The prototype for **InitCommonControlsEx( )** is shown here:

BOOL InitCommonControlsEx(LPINITCOMMONCONTROLSEX *lpcc*);

Here, *lpcc* is a pointer to an **INITCOMMONCONTROLSEX** structure that determines which controls are loaded and initialized. The function returns nonzero if successful and zero on failure.

The **INITCOMMONCONTROLSEX** structure is defined like this:

```
typedef struct tagINITCOMMONCONTROLSEX {
  DWORD dwSize;
  DWORD dwICC;
} INITCOMMONCONTROLSEX;
```

The **dwSize** member must contain the size of the **INITCOMMONCONTROLSEX** structure. The **dwICC** member specifies which control or set of controls is loaded. It must be one or more of the following values:

Macro	Loads
ICC_ANIMATE_CLASS	Animation control
ICC_BAR_CLASSES	Status bar, toolbar, tooltip, and trackbar controls
ICC_COOL_CLASSES	Rebar control
ICC_DATE_CLASSES	Date and time picker control
ICC_HOTKEY_CLASS	Hot key control
ICC_INTERNET_CLASSES	Internet address control
ICC_LISTVIEW_CLASSES	List view and header controls
ICC_PAGESCROLLER_CLASS	Page scrolling control
ICC_PROGRESS_CLASS	Progress bar
ICC_TAB_CLASSES	Tab and tooltip controls
ICC_TREEVIEW_CLASSES	Tree view and tooltip controls
ICC_UPDOWN_CLASSES	Up-down controls
ICC_USEREX_CLASSES	ComboBoxEx control
ICC_WIN95_CLASSES	Common controls supported by Windows 95

For example, the following code ensures that the toolbar control classes are loaded and initialized.

```
INITCOMMONCONTROLSEX cc;

cc.dwSize = sizeof(INITCOMMONCONTROLSEX);
cc.dwICC = ICC_BAR_CLASSES;
InitCommonControlsEx(&cc);
```

A good place to call **InitCommonControlsEx( )** is after your main window class has been registered.

10

HISTORICAL PERSPECTIVE: **InitCommonControlsEx( )** replaces the older **InitCommonControls( )** function.

Common Controls Are Windows

All of the common controls are child windows. They will be created using one of three methods: by calling **CreateWindow( )**, by calling **CreateWindowEx( )**, or by calling a control-specific API function. (The **CreateWindowEx( )** function allows extended style attributes to be specified.) Because the common controls are windows, they can be managed in more or less the same way as you manage other windows used by your program.

Many common controls send your program either **WM_COMMAND** or **WM_NOTIFY** messages when they are accessed by the user. Your program sends a control a message using the **SendMessage( )** API function, whose prototype is shown here:

LRESULT SendMessage(HWND *hwnd*, UINT *Msg*, WPARAM *wParam*,
                    LPARAM *lParam*);

Here, *hwnd* is the handle of the control, *Msg* is the message that you want to send to the control, and *wParam* and *lParam* contain any additional information associated with the message. The function returns the control's response, if any.

Using a Toolbar

One of the most important common controls is the toolbar because it can speed up menu selection when you are using a mouse. A *toolbar* is, essentially, a graphical menu. In the toolbar, menu items are represented by icons, which form graphical buttons. Often, a toolbar is used in conjunction with a standard menu. As such, it provides an alternative means of making a menu selection. In a sense, a toolbar is a menu accelerator for the mouse.

To create a toolbar, use the **CreateToolbarEx( )** function, which is shown here:

HWND CreateToolbarEx(HWND *hwnd*, DWORD *dwStyle*, UINT *ID*,
                    int *NumBitmaps*, HINSTANCE *hInst*,
                    UINT *BmpID*, LPCTBBUTTON *Buttons*,
                    int *NumButtons*,
                    int *ButtonWidth*, int *ButtonHeight*,
                    int *BmpWidth*, int *BmpHeight*,
                    UINT *Size*);

Here, *hwnd* is the handle of the parent window that owns the toolbar.

The style of the toolbar is passed in *dwStyle*. The toolbar style must include **WS_CHILD**. It can also include other standard styles, such as **WS_BORDER** or **WS_VISIBLE**. Several toolbar style options are available. Here are some of the most popular:

TBSTYLE_TOOLTIPS	Include tooltips.
TBSTYLE_WRAPABLE	Wrap a long toolbar to the next line.
TBSTYLE_FLAT	Toolbar is flat.
TBSTYLE_TRANSPARENT	Toolbar is transparent.

The identifier associated with the toolbar is passed in *ID*. The identifier of the bitmap resource that forms the toolbar is passed in *BmpID*. This bitmap contains all of the images displayed within the individual toolbar buttons. The number of individual bitmap images contained in the bitmap specified by *BmpID* is passed in *NumBitmaps*. The instance handle of the application is passed in *hInst*. If you prefer, you can pass the handle to a bitmap in *BmpID* instead of its resource ID. In that case, you must specify *hInst* as **NULL**.

Information about each button is passed in an array of **TBBUTTON** structures pointed to by *Buttons*. The number of buttons in the toolbar is specified in *NumButtons*. The width and height of the buttons are passed in *ButtonWidth* and *ButtonHeight*. The width and height of the images within each button are passed in *BmpWidth* and *BmpHeight*. These dimensions are specified in terms of pixels. The size of the **TBBUTTON** structure is passed in *Size*.

CreateToolbarEx( ) returns a handle to the toolbar window. It returns **NULL** on failure.

10

Each button has a **TBBUTTON** structure associated with it that defines its various characteristics. The **TBBUTTON** structure is shown here.

```
typedef struct _TBBUTTON {
  int iBitmap;
  int idCommand;
  BYTE fsState;
  BYTE fsStyle;
  DWORD dwData;
  int iString;
} TBBUTTON;
```

The index of the bitmap image associated with the button is contained in **iBitmap**. The buttons begin their indexing at zero and are displayed left to right.

The ID associated with the button is stored in **idCommand**. Each time the button is pressed, a **WM_COMMAND** message will be generated and sent to the parent window. The value of **idCommand** will be contained in the low-order word of **wParam**.

The initial state of the button is stored in **fsState**. It can be one (or more) of the following values:

State	Meaning
TBSTATE_CHECKED	Button is pressed.
TBSTATE_ELLIPSES	Ellipsis is shown when button text is truncated.
TBSTATE_ENABLE	Button is able to be pressed.
TBSTATE_HIDDEN	Button is hidden and inactive.
TBSTATE_INDETERMINATE	Button is gray and inactive.
TBSTATE_MARKED	Button is marked (this differs from checked).
TBSTATE_PRESSED	Button is pressed.
TBSTATE_WRAP	Following buttons are on new line.

The style of the button is contained in **fsStyle**. It can be any valid combination of the following values:

Style	Meaning
BTNS_AUTOSIZE	The text in a button determines its size. (Older compilers must use **TBSTYLE_AUTOSIZE**.)
BTNS_BUTTON	Standard button. (Older compilers must use **TBSTYLE_BUTTON**.)
BTNS_CHECK	Button toggles between checked and unchecked each time it is pressed. (Older compilers must use **TBSTYLE_CHECK**.)

Style	Meaning
BTNS_CHECKGROUP	A check button that is part of a mutually-exclusive group. (Older compilers must use **TBSTYLE_CHECKGROUP**.)
BTNS_DROPDOWN	Button is a drop-down list. (Older compilers must use **TBSTYLE_DROPDOWN**.)
BTNS_GROUP	A standard button that is part of a mutually exclusive group. (Older compilers must use **TBSTYLE_GROUP**.)
BTNS_NOPREFIX	No accelerator prefix is shown. (Older compilers must use **TBSTYLE_NOPREFIX**.)
BTNS_SEP	Separates buttons (**idCommand** must be zero when this style is used). (Older compilers must use **TBSTYLE_SEP**.)
BTNS_SHOWTEXT	Shows button text. (New for 2000.)
BTNS_WHOLEDROPDOWN	Button has drop-down arrow. (New for 2000.)

Most of the styles are self-explanatory, but a few comments are in order. First, the **BTNS_SEP** style provides a gap between buttons on the toolbar, allowing you to visually group buttons into clusters. The **BTNS_DROPDOWN** and **BTNS_WHOLEDROPDOWN** styles are used to create buttons that activate drop-down menus. When pressed, these buttons generate a **TBN_DROPDOWN** notification message rather than a **WM_COMMAND** message. The handling of this message requires the use of advanced menu techniques, which are described in Chapter 19.

10

HISTORICAL PERSPECTIVE: The toolbar style macros beginning with **BTNS** replace equivalent macros that begin with **TBSTYLE**. For example, **BTNS_SEP** used to be called **TBSTYLE_SEP**. While both versions are still supported, the recommended form is **BTNS**. However, if you are using an old compiler, then you may need to use the **TBSTYLE** forms.

The **dwData** field contains user-defined data. The **iString** field is the index of an optional string associated with the button. These fields should be zero if they are unused.

In their default configuration, toolbars are fully automated controls and require virtually no management by your program in order to use them. However, you can manually manage a toolbar if you like by sending it explicit control messages. These messages are sent to the toolbar using **SendMessage( )**. Three common toolbar messages are shown here (you will want to explore the other toolbar messages on your own):

Message	Meaning
TB_CHECKBUTTON	Presses or clears a toolbar button. *wParam* must contain the ID of the button. *lParam* must be nonzero to press or 0 to clear.
TB_ENABLEBUTTON	Enables or disables a toolbar button. *wParam* must contain the ID of the button. *lParam* must be nonzero to enable or 0 to disable.
TB_HIDEBUTTON	Hides or shows a toolbar button. *wParam* must contain the ID of the button. *lParam* must be nonzero to hide or 0 to show.

Toolbars can also generate notification messages that inform your program about various activities related to the toolbar. For simple toolbars, you won't need to worry about these messages. (The notification messages all begin with **TBN_**, and you can find information on them by examining the COMMCTRL.H header file or your API library reference.)

Adding Tooltips

As you know, some toolbars automatically pop up small text windows after the mouse pointer has paused for about one second over a toolbar button. These small text windows are called *tooltips*. Although not technically required, tooltips should be included with most toolbars because users will expect to see them. They also add polish to your application.

Tooltips are small text messages that appear when the mouse pauses over a control.

To add tooltips to a toolbar, you must first include the **TBSTYLE_TOOLTIPS** style when you create the toolbar. This enables the toolbar to send a **WM_NOTIFY** message when the mouse pointer lingers over a button for more than about one second. In general, **WM_NOTIFY** messages are generated by controls when some event occurs. In the case of tooltips, one is sent when the tooltip text needs to be displayed. When this occurs, **lParam** will point to a **NMTTDISPINFO** structure, which is defined like this:

```
typedef struct tagNMTTDISPINFO{
  NMHDR hdr;
  LPSTR lpszText;
  char szText[80];
  HINSTANCE hinst;
  UINT uFlags;
  LPARAM lParam;
} NMTTDISPINFO;
```

The first member of **NMTTDISPINFO** is an **NMHDR** structure, which is defined like this:

```
typedef struct tagNMHDR
{
  HWND  hwndFrom; // handle of control
  UINT  idFrom;   // control ID
  UINT  code;     // notification code
} NMHDR;
```

If a tooltip is being requested, then **code** will contain the notification message **TTN_GETDISPINFO,** and **idFrom** will contain the ID of the button for which the tip is needed. Since other controls can generate **WM_NOTIFY** messages and toolbars can generate other types of notification messages, you will need to check these fields to determine precisely what event has occurred.

10

HISTORICAL PERSPECTIVE: The **NMTTDISPINFO** structure used to be called **TOOLTIPTEXT**; this old name is still valid. However, new code should use **NMTTDISPINO**. The **TTN_GETDISPINFO** message used to be called **TTN_NEEDTEXT**; this old name is also still valid. However, for new code, use **TTN_GETDISPINFO**.

There are three ways to supply the required tooltip. You must either copy the tooltip text into the **szText** array of **NMTTDISPINFO**, point **lpszText** to the text, or supply the resource ID of a string resource. When using a string resource, the string ID is assigned to **lpszText**, and **hinst** must be the handle of the instance that contains the string resource (which is usually the instance handle of your program). By far the easiest way is simply to point **lpszText** to a string supplied by your program. For example, the following case responds to tooltip requests for the tooltips example program shown later.

```
case WM_NOTIFY: // respond to tooltip request
  TTtext = (LPNMTTDISPINFO) lParam;
  if(TTtext->hdr.code == TTN_GETDISPINFO)
    switch(TTtext->hdr.idFrom) {
      case IDM_OPEN: TTtext->lpszText = "Open File";
        break;
      case IDM_UPPER: TTtext->lpszText = "Uppercase";
        break;
      case IDM_LOWER: TTtext->lpszText = "Lowercase";
        break;
      case IDM_SAVE: TTtext->lpszText = "Save File";
        break;
      case IDM_HELP: TTtext->lpszText = "Help";
        break;
    }
  break;
```

Once the tooltip text has been set and control passes back to Windows, the tooltip will automatically be displayed. Your program need perform no further action. As you can see, tooltips are largely automated and easy to add to a toolbar.

The **uFlags** field of **NMTTDISPINFO** specifies whether the **idFrom** field in **hdr** contains an ID or a handle. If **uFlags** contains **TTF_IDISHWND**, then **idFrom** contains the handle of the control that requires the tooltip text. If it does not, then **idFrom** specifies the ID of the control. For tooltips for toolbars, **idFrom** will always specify an ID, and you will not need to check the contents of **uFlags**.

The **lParam** field of **NMTTDISPINFO** contains user-defined data.

Creating a Toolbar Bitmap

Before you can use a toolbar, you must create the bitmaps that form the graphical images inside each button. To do this, you must use an image editor. (The process is similar to that used with bitmaps in Chapter 7). There is one important point to remember: only one bitmap is associated with the toolbar and this bitmap must contain *all* of the button images. Thus, if your toolbar will have six buttons, then the bitmap associated with your toolbar must define six images. For example, if your toolbar images are each 16 by 16 bits and your toolbar has 6 buttons, then your toolbar bitmap will need to be 96 (6 times 16) bits long by 16 bits high.

For the toolbar example presented in this chapter, you will need five images. Each image must be 16 by 16 bits. This means that you will need to create a bitmap that is 80 by 16. Figure 10-1 shows how the toolbar bitmap used by the sample programs in this chapter looks inside the image editor. Store your bitmap in a file called TOOLBAR.BMP.

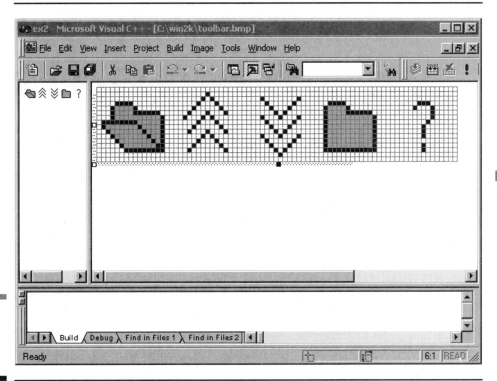

The toolbar bitmap while being edited

Figure 10-1.

10

A Toolbar Sample Program

The following program demonstrates a toolbar. It implements a very simple set of text file utilities. The program can do the following operations:

◆ Load and display a file

◆ Convert a file to uppercase

◆ Convert a file to lowercase

◆ Save the file

Once the file has been loaded, it is displayed within the client area. A vertical scroll bar is included that allows you to scroll through the file. The toolbar duplicates the menu options and includes tooltips.

When loading or saving a file, the program uses two common dialog boxes to obtain the name of the file that you wish to use. These are the standard Open and Save As dialog boxes. They are activated by calling the **GetOpenFileName( )** and **GetSaveFileName( )** API functions. The operations of these functions are described later in this chapter.

The toolbar program is shown here:

```
/* Demonstrate a toolbar with tooltips.

   This program provides a small set
   of file utilities.

*/

#include <windows.h>
#include <commctrl.h>
#include <cstring>
#include <cstdio>
#include <cctype>
#include "tb.h"

#define NUMBUTTONS 6
#define MAXSIZE 25000

LRESULT CALLBACK WindowFunc(HWND, UINT, WPARAM, LPARAM);

void InitToolbar(); // initialize the tool bar
```

```c
void display(int startY, HDC hdc); // display file

char szWinName[] = "MyWin"; // name of window class

TBBUTTON tbButtons[NUMBUTTONS];

HWND tbwnd; // toolbar handle

FILE *fp; // file pointer
char buf[MAXSIZE];  // buffer to hold the file

TEXTMETRIC tm;
SIZE size;

int SBPos = 0; // scroll bar position
int X = 5, Y = 32; // scroll coordinates
int NumLines = 0;
int ToolBarActive = 1;

HWND hwnd;

int WINAPI WinMain(HINSTANCE hThisInst, HINSTANCE hPrevInst,
                   LPSTR lpszArgs, int nWinMode)
{
  MSG msg;
  WNDCLASSEX wcl;
  HACCEL hAccel;
  INITCOMMONCONTROLSEX cc;

  // Define a window class.
  wcl.cbSize = sizeof(WNDCLASSEX);

  wcl.hInstance = hThisInst;      // handle to this instance
  wcl.lpszClassName = szWinName; // window class name
  wcl.lpfnWndProc = WindowFunc;  // window function
  wcl.style = 0;                 // default style

  wcl.hIcon = LoadIcon(NULL, IDI_APPLICATION); // large icon
  wcl.hIconSm = NULL; // use small version of large icon
  wcl.hCursor = LoadCursor(NULL, IDC_ARROW);  // cursor style

  wcl.lpszMenuName = "ShowFileMenu"; // main menu

  wcl.cbClsExtra = 0; // no extra memory needed
  wcl.cbWndExtra = 0;
```

10

```
// Make the window background white.
wcl.hbrBackground = (HBRUSH) GetStockObject(WHITE_BRUSH);

// Register the window class.
if(!RegisterClassEx(&wcl)) return 0;

/* Now that a window class has been registered, a window
   can be created. */
hwnd = CreateWindow(
  szWinName, // name of window class
  "Using a Toolbar", // title
  WS_OVERLAPPEDWINDOW, // window style - normal
  CW_USEDEFAULT, // X coordinate - let Windows decide
  CW_USEDEFAULT, // Y coordinate - let Windows decide
  CW_USEDEFAULT, // width - let Windows decide
  CW_USEDEFAULT, // height - let Windows decide
  NULL,          // no parent window
  NULL,          // no menu
  hThisInst,     // instance handle
  NULL           // no additional arguments
);

// Load the keyboard accelerators.
hAccel = LoadAccelerators(hThisInst, "ShowFileMenu");

// initialize the common controls
cc.dwSize = sizeof(INITCOMMONCONTROLSEX);
cc.dwICC = ICC_BAR_CLASSES;
InitCommonControlsEx(&cc);

InitToolbar(); // initialize the toolbar

// create the toolbar
tbwnd = CreateToolbarEx(hwnd,
                        WS_VISIBLE | WS_CHILD |
                        WS_BORDER | TBSTYLE_TOOLTIPS,
                        IDM_TOOLBAR,
                        NUMBUTTONS,
                        hThisInst,
                        IDTB_BMP,
                        tbButtons,
                        NUMBUTTONS,
                        16, 16, 16, 16,
                        sizeof(TBBUTTON));
```

```
      // Display the window.
      ShowWindow(hwnd, nWinMode);
      UpdateWindow(hwnd);

      // Create the message loop.
      while(GetMessage(&msg, NULL, 0, 0))
      {
        if(!TranslateAccelerator(hwnd, hAccel, &msg)) {
          TranslateMessage(&msg); // translate keyboard messages
          DispatchMessage(&msg); // return control to Windows 2000
        }
      }

      return msg.wParam;
    }

    /* This function is called by Windows 2000 and is passed
       messages from the message queue.
    */
    LRESULT CALLBACK WindowFunc(HWND hwnd, UINT message,
                                  WPARAM wParam, LPARAM lParam)
    {
      HDC hdc;
      PAINTSTRUCT paintstruct;
      int i, response;
      SCROLLINFO si;
      OPENFILENAME fname;
      char filename[64]; // file name
      static char fn[256]; // full path name
      char filefilter[] = "C++\0*.CPP\0C\0*.C\0\0\0";

      LPNMTTDISPINFO TTtext;
      RECT rect;

      switch(message) {
        case WM_CREATE:
          // retrieve and save the text metrics
          hdc = GetDC(hwnd);
          GetTextMetrics(hdc, &tm);
          ReleaseDC(hwnd, hdc);
          break;
        case WM_NOTIFY: // respond to tooltip request
          TTtext = (LPNMTTDISPINFO) lParam;
          if(TTtext->hdr.code == TTN_GETDISPINFO)
```

10

```
      switch(TTtext->hdr.idFrom) {
        case IDM_OPEN: TTtext->lpszText = "Open File";
          break;
        case IDM_UPPER: TTtext->lpszText = "Uppercase";
          break;
        case IDM_LOWER: TTtext->lpszText = "Lowercase";
          break;
        case IDM_SAVE: TTtext->lpszText = "Save File";
          break;
        case IDM_HELP: TTtext->lpszText = "Help";
          break;
      }
    break;
  case WM_VSCROLL:
    switch(LOWORD(wParam)) {
      case SB_LINEDOWN:
        SBPos++;
        if(SBPos>NumLines) SBPos = NumLines;
        si.cbSize = sizeof(SCROLLINFO);
        si.fMask = SIF_POS;
        si.nPos = SBPos;
        SetScrollInfo(hwnd, SB_VERT, &si, 1);
        InvalidateRect(hwnd, NULL, 1);
        break;
      case SB_LINEUP:
        SBPos--;
        if(SBPos<0) SBPos = 0;
        si.cbSize = sizeof(SCROLLINFO);
        si.fMask = SIF_POS;
        si.nPos = SBPos;
        SetScrollInfo(hwnd, SB_VERT, &si, 1);
        InvalidateRect(hwnd, NULL, 1);
        break;
      case SB_PAGEDOWN:
        /* advance by the amount of lines that will fit
           within the current window */
        GetClientRect(hwnd, &rect);

        // compensate for toolbar
        if(ToolBarActive) rect.bottom -= 32;

        // compute number of lines to advance
        SBPos += rect.bottom /
                  (tm.tmHeight+tm.tmExternalLeading);
```

```
            if(SBPos>NumLines) SBPos = NumLines;
            si.cbSize = sizeof(SCROLLINFO);
            si.fMask = SIF_POS;
            si.nPos = SBPos;
            SetScrollInfo(hwnd, SB_VERT, &si, 1);
            InvalidateRect(hwnd, NULL, 1);
            break;
          case SB_PAGEUP:
            /* backup by the amount of lines that will fit
               within the current window */
            GetClientRect(hwnd, &rect);

            // compensate for toolbar
            if(ToolBarActive) rect.bottom -= 32;

            // compute number of lines to backup
            SBPos -= rect.bottom /
                    (tm.tmHeight+tm.tmExternalLeading);

            if(SBPos<0) SBPos = 0;
            si.cbSize = sizeof(SCROLLINFO);
            si.fMask = SIF_POS;
            si.nPos = SBPos;
            SetScrollInfo(hwnd, SB_VERT, &si, 1);
            InvalidateRect(hwnd, NULL, 1);
            break;
          case SB_THUMBTRACK:
            SBPos = HIWORD(wParam); // get curent position
            if(SBPos<0) SBPos = 0;
            si.cbSize = sizeof(SCROLLINFO);
            si.fMask = SIF_POS;
            si.nPos = SBPos;
            SetScrollInfo(hwnd, SB_VERT, &si, 1);
            InvalidateRect(hwnd, NULL, 1);
            break;
        }
        break;
      case WM_COMMAND:
        switch(LOWORD(wParam)) {
          case IDM_OPEN:
            // initialize the OPENFILENAME struct
            memset(&fname, 0, sizeof(OPENFILENAME));
            fname.lStructSize = sizeof(OPENFILENAME);
            fname.hwndOwner = hwnd;
            fname.lpstrFilter = filefilter;
```

```
    fname.nFilterIndex = 1;
    fname.lpstrFile = fn;
    fname.nMaxFile = sizeof(fn);
    fname.lpstrFileTitle = filename;
    fname.nMaxFileTitle = sizeof(filename)-1;
    fname.Flags = OFN_FILEMUSTEXIST | OFN_HIDEREADONLY;

    if(!GetOpenFileName(&fname)) // get the file name
      break;

    if((fp=fopen(fn, "r"))==NULL) {
      MessageBox(hwnd, fn, "Cannot Open File", MB_OK);
      break;
    }

    for(i=0; !feof(fp) && (i < MAXSIZE-1); i++) {
      fread(&buf[i], sizeof (char), 1, fp);
    }
    buf[i] = '\0';
    fclose(fp);

    // count the number of lines
    for(NumLines=0, i=0; buf[i]; i++)
      if(buf[i] == '\n') NumLines++;

    // set scrollbar range to number of lines
    si.cbSize = sizeof(SCROLLINFO);
    si.fMask = SIF_RANGE | SIF_POS;
    si.nMin = 0; si.nMax = NumLines;
    si.nPos = 0;
    SetScrollInfo(hwnd, SB_VERT, &si, 1);

    SBPos = 0;

    if(ToolBarActive) Y = 32;
    else Y = 0;

    InvalidateRect(hwnd, NULL, 1);
    break;
  case IDM_UPPER: // uppercase file
    for(i=0; buf[i]; i++) buf[i] = toupper(buf[i]);
    InvalidateRect(hwnd, NULL, 1);
    break;
  case IDM_LOWER: // lowercase file
    for(i=0; buf[i]; i++) buf[i] = tolower(buf[i]);
```

```
      InvalidateRect(hwnd, NULL, 1);
      break;
    case IDM_SAVE:
      // initialize the OPENFILENAME struct
      memset(&fname, 0, sizeof(OPENFILENAME));
      fname.lStructSize = sizeof(OPENFILENAME);
      fname.hwndOwner = hwnd;
      fname.lpstrFilter = filefilter;
      fname.nFilterIndex = 1;
      fname.lpstrFile = fn;
      fname.nMaxFile = sizeof(fn);
      fname.lpstrFileTitle = filename;
      fname.nMaxFileTitle = sizeof(filename)-1;
      fname.Flags = OFN_HIDEREADONLY;

      if(!GetSaveFileName(&fname)) // get the file name
        break;

      if((fp=fopen(fn, "w"))==NULL) {
        MessageBox(hwnd, fn, "Cannot Open File", MB_OK);
        break;
      }

      for(i=0; buf[i]; i++) {
        fwrite(&buf[i], sizeof (char), 1, fp);
      }

      fclose(fp);
      InvalidateRect(hwnd, NULL, 1);
      break;
    case IDM_SHOW: // show toolbar
      ToolBarActive = 1;
      Y = 32; // advance past toolbar
      ShowWindow(tbwnd, SW_RESTORE);
      InvalidateRect(hwnd, NULL, 1);
      break;
    case IDM_HIDE: // hide toolbar
      ToolBarActive = 0;
      Y = 0;
      ShowWindow(tbwnd, SW_HIDE);
      InvalidateRect(hwnd, NULL, 1);
      break;
    case IDM_HELP:
      // show help button as pressed
      SendMessage(tbwnd, TB_CHECKBUTTON,
```

10

```
                        (LPARAM) IDM_HELP, (WPARAM) 1);

            MessageBox(hwnd, "F2: Open\nF3: Uppercase\n"
                    "F4: Lowercase\nF5: Save\n"
                    "F6: Show Toolbar\n"
                    "F7: Hide Toolbar\nCtrl+X: Exit",
                    "File Utilities", MB_OK);

          // reset the help button
          SendMessage(tbwnd, TB_CHECKBUTTON,
                    (LPARAM) IDM_HELP, (WPARAM) 0);
        break;
      case IDM_EXIT:
        response = MessageBox(hwnd, "Quit the Program?",
                        "Exit", MB_YESNO);
        if(response == IDYES) PostQuitMessage(0);
        break;
    }
    break;
  case WM_PAINT: // process a repaint request
    hdc = BeginPaint(hwnd, &paintstruct); // get DC
    display(SBPos, hdc);
    EndPaint(hwnd, &paintstruct); // release DC
    break;
  case WM_DESTROY: // terminate the program
    PostQuitMessage(0);
    break;
  default:
    /* Let Windows 2000 process any messages not specified in
       the preceding switch statement. */
    return DefWindowProc(hwnd, message, wParam, lParam);
}

return 0;
}

// Initialize the toolbar structures.
void InitToolbar()
{
  tbButtons[0].iBitmap = 0;
  tbButtons[0].idCommand = IDM_OPEN;
  tbButtons[0].fsState = TBSTATE_ENABLED;
  tbButtons[0].fsStyle = BTNS_BUTTON;
  tbButtons[0].dwData = 0L;
  tbButtons[0].iString = 0;
```

```
      tbButtons[1].iBitmap = 1;
      tbButtons[1].idCommand = IDM_UPPER;
      tbButtons[1].fsState = TBSTATE_ENABLED;
      tbButtons[1].fsStyle = BTNS_BUTTON;
      tbButtons[1].dwData = 0L;
      tbButtons[1].iString = 0;

      tbButtons[2].iBitmap = 2;
      tbButtons[2].idCommand = IDM_LOWER;
      tbButtons[2].fsState = TBSTATE_ENABLED;
      tbButtons[2].fsStyle = BTNS_BUTTON;
      tbButtons[2].dwData = 0L;
      tbButtons[2].iString = 0;

      tbButtons[3].iBitmap = 3;
      tbButtons[3].idCommand = IDM_SAVE;
      tbButtons[3].fsState = TBSTATE_ENABLED;
      tbButtons[3].fsStyle = BTNS_BUTTON;
      tbButtons[3].dwData = 0L;
      tbButtons[3].iString = 0;

      // button separator
      tbButtons[4].iBitmap = 0;
      tbButtons[4].idCommand = 0;
      tbButtons[4].fsState = TBSTATE_ENABLED;
      tbButtons[4].fsStyle = BTNS_SEP;
      tbButtons[4].dwData = 0L;
      tbButtons[4].iString = 0;

      tbButtons[5].iBitmap = 4;
      tbButtons[5].idCommand = IDM_HELP;
      tbButtons[5].fsState = TBSTATE_ENABLED;
      tbButtons[5].fsStyle = BTNS_BUTTON;
      tbButtons[5].dwData = 0L;
      tbButtons[5].iString = 0;
    }

  // Display the file.
  void display(int startline, HDC hdc)
  {
    register int i, j;
    int linelim;
    int lines;
    char line[256];
```

10

```
  RECT rect;
  int tempY;

  GetClientRect(hwnd, &rect); // get size of window

  // compute number of lines to display
  lines = rect.bottom /
          (tm.tmHeight+tm.tmExternalLeading);

  // find first line
  for(i=0; startline && buf[i]; i++)
    if(buf[i] == '\n')  startline--;

  tempY = Y;

  // erase old contents
  PatBlt(hdc, X, Y, rect.right, rect.bottom, PATCOPY);

  // display file
  for(linelim=lines; linelim && buf[i]; i++) {
    for(j=0; j<256 && buf[i] && buf[i]!='\n'; j++, i++)
      line[j] = buf[i];

    if(!buf[i]) break;

    TextOut(hdc, X, Y, line, j);

    // go to next line
    Y = Y + tm.tmHeight + tm.tmExternalLeading;
    linelim--;
  }
  Y = tempY;
}
```

This program requires the following resource file:

```
#include <windows.h>
#include "tb.h"

IDTB_BMP BITMAP toolbar.bmp

ShowFileMenu MENU
{
  POPUP "&File"
  {
```

```
    MENUITEM "&Open\tF2", IDM_OPEN
    MENUITEM "&Uppercase\tF3", IDM_UPPER
    MENUITEM "&Lowercase\tF4", IDM_LOWER
    MENUITEM "&Save\tF5", IDM_SAVE
    MENUITEM "E&xit\tCtrl+X", IDM_EXIT
  }
  POPUP "&Options"
  {
    MENUITEM "&Show Toolbar\tF6", IDM_SHOW
    MENUITEM "&Hide Toolbar\tF7", IDM_HIDE
  }
  MENUITEM "&Help", IDM_HELP
}

ShowFileMenu ACCELERATORS
{
  VK_F2, IDM_OPEN, VIRTKEY
  VK_F3, IDM_UPPER, VIRTKEY
  VK_F4, IDM_LOWER, VIRTKEY
  VK_F5, IDM_SAVE, VIRTKEY
  VK_F6, IDM_SHOW, VIRTKEY
  VK_F7, IDM_HIDE, VIRTKEY
  VK_F1, IDM_HELP, VIRTKEY
  "^X", IDM_EXIT
}
```

TheTB.H header file is shown here:

```
#define IDM_OPEN      100
#define IDM_UPPER     101
#define IDM_LOWER     102
#define IDM_SHOW      103
#define IDM_HIDE      104
#define IDM_SAVE      105
#define IDM_HELP      106
#define IDM_EXIT      107

#define IDM_TOOLBAR   200

#define IDTB_BMP      300
```

Sample output from the toolbar program is shown in Figure 10-2.

A Closer Look at the Toolbar Program

The toolbar program implements a very simple set of file operations. When you select the Open option (either from the menu or the toolbar), a file is opened and its contents are read into the **buf** array. The size of **buf** is arbitrary and may be changed if you like. A window's worth of this buffer is displayed by **display( )** each time a **WM_PAINT** message is received. The code within **display( )** should be familiar because it uses the same techniques as those described in Chapter 8 to output text to the window. By selecting Uppercase, you convert the contents of the buffer to uppercase. By selecting Lowercase, the buffer is converted to lowercase. You can save the contents of the buffer by selecting Save. Each of these operations can be initiated using the menu or the toolbar.

The toolbar information is held in the **tbButtons** array. This array is initialized in **InitToolBar( )**. Notice that the fifth structure is simply a button separator. In **WinMain( )**, the **InitCommonControlsEx( )** function is called. Next, the toolbar is created and a handle to it is assigned to **tbwnd**.

Each button in the toolbar corresponds to a menu entry in the main menu. Specifically, each of the buttons (other than the separator) is associated with a menu ID. When a button is pressed, its associated ID will be sent to the program as part of a **WM_COMMAND** message, just as if a menu item had been selected. In fact, the same **case** statement handles both toolbar button presses and menu selections.

Since a toolbar is a window, it may be displayed or hidden like any other window using the **ShowWindow( )** function. To hide the window, select Hide Toolbar in the Options menu. To redisplay the toolbar, select Show Toolbar. Since the toolbar overlays part of the client area of the main window, you should always allow the user to remove the toolbar if it is not needed. As the program illustrates, doing this is very easy.

Examine the code inside the **IDM_HELP** case. Notice that when Help is selected (either through the main menu or by pressing the Help button), the Help toolbar button is manually pressed by sending it a **TB_CHECKBUTTON** message. After the user closes the Help message box, the button is manually released. Thus, the Help button remains pressed while the Help message box is displayed. This is an example of how a toolbar can be manually managed by your program when necessary.

The file can be scrolled in the window using the vertical scroll bar. The operation of the scroll bar was described in Chapter 6. The function **display( )** actually displays the file. It outputs enough text to fill the window as it is currently sized. (Doing this is more efficient than outputting a screen full of information and letting Windows clip it.) The current size of the window is obtained by calling **GetClientRect( )**, described in Chapter 8, which returns the current window coordinates in a **RECT** structure. In this case, it is used to determine how much of the file can be displayed.

10

Introducing the Common Dialogs

In the toolbar example, the name of the file to open or to save is obtained using the functions **GetOpenFileName( )** and **GetSaveFileName( )**, respectively. These functions activate built-in common dialog boxes, called Open and Save As, which obtain the name of a file. Open and Save As are two specific examples of a general class of built-in dialog boxes called *common dialog boxes*. Common dialog boxes are system-defined dialog boxes that your application may use to perform various common input tasks, such as obtaining a filename, choosing a font, or setting a color.

Passing Along WM_SIZE Messages

Try the following experiment with the toolbar program. Execute the program and then increase its horizontal size. As you will see, the toolbar is *not* automatically expanded to the new size. The reason for this is that a toolbar is a child window of the program's main window. Therefore, it does not automatically receive resize messages. Instead, if you want a child window (in this case, a toolbar) to receive resize messages, you must pass that message along to it. For example, to do this in the toolbar program, add the following **case** to **WindowFunc( )**.

```
case WM_SIZE:
  // pass resize message along to toolbar
  SendMessage(tbwnd, WM_SIZE, wParam, lParam);
  break;
```

After adding this code, when you expand the main window, the toolbar will automatically be resized appropriately.

In general, each time your main window is resized, it receives a **WM_SIZE** message. The new width of the window is in **LOWORD(lParam)**. The new height of the window is in **HIWORD(lParam)**. The value in **wParam** will be one of those shown here:

wParam	Meaning
SIZE_RESTORED	Window resized
SIZE_MAXIMIZED	Window maximized
SIZE_MINIMIZED	Window minimized
SIZE_MAXHIDE	Another window has been maximized
SIZE_MAXSHOW	Another window has been restored

As a general rule, if your program contains a child window, your main window function will need to pass appropriate sizing messages along to the child window.

Common dialog
boxes are
predefined
dialog boxes
that perform
commonly
needed input
tasks.

A common dialog box is activated by calling an API function. (This process differs from that for the common controls, which are windows that must be created.) The common dialog boxes supported by Windows 2000 are shown here:

Function	Dialog Box Activated
ChooseColor( )	Activates the Color dialog. This allows the user to choose a color or create a custom control.
ChooseFont( )	Activates the Font dialog. This allows the user to select a font.
FindText( )	Activates the Find dialog, which supports text searches.
GetOpenFileName( )	Activates the Open dialog. This allows the user to select a file to open.
GetSaveFileName( )	Activates the Save As dialog. This allows the user to select a file into which information will be saved.
PageSetupDlg( )	Activates the Page Setup dialog, which is used to specify the format of a printed page.
PrintDlg( )	Activates the Print dialog, which is used to print a file.
PrintDlgEx( )	Windows 2000 version of **PrintDlg( )**.
ReplaceText( )	Activates the Replace dialog, which supports text replacements.

10

In the remainder of this chapter you will learn about the Open and the Save As dialog boxes. In Chapter 17 you will see how to use the Print common dialog box. After you understand how to employ these common dialog boxes, the others will be easy to master on your own.

While there is no technical reason for not creating your own dialog boxes to handle the types of input managed by the common dialogs, generally you should not. Instead, the common dialogs should be used by your program whenever one of the operations they perform is required. The reason for this approach is easy to understand: it is what the users of your programs have come to expect. Frankly, the common dialogs provide easy-to-use solutions to several fairly complex input situations. It is fortunate that they are built into Windows 2000.

GetOpenFileName( ) and GetSaveFileName( )

The Open dialog box is used to input the name of a file to be opened. It allows a user to select a filename either by typing it or by selecting it from a list. The user may also change directories or drives. The Open dialog box is activated by calling the **GetOpenFileName( )** API function. When called, it displays a dialog box similar to that shown here:

The Save As dialog box allows the user to select a file into which output will be written. The Save As dialog box looks like this:

The **GetOpenFileName( )** and **GetSaveFileName( )** functions have these prototypes:

BOOL GetOpenFileName(LPOPENFILENAME *lpBuf*);

BOOL GetSaveFileName(LPOPENFILENAME *lpBuf*);

Here, *lpBuf* is a pointer to a structure of type **OPENFILENAME**. These functions return nonzero if a valid filename is specified by the user, zero otherwise.

The **OPENFILENAME** structure pointed to by *lpBuf* must be initialized prior to calling either function. Upon return, the filename specified by the user, and several other pieces of information, will be contained in that structure. The **OPENFILENAME** structure is defined like this:

```
typedef struct tagOFN
{
  DWORD lStructSize;
  HWND hwndOwner;
  HINSTANCE hInstance;
  LPCSTR lpstrFilter;
  LPSTR lpstrCustomFilter;
  DWORD nMaxCustFilter;
  DWORD nFilterIndex;
  LPSTR lpstrFile;
  DWORD nMaxFile;
  LPSTR lpstrFileTitle;
  DWORD nMaxFileTitle;
  LPCSTR lpstrInitialDir;
  LPCSTR lpstrTitle;
  DWORD Flags;
  WORD nFileOffset;
  WORD nFileExtension;
  LPCSTR lpstrDefExt;
  LPARAM lCustData;
  LPOFNHOOKPROC lpfnHook;
  LPCSTR  lpTemplateName;
  void * pvReserved; // Windows 2000 only
  DWORD dwReserved;  // Windows 2000 only
  DWORD FlagsEx;     // Windows 2000 only
} OPENFILENAME;
```

10

Each element of **OPENFILENAME** is described here.

lStructSize must contain the size of the **OPENFILENAME** structure. **hwndOwner** must contain the handle of the window that owns the dialog box. If **Flags** contains either **OFN_ENABLETEMPLATE** or **OFN_ENABLETEMPLATEHANDLE**, then **hInstance** specifies a handle that defines an alternative dialog box template. Otherwise, **hInstance** is not used.

lpstrFilter must point to an array that contains pairs of strings that define a filename filter. The pairs of strings must be organized like this: "description""mask", where the description identifies the type of files matched by the mask. For example, "C Files""C.*" specifies the description *C Files* and the mask *C.*. The last two strings in the array must be null in order to terminate the list. The names of the filters are displayed in a drop-down list from which the user may choose. If this element is **NULL**, then no filename filter is used.

lpstrCustomFilter points to a static array that will be used to store a file filter entered by the user. This array must initially contain a description and file filter using the format just described. However, after the user selects a filename, the new filter is copied into the array. If **lpstrCustomFilter** is **NULL**, then this element is ignored. The array must be 40 characters (or more) long.

nMaxCustFilter specifies the size of the array pointed to by **lpstrCustomFilter**. This value is needed only if **lpstrCustomFilter** is not **NULL**.

nFilterIndex specifies which pair of strings pointed to by **lpstrFilter** will provide the initial file filter and description when the dialog box is first displayed. The value 1 corresponds to the first pair, the second pair is specified by the value 2, and so on. This value is ignored if **lpstrFilter** is **NULL**. If **nFilterIndex** is zero, the strings pointed to by **lpstrCustomFilter** are used.

lpstrFile points to an array that will receive the complete file, path, and drive of the filename selected by the user. The array may contain an initial filename that will be used to initialize the filename edit box or it may point to a null string.

nMaxFile specifies the size of the array pointed to by **lpstrFile**. The array should be at least 256 bytes long so as to accommodate the longest possible filename.

lpstrFileTitle points to an array that receives the filename (without path or drive information) of the file selected by the user. If the filename by itself is not needed, this field can be **NULL**.

nMaxFileTitle specifies the size of the array pointed to by **lpstrFileTitle**.

lpstrInitialDir points to an array that contains the directory that will first be used when the dialog box is activated. However, if a path is passed in **lpstrFile**, then that path is used and **lpstrInitialDir** is ignored. If **lpstrInitialDir** is **NULL**, then the current directory is selected. However, if no files in the current directory match the specified file filter, then the previous directory is used. (The previous directory is stored in the **LastVisited** registry entry each time the user chooses a file.) If there is no previous directory, then the user's personal files directory is used, if it exists. Otherwise, the desktop directory is displayed.

lpstrTitle points to a string that will be used as the title for the dialog box. The default title is used if **lpstrTitle** is **NULL**. For the **GetOpenFileName( )** function, the default title is "Open"; for **GetSaveFileName( )**, the default title is "Save As".

The **Flags** element is used to set various options inside the dialog box. Both **GetOpenFilename( )** and **GetSaveFilename( )** support numerous options. Several of the most commonly used are shown here (you can OR together two or more flags if necessary):

Flags	Effect
OFN_ENABLEHOOK	Allows the function pointed to by **lpfnHook** to be used.
OFN_ENABLETEMPLATE	Allows alternative dialog box template to be used. In this case, **hInstance** specifies the instance handle of the module that contains the dialog box specified by **lpTemplateName**.
OFN_ENABLETEMPLATEHANDLE	Allows alternative dialog box template to be used. In this case, **hInstance** is the handle to a region of memory that contains the dialog box template.
OFN_FILEMUSTEXIST	User may specify only existent files.

10

Flags	Effect
OFN_HIDEREADONLY	Causes the read-only check box to be suppressed.
OFN_NOCHANGEDIR	Current directory remains unchanged by user selection.
OFN_OVERWRITEPROMPT	Causes a confirmation window to be displayed if the user selects a file that already exists.
OFN_PATHMUSTEXIST	User may specify only existent paths.

The **nFileOffset** element receives the index of the start of the filename within the string returned in the array pointed to by **lpstrFile**. (Remember, this array will contain drive and path information in addition to the filename.)

nFileExtension receives the index of the file extension within the string returned in the array pointed to by **lpstrFile**.

lpstrDefExt points to an array that contains a default extension that is appended to the filename entered by the user when no extension is included. (The extension should be specified without a leading period.)

lCustData contains data that is passed to the optional function pointed to by **lpfnHook**.

lpfnHook is a pointer to a function that preempts and processes messages intended for the dialog box. This element is used only if **Flags** contains the value **OFN_ENABLEHOOK**.

lpTemplateName points to the name of an alternative dialog box template. **hInstance** must be the handle to the module that contains the dialog box resource. **lpTemplateName** is ignored unless **Flags** contains the value **OFN_ENABLETEMPLATE.**

The last three fields, **pvReserved, dwReserved2,** and **FlagsEx** are new for Windows 2000 and do not apply to other environments. Currently, the only additional flag supported by **ExtFlags** is **OFN_EX_NOPLACESBAR,** which suppresses the Explorer-style Places bar when set.

Notice how the **OPENFILENAME** structure (**fname**) is initialized within the toolbars program. Since many of the elements of the structure must be set to **NULL** if not used, it is common practice first to "zero" the entire structure using **memset( )**, as is done in the program. After **fname** has been zeroed, the essential elements are set. Pay special attention to how the array **filefilter** is initialized. Remember, the array pointed to by **lpstrFilter** must contain *pairs of strings*.

Once a filename has been obtained, it is used to open the file. Notice that in this case, the entire drive, path, and filename contained in **fn** and pointed to by **lpstrFile** are used. If you wanted to restrict files to the current directory, then the contents of **filename** (pointed to by **lpstrFileTitle**) could have been used.

You might want to try experimenting with **GetOpenFileName( )** and **GetSaveFileName( )** on your own, trying different options. For example, try using a custom file filter. These are two important built-in dialog boxes, which nearly all applications will need to use.

A Short Word on Using Files in a Windows 2000 Program

Before concluding this chapter, a short comment on using files in a Windows 2000 program is in order. Files are easily used by a Windows 2000 program. Because any C/C++ compiler that can create a Windows 2000 program will supply Windows 2000-compatible file functions and classes, such as **open( )**, **close( )**, **fopen( )**, **istream**, and **ostream**, you can generally use them to perform file I/O without any further worry. This is the approach used by the toolbar demo program. However, if you wish, you may use API functions defined by Win32, such as **CreateFile( )**, **ReadFile( )**, and **WriteFile( )**.

10

CHAPTER 11

More Common Controls: Up-Down Controls, Trackbars, and Progress Bars

This chapter explores three more of Windows 2000's common controls: the up-down controls, the trackbar, and the progress bar. These controls are particularly important because they are visually appealing, are easily incorporated into any new application, and make a convenient means of enhancing an existing program when it is ported to Windows 2000.

This chapter begins by presenting an overview of these controls. It concludes by demonstrating their use in an enhanced version of the countdown timer program developed in Chapter 6. As you will see, the addition of the new controls improves the interface to this application.

Up-Down Controls

An up-down control is essentially a compressed scroll bar. That is, it consists only of the arrows found on the ends of a scroll bar, but there is no bar between them. As you may have seen while using various Windows applications, some scrollbars are so small that the bar is essentially pointless. Also, some situations don't lend themselves to the concept of the bar, but benefit from the use of the up and down arrows. To accommodate these situations, the up-down control was invented.

An up-down control may be employed two different ways. First, it may be used more or less like a stand-alone scroll bar. Second, it can be used in conjunction with another control, called its *buddy window*. The most common buddy window is an edit box. An up-down control with an edit box is known as a *spin control* (or *spinner*). Here is the way these two controls appear. (The spin control is on the left.)

> An up-down control is essentially a scroll bar control without the bar.

> A spin control is a combination of an up-down control and an edit box.

When a spin control is used, almost all of the overhead required to manage the control is provided automatically by Windows 2000. This makes the spin control easy to add to your application. The methods for creating and

managing both a stand-alone up-down control and a spin control are discussed in the next section.

Creating an Up-Down Control

To create an up-down control, use the **CreateUpDownControl( )** function shown here:

HWND CreateUpDownControl(DWORD *Style*, int *X*, int *Y*,
               int *Width*, int *Height*, HWND *hParent*,
               int *ID*, HINSTANCE *hInst*,
               HWND *hBuddy*, int *Max*, int *Min*, int *StartPos*);

Here, *Style* specifies the style of the up-down control. This parameter must include the standard styles **WS_CHILD**, **WS_VISIBLE**, and **WS_BORDER**. It may also include one or more of the up-down styles shown in Table 11-1.

The location of the upper-left corner of the up-down control is passed in *X* and *Y*. The width and height of the control are specified in *Width* and *Height*.

The handle of the parent window is passed in *hParent*. The ID associated with the up-down control is specified in *ID*. The instance handle of the application is passed in *hInst*. The handle of the buddy window is passed in *hBuddy*. If there is no buddy window, then this parameter must be **NULL**.

The range of the control is passed in *Max* and *Min*. If *Max* is less then *Min*, then the control runs backwards. The initial position of the control (which must be within the specified range) is passed in *StartPos*. This value determines the control's initial value. It is important to be aware that an up-down control maintains an internal counter that is incremented or decremented each time one of the arrows is pressed. This internal value will always be within the range specified when the control is created.

The function returns a handle to the control. It returns **NULL** on failure.

Receiving Up-Down Control Messages

When one of the arrows of an up-down control is pressed, it sends either a **WM_VSCROLL** or a **WM_HSCROLL** message to its parent window, depending upon whether the up-down control is vertical (the default) or horizontal. The handle of the up-down control will be in *lParam*. Since there might be more than one control that generates **WM_VSCROLL** or **WM_HSCROLL** messages, you will need to check this handle to determine if it is that of the up-down control. The new value of the up-down control will be in **HIWORD(wParam)**.

Style	Meaning
UDS_ALIGNLEFT	Aligns up-down control to the left of its buddy window.
UDS_ALIGNRIGHT	Aligns up-down control to the right of its buddy window.
UDS_ARROWKEYS	Enables arrow keys. (That is, arrow keys may be used to move the control.)
TBS_AUTOBUDDY	Buddy window is previous window in z-order.
UDS_HORZ	Up-down control is horizontal. Up-down controls are vertical by default.
UDS_HOTTRACK	The arrows of the up-down control will be highlighted when the mouse is over them. Works for Windows 2000 and Windows 98 only.
UDS_NOTHOUSANDS	Commas not used in large values when displayed in buddy window. (Applies to spin controls only.)
UDS_SETBUDDYINT	Automatically sets the text within the buddy window when the control position is changed. This allows the buddy window to show the current position of the up-down control.
UDS_WRAP	Position of up-down control will "wrap around" when moved past an end.

The Up-Down
Control Styles
Table 11-1.

Sending Up-Down Control Messages

Up-down controls respond to a variety of messages. Several commonly used ones are shown in Table 11-2. For example, to obtain the value of the control (that is, its position), send the control a **UDM_GETPOS** message. The current position of the control is returned. To set the position of an up-down control, use the **UDM_SETPOS** message. Up-down controls are sent messages using **SendMessage( )**.

Creating a Spin Control

While there is nothing whatsoever wrong with creating and using a stand-alone up-down control, the up-down control is most commonly linked with an edit box. As mentioned, this combination is called a spin control.

Message	Meaning
UDM_GETBUDDY	Obtains handle of buddy window. The handle is returned. *wParam* is 0. *lParam* is 0.
UDM_GETPOS	Obtains the current position. The current position is in the low-order word of the return value. *wParam* is 0. *lParam* is 0.
UDM_GETRANGE	Obtains the current range. The maximum value is in the low-order word of the return value and the minimum value is in the high-order word of the return value. *wParam* is 0. *lParam* is 0.
UDM_SETBUDDY	Specifies a new buddy window. The handle of the old buddy window is returned. *wParam* is the handle of new buddy window. *lParam* is 0.
UDM_SETPOS	Sets the current position. *wParam* is 0. *lParam* is new current position.
UDM_SETRANGE	Sets the current range. *wParam* is 0. *lParam* is the range. Its low-order word contains maximum, high-order word contains minimum.

Common
Up-Down
Messages
Table 11-2.

Because the spin control is such a common implementation of an up-down control, Windows 2000 provides special support for it. In fact, a spin control is a completely automated control—your program incurs virtually no management overhead.

To create a spin control you must specify an edit control as a buddy window to an up-down control. After you have done this, each time the up-down control is changed, its new position is automatically displayed in the edit box. Further, if you manually change the value in the edit box, the up-down control is automatically set to reflect that value. Typically, you will define the edit box within your program's resource file. There will be an example of a spin control later in this chapter.

11

Using a Trackbar

One of the most visually appealing of the common controls is the trackbar (sometimes called a *slider control*). A trackbar is visually similar to a slider control found on various types of electronic equipment, such as stereos. It consists of a pointer that moves within a track. Although they look quite different, trackbars and scroll bars are handled in much the same way by your program. Trackbars are particularly useful when your program is emulating a real device. For example, if your program is controlling a graphic equalizer, then trackbars are an excellent choice for representing and setting the frequency curve. Here is a sample trackbar.

A trackbar is a special type of scroll bar that resembles a slider control found on electronic equipment such as stereos.

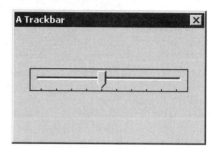

To create a trackbar, use either **CreateWindow( )** or **CreateWindowEx( )**. **CreateWindowEx( )** allows some extended style specifications. For the trackbar example in this chapter we won't need to use any extended styles, but you may find them useful in your own applications. The window class of a trackbar is **TRACKBAR_CLASS**.

Trackbar Styles

When creating the trackbar, you can specify various style options. The most common ones are shown in Table 11-3. You will almost always want to include **TBS_AUTOTICKS** because this style causes small "tick" marks to be automatically shown on the bar. The tick marks provide a scale for the bar.

Style	Effect
TBS_AUTOTICKS	Automatically adds tick marks to the trackbar.
TBS_HORZ	Trackbar is horizontal. (This is the default.)
TBS_VERT	Trackbar is vertical.
TBS_BOTTOM	Tick marks on bottom of bar. (This is the default for horizontal trackbars.)
TBS_TOP	Tick marks on top of bar.

Common Trackbar Style Options
Table 11-3.

Style	Effect
TBS_LEFT	Tick marks on left of bar.
TBS_RIGHT	Tick marks on right of bar. (This is the default for vertical trackbars.)
TBS_BOTH	Tick marks on both sides of bar.
TBS_TOOLTIPS	Trackbar includes a tooltip. By default, the tooltip displays the current position of the slider.

Common Trackbar Style Options *(continued)* **Table 11-3.**

Sending Trackbar Messages

As with the other common controls we have examined, you send a trackbar a message using the **SendMessage( )** function. Common trackbar messages are shown in Table 11-4. Two messages that you will almost always need to send to a trackbar are **TBM_SETRANGE** and **TBM_SETPOS**. These set the range of the trackbar and establish its initial position, respectively. These items cannot be set when the trackbar is created.

Notice the message **TBM_SETBUDDY**. Using this message you can add a buddy window to a trackbar. As is the case with up-down controls, trackbar buddy windows are usually edit boxes. In *lParam* specify the handle of the buddy. In *wParam*, specify its position. To position the buddy window on the right side of a horizontal bar or the bottom of a vertical bar, pass 0 in *wParam*. To position the buddy window on the left side of a horizontal bar or the top of a vertical bar, pass nonzero. Trackbars may have one or two buddy windows. When two are used, one is on each side. (See the In-Depth box entitled "Using Buddy Windows with Trackbars" later in this chapter.)

11

Message	Meaning
TBM_GETPOS	Obtains the current position. *wParam* is 0. *lParam* is 0.
TBM_GETRANGEMAX	Gets the maximum trackbar range. *wParam* is 0. *lParam* is 0.
TBM_GETRANGEMIN	Gets the minimum trackbar range. *wParam* is 0. *lParam* is 0.

Common Trackbar Messages **Table 11-4.**

Message	Meaning
TBM_SETBUDDY	Assigns the trackbar a buddy window. *wParam* specifies the location of the buddy. If it is zero, the buddy is on the right or bottom. If it is nonzero, the buddy is on the left or top. *wParam* specifies the handle of the edit box that will become the buddy window.
TBM_SETPOS	Sets the current position. *wParam* is nonzero to redraw the trackbar and zero otherwise. *lParam* contains the new position.
TBM_SETRANGE	Sets the trackbar range. *wParam* is nonzero to redraw trackbar and 0 otherwise. *lParam* contains the range. The minimum value is in the low-order word. The maximum value is in the high-order word.
TBM_SETRANGEMAX	Sets the maximum range. *wParam* is nonzero to redraw trackbar and 0 otherwise. *lParam* contains the maximum range value.
TBM_SETRANGEMIN	Sets the minimum range. *wParam* is nonzero to redraw trackbar and 0 otherwise. *lParam* contains the minimum range value.
TBM_SETTIPSIDE	Sets the location in which the tooltip for a trackbar is displayed. *wParam* must be either TBTS_TOP, TBTS_BOTTM, TBTS_LEFT, or TBTS_RIGHT. *lParam* is 0.

Common
Trackbar
Messages
(continued)
Table 11-4.

Processing Trackbar Notification Messages

When a trackbar is accessed, it generates either a **WM_HSCROLL** or a **WM_VSCROLL** scroll message, depending upon whether the trackbar is horizontal or vertical. A value describing the nature of the activity is passed in the low-order word of *wParam*. This value is referred to as a *notification message*. The handle of the trackbar that generated the message is in *lParam*. Common trackbar notification messages are shown in Table 11-5.

Message	Meaning
TB_BOTTOM	END key is pressed. Slider is moved to minimum value.
TB_ENDTRACK	End of trackbar activity.
TB_LINEDOWN	Right or down arrow key pressed.
TB_LINEUP	Left or up arrow key pressed.
TB_PAGEDOWN	PGDN (page down) key pressed or mouse click before slider.
TB_PAGEUP	PGUP (page up) key pressed or mouse click after slider.
TB_THUMBPOSITION	Slider moved using the mouse.
TB_THUMBTRACK	Slider dragged using the mouse.
TB_TOP	HOME key pressed. Slider is moved to maximum value.

Common
Trackbar
Notification
Messages
Table 11-5.

Trackbars are fully automated. For example, the trackbar will move itself when its position is changed by the user. Your program does not need to do this manually.

NOTE: When a **TB_THUMBTRACK** or **TB_THUMBPOSITION** message is received from a trackbar, the value in **HIWORD(wParam)** will contain the current position of the bar. For all other trackbar events, this value will be zero.

11

Using a Progress Bar

A progress bar indicates the degree to which a task has been completed.

A progress bar is a small horizontal window that depicts the degree of completion of a task. As the task proceeds, the bar is filled from left to right. When the bar is filled, the task is finished. The progress bar is one of the simplest of the common controls, and you have almost certainly seen one in action. Progress bars are created using either **CreateWindow( )** or **CreateWindowEx( )** by specifying the **PROGRESS_CLASS** window class.

Your program sends a progress bar a message using the **SendMessage( )** function. Progress bars do not generate messages. Generally, you will send messages to set a progress bar's range and increment its progress. Table 11-6 shows a few of the most common progress bar messages.

By default, a progress bar has the range 0 through 100. However, you can set it to any value between 0 through 65,535. Typically, you will advance the bar by sending it a **PBM_STEPIT** message. This causes the bar's current position to advance by a predetermined increment called a *step*. By default, the step increment is 10, but it may be any value you like. As you increment the bar's position, more of the bar is filled. Since a progress bar is used to display the degree of completion of a long task, the task should end when the bar is fully filled.

Originally, progress bars did not offer any style options, but two styles have recently been added. The first is **PBS_SMOOTH**. By default, progress bars display their progress in steps. By specifying **PBS_SMOOTH**, the progress is shown in a smooth, continuous fashion. The second is **PBS_VERTICAL**. It creates a vertical progress bar. Normally, progress bars advance from left to right. A vertical progress bar advances from bottom to top.

Message	Meaning
PBM_SETPOS	Sets the progress bar's position. The old position is returned. *wParam* contains the new position. *lParam* is 0.
PBM_SETRANGE	Sets the progress bar's range. The old range is returned with the maximum in the high-order word and the minimum in the low-order word. *wParam* is 0. *lParam* contains the range. The maximum value is in the high-order word. The minimum value is in the low-order word.
PBM_SETSTEP	Sets the increment (or step) value. The old increment is returned. *wParam* contains the new increment. *lParam* is 0.
PBM_STEPIT	Advances the bar's progress by the step value. *wParam* is 0. *lParam* is 0.

Progress Bar Messages.

Table 11-6.

Demonstrating a Spin Control, Trackbar, and Progress Bar

The following program demonstrates a spin control, a trackbar, and a progress bar by modifying the countdown timer program first developed in Chapter 6. Specifically, it uses the spin control to set the number of seconds to delay. It uses the trackbar to set the number of beeps that will be sounded when the timer goes off. If beeps are not selected, then a message box is displayed at the end of the period. A progress bar displays how far the countdown has advanced. The enhanced countdown timer program is shown here:

```
/* Add a spin control, trackbar, and progress bar to
   the countdown timer. */

#include <windows.h>
#include <commctrl.h>
#include <cstring>
#include <cstdio>
#include "timer.h"

#define BEEPMAX 10
#define MAXTIME 99

LRESULT CALLBACK WindowFunc(HWND, UINT, WPARAM, LPARAM);
BOOL CALLBACK DialogFunc(HWND, UINT, WPARAM, LPARAM);

char szWinName[] = "MyWin"; // name of window class

HINSTANCE hInst;

HWND hwnd;

int WINAPI WinMain(HINSTANCE hThisInst, HINSTANCE hPrevInst,
                   LPSTR lpszArgs, int nWinMode)
{
  MSG msg;
  WNDCLASSEX wcl;
  HACCEL hAccel;
  INITCOMMONCONTROLSEX cc;

  // Define a window class.
  wcl.cbSize = sizeof(WNDCLASSEX);

  wcl.hInstance = hThisInst;     // handle to this instance
```

11

```
wcl.lpszClassName = szWinName; // window class name
wcl.lpfnWndProc = WindowFunc;  // window function
wcl.style = 0;                 // default style

wcl.hIcon = LoadIcon(NULL, IDI_APPLICATION); // large icon
wcl.hIconSm = NULL; // use small version of large icon
wcl.hCursor = LoadCursor(NULL, IDC_ARROW);  // cursor style

wcl.lpszMenuName = "TimerMenu"; // main menu

wcl.cbClsExtra = 0; // no extra memory needed
wcl.cbWndExtra = 0;

// Make the window background white.
wcl.hbrBackground = (HBRUSH) GetStockObject(WHITE_BRUSH);

// Register the window class.
if(!RegisterClassEx(&wcl)) return 0;

/* Now that a window class has been registered, a window
   can be created. */
hwnd = CreateWindow(
  szWinName, // name of window class
  "Spin Controls, Trackbars, and Progress Bars", // title
  WS_OVERLAPPEDWINDOW, // window style - normal
  CW_USEDEFAULT, // X coordinate - let Windows decide
  CW_USEDEFAULT, // Y coordinate - let Windows decide
  CW_USEDEFAULT, // width - let Windows decide
  CW_USEDEFAULT, // height - let Windows decide
  NULL,          // no parent window
  NULL,          // no menu
  hThisInst,     // instance handle
  NULL           // no additional arguments
);

hInst = hThisInst; // save the current instance handle

// Load the keyboard accelerators.
hAccel = LoadAccelerators(hThisInst, "TimerMenu");

// Initialize the common controls.
cc.dwSize = sizeof(INITCOMMONCONTROLSEX);
cc.dwICC = ICC_BAR_CLASSES | ICC_UPDOWN_CLASS |
           ICC_PROGRESS_CLASS;
```

```
       InitCommonControlsEx(&cc);

       // Display the window.
       ShowWindow(hwnd, nWinMode);
       UpdateWindow(hwnd);

       // Create the message loop.
       while(GetMessage(&msg, NULL, 0, 0))
       {
         if(!TranslateAccelerator(hwnd, hAccel, &msg)) {
           TranslateMessage(&msg); // translate keyboard messages
           DispatchMessage(&msg); // return control to Windows 2000
         }
       }

       return msg.wParam;
    }

    /* This function is called by Windows 2000 and is passed
       messages from the message queue.
    */
    LRESULT CALLBACK WindowFunc(HWND hwnd, UINT message,
                                WPARAM wParam, LPARAM lParam)
    {
      int response;

      switch(message) {
        case WM_COMMAND:
          switch(LOWORD(wParam)) {
            case IDM_DIALOG:
              DialogBox(hInst, "MYDB", hwnd, (DLGPROC) DialogFunc);
              break;
            case IDM_EXIT:
              response = MessageBox(hwnd, "Quit the Program?",
                                    "Exit", MB_YESNO);
              if(response == IDYES) PostQuitMessage(0);
              break;
            case IDM_HELP:
              MessageBox(hwnd, "Try the Timer", "Help", MB_OK);
              break;
          }
          break;
        case WM_DESTROY: // terminate the program
          PostQuitMessage(0);
```

```
      break;
    default:
      /* Let Windows 2000 process any messages not specified in
         the preceding switch statement. */
      return DefWindowProc(hwnd, message, wParam, lParam);
  }
  return 0;
}

// Timer Dialog function
BOOL CALLBACK DialogFunc(HWND hdwnd, UINT message,
                          WPARAM wParam, LPARAM lParam)
{
  char str[80];

  HDC hdc;
  PAINTSTRUCT paintstruct;
  static int t;
  int i;

  static long udpos = 1;
  static long trackpos = 1;
  static HWND hEboxWnd;
  static HWND hTrackWnd;
  static HWND udWnd;
  static HWND hProgWnd;
  int low=1, high=BEEPMAX;


  switch(message) {
    case WM_INITDIALOG:
      hEboxWnd = GetDlgItem(hdwnd, IDD_EB1);
      udWnd = CreateUpDownControl(
                  WS_CHILD | WS_BORDER | WS_VISIBLE |
                  UDS_SETBUDDYINT | UDS_ALIGNRIGHT,
                  10, 10, 50, 50,
                  hdwnd,
                  IDD_UPDOWN,
                  hInst,
                  hEboxWnd,
                  MAXTIME, 1, udpos);

      // Create a track bar
      hTrackWnd = CreateWindow(TRACKBAR_CLASS,
                  "",
                  WS_CHILD | WS_VISIBLE | WS_TABSTOP |
                  TBS_AUTOTICKS | WS_BORDER,
```

```
                        2, 50,
                        200, 28,
                        hdwnd,
                        NULL,
                        hInst,
                        NULL
       );
       SendMessage(hTrackWnd, TBM_SETRANGE,
                    1, MAKELONG(low, high));
       SendMessage(hTrackWnd, TBM_SETPOS,
                    1, trackpos);

       // create progress bar
       hProgWnd = CreateWindow(PROGRESS_CLASS,
                        "",
                        WS_CHILD | WS_VISIBLE | WS_BORDER,
                        2, 84,
                        240, 12,
                        hdwnd,
                        NULL,
                        hInst,
                        NULL);

       // set step increment to 1
       SendMessage(hProgWnd, PBM_SETSTEP, 1, 0);

       // check the As-Is radio button
       SendDlgItemMessage(hdwnd, IDD_RB3, BM_SETCHECK, 1, 0);

       // set number of beeps box
       SetDlgItemInt(hdwnd, IDD_EB2, trackpos, 1);
       return 1;
     case WM_VSCROLL: // beep at each 10-second mark
       if(udWnd==(HWND)lParam) // if spin control
         if(!(HIWORD(wParam) % 10)) MessageBeep(MB_OK);
       return 1;
     case WM_HSCROLL: // track bar was activated
       if(hTrackWnd != (HWND)lParam) break; // not track bar

       switch(LOWORD(wParam)) {
         case TB_TOP:
         case TB_BOTTOM:        // For this example
         case TB_LINEUP:        // all messages will be
         case TB_LINEDOWN:      // processed in the same
         case TB_THUMBPOSITION: // way.
         case TB_THUMBTRACK:
         case TB_PAGEUP:
```

11

```
      case TB_PAGEDOWN:
        trackpos = SendMessage(hTrackWnd, TBM_GETPOS,
                          0, 0);
        SetDlgItemInt(hdwnd, IDD_EB2, trackpos, 1);
        return 1;
    }
    break;
  case WM_COMMAND:
    switch(LOWORD(wParam)) {
      case IDCANCEL:
        KillTimer(hdwnd, IDD_TIMER);
        EndDialog(hdwnd, 0);
        return 1;
      case IDD_EB2:
        /* Update trackbar if user enters number
           of beeps into the Beeps edit box. */
        trackpos = GetDlgItemInt(hdwnd, IDD_EB2, NULL, 1);
        SendMessage(hTrackWnd, TBM_SETPOS, 1, trackpos);
        return 1;
      case IDD_START: // start the timer
        SetTimer(hdwnd, IDD_TIMER, 1000, NULL);

        // get number of seconds to delay
        t = udpos = SendMessage(udWnd, UDM_GETPOS, 0, 0);

        // initialize progress bar
        SendMessage(hProgWnd, PBM_SETRANGE, 0,
                    MAKELONG(0, udpos));
        SendMessage(hProgWnd, PBM_SETPOS, 0, 0);

        if(SendDlgItemMessage(hdwnd,
                  IDD_RB1, BM_GETCHECK, 0, 0))
          ShowWindow(hwnd, SW_MINIMIZE);
        else
          if(SendDlgItemMessage(hdwnd,
                  IDD_RB2, BM_GETCHECK, 0, 0))
            ShowWindow(hwnd, SW_MAXIMIZE);
        return 1;
    }
    break;
  case WM_TIMER: // timer went off
    if(t==0) {
      KillTimer(hdwnd, IDD_TIMER);

      // beep or display message box?
```

```
       if(SendDlgItemMessage(hdwnd,
                 IDD_CB2, BM_GETCHECK, 0, 0)) {

          // beep and move track bar with each beep
          for(i=trackpos; i; i--) {
            MessageBeep(MB_OK);
            Sleep(1000);
            SendMessage(hTrackWnd, TBM_SETPOS, 1, i-1);
          }

          // reset track bar after countdown
          SendMessage(hTrackWnd, TBM_SETPOS, 1, trackpos);
        }
        else MessageBox(hdwnd, "Timer Went Off", "Timer", MB_OK);

        SetDlgItemInt(hdwnd, IDD_EB1, udpos, 1);
        ShowWindow(hwnd, SW_RESTORE);
        return 1;
      }
      t--;

      // advance progress bar
      SendMessage(hProgWnd, PBM_STEPIT, 0, 0);

      // see if count down is to be displayed
      if(SendDlgItemMessage(hdwnd,
                 IDD_CB1, BM_GETCHECK, 0, 0)) {
          SetDlgItemInt(hdwnd, IDD_EB1, t, 1);
      }
      return 1;
    case WM_PAINT:
      hdc = BeginPaint(hdwnd, &paintstruct);
      SetBkMode(hdc, TRANSPARENT);
      sprintf(str, "Seconds");
      TextOut(hdc, 44, 6, str, strlen(str));
      sprintf(str, "Beeps");
      TextOut(hdc, 186, 6, str, strlen(str));
      sprintf(str, "Set Number of Beeps");
      TextOut(hdc, 30, 32, str, strlen(str));
      EndPaint(hdwnd, &paintstruct);
      return 1;
  }

  return 0;
}
```

11

This program uses the following resource file. The edit box identified as **IDD_EB1** is linked to the up-down control to form the spin control.

```
// Demonstrate a Spin Control and a Trackbar
#include <windows.h>
#include "timer.h"
TimerMenu MENU
{
  POPUP "&Options"
  {
    MENUITEM "&Timer\tF2", IDM_DIALOG
    MENUITEM "E&xit\tCtrl+X", IDM_EXIT
  }
  MENUITEM "&Help", IDM_HELP
}


TimerMenu ACCELERATORS
{
  VK_F2, IDM_DIALOG, VIRTKEY
  VK_F1, IDM_HELP, VIRTKEY
  "^X", IDM_EXIT
}


MYDB DIALOGEX 18, 18, 144, 100
CAPTION "A Countdown Timer"
STYLE DS_MODALFRAME | WS_POPUP | WS_CAPTION | WS_SYSMENU
{
  PUSHBUTTON "Start", IDD_START, 30, 80, 30, 14
  PUSHBUTTON "Cancel", IDCANCEL, 70, 80, 30, 14
  EDITTEXT IDD_EB1, 1, 1, 20, 12, ES_LEFT | WS_CHILD |
           WS_VISIBLE | WS_BORDER
  EDITTEXT IDD_EB2, 80, 1, 12, 12, ES_LEFT | WS_CHILD |
           WS_VISIBLE | WS_BORDER
  AUTOCHECKBOX "Show Countdown", IDD_CB1, 1, 48, 70, 10
  AUTOCHECKBOX "Beep At End", IDD_CB2, 1, 58, 50, 10
  AUTORADIOBUTTON "Minimize", IDD_RB1, 80, 48, 50, 10
  AUTORADIOBUTTON "Maximize", IDD_RB2, 80, 58, 50, 10
  AUTORADIOBUTTON "As-Is", IDD_RB3, 80, 68, 50, 10
}
```

The header file TIMER.H is shown here:

```
#define IDM_DIALOG    100
#define IDM_EXIT      101
```

```
#define IDM_HELP        102

#define IDD_START       300
#define IDD_TIMER       301

#define IDD_CB1         400
#define IDD_CB2         401
#define IDD_RB1         402
#define IDD_RB2         403
#define IDD_RB3         404

#define IDD_EB1         500
#define IDD_EB2         501

#define IDD_UPDOWN      602
```

Sample output from the program is shown in Figure 11-1. When the timer is started (by pressing Start), the currently specified delay time is retrieved from the spin control. If the Show Countdown option is checked, then the time remaining is updated in the spin control each time the timer goes off. When the end of the time period has been reached, the specified number of beeps are sounded (if the Beep At End option was selected). Also, the trackbar is moved left one position each time a beep sounds. Let's take a closer look at the enhanced countdown program now.

11

Sample output from the enhanced timer program

Figure 11-1.

The Sleep( ) Function

In the countdown program, the **Sleep( )** function provides a slight delay between beeps when the timer goes off. If a short delay does not separate each beep, then only one long, continuous sound is heard instead of the individual beeps that are desired. In the past, such a delay was generally achieved through the use of some sort of software-based delay loop, such as:

```
for(x=0; x<100000; x++) ; // a simple delay loop
```

However, such software methods are problematic for two reasons. First, software delay loops are imprecise. Specifically, the length of the delay is affected by the speed of the CPU. On a fast computer, the delay will be shorter. On a slow computer, the delay will be longer. Further, even with equivalent CPU speeds, different compilers will use different machine instructions when compiling the preceding loop. This could lead to differences in the length of the delay. The second reason software delay loops can cause problems is that they are CPU intensive. That is, even though they do nothing, they are using CPU time that could be allocated to other processes running in your system. To prevent inconsistent delays and CPU intensive code, your Windows 2000 programs should use the **Sleep( )** function to provide a delay.

The **Sleep( )** function suspends the execution of your program for a specified number of milliseconds. Its prototype is shown here:

VOID Sleep(DWORD *delay*);

Here, *delay* specifies the number of milliseconds that the calling thread will suspend. While your program is asleep, CPU time is allocated to other processes running in the system.

Creating the Spin Control, Trackbar, and Progress Bar

The spin control, trackbar, and progress bar are created each time **DialogFunc( )** receives a **WM_INITDIALOG** message, using the code shown here:

```
case WM_INITDIALOG:
  hEboxWnd = GetDlgItem(hdwnd, IDD_EB1);
  udWnd = CreateUpDownControl(
                WS_CHILD | WS_BORDER | WS_VISIBLE |
                UDS_SETBUDDYINT | UDS_ALIGNRIGHT,
                10, 10, 50, 50,
                hdwnd,
                IDD_UPDOWN,
                hInst,
                hEboxWnd,
                MAXTIME, 1, udpos);

  // Create a track bar
  hTrackWnd = CreateWindow(TRACKBAR_CLASS,
                "",
                WS_CHILD | WS_VISIBLE | WS_TABSTOP |
                TBS_AUTOTICKS | WS_BORDER,
                2, 50,
                200, 28,
                hdwnd,
                NULL,
                hInst,
                NULL
  );
  SendMessage(hTrackWnd, TBM_SETRANGE,
                1, MAKELONG(low, high));
  SendMessage(hTrackWnd, TBM_SETPOS,
                1, trackpos);

  // create progress bar
  hProgWnd = CreateWindow(PROGRESS_CLASS,
                "",
                WS_CHILD | WS_VISIBLE | WS_BORDER,
```

11

```
            2, 84,
            240, 12,
            hdwnd,
            NULL,
            hInst,
            NULL);

// set step increment to 1
SendMessage(hProgWnd, PBM_SETSTEP, 1, 0);

// check the As-Is radio button
SendDlgItemMessage(hdwnd, IDD_RB3, BM_SETCHECK, 1, 0);

// set number of beeps box
SetDlgItemInt(hdwnd, IDD_EB2, trackpos, 1);
return 1;
```

Look first at the call to **CreateUpDownControl( )**. This creates a spin
control that is at location 10, 10 within the dialog box. The control is 50
pixels wide and 50 pixels tall. Because the control is a child window of the
dialog box, the dialog box's handle (**hdwnd**) is passed as the parent handle.
The ID of the up-down control is **IDD_UPDOWN**. **hInst** is the instance
handle of the program. The buddy window is specified by **hEboxWnd**. This
is the handle of the edit box that will be linked to the up-down control. The
range of the up-down control is 1 to **MAXTIME**, and the initial position is 1.

Since the edit box that is part of the spin control is defined in the resource
file, the program must call **GetDlgItem( )** to obtain its handle.
(**GetDlgItem( )** was described in Chapter 5.) Once the handle of the edit
box has been obtained, it is passed as the buddy window to the
CreateUpDownControl( ) function. After the up-down control has been
created with an edit box as its buddy window, the two controls are
automatically linked together, forming the spin control.

Next, examine how the trackbar is created. It is located at 2, 50 and is 200
pixels long by 28 pixels high. The handle of the trackbar is stored in
hTrackWnd. After the trackbar is created, its range is set to 1 through
BEEPMAX. Its initial position is set at 1. Notice that the range is set
using the macro **MAKELONG( )**. This macro assembles two integers into
a long integer. It has this prototype:

DWORD MAKELONG(WORD *low*, WORD *high*);

The low-order part of the double word value is specified in *low* and the high-order portion is specified in *high*. **MAKELONG( )** is quite useful when you need to encode two word values into a long integer.

Finally, the progress bar is created. It is located beneath the trackbar. Its step increment is set to one. The progress bar will be updated each time the timer goes off, showing the current state of the countdown.

Managing the Spin Control

Each time the spin control is accessed, a **WM_VSCROLL** message is sent to the dialog box. The handle of the up-down control is contained in **lParam**. This handle is tested against that returned by **CreateUpDownControl( )** to confirm that it is the up-down control that generated the message. While there is only one control in this example, real world applications may have several controls capable of generating a **WM_VSCROLL** message, so you should always confirm which control has been accessed. The new position of the spin control is contained in **HIWORD(wParam)**. If this value is a multiple of ten, then a beep is sounded. That is, as the user increases (or decreases) the timing interval, a beep is sounded as each multiple of ten is passed. This feature can be useful when setting a large delay period.

Since a spin control is completely automated, there is no need to perform any other actions when the **WM_VSCROLL** message is received. Except for sounding the beep at each 10-second interval, there is no need to handle **WM_VSCROLL** messages, at all. In fact, most programs that use spin controls don't interact with the control until its current setting is required.

Inside the **IDD_START** handler, the current value of the spin control is obtained by sending a **UDM_GETPOS** message. When this message is received, the spin control returns the value shown in its buddy window. Remember, the value in the edit box always reflects the current value of the spin control. This is true even if the user changes this value, manually, by entering a new number.

11

Managing the Trackbar

Whenever the trackbar is moved, a **WM_HSCROLL** message is received and processed by the following code:

```
case WM_HSCROLL: // track bar was activated
  if(hTrackWnd != (HWND)lParam) break; // not track bar
```

```
switch(LOWORD(wParam)) {
  case TB_TOP:
  case TB_BOTTOM:        // For this example
  case TB_LINEUP:        // all messages will be
  case TB_LINEDOWN:      // processed in the same
  case TB_THUMBPOSITION: // way.
  case TB_THUMBTRACK:
  case TB_PAGEUP:
  case TB_PAGEDOWN:
    trackpos = SendMessage(hTrackWnd, TBM_GETPOS,
                   0, 0);
    SetDlgItemInt(hwnd, IDD_EB2, trackpos, 1);
    return 1;
}
break;
```

When the user moves the slider within the trackbar, the trackbar's position is automatically updated—your program does not have to do this itself. After the trackbar has been moved, the program obtains its new value and then uses this value to update the edit box that displays the number of beeps.

The current value of the trackbar is displayed inside the Beeps edit box using **SetDlgItemInt( )**. This function displays an integer inside an edit box. It has the following prototype:

BOOL SetDlgItemInt(HWND *hDialog*, int *ID*, UINT *value*, BOOL *signed*);

The handle of the dialog box that contains the edit control is passed in *hDialog*. The ID of the dialog box is passed in *ID*. The value to put into the edit box is passed in *value*. If *signed* is a nonzero value, then negative values are allowed. Otherwise, an unsigned value is assumed. The function returns nonzero if successful and zero on failure.

The user may also manually set the number of beeps using the Beeps edit box. When this is done, the trackbar is automatically adjusted to reflect the value entered by the user, using the sequence shown here:

```
case IDD_EB2:
  /* Update trackbar if user enters number
     of beeps into the Beeps edit box. */
  trackpos = GetDlgItemInt(hwnd, IDD_EB2, NULL, 1);
  SendMessage(hTrackWnd, TBM_SETPOS, 1, trackpos);
  return 1;
```

Notice that the value inside the edit box is retrieved by calling **GetDlgItemInt( )**. This function returns the integer equivalent of the string currently inside the box. For example, if the box contains the string 102, then **GetDlgItemInt( )** will return the value 102. For obvious reasons, this function applies only to edit boxes that contain numeric values. The prototype for **GetDlgItemInt( )** is shown here:

UINT GetDlgItemInt(HWND *hDialog*, int *ID*, BOOL *error, BOOL *signed*);

The handle of the dialog box that contains the edit control is passed in *hDialog*. The ID of the dialog box is passed in *ID*. If the edit box does not contain a valid numeric string, zero is returned. However, zero is also a valid value. For this reason, the success or failure of the function is returned in the variable pointed to by *error*. After the call, the variable pointed to by *error* will be nonzero if the return value is valid. It will be zero if an error occurred. If you don't care about errors, you can use **NULL** for this parameter. If *signed* is a nonzero value, then a signed value will be returned by **GetDlgItemInt( )**. Otherwise, an unsigned value is returned.

In this example, the trackbar may be moved using either the mouse or the keyboard. In fact, the reason that so many **TB_** messages are included is to support the keyboard interface. You might want to try taking some of these messages out and observing the results.

Managing the Progress Bar

The progress bar shows how far the countdown has advanced. To accurately reflect the progress of the countdown, the range of the bar must be initialized so that its maximum value is equal to the number of seconds in the countdown. The bar's initial position must be set to zero. This is done inside the **IDD_START** case, which is executed when the user presses the Start button, using the code sequence shown here.

11

```
// initialize progress bar
SendMessage(hProgWnd, PBM_SETRANGE, 0,
          MAKELONG(0, udpos));
SendMessage(hProgWnd, PBM_SETPOS, 0, 0);
```

Here, **udpos** contains the number of seconds specified in the spin control.

Each time the timer goes off, the bar is updated by the following statement:

```
// advance progress bar
SendMessage(hProgWnd, PBM_STEPIT, 0, 0);
```

This statement causes the bar to be advanced one step position.

Large Reward, Little Effort

As you have seen, incorporating an up-down control, trackbar, or progress bar into your application requires very little effort. Yet, the reward is quite large. If you compare the look and feel of the original countdown program in Chapter 6 with that of the enhanced version just shown, it is obvious which has the more appealing interface.

IN DEPTH

Using Buddy Windows with Trackbars

As explained, a recent enhancement to the trackbar is the ability to add a buddy window. As is the case with up-down controls, trackbar buddy windows are usually edit boxes. To add a buddy window to a trackbar, send the trackbar a **TBM_SETBUDDY** message after it has been created. In *lParam* specify the handle of the buddy. In *wParam*, specify its position. To position the buddy window on the right side of a horizontal bar or the bottom of a vertical bar, pass 0 in *wParam*. To position the buddy window on the left side of a horizontal bar or the top of a vertical bar, pass nonzero. Trackbars may have one or two buddy windows. When two are used, one is on each side.

You can try using a buddy window with a trackbar by changing the example in this chapter so that it uses the Beeps edit control as a buddy window for the trackbar. First, remove these lines from the **WM_PAINT** handler because they are no longer needed.

```
sprintf(str, "Beeps");
TextOut(hdc, 186, 6, str, strlen(str));
```

Next, send this **TBM_SETBUDDY** message to the trackbar after it has been created.

```
SendMessage(hTrackWnd, TBM_SETBUDDY, 0, (LPARAM)
            GetDlgItem(hdwnd, IDD_EB2));
```

Here, the call to **GetDlgItem( )** returns the handle of the Beeps edit box, which becomes the buddy window of the Beeps trackbar. After making these changes, the trackbar will look like the one shown here:

11

CHAPTER 12

Status Windows, Tab Controls, and the Tree-Views

This chapter continues our look at the Windows 2000 common controls. We will examine the status window, the tab control, and the tree-view control.

Using a Status Window

Frequently an application will need to keep the user informed of the status of certain program variables, attributes, or parameters. Windows 2000 includes a standard control for this purpose, called the *status window* or *status bar*. A status window is a bar that (typically) is displayed along the bottom of a window. It is used to display information related to the program.

As you will see, status bars are easy to implement. If you make a status bar a standard feature of each application that you write, then you will be providing status information in a consistent and easily recognizable manner.

Creating a Status Window

To create a status window, you can use **CreateStatusWindow( )**, shown here.

> HWND CreateStatusWindow(LONG *WinStyle*, LPCSTR *lpszFirstPart*,
> HWND *hParent*, UINT *ID*);

Here, *WinStyle* specifies the style of the status bar. It must include **WS_CHILD,** and it usually includes the **WS_VISIBLE** style so that it is automatically displayed. A status window can consist of two or more partitions in which text is displayed. A pointer to the string that will be displayed in the first part of the status bar is passed in *lpszFirstPart*. This parameter can be **NULL** if this text will be set later. The handle of the parent window is passed in *hParent*, and the ID of the status bar is passed in *ID*. The handle to the status bar is returned. **NULL** is returned on failure.

Notice that you don't pass the dimensions or location of the status window when it is created. The reason for this is that it is automatically sized to fit its parent window and positioned along the bottom of the parent window. If you want to display the status bar at the top of the parent window, include the **CCS_TOP** style in the *WinStyle* parameter. Tooltips are enabled if you include the **SBARS_TOOLTIPS** style. (The older macro **SBT_TOOLTIPS** can also be used.)

NOTE: You can also create a status bar by using either **CreateWindow( )** or **CreateWindowEx( )** and specifying the window class **STATUSCLASSNAME**. But, **CreateStatusWindow( )** is easier.

A status window is generally divided into two or more parts. (However, a single-part status window is perfectly acceptable.) Once the parts have been established, you can write text to each part individually. Each part is referred to by its index. The first part has an index value of 0. As just described, you can set the text in the first part when the status bar is created.

Status Window Messages

A status window does not generate messages, but your program will send it messages using the **SendMessage( )** function. Common status window messages are shown in Table 12-1.

Almost all applications will send **SB_SETPARTS**, which sets the number of parts to the status bar, and **SB_SETTEXT**, which writes text to a part. The general procedure for creating a status bar is described here:

1. Create the status window.
2. Set the number of parts by sending an **SB_SETPARTS** message.
3. Set the text in each part by sending an **SB_SETTEXT** message.

Message	Meaning
SB_GETPARTS	Obtains the X coordinate of the right edge of the parts in a status bar. The number of parts in the status bar is returned. (Zero is returned on failure.) *wParam* specifies the number of parts to obtain. *lParam* is a pointer to an integer array that will receive the X coordinate of the right edge of each part. The array must be at least as large as the number of parts requested. If an edge is bounded by the border of the window, its X coordinate will be −1.
SB_GETTEXT	Obtains the text from the specified part. The low-order word of the return value contains the number of characters in the text. The high-order word contains a value that describes how the text is displayed. If it is 0, the text appears beneath the level of the window. If it is **SBT_POPOUT**, the text appears above the level of the window. If it is **SBT_NOBORDERS**, the text is displayed without a border. If it is **SBT_RTLREADING**, the text is displayed right to left. *wParam* specifies the index of the desired part. *lParam* points to a character array that will receive the text. (Make sure that this array is large enough to hold the text contained in the part.)

Commonly Used Status Bar Messages
Table 12-1.

12

Message	Meaning
SB_SETPARTS	Specifies the number of parts in a status bar. It returns nonzero if successful and zero on failure. *wParam* specifies the number of parts. *lParam* is a pointer to an array of integers that contains the X coordinate of the right edge of each part. A value of −1 specifies the right boundary of the parent window.
SB_SETTEXT	Outputs text to a part. It returns nonzero if successful and zero on failure. *wParam* specifies the index of the part that will receive the text ORed with a value that determines how the text will be displayed. If the display value is zero, then the text appears beneath the level of the window. (This is the default.) If the display value is **SBT_POPOUT**, the text appears above the level of the window. If it is **SBT_NOBORDERS**, the text is displayed without a border. If the display value is **SBT_OWNERDRAW** the parent window displays the text. If it **SBT_RTLREADING**, the text is displayed right to left. *lParam* is a pointer to the string to be displayed.
SB_SETTIPTEXT	Sets the tooltip text. *wParam* specifies the index of the part for which the tooltip text is being set. *lParam* is a pointer to the string that contains text.

Commonly
Used Status
Bar Messages
(continued)

Table 12-1.

Once a status bar has been initialized, you can update each part as needed by sending an **SB_SETTEXT** message.

Using a Status Bar

The following program uses a status bar to report the settings within a dialog box. The dialog box contains a spin control, three check boxes, and two radio buttons. The status bar shows the current setting of each control. When compiling, remember to include COMCTL32.LIB in the link. Sample output from the program is shown in Figure 12-1.

Sample output
from the Status
Bar program
Figure 12-1.

```
// Demonstrate a status bar.

#include <windows.h>
#include <commctrl.h>
#include <cstdio>
#include "status.h"

#define NUMPARTS 5

LRESULT CALLBACK WindowFunc(HWND, UINT, WPARAM, LPARAM);
BOOL CALLBACK DialogFunc(HWND, UINT, WPARAM, LPARAM);
void InitStatus(HWND hwnd);

char szWinName[] = "MyWin"; // name of window class

HINSTANCE hInst;
HWND hwnd;
HWND hStatusWnd;

int parts[NUMPARTS];

int WINAPI WinMain(HINSTANCE hThisInst, HINSTANCE hPrevInst,
                   LPSTR lpszArgs, int nWinMode)
```

12

```
{
  MSG msg;
  WNDCLASSEX wcl;
  HACCEL hAccel;
  INITCOMMONCONTROLSEX cc;

  // Define a window class.
  wcl.cbSize = sizeof(WNDCLASSEX);

  wcl.hInstance = hThisInst;      // handle to this instance
  wcl.lpszClassName = szWinName; // window class name
  wcl.lpfnWndProc = WindowFunc;  // window function
  wcl.style = 0;                  // default style

  wcl.hIcon = LoadIcon(NULL, IDI_APPLICATION); // large icon
  wcl.hIconSm = NULL; // use small version of large icon
  wcl.hCursor = LoadCursor(NULL, IDC_ARROW);   // cursor style

  wcl.lpszMenuName = "StatusMenu"; // main menu

  wcl.cbClsExtra = 0; // no extra memory needed
  wcl.cbWndExtra = 0;

  // Make the window background white.
  wcl.hbrBackground = (HBRUSH) GetStockObject(WHITE_BRUSH);

  // Register the window class.
  if(!RegisterClassEx(&wcl)) return 0;

  /* Now that a window class has been registered, a window
     can be created. */
  hwnd = CreateWindow(
    szWinName, // name of window class
    "Using a Status Bar", // title
    WS_OVERLAPPEDWINDOW, // window style - normal
    CW_USEDEFAULT, // X coordinate - let Windows decide
    CW_USEDEFAULT, // Y coordinate - let Windows decide
    CW_USEDEFAULT, // width - let Windows decide
    CW_USEDEFAULT, // height - let Windows decide
    NULL,          // no parent window
    NULL,          // no menu
    hThisInst,     // instance handle
    NULL           // no additional arguments
  );
```

```
      hInst = hThisInst; // save the current instance handle

      // Load the keyboard accelerators.
      hAccel = LoadAccelerators(hThisInst, "StatusMenu");

      // Initialize the common controls.
      cc.dwSize = sizeof(INITCOMMONCONTROLSEX);
      cc.dwICC = ICC_BAR_CLASSES | ICC_UPDOWN_CLASS;
      InitCommonControlsEx(&cc);

      // Display the window.
      ShowWindow(hwnd, nWinMode);
      UpdateWindow(hwnd);

      // Create the message loop.
      while(GetMessage(&msg, NULL, 0, 0))
      {
        if(!TranslateAccelerator(hwnd, hAccel, &msg)) {
          TranslateMessage(&msg); // translate keyboard messages
          DispatchMessage(&msg); // return control to Windows 2000
        }
      }

      return msg.wParam;
    }

    /* This function is called by Windows 2000 and is passed
       messages from the message queue.
    */
    LRESULT CALLBACK WindowFunc(HWND hwnd, UINT message,
                                WPARAM wParam, LPARAM lParam)
    {
      int response;

      switch(message) {
        case WM_COMMAND:
          switch(LOWORD(wParam)) {
            case IDM_DIALOG:
              DialogBox(hInst, "StatusDB", hwnd, (DLGPROC) DialogFunc);
              break;
            case IDM_EXIT:
              response = MessageBox(hwnd, "Quit the Program?",
                                    "Exit", MB_YESNO);
              if(response == IDYES) PostQuitMessage(0);
              break;
```

12

```
      case IDM_HELP:
        MessageBox(hwnd, "Try the Dialog Box",
                   "Help", MB_OK);
        break;
    }
    break;
  case WM_DESTROY: // terminate the program
    PostQuitMessage(0);
    break;
  default:
    /* Let Windows 2000 process any messages not specified in
       the preceding switch statement. */
    return DefWindowProc(hwnd, message, wParam, lParam);
  }

  return 0;
}

// Status bar demo dialog function.
BOOL CALLBACK DialogFunc(HWND hdwnd, UINT message,
                         WPARAM wParam, LPARAM lParam)
{
  static long udpos = 0;
  static char str[80];
  static HWND hEboxWnd;
  static HWND udWnd;
  static statusCB1, statusCB2;
  static statusRB1;
  int low=0, high=10;

  switch(message) {
    case WM_INITDIALOG:
      InitStatus(hdwnd); // initialize the status bar

      hEboxWnd = GetDlgItem(hdwnd, ID_EB1);
      udWnd = CreateUpDownControl(
                WS_CHILD | WS_BORDER | WS_VISIBLE |
                UDS_SETBUDDYINT | UDS_ALIGNRIGHT,
                10, 10, 50, 50,
                hdwnd,
                ID_UPDOWN,
                hInst,
                hEboxWnd,
                high, low, high/2);
```

```
      // Initialize radio buttons
      SendDlgItemMessage(hdwnd, ID_RB2, BM_SETCHECK,
                         BST_CHECKED, 0);
    return 1;
  case WM_VSCROLL: // process up-down control
    if(udWnd==(HWND)lParam) {
      udpos = GetDlgItemInt(hdwnd, ID_EB1, NULL, 1);
      sprintf(str, "Power: %d", udpos);
      SendMessage(hStatusWnd, SB_SETTEXT,
                  (WPARAM) 0, (LPARAM) str);
    }
    return 1;
  case WM_COMMAND:
    switch(LOWORD(wParam)) {
      case ID_CB1: // process Optimize checkbox
        statusCB1 = SendDlgItemMessage(hdwnd, ID_CB1,
                    BM_GETCHECK, 0, 0);
        if(statusCB1) sprintf(str, "Optimize: Yes");
        else sprintf(str, "Optimize: No");
        SendMessage(hStatusWnd, SB_SETTEXT,
                    (WPARAM) 1, (LPARAM) str);
        return 1;
      case ID_CB2: // process Debug checkbox
        statusCB2 = SendDlgItemMessage(hdwnd, ID_CB2,
                    BM_GETCHECK, 0, 0);
        if(statusCB2) sprintf(str, "Debug: Yes");
        else sprintf(str, "Debug: No");
        SendMessage(hStatusWnd, SB_SETTEXT,
                    (WPARAM) 2, (LPARAM) str);
        return 1;
      case ID_CB3: // process NT 4 checkbox
        statusCB2 = SendDlgItemMessage(hdwnd, ID_CB3,
                    BM_GETCHECK, 0, 0);
        if(statusCB2) sprintf(str, "NT 4: Yes");
        else sprintf(str, "NT 4: No");
        SendMessage(hStatusWnd, SB_SETTEXT,
                    (WPARAM) 3, (LPARAM) str);
        return 1;
      case ID_RB1: // process radio buttons
      case ID_RB2:
        statusRB1 = SendDlgItemMessage(hdwnd, ID_RB1,
                    BM_GETCHECK, 0, 0);
        if(statusRB1) sprintf(str, "Using C");
        else sprintf(str, "Using C++");
        SendMessage(hStatusWnd, SB_SETTEXT,
```

```
                          (WPARAM) 4, (LPARAM) str);
              return 1;
          case ID_RESET: // reset options
            SendMessage(udWnd, UDM_SETPOS, 0, (LPARAM) high /2);
            SendMessage(hStatusWnd, SB_SETTEXT, (WPARAM) 0,
                (LPARAM) "Power: 5");
            SendDlgItemMessage(hdwnd, ID_CB1,
                    BM_SETCHECK, 0, 0);
            SendDlgItemMessage(hdwnd, ID_CB2,
                    BM_SETCHECK, 0, 0);
            SendDlgItemMessage(hdwnd, ID_CB3,
                    BM_SETCHECK, 0, 0);
            SendMessage(hStatusWnd, SB_SETTEXT, (WPARAM) 1,
                (LPARAM) "Optimize: No");
            SendMessage(hStatusWnd, SB_SETTEXT, (WPARAM) 2,
                (LPARAM) "Debug: No");
            SendMessage(hStatusWnd, SB_SETTEXT, (WPARAM) 3,
                (LPARAM) "NT 4: No");
            SendMessage(hStatusWnd, SB_SETTEXT, (WPARAM) 4,
                (LPARAM) "Using C++");
            return 1;
          case IDCANCEL:
          case IDOK:
            EndDialog(hdwnd, 0);
            return 1;
      }
  }
  return 0;
}

// Initialize the status bar.
void InitStatus(HWND hwnd)
{
  RECT WinDim;
  int i;

  GetClientRect(hwnd, &WinDim);

  for(i=1; i<=NUMPARTS; i++)
    parts[i-1] = WinDim.right/NUMPARTS * i;

  // Create a status bar
  hStatusWnd = CreateStatusWindow(
              WS_CHILD | WS_VISIBLE,
              "Power: 5", hwnd,
              ID_STATUSWIN);
```

```
SendMessage(hStatusWnd, SB_SETPARTS,
            (WPARAM) NUMPARTS, (LPARAM) parts);

SendMessage(hStatusWnd, SB_SETTEXT, (WPARAM) 1,
            (LPARAM) "Optimize: No");
SendMessage(hStatusWnd, SB_SETTEXT, (WPARAM) 2,
            (LPARAM) "Debug: No");
SendMessage(hStatusWnd, SB_SETTEXT, (WPARAM) 3,
            (LPARAM) "NT 4: No");
SendMessage(hStatusWnd, SB_SETTEXT, (WPARAM) 4,
            (LPARAM) "Using C++");
}
```

The status bar program requires the following resource file.

```
#include <windows.h>
#include "status.h"

StatusMenu MENU
{
  POPUP "&Options" {
    MENUITEM "&Dialog\tF2", IDM_DIALOG
    MENUITEM "E&xit\tCtrl+X", IDM_EXIT
  }
  MENUITEM "&Help", IDM_HELP
}

StatusMenu ACCELERATORS
{
  VK_F1, IDM_HELP, VIRTKEY
  VK_F2, IDM_DIALOG, VIRTKEY
  "^X", IDM_EXIT
}

StatusDB DIALOGEX 18, 18, 180, 92
CAPTION "Demonstrate a Status Bar"
STYLE DS_MODALFRAME | WS_POPUP | WS_CAPTION | WS_SYSMENU
{
  PUSHBUTTON "Reset", ID_RESET, 112, 40, 37, 14
  PUSHBUTTON "OK", IDOK, 112, 60, 37, 14
  EDITTEXT ID_EB1, 10, 10, 20, 12, ES_LEFT |
          WS_BORDER | WS_TABSTOP
  LTEXT "Power Factor", ID_STEXT1, 36, 12, 50, 12
  AUTOCHECKBOX "Optimize", ID_CB1, 10, 35, 48, 12
  AUTOCHECKBOX "Debug Info", ID_CB2, 10, 50, 48, 12
```

12

```
  AUTOCHECKBOX "NT 4 Compatible", ID_CB3, 10, 65, 70, 12
  AUTORADIOBUTTON "C", ID_RB1, 112, 8, 20, 12
  AUTORADIOBUTTON "C++", ID_RB2, 112, 20, 28, 12
  LTEXT "Language", ID_STEXT2, 140, 14, 40, 12
}
```

The header file STATUS.H is shown here:

```
#define IDM_DIALOG    100
#define IDM_EXIT      101
#define IDM_HELP      102
#define ID_UPDOWN     103
#define ID_EB1        104
#define ID_EB2        105
#define ID_CB1        106
#define ID_CB2        107
#define ID_CB3        108
#define ID_RB1        109
#define ID_RB2        110
#define ID_RESET      111

#define ID_STATUSWIN 200

#define ID_STEXT1     300
#define ID_STEXT2     301
```

In the program, the function **InitStatus( )** creates and initializes the status window. First, the dimensions of the dialog box are obtained using **GetClientRect( )**. The width of the window is divided by **NUMPARTS** (which is defined as 5) to determine the right endpoints for the status bar parts, and these values are put into the **parts** array. Remember, the end point of each part—not the width of each part—must be passed to the status window. Next, the status window is created. Then, its partitions are set. Finally, the initial text to each part is set. (The text for the first part is passed in **CreateStatusWindow( )**.)

Within **DialogFunc( )**, the text within the status bar is updated each time a control is changed. This is accomplished by sending an **SB_SETTEXT** message to the part of the bar associated with the control that has changed its state. One last point: the text written to a status bar part will be automatically truncated to fit within that part. Text will not spill over into the next part.

Resizing a Status Bar

Although a status bar will initially size itself to fit its parent window, it will not automatically change its size when the parent window does. Recall that a window receives a **WM_SIZE** message after its size has been changed. To allow a child status window to be resized with its parent, you must pass the **WM_SIZE** message received by the parent window to the status window using the **SendMessage( )** function. (This process is similar to that used to resize a toolbar, as described in Chapter 10.)

For example, to allow the status window in the preceding example to be automatically resized when the size of its parent dialog box is changed, add the following case to **DialogFunc( )**. It passes along the **WM_SIZE** message and then resets the dimensions of the status bar partitions.

```
case WM_SIZE:
  SendMessage(hStatusWnd, WM_SIZE, wParam, lParam);
  GetClientRect(hdwnd, &WinDim);
  for(i=1; i<=NUMPARTS; i++)
    parts[i-1] = WinDim.right/NUMPARTS * i;
  SendMessage(hStatusWnd, SB_SETPARTS,
              (WPARAM) NUMPARTS, (LPARAM) parts);
  return 1;
```

You must also add

```
RECT WinDim;
int i;
```

to **DialogFunc( )**. Finally, in order for the dialog box to be capable of being resized, it must be created with the **WS_SIZEBOX** style, also included. Once you have made these modifications, execute the status bar program and then try resizing the status dialog box. As you will see, the status bar is automatically resized too. For example, here is the dialog box after it has been lengthened:

12

Introducing Tab Controls

One of the more visually interesting common controls is the *tab control*. A tab control emulates the tabs on a set of file folders. Each time a tab is selected, its associated folder comes to the surface. While tab controls are easy to use, it is somewhat complicated to program for them. In this section, tab control basics are introduced. In the next section, additional tab control features are discussed.

Creating a Tab Control

To create a tab control, you use either **CreateWindow( )** or **CreateWindowEx( )**, specifying the window class **WC_TABCONTROL**. Typically, a tab control will be a child window. It is also usually created using the **WS_VISIBLE** style, so that it is automatically displayed. For example, the following creates a tab control:

```
hTabWnd = CreateWindow(
            WC_TABCONTROL,
            "",
            WS_VISIBLE | WS_TABSTOP | WS_CHILD,
            0, 0, 100, 100,
            hwnd, // handle of parent
            NULL,
            hInst, // instance handle
            NULL
        );
```

There are various tab control-specific styles, such as **TCS_BUTTONS** (which creates button tabs), but for most applications the default tab control style is adequate. Once created, a tab control can be sent messages by your application or generate messages when it is accessed.

After a tab control has been created, it is empty. Before it can be used, you must insert tabs into it. Each tab is defined by a **TCITEM** structure, which is shown here:

```
typedef struct tagTCITEM
{
  UINT mask;
  DWORD dwState;
  DWORD dwStateMask
  LPSTR pszText;
  int cchTextMax;
```

```
    int iImage;
    LPARAM lParam;
} TCITEM;
```

In this structure, the value contained in **mask** determines whether the **dwState**, **pszText**, **iImage**, or **lParam** members of the structure contain valid data. **mask** can contain one or more of the following values:

Value in mask	Meaning
TCIF_IMAGE	**iImage** contains data.
TCIF_PARAM	**lParam** contains data.
TCIF_STATE	**dwState** contains data.
TCIF_TEXT	**pszText** contains data.

mask may also contain the value **TCIF_RTLREADING**, which means that the text should be displayed right to left.

When a tab is being created, the value of **dwState** is not used. When information is being obtained about an existing tab, **dwState** indicates its state. It will be either zero, **TCIS_BUTTONPRESSED** (applies to button tabs only), or **TCIS_HIGHLIGHTED** (the tab is highlighted). The value of **dwStateMask** determines which bits in **dwState** are valid. This field is not used when inserting items.

When a tab is being set, **pszText** points to the string that will be displayed within the tab. When information about a tab is being obtained, **pszText** must point to an array that will receive the text. In this case, the value of **cchTextMax** specifies the size of the array pointed to by **pszText**.

If there is an image list associated with the tab control, then **iImage** will contain the index of the image associated with the specified tab. If there is no image list associated with the tab control, **iImage** should be –1. We won't be using images in the tab control examples shown in this chapter, but you might find them useful for your applications.

12

lParam contains application-defined data.

HISTORICAL PERSPECTIVE: The **TCITEM** structure replaces the older **TC_ITEM** structure. In **TC_ITEM**, **dwState** and **dwStateMask** were reserved fields.

Sending Tab Control Messages

You can send a tab control several different types of messages using the
SendMessage( ) function. Several commonly used tab control messages are
shown in Table 12-2. As an alternative to using **SendMessage( )**, special
macros were created that simplify the process of sending messages to tab
controls. The tab control macros corresponding to the messages in Table 12-2
are shown here. In all cases, *hTabWnd* is the handle of the tab control.

```
VOID TabCtrl_AdjustRect(HWND hTabWnd, BOOL operation, RECT *lpRect);
BOOL TabCtrl_DeleteAllItems(HWND hTabWnd);
BOOL TabCtrl_DeleteItem(HWND hTabWnd, int index);
int TabCtrl_GetCurSel(HWND hTabWnd);
BOOL TabCtrl_GetItem(HWND hTabWnd, int index, TCITEM *lpitem);
int TabCtrl_GetItemCount(HWND hTabWnd);
int TabCtrl_InsertItem(HWND hTabWnd, int index, CONST TCITEM *lpitem);
int TabCtrl_SetCurSel(HWND hTabWnd, int index);
BOOL TabCtrl_SetItem(HWND hTabWnd, int index, TCITEM *lpitem);
```

In general, the macros are easier to use than the equivalent calls to
SendMessage( ).

When a tab control is created, it has no tabs. Therefore, your program will
always send at least one **TCM_INSERTITEM** message to it. Although neither
of the examples in this chapter require its use, one message that your real
world applications will probably employ is **TCM_ADJUSTRECT**. This message
obtains the dimensions of the display area of a tab control. Remember,
when you create a tab control, its window contains the tabs themselves, as
well as the area in which you will display information or pop up a dialog
box. The display area is the part of a tab control window that excludes the tabs.
(That is, the display area is the part of the tab control window that you
can use to display other items.) Since it is the display area that will contain
the information associated with the tab, you will often need to know
its dimensions.

Tab Notification Messages

When a tab control is accessed by the user a **WM_NOTIFY** message is
generated. Tab controls can generate two selection-change notification codes:
TCN_SELCHANGE and **TCN_SELCHANGING**. **TCN_SELCHANGING** is
sent when a tab selection is about to change. **TCN_SELCHANGE** is sent after
a new tab is selected.

Message	Meaning
TCM_ADJUSTRECT	Translates between the dimensions of the tab control's display area and its window. *wParam* specifies the operation. If it is nonzero, then, given the dimensions of a tab control's display area, the dimensions of the window rectangle are obtained. If it is zero, then, given the dimensions of the window rectangle, the display area of the tab control is obtained. *lParam* points to a **RECT** structure that contains the coordinates of the region to be translated (that is, either the window or the tab control's display area). On return, this structure will contain the translated coordinates.
TCM_DELETEALLITEMS	Deletes all tabs in the control. Returns nonzero if successful and zero on failure. *wParam* is 0. *lParam* is 0.
TCM_DELETEITEM	Deletes a specified tab. Returns nonzero if successful and zero on failure. *wParam* specifies the index of the tab to remove. *lParam* is 0.
TCM_GETCURSEL	Returns the index of the currently selected tab or −1 if no tab is selected. *wParam* is 0. *lParam* is 0.
TCM_GETITEM	Obtains information about the specified tab. Returns nonzero if successful and zero on failure. *wParam* specifies the index of the tab. *lParam* is a pointer to a **TCITEM** structure that receives the information about the item.
TCM_GETITEMCOUNT	Returns the number of tabs. *wParam* is 0. *lParam* is 0.
TCM_INSERTITEM	Creates (that is, inserts) a new tab. Returns the index of the item being inserted or −1 on failure. *wParam* specifies the index of the tab. *lParam* is a pointer to a **TCITEM** structure that describes the tab.
TCM_SETCURSEL	Selects a tab. Returns the index of the previously selected tab or −1 if no tab was previously selected. *wParam* specifies the index of the tab being selected. *lParam* is 0.
TCM_SETITEM	Sets information about the specified tab. Returns nonzero if successful and zero on failure. *wParam* specifies the index of the tab. *lParam* is a pointer to a **TCITEM** structure that contains the information about the item.

12

Commonly
Used Tab
Control
Messages
Table 12-2.

When a **WM_NOTIFY** message is received, *lParam* will point to a **NMHDR** structure (discussed in Chapter 10). The notification code will be contained in the **code** field of the **NMHDR** structure. The handle of the tab control that generates the message is found in the **hwndFrom** field.

A Simple Tab Demonstration Program

The following short program demonstrates the tab control. It creates a tab control that has three tabs, labeled Options, View, and Errors. Each time a new tab is selected, a message is displayed reporting this fact. Sample output is shown in Figure 12-2.

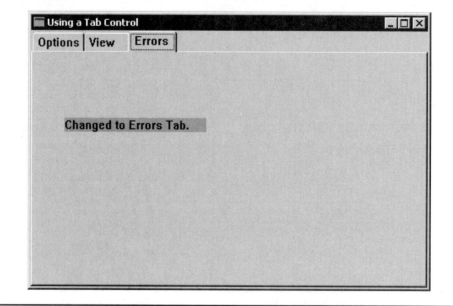

Sample output
from the first
tab control
program

Figure 12-2.

```
// A simple tab control demonstration.

#include <windows.h>
#include <commctrl.h>
#include <cstdio>

LRESULT CALLBACK WindowFunc(HWND, UINT, WPARAM, LPARAM);

char szWinName[] = "MyWin"; // name of window class

HINSTANCE hInst;
HWND hwnd;
HWND hTabWnd;

char TabName[][40] = {
  "Options",
  "View",
  "Errors"
};

int WINAPI WinMain(HINSTANCE hThisInst, HINSTANCE hPrevInst,
                   LPSTR lpszArgs, int nWinMode)
{
  MSG msg;
  WNDCLASSEX wcl;
  INITCOMMONCONTROLSEX cc;

  // Define a window class.
  wcl.cbSize = sizeof(WNDCLASSEX);

  wcl.hInstance = hThisInst;      // handle to this instance
  wcl.lpszClassName = szWinName; // window class name
  wcl.lpfnWndProc = WindowFunc;   // window function
  wcl.style = 0;                  // default style

  wcl.hIcon = LoadIcon(NULL, IDI_APPLICATION); // large icon
  wcl.hIconSm = NULL; // use small version of large icon
  wcl.hCursor = LoadCursor(NULL, IDC_ARROW);   // cursor style
```

12

```
wcl.lpszMenuName = NULL; // no class menu
wcl.cbClsExtra = 0; // no extra memory needed
wcl.cbWndExtra = 0;

// Make the window background white.
wcl.hbrBackground = (HBRUSH) GetStockObject(WHITE_BRUSH);

// Register the window class.
if(!RegisterClassEx(&wcl)) return 0;

/* Now that a window class has been registered, a window
   can be created. */
hwnd = CreateWindow(
  szWinName, // name of window class
  "Using a Tab Control", // title
  WS_OVERLAPPEDWINDOW, // window style - normal
  CW_USEDEFAULT, // X coordinate - let Windows decide
  CW_USEDEFAULT, // Y coordinate - let Windows decide
  CW_USEDEFAULT, // width - let Windows decide
  CW_USEDEFAULT, // height - let Windows decide
  NULL,          // no parent window
  NULL,          // no menu
  hThisInst,     // instance handle
  NULL           // no additional arguments
);

// Initialize the common controls.
cc.dwSize = sizeof(INITCOMMONCONTROLSEX);
cc.dwICC = ICC_TAB_CLASSES;
InitCommonControlsEx(&cc);

// Display the window.
ShowWindow(hwnd, nWinMode);
UpdateWindow(hwnd);

// Create the message loop.
while(GetMessage(&msg, NULL, 0, 0))
{
  TranslateMessage(&msg); // translate keyboard messages
  DispatchMessage(&msg); // return control to Windows 2000
}

return msg.wParam;
}

/* This function is called by Windows 2000 and is passed
   messages from the message queue.
```

```
*/
LRESULT CALLBACK WindowFunc(HWND hwnd, UINT message,
                            WPARAM wParam, LPARAM lParam)
{
  NMHDR *nmptr;
  int tabnumber;
  HDC hdc;
  char str[80];
  RECT WinDim;
  TCITEM tci;

  switch(message) {
    case WM_CREATE:
      // get size of parent window
      GetClientRect(hwnd, &WinDim);

      // create a tab control
      hTabWnd = CreateWindow(
              WC_TABCONTROL,
              "",
              WS_VISIBLE | WS_TABSTOP | WS_CHILD,
              0, 0, WinDim.right, WinDim.bottom,
              hwnd,
              NULL,
              hInst,
              NULL
            );

      tci.mask = TCIF_TEXT;
      tci.iImage = -1;

      tci.pszText = TabName[0];
      TabCtrl_InsertItem(hTabWnd, 0, &tci);

      tci.pszText = TabName[1];
      TabCtrl_InsertItem(hTabWnd, 1, &tci);

      tci.pszText = TabName[2];
      TabCtrl_InsertItem(hTabWnd, 2, &tci);
      break;
    case WM_NOTIFY: // process a tab change
      nmptr = (LPNMHDR) lParam;
      if(nmptr->code == TCN_SELCHANGE) {
        tabnumber = TabCtrl_GetCurSel((HWND)nmptr->hwndFrom);
        hdc = GetDC(hTabWnd);
        sprintf(str, "Changed to %s Tab.      ",
                TabName[tabnumber]);
```

12

```
        SetBkColor(hdc, RGB(200, 200, 200));
        TextOut(hdc, 40, 100, str, strlen(str));
        ReleaseDC(hTabWnd, hdc);
      }
      break;
    case WM_DESTROY: // terminate the program
      PostQuitMessage(0);
      break;
    default:
      /* Let Windows 2000 process any messages not specified in
         the preceding switch statement. */
      return DefWindowProc(hwnd, message, wParam, lParam);
  }

  return 0;
}
```

In the program, just before the tab control is created, a call is made to
GetClientRect( ) to obtain the size of the main window. When the tab
control is created, it is sized to fill the entire client area of its parent window.
While this is arbitrary, it is not uncommon. After the tab control has been
constructed, its three tabs are created.

Each time a **WM_NOTIFY** message contains the **TCN_SELCHANGE** code, a
message is displayed within the tab control display area, indicating that the
selection has changed to the specified tab. The index of the newly selected
tab is obtained by sending a **TCM_GETCURSEL** message.

Using Tab Controls

*Tab control
dialog boxes
must be
modeless.*

While tab controls are quite easy to create, they are a bit tricky to use because
each tab will typically have a dialog box associated with it. Each time a new tab
is selected, the currently displayed dialog box must be removed and the new
dialog box displayed. Also, you will generally want to fit each dialog box to the
display area of the tab control. Frankly, there are many other subtle issues
associated with tab controls and their associated dialog boxes that are simply
beyond the scope of this book. In this section you will learn the general method
of applying a tab control to your application. Once you understand the basics,
you will be able to add other features to your tab controls on your own.

Since a new tab may be selected at any time, modeless (rather than modal)
dialog boxes must be used. As you should recall, a modeless dialog box allows
other parts of your application to be activated without deactivating the
dialog box. (This differs from modal dialog boxes, which must be closed by
the user before other parts of the program can be used.) Typically, when a

new tab is selected, your application will close the currently displayed dialog box and then activate the next one. Because a dialog box may be closed at any time, your program must take appropriate action (such as saving its settings) before displaying the new box.

The following program creates a tab control that adds dialog boxes to the three tabs created by the preceding example. Each tab is associated with its own modeless dialog box. The first dialog box is the one created for the status bar example earlier in this chapter. The other two are simply placeholders used for the sake of illustration. Sample output from this program is shown in Figure 12-3.

Sample output from the second tab control program

Figure 12-3.

12

```
// Demonstrate a tab control.

#include <windows.h>
#include <commctrl.h>
#include <cstdio>
#include "tab.h"

#define NUMPARTS 5

LRESULT CALLBACK WindowFunc(HWND, UINT, WPARAM, LPARAM);
BOOL CALLBACK DialogFunc1(HWND, UINT, WPARAM, LPARAM);
BOOL CALLBACK DialogFunc2(HWND, UINT, WPARAM, LPARAM);
BOOL CALLBACK DialogFunc3(HWND, UINT, WPARAM, LPARAM);
void InitStatus(HWND hwnd);

char szWinName[] = "MyWin"; // name of window class

HINSTANCE hInst;
HWND hwnd;
HWND hStatusWnd;
HWND hTabWnd;

int parts[NUMPARTS];

HWND hDlg = (HWND) NULL;

char TabName[][40] = {
  "Options",
  "View",
  "Errors"
};

int WINAPI WinMain(HINSTANCE hThisInst, HINSTANCE hPrevInst,
                   LPSTR lpszArgs, int nWinMode)
{
  MSG msg;
  WNDCLASSEX wcl;
  INITCOMMONCONTROLSEX cc;

  // Define a window class.
  wcl.cbSize = sizeof(WNDCLASSEX);

  wcl.hInstance = hThisInst;      // handle to this instance
  wcl.lpszClassName = szWinName;  // window class name
  wcl.lpfnWndProc = WindowFunc;   // window function
```

```
wcl.style = 0;                       // default style

wcl.hIcon = LoadIcon(NULL, IDI_APPLICATION); // large icon
wcl.hIconSm = NULL; // use small version of large icon
wcl.hCursor = LoadCursor(NULL, IDC_ARROW);   // cursor style

wcl.lpszMenuName = NULL; // no class menu
wcl.cbClsExtra = 0; // no extra memory needed
wcl.cbWndExtra = 0;

// Make the window background white.
wcl.hbrBackground = (HBRUSH) GetStockObject(WHITE_BRUSH);

// Register the window class.
if(!RegisterClassEx(&wcl)) return 0;

/* Now that a window class has been registered, a window
   can be created. */
hwnd = CreateWindow(
  szWinName, // name of window class
  "Using a Tab Control", // title
  WS_OVERLAPPEDWINDOW, // window style - normal
  CW_USEDEFAULT, // X coordinate - let Windows decide
  CW_USEDEFAULT, // Y coordinate - let Windows decide
  CW_USEDEFAULT, // width - let Windows decide
  CW_USEDEFAULT, // height - let Windows decide
  NULL,          // no parent window
  NULL,          // no menu
  hThisInst,     // instance handle
  NULL           // no additional arguments
);

// Initialize the common controls.
cc.dwSize = sizeof(INITCOMMONCONTROLSEX);
cc.dwICC = ICC_TAB_CLASSES | ICC_UPDOWN_CLASS;
InitCommonControlsEx(&cc);

hInst = hThisInst; // save the current instance handle

// Display the window.
ShowWindow(hwnd, nWinMode);
UpdateWindow(hwnd);

// Create the message loop.
while(GetMessage(&msg, NULL, 0, 0))
```

12

```
    {
      if(!hDlg || !IsDialogMessage(hDlg, &msg)) {
        TranslateMessage(&msg); // translate keyboard messages
        DispatchMessage(&msg); // return control to Windows 2000
      }
    }

    return msg.wParam;
}

/* This function is called by Windows 2000 and is passed
   messages from the message queue.
*/
LRESULT CALLBACK WindowFunc(HWND hwnd, UINT message,
                                WPARAM wParam, LPARAM lParam)
{
  NMHDR *nmptr;
  int tabnumber = 0;
  TCITEM tci;

  switch(message) {
    case WM_CREATE:
      hTabWnd = CreateWindow(
                  WC_TABCONTROL,
                  "",
                  WS_VISIBLE | WS_TABSTOP | WS_CHILD,
                  20, 20, 368, 220,
                  hwnd,
                  NULL,
                  hInst,
                  NULL
                );

      tci.mask = TCIF_TEXT;
      tci.iImage = -1;

      tci.pszText = TabName[0];
      TabCtrl_InsertItem(hTabWnd, 0, &tci);

      tci.pszText = TabName[1];
      TabCtrl_InsertItem(hTabWnd, 1, &tci);

      tci.pszText = TabName[2];
      TabCtrl_InsertItem(hTabWnd, 2, &tci);
```

```
          hDlg = CreateDialog(hInst, "TabDB1", hTabWnd,
                             (DLGPROC) DialogFunc1);
        break;
      case WM_NOTIFY:
        nmptr = (LPNMHDR) lParam;
        if(nmptr->code == TCN_SELCHANGE) {
          if(hDlg) DestroyWindow(hDlg);
          tabnumber = TabCtrl_GetCurSel((HWND)nmptr->hwndFrom);
          switch(tabnumber) {
            case 0:
              hDlg = CreateDialog(hInst, "TabDB1",
                          hTabWnd, (DLGPROC) DialogFunc1);
              break;
            case 1:
              hDlg = CreateDialog(hInst, "TabDB2",
                          hTabWnd, (DLGPROC) DialogFunc2);
              break;
            case 2:
              hDlg = CreateDialog(hInst, "TabDB3",
                          hTabWnd, (DLGPROC) DialogFunc3);
              break;
          }
        }
        break;
      case WM_DESTROY: // terminate the program
        if(hDlg) DestroyWindow(hDlg);
        PostQuitMessage(0);
        break;
      default:
        /* Let Windows 2000 process any messages not specified in
           the preceding switch statement. */
        return DefWindowProc(hwnd, message, wParam, lParam);
  }
  return 0;
}

// Options dialog function.
BOOL CALLBACK DialogFunc1(HWND hdwnd, UINT message,
                          WPARAM wParam, LPARAM lParam)
{
  static long udpos = 0;
  static char str[80];
  static HWND hEboxWnd;
  static HWND udWnd;
  static statusCB1, statusCB2;
```

12

```
static statusRB1;
int low=0, high=10;

switch(message) {
  case WM_INITDIALOG:
    InitStatus(hdwnd); // initialize the status bar

    hEboxWnd = GetDlgItem(hdwnd, ID_EB1);
    udWnd = CreateUpDownControl(
                WS_CHILD | WS_BORDER | WS_VISIBLE |
                UDS_SETBUDDYINT | UDS_ALIGNRIGHT,
                10, 10, 50, 50,
                hdwnd,
                ID_UPDOWN,
                hInst,
                hEboxWnd,
                high, low, high/2);

    // Initialize radio buttons
    SendDlgItemMessage(hdwnd, ID_RB2, BM_SETCHECK,
                BST_CHECKED, 0);
    return 1;
  case WM_VSCROLL: // process up-down control
    if(udWnd==(HWND)lParam) {
      udpos = GetDlgItemInt(hdwnd, ID_EB1, NULL, 1);
      sprintf(str, "Power: %d", udpos);
      SendMessage(hStatusWnd, SB_SETTEXT,
                (WPARAM) 0, (LPARAM) str);
    }
    return 1;
  case WM_COMMAND:
    switch(LOWORD(wParam)) {
      case ID_CB1: // process Optimize checkbox
        statusCB1 = SendDlgItemMessage(hdwnd, ID_CB1,
                BM_GETCHECK, 0, 0);
        if(statusCB1) sprintf(str, "Optimize: Yes");
        else sprintf(str, "Optimize: No");
        SendMessage(hStatusWnd, SB_SETTEXT,
                (WPARAM) 1, (LPARAM) str);
        return 1;
      case ID_CB2: // process Debug checkbox
        statusCB2 = SendDlgItemMessage(hdwnd, ID_CB2,
                BM_GETCHECK, 0, 0);
        if(statusCB2) sprintf(str, "Debug: Yes");
        else sprintf(str, "Debug: No");
```

```
        SendMessage(hStatusWnd, SB_SETTEXT,
                (WPARAM) 2, (LPARAM) str);
      return 1;
    case ID_CB3: // process NT 4 checkbox
      statusCB2 = SendDlgItemMessage(hdwnd, ID_CB3,
              BM_GETCHECK, 0, 0);
      if(statusCB2) sprintf(str, "NT 4: Yes");
      else sprintf(str, "NT 4: No");
      SendMessage(hStatusWnd, SB_SETTEXT,
              (WPARAM) 3, (LPARAM) str);
      return 1;
    case ID_RB1: // process radio buttons
    case ID_RB2:
      statusRB1 = SendDlgItemMessage(hdwnd, ID_RB1,
              BM_GETCHECK, 0, 0);
      if(statusRB1) sprintf(str, "Using C");
      else sprintf(str, "Using C++");
      SendMessage(hStatusWnd, SB_SETTEXT,
              (WPARAM) 4, (LPARAM) str);
      return 1;
    case ID_RESET: // reset options
      SendMessage(udWnd, UDM_SETPOS, 0, (LPARAM) high /2);
      SendMessage(hStatusWnd, SB_SETTEXT, (WPARAM) 0,
          (LPARAM) "Power: 5");
      SendDlgItemMessage(hdwnd, ID_CB1,
              BM_SETCHECK, 0, 0);
      SendDlgItemMessage(hdwnd, ID_CB2,
              BM_SETCHECK, 0, 0);
      SendDlgItemMessage(hdwnd, ID_CB3,
              BM_SETCHECK, 0, 0);
      SendMessage(hStatusWnd, SB_SETTEXT, (WPARAM) 1,
          (LPARAM) "Optimize: No");
      SendMessage(hStatusWnd, SB_SETTEXT, (WPARAM) 2,
          (LPARAM) "Debug: No");
      SendMessage(hStatusWnd, SB_SETTEXT, (WPARAM) 3,
          (LPARAM) "NT 4: No");
      SendMessage(hStatusWnd, SB_SETTEXT, (WPARAM) 4,
          (LPARAM) "Using C++");
      return 1;
    case IDCANCEL:
    case IDOK:
      PostQuitMessage(0);
      return 1;
  }
}
```

12

```
    return 0;
}

// Second dialog function. This is just a placeholder.
BOOL CALLBACK DialogFunc2(HWND hdwnd, UINT message,
                          WPARAM wParam, LPARAM lParam)
{
  switch(message) {
    case WM_COMMAND:
      switch(LOWORD(wParam)) {
        case IDCANCEL:
        case IDOK:
          PostQuitMessage(0);
          return 1;
      }
  }
  return 0;
}

// Third dialog function. This is just a placeholder.
BOOL CALLBACK DialogFunc3(HWND hdwnd, UINT message,
                          WPARAM wParam, LPARAM lParam)
{
  switch(message) {
    case WM_COMMAND:
      switch(LOWORD(wParam)) {
        case IDCANCEL:
        case IDOK:
          PostQuitMessage(0);
          return 1;
      }
  }
  return 0;
}

// Initialize the status bar.
void InitStatus(HWND hwnd)
{
  RECT WinDim;
  int i;

  GetClientRect(hwnd, &WinDim);

  for(i=1; i<=NUMPARTS; i++)
    parts[i-1] = WinDim.right/NUMPARTS * i;
```

```
        // Create a status bar
        hStatusWnd = CreateStatusWindow(
                    WS_CHILD | WS_VISIBLE,
                    "Power: 5", hwnd,
                    ID_STATUSWIN);

        SendMessage(hStatusWnd, SB_SETPARTS,
                    (WPARAM) NUMPARTS, (LPARAM) parts);

        SendMessage(hStatusWnd, SB_SETTEXT, (WPARAM) 1,
                    (LPARAM) "Optimize: No");
        SendMessage(hStatusWnd, SB_SETTEXT, (WPARAM) 2,
                    (LPARAM) "Debug: No");
        SendMessage(hStatusWnd, SB_SETTEXT, (WPARAM) 3,
                    (LPARAM) "NT 4: No");
        SendMessage(hStatusWnd, SB_SETTEXT, (WPARAM) 4,
                    (LPARAM) "Using C++");
}
```

This program requires the following resource file. Notice that the dialog boxes do not have borders.

```
#include <windows.h>
#include "tab.h"

TabDB1 DIALOGEX 2, 16, 180, 92
STYLE  WS_CHILD | WS_VISIBLE
{
  PUSHBUTTON "Reset", ID_RESET, 112, 40, 37, 14
  PUSHBUTTON "OK", IDOK, 112, 60, 37, 14
  EDITTEXT ID_EB1, 10, 10, 20, 12, ES_LEFT |
          WS_TABSTOP | WS_BORDER
  LTEXT "Power Factor", ID_STEXT1, 36, 12, 50, 12
  AUTOCHECKBOX "Optimize", ID_CB1, 10, 35, 48, 12
  AUTOCHECKBOX "Debug Info", ID_CB2, 10, 50, 48, 12
  AUTOCHECKBOX "NT 4 Compatible", ID_CB3, 10, 65, 70, 12
  AUTORADIOBUTTON "C", ID_RB1, 112, 8, 20, 12
  AUTORADIOBUTTON "C++", ID_RB2, 112, 20, 28, 12
  LTEXT "Language", ID_STEXT2, 140, 14, 40, 12
}

TabDB2 DIALOGEX 2, 16, 180, 92
STYLE WS_CHILD | WS_VISIBLE
{
  PUSHBUTTON "OK", IDOK, 82, 43, 37, 14
  PUSHBUTTON "CANCEL", IDCANCEL, 132, 43, 37, 14
```

```
   LTEXT "Show contents of", ID_STEXT3, 10, 10, 60, 12
   AUTORADIOBUTTON "Registers", ID_RB3, 10, 30, 48, 12
   AUTORADIOBUTTON "Variables", ID_RB4, 10, 50, 52, 12
   AUTORADIOBUTTON "Stack", ID_RB5, 10, 70, 48, 12
}

TabDB3 DIALOGEX  2, 16, 180, 92
STYLE WS_CHILD | WS_VISIBLE
{
   PUSHBUTTON "OK", IDOK, 82, 43, 37, 14
   PUSHBUTTON "CANCEL", IDCANCEL, 132, 43, 37, 14
   LTEXT "Report", ID_STEXT4, 10, 10, 60, 12
   AUTOCHECKBOX "Syntax errors", ID_CB4, 10, 30, 60, 12
   AUTOCHECKBOX "Warnings", ID_CB5, 10, 50, 60, 12
   AUTOCHECKBOX "ANSI Violations", ID_CB6, 10, 70, 60, 12
}
```

The header file TAB.H is shown here:

```
#define IDM_DIALOG    100
#define IDM_EXIT      101
#define IDM_HELP      102
#define ID_UPDOWN     103
#define ID_EB1        104
#define ID_EB2        105
#define ID_CB1        106
#define ID_CB2        107
#define ID_CB3        108
#define ID_CB4        109
#define ID_CB5        110
#define ID_CB6        111
#define ID_RB1        112
#define ID_RB2        113
#define ID_RB3        114
#define ID_RB4        115
#define ID_RB5        116
#define ID_RESET      117

#define ID_STATUSWIN 200

#define ID_STEXT1     300
#define ID_STEXT2     301
#define ID_STEXT3     302
#define ID_STEXT4     303
```

The interesting portion of this program occurs inside the **WM_NOTIFY** case of **WindowFunc( )**. It is shown here for your convenience:

```
case WM_NOTIFY:
  nmptr = (LPNMHDR) lParam;
  if(nmptr->code == TCN_SELCHANGE) {
    if(hDlg) DestroyWindow(hDlg);
    tabnumber = TabCtrl_GetCurSel((HWND)nmptr->hwndFrom);
    switch(tabnumber) {
      case 0:
        hDlg = CreateDialog(hInst, "TabDB1",
                    hTabWnd, (DLGPROC) DialogFunc1);
        break;
      case 1:
        hDlg = CreateDialog(hInst, "TabDB2",
                    hTabWnd, (DLGPROC) DialogFunc2);
        break;
      case 2:
        hDlg = CreateDialog(hInst, "TabDB3",
                    hTabWnd, (DLGPROC) DialogFunc3);
        break;
    }
  }
  break;
```

Each time a new tab is selected two events occur. First, the dialog box associated with the currently selected tab is removed by calling **DestroyWindow( )**. (As you may recall, to close a modeless dialog box, you must call **DestroyWindow( )** rather than **EndDialog( )**, which is used for modal dialog boxes.) Next, the current tab selection is obtained and its dialog box is created using **CreateDialog( )**. (Remember, **CreateDialog( )** creates modeless dialog boxes.) This general procedure is the one you should follow with your own tab control dialog boxes.

Before moving on, you should experiment with this program. Try making changes to the dialog boxes or to the tab control. Also, tab controls may also have tooltips associated with them. As a challenge, you might want to try adding tooltips to the preceding example.

12

Tree-View Controls

Tree-view controls are used to display information using a tree structure. For example, the folders list used by Windows 2000's Explorer is an example of a tree-view control. Because trees imply a hierarchy, tree-view controls should

Tree-view
controls display
hierarchical
information in
a "tree-like"
manner.

be used to display only hierarchical information. Tree-view controls are very powerful and support a large number of different options. In fact, one could easily write a book about tree-view controls, alone! For this reason, this section discusses only tree-view fundamentals. Once you understand the basics, you will be able to easily incorporate the other tree-view features on your own.

Create a Tree-View Control

A tree-view control is a window that is created using either **CreateWindow( )** or **CreateWindowEx( )** and specifying the **WC_TREEVIEW** class. Typically, a tree-view control will be a child window, so the **WS_CHILD** style is needed. It is usually created using the **WS_VISIBLE** style, so that it is automatically displayed. **WS_TABSTOP** is also commonly included. Tree-view controls allow additional tree-related styles, which include the following, to be specified when they are created:

Style	Meaning
TVS_HASLINES	Lines link branches in the tree.
TVS_LINESATROOT	Lines link root to the branches.
TVS_HASBUTTONS	Expand/Collapse buttons included to the left of each branch.

Including the **TVS_HASLINES** and **TVS_LINESATROOT** styles causes lines to be drawn to each item in the tree. This gives the tree-view control its "tree-like" look. Including **TVS_HASBUTTONS** causes the standard expand/collapse buttons to be added. These buttons contain a + if the branch can be expanded at least one more level and a – if the branch is fully expanded. You may also click on these buttons to expand or collapse a branch. Typically, all three of these styles are included when a tree-view control is created. For example, the following creates a standard tree-view window.

```
hTreeWndCtrl = CreateWindow(
           WC_TREEVIEW,
           "",
           WS_VISIBLE | WS_TABSTOP | WS_CHILD |
```

```
                              TVS_HASLINES | TVS_HASBUTTONS |
                              TVS_LINESATROOT,
                              0, 0, 100, 100,
                              hwnd, // handle of parent
                              NULL,
                              hInst, // instance handle
                              NULL
              );
```

When the tree-view control is first created, it is empty. You must add each item in the tree, as described in the next section.

Sending Tree-View Messages

Tree-view controls respond to several messages. Several commonly used tree-view control messages are shown in Table 12-3. You can send messages using **SendMessage( )** or by using special macros created expressly for this purpose. Tree-view control macros corresponding to the messages in Table 12-3 are shown here. In all cases, *hTreeWnd* is the handle of the tree-view control.

BOOL TreeView_DeleteItem(HWND *hTreeWnd*, HTREEITEM *hItem*)

BOOL TreeView_Expand(HWND *hTreeWnd*, HTREEITEM *hItem*,
                     UINT *action*)

BOOL TreeView_GetItem(HWND *hTreeWnd*, TVITEM **lpItem*)

HTREEVIEW TreeView_InsertItem(HWND *hTreeWnd*,
                              TVINSERTSTRUCT **lpitem*)

BOOL TreeView_Select(HWND *hTreeWnd*, HTREEITEM *hItem*,
                     UINT *action*)

12

The only messages used by the example in this chapter are **TVM_INSERTITEM** and **TVM_EXPAND**, but your applications will probably use others.

Message	Meaning
TVM_DELETEITEM	Deletes an item from the tree list. Returns nonzero if successful and zero on failure. *wParam* is 0. *lParam* specifies the handle of the item to delete.
TVM_EXPAND	Expands or collapses the tree list one level. Returns nonzero if successful and zero on failure. *wParam* specifies the operation. It must be **TVE_COLLAPSE** (collapses tree), **TVE_COLLAPSERESET** (collapses tree and deletes child items), **TVE_EXPAND** (expands a tree), **TVE_EXPANDPARTIAL** (partially expands a tree), or **TVE_TOGGLE** (toggles state). **TVE_COLLAPSERESET** must be used in conjunction with **TVE_COLLAPSE**. **TVE_EXPANDPARTIAL** must be used with **TVE_EXPAND**. *lParam* specifies the handle of the parent of the branch.
TVM_GETITEM	Obtains an item's attributes. Returns nonzero if successful and zero on failure. *wParam* is 0. *lParam* specifies a pointer to a **TVITEM** structure that receives information about the item.
TVM_INSERTITEM	Inserts an item into the tree. Returns a handle to the item being inserted or **NULL** on failure. *wParam* is 0. *lParam* specifies a pointer to a **TVINSERTSTRUCT** that contains information about the item.
TVM_SELECTITEM	Selects a tree-view item. Returns nonzero if successful and zero on failure. *wParam* specifies the action. If it is **TVGN_CARET**, the item is selected. If it is **TVGN_DROPHILITE**, the item is highlighted for a drag-drop operation. If it is **TVGN_FIRSTVISIBLE**, the tree-view is scrolled so that the specified item is the first visible item. *lParam* specifies the handle of the item.

Commonly
Used
Tree-view
Control
Messages

Table 12-3.

When an item is inserted, the item's information is contained in a
TVINSERTSTRUCT structure, which is shown here:

```
typedef struct tagTVINSERTSTRUCT {
  HTREEITEM hParent;
  HTREEITEM hInsertAfter;
  union {
    TVITEMEX item;
    TVITEM item;
  }
} TVINSERTSTRUCT;
```

Here, **hParent** is the handle to the parent of the item. If the item has no
parent, then this field should contain **TVI_ROOT**. The value in
hInsertAfter determines how the new item will be inserted into the tree. If
it contains the handle of an item, the new item will be inserted after that
item. Otherwise, **hInsertAfter** can be one of the following values:

TVI_FIRST	Insert at beginning of list.
TVI_LAST	Insert at end of list.
TVI_ROOT	Insert at root.
TVI_SORT	Insert in alphabetical order.

The contents of **item** describe the item. This field must be either a **TVITEM**
or a **TVITEMEX** structure. **TVITEMEX** is an expanded version of **TVITEM**
that provides some special capabilities not required by the examples in this
chapter. **TVITEM** is shown here.

```
typedef struct tagTVITEM {
  UINT mask;
  HTREEITEM hItem;
  UINT state;
  UINT stateMask;
  LPSTR pszText;
  int cchTextMax;
  int iImage;
  int iSelectedImage;
  int cChildren;
  LPARAM lParam;
} TVITEM;
```

12

Here, the values in **mask** determine which of the other members of **TVITEM** contain valid data when this structure receives information from the tree-view control. The values that it may contain are shown here:

Value in Mask	Meaning
TVIF_HANDLE	**hItem** contains data.
TVIF_STATE	**state** and **stateMask** contain data.
TVIF_TEXT	**pszText** and **cchTextMax** contain data.
TVIF_IMAGE	**iImage** contains data.
TVIF_SELECTEDIMAGE	**iSelectedImage** contains data.
TVIF_CHILDREN	**cChildren** contains data.
TVIF_PARAM	**lParam** contains data.

The **hItem** field contains the handle of the item.

The **state** member contains the state of the tree-view control. Here are some common tree state values:

State	Meaning
TVIS_DROPHILITED	Item is highlighted as the target of drag/drop operation.
TVIS_EXPANDED	Branch descending from item is fully expanded. (Applies to parent items only.)
TVIS_EXPANDEDONCE	Branch descending from item is expanded one (or more) levels. (Applies to parent items only.)
TVIS_EXPANDPARTIAL	Branch descending from item is partially expanded.
TVIS_SELECTED	Item is selected.

The **stateMask** determines which tab state to set or obtain. It will also be one or more of the preceding values.

When an item is being inserted into the tree, **pszText** points to the string that will be displayed in the tree. When information about an item is being obtained, **pszText** must point to an array that will receive its text. In this case, the value of **cchTextMax** specifies the size of the array pointed to by **pszText**. Otherwise, **cchTextMax** is ignored.

If there is an image list associated with the tree-view control, then **iImage** will contain the index of the image associated with the item when it is not selected. **iImageSelected** contains the index of the image used by the item when it is selected. (We won't be using images in the tree-view created in this chapter.)

cChildren will contain 1 if the item has child items and zero if it does not.

lParam contains application-defined data.

Tree-View Notification Messages

When a tree-view control is accessed, it generates a **WM_NOTIFY** message. There are several notification messages associated with tree-view controls. Some commonly used ones are shown here:

Notification Message	Meaning
TVN_DELETEITEM	An item has been deleted.
TVN_ITEMEXPANDING	A branch is about to expand or collapse.
TVN_ITEMEXPANDED	A branch has expanded or collapsed.
TVN_SELCHANGING	A new item is about to be selected.
TVN_SELCHANGED	A new item has been selected.

For these notification messages, when the **WM_NOTIFY** message is received, *lParam* will point to a **NMTREEVIEW** structure. The **NMTREEVIEW** structure is shown here:

```
typedef struct tagNMTREEVIEW {
  NMHDR hdr;
  UINT action;
  TVITEM itemOld;
  TVITEM itemNew;
  POINT ptDrag;
} NMTREEVIEW;
```

12

The first field in **NMTREEVIEW** is the standard **NMHDR** structure. The notification code will be contained in the **hdr.code**. The handle of the tree control that generates the message is found in the **hdr.hwndFrom** field.

The **action** field contains notification-specific information. The structures **itemOld** and **itemNew** contain information about the previously selected item (if applicable) and the newly selected item (again, if applicable). The location of the mouse at the time the message was generated is contained in **ptDrag**.

For **TVN_SELCHANGING** and **TVN_SELCHANGED**, **itemOld** describes the previously selected item and **itemNew** describes the newly selected item. For **TVN_ITEMEXPANDING** and **TVN_ITEMEXPANDED**, **itemNew** describes the item that is the parent of the branch that is expanding. For **TVN_DELETEITEM**, **itemOld** describes the item that was deleted.

HISTORICAL PERSPECTIVE: The structures associated with a tree-view control have undergone a name change. Table 12-4 lists the old and new names of the tree-view structures used in this chapter. At the time of this writing, the old names are still valid. However, you should use the new names for new programs or when updating old ones.

A Tree-View Demonstration Program

The following program demonstrates a tree-view control. The program builds a simple tree and allows you to expand a branch, expand the entire tree, or collapse a branch. Each time a new tree-view item is chosen, the selection is displayed in the program's window. Sample output from the program is shown in Figure 12-4.

Old and New Names of Tree-view Structures

Table 12-4.

Old Name	New Name
TV_ITEM	TVITEM
TV_INSERTSTRUCT	TVINSERTSTRUCT
NM_TREEVIEW	NMTREEVIEW
NM_DISPINFO	NMTVDISPINFO

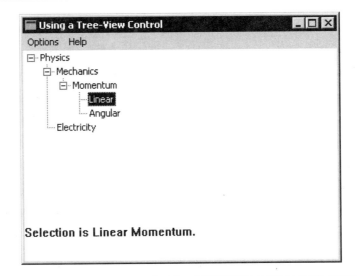

Sample output
from the
tree-view
control
program
Figure 12-4.

```
// Demonstrate a tree-view control.

#include <windows.h>
#include <commctrl.h>
#include "tree.h"

#define NUM 6

LRESULT CALLBACK WindowFunc(HWND, UINT, WPARAM, LPARAM);
BOOL CALLBACK DialogFunc(HWND, UINT, WPARAM, LPARAM);
void InitTree(void);
void report(HDC hdc, char *s);

char szWinName[] = "MyWin"; // name of window class

HINSTANCE hInst;
HWND hwnd;
HWND hTreeWndCtrl;
HTREEITEM hTreeWnd[NUM];
HTREEITEM hTreeCurrent;

int WINAPI WinMain(HINSTANCE hThisInst, HINSTANCE hPrevInst,
                   LPSTR lpszArgs, int nWinMode)
{
```

12

```
   MSG msg;
   WNDCLASSEX wcl;
   HACCEL hAccel;
   INITCOMMONCONTROLSEX cc;

   // Define a window class.
   wcl.cbSize = sizeof(WNDCLASSEX);

   wcl.hInstance = hThisInst;       // handle to this instance
   wcl.lpszClassName = szWinName;   // window class name
   wcl.lpfnWndProc = WindowFunc;    // window function
   wcl.style = 0;                   // default style

   wcl.hIcon = LoadIcon(NULL, IDI_APPLICATION); // large icon
   wcl.hIconSm = NULL; // use small version of large icon
   wcl.hCursor = LoadCursor(NULL, IDC_ARROW);   // cursor style

   wcl.lpszMenuName = "TreeViewMenu"; // menu

   wcl.cbClsExtra = 0; // no extra memory needed
   wcl.cbWndExtra = 0;

   // Make the window background white.
   wcl.hbrBackground = (HBRUSH) GetStockObject(WHITE_BRUSH);

   // Register the window class.
   if(!RegisterClassEx(&wcl)) return 0;

   /* Now that a window class has been registered, a window
      can be created. */
   hwnd = CreateWindow(
     szWinName, // name of window class
     "Using a Tree-View Control", // title
     WS_OVERLAPPEDWINDOW, // window style - normal
     CW_USEDEFAULT, // X coordinate - let Windows decide
     CW_USEDEFAULT, // Y coordinate - let Windows decide
     CW_USEDEFAULT, // width - let Windows decide
     CW_USEDEFAULT, // height - let Windows decide
     NULL,          // no parent window
     NULL,          // no menu
     hThisInst,     // instance handle
     NULL           // no additional arguments
   );

   hInst = hThisInst; // save the current instance handle
```

```
      // Load the keyboard accelerators.
      hAccel = LoadAccelerators(hThisInst, "TreeViewMenu");

      // Initialize the common controls.
      cc.dwSize = sizeof(INITCOMMONCONTROLSEX);
      cc.dwICC = ICC_TREEVIEW_CLASSES;
      InitCommonControlsEx(&cc);

      // Display the window.
      ShowWindow(hwnd, nWinMode);
      UpdateWindow(hwnd);

      // Create the message loop.
      while(GetMessage(&msg, NULL, 0, 0))
      {
        if(!TranslateAccelerator(hwnd, hAccel, &msg)) {
          TranslateMessage(&msg); // translate keyboard messages
          DispatchMessage(&msg); // return control to Windows 2000
        }
      }

      return msg.wParam;
}

/* This function is called by Windows 2000 and is passed
   messages from the message queue.
*/
LRESULT CALLBACK WindowFunc(HWND hwnd, UINT message,
                             WPARAM wParam, LPARAM lParam)
{
  HDC hdc;
  static char selection[80] = "";
  NMTREEVIEW *nmptr;
  PAINTSTRUCT paintstruct;
  int i, response;
  RECT WinDim;

  switch(message) {
    case WM_CREATE:
      // get size of parent window
      GetClientRect(hwnd, &WinDim);

      // create a tree-view control
      hTreeWndCtrl = CreateWindow(
                    WC_TREEVIEW,
```

. **12**

```
                              "",
                              WS_VISIBLE | WS_TABSTOP | WS_CHILD |
                              TVS_HASLINES | TVS_HASBUTTONS |
                              TVS_LINESATROOT,
                              0, 0, 200, 200,
                              hwnd,
                              NULL,
                              hInst,
                              NULL
                         );

    InitTree();
    break;
  case WM_COMMAND:
    switch(LOWORD(wParam)) {
      case IDM_EXPAND:
        TreeView_Expand(hTreeWndCtrl, hTreeCurrent,
                        TVE_EXPAND);
        break;
      case IDM_EXPANDALL:
        for(i=0; i<NUM; i++)
          TreeView_Expand(hTreeWndCtrl, hTreeWnd[i],
                          TVE_EXPAND);
        break;
      case IDM_COLLAPSE:
        TreeView_Expand(hTreeWndCtrl, hTreeCurrent,
                        TVE_COLLAPSE);
        break;
      case IDM_EXIT:
        response = MessageBox(hwnd, "Quit the Program?",
                             "Exit", MB_YESNO);
        if(response == IDYES) PostQuitMessage(0);
        break;
      case IDM_HELP:
        MessageBox(hwnd, "Try the Tree View",
                   "Help", MB_OK);
        break;
    }
    break;
  case WM_NOTIFY:
    nmptr = (LPNMTREEVIEW) lParam;
    if(nmptr->hdr.code == TVN_SELCHANGED) {
      InvalidateRect(hwnd, NULL, 1);
      if(nmptr->itemNew.hItem == hTreeWnd[0])
        strcpy(selection, "Physics.");
```

```
            else if(nmptr->itemNew.hItem == hTreeWnd[1])
              strcpy(selection, "Mechanics.");
            else if(nmptr->itemNew.hItem == hTreeWnd[2])
              strcpy(selection, "Electricity.");
            else if(nmptr->itemNew.hItem == hTreeWnd[3])
              strcpy(selection, "Momentum.");
            else if(nmptr->itemNew.hItem == hTreeWnd[4])
              strcpy(selection, "Linear Momentum.");
            else if(nmptr->itemNew.hItem == hTreeWnd[5])
              strcpy(selection, "Angular Momentum.");

            hTreeCurrent = nmptr->itemNew.hItem;
          }
          break;
        case WM_PAINT:
          hdc = BeginPaint(hwnd, &paintstruct);
          report(hdc, selection);
          EndPaint(hwnd, &paintstruct);
          break;
        case WM_DESTROY: // terminate the program
          PostQuitMessage(0);
          break;
        default:
          /* Let Windows 2000 process any messages not specified in
             the preceding switch statement. */
          return DefWindowProc(hwnd, message, wParam, lParam);
      }
      return 0;
}

// Report Selection
void report(HDC hdc, char *s)
{
  char str[80];

  if(*s) {
    strcpy(str, "Selection is ");
    strcat(str, s);
  }
  else strcpy(str, "No selection has been made.");
  TextOut(hdc, 0, 200, str, strlen(str));
}

// Initialize the tree list.
void InitTree(void)
```

12

```
{
  TVINSERTSTRUCT tvs;
  TVITEM tvi;

  tvs.hInsertAfter = TVI_LAST; // make tree in order given
  tvi.mask = TVIF_TEXT;

  tvi.pszText = "Physics";
  tvs.hParent = TVI_ROOT;
  tvs.item = tvi;
  hTreeWnd[0] = TreeView_InsertItem(hTreeWndCtrl, &tvs);
  hTreeCurrent = hTreeWnd[0];

  tvi.pszText = "Mechanics";
  tvs.hParent = hTreeWnd[0];
  tvs.item = tvi;
  hTreeWnd[1] = TreeView_InsertItem(hTreeWndCtrl, &tvs);

  tvi.pszText = "Electricity";
  tvs.item = tvi;
  tvs.hParent = hTreeWnd[0];
  hTreeWnd[2] = TreeView_InsertItem(hTreeWndCtrl, &tvs);

  tvi.pszText = "Momentum";
  tvs.item = tvi;
  tvs.hParent = hTreeWnd[1];
  hTreeWnd[3] = TreeView_InsertItem(hTreeWndCtrl, &tvs);

  tvi.pszText = "Linear";
  tvs.item = tvi;
  tvs.hParent = hTreeWnd[3];
  hTreeWnd[4] = TreeView_InsertItem(hTreeWndCtrl, &tvs);

  tvi.pszText = "Angular";
  tvs.item = tvi;
  tvs.hParent = hTreeWnd[3];
  hTreeWnd[5] = TreeView_InsertItem(hTreeWndCtrl, &tvs);
}
```

The program requires the following resource file:

```
#include <windows.h>
#include "tree.h"

TreeViewMenu MENU
```

```
{
  POPUP "&Options" {
    MENUITEM "&Expand One\tF2", IDM_EXPAND
    MENUITEM "Expand &All\tF3", IDM_EXPANDALL
    MENUITEM "&Collapse\tF4", IDM_COLLAPSE
    MENUITEM "E&xit\tCtrl+X", IDM_EXIT
  }
  MENUITEM "&Help", IDM_HELP
}

TreeViewMenu ACCELERATORS
{
  VK_F1, IDM_HELP, VIRTKEY
  VK_F2, IDM_EXPAND, VIRTKEY
  VK_F3, IDM_EXPANDALL, VIRTKEY
  VK_F4, IDM_COLLAPSE, VIRTKEY
  "^X", IDM_EXIT
}
```

The TREE.H header file is shown here:

```
#define IDM_EXPAND     100
#define IDM_EXPANDALL  101
#define IDM_COLLAPSE   102
#define IDM_EXIT       103
#define IDM_HELP       104
```

In the program, the function **InitTree( )** initializes the tree-view control. Notice that the handle of each item is stored in the **hTreeWnd** array. These handles are used to identify items when they are selected in the tree list. The **hTreeCurrent** identifies the currently selected item. This handle is used when the user expands or collapses a branch using the menu.

Inside **WindowFunc( )**, each time a new item is selected, a **WM_NOTIFY** message is received and processed. The value of **itemNew** is checked against the list of item handles stored in the **hTreeWnd** array. When the matching handle is found, the new selection is reported.

12

While this example illustrates the essential aspects of tree-view controls, it just scratches the surface of their power. For example, using a tree-view, you can drag and drop an item from one tree to another. You will want to explore this feature and others on your own.

Editing Tree-View Labels

It is possible to create a tree-view that allows the user to modify the labels in the tree. To do so, you must include the **TVS_EDITLABELS** style when you create a tree-view control. You must also handle these two notification messages: **TVN_BEGINLABELEDIT** and **TVN_ENDLABELEDIT**. (Remember, notification messages are sent via the **WM_NOTIFY** message.) For both messages, *lParam* points to a **NMTVDISPINFO** structure, shown here:

```
typedef struct tagNMTVDISPINFO {
  NMHDR hdr;
  TVITEM item;
} NMTVDISPINFO;
```

When the user begins editing a label, your program will receive a **TVN_BEGINLABELEDIT** notification message. To allow the user to edit the label, your program must return zero. To disallow editing, return nonzero.

When the user finishes editing, your program receives a **TVN_ENDLABELEDIT** notification message. If the editing was cancelled by the user, then the **pszText** field of **item** will be **NULL**. Otherwise, it will point to the new label. If editing was cancelled, your program should return zero, causing the original label to remain. Otherwise, return nonzero to cause the new label to be used.

To experiment with editing tree-view labels, add the **TVS_EDITLABELS** style to the tree-view control created in the example program and then substitute the following **WM_NOTIFY** case into **WindowFunc( )**.

```
case WM_NOTIFY:
  nmptr = (LPNMTREEVIEW) lParam;
  switch(nmptr->hdr.code) {
    case TVN_BEGINLABELEDIT:
      return 0;
    case TVN_ENDLABELEDIT:
      if(((NMTVDISPINFO *) nmptr)->item.pszText)
        return 1; // label was edited
      else
        return 0; // user cancelled
  }
  break;
```

After making these changes, you can alter the contents of a tree-view label.

CHAPTER 13

Property Sheets
and Wizards

425

This chapter describes how to create one of Windows' most exciting controls: the *wizard*. As you probably know, a wizard is a sequenced set of dialog boxes that guide the user through a complex group of selections. The dialog boxes that constitute the wizard must be accessed in the order in which they are presented by the wizard. Wizards are used frequently in Windows 2000. For example, when you install a new printer, the printer installation wizard is activated.

As you will soon see, wizards are built upon another common control element: the *property sheet*. A property sheet is typically used to view and set various properties associated with some item. Although they look like the tab control described in the preceding chapter, property sheets are much more powerful.

Since property sheets underpin wizards, we will begin there.

Property Sheet Basics

A property sheet provides a convenient way of managing the properties associated with some item.

Property sheets allow the user to examine or alter various properties associated with some item. For example, a property sheet is typically used to set printer options or a modem configuration. From the user's perspective, a property sheet consists of one or more *pages*. Each page has a tab associated with it. A page is activated by selecting its tab. A sample property sheet is shown in Figure 13-1.

From the programmer's perspective, a property sheet is a collection of one or more modeless dialog boxes. That is, each page in a property sheet is defined by a dialog box template, and interaction with the page is handled by a dialog function. Most commonly, each dialog box template is specified in your application's resource file.

All property sheets contain two buttons: OK and Cancel. Usually a third button called Apply is also included. It is also possible to include a Help button. It is important to understand that although the dialog functions associated with each page provide the mechanism by which the user sets or views the properties, only the property sheet control itself can accept or cancel the user's changes. Put differently, no page dialog function should include an OK or Cancel button. These two operations are provided by the property sheet control.

The dialog boxes that constitute the property sheet are enclosed within the property sheet control. The property sheet control manages interaction with and between the individual pages. As a general rule, each dialog box function responds to its own controls in the normal fashion. That is, the individual controls that make up each page are handled in the standard way by the

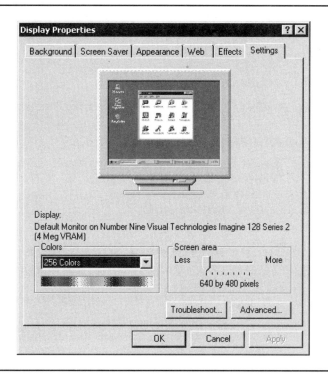

A sample
property sheet
Figure 13-1.

page's dialog box function. However, each page must also respond to messages generated by the enclosing property sheet. When the property sheet needs to communicate with a page, it does so by sending it a **WM_NOTIFY** message. Each page in a property sheet must be able to respond to this message. (The details of this process are discussed shortly.)

There is one very important requirement that you must follow when creating a property sheet: The modeless dialog box function associated with each page must *not* close its dialog box. That is, it must not call **DestroyWindow( )**. Instead, the enclosing property sheet control will take care of this. (If you do close one of the page dialog boxes, that dialog box will then be empty. This condition is a violation of Windows 2000 style rules, to say the least!)

REMEMBER: Since a property sheet is a common control, you must include the header file COMMCTRL.H in your program and link in COMCTL32.LIB.

13

Creating a Property Sheet

There are four basic steps required to create a property sheet:

1. Store information about each page in the control in a
   PROPSHEETPAGE structure.
2. Create each page by calling **CreatePropertySheetPage( )**.
3. Store information about the property sheet itself in a
   PROPSHEETHEADER structure.
4. Create and display the property sheet control by calling
   PropertySheet( ).

Let's look at each step, now.

Defining a Property Sheet Page

Each page in a property sheet must be defined in a **PROPSHEETPAGE**
structure. **PROPSHEETPAGE** is defined like this:

```
typedef struct _PROPSHEETPAGE {
  DWORD dwSize;
  DWORD dwFlags;
  HINSTANCE hInstance;
  union {
    LPCSTR pszTemplate;
    LPCDLGTEMPLATE pResource;
  };
  union {
    HICON hIcon;
    LPCSTR pszIcon;
  };
  LPCSTR pszTitle;
  DLGPROC pfnDlgProc;
  LPARAM lParam;
  LPFNPSPCALLBACK pfnCallback;
  UINT FAR *pcRefParent;
  LPCSTR pszHeaderTitle;
  LPCSTR pszHeaderSubTitle;
} PROPSHEETPAGE;
```

Here, **dwSize** must contain the size, in bytes, of the **PROPSHEETPAGE**
structure.

The value of **dwFlags** determines which of the remaining members contain valid information. It must be a combination of one or more of the flags shown in Table 13-1. The flags can be combined by ORing them together.

hInstance specifies the instance handle of the application. **pszTemplate** specifies the name or ID of the dialog box template associated with this page. However, if the **PSP_DLGINDIRECT** flag is included, then **pszTemplate** is ignored and the dialog box described by **pResource** is used.

If you wish to include a small icon in the tab associated with a page, it must be specified in either the **hIcon** or the **pszIcon** member. You must also

Flag	Meaning
PSP_DEFAULT	Uses defaults.
PSP_DLGINDIRECT	Uses **pResource**, not **pszTemplate**.
PSP_HASHELP	Displays Help button.
PSP_HIDEHEADER	The wizard header is not displayed. (Applies to wizards only.)
PSP_PREMATURE	Creates page when property sheet control is created. Normally, the page is not created until it is first activated.
PSP_RTLREADING	Displays text right to left. (Provides support for Hebrew or Arabic.)
PSP_USECALLBACK	Enables **pfnCallback.**
PSP_USEHEADERTITLE	Enables **pszHeaderTitle.** (Applies to wizards only.)
PSP_USEHEADERSUBTITLE	Enables **pszHeaderSubTitle.** (Applies to wizards only.)
PSP_USEHICON	Enables **hIcon**.
PSP_USEICONID	Enables **pszIcon**.
PSP_USEREFPARENT	Enables reference counting.
PSP_USETITLE	Uses title specified by **pszTitle** rather than the one defined by the page's dialog box template.

The Valid Values for the **dwFlags** Member of **PROPSHEET-PAGE** Table 13-1.

13

include the appropriate flag. **hIcon** specifies an icon handle. **pszIcon** specifies the name or ID of the icon as specified in a resource file.

Normally, the title of the dialog box associated with a page becomes the title of the page. This title is displayed in the tab associated with the page. However, you can specify a different title by storing a pointer to the new title in **pszTitle.** Of course, you must also include the **PSP_USETITLE** flag.

The address of the modeless dialog box function that is associated with the page must be stored in **pfnDlgProc**.

lParam is used for application-specific data.

When **pfnCallback** is enabled, it specifies a callback function that is called whenever the page is created or destroyed. This function is not needed by the examples in this chapter. However, if your application requires this function, it must have the following prototype:

UINT CALLBACK PropPageFunc(HWND *hwnd*, UINT *message*,
  LPPROPSHEETPAGE *lpPropSheet*);

When called, *hwnd* will be **NULL**. The value of *message* will be either **PSPCB_ADDREF** (page is being created), **PSPCB_CREATE** (page is being created), or **PSPCB_RELEASE** (page is being released). *lpPropSheet* points to the **PROPSHEETPAGE** structure of the page being affected. If *message* is **PSPCB_CREATE,** then the function must return nonzero to enable page creation or zero to cancel the creation of the page. If *message* is **PSPCB_ADDREF** or **PSPCB_RELEASE**, the return value is not used.

pcRefParent specifies the address of a reference count variable. This member is active only if **PSP_USEREFPARENT** is specified.

The **pszHeaderTitle** and **pszHeaderSubTitle** fields apply only to wizards. They contain pointers to the strings used as the title and subtitle. These are displayed in the header area of a wizard. They are ignored unless **dwFlags** includes **PSP_USEHEADERTITLE** or **PSP_USEHEADERSUBTITLE**, respectively.

 HISTORICAL PERSPECTIVE: The original versions of **PROPSHEETPAGE** did not include the fields **pszHeaderTitle** or **pszHeaderSubTitle** or their associated flags.

Initializing Each Page

After you have loaded a **PROPSHEETPAGE** structure with the necessary information, you must create the page by calling **CreatePropertySheetPage( )**. Its prototype is shown here.

```
HPROPSHEETPAGE CreatePropertySheetPage(
                            LPCPPROPSHEETPAGE lpPage);
```

Here, *lpPage* is a pointer to a **PROPSHEETPAGE** structure. The function returns a handle to the newly created page. You will usually want to store this handle because it is needed for some property sheet operations. The function returns **NULL** if the page cannot be created.

Initializing the PROPSHEETHEADER structure

After you have created each page, you must initialize the **PROPSHEETHEADER** structure associated with the property sheet. This structure is defined like this:

```
typedef struct _PROPSHEETHEADER {
  DWORD dwSize;
  DWORD dwFlags;
  HWND  hwndParent;
  HINSTANCE hInstance;
  union {
    HICON hIcon;
    LPCSTR pszIcon;
  };
  LPCSTR pszCaption;
  UINT nPages;
  union {
    UINT nStartPage;
    LPCSTR pStartPage;
  };
  union {
    LPCPROPSHEETPAGE ppsp;
    HPROPSHEETPAGE FAR *phpage;
  };
  PFNPROPSHEETCALLBACK pfnCallback;
  union {
    HBITMAP hbmWatermark;
    LPCSTR pszbmWatermark;
  }
```

13

```
  HPALETTE hplWatermark;
  union {
    HBITMAP hbmHeader;
    LPCSTR pszbmHeader;
  }
} PROPSHEETHEADER;
```

Here, **dwSize** must contain the size, in bytes, of the **PROPSHEETHEADER** structure.

The value of **dwFlags** determines which of the remaining members contain valid information. It must be a combination of one or more of the flags shown in Table 13-2. The flags can be combined by ORing them together.

Flag	Meaning
PSH_DEFAULT	Uses defaults.
PSH_HASHELP	Enables Help button.
PSH_HEADER	Displays a header bitmap. (Applies to wizards only.)
PSH_MODELESS	Creates a modeless property sheet control. By default, property sheet controls are modal.
PSH_NOAPPLYNOW	Suppresses the Apply button.
PSH_NOCONTEXTHELP	Suppresses the context-help "?" (for property sheets only).
PSH_PROPSHEETPAGE	Enables the **ppsp** member and disables **phpage**.
PSH_PROPTITLE	Appends the word "Properties" to the title specified by **pszCaption**.
PSH_RTLREADING	Displays text right to left. (Provides support for Hebrew or Arabic.)
PSH_USECALLBACK	Enables **pfnCallback**.
PSH_USEHBMHEADER	Enables **hbmHeader**; otherwise, **pszbmHeader** is used. (Applies to wizards only.)

Flag	Meaning
PSH_USEHBMWATERMARK	Enables **hbmWaterMark**; otherwise **pszbmWatermark** is used. (Applies to wizards only.)
PSH_USEHICON	Enables **hIcon**.
PSH_USEICONID	Enables **pszIcon**.
PSH_USEHPLWATERMARK	Enables **hplWatermark**. (Applies to wizards only.)
PSH_USEPAGELANG	The language is determined by page zero.
PSH_USEPSTARTPAGE	Enables **pStartPage** and disables **nStartPage**.
PSH_WATERMARK	Includes a watermark. (Applies to wizards only.)
PSH_WIZARD	Creates a wizard.
PSH_WIZARD97	Creates a wizard that can include a header title and subtitle, watermark, and header bitmap. This is the type of wizard used by Windows 2000.
PSH_WIZARDCONTEXTHELP	Wizard supports context help. (Applies to wizards only.)
PSH_WIZARDHASFINISH	Includes Finish button on all wizard pages. (Applies to wizards only.)
PSH_WIZARD_LITE	A simplified wizard that is similar to those created by PSH_WIZARD97.

The Valid Values for the **dwFlags** Member of **PROPSHEET-HEADER** *(continued)* **Table 13-2.**

hwndParent specifies the handle of the parent window, which is usually the window that activates the property sheet. **hInstance** specifies the instance handle of the application.

If you wish to include a small icon in the title bar of the property sheet, it must be specified in either the **hIcon** or the **pszIcon** member. You must also include the appropriate flag. **hIcon** specifies an icon handle. **pszIcon** specifies the name or ID of the icon as specified in a resource file.

The title of the property sheet control window is pointed to by **pszCaption**. The number of pages in the property sheet is specified by **nPages**.

13

The index of the first page displayed when the property sheet control is activated is specified by either **nStartPage** or **pStartPage**. By default, **nStartPage** is used. **nStartPage** specifies the index of the first page. All page indexes begin at zero. If you include the flag **PSH_USEPSTARTPAGE**, you must specify the name or the ID of the page in **pStartPage**.

phpage must contain a pointer to an array of property sheet page handles. These handles are created by calling **CreatePropertySheetPage( )**, described earlier. However, if you specify the **PSH_PROPSHEETPAGE** flag, you can instead specify the address of an array of **PROPSHEETPAGE** structures in the **ppsp** member. In this case, the handles will be created automatically and there is no need to call **CreatePropertySheetPage( )**. However, since the page handles are useful for some other operations, you will usually want to create them explicitly.

When **pfnCallback** is enabled, it specifies a callback function that is called whenever the property sheet is created. Although not used by the examples in this chapter, such a function may need to be created by your applications. If so, it must have the following prototype:

int CALLBACK PropSheetFunc(HWND *hdwnd*, UINT *message*,
                 LPARAM *lParam*);

When called, *hdwnd* will contain the handle of the property sheet control. The value of *message* will be either **PSCB_INITIALIZED**, which means that the property sheet is being initialized, or **PSCB_PRECREATE**, which means that the property sheet is about to be initialized. For **PSCB_INITIALIZED**, *lParam* will be zero. For **PSCB_PRECREATE**, *lParam* points to the dialog box template, and *hdwnd* is **NULL**. In either case, the function must return zero.

Wizards can specify a watermark and a header bitmap. The watermark is a bitmap that is displayed on the left side of a page, and the header bitmap is displayed on the right side of a wizard header. For these items to appear, their respective flags must be set and the **PSH_WIZARD97** flag must be included. Since **PSH_WIZARD97** is the style recommended for use with Windows 2000, these elements are present in all Windows 2000-style wizards.

hbmWatermark specifies the handle of the bitmap to be used as a watermark. Alternatively, you can specify the name of this bitmap using **pszbmWatermark**. Normally, the default palette is used to draw the watermark, but you can specify the handle to a palette in the **hplWatermark** field. In each case the appropriate flags must be set.

The handle to the bitmap used for a header is passed in **hbmHeader**. Alternatively, you can specify the resource name of the header in **pszbmHeader**. Of course, the appropriate flags must be set.

HISTORICAL PERSPECTIVE: The original versions of **PROPSHEETHEADER** did not include the fields **hbmWatermark**, **pszbmWatermark**, **hplWatermark**, **bhmHeader**, or **pszbmHeader**. Also, the flags that enable or affect these fields were not defined.

Creating the Property Sheet Control

After the property sheet pages have been defined and the **PROPSHEETHEADER** structure has been initialized, the property sheet control can be created. This is done by calling **PropertySheet( )**, whose prototype is shown here:

    int PropertySheet(LPCPPROPSHEETHEADER *lpHeader*);

Here, *lpHeader* is a pointer to the property sheet header structure. The function returns −1 if an error occurs or a positive value if successful. When creating a modeless property sheet control (that is, one in which you have included the **PSH_MODELESS** flag), then a handle to the property sheet is returned.

Processing Property Sheet Messages

As mentioned, a property sheet control sends messages to the page dialog box functions using the **WM_NOTIFY** message. For most notifications, the value of **lParam** is a pointer to a **PSHNOTIFY** structure, which is defined like this:

```
typedef struct _PSHNOTIFY {
  NMHDR hdr;
  LPARAM lParam;
} PSHNOTIFY;
```

The first member is the standard **NMHDR** structure that described the notification message. Recall that the **NMHDR** structure is defined like this:

13

```
typedef struct tagNMHDR
{
  HWND hwndFrom;
  UINT idFrom;
  UINT code;
} NMHDR;
```

For **WM_NOTIFY** messages associated with property sheets, **hwndFrom** is the handle of the property sheet control. The value of **code** contains the *notification code*, which describes what action has taken place.

The **lParam** field of **PSHNOTIFY** is not used by all messages. When used, it contains additional information associated with the message. We won't need to use the value in **lParam** for the example in this chapter. The information in **hdr** is sufficient.

The property sheet control uses the notification messages to inform individual dialog boxes about various events. For example, notification messages are sent when a page is selected, when the user presses one of the property sheet buttons, or when the page is being deselected. The notification code specifies the precise nature of the event. Commonly used notification codes are shown in Table 13-3.

In some cases, your dialog box function must respond to a notification message by returning a value to the property sheet control. To accomplish this you will need to use the **SetWindowLong( )** function. This function sets various attributes associated with a window. The prototype for **SetWindowLong( )** is shown here:

LONG SetWindowLong(HANDLE *hwnd*, int *index*, LONG *value*);

Here, *hwnd* is the handle of the dialog box; *index* specifies the attribute to set. To return a value to a property sheet, the value of *index* will be **DWL_MSGRESULT**. The value to return is passed in *value*. Remember, your dialog box function must still return true if it processes a message or false if it does not. The return value specified using **SetWindowLong( )** specifies the outcome of a **WM_NOTIFY** message only.

Sending Messages to the Property Sheet

In addition to receiving messages, your application can send messages to the property sheet control. This can be accomplished using the **SendMessage( )** function, specifying the handle of the property sheet control as the recipient

Notification Code	Meaning	Expected Return Value
PSN_APPLY	Sent when user presses the Apply or OK button.	**PSNRET_NOERROR** (zero) to apply changes. **PSNRET_INVALID_NO-CHANGEPAGE** to prevent changes.
PSN_HELP	Sent when user presses the Help button.	None.
PSN_KILLACTIVE	Sent when a page is losing focus or the OK button has been pressed.	Zero to allow deactivation. Nonzero to prevent deactivation.
PSN_QUERYCANCEL	Sent when user presses Cancel button.	Zero to allow cancellation. Nonzero to prevent cancellation.
PSN_RESET	Sent when user presses Cancel button.	None.
PSN_SETACTIVE	Sent when page gains focus (that is, when activated).	Zero to allow activation. Otherwise, return the ID of page to activate.
PSN_WIZBACK	Sent when user presses the Back button (wizards only).	Zero to activate previous page. −1 to prevent activation of previous page, or the ID of the page to activate.
PSN_WIZFINISH	Sent when user presses the Finish button (wizards only).	Zero to terminate wizard; nonzero otherwise.
PSN_WIZNEXT	Sent when user presses the Next button (wizards only).	Zero to activate next page. −1 to prevent activation of next page, or the ID of the page to activate.

Common Property Sheet Notification Codes
Table 13-3.

13

of the message. All property sheet messages begin with the prefix **PSM_**. Some of the most common ones are shown in Table 13-4.

Message Macro	Meaning
PSM_APPLY	Sends **PSN_APPLY** message. *lParam* is zero. *wParam* is zero. Returns nonzero if successful and zero on failure.
PSM_CHANGED	Enables Apply button. *lParam* is zero. *wParam* contains the handle of page dialog box. No return value.
PSM_SETCURSEL	Changes page. *lParam* contains the handle of the new page. *wParam* contains the index of new page. Returns nonzero if successful and zero on failure.
PSM_SETWIZBUTTONS	Enables wizard buttons (Applies only to wizards.) *lParam* must contain one or more of the following flags: **PSWIZB_BACK**, **PSWIZB_NEXT**, **PSWIZB_FINISH**, or **PSWIZB_DISABLEDFINISH**. *wParam* is zero. No return value.
PSM_UNCHANGED	Disables Apply button. *lParam* is zero. *wParam* contains the handle of page dialog box. No return value.

Common
Property Sheet
Messages
Table 13-4.

Windows also provides a set of macros to facilitate the sending of property sheet messages. The macros for the messages in Table 13-4 are shown here.

BOOL PropSheet_Apply(*hPropSheet*);

BOOL PropSheet_Changed(*hPropSheet*, *hPageDialog*);

BOOL PropSheet_SetCurSel(*hPropSheet*, *hPage*, *Index*);

VOID PropSheet_SetWizButtons(*hPropSheet*, *Flags*);

VOID PropSheet_Unchanged(*hPropSheet*, *hPageDialog*);

Here, *hPropSheet* is the handle of the property sheet control being sent the message. *hPageDialog* is the handle of the page dialog function sending the

Your application
should send a
PSM_CHANGED
message
whenever a
property
changes.

message. *Index* is the zero-based index of the next page to select. *hPage*
specifies the handle of a page. *Flags* specify which wizard buttons
will be enabled. Remember that the **PropSheet_SetWizButtons( )**
macro applies only to wizards and is discussed in detail later in
this chapter.

The **PSM_CHANGED** message is particularly important because it enables
the Apply button. Your application should send this message whenever the
user changes anything within a property sheet.

Property Sheet Dialog Dimensions

It is best
to use
standard
size property
sheets.

The dialog box that underlies a property sheet can be of any size. However, it
is recommended that your property sheets be of one of the standard sizes
defined by Microsoft. The standard sizes are shown here:

Size	Width	Height
Small	PROP_SM_CXDLG	PROP_SM_CYDLG
Medium	PROP_MED_CXDLG	PROP_MED_CYDLG
Large	PROP_LG_CXDLG	PROP_LG_CYDLG

These macros are defined by including COMMCTRL.H. They are specified in
terms of dialog box units and should be used in the DIALOG descriptions
within your application's resource file.

A Property Sheet Demonstration Program

The following program displays a property sheet that contains three pages.
Although the property sheet does not actually set any real properties, it does
demonstrate the necessary procedures to create and display a property sheet.
Sample output is shown in Figure 13-2.

13

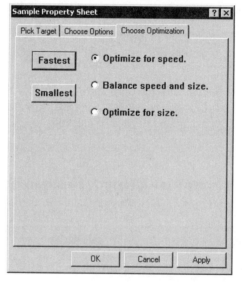

Sample output
from the
property sheet
demonstration
program

Figure 13-2.

```
// Demonstrate a Property Sheet

#include <windows.h>
#include <cstdio>
#include <commctrl.h>
#include "prop.h"

#define NUMSTRINGS 5
#define NUMPAGES 3

LRESULT CALLBACK WindowFunc(HWND, UINT, WPARAM, LPARAM);
BOOL CALLBACK DialogFunc1(HWND, UINT, WPARAM, LPARAM);
BOOL CALLBACK DialogFunc2(HWND, UINT, WPARAM, LPARAM);
BOOL CALLBACK DialogFunc3(HWND, UINT, WPARAM, LPARAM);

char szWinName[] = "MyWin"; // name of window class

HINSTANCE hInst;

HWND hDlg; // dialog box handle
HPROPSHEETPAGE hPs[NUMPAGES];
HWND hPropSheet;
HWND hPage[NUMPAGES];

char list[][40] = {
  "Windows 2000",
  "Windows NT 4",
  "Windows 98",
  "Windows 95",
  "Windows 3.1"
};

int cb1=0, cb2=0, cb3=0;
int rb1=1, rb2=0, rb3=0;
int lb1sel=0;

int WINAPI WinMain(HINSTANCE hThisInst, HINSTANCE hPrevInst,
                   LPSTR lpszArgs, int nWinMode)
{
  HWND hwnd;
  MSG msg;
  WNDCLASSEX wcl;
```

```
HACCEL hAccel;
INITCOMMONCONTROLSEX cc;

// Define a window class.
wcl.cbSize = sizeof(WNDCLASSEX);

wcl.hInstance = hThisInst;      // handle to this instance
wcl.lpszClassName = szWinName;  // window class name
wcl.lpfnWndProc = WindowFunc;   // window function
wcl.style = 0;                  // default style

wcl.hIcon = LoadIcon(NULL, IDI_APPLICATION); // large icon
wcl.hIconSm = NULL; // use small version of large icon
wcl.hCursor = LoadCursor(NULL, IDC_ARROW);   // cursor style

wcl.lpszMenuName = "PropSheetMenu"; // main menu

wcl.cbClsExtra = 0; // no extra memory needed
wcl.cbWndExtra = 0;

// Make the window background white.
wcl.hbrBackground = (HBRUSH) GetStockObject(WHITE_BRUSH);

// Register the window class.
if(!RegisterClassEx(&wcl)) return 0;

/* Now that a window class has been registered, a window
   can be created. */
hwnd = CreateWindow(
  szWinName, // name of window class
  "Demonstrate a Property Sheet", // title
  WS_OVERLAPPEDWINDOW, // window style - normal
  CW_USEDEFAULT, // X coordinate - let Windows decide
  CW_USEDEFAULT, // Y coordinate - let Windows decide
  CW_USEDEFAULT, // width - let Windows decide
  CW_USEDEFAULT, // height - let Windows decide
  NULL,          // no parent window
  NULL,          // no menu
  hThisInst,     // instance handle
  NULL           // no additional arguments
);

hInst = hThisInst; // save the current instance handle
```

```
  // Load the keyboard accelerators.
  hAccel = LoadAccelerators(hThisInst, "PropSheetMenu");

  // Initialize the common controls.
  cc.dwSize = sizeof(INITCOMMONCONTROLSEX);
  cc.dwICC = ICC_TAB_CLASSES;
  InitCommonControlsEx(&cc);

  // Display the window.
  ShowWindow(hwnd, nWinMode);
  UpdateWindow(hwnd);

  // Create the message loop.
  while(GetMessage(&msg, NULL, 0, 0))
  {
    if(!TranslateAccelerator(hwnd, hAccel, &msg)) {
      TranslateMessage(&msg); // translate keyboard messages
      DispatchMessage(&msg); // return control to Windows 2000
    }
  }

  return msg.wParam;
}

/* This function is called by Windows 2000 and is passed
   messages from the message queue.
*/
LRESULT CALLBACK WindowFunc(HWND hwnd, UINT message,
                            WPARAM wParam, LPARAM lParam)
{
  int response;
  PROPSHEETPAGE PropSheet[NUMPAGES];
  PROPSHEETHEADER PropHdr;

  switch(message) {
    case WM_COMMAND:
      switch(LOWORD(wParam)) {
        case IDM_DIALOG:
          PropSheet[0].dwSize = sizeof(PROPSHEETPAGE);
          PropSheet[0].dwFlags = PSP_DEFAULT;
          PropSheet[0].hInstance = hInst;
          PropSheet[0].pszTemplate = "PropSheetDB1";
          PropSheet[0].pszIcon = NULL;
```

13

```
      PropSheet[0].pfnDlgProc = (DLGPROC) DialogFunc1;
      PropSheet[0].pszTitle = "";
      PropSheet[0].lParam = 0;
      PropSheet[0].pfnCallback = NULL;

      PropSheet[1].dwSize = sizeof(PROPSHEETPAGE);
      PropSheet[1].dwFlags = PSP_DEFAULT;
      PropSheet[1].hInstance = hInst;
      PropSheet[1].pszTemplate = "PropSheetDB2";
      PropSheet[1].pszIcon = NULL;
      PropSheet[1].pfnDlgProc = (DLGPROC) DialogFunc2;
      PropSheet[1].pszTitle = "";
      PropSheet[1].lParam = 0;
      PropSheet[1].pfnCallback = NULL;

      PropSheet[2].dwSize = sizeof(PROPSHEETPAGE);
      PropSheet[2].dwFlags = PSP_DEFAULT;
      PropSheet[2].hInstance = hInst;
      PropSheet[2].pszTemplate = "PropSheetDB3";
      PropSheet[2].pszIcon = NULL;
      PropSheet[2].pfnDlgProc = (DLGPROC) DialogFunc3;
      PropSheet[2].pszTitle = "";
      PropSheet[2].lParam = 0;
      PropSheet[2].pfnCallback = NULL;

      hPs[0] = CreatePropertySheetPage(&PropSheet[0]);
      hPs[1] = CreatePropertySheetPage(&PropSheet[1]);
      hPs[2] = CreatePropertySheetPage(&PropSheet[2]);

      PropHdr.dwSize = sizeof(PROPSHEETHEADER);
      PropHdr.dwFlags = PSH_DEFAULT;
      PropHdr.hwndParent = hwnd;
      PropHdr.hInstance = hInst;
      PropHdr.pszIcon = NULL;
      PropHdr.pszCaption = "Sample Property Sheet";
      PropHdr.nPages = NUMPAGES;
      PropHdr.nStartPage = 0;
      PropHdr.phpage = hPs;
      PropHdr.pfnCallback = NULL;

      PropertySheet(&PropHdr);
      break;
    case IDM_EXIT:
      response = MessageBox(hwnd, "Quit the Program?",
                            "Exit", MB_YESNO);
```

```
         if(response == IDYES) PostQuitMessage(0);
         break;
       case IDM_HELP:
         MessageBox(hwnd, "Try the Property Sheet", "Help", MB_OK);
         break;
     }
     break;
   case WM_DESTROY: // terminate the program
     PostQuitMessage(0);
     break;
   default:
     /* Let Windows 2000 process any messages not specified in
        the preceding switch statement. */
     return DefWindowProc(hwnd, message, wParam, lParam);
 }

 return 0;
}

// The first dialog function.
BOOL CALLBACK DialogFunc1(HWND hdwnd, UINT message,
                          WPARAM wParam, LPARAM lParam)
{
  static long index;
  int i;
  char str[80];

  switch(message) {
    case WM_NOTIFY:
      switch(((NMHDR *) lParam)->code) {
        case PSN_SETACTIVE: // page gaining focus
          hPropSheet = ((NMHDR *) lParam)->hwndFrom;
          SetWindowLong(hdwnd, DWL_MSGRESULT, 0);
          index = lb1sel;
          return 1;
        case PSN_KILLACTIVE: // page losing focus
          lb1sel = index;
          SetWindowLong(hdwnd, DWL_MSGRESULT, 0);
          return 1;
      }
      break;
    case WM_COMMAND:
      switch(LOWORD(wParam)) {
        case IDD_OPTIONS:
          PropSheet_SetCurSel(hPropSheet, hPs[1], 1);
```

13

```
        return 1;
      case IDD_OPTIMIZE:
        PropSheet_SetCurSel(hPropSheet, hPs[2], 2);
        return 1;
      case IDD_LB1: // process a list box LBN_DBLCLK
        PropSheet_Changed(hPropSheet, hdwnd);
        // see if user made a selection
        if(HIWORD(wParam)==LBN_DBLCLK) {
          index = SendDlgItemMessage(hdwnd, IDD_LB1,
                  LB_GETCURSEL, 0, 0);  // get index
          sprintf(str, "%s", list[index]);

          MessageBox(hdwnd, str, "Selection Made", MB_OK);
        }
        return 1;
    }
    break;
  case WM_INITDIALOG: // initialize list box
    for(i=0; i<NUMSTRINGS; i++)
      SendDlgItemMessage(hdwnd, IDD_LB1,
                LB_ADDSTRING, 0, (LPARAM)list[i]);

    // select first item
    SendDlgItemMessage(hdwnd, IDD_LB1, LB_SETCURSEL, lb1sel, 0);

    return 1;
  }

  return 0;
}

// The Second dialog function.
BOOL CALLBACK DialogFunc2(HWND hdwnd, UINT message,
                          WPARAM wParam, LPARAM lParam)
{
  switch(message) {
    case WM_NOTIFY:
      switch(((NMHDR *) lParam)->code) {
        case PSN_SETACTIVE:// page gaining focus
          hPropSheet = ((NMHDR *) lParam)->hwndFrom;
          SetWindowLong(hdwnd, DWL_MSGRESULT, 0);
          return 1;
        case PSN_KILLACTIVE: // page losing focus
          cb1 = SendDlgItemMessage(hdwnd, IDD_CB1,
                          BM_GETCHECK, 0, 0);
```

```
            cb2 = SendDlgItemMessage(hdwnd, IDD_CB2,
                            BM_GETCHECK, 0, 0);
            cb3 = SendDlgItemMessage(hdwnd, IDD_CB3,
                            BM_GETCHECK, 0, 0);
            SetWindowLong(hdwnd, DWL_MSGRESULT, 0);
            return 1;
        }
      break;
    case WM_COMMAND:
      switch(LOWORD(wParam)) {
        case IDD_CB1:
        case IDD_CB2:
        case IDD_CB3:
          PropSheet_Changed(hPropSheet, hdwnd);
          return 1;
        case IDD_ALL:
          PropSheet_Changed(hPropSheet, hdwnd);
          SendDlgItemMessage(hdwnd, IDD_CB1, BM_SETCHECK,
                            BST_CHECKED, 0);
          SendDlgItemMessage(hdwnd, IDD_CB2, BM_SETCHECK,
                            BST_CHECKED, 0);
          SendDlgItemMessage(hdwnd, IDD_CB3, BM_SETCHECK,
                            BST_CHECKED, 0);
          return 1;
        }
      break;
    case WM_INITDIALOG: // initialize check boxes
      SendDlgItemMessage(hdwnd, IDD_CB1, BM_SETCHECK, cb1, 0);
      SendDlgItemMessage(hdwnd, IDD_CB2, BM_SETCHECK, cb2, 0);
      SendDlgItemMessage(hdwnd, IDD_CB3, BM_SETCHECK, cb3, 0);
      return 1;
  }

  return 0;
}

// The Third dialog function.
BOOL CALLBACK DialogFunc3(HWND hdwnd, UINT message,
                          WPARAM wParam, LPARAM lParam)
{
  switch(message) {
    case WM_NOTIFY:
      switch(((NMHDR *) lParam)->code) {
        case PSN_SETACTIVE: // page gaining focus
          hPropSheet = ((NMHDR *) lParam)->hwndFrom;
```

13

```
          SetWindowLong(hdwnd, DWL_MSGRESULT, 0);
          return 1;
       case PSN_KILLACTIVE: // page losing focus
          rb1 = SendDlgItemMessage(hdwnd, IDD_RB1,
                         BM_GETCHECK, 0, 0);
          rb2 = SendDlgItemMessage(hdwnd, IDD_RB2,
                         BM_GETCHECK, 0, 0);
          rb3 = SendDlgItemMessage(hdwnd, IDD_RB3,
                         BM_GETCHECK, 0, 0);
          SetWindowLong(hdwnd, DWL_MSGRESULT, 0);
          return 1;
     }
     break;
   case WM_COMMAND:
     switch(LOWORD(wParam)) {
       case IDD_RB1:
       case IDD_RB2:
       case IDD_RB3:
         PropSheet_Changed(hPropSheet, hdwnd);
         return 1;
       case IDD_FASTEST:
         PropSheet_Changed(hPropSheet, hdwnd);
         SendDlgItemMessage(hdwnd, IDD_RB2, BM_SETCHECK, 0, 0);
         SendDlgItemMessage(hdwnd, IDD_RB3, BM_SETCHECK, 0, 0);
         SendDlgItemMessage(hdwnd, IDD_RB1, BM_SETCHECK, 1, 0);
         return 1;
       case IDD_SMALLEST:
         PropSheet_Changed(hPropSheet, hdwnd);
         SendDlgItemMessage(hdwnd, IDD_RB1, BM_SETCHECK, 0, 0);
         SendDlgItemMessage(hdwnd, IDD_RB2, BM_SETCHECK, 0, 0);
         SendDlgItemMessage(hdwnd, IDD_RB3, BM_SETCHECK, 1, 0);
         return 1;
     }
     break;
   case WM_INITDIALOG: // initialize radio buttons
     SendDlgItemMessage(hdwnd, IDD_RB1, BM_SETCHECK, rb1, 0);
     SendDlgItemMessage(hdwnd, IDD_RB2, BM_SETCHECK, rb2, 0);
     SendDlgItemMessage(hdwnd, IDD_RB3, BM_SETCHECK, rb3, 0);
     return 1;
  }

  return 0;
}
```

The program requires the following resource file:

```
// Property sheet dialog boxes.
#include <windows.h>
#include <commctrl.h>
#include "prop.h"

PropSheetMenu MENU
{
  POPUP "&Property Sheet"
  {
    MENUITEM "&Activate\tF2", IDM_DIALOG
    MENUITEM "E&xit\tCtrl+X", IDM_EXIT
  }
  MENUITEM "&Help", IDM_HELP
}

PropSheetMenu ACCELERATORS
{
  VK_F2, IDM_DIALOG, VIRTKEY
  VK_F1, IDM_HELP, VIRTKEY
  "^X", IDM_EXIT
}

PropSheetDB1 DIALOGEX 0, 0, PROP_SM_CXDLG, PROP_SM_CYDLG
CAPTION "Pick Target"
{
  PUSHBUTTON "Options", IDD_OPTIONS, 11, 24, 34, 14
  PUSHBUTTON "Optimize", IDD_OPTIMIZE, 11, 48, 34, 14
  CTEXT "Target OS", 1, 66, 14, 60, 14
  LISTBOX IDD_LB1, 66, 30, 60, 44, LBS_NOTIFY |
            WS_BORDER | WS_VSCROLL | WS_TABSTOP
}

PropSheetDB2 DIALOGEX 0, 0, PROP_SM_CXDLG, PROP_SM_CYDLG
CAPTION "Choose Options"
{
  DEFPUSHBUTTON "All", IDD_ALL, 11, 10, 34, 14
  AUTOCHECKBOX "Check for stack overflows.", IDD_CB1,
            56, 10, 92, 10
  AUTOCHECKBOX "Check array boundaries.", IDD_CB2,
            56, 30, 90, 10
```

13

```
      AUTOCHECKBOX "Prevent assignment to null.", IDD_CB3,
                56, 50, 100, 10
}

PropSheetDB3 DIALOGEX 0, 0, PROP_SM_CXDLG, PROP_SM_CYDLG
CAPTION "Choose Optimization"
{
  DEFPUSHBUTTON "Fastest", IDD_FASTEST, 11, 10, 34, 14
  PUSHBUTTON "Smallest", IDD_SMALLEST, 11, 34, 34, 14
  AUTORADIOBUTTON "Optimize for speed.", IDD_RB1,
                56, 10, 90, 10
  AUTORADIOBUTTON "Balance speed and size.", IDD_RB2,
                56, 30, 90, 10
  AUTORADIOBUTTON "Optimize for size.", IDD_RB3,
                56, 50, 90, 10
}
```

The header file PROP.H is shown here:

```
#define IDM_DIALOG    100
#define IDM_EXIT      101
#define IDM_HELP      102

#define IDD_OPTIONS   201
#define IDD_OPTIMIZE  202
#define IDD_FASTEST   204
#define IDD_SMALLEST  205
#define IDD_ALL       207

#define IDD_LB1       301

#define IDD_EB1       401

#define IDD_CB1       501
#define IDD_CB2       502
#define IDD_CB3       503

#define IDD_RB1       601
#define IDD_RB2       602
#define IDD_RB3       603

#define IDD_STEXT1    700
```

In all three page dialog boxes there is one important thing to notice: each time one is changed by the user, a **PSM_CHANGED** message is sent. For example, when the user alters the state of a check box in the Options dialog box, **PropSheet_Changed( )** is called. Once a **PSM_CHANGED** message has been sent, the Apply button will change from inactive to active. In general, you must notify the property sheet control whenever a property changes.

On the first page of the property sheet, the push buttons Options and Optimize demonstrate how pages can be selected under program control. That is, pressing Options selects the second page and pressing Optimize selects the third page. While there is no need for these push buttons in this example (since you can simply click on a page's tab to select it) these buttons illustrate the **PSM_SETCURSEL** message.

While the dialog boxes in this example are only placeholders, they demonstrate the effect of using a property sheet. For example, if the user presses OK or moves to another page, then a **PSN_KILLACTIVE** message is received and any changes made by the user are saved. However, if the user presses Cancel, any changes made to the current page are ignored. As the program is written, pressing Cancel does not undo any changes made to other pages. You might want to try adding this feature on your own. You should also try handling the **PSN_APPLY** message.

IN DEPTH

Responding to PSN_HELP

If you include the **PSP_HASHELP** flag when you create a property sheet page, then the Help button will be included in the property sheet control whenever that page is active. Pressing this button causes the **PSN_HELP** notification message to be sent. For most applications you will want to activate the Windows help system, which is described in Chapter 16, to provide online help relating to the property sheet control. However, the Windows help system is as complex as it is sophisticated. Fortunately, for very limited property sheets, you can respond to a **PSN_HELP** message by simply displaying a message box.

To experiment with the Help button, try adding it to the property sheet example. First, add **PSH_HASHELP** to the **PropHdr** structure as shown here:

```
PropHdr.dwFlags = PSH_DEFAULT | PSH_HASHELP;
```

13

Next, add **PSP_HASHELP** to each property sheet page. For example, here it is added to the first page:

```
PropSheet[0].dwFlags = PSP_DEFAULT | PSP_HASHELP;
```

Finally, add a handler for **PSN_HELP** to each property page dialog box function under the **WM_NOTIFY** case. For example, here is the handler for the first dialog box:

```
case PSN_HELP:
  MessageBox(hdwnd,
        "Pick Target allows you to choose\n"
        "the target operating system.",
        "Target", MB_OK);
  return 1;
```

Here is the way the Pick Target page looks with the addition of the Help button:

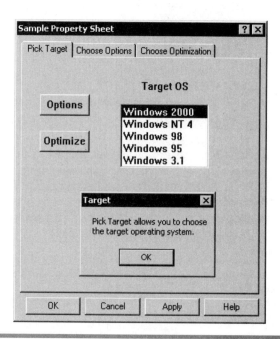

Creating a Wizard

From the programmer's point of view, a wizard is simply a set of sequenced property sheets. It is defined using the **PROPSHEETPAGE** and **PROPSHEETHEADER** structures and created using the **CreatePropertySheetPage( )** and **PropertySheet( )** functions discussed earlier. To create a wizard, you must specify one of the following flags in the **dwFlags** field of the **PROPSHEETHEADER** structure.

PSH_WIZARD97	Creates new-style wizard
PSH_WIZARD	Creates old-style wizard
PSH_WIZARD_LITE	Creates a simplified wizard

When one of these styles is included, the dialog boxes will automatically be sequenced from first to last, forming a wizard. The type of wizard used by Windows 2000 is based on the Wizard 97 specification from Microsoft and is created by including the **PSH_WIZARD97** style. This is the only type of wizard examined in this chapter.

The Wizard 97 Specification

When wizards were first created several years ago there was no clear, coherent specification for how wizards should look or how their various elements should be arranged. To remedy this, Microsoft created the Wizard 97 specification, which among other things dictates the size and placement of various items, states how the first and last page of the wizard should look, and defines a title and subtitle for each page. While not complicated, the Wizard 97 specification contains many details, and a full discussion is beyond the scope of this chapter. However, in the sections that follow the main constraints to which a wizard must adhere are described.

As mentioned, Windows 2000 uses Wizard 97-style wizards, and applications designed for use with Windows 2000 should do the same. Wizard 97-style wizards are also compatible with any system that is running Internet Explorer 5 or later. If you want to create a wizard that is backward compatible with older systems, refer to my earlier programming books, such as *Windows NT 4 Programming From the Ground Up* or *Windows 98 Programming From the Ground Up*.

Exterior and Interior Pages

Windows 2000-style wizards contain two types of pages: interior and exterior. The exterior pages begin and end the wizard. Thus, they frame the interior

13

The Welcome
and Completion
pages of
a wizard
are called
exterior pages.

pages. There are two exterior pages: Welcome and Completion. The Welcome
page identifies the wizard. The Completion page signals the end of the
wizard. An example of a Welcome page is shown in Figure 13-3.

The interior pages contain the dialog boxes that perform the "work" of the
wizard. They also contain a header title, subtitle, and bitmap. An example of
an interior page is shown in Figure 13-4.

The interior
pages provide the
functionality of
the wizard.

The Organization of Exterior Pages

Exterior pages typically contain no controls. They are used to display text
that either identifies the wizard or signals its end. The Welcome page should
contain a large, bold title that begins with "Welcome to the". For example, if
you are creating a wizard that configures an industrial robot, then your title
might read "Welcome to the Robot Configuration Wizard." According to the
Wizard 97 specification, the title should be in the Verdana bold font and 12
points high. However, the 12 points refers to dialog units and this value will
need to be converted to pixels. (You will see how to do this in the program

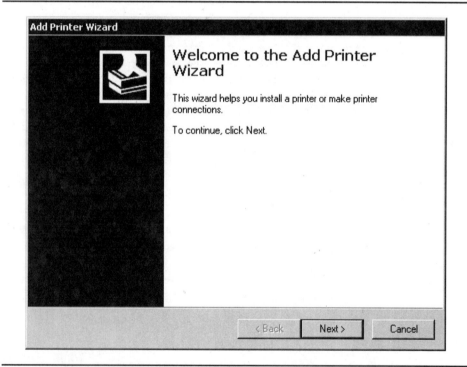

The Welcome
page from
the Windows
2000 Printer
wizard

Figure 13-3.

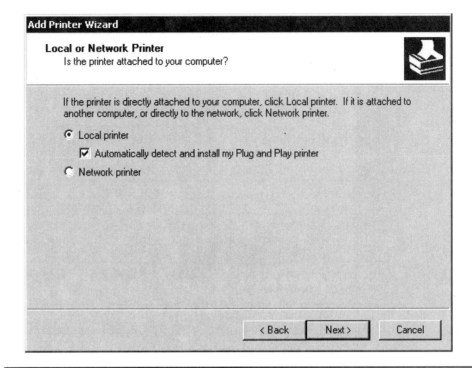

An interior
page from
the Windows
2000 Printer
wizard

Figure 13-4.

that follows.) The title should start at location 115, 8 (in dialog units). Starting at 115 leaves room for the watermark.

After any other remarks that you want to put on the Welcome page, you should conclude with a phrase similar to "To continue, click Next." This and any other text should be in the "MS Shell Dlg" font and be 8 points high. To specify this font, include the following statement as part of the DIALOGEX statement.

```
FONT 8, "MS Shell Dlg"
```

All additional text should begin at location 115, 40 (in dialog units).

The dimensions of the underlying dialog boxes that support the Welcome and Completion pages must be 317 × 193.

The Organization of Interior Pages

Interior pages have a header area that contains a title, subtitle, and bitmap. These are supplied automatically when the **PSH_WIZARD97** style is used.

13

The dimensions of the underlying dialog boxes that are used in interior pages must be 317 ×143. It is here that you can position your controls. For most purposes, interior pages leave a boundary of 1 dialog unit at the top and 21 dialog units on the sides. If you need the extra horizontal space, then you reduce the horizontal border to 7.

The title and subtitle for each interior page is specified in the **pszHeaderTitle** and **pszHeaderSubTitle** of the **PROPSHEETPAGE** structure. To enable these fields, you must include the **PSP_USEHEADERTITLE** and **PSP_USEHEADERSUBTITLE** style flags.

The Watermark and Header Bitmaps

Wizards specify a large bitmap on the left side of the Welcome and Completion pages. It is not used on interior pages. This bitmap serves to identify the wizard. While not technically required, the bitmap is highly recommended since it is mandated by the Wizard 97 specification. This bitmap must be 164 x 314 pixels in size. The watermark bitmap is specified in the **pszbmWatermark** field of the **PROPSHEETHEADER** structure. To try the example that follows, you will need to create a watermark bitmap, storing it in a file called BP1.BMP.

The header bitmap is shown in the header of interior pages. This bitmap is a 49 x 49 pixels square. Again, while not technically required, it should be included because it is part of the Wizard 97 specification. The header bitmap is specified in the **pszbmHeader** field of the **PROPSHEETHEADER** structure. For the example that follows, you will need to create a header bitmap, storing it in a file called BP2.BMP.

Enabling Wizard Buttons

Although including **PSH_WIZARD97** automatically transforms your property sheet into a wizard, there are a few more steps that you will need to take in order for your wizard to perform correctly. First, you will need to enable and disable certain buttons manually. For example, on the Welcome page, you will need to enable the Next button, but disable the Back button. On the Completion page, you will need to enable the Back button and the Finish button. On the interior pages, the Next and Back buttons will have to be enabled. To accomplish this, either send a **PSM_SETWIZBUTTONS** message or use the **PropSheet_SetWizButtons( )** macro. As shown earlier, **PropSheet_SetWizButtons( )** has this general form:

VOID PropSheet_SetWizButtons(*hPropSheet, Flags*);

Here, *hPropSheet* is the handle of the property sheet control. In the *Flags* parameter, specify the button or buttons that you want to enable. Only those buttons that you specify will be enabled. The others will be disabled. The button macros are shown here:

PSWIZB_BACK	PSWIZB_NEXT
PSWIZB_FINISH	PSWIZB_DISABLEDFINISH

PSWIZB_DISABLEDFINISH creates a disabled Finish button. You might pass this value when the user has failed to enter some piece of necessary information. You can OR together two or more buttons. Therefore, to enable the Back and Finish buttons, you would use this statement:

```
PropSheet_SetWizButtons(PSWIZB_BACK | PSWIZB_FINISH);
```

A Wizard Demonstration Program

The following program demonstrates a wizard. It does so by converting the previous property sheet example into a wizard. Sample output is shown in Figure 13-5.

Sample output from the wizard program

Figure 13-5.

13

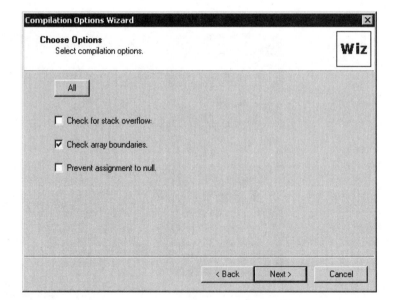

Sample output
from the
wizard
program
(continued)

Figure 13-5.

Sample output
from the
wizard
program
(continued)

Figure 13-5.

13

```
// Demonstrate a Wizard

#include <windows.h>
#include <cstring>
#include <cstdio>
#include <commctrl.h>
#include "wiz.h"

#define NUMSTRINGS 5
#define NUMPAGES 5

LRESULT CALLBACK WindowFunc(HWND, UINT, WPARAM, LPARAM);
BOOL CALLBACK DialogFunc0(HWND, UINT, WPARAM, LPARAM);
BOOL CALLBACK DialogFunc1(HWND, UINT, WPARAM, LPARAM);
BOOL CALLBACK DialogFunc2(HWND, UINT, WPARAM, LPARAM);
BOOL CALLBACK DialogFuncWel(HWND, UINT, WPARAM, LPARAM);
BOOL CALLBACK DialogFuncComp(HWND, UINT, WPARAM, LPARAM);

char szWinName[] = "MyWin"; // name of window class

HINSTANCE hInst;

HWND hDlg; // dialog box handle
HPROPSHEETPAGE hPs[NUMPAGES];
HWND hPropSheet;
HWND hPage[NUMPAGES];

char list[][40] = {
  "Windows 2000",
  "Windows NT 4",
  "Windows 98",
  "Windows 95",
  "Windows 3.1"
};

int cb1=0, cb2=0, cb3=0;
int rb1=1, rb2=0, rb3=0;
int lb1sel=0;

int WINAPI WinMain(HINSTANCE hThisInst, HINSTANCE hPrevInst,
                   LPSTR lpszArgs, int nWinMode)
```

```
{
  HWND hwnd;
  MSG msg;
  WNDCLASSEX wcl;
  HACCEL hAccel;
  INITCOMMONCONTROLSEX cc;

  // Define a window class.
  wcl.cbSize = sizeof(WNDCLASSEX);

  wcl.hInstance = hThisInst;      // handle to this instance
  wcl.lpszClassName = szWinName; // window class name
  wcl.lpfnWndProc = WindowFunc;  // window function
  wcl.style = 0;                  // default style

  wcl.hIcon = LoadIcon(NULL, IDI_APPLICATION); // large icon
  wcl.hIconSm = NULL; // use small version of large icon
  wcl.hCursor = LoadCursor(NULL, IDC_ARROW);  // cursor style

  wcl.lpszMenuName = "PropSheetMenu"; // main menu

  wcl.cbClsExtra = 0; // no extra memory needed
  wcl.cbWndExtra = 0;

  // Make the window background white.
  wcl.hbrBackground = (HBRUSH) GetStockObject(WHITE_BRUSH);

  // Register the window class.
  if(!RegisterClassEx(&wcl)) return 0;

  /* Now that a window class has been registered, a window
     can be created. */
  hwnd = CreateWindow(
    szWinName, // name of window class
    "Demonstrate a Wizard", // title
    WS_OVERLAPPEDWINDOW, // window style - normal
    CW_USEDEFAULT, // X coordinate - let Windows decide
    CW_USEDEFAULT, // Y coordinate - let Windows decide
    CW_USEDEFAULT, // width - let Windows decide
    CW_USEDEFAULT, // height - let Windows decide
    NULL,           // no parent window
```

13

```
     NULL,             // no menu
     hThisInst,        // instance handle
     NULL              // no additional arguments
  );

  hInst = hThisInst; // save the current instance handle

  // Load the keyboard accelerators.
  hAccel = LoadAccelerators(hThisInst, "PropSheetMenu");

  // Initialize the common controls.
  cc.dwSize = sizeof(INITCOMMONCONTROLSEX);
  cc.dwICC = ICC_TAB_CLASSES;
  InitCommonControlsEx(&cc);

  // Display the window.
  ShowWindow(hwnd, nWinMode);
  UpdateWindow(hwnd);

  // Create the message loop.
  while(GetMessage(&msg, NULL, 0, 0))
  {
    if(!TranslateAccelerator(hwnd, hAccel, &msg)) {
      TranslateMessage(&msg); // translate keyboard messages
      DispatchMessage(&msg); // return control to Windows 2000
    }
  }

  return msg.wParam;
}

/* This function is called by Windows 2000 and is passed
   messages from the message queue.
*/
LRESULT CALLBACK WindowFunc(HWND hwnd, UINT message,
                            WPARAM wParam, LPARAM lParam)
{
  int response;
  PROPSHEETPAGE PropSheet[NUMPAGES];
  PROPSHEETHEADER PropHdr;

  switch(message) {
    case WM_CREATE:
      break;
    case WM_COMMAND:
```

```
switch(LOWORD(wParam)) {
  case IDM_DIALOG:
    PropSheet[0].dwSize = sizeof(PROPSHEETPAGE);
    PropSheet[0].dwFlags = PSP_DEFAULT | PSP_HIDEHEADER;
    PropSheet[0].hInstance = hInst;
    PropSheet[0].pszTemplate = "WelcomeDB";
    PropSheet[0].pszIcon = NULL;
    PropSheet[0].pfnDlgProc = (DLGPROC) DialogFuncWel;
    PropSheet[0].pszTitle = "";
    PropSheet[0].lParam = 0;
    PropSheet[0].pfnCallback = NULL;

    PropSheet[1].dwSize = sizeof(PROPSHEETPAGE);
    PropSheet[1].dwFlags = PSP_DEFAULT |
                           PSP_USEHEADERTITLE |
                           PSP_USEHEADERSUBTITLE;
    PropSheet[1].hInstance = hInst;
    PropSheet[1].pszTemplate = "PropSheetDB1";
    PropSheet[1].pszIcon = NULL;
    PropSheet[1].pfnDlgProc = (DLGPROC) DialogFunc0;
    PropSheet[1].pszTitle = "";
    PropSheet[1].lParam = 0;
    PropSheet[1].pfnCallback = NULL;
    PropSheet[1].pszHeaderTitle = "Pick Target";
    PropSheet[1].pszHeaderSubTitle = "Choose a target operating system.";

    PropSheet[2].dwSize = sizeof(PROPSHEETPAGE);
    PropSheet[2].dwFlags = PSP_DEFAULT   |
                           PSP_USEHEADERTITLE |
                           PSP_USEHEADERSUBTITLE;;
    PropSheet[2].hInstance = hInst;
    PropSheet[2].pszTemplate = "PropSheetDB2";
    PropSheet[2].pszIcon = NULL;
    PropSheet[2].pfnDlgProc = (DLGPROC) DialogFunc1;
    PropSheet[2].pszTitle = "";
    PropSheet[2].lParam = 0;
    PropSheet[2].pfnCallback = NULL;
    PropSheet[2].pszHeaderTitle = "Choose Options";
    PropSheet[2].pszHeaderSubTitle = "Select compilation options.";

    PropSheet[3].dwSize = sizeof(PROPSHEETPAGE);
    PropSheet[3].dwFlags = PSP_DEFAULT   |
                           PSP_USEHEADERTITLE |
                           PSP_USEHEADERSUBTITLE;
    PropSheet[3].hInstance = hInst;
```

13

```
    PropSheet[3].pszTemplate = "PropSheetDB3";
    PropSheet[3].pszIcon = NULL;
    PropSheet[3].pfnDlgProc = (DLGPROC) DialogFunc2;
    PropSheet[3].pszTitle = "";
    PropSheet[3].lParam = 0;
    PropSheet[3].pfnCallback = NULL;
    PropSheet[3].pszHeaderTitle = "Choose Optimizations";
    PropSheet[3].pszHeaderSubTitle = "Determine how to optimize.";

    PropSheet[4].dwSize = sizeof(PROPSHEETPAGE);
    PropSheet[4].dwFlags = PSP_DEFAULT | PSP_HIDEHEADER;;
    PropSheet[4].hInstance = hInst;
    PropSheet[4].pszTemplate = "CompletionDB";
    PropSheet[4].pszIcon = NULL;
    PropSheet[4].pfnDlgProc = (DLGPROC) DialogFuncComp;
    PropSheet[4].pszTitle = "";
    PropSheet[4].lParam = 0;
    PropSheet[4].pfnCallback = NULL;

    hPs[0] = CreatePropertySheetPage(&PropSheet[0]);
    hPs[1] = CreatePropertySheetPage(&PropSheet[1]);
    hPs[2] = CreatePropertySheetPage(&PropSheet[2]);
    hPs[3] = CreatePropertySheetPage(&PropSheet[3]);
    hPs[4] = CreatePropertySheetPage(&PropSheet[4]);

    PropHdr.dwSize = sizeof(PROPSHEETHEADER);
    PropHdr.dwFlags = PSH_WIZARD97 | // specify wizard
                      PSH_HEADER |
                      PSH_WATERMARK;
    PropHdr.hwndParent = hwnd;
    PropHdr.hInstance = hInst;
    PropHdr.pszIcon = NULL;
    PropHdr.pszCaption = "";
    PropHdr.nPages = NUMPAGES;
    PropHdr.nStartPage = 0;
    PropHdr.phpage = hPs;
    PropHdr.pfnCallback = NULL;
    PropHdr.pszbmWatermark = "wizbmp1";
    PropHdr.pszbmHeader = "wizbmp2";

    PropertySheet(&PropHdr);
    break;
  case IDM_EXIT:
    response = MessageBox(hwnd, "Quit the Program?",
                          "Exit", MB_YESNO);
```

```
            if(response == IDYES) PostQuitMessage(0);
            break;
          case IDM_HELP:
            MessageBox(hwnd, "Try the Wizard", "Help", MB_OK);
            break;
        }
        break;
      case WM_DESTROY: // terminate the program
        PostQuitMessage(0);
        break;
      default:
        /* Let Windows 2000 process any messages not specified in
           the preceding switch statement. */
        return DefWindowProc(hwnd, message, wParam, lParam);
  }
  return 0;
}

// The first dialog function.
BOOL CALLBACK DialogFunc0(HWND hdwnd, UINT message,
                          WPARAM wParam, LPARAM lParam)
{
  static long index;
  int i;
  char str[80];

  switch(message) {
    case WM_NOTIFY:
      switch(((NMHDR *) lParam)->code) {
        case PSN_SETACTIVE: // page gaining focus
          hPropSheet = ((NMHDR *) lParam)->hwndFrom;
          index = lb1sel;
          PropSheet_SetWizButtons(hPropSheet, PSWIZB_NEXT | PSWIZB_BACK);
          SetWindowLong(hdwnd, DWL_MSGRESULT, 0);
          return 1;
        case PSN_KILLACTIVE: // page losing focus
          lb1sel = index;
          SetWindowLong(hdwnd, DWL_MSGRESULT, 0);
          return 1;
      }
      break;
    case WM_COMMAND:
      switch(LOWORD(wParam)) {
        case IDD_LB1: // process a list box LBN_DBLCLK
          PropSheet_Changed(hPropSheet, hdwnd);
```

13

```
      // see if user made a selection
      if(HIWORD(wParam)==LBN_DBLCLK) {
        index = SendDlgItemMessage(hdwnd, IDD_LB1,
               LB_GETCURSEL, 0, 0);  // get index
        sprintf(str, "%s", list[index]);

        MessageBox(hdwnd, str, "Selection Made", MB_OK);
      }
      return 1;
    }
    break;
  case WM_INITDIALOG: // initialize list box
    for(i=0; i<NUMSTRINGS; i++)
      SendDlgItemMessage(hdwnd, IDD_LB1,
               LB_ADDSTRING, 0, (LPARAM)list[i]);

    // select first item
    SendDlgItemMessage(hdwnd, IDD_LB1, LB_SETCURSEL, lb1sel, 0);

    return 1;
  }

  return 0;
}

// The Second dialog function.
BOOL CALLBACK DialogFunc1(HWND hdwnd, UINT message,
                       WPARAM wParam, LPARAM lParam)
{
  switch(message) {
    case WM_NOTIFY:
      switch(((NMHDR *) lParam)->code) {
        case PSN_SETACTIVE:// page gaining focus
          hPropSheet = ((NMHDR *) lParam)->hwndFrom;
          PropSheet_SetWizButtons(hPropSheet,
                       PSWIZB_NEXT | PSWIZB_BACK);
          SetWindowLong(hdwnd, DWL_MSGRESULT, 0);
          return 1;
        case PSN_KILLACTIVE: // page losing focus
          cb1 = SendDlgItemMessage(hdwnd, IDD_CB1,
                       BM_GETCHECK, 0, 0);
          cb2 = SendDlgItemMessage(hdwnd, IDD_CB2,
                        BM_GETCHECK, 0, 0);
          cb3 = SendDlgItemMessage(hdwnd, IDD_CB3,
                        BM_GETCHECK, 0, 0);
```

```
              SetWindowLong(hdwnd, DWL_MSGRESULT, 0);
            return 1;
          }
          break;
        case WM_COMMAND:
          switch(LOWORD(wParam)) {
            case IDD_CB1:
            case IDD_CB2:
            case IDD_CB3:
              PropSheet_Changed(hPropSheet, hdwnd);
              return 1;
            case IDD_ALL:
              PropSheet_Changed(hPropSheet, hdwnd);
              SendDlgItemMessage(hdwnd, IDD_CB1, BM_SETCHECK,
                                 BST_CHECKED, 0);
              SendDlgItemMessage(hdwnd, IDD_CB2, BM_SETCHECK,
                                 BST_CHECKED, 0);
              SendDlgItemMessage(hdwnd, IDD_CB3, BM_SETCHECK,
                                 BST_CHECKED, 0);
              return 1;
          }
          break;
        case WM_INITDIALOG: // initialize check boxes
          SendDlgItemMessage(hdwnd, IDD_CB1, BM_SETCHECK, cb1, 0);
          SendDlgItemMessage(hdwnd, IDD_CB2, BM_SETCHECK, cb2, 0);
          SendDlgItemMessage(hdwnd, IDD_CB3, BM_SETCHECK, cb3, 0);
          return 1;
      }

      return 0;
    }


    // The Third dialog function.
    BOOL CALLBACK DialogFunc2(HWND hdwnd, UINT message,
                              WPARAM wParam, LPARAM lParam)
    {
      switch(message) {
        case WM_NOTIFY:
          switch(((NMHDR *) lParam)->code) {
            case PSN_SETACTIVE: // page gaining focus
              hPropSheet = ((NMHDR *) lParam)->hwndFrom;
              PropSheet_SetWizButtons(hPropSheet,
                              PSWIZB_BACK | PSWIZB_NEXT);
              SetWindowLong(hdwnd, DWL_MSGRESULT, 0);
              return 1;
```

13

```
      case PSN_WIZFINISH: // Finish button pressed
      case PSN_KILLACTIVE: // page losing focus
        rb1 = SendDlgItemMessage(hdwnd, IDD_RB1,
                          BM_GETCHECK, 0, 0);
        rb2 = SendDlgItemMessage(hdwnd, IDD_RB2,
                          BM_GETCHECK, 0, 0);
        rb3 = SendDlgItemMessage(hdwnd, IDD_RB3,
                          BM_GETCHECK, 0, 0);
        SetWindowLong(hdwnd, DWL_MSGRESULT, 0);
        return 1;
    }
    break;
  case WM_COMMAND:
    switch(LOWORD(wParam)) {
      case IDD_RB1:
      case IDD_RB2:
      case IDD_RB3:
        PropSheet_Changed(hPropSheet, hdwnd);
        return 1;
      case IDD_FASTEST:
        PropSheet_Changed(hPropSheet, hdwnd);
        SendDlgItemMessage(hdwnd, IDD_RB2, BM_SETCHECK, 0, 0);
        SendDlgItemMessage(hdwnd, IDD_RB3, BM_SETCHECK, 0, 0);
        SendDlgItemMessage(hdwnd, IDD_RB1, BM_SETCHECK, 1, 0);
        return 1;
      case IDD_SMALLEST:
        PropSheet_Changed(hPropSheet, hdwnd);
        SendDlgItemMessage(hdwnd, IDD_RB1, BM_SETCHECK, 0, 0);
        SendDlgItemMessage(hdwnd, IDD_RB2, BM_SETCHECK, 0, 0);
        SendDlgItemMessage(hdwnd, IDD_RB3, BM_SETCHECK, 1, 0);
        return 1;
    }
    break;
  case WM_INITDIALOG: // initialize radio buttons
    SendDlgItemMessage(hdwnd, IDD_RB1, BM_SETCHECK, rb1, 0);
    SendDlgItemMessage(hdwnd, IDD_RB2, BM_SETCHECK, rb2, 0);
    SendDlgItemMessage(hdwnd, IDD_RB3, BM_SETCHECK, rb3, 0);
    return 1;
  }
  return 0;
}

// Welcome Dialog box.
BOOL CALLBACK DialogFuncWel(HWND hdwnd, UINT message,
                            WPARAM wParam, LPARAM lParam)
```

```
{
  PAINTSTRUCT ps;
  HDC dc;
  static HFONT hFontTitle;
  static char *welcomeStr = "Welcome to the Wizard";
  RECT r;

  switch(message) {
    case WM_PAINT:
      dc = BeginPaint(hdwnd, &ps);
      r.right = 115; r.bottom = 8;
      MapDialogRect(hdwnd, &r); // convert to pixels
      SelectObject(dc, hFontTitle); // select large font
      TextOut(dc, r.right, r.bottom, welcomeStr,
              strlen(welcomeStr));
      EndPaint(hdwnd, &ps);
      break;
    case WM_NOTIFY:
      switch(((NMHDR *) lParam)->code) {
        case PSN_SETACTIVE:// page gaining focus
          r.bottom = 12;
          MapDialogRect(hdwnd, &r); // convert to pixels
          // create wizard title font
          hFontTitle = CreateFont(r.bottom, 0, 0, 0, FW_MEDIUM,
                          0, 0, 0, ANSI_CHARSET,
                          OUT_DEFAULT_PRECIS,
                          CLIP_DEFAULT_PRECIS,
                          DEFAULT_QUALITY,
                          DEFAULT_PITCH | FF_DONTCARE,
                          "Verdana");

          hPropSheet = ((NMHDR *) lParam)->hwndFrom;
          PropSheet_SetWizButtons(hPropSheet,
                          PSWIZB_NEXT);
          SetWindowLong(hdwnd, DWL_MSGRESULT, 0);
          return 1;
        case PSN_KILLACTIVE: // page losing focus
          SetWindowLong(hdwnd, DWL_MSGRESULT, 0);
          DeleteObject(hFontTitle);
          return 1;
      }
      break;
  }

  return 0;
```

13

```
}

// Completion Dialog box.
BOOL CALLBACK DialogFuncComp(HWND hdwnd, UINT message,
                             WPARAM wParam, LPARAM lParam)
{
  PAINTSTRUCT ps;
  HDC dc;
  static HFONT hFontTitle;
  static char *compStr = "Completing the Wizard.";
  RECT r;

  switch(message) {
    case WM_PAINT:
      dc = BeginPaint(hdwnd, &ps);
      r.right = 115; r.bottom = 8;
      MapDialogRect(hdwnd, &r); // convert to pixels
      SelectObject(dc, hFontTitle); // select large font
      TextOut(dc, r.right, r.bottom, compStr,
              strlen(compStr));
      EndPaint(hdwnd, &ps);
      break;
    case WM_NOTIFY:
      switch(((NMHDR *) lParam)->code) {
        case PSN_SETACTIVE:// page gaining focus
          r.bottom = 12;
          MapDialogRect(hdwnd, &r); // convert to pixels
          // create wizard title font
          hFontTitle = CreateFont(r.bottom, 0, 0, 0, FW_MEDIUM,
                        0, 0, 0, ANSI_CHARSET,
                        OUT_DEFAULT_PRECIS,
                        CLIP_DEFAULT_PRECIS,
                        DEFAULT_QUALITY,
                        DEFAULT_PITCH | FF_DONTCARE,
                        "Verdana");

          hPropSheet = ((NMHDR *) lParam)->hwndFrom;
          PropSheet_SetWizButtons(hPropSheet,
                        PSWIZB_BACK | PSWIZB_FINISH);
          SetWindowLong(hdwnd, DWL_MSGRESULT, 0);
          return 1;
        case PSN_KILLACTIVE: // page losing focus
          SetWindowLong(hdwnd, DWL_MSGRESULT, 0);
          DeleteObject(hFontTitle);
          return 1;
```

```
      }
      break;
  }

  return 0;
}
```

The wizard program uses the following resource file. Notice the addition of the two bitmaps. As explained, BP1.BMP contains the watermark and BP2.BMP contains the header bitmap. Remember to create these before compiling the wizard.

```
// Wizard resource file.
#include <windows.h>
#include <commctrl.h>
#include "wiz.h"

wizbmp1 BITMAP bp1.bmp
wizbmp2 BITMAP bp2.bmp

PropSheetMenu MENU
{
  POPUP "&Wizard Demo"
  {
    MENUITEM "&Start Wizard\tF2", IDM_DIALOG
    MENUITEM "E&xit\tCtrl+X", IDM_EXIT
  }
  MENUITEM "&Help", IDM_HELP
}

PropSheetMenu ACCELERATORS
{
  VK_F2, IDM_DIALOG, VIRTKEY
  VK_F1, IDM_HELP, VIRTKEY
  "^X", IDM_EXIT
}

WelcomeDB DIALOGEX 0, 0, 317, 193
CAPTION "Compilation Options Wizard"
FONT 8, "MS Shell Dlg"
{
  LTEXT "To continue, click Next.", IDD_STEXT2, 115, 40, 100, 14
}
```

13

```
PropSheetDB1 DIALOGEX 0, 0, 317, 143
CAPTION "Compilation Options Wizard"
FONT 8, "MS Shell Dlg"
{
  CTEXT "Choose Target OS", IDD_STEXT1, 21, 1, 60, 14
  LISTBOX IDD_LB1, 21, 24, 60, 52, LBS_NOTIFY |
             WS_BORDER | WS_VSCROLL | WS_TABSTOP
}

PropSheetDB2 DIALOGEX 0, 0, 317, 143
CAPTION "Compilation Options Wizard"
FONT 8, "MS Shell Dlg"
{
  DEFPUSHBUTTON "All", IDD_ALL, 21, 1, 34, 14
  AUTOCHECKBOX "Check for stack overflows.", IDD_CB1,
             21, 31, 92, 10
  AUTOCHECKBOX "Check array boundaries.", IDD_CB2,
             21, 51, 92, 10
  AUTOCHECKBOX "Prevent assignment to null.", IDD_CB3,
             21, 71, 100, 10
}

PropSheetDB3 DIALOGEX 0, 0, 317, 143
CAPTION "Compilation Options Wizard"
FONT 8, "MS Shell Dlg"
{
  DEFPUSHBUTTON "Fastest", IDD_FASTEST, 21, 1, 34, 14
  PUSHBUTTON "Smallest", IDD_SMALLEST, 21, 25, 34, 14
  AUTORADIOBUTTON "Optimize for speed.", IDD_RB1,
                66, 1, 90, 10
  AUTORADIOBUTTON "Balance speed and size.", IDD_RB2,
                66, 21, 90, 10
  AUTORADIOBUTTON "Optimize for size.", IDD_RB3,
                66, 41, 90, 10
}

CompletionDB DIALOGEX 0, 0, 317, 193
CAPTION "Compilation Options Wizard"
FONT 8, "MS Shell Dlg"
{
  LTEXT "To close, click Finish.", IDD_STEXT3, 115, 40, 100, 14
}
```

The header file WIZ.H is shown here.

```
#define IDM_DIALOG     100
#define IDM_EXIT       101
#define IDM_HELP       102

#define IDD_OPTIONS    201
#define IDD_OPTIMIZE   202
#define IDD_FASTEST    204
#define IDD_SMALLEST   205
#define IDD_ALL        207

#define IDD_LB1        301

#define IDD_EB1        401

#define IDD_CB1        501
#define IDD_CB2        502
#define IDD_CB3        503

#define IDD_RB1        601
#define IDD_RB2        602
#define IDD_RB3        603

#define IDD_STEXT1     700
#define IDD_STEXT2     701
#define IDD_STEXT3     702
```

A Closer Look at the Wizard Example

Much of the wizard program is similar to the property sheet example.
However, a number of changes were made. First, notice the addition of
PSH_WIZARD97 to the **dwFlags** field of the **PropHdr** structure. As
explained, this flag transforms a property sheet into a modern-style wizard.
Also, the watermark and header bitmaps were added to the **PropHdr**
structure along with the appropriate flags.

To comply with the Wizard 97 specification, Welcome and Completion
dialog boxes were added to the resource file and dialog box functions were
added to the program to handle them. This means that there are five, not
three, dialog boxes that need to be included in the wizard and handled by
the program. Thus, the macro **NUMPAGES** is changed from 3 to 5. The
Welcome and Completion pages are handled by the **DialogFuncWel( )** and
DialogFuncComp( ) functions, respectively. Also, the position of the
various controls within the previously defined dialog boxes that comprise the
interior pages were altered slightly to meet the Wizard 97 specification.

13

The program now activates the appropriate buttons each time a new page is activated. That is, the program enables the Back, Next, and Finish buttons, as needed. Notice how the code for this has been added to the **WM_NOTIFY** handlers.

Since wizards are activated in a strictly linear sequence, the Options and Optimize push buttons are no longer included on the Pick Target page. Remember, it is not proper style to activate pages out of sequence when using a wizard.

Displaying the Welcome and Completion Page Title

As previously mentioned, the title on the exterior pages must be a 12 point, bold, Verdana font, with the point size referring to dialog units. To translate dialog units into pixels, the program calls **MapDialogRect( )**. The prototype for **MapDialogRect( )** is shown here:

BOOL MapDialogRect(HWND *hDialog*, RECT **rect*);

The handle of the dialog box is passed in *hDialog*. The dialog dimensions to be converted into pixels are passed in the structure pointed to by *rect*. Nonzero is returned on success, and zero is returned on failure.

To convert the value 12 from dialog units to pixels, the program assigns 12 to the **bottom** field of a **RECT** structure and then calls **MapDialogRect( )**. On return, **bottom** will contain the height of the font in pixels. This value is then used to create the title font. Notice that the title font is created each time that an exterior page is activated and is destroyed when the page is left. This procedure is necessary since fonts are resources that must be deleted when no longer needed.

A conversion from dialog units to pixels must also occur when the title is output. As explained, the title must be displayed at the dialog location of 115, 8. The program again uses **MapDialogRect( )** to translate this location into pixels.

Worth the Effort

Property sheets and wizards are two of Windows 2000's more sophisticated controls. Although they require a bit of work to set up, they are worth the effort because they help you handle complex input situations. In particular, wizards enable you to guide a user through a complex set of options and selections that require more than one screen full of controls. Now that you know how to handle wizards, you should use one whenever a complicated input operation is required.

CHAPTER 14

Using the Header and Month Calendar Controls

This chapter concludes our exploration of the common controls by examining the header and the month calendar controls. A header control is a bar consisting of column headings that helps you display information in a tabular form. The month calendar is a relatively new control that displays a full month in calendar format and allows the user to pick a date. The month calendar control is as visually appealing as it is practical.

Header Controls

A header control helps you organize and manage columns of information.

A *header control* is a bar that consists of column headings. You have undoubtedly seen header controls when using Windows 2000. For example, when using the Explorer, the detailed view of files is presented using a header control. A header control is not, however, just a set of passive column headings. The user can adjust the width of each column, and it is also possible to make the header control respond to mouse clicks. As you will see, the header control is one of the more useful of the common controls because it gives you a standardized way of displaying and managing columns of information.

Creating a Header Control

A header control is created using **CreateWindow( )** or **CreateWindowEx( )**, specifying the **WC_HEADER** window class. A header control should also include the **WS_CHILD** style. Generally, a header control is created with zero width and height. The reason for this is that the control will need to be sized to fit the client area of its parent window. It must also be sized appropriately for the currently selected font. Fortunately, the header control has a mechanism that will determine its correct dimensions after it has been created, so you do not need to handle these matters manually.

Since a header control will be resized after it is created, you can use the following call to **CreateWindow( )** to create nearly any type of header control:

```
hHeadWnd = CreateWindow(WC_HEADER, NULL,
               WS_CHILD | WS_BORDER,
               CW_USEDEFAULT, CW_USEDEFAULT,
               0, 0, hParent,
               (HMENU) ID_HEADCONTROL,
               hInst, NULL);
```

Here, **hParent** is the handle of the parent window, and **hInst** is the instance handle of the application. The ID of the header control is specified by **ID_HEADCONTROL** (which is a value that you define). The dimensions of the control are irrelevant, and the control is not initially visible.

By default, the header control contains only labels and dividers. However, if you include the **HDS_BUTTONS** style when you create the control, then each heading will consist of a push button. You will see an example that makes use of this feature later in this chapter.

A header control is empty when it is first created. Each heading must be added individually. As just mentioned, the control must also be sized to fit the parent window. For these reasons, the header control should initially be invisible. It should be displayed only after it has been given headings and its size has been adjusted. Thus, follow these steps when using a header control.

1. Obtain the proper dimensions for the header control and resize the control.
2. Add each heading to the control.
3. Make the header control visible.

To accomplish these steps, you will send various messages to the control, as described next.

Sending Messages to a Header Control

A header control responds to various messages. Some of the most frequently used messages are shown in Table 14-1. You can send a header control a message using **SendMessage( )**, specifying the handle of the control as the target. There are also predefined macros that are more convenient to use. The macros that correspond to the messages in Table 14-1 are shown here:

BOOL Header_DeleteItem(HWND *hHeadWnd*, int *index*);

BOOL Header_GetItem(HWND *hHeadWnd*, int *index*,
                    HDITEM **HdItemPtr*);

int Header_GetItemCount(HWND *hHeadWnd*);

int Header_InsertItem(HWND *hHeadWnd*, int *index*,
                      HDITEM * *HdItemPtr*);

BOOL Header_Layout(HWND *hHeadWnd*, HDLAYOUT **LayoutPtr*);

14

BOOL Header_SetItem(HWND *hHeadWnd*, int *index*,
HDITEM * *HdItemPtr*);

In all cases, *hHeadWnd* is the handle of the header control, and *index* is the index of the specific heading being affected. *HdItemPtr* is a pointer to an **HDITEM** structure. *LayoutPtr* is a pointer to an **HDLAYOUT** structure. Since these structures are crucial to creating and using a header control, let's examine them now.

Message	Meaning
HDM_DELETEITEM	Deletes a heading. Returns nonzero if successful and zero on failure. *wParam* specifies the index of the heading. *lParam* is zero.
HDM_GETITEM	Obtains heading information. Returns nonzero if successful and zero on failure. *wParam* specifies the index of the heading. *lParam* is a pointer to an **HDITEM** structure that receives the information. The value of the **mask** member of **HDITEM** specifies what information is obtained.
HDM_GETITEMCOUNT	Returns the number of headings or –1 on failure. *wParam* is zero. *lParam* is zero.
HDM_HITTEST	Given a point, returns index of heading that contains that point or –1 if specified point is not in a heading. *wParam* is zero. *lParam* is a pointer to an **HDHITTESTINFO** structure that defines the point.
HDM_INSERTITEM	Inserts a heading. Returns index of item being inserted if successful and –1 on failure. *wParam* specifies the index after which the new heading is inserted. To insert the first heading, use zero for the index. To insert a heading at the end, specify an index that is greater than the number of headings currently in the header control. *lParam* is a pointer to an **HDITEM** structure that contains the heading being inserted.

Several Commonly Used Header Control Messages

Table 14-1.

Message	Meaning
HDM_LAYOUT	Obtains appropriate dimensions for the header control given the dimensions of its parent window's client area. Returns nonzero if successful and zero on failure. *wParam* is zero. *lParam* is a pointer to an **HDLAYOUT** structure. Its **prc** member contains the dimensions of the parent window's client area when sent. On return, its **pwpos** member contains the suggested dimensions for the header control.
HDM_SETITEM	Sets heading information. Returns nonzero if successful and zero on failure. *wParam* specifies the index of the heading. *lParam* is a pointer to an **HDITEM** structure that contains the heading's information. The value of the **mask** member of **HDITEM** specifies what information is set.

Several Commonly Used Header Control Messages *(continued)*

Table 14-1.

The HDITEM Structure

Each header item (that is, heading) in a header control is defined by an **HDITEM** structure. This structure is shown here:

```
typedef struct _HDITEM
{
  UINT mask;
  int cxy;
  LPSTR pszText;
  HBITMAP hbm;
  int cchTextMax;
  int fmt;
  LPARAM lParam;
  int iImage;
  int iOrder;
  UINT type; // new for Windows 2000
  LPVOID pvFilter; // new for Windows 2000
} HDITEM;
```

The value of **mask** determines which of the other members of **HDITEM** contain information. It can be any combination of the following values:

14

Value	Meaning
HDI_BITMAP	**hbm** contains the handle of a bitmap.
HDI_FILTER	**type** and **pvFilter** contain information. (New for Windows 2000.)
HDI_FORMAT	**fmt** contains format flags.
HDI_HEIGHT	**cxy** contains the height of the header.
HDI_WIDTH	**cxy** contains the width of the header.
HDI_LPARAM	**lParam** contains information.
HDI_TEXT	**pszText** and **cchTextMax** contain information.
HDI_IMAGE	**iImage** contains information.
HDI_ORDER	**iOrder** contains information.

The **cxy** member contains the width or height of the heading, depending upon whether **HDI_WIDTH** or **HDI_HEIGHT** is specified in **mask**.

pszText points to a string that acts as a column label. **cchTextMax** specifies the length of the string.

If a bitmap will be displayed in the heading, then the handle of the bitmap must be specified in **hbm**.

The value contained in **fmt** determines how the header is displayed. It contains a combination of one justification value and one content value. The content values are

HDF_STRING	Header displays a string.
HDF_BITMAP	Header displays a bitmap.
HDF_BITMAP_ON_RIGHT	Bitmap goes to right of text.
HDF_OWNERDRAW	Owner draws.

The justification values are

HDF_LEFT	Left justify
HDF_CENTER	Center
HDF_RIGHT	Right justify

You can also include one or more of the following values:

HDF_IMAGE	Header uses an image list.
HDF_RTLREADING	Text is displayed right to left.

The value in **lParam** is application-dependent.

If the header includes an image list, then the contents of **iImage** specify the index of an image. The example in this chapter will not use an image list.

When obtaining information about an item, the position of the item, beginning at 0 and moving from left to right, is contained in the **iOrder** field.

The fields **type** and **pvFilter** are new for Windows 2000. These fields are used to create data filters. They are not used by the examples in this chapter.

HISTORICAL PERSPECTIVE: The **HDITEM** structure was formerly called **HD_ITEM**.

The HDLAYOUT Structure

The **HDLAYOUT** structure is used by the **HDM_LAYOUT** message to obtain appropriate dimensions for a header control, given the dimensions of a bounding rectangle that is usually the client area of the header control's parent window. **HDLAYOUT** is defined like this:

```
typedef struct _HDLAYOUT
{
  RECT *prc;
  WINDOWPOS *pwpos;
} HDLAYOUT;
```

Here, **prc** is a pointer to a **RECT** structure that specifies the size of the area in which the header control will be used. These dimensions are processed by the header control, which determines what its size must be to fit within the specified region. The adjusted dimensions are returned in the **WINDOWPOS** structure pointed to by **pwpos**.

You are already familiar with the **RECT** structure. The **WINDOWPOS** structure is defined like this:

```
typedef struct tagWINDOWPOS {
  HWND hwnd;
```

14

```
    HWND hwndInsertAfter;
    int x;
    int y;
    int cx;
    int cy;
    UINT flags;
} WINDOWPOS;
```

Here, **hwnd** is the handle of the header control. **hwndInsertAfter** is the handle of the previous window in the Z-order. The upper-left corner of the window is specified by **x** and **y**. The width is contained in **cx**, and the height is contained in **cy**. The value in **flags** specifies various attributes associated with the window. For our purposes, the **WINDOWPOS** structure is initialized by the header control. There is no reason to alter the contents of this structure.

HISTORICAL PERSPECTIVE: The **HDLAYOUT** structure was formerly called **HD_LAYOUT**.

Sizing the Header

To resize a header control after it has been initialized, send an **HDM_LAYOUT** message (or use the **Header_Layout( )** macro). You then use the dimensions and coordinates returned by this message to adjust the size of the header control. For example, here is one way to accomplish this.

```
RECT rect;
HDLAYOUT layout;
WINDOWPOS winpos;

// get size of parent window
GetClientRect(hParent, &rect);

// get header control layout that will fit client area
layout.pwpos = &winpos;
layout.prc = &rect;
Header_Layout(hHeadWnd, &layout);

// dimension header to fit current size of client area
```

```
MoveWindow(hHeadWnd, winpos.x, winpos.y,
          winpos.cx, winpos.cy, 0);
```

First, the size of the window in which the header control must fit is obtained by calling **GetClientRect( )**. Then, these dimensions are passed to the header control using **Header_Layout( )**. On return, the **pwpos** member will contain the appropriate dimensions for the header control. These dimensions are then used in a call to **MoveWindow( )**, which resizes and positions the header control as specified. (See the In Depth box.)

As mentioned earlier, at this point the header control is still not visible. It should not be made visible until after the actual headings have been inserted in the control.

IN DEPTH

Moving a Window

Sometimes you will want to change the position or the size of a window. To accomplish this, you can use the **MoveWindow( )** API function. Its prototype is shown here:

BOOL MoveWindow(HWND *hwnd*, int *NewX*, int *NewY*, int *NewWidth*,
          int *NewHeight*, BOOL *Repaint*);

Here, *hwnd* is the handle of the window being affected. The desired location of its upper-left corner is passed in *NewX* and *NewY*. The new width and height are specified in *NewWidth* and *NewHeight*. If *Repaint* is nonzero, the window will be repainted immediately after it has been resized. Otherwise, a repainting request will be put in the window's message queue for later processing. **MoveWindow( )** returns nonzero if successful and zero on failure.

While the **MoveWindow( )** function can change the size and location of a window, it cannot change its Z-order (that is, the order of the

14

window in the stack of windows). If you wish to change a window's Z-order, then you will need to use **SetWindowPos( )**. It has the following prototype:

```
BOOL SetWindowPos(HWND hwnd, HWND hWhere, int NewX,
                  int NewY,
                  int NewWidth, int NewHeight, UINT How);
```

Here, *hwnd* is the handle of the window being affected. *hWhere* specifies where in the Z-order the window will be placed. *hWhere* can be either the handle of the window that will precede *hwnd* in the Z-order or a value that specifies an absolute location. For example, to specify the topmost window, use **HWND_TOP**. To put *hwnd* on the bottom, use **HWND_BOTTOM**. The desired location of its upper-left corner is passed in *NewX* and *NewY*. The new width and height are specified in *NewWidth* and *NewHeight*. The value of *How* determines precisely what occurs when the window is repositioned. For example, **SWP_HIDEWINDOW** hides the window and **SWP_SHOWWINDOW** makes the window visible. **SetWindowPos( )** returns nonzero if successful and zero on failure.

The coordinates that you pass in *NewX* and *NewY* have different meanings depending upon whether the window being affected is a top-level window or a child window. For child windows, the coordinates are relative to the parent window's client area. For top-level windows, the coordinates apply to the screen.

Both **MoveWindow( )** and **SetWindowPos( )** are interesting and useful functions that can help you solve a variety of problems. You might want to experiment with them a bit.

Inserting Headings into the Header Control

After the header control has been appropriately sized, you can insert headings into it. Each heading defines one column. To insert a heading, you must first load an **HDITEM** structure with information about the heading and then call **HeaderInsertItem( )**. For example, the following fragment inserts the first column's heading into a header control.

```
HDITEM hditem;

hditem.mask = HDI_FORMAT | HDI_WIDTH | HDI_TEXT;
hditem.pszText = "Heading #1";
hditem.cchTextMax = strlen(hditem.pszText);
hditem.cxy = 100;
hditem.fmt = HDF_STRING | HDF_LEFT;
Header_InsertItem(hHeadWnd, 0, &hditem);
```

In this example, the header displays a string, which, in this case, is "Heading #1". The string is left justified. The width of the item is specified as 100, which is arbitrary in this case.

Remember, each time you insert an item, you must specify the index of the item that the new header will follow.

Displaying the Header Control

Header controls are usually invisible when created and must be shown after they are sized and initialized.

Once you have inserted all the headings, you can finally display the header control by calling **ShowWindow( )**. For example, to display the header control whose handle is **hHeadWnd**, use the following call:

```
ShowWindow(hHeadWnd, SW_SHOW); // display the header control
```

Keep in mind that, at this point, you have created only the header control, which defines headings for columns of data. You have not displayed any data. This will be done by other parts of your program. However, before you can use the header control, you will need to learn about the various notification messages that it can generate.

Header Notification Messages

Header controls are active rather than passive. That is, they generate messages when they are accessed by the user. For example, when the user resizes a heading, your program will be sent a message describing this event and will need to respond appropriately. The header control generates several different messages. Which messages your program responds to is determined by how you utilize the control.

A header control sends a message to your program through the **WM_NOTIFY** message. When **WM_NOTIFY** is received, **wParam** contains the ID of the control generating the message. For most header control notification messages, **lParam** points to an **NMHEADER** structure, which is defined like this:

```
typedef struct tagNMHEADER
{
  NMHDR hdr;
  int iItem;
  int iButton;
  HDITEM *pitem;
} NMHEADER;
```

*When a header control is clicked, the **pitem** member of HDITEM will be NULL.*

The **hdr** member is the standard **NMHDR** structure that we have been using. For **WM_NOTIFY** messages associated with header controls, **hdr.hwndFrom** is the handle of the header control that generated the message. **hdr.idFrom** is the header control's ID. The value of **hdr.code** contains the notification code, which describes what action has taken place. Several frequently used header control notification codes are shown in Table 14-2.

The **iItem** member of **NMHEADER** specifies the index of the heading that was accessed. **iButton** specifies which mouse button was pressed. For most applications this is not of interest.

The **pitem** member points to an **HDITEM** structure that describes the heading that was accessed. However, when an **HDN_ITEMCLICK** or **HDN_ITEMDBLCLICK** notification is received, **pitem** is **NULL.**

HISTORICAL PERSPECTIVE: The **NMHEADER** structure was formerly called **HD_NOTIFY**. Some compilers may require the old name.

A Simple Header Control Example

Now that you have seen all the pieces, a simple header control example can be assembled. The following program creates a header control that has five columns. The control is used to manage a simple mailing list that stores name and address information. The entire header control program is shown next. Sample output is shown in Figure 14-1.

Code	Meaning
HDN_BEGINTRACK	User has started to resize a column heading. Your handler must return zero to enable tracking or nonzero to disable it.
HDN_DIVIDERDBLCLICK	User double-clicked on divider.
HDN_ENDTRACK	User has finished resizing a column heading.
HDN_ITEMCHANGED	A heading has been changed.
HDN_ITEMCHANGING	A heading is going to change. Your handler must return zero to allow a change to occur or nonzero to disallow the change.
HDN_ITEMCLICK	User clicked on a heading. Applies only to button-style headers.
HDN_ITEMDBLCLICK	User double-clicked on a heading. Applies only to button-style headers.
HDN_TRACK	User is in the process of resizing a column heading. Your handler must return zero to allow tracking to proceed or nonzero to stop tracking.

Some Commonly Used Header Control Notification Codes

Table 14-2.

Sample output from the first header control example program

Figure 14-1.

14

```
// A simple header control example.

#include <windows.h>
#include <commctrl.h>
#include <cstring>
#include <cstdio>
#include "head.h"

#define NUMCOLS 5
#define DEFWIDTH 100
#define MINWIDTH 20
#define SPACING 8
#define NUMENTRIES 7

LRESULT CALLBACK WindowFunc(HWND, UINT, WPARAM, LPARAM);
HWND InitHeader(HWND hParent);
void InitDatabase(void);

char szWinName[] = "MyWin"; // name of window class

HINSTANCE hInst;
HWND hHeadWnd;

int HeaderHeight;

int columns[NUMCOLS] = {DEFWIDTH, DEFWIDTH,
                        DEFWIDTH, DEFWIDTH,
                        DEFWIDTH};

struct MailList {
  char name[40];
  char street[40];
  char city[40];
  char state[3];
  char code[11];
} data[NUMENTRIES];

int WINAPI WinMain(HINSTANCE hThisInst, HINSTANCE hPrevInst,
                   LPSTR lpszArgs, int nWinMode)
{
  MSG msg;
  WNDCLASSEX wcl;
  HACCEL hAccel;
  HWND hwnd;
  INITCOMMONCONTROLSEX cc;
```

```
// Define a window class.
wcl.cbSize = sizeof(WNDCLASSEX);

wcl.hInstance = hThisInst;      // handle to this instance
wcl.lpszClassName = szWinName; // window class name
wcl.lpfnWndProc = WindowFunc;   // window function
wcl.style = 0;                  // default style

wcl.hIcon = LoadIcon(NULL, IDI_APPLICATION); // large icon
wcl.hIconSm = NULL; // use small version of large icon
wcl.hCursor = LoadCursor(NULL, IDC_ARROW);  // cursor style

wcl.lpszMenuName = "HeaderMenu"; // main menu

wcl.cbClsExtra = 0; // no extra memory needed
wcl.cbWndExtra = 0;

// Make the window background white.
wcl.hbrBackground = (HBRUSH) GetStockObject(WHITE_BRUSH);

// Register the window class.
if(!RegisterClassEx(&wcl)) return 0;

/* Now that a window class has been registered, a window
   can be created. */
hwnd = CreateWindow(
  szWinName, // name of window class
  "Using a Header Control", // title
  WS_OVERLAPPEDWINDOW, // window style - normal
  CW_USEDEFAULT, // X coordinate - let Windows decide
  CW_USEDEFAULT, // Y coordinate - let Windows decide
  CW_USEDEFAULT, // width - let Windows decide
  CW_USEDEFAULT, // height - let Windows decide
  NULL,          // no parent window
  NULL,          // no menu
  hThisInst,     // instance handle
  NULL           // no additional arguments
);

hInst = hThisInst; // save the current instance handle

// Load the keyboard accelerators.
hAccel = LoadAccelerators(hThisInst, "HeaderMenu");
```

14

```
      // Initialize the common controls.
      cc.dwSize = sizeof(INITCOMMONCONTROLSEX);
      cc.dwICC = ICC_LISTVIEW_CLASSES;
      InitCommonControlsEx(&cc);

      // Display the window.
      ShowWindow(hwnd, nWinMode);
      UpdateWindow(hwnd);

      // Create the message loop.
      while(GetMessage(&msg, NULL, 0, 0))
      {
        if(!TranslateAccelerator(hwnd, hAccel, &msg)) {
          TranslateMessage(&msg); // translate keyboard messages
          DispatchMessage(&msg); // return control to Windows 2000
        }
      }

      return msg.wParam;
}

/* This function is called by Windows 2000 and is passed
   messages from the message queue.
*/
LRESULT CALLBACK WindowFunc(HWND hwnd, UINT message,
                            WPARAM wParam, LPARAM lParam)
{
  int response;
  RECT rect;
  HDLAYOUT layout;
  WINDOWPOS winpos;
  NMHEADER *hdnptr;
  HDITEM *hdiptr;
  PAINTSTRUCT ps;
  TEXTMETRIC tm;
  SIZE size;

  char str[80];
  int i, j, ColStart, chrs;
  int entry;
  int linespacing;

  HDC hdc;

  switch(message) {
```

```
        case WM_CREATE:
          hHeadWnd = InitHeader(hwnd);
          InitDatabase();
          break;
        case WM_COMMAND:
          switch(LOWORD(wParam)) {
            case IDM_EXIT:
              response = MessageBox(hwnd, "Quit the Program?",
                                    "Exit", MB_YESNO);
              if(response == IDYES) PostQuitMessage(0);
              break;
            case IDM_HELP:
              MessageBox(hwnd, "Try resizing the header.",
                         "Help", MB_OK);
              break;
          }
          break;
        case WM_SIZE:
          /* Resize the header control when its parent window
             changes size. */
          GetClientRect(hwnd, &rect);
          layout.prc = &rect;
          layout.pwpos = &winpos;
          Header_Layout(hHeadWnd, &layout);

          MoveWindow(hHeadWnd, winpos.x, winpos.y,
                     winpos.cx, winpos.cy, 1);
          break;
        case WM_NOTIFY:
          if(LOWORD(wParam) == ID_HEADCONTROL) {
            hdnptr = (NMHEADER *) lParam;
            hdiptr = (HDITEM *) hdnptr->pitem;
            switch(hdnptr->hdr.code) {
              case HDN_ENDTRACK: // user changed column width
                if(hdiptr->cxy < MINWIDTH) {
                  hdiptr->cxy = MINWIDTH;
                  columns[hdnptr->iItem] = MINWIDTH;
                }
                else
                  columns[hdnptr->iItem] = hdiptr->cxy;
                InvalidateRect(hwnd, NULL, 1);
                break;
            }
          }
          break;
```

14

```
case WM_PAINT:
  hdc = BeginPaint(hwnd, &ps);

  GetTextMetrics(hdc, &tm);
  linespacing = tm.tmHeight + tm.tmInternalLeading;

  for(entry = 0; entry < NUMENTRIES; entry++) {
    ColStart = 0;
    for(i=0; i<NUMCOLS; i++) {
      switch(i) {
        case 0: strcpy(str, data[entry].name);
          break;
        case 1: strcpy(str, data[entry].street);
          break;
        case 2: strcpy(str, data[entry].city);
          break;
        case 3: strcpy(str, data[entry].state);
          break;
        case 4: strcpy(str, data[entry].code);
          break;
      }

      // add ... to truncated entries
      GetTextExtentPoint32(hdc, str, strlen(str), &size);
      j = 2;
      while((columns[i]-SPACING) < size.cx) {
        chrs = columns[i] / tm.tmAveCharWidth;
        strcpy(&str[chrs-j], "...");
        GetTextExtentPoint32(hdc, str, strlen(str), &size);
        j++;
      }

      TextOut(hdc, ColStart+SPACING,
              HeaderHeight+(entry*linespacing),
              str, strlen(str));

      ColStart += columns[i];
    }
  }
  EndPaint(hwnd, &ps);
  break;
case WM_DESTROY: // terminate the program
  PostQuitMessage(0);
  break;
default:
```

```
            /* Let Windows 2000 process any messages not specified in
               the preceding switch statement. */
            return DefWindowProc(hwnd, message, wParam, lParam);
      }

   return 0;
}

// Initialize the header control.
HWND InitHeader(HWND hParent)
{
   HWND hHeadWnd;
   RECT rect;
   HDLAYOUT layout;
   WINDOWPOS winpos;
   HDITEM hditem;

   GetClientRect(hParent, &rect);

   // create the header control
   hHeadWnd = CreateWindow(WC_HEADER, NULL,
                   WS_CHILD | WS_BORDER,
                   CW_USEDEFAULT, CW_USEDEFAULT,
                   0, 0, hParent,
                   (HMENU) ID_HEADCONTROL,
                   hInst, NULL);

   // get header control layout that will fit client area
   layout.pwpos = &winpos;
   layout.prc = &rect;
   Header_Layout(hHeadWnd, &layout);

   // dimension header to fit current size of client area
   MoveWindow(hHeadWnd, winpos.x, winpos.y,
              winpos.cx, winpos.cy, 0);

   HeaderHeight = winpos.cy; // save height of header

   // insert items into the header
   hditem.mask = HDI_FORMAT | HDI_WIDTH | HDI_TEXT;
   hditem.pszText = "Name";
   hditem.cchTextMax = strlen(hditem.pszText);
   hditem.cxy = DEFWIDTH;
   hditem.fmt = HDF_STRING | HDF_LEFT;
   Header_InsertItem(hHeadWnd, 0, &hditem);
```

14

```
    hditem.pszText = "Street";
    hditem.cchTextMax = strlen(hditem.pszText);
    Header_InsertItem(hHeadWnd, 1, &hditem);

    hditem.pszText = "City";
    hditem.cchTextMax = strlen(hditem.pszText);
    Header_InsertItem(hHeadWnd, 2, &hditem);

    hditem.pszText = "State";
    hditem.cchTextMax = strlen(hditem.pszText);
    Header_InsertItem(hHeadWnd, 3, &hditem);

    hditem.pszText = "Postal Code";
    hditem.cchTextMax = strlen(hditem.pszText);
    Header_InsertItem(hHeadWnd, 4, &hditem);

    ShowWindow(hHeadWnd, SW_SHOW); // display the header control

    return hHeadWnd;
}

// Sample data to illustrate the header control.
void InitDatabase(void)
{
    strcpy(data[0].name, "Stan Jones");
    strcpy(data[0].street, "1101 Elm St. S.W.");
    strcpy(data[0].city, "Carlsburg");
    strcpy(data[0].state, "MT");
    strcpy(data[0].code, "59345-0089");

    strcpy(data[1].name, "Ralph Johnson");
    strcpy(data[1].street, "23978 N. Wesley Blvd.");
    strcpy(data[1].city, "Laguna Hills");
    strcpy(data[1].state, "FL");
    strcpy(data[1].code, "32465");

    strcpy(data[2].name, "Chris Thomas");
    strcpy(data[2].street, "1911 Robin Way");
    strcpy(data[2].city, "St. John");
    strcpy(data[2].state, "MN");
    strcpy(data[2].code, "55576");

    strcpy(data[3].name, "R. W. Ridgeway");
    strcpy(data[3].street, "P.O. Box 587");
```

```
      strcpy(data[3].city, "Goldsberry");
      strcpy(data[3].state, "MO");
      strcpy(data[3].code, "65345");

      strcpy(data[4].name, "Warren Clarence");
      strcpy(data[4].street, "3546 Newton Lane");
      strcpy(data[4].city, "Longtree");
      strcpy(data[4].state, "OH");
      strcpy(data[4].code, "43556-0234");

      strcpy(data[5].name, "William Spinoza");
      strcpy(data[5].street, "412 Monad Ave.");
      strcpy(data[5].city, "Marshall");
      strcpy(data[5].state, "SD");
      strcpy(data[5].code, "57345");

      strcpy(data[6].name, "W.S. Tempest");
      strcpy(data[6].street, "19 Water St. Apt 2A");
      strcpy(data[6].city, "Rushville");
      strcpy(data[6].state, "WI");
      strcpy(data[6].code, "53576");
    }
```

The program uses the following resource file:

```
// Demonstrate a header control.
#include <windows.h>
#include "head.h"

HeaderMenu MENU
{
  POPUP "&Options"
  {
    MENUITEM "E&xit\tCtrl+X", IDM_EXIT
  }
  MENUITEM "&Help", IDM_HELP
}

HeaderMenu ACCELERATORS
{
  "^X", IDM_EXIT
  VK_F1, IDM_HELP, VIRTKEY
}
```

14

The header file HEAD.H is shown here. It contains values used by this and the subsequent example program.

```
#define IDM_EXIT        100
#define IDM_HELP        101
#define IDM_RESET       102

#define ID_HEADCONTROL  500
```

A Closer Look at the First Header Control Example

When the program receives the **WM_CREATE** message, two functions are called: **InitHeader( )** and **InitDatabase( )**. The program uses the function **InitHeader( )** to construct and initialize the header control. It is passed the handle of its parent window. It returns a handle to the header control. The header control is given an ID value of **ID_HEADCONTROL**. This value is defined in the program's resource file and identifies the header control when a **WM_NOTIFY** message is received. (Remember, other types of controls also generate **WM_NOTIFY** messages.) Most of the other elements inside the function should be clear because they implement the steps described earlier in this chapter. In this example, all columns are given the same default width, which is 100. Of course, the columns' widths may be adjusted dynamically by the user. The size of each column is stored in the **columns** array.

Notice that the height of the header control is saved in the global variable **HeaderHeight**. Since the header control occupies space at the top of the client area of the parent window, **HeaderHeight** is used as an offset when information is displayed in the main window.

Once the header control has been constructed, the mailing list is initialized using **InitDatabase( )**. The database is stored in an array of **MailList** structures called **data**. The **MailList** structure contains character arrays that hold name and address information. The contents of the **data** array are displayed each time a **WM_PAINT** message is received.

The only header control message that the program responds to is **HDN_ENDTRACK**. This message is sent when the user has finished resizing a column header (by dragging the divider on its right side). Since the width of the column has been changed, the information displayed under the header control must be updated to reflect this change. This change is made by updating the value in **columns** so that it contains the new width of the header and then forcing a repaint. Notice that the user cannot reduce the size of a column to less than **MINWIDTH**. This restriction ensures that there is always a small part of the column heading showing.

There is one thing to note inside the **WM_PAINT** handler. If the information to be displayed in a column is longer than the current width of the column, then the information is truncated and an ellipsis is added. This tells the user that more information is available than can currently be displayed.

There is one other point of interest in this program. Examine the code under the **WM_SIZE** case. As you probably know, a window receives a **WM_SIZE** message when its size is changed. The program responds to this message by altering the size of the header control so that it continues to fit its parent window. Keep in mind that this step is not technically necessary. In fact, there are applications of a header control in which you will want its size to remain fixed. However, in this example, the header control is resized to fit the new dimensions of the window.

Enhancing the Header Control

The preceding example illustrated the basic elements necessary to create a simple header control. By employing some of the header control's other capabilities, you can greatly expand its power and utility. In this section, some of these features will be used to enhance the functionality of the header control. Specifically, the following features will be added to the preceding program:

◆ Button headers are used, allowing the header to respond to mouse events.

◆ When a button heading is clicked, the column will double its width.

◆ When a button heading is double-clicked, the column will return to its default width.

◆ When a heading is resized, the information in the column below the heading will expand or contract as the heading changes size.

Let's look at each of these options now.

Creating Button Headers

It is quite easy to create button headers. Just include the header style **HDS_BUTTONS** when you create the header control. Once you have done this, each heading will become a push button that is capable of responding to

14

The **HDS_BUTTONS** style causes the column headings to become push buttons.

mouse events. It also retains all other attributes of a standard heading. For example, you can still resize a header button by dragging its divider.

Responding to Mouse Events

When a button header is clicked by the mouse, it sends an **HDN_ITEMCLICK** message. When the button is double-clicked, it sends an **HDN_ITEMDBLCLICK** message. Your program can respond to these messages any way it chooses. There is no prescribed meaning to these events.

Using the HDN_TRACK Message

When the user first begins to resize a heading, the header control sends an **HDN_BEGINTRACK** message. When the user finishes resizing, the control sends **HDN_ENDTRACK**. During the resizing, the control sends a stream of **HDN_TRACK** messages. These messages can be used by your program to continually update the information displayed in the column that is being resized. Doing so allows the user to immediately see the effects of the changes being made.

An Enhanced Header Control Example

The following program incorporates the enhancements just described into the header control example. Sample output is shown in Figure 14-2.

Sample output from the enhanced header control program

Figure 14-2.

```
// Enhancing the header control.

#include <windows.h>
#include <commctrl.h>
#include <cstring>
#include <cstdio>
#include "head.h"

#define NUMCOLS 5
#define DEFWIDTH 100
#define MINWIDTH 20
#define MAXWIDTH 400
#define SPACING 8
#define NUMENTRIES 7

LRESULT CALLBACK WindowFunc(HWND, UINT, WPARAM, LPARAM);
HWND InitHeader(HWND hParent);
void InitDatabase(void);

char szWinName[] = "MyWin"; // name of window class

HINSTANCE hInst;
HWND hHeadWnd;

int HeaderHeight;

int columns[NUMCOLS] = {DEFWIDTH, DEFWIDTH,
                        DEFWIDTH, DEFWIDTH,
                        DEFWIDTH};

struct MailList {
  char name[40];
  char street[40];
  char city[40];
  char state[3];
  char code[11];
} data[NUMENTRIES];

int WINAPI WinMain(HINSTANCE hThisInst, HINSTANCE hPrevInst,
                   LPSTR lpszArgs, int nWinMode)
{
  MSG msg;
  WNDCLASSEX wcl;
  HACCEL hAccel;
  HWND hwnd;
```

14

```
INITCOMMONCONTROLSEX cc;

// Define a window class.
wcl.cbSize = sizeof(WNDCLASSEX);

wcl.hInstance = hThisInst;      // handle to this instance
wcl.lpszClassName = szWinName; // window class name
wcl.lpfnWndProc = WindowFunc;   // window function
wcl.style = 0;                  // default style

wcl.hIcon = LoadIcon(NULL, IDI_APPLICATION); // large icon
wcl.hIconSm = NULL; // use small version of large icon
wcl.hCursor = LoadCursor(NULL, IDC_ARROW);   // cursor style

wcl.lpszMenuName = "HeaderMenuEnhanced"; // main menu

wcl.cbClsExtra = 0; // no extra memory needed
wcl.cbWndExtra = 0;

// Make the window background white.
wcl.hbrBackground = (HBRUSH) GetStockObject(WHITE_BRUSH);

// Register the window class.
if(!RegisterClassEx(&wcl)) return 0;

/* Now that a window class has been registered, a window
   can be created. */
hwnd = CreateWindow(
  szWinName, // name of window class
  "An Enhanced Header Control", // title
  WS_OVERLAPPEDWINDOW, // window style - normal
  CW_USEDEFAULT, // X coordinate - let Windows decide
  CW_USEDEFAULT, // Y coordinate - let Windows decide
  CW_USEDEFAULT, // width - let Windows decide
  CW_USEDEFAULT, // height - let Windows decide
  NULL,          // no parent window
  NULL,          // no menu
  hThisInst,     // instance handle
  NULL           // no additional arguments
);

hInst = hThisInst; // save the current instance handle

// Load the keyboard accelerators.
hAccel = LoadAccelerators(hThisInst, "HeaderMenuEnhanced");
```

```
    // Initialize the common controls.
    cc.dwSize = sizeof(INITCOMMONCONTROLSEX);
    cc.dwICC = ICC_LISTVIEW_CLASSES;
    InitCommonControlsEx(&cc);

    // Display the window.
    ShowWindow(hwnd, nWinMode);
    UpdateWindow(hwnd);

    // Create the message loop.
    while(GetMessage(&msg, NULL, 0, 0))
    {
      if(!TranslateAccelerator(hwnd, hAccel, &msg)) {
        TranslateMessage(&msg); // translate keyboard messages
        DispatchMessage(&msg); // return control to Windows 2000
      }
    }

    return msg.wParam;
}

/* This function is called by Windows 2000 and is passed
   messages from the message queue.
*/
LRESULT CALLBACK WindowFunc(HWND hwnd, UINT message,
                                WPARAM wParam, LPARAM lParam)
{
    int response;
    RECT rect;
    HDLAYOUT layout;
    WINDOWPOS winpos;
    NMHEADER *hdnptr;
    HDITEM *hdiptr, hditem;
    PAINTSTRUCT ps;
    TEXTMETRIC tm;
    SIZE size;

    char str[80];
    int i, j, ColStart, chrs;
    int entry;
    int linespacing;

    HDC hdc;
```

14

```
switch(message) {
  case WM_CREATE:
    hHeadWnd = InitHeader(hwnd);
    InitDatabase();
    break;
  case WM_COMMAND:
    switch(LOWORD(wParam)) {
      case IDM_RESET: // restore default widths
        hditem.mask = HDI_WIDTH;
        for(i=0; i<NUMCOLS; i++) {
          Header_GetItem(hHeadWnd, i, &hditem);
          hditem.cxy = DEFWIDTH;
          columns[i] = DEFWIDTH;
          Header_SetItem(hHeadWnd, i, &hditem);
        }
        InvalidateRect(hwnd, NULL, 1);
        break;
      case IDM_EXIT:
        response = MessageBox(hwnd, "Quit the Program?",
                              "Exit", MB_YESNO);
        if(response == IDYES) PostQuitMessage(0);
        break;
      case IDM_HELP:
        MessageBox(hwnd, "Try resizing the header.",
                   "Help", MB_OK);
        break;
    }
    break;
  case WM_SIZE:
    /* Resize the header control when its parent window
       changes size. */
    GetClientRect(hwnd, &rect);
    layout.prc = &rect;
    layout.pwpos = &winpos;
    Header_Layout(hHeadWnd, &layout);

    MoveWindow(hHeadWnd, winpos.x, winpos.y,
           winpos.cx, winpos.cy, 1);
    break;
  case WM_NOTIFY:
    if(LOWORD(wParam) == ID_HEADCONTROL) {
      hdnptr = (NMHEADER *) lParam;
      hdiptr = (HDITEM *) hdnptr->pitem;
      switch(hdnptr->hdr.code) {
        case HDN_ENDTRACK: // user changed column width
```

```
            if(hdiptr->cxy < MINWIDTH) {
              hdiptr->cxy = MINWIDTH;
              columns[hdnptr->iItem] = MINWIDTH;
            }
            else
              columns[hdnptr->iItem] = hdiptr->cxy;
            InvalidateRect(hwnd, NULL, 1);
            break;
        case HDN_TRACK: // user changing column width
          GetClientRect(hwnd, &rect);
            if(hdiptr->cxy < MINWIDTH) {
              hdiptr->cxy = MINWIDTH;
              columns[hdnptr->iItem] = MINWIDTH;
            }
            else
              columns[hdnptr->iItem] = hdiptr->cxy;
            rect.top = HeaderHeight;
            InvalidateRect(hwnd, &rect, 1);
            break;
        case HDN_ITEMDBLCLICK: // user double-clicked header
          // return to default width
          hditem.mask = HDI_WIDTH;
          Header_GetItem(hHeadWnd, hdnptr->iItem, &hditem);
          hditem.cxy = DEFWIDTH;
          columns[hdnptr->iItem] = DEFWIDTH;
          Header_SetItem(hHeadWnd, hdnptr->iItem, &hditem);
          InvalidateRect(hwnd, NULL, 1);
          break;
        case HDN_ITEMCLICK: // user clicked header button
          // double width of button
          hditem.mask = HDI_WIDTH;
          Header_GetItem(hHeadWnd, hdnptr->iItem, &hditem);
          hditem.cxy += hditem.cxy;
          if(hditem.cxy > MAXWIDTH) hditem.cxy = MAXWIDTH;
          columns[hdnptr->iItem] = hditem.cxy;
          Header_SetItem(hHeadWnd, hdnptr->iItem, &hditem);
          InvalidateRect(hwnd, NULL, 1);
          break;
      }
    }
    break;
  case WM_PAINT:
    hdc = BeginPaint(hwnd, &ps); // get DC
```

14

```
     GetTextMetrics(hdc, &tm);
     linespacing = tm.tmHeight + tm.tmInternalLeading;

     for(entry = 0; entry < NUMENTRIES; entry++) {
       ColStart = 0;
       for(i=0; i<NUMCOLS; i++) {
         switch(i) {
           case 0: strcpy(str, data[entry].name);
             break;
           case 1: strcpy(str, data[entry].street);
             break;
           case 2: strcpy(str, data[entry].city);
             break;
           case 3: strcpy(str, data[entry].state);
             break;
           case 4: strcpy(str, data[entry].code);
             break;
         }

         // add ... to truncated entries
         GetTextExtentPoint32(hdc, str, strlen(str), &size);
         j = 2;
         while((columns[i]-SPACING) < size.cx) {
           chrs = columns[i] / tm.tmAveCharWidth;
           strcpy(&str[chrs-j], "...");
           GetTextExtentPoint32(hdc, str, strlen(str), &size);
           j++;
         }

         TextOut(hdc, ColStart+SPACING,
                 HeaderHeight+(entry*linespacing),
                 str, strlen(str));

         ColStart += columns[i];
       }
     }
     EndPaint(hwnd, &ps); // release DC
     break;
   case WM_DESTROY: // terminate the program
     PostQuitMessage(0);
     break;
   default:
     /* Let Windows 2000 process any messages not specified in
        the preceding switch statement. */
     return DefWindowProc(hwnd, message, wParam, lParam);
```

```
    }
    return 0;
}

// Initialize the header control.
HWND InitHeader(HWND hParent)
{
    HWND hHeadWnd;
    RECT rect;
    HDLAYOUT layout;
    WINDOWPOS winpos;
    HDITEM hditem;

    GetClientRect(hParent, &rect);

    // create the header control
    hHeadWnd = CreateWindow(WC_HEADER, NULL,
                WS_CHILD | WS_BORDER | HDS_BUTTONS,
                CW_USEDEFAULT, CW_USEDEFAULT,
                0, 0, hParent,
                (HMENU) ID_HEADCONTROL,
                hInst, NULL);

    // get header control layout that will fit client area
    layout.pwpos = &winpos;
    layout.prc = &rect;
    Header_Layout(hHeadWnd, &layout);

    // dimension header to fit current size of client area
    MoveWindow(hHeadWnd, winpos.x, winpos.y,
                winpos.cx, winpos.cy, 0);

    HeaderHeight = winpos.cy; // save height of header

    // insert items into the header
    hditem.mask = HDI_FORMAT | HDI_WIDTH | HDI_TEXT;
    hditem.pszText = "Name";
    hditem.cchTextMax = strlen(hditem.pszText);
    hditem.cxy = DEFWIDTH;
    hditem.fmt = HDF_STRING | HDF_LEFT;
    Header_InsertItem(hHeadWnd, 0, &hditem);

    hditem.pszText = "Street";
    hditem.cchTextMax = strlen(hditem.pszText);
    Header_InsertItem(hHeadWnd, 1, &hditem);
```

14

```
    hditem.pszText = "City";
    hditem.cchTextMax = strlen(hditem.pszText);
    Header_InsertItem(hHeadWnd, 2, &hditem);

    hditem.pszText = "State";
    hditem.cchTextMax = strlen(hditem.pszText);
    Header_InsertItem(hHeadWnd, 3, &hditem);

    hditem.pszText = "Postal Code";
    hditem.cchTextMax = strlen(hditem.pszText);
    Header_InsertItem(hHeadWnd, 4, &hditem);

    ShowWindow(hHeadWnd, SW_SHOW); // display the header control

    return hHeadWnd;
}

// Sample data to illustrate the header control.
void InitDatabase(void)
{
  strcpy(data[0].name, "Stan Jones");
  strcpy(data[0].street, "1101 Elm St. S.W.");
  strcpy(data[0].city, "Carlsburg");
  strcpy(data[0].state, "MT");
  strcpy(data[0].code, "59345-0089");

  strcpy(data[1].name, "Ralph Johnson");
  strcpy(data[1].street, "23978 N. Wesley Blvd.");
  strcpy(data[1].city, "Laguna Hills");
  strcpy(data[1].state, "FL");
  strcpy(data[1].code, "32465");

  strcpy(data[2].name, "Chris Thomas");
  strcpy(data[2].street, "1911 Robin Way");
  strcpy(data[2].city, "St. John");
  strcpy(data[2].state, "MN");
  strcpy(data[2].code, "55576");

  strcpy(data[3].name, "R. W. Ridgeway");
  strcpy(data[3].street, "P.O. Box 587");
  strcpy(data[3].city, "Goldsberry");
  strcpy(data[3].state, "MO");
  strcpy(data[3].code, "65345");
```

```
      strcpy(data[4].name, "Warren Clarence");
      strcpy(data[4].street, "3546 Newton Lane");
      strcpy(data[4].city, "Longtree");
      strcpy(data[4].state, "OH");
      strcpy(data[4].code, "43556-0234");

      strcpy(data[5].name, "William Spinoza");
      strcpy(data[5].street, "412 Monad Ave.");
      strcpy(data[5].city, "Marshall");
      strcpy(data[5].state, "SD");
      strcpy(data[5].code, "57345");

      strcpy(data[6].name, "W.S. Tempest");
      strcpy(data[6].street, "19 Water St. Apt 2A");
      strcpy(data[6].city, "Rushville");
      strcpy(data[6].state, "WI");
      strcpy(data[6].code, "53576");
}
```

This program uses the same HEAD.H file shown earlier. It uses the following resource file.

```
// Demonstrate an enhanced header control.
#include <windows.h>
#include "head.h"

HeaderMenuEnhanced MENU
{
  POPUP "&Options"
  {
    MENUITEM "&Reset\tF2", IDM_RESET
    MENUITEM "E&xit\tCtrl+X", IDM_EXIT
  }
  MENUITEM "&Help", IDM_HELP
}

HeaderMenuEnhanced ACCELERATORS
{
  VK_F2, IDM_RESET, VIRTKEY
  "^X", IDM_EXIT
  VK_F1, IDM_HELP, VIRTKEY
}
```

14

A Closer Look at the Enhanced Header Control Program

Most of the code in this program is similar to that found in the first header control program and will already be familiar to you. However, pay special attention to the changes. First, notice that the header control is now created with the **HDS_BUTTONS** style. This creates button headers. Next, look closely at the **WM_NOTIFY** message. It is here that most of the enhancements take place. It is shown here for your convenience.

```
case WM_NOTIFY:
  if(LOWORD(wParam) == ID_HEADCONTROL) {
    hdnptr = (NMHEADER *) lParam;
    hdiptr = (HDITEM *) hdnptr->pitem;
    switch(hdnptr->hdr.code) {
      case HDN_ENDTRACK: // user changed column width
        if(hdiptr->cxy < MINWIDTH) {
          hdiptr->cxy = MINWIDTH;
          columns[hdnptr->iItem] = MINWIDTH;
        }
        else
          columns[hdnptr->iItem] = hdiptr->cxy;
        InvalidateRect(hwnd, NULL, 1);
        break;
      case HDN_TRACK: // user changing column width
        GetClientRect(hwnd, &rect);
        if(hdiptr->cxy < MINWIDTH) {
          hdiptr->cxy = MINWIDTH;
          columns[hdnptr->iItem] = MINWIDTH;
        }
        else
          columns[hdnptr->iItem] = hdiptr->cxy;
        rect.top = HeaderHeight;
        InvalidateRect(hwnd, &rect, 1);
        break;
      case HDN_ITEMDBLCLICK: // user double-clicked header button
        // return to default width
        hditem.mask = HDI_WIDTH;
        Header_GetItem(hHeadWnd, hdnptr->iItem, &hditem);
        hditem.cxy = DEFWIDTH;
        columns[hdnptr->iItem] = DEFWIDTH;
        Header_SetItem(hHeadWnd, hdnptr->iItem, &hditem);
        InvalidateRect(hwnd, NULL, 1);
        break;
```

```
     case HDN_ITEMCLICK: // user clicked header button
        // double width of button
        hditem.mask = HDI_WIDTH;
        Header_GetItem(hHeadWnd, hdnptr->iItem, &hditem);
        hditem.cxy += hditem.cxy;
        if(hditem.cxy > MAXWIDTH) hditem.cxy = MAXWIDTH;
        columns[hdnptr->iItem] = hditem.cxy;
        Header_SetItem(hHeadWnd, hdnptr->iItem, &hditem);
        InvalidateRect(hwnd, NULL, 1);
        break;
  }
 }
 break;
```

Let's look at how each notification message is processed.

The **HDN_ENDTRACK** message is handled the same as it was in the first program.

Each time that an **HDN_TRACK** message is received, the program uses the new width of the header to adjust the contents of the information displayed in the columns. It does this by updating the **columns** array with the new column width and then forcing a repaint (by calling **InvalidateRect( )**). Thus, as the user drags the divider, the information in the columns below the header control will be dynamically updated, allowing the user to see the effects of expanding or contracting a column as they are occurring. This process makes it easy for the user to set each column width appropriately because it eliminates guesswork.

When the user clicks on a header button, the **HDN_ITEMCLICK** message is sent. The program responds by doubling the width of the column. Notice that the item must be obtained using **Header_GetItem( )** and reset using **Header_SetItem( )**. This procedure is required because, when an **HDN_ITEMCLICK** message is received, the value of the **pitem** member of **NMHEADER** is **NULL**. That is, it does not point to the item that was clicked.

When the user double-clicks on a header button, an **HDN_ITEMDBLCLICK** message is sent. The program responds by setting the width of the item to its default width. Again, notice that the item must be obtained using **Header_GetItem( )** and reset using **Header_SetItem( )**.

There is one other enhancement in the program. When the user selects Reset from the Options menu, all columns are returned to their default widths.

14

Some Things to Try

It is possible to dynamically add or delete column headers. Doing this might be useful when presenting information in various formats. For example, you could give the user the choice of what items he or she wanted to see and then adjust the header appropriately. You might want to try adding this option to the examples.

Another thing to try is giving the user the option of hiding the header control. For example, the user could use the header control to adjust the size of the columns and then remove the control from the screen. In this way, more information could be displayed.

The Month Calendar Control

One very useful common control is the month calendar. The month calendar control displays one or more months of a calendar and allows you to pick a date. By default, it displays and selects the current date. The user may change the month or year of the calendar. Various pop-up menus, up-down controls, and arrows are automatically supplied to make using the control exceedingly convenient. In fact, the month calendar control is so well designed that, although it allows a number of interesting variations, its default mode of operation is what you will usually want. It is also visually appealing and adds professionalism to any application that needs to work with dates.

A month calendar control displays a calendar and allows the user to pick a date.

Creating a Month Calendar

To create a month calendar you will use either **CreateWindow( )** or **CreateWindowEx( )**, specifying the **MONTHCAL_CLASS** window class. The control should include the **WS_CHILD** style. It will usually include the **WS_VISIBLE** and **WS_BORDER** styles, too. The month calendar is usually created with zero dimensions because its precise size can only be determined at run time. (Its size is partially determined by the type font, for example.)

The month calendar supports a number of style options that can be specified when it is created. We won't be using any, but they are shown in Table 14-3 for your information.

Sending Messages to a Month Calendar

A month calendar control responds to various messages. Several commonly used ones are shown in Table 14-4. You can send a month calendar control a message using **SendMessage( )**, specifying the handle of the control as the target. However, macros are defined for this purpose and are more

Style	Effect
MCS_DAYSTATE	Calendar will request information about which days should be marked as special (such as holidays, and so forth).
MCS_MULTISELECT	Allows a range of dates to be selected.
MCS_NOTODAY	The current date is not shown.
MCS_NOTODAYCIRCLE	The current date is not circled.
MCS_WEEKNUMBERS	The number of each week is displayed.

convenient to use. The macros corresponding to the messages in Table 14-4 are shown here:

BOOL MonthCal_GetCurSel(HWND *hCal*, SYSTEMTIME **st*);

BOOL MonthCal_GetMaxTodayWidth(HWND *hCal*);

BOOL MonthCal_GetMinReqRect(HWND *hCal*, RECT **rect*);

BOOL MonthCal_GetToday(HWND *hCal*, SYSTEMTIME **st*);

BOOL MonthCal_SetCurSel(HWND *hCal*, SYSTEMTIME **st*);

VOID MonthCal_SetToday(HWND *hCal*, SYSTEMTIME **st*);

Message	Meaning
MCM_GETCURSEL	Obtains the currently selected date. Returns nonzero if successful and zero on failure. *wParam* is zero. *lParam* is a pointer to a **SYSTEMTIME** structure that receives the currently selected date.
MCM_GETMAXTODAYWIDTH	Returns the width of the "today" string. Both *wParam* and *lParam* are zero.
MCM_GETMINREQRECT	Obtains the dimensions for the smallest window that can hold one month. Returns nonzero if successful and zero on failure. *wParam* is zero. *lParam* points to a **RECT** structure that receives the dimensions.

14

Message	Meaning
MCM_GETTODAY	Obtains the current date. Returns nonzero if successful and zero on failure. *wParam* is zero. *lParam* points to a **SYSTEMTIME** structure that receives the current date.
MCM_SETCURSEL	Selects a date. Returns nonzero if successful and zero on failure. *wParam* is zero. *lParam* is a pointer to a **SYSTEMTIME** structure that specifies the desired date.
MCM_SETTODAY	Sets the current date. No return value. *wParam* is zero. *lParam* points to a **SYSTEMTIME** structure that specifies the current date.

Commonly
Used Month
Calendar
Messages
(continued)
Table 14-4.

When setting or getting a date, the date is stored in a **SYSTEMTIME** structure, which is defined like this:

```
typedef struct _SYSTEMTIME {
  WORD wYear;          // year
  WORD wMonth;         // month (1 through 12)
  WORD wDayOfWeek;     // day of week (0 through 6)
  WORD wDay;           // day of month (1 through 31)
  WORD wHour;          // hour
  WORD wMinute;        // minutes
  WORD wSecond;        // seconds
  WORD wMilliseconds;  // milliseconds
} SYSTEMTIME;
```

As you can see, **SYSTEMTIME** includes both date and time members. Although the calendar control does not actually deal with times, it will handle them for you. For example, when the control is created, the current time is also stored in the current date.

Month Calendar Notification Messages

A month calendar is mostly a passive control. However, it can generate the following notification messages via **WM_NOTIFY**.

MCN_GETDAYSTATE	Sent to determine how to display a date. For example, holidays can be displayed in bold.
MCN_SELCHANGE	The selected date was changed.
MCN_SELECT	The user selected a date.

We won't be using any of these messages in the month calendar example, but they may be valuable to your own applications.

Sizing the Month Calendar Control

As explained, you will normally create a month calendar with zero dimensions and then resize it to fit its minimum dimensions. To obtain the dimensions of the smallest rectangle that can hold one month, send a **MCM_GETMINREQRECT** message. It returns in a **RECT** structure the minimum bounding rectangle that will fit the calendar. Next, you must obtain the length of the "today" string. This is the string that shows the current date. The width of the month calendar control must be the larger of the width of the "today" string or the width obtained by **MCM_GETMINREQRECT**. (Usually the "today" string is the smaller value, but for maximum portability, you should not count on this.) Using the proper dimensions, you can resize the month calendar using a function such as **MoveWindow( )**, described earlier. Here is the sequence used to accomplish these steps by the example program.

```
hCal = CreateWindow(MONTHCAL_CLASS,
            "Month Calendar", // not used
            WS_BORDER | WS_VISIBLE | WS_CHILD,
            0, 0, 0, 0,
            hdwnd, NULL, hInst, NULL);

// size the calendar
MonthCal_GetMinReqRect(hCal, &rect); // get min size

// now, check that "today" string fits
todaywidth = MonthCal_GetMaxTodayWidth(hCal);
if(todaywidth > rect.right) rect.right = todaywidth;

// finally, resize the control
MoveWindow(hCal, 0, 0, rect.right, rect.bottom, 1);
```

14

After this sequence has executed, the control will be precisely large enough to hold one month's worth of dates, plus all of the menus and controls required by the calendar.

Demonstrating a Month Calendar Control

The following program demonstrates a month calendar. The main menu allows you to activate the calendar or to display the currently selected date. The calendar is displayed within a dialog box. In addition to the calendar itself, the dialog box holds three buttons: Show Date, OK, and Cancel. Pressing Show Date shows the currently selected date. Pressing OK stores the currently selected date in the global variable **st**. Pressing Cancel leaves the previous contents of **st** unchanged. The contents of **st** are used to display the currently selected date from the main menu. Sample output is shown in Figure 14-3.

```
// Demonstrate a month calendar.

#include <windows.h>
#include <commctrl.h>
#include <cstdio>
#include "cal.h"


LRESULT CALLBACK WindowFunc(HWND, UINT, WPARAM, LPARAM);
BOOL CALLBACK DialogFunc(HWND, UINT, WPARAM, LPARAM);

char szWinName[] = "MyWin"; // name of window class
```

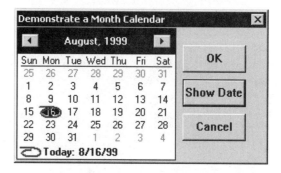

Sample output from the month calendar control

Figure 14-3.

```
HINSTANCE hInst;
HWND hCal;
SYSTEMTIME st;
int dateset = 0;

int WINAPI WinMain(HINSTANCE hThisInst, HINSTANCE hPrevInst,
                   LPSTR lpszArgs, int nWinMode)
{
  MSG msg;
  HWND hwnd;
  WNDCLASSEX wcl;
  HACCEL hAccel;
  INITCOMMONCONTROLSEX cc;

  // Define a window class.
  wcl.cbSize = sizeof(WNDCLASSEX);

  wcl.hInstance = hThisInst;      // handle to this instance
  wcl.lpszClassName = szWinName;  // window class name
  wcl.lpfnWndProc = WindowFunc;   // window function
  wcl.style = 0;                  // default style

  wcl.hIcon = LoadIcon(NULL, IDI_APPLICATION); // large icon
  wcl.hIconSm = NULL; // use small version of large icon
  wcl.hCursor = LoadCursor(NULL, IDC_ARROW);   // cursor style

  wcl.lpszMenuName = "MonthCalMenu"; // main menu

  wcl.cbClsExtra = 0; // no extra memory needed
  wcl.cbWndExtra = 0;

  // Make the window background white.
  wcl.hbrBackground = (HBRUSH) GetStockObject(WHITE_BRUSH);

  // Register the window class.
  if(!RegisterClassEx(&wcl)) return 0;

  /* Now that a window class has been registered, a window
     can be created. */
  hwnd = CreateWindow(
    szWinName, // name of window class
    "Using a Month Calendar", // title
    WS_OVERLAPPEDWINDOW, // window style - normal
    CW_USEDEFAULT, // X coordinate - let Windows decide
    CW_USEDEFAULT, // Y coordinate - let Windows decide
```

14

```
    CW_USEDEFAULT, // width - let Windows decide
    CW_USEDEFAULT, // height - let Windows decide
    NULL,          // no parent window
    NULL,          // no menu
    hThisInst,     // instance handle
    NULL           // no additional arguments
  );

  hInst = hThisInst; // save the current instance handle

  // Load the keyboard accelerators.
  hAccel = LoadAccelerators(hThisInst, "MonthCalMenu");

  // Initialize the common controls.
  cc.dwSize = sizeof(INITCOMMONCONTROLSEX);
  cc.dwICC = ICC_DATE_CLASSES;
  InitCommonControlsEx(&cc);

  // Display the window.
  ShowWindow(hwnd, nWinMode);
  UpdateWindow(hwnd);

  // Create the message loop.
  while(GetMessage(&msg, NULL, 0, 0))
  {
    if(!TranslateAccelerator(hwnd, hAccel, &msg)) {
      TranslateMessage(&msg); // translate keyboard messages
      DispatchMessage(&msg); // return control to Windows 2000
    }
  }

  return msg.wParam;
}

/* This function is called by Windows 2000 and is passed
   messages from the message queue.
*/
LRESULT CALLBACK WindowFunc(HWND hwnd, UINT message,
                            WPARAM wParam, LPARAM lParam)
{
  int response;
  char str[255];

  switch(message) {
    case WM_COMMAND:
```

```
          switch(LOWORD(wParam)) {
            case IDM_DIALOG:
              DialogBox(hInst, "MonthCalDB", hwnd,
                        (DLGPROC) DialogFunc);
              break;
            case IDM_GETDATE:
              if(dateset) {
                sprintf(str, "%d/%d/%d",
                        st.wMonth, st.wDay, st.wYear);
                MessageBox(hwnd, str, "Date Selected", MB_OK);
              } else
                MessageBox(hwnd, "Date not set", "Error", MB_OK);
              break;
            case IDM_EXIT:
              response = MessageBox(hwnd, "Quit the Program?",
                                    "Exit", MB_YESNO);
              if(response == IDYES) PostQuitMessage(0);
              break;
            case IDM_HELP:
              MessageBox(hwnd, "Try the calendar.", "Help", MB_OK);
              break;
          }
          break;
        case WM_DESTROY: // terminate the program
          PostQuitMessage(0);
          break;
        default:
          /* Let Windows 2000 process any messages not specified in
             the preceding switch statement. */
          return DefWindowProc(hwnd, message, wParam, lParam);
      }

      return 0;
    }


    // Dialog function.
    BOOL CALLBACK DialogFunc(HWND hdwnd, UINT message,
                             WPARAM wParam, LPARAM lParam)
    {
      static HWND hCal;
      RECT rect;
      int todaywidth;
      char str[255];
      SYSTEMTIME tempst;
```

14

```
      switch(message) {
        case WM_INITDIALOG:
          hCal = CreateWindow(MONTHCAL_CLASS,
                     "Month Calendar", // not used
                     WS_BORDER | WS_VISIBLE | WS_CHILD,
                     0, 0, 0, 0,
                     hdwnd, NULL, hInst, NULL);

          // now, size the calendar
          MonthCal_GetMinReqRect(hCal, &rect); // get min size
          todaywidth = MonthCal_GetMaxTodayWidth(hCal);
          if(todaywidth > rect.right) rect.right = todaywidth;
          MoveWindow(hCal, 0, 0, rect.right, rect.bottom, 1);
          return 1;
        case WM_COMMAND:
          switch(LOWORD(wParam)) {
            case ID_GETDATE:
              MonthCal_GetCurSel(hCal, &tempst);
              sprintf(str, "%d/%d/%d", tempst.wMonth,
                      tempst.wDay, tempst.wYear);
              MessageBox(hdwnd, str, "Date Selected", MB_OK);
              return 1;
            case IDOK:
              MonthCal_GetCurSel(hCal, &st);
              dateset = 1;
            case IDCANCEL:
              EndDialog(hdwnd, 0);
              return 1;
          }
      }

      return 0;
}
```

The program uses the following resource file:

```
#include <windows.h>
#include "cal.h"

MonthCalMenu MENU
{
  POPUP "&Calendar" {
    MENUITEM "&Calendar\tF2", IDM_DIALOG
    MENUITEM "&Get Selected Date\tF3", IDM_GETDATE
    MENUITEM "E&xit\tCtrl+X", IDM_EXIT
```

```
  }
  MENUITEM "&Help", IDM_HELP
}

MonthCalMenu ACCELERATORS
{
  VK_F2, IDM_DIALOG, VIRTKEY
  VK_F3, IDM_GETDATE, VIRTKEY
  "^X", IDM_EXIT
  VK_F1, IDM_HELP, VIRTKEY
}

MonthCalDB DIALOGEX 18, 18, 150, 78
CAPTION "Demonstrate a Month Calendar"
STYLE DS_MODALFRAME | WS_POPUP | WS_CAPTION | WS_SYSMENU
{
  DEFPUSHBUTTON "OK", IDOK, 100, 10, 38, 16
  PUSHBUTTON "Show Date", ID_GETDATE, 100, 30, 38, 16
  PUSHBUTTON "Cancel", IDCANCEL, 100, 50, 38, 16
}
```

The header file CAL.H is shown here:

```
#define IDM_DIALOG  100
#define IDM_GETDATE 101
#define IDM_EXIT    102
#define IDM_HELP    103

#define ID_GETDATE  201
```

Common Control Wrap-up

The preceding five chapters have explored several of the most popular common controls. If you can apply these controls, you will have no trouble learning to use the remaining ones on your own. Just remember that, in general, using a common control involves these basic mechanisms:

◆ Creation and initialization

◆ Sending messages to the control

◆ Handling messages from the control

As stated in the beginning of Chapter 10, the common controls give your application a modern, sophisticated look. You should take advantage of them whenever you can.

14

CHAPTER 15

Thread-based
Multitasking

This chapter describes Windows 2000's thread-based multitasking system. As mentioned at the start of this book, Windows 2000 supports two forms of multitasking. The first type is process-based. This is the type of multiprocessing that Windows has supported from its inception. A *process* is, essentially, a program that is executing. In process-based multitasking, two or more processes can execute concurrently. The second type of multitasking is thread-based. A *thread* is a path of execution within a process. In Windows 2000, each process has at least one thread, but it may have two or more. Thread-based multitasking allows two or more parts of a single program to execute concurrently. This added dimension allows extremely efficient programs to be written because you, the programmer, can define the separate threads of execution and thus manage the way that your program executes.

The inclusion of thread-based multitasking has increased the need for a special type of multitasking feature called *synchronization*, which allows the execution of threads (and processes) to be coordinated in certain well-defined ways. Windows 2000 has a complete subsystem devoted to synchronization, and its key features are discussed in this chapter.

HISTORICAL PERSPECTIVE: 16-bit Windows 3.1 does not support thread-based multitasking.

Creating a Multithreaded Program

If you have never programmed for a multithreaded environment before, then you are in for a pleasant surprise. Multithreaded multitasking adds a new dimension to your programming because it lets you, the programmer, more fully control how pieces of your program execute. This allows you to implement more efficient programs. For example, you could assign one thread the job of sorting a file, a second thread the job of gathering information from some remote source, and a third thread the task of performing user input. Because of multithreaded multitasking, each thread can execute concurrently, with little wasted CPU time.

The thread of execution created when a program begins is called its main thread.

It is important to understand that all processes have at least one thread of execution. For the sake of discussion, this is called the *main thread*. The main thread is the thread created when your program begins. From within the main thread it is possible to create one or more other threads. In general, once a new thread is created, it also begins execution. Thus, each process starts with one thread of execution and may create one or more additional threads.

Creating a Thread

To create a thread, use the API function **CreateThread( )**. Its prototype is shown here:

HANDLE CreateThread(LPSECURITY_ATTRIBUTES *lpSecAttr,*
                  DWORD *dwStackSize,*
                  LPTHREAD_START_ROUTINE *lpThreadFunc,*
                  LPVOID *lpParam,*
                  DWORD *dwFlags,*
                  LPDWORD *lpdwThreadID*);

Here, *lpSecAttr* is a pointer to a set of security attributes pertaining to the thread. However, if *lpSecAttr* is **NULL**, then the default security descriptor is used.

NOTE: Windows 2000's security system is discussed in Chapter 20. For the purposes of this chapter, the default security descriptor is always used.

Each thread has its own stack. You can specify the size of the new thread's stack, in bytes, using the *dwStackSize* parameter. If this value is zero, then the thread will be given a stack that is the same size as the creating thread. In this case, the stack will be expanded, if necessary. (Specifying zero is the common approach taken to thread stack size.)

Each thread of execution begins with a call to a function, called the *thread function*, within the creating process. Execution of the thread continues until the thread function returns. The address of this function (that is, the entry point to the thread) is specified in *lpThreadFunc*. All thread functions must have this prototype:

DWORD WINAPI threadfunc(LPVOID *param*);

The thread function is the entry point to a new thread of execution.

Any argument that you need to pass to the new thread is specified in **CreateThread( )**'s *lpParam*. This 32-bit value is received by the thread function in its parameter. This parameter may be used for any purpose. The function returns its exit status.

The *dwFlags* parameter determines the execution state of the thread. If it is zero, the thread begins execution immediately. If it is **CREATE_SUSPEND**, the thread is created in a suspended state, awaiting execution. (It may be started using a call to **ResumeThread( )**, discussed later.)

The identifier associated with the thread is returned in the double word pointed to by *lpdwThreadID*.

The function returns a handle to the thread if successful or **NULL** if a failure occurs. The thread handle can be explicitly destroyed by calling **CloseHandle( )**. Otherwise, it will be destroyed automatically when the parent process ends.

Terminating a Thread

As stated, a thread of execution terminates when its entry function returns. The process may also terminate the thread manually, using either **TerminateThread( )** or **ExitThread( )**, whose prototypes are shown here:

    BOOL TerminateThread(HANDLE *hThread*, DWORD *dwStatus*);

    VOID ExitThread(DWORD *dwStatus*);

For **TerminateThread( )**, *hThread* is the handle of the thread to be terminated. **ExitThread( )** can only be used to terminate the thread that calls **ExitThread( )**. For both functions, *dwStatus* is the termination status. **TerminateThread( )** returns nonzero if successful and zero otherwise.

Calling **ExitThread( )** is functionally equivalent to allowing a thread function to return normally. This means that the stack is properly reset. When a thread is terminated using **TerminateThread( )**, it is stopped immediately and does not perform any special cleanup activities. Also, **TerminateThread( )** may stop a thread during an important operation. For these reasons, it is usually best (and easiest) to let a thread terminate normally when its entry function returns. This is the approach used by most of the example programs in this chapter.

A Multithreaded Example

The following program creates two threads each time the Demonstrate Thread menu option is selected. Each thread iterates a **for** loop 5,000 times, displaying the number of the iteration each time the loop repeats. As you will see when you run the program, both threads appear to execute concurrently.

```
// A simple multithreaded program.

#include <windows.h>
#include <cstring>
#include <cstdio>
#include "thread.h"

#define MAX 5000

LRESULT CALLBACK WindowFunc(HWND, UINT, WPARAM, LPARAM);
DWORD WINAPI MyThread1(LPVOID param);
DWORD WINAPI MyThread2(LPVOID param);

char szWinName[] = "MyWin"; // name of window class

char str[255]; // holds output strings

DWORD Tid1, Tid2; // thread IDs

int WINAPI WinMain(HINSTANCE hThisInst, HINSTANCE hPrevInst,
                   LPSTR lpszArgs, int nWinMode)
{
  HWND hwnd;
  MSG msg;
  WNDCLASSEX wcl;
  HACCEL hAccel;

  // Define a window class.
  wcl.cbSize = sizeof(WNDCLASSEX);

  wcl.hInstance = hThisInst;      // handle to this instance
  wcl.lpszClassName = szWinName; // window class name
  wcl.lpfnWndProc = WindowFunc;  // window function
  wcl.style = 0;                 // default style

  wcl.hIcon = LoadIcon(NULL, IDI_APPLICATION); // large icon
  wcl.hIconSm = NULL; // use small version of large icon
  wcl.hCursor = LoadCursor(NULL, IDC_ARROW);  // cursor style

  wcl.lpszMenuName = "ThreadMenu"; // main menu

  wcl.cbClsExtra = 0; // no extra memory needed
  wcl.cbWndExtra = 0;

  // Make the window background white.
```

```
    wcl.hbrBackground = (HBRUSH) GetStockObject(WHITE_BRUSH);

    // Register the window class.
    if(!RegisterClassEx(&wcl)) return 0;

    /* Now that a window class has been registered, a window
       can be created. */
    hwnd = CreateWindow(
      szWinName, // name of window class
      "Demonstrate Threads", // title
      WS_OVERLAPPEDWINDOW, // window style - normal
      CW_USEDEFAULT, // X coordinate - let Windows decide
      CW_USEDEFAULT, // Y coordinate - let Windows decide
      CW_USEDEFAULT, // width - let Windows decide
      CW_USEDEFAULT, // height - let Windows decide
      NULL,          // no parent window
      NULL,          // no override of class menu
      hThisInst,     // instance handle
      NULL           // no additional arguments
    );

    // Load the keyboard accelerators.
    hAccel = LoadAccelerators(hThisInst, "ThreadMenu");

    // Display the window.
    ShowWindow(hwnd, nWinMode);
    UpdateWindow(hwnd);

    // Create the message loop.
    while(GetMessage(&msg, NULL, 0, 0))
    {
      if(!TranslateAccelerator(hwnd, hAccel, &msg)) {
        TranslateMessage(&msg); // translate keyboard messages
        DispatchMessage(&msg); // return control to Windows 2000
      }
    }

    return msg.wParam;
}

/* This function is called by Windows 2000 and is passed
   messages from the message queue.
*/
LRESULT CALLBACK WindowFunc(HWND hwnd, UINT message,
                            WPARAM wParam, LPARAM lParam)
```

```
      {
        int response;

        switch(message) {
          case WM_COMMAND:
            switch(LOWORD(wParam)) {
              case IDM_THREAD: // create the threads
                CreateThread(NULL, 0,
                             (LPTHREAD_START_ROUTINE)MyThread1,
                             (LPVOID) hwnd, 0, &Tid1);
                CreateThread(NULL, 0,
                             (LPTHREAD_START_ROUTINE)MyThread2,
                             (LPVOID) hwnd, 0, &Tid2);
                break;
              case IDM_EXIT:
                response = MessageBox(hwnd, "Quit the Program?",
                                      "Exit", MB_YESNO);
                if(response == IDYES) PostQuitMessage(0);
                break;
              case IDM_HELP:
                MessageBox(hwnd,
                           "F1: Help\nF2: Demonstrate Threads",
                           "Help", MB_OK);
                break;
            }
            break;
          case WM_DESTROY: // terminate the program
            PostQuitMessage(0);
            break;
          default:
            /* Let Windows 2000 process any messages not specified in
               the preceding switch statement. */
            return DefWindowProc(hwnd, message, wParam, lParam);
        }
        return 0;
      }

      // A thread of execution within the process.
      DWORD WINAPI MyThread1(LPVOID param)
      {
        int i;
        HDC hdc;

        for(i=0; i<MAX; i++) {
          sprintf(str, "Thread 1: loop # %5d ", i);
```

15

```
      hdc = GetDC((HWND) param);
      TextOut(hdc, 1, 1, str, strlen(str));
      ReleaseDC((HWND) param, hdc);
    }
  return 0;
}

// Another thread of execution within the process.
DWORD WINAPI MyThread2(LPVOID param)
{
  int i;
  HDC hdc;

  for(i=0; i<MAX; i++) {
    sprintf(str, "Thread 2: loop # %5d ", i);
    hdc = GetDC((HWND) param);
    TextOut(hdc, 1, 20, str, strlen(str));
    ReleaseDC((HWND) param, hdc);
  }
  return 0;
}
```

This program uses the THREAD.H file shown here:

```
#define IDM_THREAD 100
#define IDM_HELP   101
#define IDM_EXIT   102
```

The program also requires this resource file:

```
#include <windows.h>
#include "thread.h"

ThreadMenu MENU
{
  POPUP "&Threads" {
    MENUITEM "Demonstrate &Threads\tF2", IDM_THREAD
    MENUITEM "E&xit\tCtrl+X", IDM_EXIT
  }
  MENUITEM "&Help", IDM_HELP
}

ThreadMenu ACCELERATORS
{
```

```
  VK_F1, IDM_HELP, VIRTKEY
  VK_F2, IDM_THREAD, VIRTKEY
  "^X", IDM_EXIT
}
```

Sample output from the program is shown in Figure 15-1.

A Closer Look at the Multithreaded Program

Each time the Demonstrate Threads option is chosen, the following code
executes:

```
case IDM_THREAD: // create the threads
  CreateThread(NULL, 0,
               (LPTHREAD_START_ROUTINE)MyThread1,
               (LPVOID) hwnd, 0, &Tid1);
  CreateThread(NULL, 0,
               (LPTHREAD_START_ROUTINE)MyThread2,
               (LPVOID) hwnd, 0, &Tid2);
  break;
```

As you can see, the first call to **CreateThread( )** activates **MyThread1( )**,
and the second call activates **MyThread2( ).** Notice that the handle of the
main window (**hwnd**) is passed as a parameter to each thread function. This
handle is used by the threads to obtain a device context so that they can
output information to the main window.

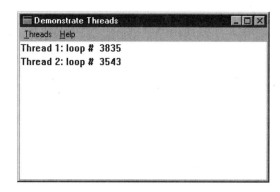

Sample output
from the
multithreaded
program
Figure 15-1.

Once started, each thread of execution (including the main thread) runs independently. For example, while the threads are executing, you may activate the Help message box, exit the program, or even start another set of threads. If you exit the program, then any child threads will be automatically terminated.

Before continuing, you might want to experiment with this program. For example, as it now stands, each thread terminates when its associated function terminates. Try terminating a thread early, using **ExitThread( )**. Also, try starting multiple instances of each thread.

Alternatives to CreateThread( ) and ExitThread( )

Depending upon what C/C++ compiler you are using and what C/C++ standard library functions are employed in your program, you may need to avoid the use of **CreateThread( )** and **ExitThread( )** because they may result in small memory leaks. A *memory leak* is the loss of a small amount of memory. It is usually caused when a portion of memory allocated by a program is not released. For many C/C++ compilers, including Microsoft Visual C++, if a multithreaded program utilizes standard C/C++ library functions and uses **CreateThread( )** and **ExitThread( )**, then small amounts of memory will be lost. (If your program does not use the C/C++ standard library, then no such losses will occur.) To eliminate this problem, you must use functions defined by the C/C++ runtime library, rather than those specified by the Win32 API, to start and stop threads.

A memory leak is the loss of a small amount of memory.

In this section we will examine the alternative thread creation and termination functions provided by Microsoft. If you are using a different compiler, check your user manual to determine if you need to bypass **CreateThread( )** and **ExitThread( )** and how to do so, if necessary.

The Microsoft Alternatives

The Microsoft Visual C++ alternatives to **CreateThread( )** and **ExitThread( )** are **_beginthreadex( )** and **_endthreadex( )**. They use the header file PROCESS.H. Here is the prototype for **_beginthreadex( )**:

```
unsigned long _beginthreadex(void *secAttr, unsigned stackSize,
                    unsigned (__stdcall *threadFunc)(void *),
                    void *param, unsigned flags,
                    unsigned *threadID);
```

As you can see, the parameters to **_beginthreadex( )** parallel those to **CreateThread( )**. Further, they have the same meaning as those specified by **CreateThread( )**. *secAttr* is a pointer to a set of security attributes pertaining to the thread. However, if *secAttr* is **NULL**, then the default security descriptor is used. The size of the new thread's stack, in bytes, is passed in *stackSize* parameter. If this value is zero, then the thread will be given a stack that is the same size as the main thread of the process that creates it and will be expanded, if necessary.

The address of the thread function (that is, the entry point to the thread) is specified in *threadFunc*. For **_beginthreadex( )**, a thread function must have this prototype:

    unsigned __stdcall threadfunc(void * *param*);

This prototype is functionally equivalent to the one for **CreateThread( )**, but it uses different type names. Any argument that you need to pass to the new thread is specified in **CreateThread( )**'s *param* parameter.

The *flags* parameter determines the execution state of the thread. If it is zero, the thread begins execution immediately. If it is **CREATE_SUSPEND**, the thread is created in a suspended state, awaiting execution. (It may be started using a call to **ResumeThread( )**.) The identifier associated with a thread is returned in the double word pointed to by *threadID*.

The function returns a handle to the thread if successful or zero if a failure occurs.

The prototype for **_endthreadex( )** is shown here:

    void _endthreadex(unsigned *status*);

It functions just like **ExitThread( )** by stopping the thread and returning the exit code specified in *status*.

When using **_beginthreadex( )** and **_endthreadex( )**, you must remember to link in the multithreaded library.

NOTE: Microsoft also supplies the functions **_beginthread( )** and **_endthread( )**, which are used to create and terminate a thread. However, **_beginthread( )** is a generic thread function that does not provide the detailed level of control available in **CreateThread( )**.

15

Using the Microsoft C/C++ Thread Functions

To demonstrate the use of the C/C++ library thread functions, the preceding thread program will be converted so that it uses Microsoft's **_beginthreadex( )** function. Since the meaning and order of the parameters are the same for both **CreateThread( )** and **_beginthreadex( )**, this is a simple matter. The three changes that need to be made are

◆ PROCESS.H must be included in the program.

◆ The prototypes of the thread functions must be changed to reflect the type names used by **_beginthreadex( )**.

◆ The calls to **CreateThread( )** need to be replaced by calls to **_beginthreadex( )**.

You must also link your program with the multithreaded library. (To do so, first activate the Project Settings property sheet. Then, select the C/C++ tab. Next, select Code Generation from the Category list box and then choose Multithreaded in the Use runtime library list box.) The following program reflects these changes:

```
// Use Microsoft's _beginthreadex() function.

#include <windows.h>
#include <cstring>
#include <cstdio>
#include <process.h>
#include "thread.h"

#define MAX 5000

LRESULT CALLBACK WindowFunc(HWND, UINT, WPARAM, LPARAM);

// use type names required by _beginthreadex()
unsigned __stdcall MyThread1(void * param);
unsigned __stdcall MyThread2(void * param);

char szWinName[] = "MyWin"; // name of window class

char str[255]; // holds output strings

DWORD Tid1, Tid2; // thread IDs

int WINAPI WinMain(HINSTANCE hThisInst, HINSTANCE hPrevInst,
```

```
                     LPSTR lpszArgs, int nWinMode)
{
  HWND hwnd;
  MSG msg;
  WNDCLASSEX wcl;
  HACCEL hAccel;

  // Define a window class.
  wcl.cbSize = sizeof(WNDCLASSEX);

  wcl.hInstance = hThisInst;     // handle to this instance
  wcl.lpszClassName = szWinName; // window class name
  wcl.lpfnWndProc = WindowFunc;  // window function
  wcl.style = 0;                 // default style

  wcl.hIcon = LoadIcon(NULL, IDI_APPLICATION); // large icon
  wcl.hIconSm = NULL; // use small version of large icon
  wcl.hCursor = LoadCursor(NULL, IDC_ARROW);  // cursor style

  wcl.lpszMenuName = "ThreadMenu"; // main menu

  wcl.cbClsExtra = 0; // no extra memory needed
  wcl.cbWndExtra = 0;

  // Make the window background white.
  wcl.hbrBackground = (HBRUSH) GetStockObject(WHITE_BRUSH);

  // Register the window class.
  if(!RegisterClassEx(&wcl)) return 0;

  /* Now that a window class has been registered, a window
     can be created. */
  hwnd = CreateWindow(
    szWinName, // name of window class
    "Demonstrate Threads", // title
    WS_OVERLAPPEDWINDOW, // window style - normal
    CW_USEDEFAULT, // X coordinate - let Windows decide
    CW_USEDEFAULT, // Y coordinate - let Windows decide
    CW_USEDEFAULT, // width - let Windows decide
    CW_USEDEFAULT, // height - let Windows decide
    NULL,          // no parent window
    NULL,          // no override of class menu
    hThisInst,     // instance handle
    NULL           // no additional arguments
  );
```

15

```
      // Load the keyboard accelerators.
      hAccel = LoadAccelerators(hThisInst, "ThreadMenu");

      // Display the window.
      ShowWindow(hwnd, nWinMode);
      UpdateWindow(hwnd);

      // Create the message loop.
      while(GetMessage(&msg, NULL, 0, 0))
      {
        if(!TranslateAccelerator(hwnd, hAccel, &msg)) {
          TranslateMessage(&msg); // translate keyboard messages
          DispatchMessage(&msg); // return control to Windows 2000
        }
      }

      return msg.wParam;
}

/* This function is called by Windows 2000 and is passed
   messages from the message queue.
*/
LRESULT CALLBACK WindowFunc(HWND hwnd, UINT message,
                            WPARAM wParam, LPARAM lParam)
{
  int response;

  switch(message) {
    case WM_COMMAND:
      switch(LOWORD(wParam)) {
        case IDM_THREAD:
          // create threads using _beginthreadex()
          _beginthreadex(NULL, 0, MyThread1,
                    (LPVOID) hwnd, 0,
                    (unsigned *) &Tid1);
          _beginthreadex(NULL, 0, MyThread2,
                    (LPVOID) hwnd, 0,
                    (unsigned *) &Tid2);
          break;
        case IDM_EXIT:
          response = MessageBox(hwnd, "Quit the Program?",
                          "Exit", MB_YESNO);
          if(response == IDYES) PostQuitMessage(0);
          break;
```

```
          case IDM_HELP:
            MessageBox(hwnd,
                       "F1: Help\nF2: Demonstrate Threads",
                       "Help", MB_OK);
            break;
        }
        break;
      case WM_DESTROY: // terminate the program
        PostQuitMessage(0);
        break;
      default:
        /* Let Windows 2000 process any messages not specified in
           the preceding switch statement. */
        return DefWindowProc(hwnd, message, wParam, lParam);
    }

    return 0;
}

// A thread of execution within the process.
unsigned __stdcall MyThread1(void * param)
{
  int i;
  HDC hdc;

  for(i=0; i<MAX; i++) {
    sprintf(str, "Thread 1: loop # %5d ", i);
    hdc = GetDC((HWND) param);
    TextOut(hdc, 1, 1, str, strlen(str));
    ReleaseDC((HWND) param, hdc);
  }

  return 0;
}

// Another thread of execution within the process.
unsigned __stdcall MyThread2(void * param)
{
  int i;
  HDC hdc;

  for(i=0; i<MAX; i++) {
    sprintf(str, "Thread 2: loop # %5d ", i);
    hdc = GetDC((HWND) param);
    TextOut(hdc, 1, 20, str, strlen(str));
```

15

```
    ReleaseDC((HWND) param, hdc);
  }

  return 0;
}
```

Avoiding the C Library Functions

For many multithreaded programs, it is possible to avoid the use of the C/C++ standard library. In such cases, you can use **CreateThread( )** and **ExitThread( )** without the potential for incurring memory leaks. For example, many of the programs in this book use only two C library functions: **sprintf( )** and **strlen( )**. Win32 contains substitutes for these functions called **wsprintf( )** and **lstrlen( )**, respectively. These functions contain some additional functionality that allow them to handle Unicode characters, but for the most part they work the same as their C/C++ library relatives.

wsprintf( ) and lstrlen( ) are Win32 functions that can be substituted for the standard C functions sprintf( ) and strlen( ).

Win32 also contains substitutes for several other C/C++ string-handling functions, including, **lstrcat( )**, **lstrcmp( )**, and **lstrcpy( )**. Various character functions are also provided, such as **CharUpper( )**, **CharLower( )**, **IsCharAlpha( )**, and **IsCharAlphaNumeric( )**. In general, if you are using the C/C++ standard library only for simple character handling, you can probably bypass it by using the functions built into Win32.

In the remaining examples in this chapter, threads will be created using **CreateThread( )**. The functions **wsprintf( )** and **lstrlen( )** will be substituted for **sprintf( )** and **strlen( )** in order to avoid the C/C++ standard library. Therefore, the examples that follow should be able to be compiled and correctly executed by any C/C++ compiler capable of creating Windows 2000 programs.

Suspending and Resuming a Thread

A thread of execution can be suspended by calling **SuspendThread( )**. It can be resumed by calling **ResumeThread( )**. The prototypes for these functions are shown here:

DWORD SuspendThread(HANDLE *hThread*);

DWORD ResumeThread(HANDLE *hThread*);

A thread will be resumed only after its suspend count reaches zero.

For both functions, the handle to the thread is passed in *hThread*.

Each thread of execution has associated with it a *suspend count*. If this count is zero, then the thread is not suspended. If it is nonzero, the thread is in a suspended state. Each call to **SuspendThread( )** increments the suspend count. Each call to **ResumeThread( )** decrements the suspend count. A suspended thread will resume only after its suspend count has reached zero. Therefore, to resume a suspended thread implies that there must be the same number of calls to **ResumeThread( )** as there have been calls to **SuspendThread( )**.

Both functions return the thread's previous suspend count or –1 if an error occurs.

Thread Priorities

Each thread has associated with it a priority setting. A thread's priority determines how much CPU time a thread receives. Low priority threads receive little. High priority threads receive a lot. Of course, how much CPU time a thread receives has a profound impact on its execution characteristics and its interaction with other threads concurrently executing in the system.

A thread's priority determines how much CPU time it receives.

A thread's priority setting is the combination of two values: the overall priority class of the process and the priority setting of the individual thread relative to that priority class. That is, a thread's actual priority is determined by combining the process's priority class with the thread's individual priority level. Each priority component is examined next.

Priority Classes

You can obtain the current priority class by calling **GetPriorityClass( )**, and you can set the priority class by calling **SetPriorityClass( )**. The prototypes for these functions are shown here:

DWORD GetPriorityClass(HANDLE *hApp*);

BOOL SetPriorityClass(HANDLE *hApp*, DWORD *dwPriority*);

Here, *hApp* is the handle of the process. **GetPriorityClass( )** returns the priority class of the application or zero on failure. For **SetPriorityClass( )**, *dwPriority* specifies the process's new priority class. The priority class values are shown here, in order of highest to lowest priority:

REALTIME_PRIORITY_CLASS
HIGH_PRIORITY_CLASS
ABOVE_NORMAL_PRIORITY_CLASS (new for 2000)
NORMAL_PRIORITY_CLASS
BELOW_NORMAL_PRIORITY_CLASS (new for 2000)
IDLE_PRIORITY_CLASS

Programs are given the **NORMAL_PRIORITY_CLASS** by default. Usually, you won't need to alter the priority class of your program. In fact, changing a process's priority class can have negative consequences on the overall performance of the computer system. For example, if you increase a program's priority class to **REALTIME_PRIORITY_CLASS**, it will dominate the CPU. For some specialized applications, you may need to increase an application's priority class, but usually you won't. For the purposes of this chapter, the default priority setting of a process will be used.

NEW FOR 2000:   There are two new priority classes for Windows 2000: **ABOVE_NORMAL_PRIORITY_CLASS** and **BELOW_NORMAL_PRIORITY_CLASS**. These additions give Windows 2000 more finely grained control over priorities than was previously available.

Thread Priorities

For any given priority class, each individual thread's priority determines how much CPU time it receives within its process. When a thread is first created, it is given normal priority, but you can change a thread's priority—even while it is executing.

You can obtain a thread's priority setting by calling **GetThreadPriority( )**. You can increase or decrease a thread's priority using **SetThreadPriority( )**. The prototypes for these functions are shown here:

    BOOL SetThreadPriority(HANDLE *hThread*, int *Priority*);

    int GetThreadPriority(HANDLE *hThread*);

For both functions, *hThread* is the handle of the thread. For
SetThreadPriority( ), *Priority* is the new priority setting. For
GetThreadPriority( ), the current priority setting is returned.
The priority settings are shown here, in order of highest to lowest:

Thread Priority	Value
THREAD_PRIORITY_TIME_CRITICAL	15
THREAD_PRIORITY_HIGHEST	2
THREAD_PRIORITY_ABOVE_NORMAL	1
THREAD_PRIORITY_NORMAL	0
THREAD_PRIORITY_BELOW_NORMAL	–1
THREAD_PRIORITY LOWEST	–2
THREAD_PRIORITY_IDLE	–15

These values are actually increments or decrements that are applied relative to
the priority class of the process. Through the combination of a process' priority
class and thread priority, Windows 2000 supports several different priority
settings for application programs.

GetThreadPriority( ) returns **THREAD_PRIORITY_ERROR_RETURN**
if an error occurs.

For the most part, if a thread has the normal priority class, you can freely
experiment with changing its priority setting without fear of negatively
affecting overall system performance. As you will see, the thread control panel
developed in the next section allows you to alter the priority setting of threads
within a process (but does not change their priority class).

Creating a Thread Control Panel

When developing multithreaded programs, it is often useful to experiment
with various priority settings. It is also useful to be able to dynamically
suspend and resume a thread, or even to terminate a thread. As you will see,
it is quite easy, using the functions just described, to create a thread control
panel that allows you to accomplish these things. Further, you can use the
control panel while your multithreaded program is running. The dynamic
nature of the thread control panel allows you to easily change the execution
profile of a thread and observe the results.

The thread control panel developed in this section is capable of controlling two threads. For the sake of simplicity the control panel is implemented as a modal dialog box that is executed as part of the program's main thread. It relies upon global thread handles, which must be defined by any program that uses the control panel.

The thread control panel is capable of performing the following actions:

◆ Setting a thread's priority

◆ Suspending a thread

◆ Resuming a thread

◆ Terminating a thread

It also displays the current priority setting of each thread.

As stated, the control panel is a modal dialog box. As you know, when a modal dialog box is activated, it usually implies that the rest of the application is suspended until the user closes the box. However, in a multithreaded program, it is possible for a modal dialog box to run in its own thread. When this is the case, the other threads in the program remain active. As mentioned, the thread control panel will be executed by the main thread of any program that uses it. Therefore, it will be executing in its own thread of execution. The advantage of this approach is that modal dialog boxes are a little easier to create than are modeless ones. Also, since the dialog box may run in its own thread, there is no particular advantage, in this case, to using a modeless dialog box. As you become more familiar with multithreaded programming, you will find that it simplifies several previously difficult programming situations.

A Thread Control Panel Program

Here is a program that includes the thread control panel and demonstrates its use. It does so by adding the panel to the thread demonstration program shown earlier. Sample output is contained in Figure 15-2. To use the program, first begin execution of the threads (by selecting Start Threads from the Threads menu) and then activate the thread control panel. Once the control panel is active, you can experiment with different priority settings, among other things.

```
// Using a thread control panel.

#include <windows.h>
#include "panel.h"
```

```
#define MAX 50000

#define NUMPRIORITIES 5
#define OFFSET 2

LRESULT CALLBACK WindowFunc(HWND, UINT, WPARAM, LPARAM);
LRESULT CALLBACK ThreadPanel(HWND, UINT, WPARAM, LPARAM);

DWORD WINAPI MyThread1(LPVOID param);
DWORD WINAPI MyThread2(LPVOID param);

char szWinName[] = "MyWin"; // name of window class

char str[255]; // holds output strings

DWORD Tid1, Tid2; // thread IDs
HANDLE hThread1, hThread2; // thread handles

int ThPriority1, ThPriority2;   // thread priorities
int suspend1 = 0, suspend2 = 0; // thread states

char priorities[NUMPRIORITIES][80] = {
  "Lowest",
  "Below Normal",
  "Normal",
  "Above Normal",
  "Highest"
};

HINSTANCE hInst;

int WINAPI WinMain(HINSTANCE hThisInst, HINSTANCE hPrevInst,
                   LPSTR lpszArgs, int nWinMode)
{
  HWND hwnd;
  MSG msg;
  WNDCLASSEX wcl;
  HACCEL hAccel;

  // Define a window class.
  wcl.cbSize = sizeof(WNDCLASSEX);

  wcl.hInstance = hThisInst;      // handle to this instance
  wcl.lpszClassName = szWinName; // window class name
  wcl.lpfnWndProc = WindowFunc;  // window function
```

```
    wcl.style = 0;                      // default style

    wcl.hIcon = LoadIcon(NULL, IDI_APPLICATION); // large icon
    wcl.hIconSm = NULL; // use small version of large icon
    wcl.hCursor = LoadCursor(NULL, IDC_ARROW);   // cursor style

    wcl.lpszMenuName = "ThreadPanelMenu"; // main menu

    wcl.cbClsExtra = 0; // no extra memory needed
    wcl.cbWndExtra = 0;

    // Make the window background white.
    wcl.hbrBackground = (HBRUSH) GetStockObject(WHITE_BRUSH);

    // Register the window class.
    if(!RegisterClassEx(&wcl)) return 0;

    /* Now that a window class has been registered, a window
       can be created. */
    hwnd = CreateWindow(
      szWinName, // name of window class
      "Using a Thread Control Panel", // title
      WS_OVERLAPPEDWINDOW, // window style - normal
      CW_USEDEFAULT, // X coordinate - let Windows decide
      CW_USEDEFAULT, // Y coordinate - let Windows decide
      CW_USEDEFAULT, // width - let Windows decide
      CW_USEDEFAULT, // height - let Windows decide
      NULL,          // no parent window
      NULL,          // no override of class menu
      hThisInst,     // instance handle
      NULL           // no additional arguments
    );

    hInst = hThisInst; // save instance handle

    // Load the keyboard accelerators.
    hAccel = LoadAccelerators(hThisInst, "ThreadPanelMenu");

    // Display the window.
    ShowWindow(hwnd, nWinMode);
    UpdateWindow(hwnd);

    // Create the message loop.
    while(GetMessage(&msg, NULL, 0, 0))
    {
```

```
      if(!TranslateAccelerator(hwnd, hAccel, &msg)) {
        TranslateMessage(&msg); // translate keyboard messages
        DispatchMessage(&msg); // return control to Windows 2000
      }
    }

    return msg.wParam;
}

/* This function is called by Windows 2000 and is passed
   messages from the message queue.
*/
LRESULT CALLBACK WindowFunc(HWND hwnd, UINT message,
                            WPARAM wParam, LPARAM lParam)
{
    int response;

    switch(message) {
      case WM_COMMAND:
        switch(LOWORD(wParam)) {
          case IDM_THREAD: // create the threads
            suspend1 = suspend2 = 0;
            hThread1 = CreateThread(NULL, 0,
                          (LPTHREAD_START_ROUTINE)MyThread1,
                          (LPVOID) hwnd, 0, &Tid1);
            hThread2 = CreateThread(NULL, 0,
                          (LPTHREAD_START_ROUTINE)MyThread2,
                          (LPVOID) hwnd, 0, &Tid2);
            break;
          case IDM_PANEL: // activate control panel
            DialogBox(hInst, "ThreadPanelDB", hwnd,
                          (DLGPROC) ThreadPanel);
            break;
          case IDM_EXIT:
            response = MessageBox(hwnd, "Quit the Program?",
                              "Exit", MB_YESNO);
            if(response == IDYES) PostQuitMessage(0);
            break;
          case IDM_HELP:
            MessageBox(hwnd,
                      "F1: Help\nF2: Start Threads\nF3: Panel",
                      "Help", MB_OK);
            break;
        }
        break;
```

```
      case WM_DESTROY: // terminate the program
        PostQuitMessage(0);
        break;
      default:
        /* Let Windows 2000 process any messages not specified in
           the preceding switch statement. */
        return DefWindowProc(hwnd, message, wParam, lParam);
    }

  return 0;
}

// A thread of execution within the process.
DWORD WINAPI MyThread1(LPVOID param)
{
  int i;
  HDC hdc;

  for(i=0; i<MAX; i++) {
    wsprintf(str, "Thread 1: loop # %5d ", i);
    hdc = GetDC((HWND) param);
    TextOut(hdc, 1, 1, str, lstrlen(str));
    ReleaseDC((HWND) param, hdc);
  }

  return 0;
}

// Another thread of execution within the process.
DWORD WINAPI MyThread2(LPVOID param)
{
  int i;
  HDC hdc;

  for(i=0; i<MAX; i++) {
    wsprintf(str, "Thread 2: loop # %5d ", i);
    hdc = GetDC((HWND) param);
    TextOut(hdc, 1, 20, str, lstrlen(str));
    ReleaseDC((HWND) param, hdc);
  }

  return 0;
}

// Thread control panel dialog box.
```

```
LRESULT CALLBACK ThreadPanel(HWND hdwnd, UINT message,
                             WPARAM wParam, LPARAM lParam)
{
  long i;
  HWND hpbRes, hpbSus;

  switch(message) {
    case WM_INITDIALOG:
      // initialize list boxes
      for(i=0; i<NUMPRIORITIES; i++) {
        SendDlgItemMessage(hdwnd, IDD_LB1,
            LB_ADDSTRING, 0, (LPARAM) priorities[i]);
        SendDlgItemMessage(hdwnd, IDD_LB2,
            LB_ADDSTRING, 0, (LPARAM) priorities[i]);
      }

      // get current priority
      ThPriority1 = GetThreadPriority(hThread1) + OFFSET;
      ThPriority2 = GetThreadPriority(hThread2) + OFFSET;

      // update list box
      SendDlgItemMessage(hdwnd, IDD_LB1, LB_SETCURSEL,
                         (WPARAM) ThPriority1, 0);
      SendDlgItemMessage(hdwnd, IDD_LB2, LB_SETCURSEL,
                         (WPARAM) ThPriority2, 0);

      // set suspend and resume buttons for first thread
      hpbSus = GetDlgItem(hdwnd, IDD_SUSPEND1);
      hpbRes = GetDlgItem(hdwnd, IDD_RESUME1);
      if(suspend1) {
        EnableWindow(hpbSus, 0); // disable Suspend
        EnableWindow(hpbRes, 1); // enable Resume
      }
      else {
        EnableWindow(hpbSus, 1); // enable Suspend
        EnableWindow(hpbRes, 0); // disable Resume
      }

      // set suspend and resume buttons for second thread
      hpbSus = GetDlgItem(hdwnd, IDD_SUSPEND2);
      hpbRes = GetDlgItem(hdwnd, IDD_RESUME2);
      if(suspend2) {
        EnableWindow(hpbSus, 0); // disable Suspend
        EnableWindow(hpbRes, 1); // enable Resume
      }
```

15

```
      else {
        EnableWindow(hpbSus, 1); // enable Suspend
        EnableWindow(hpbRes, 0); // disable Resume
      }

      return 1;
    case WM_COMMAND:
      switch(wParam) {
        case IDD_TERMINATE1:
          TerminateThread(hThread1, 0);
          return 1;
        case IDD_TERMINATE2:
          TerminateThread(hThread2, 0);
          return 1;
        case IDD_SUSPEND1:
          SuspendThread(hThread1);
          hpbSus = GetDlgItem(hdwnd, IDD_SUSPEND1);
          hpbRes = GetDlgItem(hdwnd, IDD_RESUME1);
          EnableWindow(hpbSus, 0); // disable Suspend
          EnableWindow(hpbRes, 1); // enable Resume
          suspend1 = 1;
          return 1;
        case IDD_RESUME1:
          ResumeThread(hThread1);
          hpbSus = GetDlgItem(hdwnd, IDD_SUSPEND1);
          hpbRes = GetDlgItem(hdwnd, IDD_RESUME1);
          EnableWindow(hpbSus, 1); // enable Suspend
          EnableWindow(hpbRes, 0); // disable Resume
          suspend1 = 0;
          return 1;
        case IDD_SUSPEND2:
          SuspendThread(hThread2);
          hpbSus = GetDlgItem(hdwnd, IDD_SUSPEND2);
          hpbRes = GetDlgItem(hdwnd, IDD_RESUME2);
          EnableWindow(hpbSus, 0); // disable Suspend
          EnableWindow(hpbRes, 1); // enable Resume
          suspend2 = 1;
          return 1;
        case IDD_RESUME2:
          ResumeThread(hThread2);
          hpbSus = GetDlgItem(hdwnd, IDD_SUSPEND2);
          hpbRes = GetDlgItem(hdwnd, IDD_RESUME2);
          EnableWindow(hpbSus, 1); // enable Suspend
          EnableWindow(hpbRes, 0); // disable Resume
```

```
                    suspend2 = 0;
                    return 1;
                  case IDOK: // actually change priorities
                    ThPriority1 = SendDlgItemMessage(hdwnd, IDD_LB1,
                                   LB_GETCURSEL, 0, 0);
                    ThPriority2 = SendDlgItemMessage(hdwnd, IDD_LB2,
                                   LB_GETCURSEL, 0, 0);
                    SetThreadPriority(hThread1, ThPriority1-OFFSET);
                    SetThreadPriority(hThread2, ThPriority2-OFFSET);
                    return 1;
                  case IDCANCEL:
                    EndDialog(hdwnd, 0);
                    return 1;
              }
          }
      return 0;
}
```

This program requires the header file PANEL.H, shown here:

```
#define IDM_THREAD     100
#define IDM_HELP       101
#define IDM_PANEL      102
#define IDM_EXIT       103

#define IDD_LB1        200
#define IDD_LB2        201
#define IDD_TERMINATE1 202
#define IDD_TERMINATE2 203
#define IDD_SUSPEND1   204
#define IDD_SUSPEND2   205
#define IDD_RESUME1    206
#define IDD_RESUME2    207
#define IDD_TEXT1      208
#define IDD_TEXT2      209
#define IDD_TEXT3      210
```

The resource file required by the program is shown here:

```
#include <windows.h>
#include "panel.h"

ThreadPanelMenu MENU
```

15

```
    {
      POPUP "&Threads" {
        MENUITEM "&Start Threads\tF2", IDM_THREAD
        MENUITEM "&Control Panel\tF3", IDM_PANEL
        MENUITEM "E&xit\tCtrl+X", IDM_EXIT
      }
      MENUITEM "&Help", IDM_HELP
    }

ThreadPanelDB DIALOGEX 20, 20, 170, 140
CAPTION "Thread Control Panel"
STYLE DS_MODALFRAME | WS_POPUP | WS_CAPTION | WS_SYSMENU
{
    DEFPUSHBUTTON "Change", IDOK, 80, 105, 33, 14
    PUSHBUTTON "Done", IDCANCEL, 15, 120, 33, 14
    PUSHBUTTON "Terminate 1", IDD_TERMINATE1, 10, 10, 42, 12
    PUSHBUTTON "Terminate 2", IDD_TERMINATE2, 10, 60, 42, 12
    PUSHBUTTON "Suspend 1", IDD_SUSPEND1, 10, 25, 42, 12
    PUSHBUTTON "Resume 1", IDD_RESUME1, 10, 40, 42, 12
    PUSHBUTTON "Suspend 2", IDD_SUSPEND2, 10, 75, 42, 12
    PUSHBUTTON "Resume 2", IDD_RESUME2, 10, 90, 42, 12
    LISTBOX IDD_LB1, 65, 11, 63, 42, LBS_NOTIFY | WS_VISIBLE |
            WS_BORDER | WS_VSCROLL | WS_TABSTOP
    LISTBOX IDD_LB2, 65, 61, 63, 42, LBS_NOTIFY | WS_VISIBLE |
            WS_BORDER | WS_VSCROLL | WS_TABSTOP
    CTEXT "Thread 1", IDD_TEXT1, 140, 22, 24, 18
    CTEXT "Thread 2", IDD_TEXT2, 140, 73, 24, 18
    CTEXT "Thread Priority", IDD_TEXT3, 65, 0, 64, 10
}

ThreadPanelMenu ACCELERATORS
{
  VK_F1, IDM_HELP, VIRTKEY
  VK_F2, IDM_THREAD, VIRTKEY
  VK_F3, IDM_PANEL, VIRTKEY
  "^X", IDM_EXIT
}
```

Sample output
from the
thread control
panel sample
program

Figure 15-2.

A Closer Look at the Thread Control Panel

Let's take a closer look at the thread control panel. To begin, notice that the
program defines several global variables that are used by the control panel.
They are

```
DWORD Tid1, Tid2; // thread IDs
HANDLE hThread1, hThread2; // thread handles

int ThPriority1, ThPriority2;   // thread priorities
int suspend1 = 0, suspend2 = 0; // thread states

char priorities[NUMPRIORITIES][80] = {
  "Lowest",
  "Below Normal",
  "Normal",
  "Above Normal",
  "Highest"
};
```

Here, **Tid1** and **Tid2** will hold the IDs of the two threads. **hThread1** and **hThread2** are the handles to the two threads of execution. These handles store the values returned by **CreateThread( )** when the threads are created. **ThPriority1** and **ThPriority2** hold the current priority settings of the threads. The variables **suspend1** and **suspend2** are used by the control panel to store the state of each thread. The **priorities** array holds strings that will be used to initialize the list boxes used inside the control panel dialog box. These describe the priority settings of each string.

The program also defines the following macros:

```
#define NUMPRIORITIES 5
#define OFFSET 2
```

NUMPRIORITIES defines the number of priority settings. Using the control panel you can set a thread to one of the following priorities:

THREAD_PRIORITY_HIGHEST

THREAD_PRIORITY_ABOVE_NORMAL

THREAD_PRIORITY_NORMAL

THREAD_PRIORITY_BELOW_NORMAL

THREAD_PRIORITY LOWEST

The other two thread priority settings

THREAD_PRIORITY_TIME_CRITICAL

THREAD_PRIORITY_IDLE

are not supported because, relative to the control panel, they are of little practical value. For example, if you want to create a time-critical application, you are better off making its priority class time-critical.

OFFSET defines an offset that will be used to translate between list box indexes and thread priorities. You should recall that normal priority has the value zero. In this example, the highest priority is **THREAD_PRIORITY_HIGHEST**, which is 2. The lowest priority is **THREAD_PRIORITY_LOWEST**, which is –2. Since list box indexes begin at zero, the offset is used to convert between indexes and priority settings.

The thread control panel is handled by the dialog function shown here:

```
// Thread control panel dialog box.
LRESULT CALLBACK ThreadPanel(HWND hdwnd, UINT message,
                                    WPARAM wParam, LPARAM lParam)
{
  long i;
  HWND hpbRes, hpbSus;

  switch(message) {
    case WM_INITDIALOG:
      // initialize list boxes
      for(i=0; i<NUMPRIORITIES; i++) {
        SendDlgItemMessage(hdwnd, IDD_LB1,
            LB_ADDSTRING, 0, (LPARAM) priorities[i]);
        SendDlgItemMessage(hdwnd, IDD_LB2,
            LB_ADDSTRING, 0, (LPARAM) priorities[i]);
      }

      // get current priority
      ThPriority1 = GetThreadPriority(hThread1) + OFFSET;
      ThPriority2 = GetThreadPriority(hThread2) + OFFSET;

      // update list box
      SendDlgItemMessage(hdwnd, IDD_LB1, LB_SETCURSEL,
                        (WPARAM) ThPriority1, 0);
      SendDlgItemMessage(hdwnd, IDD_LB2, LB_SETCURSEL,
                        (WPARAM) ThPriority2, 0);

      // set suspend and resume buttons for first thread
      hpbSus = GetDlgItem(hdwnd, IDD_SUSPEND1);
      hpbRes = GetDlgItem(hdwnd, IDD_RESUME1);
      if(suspend1) {
        EnableWindow(hpbSus, 0); // disable Suspend
        EnableWindow(hpbRes, 1); // enable Resume
      }
      else {
        EnableWindow(hpbSus, 1); // enable Suspend
        EnableWindow(hpbRes, 0); // disable Resume
```

15

```
    }

    // set suspend and resume buttons for second thread
    hpbSus = GetDlgItem(hdwnd, IDD_SUSPEND2);
    hpbRes = GetDlgItem(hdwnd, IDD_RESUME2);
    if(suspend2) {
      EnableWindow(hpbSus, 0); // disable Suspend
      EnableWindow(hpbRes, 1); // enable Resume
    }
    else {
      EnableWindow(hpbSus, 1); // enable Suspend
      EnableWindow(hpbRes, 0); // disable Resume
    }

    return 1;
case WM_COMMAND:
  switch(wParam) {
    case IDD_TERMINATE1:
      TerminateThread(hThread1, 0);
      return 1;
    case IDD_TERMINATE2:
      TerminateThread(hThread2, 0);
      return 1;
    case IDD_SUSPEND1:
      SuspendThread(hThread1);
      hpbSus = GetDlgItem(hdwnd, IDD_SUSPEND1);
      hpbRes = GetDlgItem(hdwnd, IDD_RESUME1);
      EnableWindow(hpbSus, 0); // disable Suspend
      EnableWindow(hpbRes, 1); // enable Resume
      suspend1 = 1;
      return 1;
    case IDD_RESUME1:
      ResumeThread(hThread1);
      hpbSus = GetDlgItem(hdwnd, IDD_SUSPEND1);
      hpbRes = GetDlgItem(hdwnd, IDD_RESUME1);
      EnableWindow(hpbSus, 1); // enable Suspend
      EnableWindow(hpbRes, 0); // disable Resume
      suspend1 = 0;
      return 1;
    case IDD_SUSPEND2:
      SuspendThread(hThread2);
      hpbSus = GetDlgItem(hdwnd, IDD_SUSPEND2);
```

```
         hpbRes = GetDlgItem(hdwnd, IDD_RESUME2);
         EnableWindow(hpbSus, 0); // disable Suspend
         EnableWindow(hpbRes, 1); // enable Resume
         suspend2 = 1;
         return 1;
       case IDD_RESUME2:
         ResumeThread(hThread2);
         hpbSus = GetDlgItem(hdwnd, IDD_SUSPEND2);
         hpbRes = GetDlgItem(hdwnd, IDD_RESUME2);
         EnableWindow(hpbSus, 1); // enable Suspend
         EnableWindow(hpbRes, 0); // disable Resume
         suspend2 = 0;
         return 1;
       case IDOK: // actually change priorities
         ThPriority1 = SendDlgItemMessage(hdwnd, IDD_LB1,
                            LB_GETCURSEL, 0, 0);
         ThPriority2 = SendDlgItemMessage(hdwnd, IDD_LB2,
                            LB_GETCURSEL, 0, 0);
         SetThreadPriority(hThread1, ThPriority1-OFFSET);
         SetThreadPriority(hThread2, ThPriority2-OFFSET);
         return 1;
       case IDCANCEL:
         EndDialog(hdwnd, 0);
         return 1;
     }
   }
   return 0;
}
```

When the control panel begins, it performs the following sequence:

1. It initializes the two list boxes used by the panel.
2. It obtains the current priority setting for each thread.
3. It highlights each thread's priority within the list boxes.
4. If a thread is suspended, then the appropriate Suspend push button is disabled. Otherwise, the corresponding Resume button is disabled.

After the dialog box has been initialized, you can change a thread's priority by first selecting the new setting in its priorities list box and then pressing the Change button. Remember, the new priority setting that you select does not become active until you press Change.

You can suspend a thread by pressing its Suspend push button. The global variables **suspend1** and **suspend2** hold the current suspend status of each thread. Zero means the thread is running. Nonzero means that the thread is suspended. To resume a suspended thread, press its Resume button. The purpose of **suspend1** and **suspend2** is to disable the Suspend buttons when the dialog box is initialized. Remember, for any given thread, there must be one call to **ResumeThread( )** for each call to **SuspendThread( )** in order to restart it. By disabling a thread's Suspend button after it has been suspended, you can prevent multiple calls to **SuspendThread( )**. Since the control panel can be closed and then reopened during the execution of the threads, the state of the Suspend and Resume buttons must be set whenever the panel is initialized. These variables are reset each time a new set of threads is started.

You can terminate a thread by pressing its Terminate button. Once a thread has been terminated, it cannot be resumed. Notice that the control panel uses **TerminateThread( )** to halt execution of a thread. As mentioned earlier, this function must be used with care. If you use the control panel to experiment with threads of your own, then you will want to make sure that no harmful side effects are possible.

Before moving on, you might want to experiment with the preceding program, noticing the effects of the different priority settings.

Synchronization

Synchronization is the mechanism that allows you to control the execution of two or more threads.

When using multiple threads or processes it is sometimes necessary to coordinate the activities of two or more of them. This process is called *synchronization*. The most common use of synchronization is when two or more threads need access to a shared resource that must be used by only one thread at a time. For example, when one thread is writing to a file, a second thread must be prevented from doing so at the same time. The mechanism that prevents this is called *serialization*. Another situation requiring synchronization is when one thread is waiting for an event that is caused by another thread. In this case, there must be some means by which the first thread is held in a suspended state until the event has occurred. Then, the waiting thread must resume execution.

Changing the Main Thread's Priority

A thought may have occurred to you while using or reading about the thread control panel. You may have wondered why the control panel controls only two threads—those created by the program—and not all three. As you know, all programs have at least one thread of execution, the main thread. In the example, the main thread is the third thread concurrently executing when the program is run. However, the main thread cannot be affected by the control panel. The reason for this is twofold. First, generally, you will not want to affect the priority of the main thread. It is usually better to initiate additional threads for this purpose. The second reason is that not all operations are applicable to the main thread. For example, if you suspend the execution of the main thread, your program cannot be terminated! Furthermore, since the dialog box that supports the control panel is part of the main thread, there is no way to restart it if you do suspend it. For these reasons, it is usually best to simply let the main thread execute at its default priority setting, which is **THREAD_PRIORITY_NORMAL**.

The preceding disclaimer notwithstanding, it is possible to monitor and adjust the priority setting of the main thread. To do so, you will need to acquire a handle to the thread. The easiest way to do this is to call **GetCurrentThread( )**, whose prototype is shown here:

```
HANDLE GetCurrentThread(void);
```

This function returns a pseudohandle to the current thread. The pseudohandle returned by **GetCurrentThread( )** can, however, be used any place that a normal thread handle can.

To see the effects of adjusting the priorities of the main thread, try altering the code inside the **IDM_THREAD** case of the preceding program so that **hThread2** is assigned the handle of the main thread. This change is shown here:

```
hThread1 = CreateThread(NULL, 0,
                (LPTHREAD_START_ROUTINE)MyThread1,
                (LPVOID) hwnd, 0, &Tid1);
            CreateThread(NULL, 0,
```

15

IN DEPTH

CONTINUED

```
                      (LPTHREAD_START_ROUTINE)MyThread2,
                      (LPVOID) hwnd, 0, &Tid2);

// assign hThread2 the handle of the main thread
hThread2 = GetCurrentThread();
```

After making this change, when you activate the thread control panel, Thread 2 will be the main thread. Be careful, however—if you suspend the main thread, you will not be able to remove your program from memory without resorting to the Task Manager!

Let's begin by defining some terms. There are two general states that a task may be in. First, it may be *executing* (or, ready to execute as soon as it obtains its time slice). Second, a task may be *blocked*, awaiting some resource or event, in which case execution is *suspended* until the needed resource is available or the event occurs.

If you are not familiar with the synchronization/serialization problem, you can read about the most common solution, the semaphore, in the next section. (If this is familiar territory for you, skip ahead.)

Understanding the Synchronization Problem

Windows 2000 must provide special services that allow access to a shared resource to be serialized because, without help from the operating system, there is no way for one process or thread to know that it has sole access to a resource. To understand this problem, imagine that you are writing programs for a multitasking operating system that does not provide any synchronization support. Further imagine that you have two concurrently executing processes, A and B, both of which require access from time to time to some resource R (such as a disk file) that can be accessed by only one task at a time. As a means of preventing one program from accessing R while the other is using it, try the following solution. First, establish a variable called **flag** that can be accessed by both programs. Your programs initialize **flag** to 0. Next, before using each piece of code that accesses R, you wait for **flag** to be cleared, then set **flag**, access R, and finally clear **flag**. That is, before either program accesses R it executes this piece of code:

```
while(flag) ; // wait for flag to be cleared
flag = 1; // set flag

// ... access resource R ...

flag = 0; // clear the flag
```

The idea behind this code is that neither process will access R if **flag** is set. Conceptually, this approach is in the spirit of the correct solution. However, in actual fact it leaves much to be desired for one simple reason: it won't always work! Let's see why.

Using the code just given, it is possible for both processes to access R at the same time. The **while** loop is, in essence, performing repeated load and compare instructions on **flag;** in other words, it is testing **flag**'s value. When **flag** is cleared, the next line of code sets **flag**'s value. The trouble is that it is possible for these two operations to be performed in two different time slices. Between the two time slices, the value of **flag** might have been accessed by the other process, thus allowing R to be used by both processes at the same time. To help understand this situation, imagine that process A enters the **while** loop and finds that **flag** is zero, which is the green light to access R. However, before it can set **flag** to 1, its time slice expires and process B resumes execution. If B executes its **while**, it too will find that **flag** is not set and assume that it is safe to access R. However, when A resumes it will also begin accessing R. The crucial aspect of the problem is that the testing and setting of **flag** do not comprise one uninterruptable operation. Rather, as just illustrated, they can be separated by a time slice. No matter how you try, there is no way, using only application-level code, that you can absolutely guarantee that one and only one process will access R at one time.

The solution to the synchronization problem is as elegant as it is simple. The operating system (in this case Windows 2000) provides a routine that in one uninterrupted operation tests and, if possible, sets a flag. In the language of operating systems engineers, this is called a *test and set* operation. For historical reasons, the flags used to control serialization and provide synchronization between threads (and processes) are called *semaphores*. The semaphore is at the core of the Windows 2000 synchronization system.

A semaphore synchronizes access to a resource.

15

Windows 2000 Synchronization Objects

Windows 2000 supports five types of synchronization objects. The first type is the classic semaphore. A semaphore can be used to allow a limited number of processes or threads access to a resource. When using a semaphore, the resource can be completely serialized, in which case one and only one thread or process can access it at any one time, or the semaphore can be used to allow no more than a small number of processes or threads access at any one time. Semaphores are implemented using a counter that is decremented when a task is granted the semaphore and incremented when the task releases it.

The second synchronization object is the *mutex semaphore*. A mutex semaphore is used to serialize a resource so that one and only one thread or process can access it at any one time. In essence, a mutex semaphore is a special case version of a standard semaphore.

The third synchronization object is the *event object*. It can be used to block access to a resource until some other thread or process signals that it can be used. (That is, an event object signals that a specified event has occurred.)

The fourth synchronization object is the *waitable timer*. A waitable timer blocks a thread's execution until a specific time. Waitable timers offer some exciting possibilities, especially for background tasks.

You can prevent a section of code from being used by more than one thread at a time by making it into a *critical section,* using a critical section object. Once a critical section is entered by one thread, no other thread can use it until the first thread has left the critical section. (Critical sections apply only to threads within a process.)

With the exception of critical sections, the other synchronization objects can themselves be used to serialize threads within a process or processes. In fact, semaphores are a common and simple means of interprocess communication.

This chapter describes how to create and use a semaphore, an event object, and a waitable timer. After you understand these synchronization objects, the mutex semaphore and the critical section will be easy for you to master on your own. Remember, at the core of all of synchronization, in one way or another, either implicitly or explicitly, is the concept of the semaphore, so we will begin with it.

Using a Semaphore to Synchronize Threads

Before you can use a semaphore, you must create one using
CreateSemaphore( ), whose prototype is shown here:

HANDLE CreateSemaphore(LPSECURITY_ATTRIBUTES *lpSecAttr*,
                             LONG *InitialCount*,
                             LONG *MaxCount*,
                             LPCSTR *lpszName*);

Here, *lpSecAttr* is a pointer to the security attributes. If *lpSecAttr* is **NULL**, the
default security descriptor is used.

A semaphore can allow one or more tasks access to an object. The number of
tasks allowed to simultaneously access an object is determined by the value
of *MaxCount*. If this value is 1, then the semaphore acts much like a mutex
semaphore, allowing one and only one thread or process access to the
resource at any one time.

Semaphores use a counter to keep track of how many tasks have currently
been granted access. If the count is zero, then no further access can be granted
until a task releases the semaphore. If the count is greater than zero, then the
semaphore is said to be *signaled,* which means that another thread can be
granted access. Each time a thread is granted access, the count is decremented.
The initial count of the semaphore is specified in *InitialCount.* If this value is
zero, then initially all objects waiting on the semaphore will be blocked until
the semaphore is released elsewhere by your program. Typically, this value is set
initially to 1 or more, indicating that the semaphore can be granted to at least
one task. In any event, *InitialCount* must be non-negative and less than or equal
to the value specified in *MaxCount.*

lpszName points to a string that becomes the name of the semaphore
object. Semaphores are global objects that may be used by other processes.
As such, when two processes each open a semaphore using the same name,
both are referring to the same semaphore. In this way, two processes can be
synchronized. The name may also be **NULL**, in which case, the semaphore
is localized to one process. If *lpszName* specifies the name of an already
existent semaphore, then *InitialCount* and *MaxCount* are not used.

The **CreateSemaphore( )** function returns a handle to the semaphore if
successful or **NULL** on failure.

Once you have created a semaphore, you use it by calling two related functions: **WaitForSingleObject( )** and **ReleaseSemaphore( )**. The prototypes for these functions are shown here:

DWORD WaitForSingleObject(HANDLE *hObject*, DWORD *dwHowLong*);

BOOL ReleaseSemaphore(HANDLE *hSema*, LONG *Count*,
                       LPLONG *lpPrevCount*);

WaitForSingleObject( ) waits on a semaphore (or other type of synchronization object). It does not return until the object it is waiting on becomes available or a time-out occurs. For semaphores, *hObject* is the handle to a semaphore created earlier. The *dwHowLong* parameter specifies, in milliseconds, how long the calling routine will wait. Once that time has elapsed, a time-out error will be returned. To wait indefinitely, use the value **INFINITE**. The function returns **WAIT_OBJECT_0** when successful (that is, when access is granted). It returns **WAIT_TIMEOUT** when time-out is reached. Each time **WaitForSingleObject( )** succeeds, the counter associated with the semaphore is decremented.

ReleaseSemaphore( ) releases the semaphore and allows another thread to use it. Here, *hSema* is the handle to the semaphore. *Count* determines what value will be added to the semaphore counter. Typically, this value is 1. The *lpPrevCount* parameter points to a variable that will contain the previous semaphore count. If you don't need this count, pass **NULL** for this parameter. The function returns nonzero if successful and zero on failure.

The following program demonstrates how to use a semaphore. It reworks the first multithreaded example program so that the two threads will not execute concurrently. That is, it forces the threads to be serialized. Notice that the semaphore handle is a global variable that is created when the window is first created, thereby capable of being used by all threads (including the main thread) in the program. The program uses the same header and resource file as shown earlier.

```
// A multithreaded program that uses a semaphore.

#include <windows.h>
#include "thread.h"

#define MAX 5000

LRESULT CALLBACK WindowFunc(HWND, UINT, WPARAM, LPARAM);
```

```
DWORD WINAPI MyThread1(LPVOID param);
DWORD WINAPI MyThread2(LPVOID param);

char szWinName[] = "MyWin"; // name of window class

char str[255]; // holds output strings

DWORD Tid1, Tid2; // thread IDs

HANDLE hSema; // handle to semaphore

int WINAPI WinMain(HINSTANCE hThisInst, HINSTANCE hPrevInst,
                   LPSTR lpszArgs, int nWinMode)
{
  HWND hwnd;
  MSG msg;
  WNDCLASSEX wcl;
  HACCEL hAccel;

  // Define a window class.
  wcl.cbSize = sizeof(WNDCLASSEX);

  wcl.hInstance = hThisInst;      // handle to this instance
  wcl.lpszClassName = szWinName; // window class name
  wcl.lpfnWndProc = WindowFunc;  // window function
  wcl.style = 0;                 // default style

  wcl.hIcon = LoadIcon(NULL, IDI_APPLICATION); // large icon
  wcl.hIconSm = NULL; // use small version of large icon
  wcl.hCursor = LoadCursor(NULL, IDC_ARROW);   // cursor style

  wcl.lpszMenuName = "ThreadMenu"; // main menu

  wcl.cbClsExtra = 0; // no extra memory needed
  wcl.cbWndExtra = 0;

  // Make the window background white.
  wcl.hbrBackground = (HBRUSH) GetStockObject(WHITE_BRUSH);

  // Register the window class.
  if(!RegisterClassEx(&wcl)) return 0;

  /* Now that a window class has been registered, a window
     can be created. */
  hwnd = CreateWindow(
```

15

```
  szWinName, // name of window class
  "Use a Semaphore", // title
  WS_OVERLAPPEDWINDOW, // window style - normal
  CW_USEDEFAULT, // X coordinate - let Windows decide
  CW_USEDEFAULT, // Y coordinate - let Windows decide
  CW_USEDEFAULT, // width - let Windows decide
  CW_USEDEFAULT, // height - let Windows decide
  NULL,          // no parent window
  NULL,          // no override of class menu
  hThisInst,     // instance handle
  NULL           // no additional arguments
);

// Load the keyboard accelerators.
hAccel = LoadAccelerators(hThisInst, "ThreadMenu");

// Display the window.
ShowWindow(hwnd, nWinMode);
UpdateWindow(hwnd);

// Create the message loop.
while(GetMessage(&msg, NULL, 0, 0))
{
  if(!TranslateAccelerator(hwnd, hAccel, &msg)) {
    TranslateMessage(&msg); // translate keyboard messages
    DispatchMessage(&msg); // return control to Windows 2000
  }
}

return msg.wParam;
}

/* This function is called by Windows 2000 and is passed
   messages from the message queue.
*/
LRESULT CALLBACK WindowFunc(HWND hwnd, UINT message,
                             WPARAM wParam, LPARAM lParam)
{
  int response;

  switch(message) {
    case WM_CREATE:
      hSema = CreateSemaphore(NULL, 1, 1, NULL);
      break;
    case WM_COMMAND:
```

```
        switch(LOWORD(wParam)) {
          case IDM_THREAD:
            CreateThread(NULL, 0, (LPTHREAD_START_ROUTINE)MyThread1,
                        (LPVOID) hwnd, 0, &Tid1);
            CreateThread(NULL, 0, (LPTHREAD_START_ROUTINE)MyThread2,
                        (LPVOID) hwnd, 0, &Tid2);
            break;
          case IDM_EXIT:
            response = MessageBox(hwnd, "Quit the Program?",
                                  "Exit", MB_YESNO);
            if(response == IDYES) PostQuitMessage(0);
            break;
          case IDM_HELP:
            MessageBox(hwnd,
                      "F1: Help\nF2: Demonstrate Threads",
                      "Help", MB_OK);
            break;
        }
        break;
      case WM_DESTROY: // terminate the program
        PostQuitMessage(0);
        break;
      default:
        /* Let Windows 2000 process any messages not specified in
           the preceding switch statement. */
        return DefWindowProc(hwnd, message, wParam, lParam);
  }

  return 0;
}

// A thread of execution within the process.
DWORD WINAPI MyThread1(LPVOID param)
{
  int i;
  HDC hdc;

  // wait for access to be granted
  if(WaitForSingleObject(hSema, 10000)==WAIT_TIMEOUT) {
    MessageBox((HWND)param, "Time Out Thread 1",
              "Semaphore Error", MB_OK);
    return 0;
  }

  for(i=0; i<MAX; i++) {
```

15

```
    if(i==MAX/2) {
      /* Release at half way point.  This allows
         MyThread2 to run. */
      ReleaseSemaphore(hSema, 1, NULL);

      // Next, once again wait for access to be granted.
      if(WaitForSingleObject(hSema, 10000)==WAIT_TIMEOUT) {
        MessageBox((HWND)param, "Time Out Thread 1",
                   "Semaphore Error", MB_OK);
        return 0;
      }
    }

    wsprintf(str, "Thread 1: loop # %5d ", i);
    hdc = GetDC((HWND) param);
    TextOut(hdc, 1, 1, str, lstrlen(str));
    ReleaseDC((HWND) param, hdc);
  }

  ReleaseSemaphore(hSema, 1, NULL);

  return 0;
}

// Another thread of execution within the process.
DWORD WINAPI MyThread2(LPVOID param)
{
  int i;
  HDC hdc;

  // wait for access to be granted
  if(WaitForSingleObject(hSema, 10000)==WAIT_TIMEOUT) {
    MessageBox((HWND)param, "Time Out Thread 2",
               "Semaphore Error", MB_OK);
    return 0;
  }

  for(i=0; i<MAX; i++) {
    wsprintf(str, "Thread 2: loop # %5d ", i);
    hdc = GetDC((HWND) param);
    TextOut(hdc, 1, 20, str, lstrlen(str));
    ReleaseDC((HWND) param, hdc);
  }
```

```
ReleaseSemaphore(hSema, 1, NULL);

return 0;
}
```

A Closer Look at the Semaphore Program

In the program, **hSema** holds the handle to a semaphore that is used to serialize the two threads. When execution begins, **MyThread1( )** is activated before **MyThread2( )**. Therefore, when **MyThread1( )** is created, it immediately acquires the semaphore and begins execution. When **MyThread2( )** is created, it cannot acquire the semaphore, so it enters a wait state. Meanwhile, when the **for** loop inside **MyThread1( )** reaches **MAX**/2, it releases the semaphore, thereby allowing **MyThread2( )** to acquire it and begin execution. **MyThread1( )** then enters a wait state. Finally, **MyThread2( )** finishes and releases the semaphore. This allows **MyThread1( )** to resume.

Here are some experiments to try. First, since the semaphore allows only one thread access to it at any one time, try substituting a mutex semaphore. Second, try allowing multiple instances of the threads to execute by increasing the count associated with **hSema** to 2 or 3. Observe the effects.

Using an Event Object

As explained earlier, an event object is used to notify one thread or process when an event has occurred. To create an event object, use the **CreateEvent( )** API function shown here:

HANDLE CreateEvent(LPSECURITY_ATTRIBUTES *lpSecAttr*,
                      BOOL *Manual*,
                      BOOL *Initial*,
                      LPCSTR *lpszName*);

Here, *lpSecAttr* is a pointer to security attributes or **NULL**, in which case the default security descriptor is used. The value of *Manual* determines how the event object will be affected after the event has occurred. If *Manual* is nonzero, the event object is reset only by a call to the **ResetEvent( )** function. Otherwise, the event object is reset automatically after a blocked thread is granted access. The value of *Initial* specifies the initial state of the object. If it is nonzero, the event object is set (the event is signaled). If it is zero, the event object is cleared (the event is not signaled).

15

lpszName points to a string that becomes the name of the event object. Event objects are global objects that may be used by other processes. As such, when two processes each open an event object using the same name, both are referring to the same object. In this way, two processes can be synchronized. The name can also be **NULL**, in which case the object is localized to one process.

CreateEvent( ) returns a handle to the event object if successful and **NULL** otherwise.

Once an event object has been created, the thread (or process) that is waiting for the event to occur simply calls **WaitForSingleObject( )** using the handle of the event object as the first parameter. This causes execution of that thread or process to suspend until the event occurs.

To signal that an event has occurred, use the **SetEvent( )** function, shown here:

    BOOL SetEvent(HANDLE *hEventObject*);

Here, *hEventObject* is the handle of a previously created event object. When this function is called, the first thread or process waiting for the event will return from **WaitForSingleObject( )** and begin execution.

To see how an event object operates, modify the preceding program as follows. First, declare a global handle called **hEvent**. Next, add the following line inside the **WM_CREATE** case statement:

```
hEvent = CreateEvent(NULL, FALSE, FALSE, NULL);
```

Finally, change **MyThread1( )** and **MyThread2( )** to that shown here:

```
// First thread of execution.
DWORD WINAPI MyThread1(LPVOID param)
{
  int i;
  HDC hdc;

  // wait for access to be granted
  if(WaitForSingleObject(hEvent, 10000)==WAIT_TIMEOUT) {
    MessageBox((HWND)param, "Time Out Thread 1",
               "Event Error", MB_OK);
```

```
      return 0;
  }

  for(i=0; i<MAX; i++) {
    wsprintf(str, "Thread 1: loop # %5d ", i);
    hdc = GetDC((HWND) param);
    TextOut(hdc, 1, 1, str, lstrlen(str));
    ReleaseDC((HWND) param, hdc);
  }

  return 0;
}

// Second thread of execution.
DWORD WINAPI MyThread2(LPVOID param)
{
  int i;
  HDC hdc;

  for(i=0; i<MAX; i++) {
    wsprintf(str, "Thread 2: loop # %5d ", i);
    hdc = GetDC((HWND) param);
    TextOut(hdc, 1, 20, str, lstrlen(str));
    ReleaseDC((HWND) param, hdc);
  }

  // send event notification
  SetEvent(hEvent);

  return 0;
}
```

Now, when the program executes, **MyThread1( )** is blocked until
MyThread2( ) completes and signals that it is done.

Using a Waitable Timer

Although timers are available for all versions of Windows, the waitable timer
is a recent addition. While it is possible to link a semaphore with a standard
timer, the waitable timer makes this process much more convenient.
Waitable timers are exciting because they will make it easier to automate
all types of background tasks.

HISTORICAL PERSPECTIVE: Waitable timers were first added by Windows NT 4. They are not supported by Windows NT 3.51, Windows 95, or Windows 3.1. They are supported by Windows 98.

When you create a waitable timer, you are creating a timer that will run in the background until a predetermined time is reached. A thread can wait on that timer using the standard **WaitForSingleObject( )** function. The thread will be blocked until the timer goes off.

Waitable timers are created using the **CreateWaitableTimer( )** function, shown here:

       HANDLE CreateWaitableTimer(LPSECURITY_ATTRIBUTES *lpSecAttr*,
                               BOOL *manual*, LPCSTR *lpszName*);

Here, *lpSecAttr* points to the security descriptor to be associated with the waitable timer. If this parameter is **NULL**, the default descriptor is used. If *manual* is nonzero, the timer must be manually reset after each timing period. If it is zero, the timer is automatically reset. *lpszName* points to the name of the timer. To create an unnamed timer, pass **NULL** for this parameter. Named timers can be shared with other processes. Unnamed ones are local to the process in which they were created. The function returns a handle to the waitable timer if successful or **NULL** on failure.

Once a timer has been created, it is inactive. To set the timer, call **SetWaitableTimer( )**. Its prototype is shown here:

       BOOL SetWaitableTimer(HANDLE *hWaitTimer*,
                      const LARGE_INTEGER **TargetTime*,
                      LONG *period*,
                      PTIMERAPCROUTINE *lpTimerFunc*,
                      LPVOID *param*,
                      BOOL *Unsuspend*);

Here, *hWaitTimer* is the handle of the timer object. *TargetTime* specifies the time at which the timer will go off. The value in *period* specifies the length of time, in milliseconds, between timer activations. If *period* is zero, then the timer goes off only once. *lpTimerFunc* points to a function that will be called when the timer goes off. This function is optional. If no such function is needed, specify **NULL** for *lpTimerFunc*. The value specified by *param* is passed to the timer function. If *Unsuspend* is nonzero, then a computer that has been operating in low-power mode will be resumed. **SetWaitableTimer( )** returns nonzero if successful and zero on failure.

Timer functions pointed to by *lpTimerFunc* must have this prototype:

VOID CALLBACK *TimerFunc*(LPVOID *param*, DWORD *dwLowTime*,
                              DWORD *dwHighTime*);

Here, *param* is the value passed by **SetWaitableTimer( )**. The values in *dwLowTime* and *dwHighTime* contain the termination time in the format compatible with that contained in a **FILETIME** structure. (Time formats are described below.) Frankly, most applications of a waitable timer will not need to use a timer function.

When calling **SetWaitableTimer( )**, the target time is specified as a **LARGE_INTEGER**. This union represents time as a 64-bit integer that is compatible with the way time is represented in a **FILETIME** structure. Both are shown here:

```
typedef struct _FILETIME {
  DWORD dwLowDateTime;   // low-order 32-bits
  DWORD dwHightDateTime; // high-order 32-bits
} FILETIME;

typedef union _LARGE_INTEGER {
  struct {
    DWORD LowPart;
    LONG HighPart;
  };
  LONGLONG QuadPart;
} LARGE_INTEGER;
```

A **FILETIME** structure contains the number of 100 nanosecond units that have passed since January 1, 1601.

Win32 provides functions to convert time as represented by a **FILETIME** structure from or to a more convenient form. Perhaps the easiest way to set the target time of a waitable timer is to first describe the time using a **SYSTEMTIME** structure and then convert that structure into a **FILETIME** structure (which can be assigned to a **LARGE_INTEGER**). Recall from Chapter 14 that the **SYSTEMTIME** structure is defined like this:

```
typedef struct _SYSTEMTIME {
  WORD wYear;          // year
```

15

```
  WORD wMonth;            // month (1 through 12)
  WORD wDayOfWeek;        // day of week (0 through 6)
  WORD wDay;              // day of month (1 through 31)
  WORD wHour;             // hour
  WORD wMinute;           // minutes
  WORD wSecond;           // seconds
  WORD wMilliseconds;     // milliseconds
} SYSTEMTIME;
```

Once you have initialized the fields of a **SYSTEMTIME** structure to the desired target time, you can then call **SystemTimeToFileTime( )** to convert the time into a **FILETIME** structure. The prototype for **SystemTimeToFileTime( )** is shown here:

BOOL SystemTimeToFileTime(CONST SYSTEMTIME *lpSysTime,
                                   FILETIME *lpFileTime);

The function returns nonzero if successful and zero on failure.

For most uses of a waitable timer, you will not actually have to manually set all of the fields in the **SYSTEMTIME** structure. Usually, you can obtain the current system time and then just advance the time by the desired amount. For example, if you wanted to create a timer that would go off in one hour, you would first obtain the current time and then increase the **wHour** field appropriately. To obtain the current system time, use **GetSystemTime( )**, shown here.

VOID GetSystemTime(SYSTEMTIME *lpSysTime);

The current time of the system is returned in the structure pointed to by *lpSysTime*. The time is specified in UTC (Coordinated Universal Time), which is essentially Greenwich Mean Time.

The following program demonstrates the use of a waitable timer. Each time you press F2, a thread of execution is created. Inside this thread, a waitable timer is created and given a target time that is ten seconds in the future. Next, the window is minimized and the thread waits on that timer. When the time interval has elapsed, the window is restored and the thread resumes execution. Notice the definition of **_WIN32_WINNT** at the top of the program. Since waitable timers are relatively new, this definition may be required by some compilers to ensure that the appropriate header information is included.

```
// Demonstrate a waitable timer

/* The following is needed to ensure that the waitable
   timer API functions are available. */
#define _WIN32_WINNT 0x0400

#include <windows.h>
#include "thread.h"

#define MAX 10000

LRESULT CALLBACK WindowFunc(HWND, UINT, WPARAM, LPARAM);
DWORD WINAPI MyThread1(LPVOID param);

char szWinName[] = "MyWin"; // name of window class

char str[255]; // holds output strings

DWORD Tid1; // thread IDs

HANDLE hWaitTimer; // handle to semaphore

int WINAPI WinMain(HINSTANCE hThisInst, HINSTANCE hPrevInst,
                   LPSTR lpszArgs, int nWinMode)
{
  HWND hwnd;
  MSG msg;
  WNDCLASSEX wcl;
  HACCEL hAccel;

  // Define a window class.
  wcl.cbSize = sizeof(WNDCLASSEX);

  wcl.hInstance = hThisInst;      // handle to this instance
  wcl.lpszClassName = szWinName; // window class name
  wcl.lpfnWndProc = WindowFunc;   // window function
  wcl.style = 0;                  // default style

  wcl.hIcon = LoadIcon(NULL, IDI_APPLICATION); // large icon
  wcl.hIconSm = NULL; // use small version of large icon
  wcl.hCursor = LoadCursor(NULL, IDC_ARROW);   // cursor style

  wcl.lpszMenuName = "WaitTimerMenu"; // main menu

  wcl.cbClsExtra = 0; // no extra memory needed
```

15

```
   wcl.cbWndExtra = 0;

   // Make the window background white.
   wcl.hbrBackground = (HBRUSH) GetStockObject(WHITE_BRUSH);

   // Register the window class.
   if(!RegisterClassEx(&wcl)) return 0;

   /* Now that a window class has been registered, a window
      can be created. */
   hwnd = CreateWindow(
     szWinName, // name of window class
     "Use a Waitable Timer", // title
     WS_OVERLAPPEDWINDOW, // window style - normal
     CW_USEDEFAULT, // X coordinate - let Windows decide
     CW_USEDEFAULT, // Y coordinate - let Windows decide
     CW_USEDEFAULT, // width - let Windows decide
     CW_USEDEFAULT, // height - let Windows decide
     NULL,          // no parent window
     NULL,          // no override of class menu
     hThisInst,     // instance handle
     NULL           // no additional arguments
   );

   // Load the keyboard accelerators.
   hAccel = LoadAccelerators(hThisInst, "WaitTimerMenu");

   // Display the window.
   ShowWindow(hwnd, nWinMode);
   UpdateWindow(hwnd);

   // Create the message loop.
   while(GetMessage(&msg, NULL, 0, 0))
   {
     if(!TranslateAccelerator(hwnd, hAccel, &msg)) {
       TranslateMessage(&msg); // translate keyboard messages
       DispatchMessage(&msg); // return control to Windows 2000
     }
   }

   return msg.wParam;
}

/* This function is called by Windows 2000 and is passed
   messages from the message queue.
*/
```

```
LRESULT CALLBACK WindowFunc(HWND hwnd, UINT message,
                            WPARAM wParam, LPARAM lParam)
{
  int response;

  switch(message) {
    case WM_CREATE:
      // create the timer
      hWaitTimer = CreateWaitableTimer(NULL, 1, NULL);
      break;
    case WM_COMMAND:
      switch(LOWORD(wParam)) {
        case IDM_THREAD:
          CreateThread(NULL, 0, (LPTHREAD_START_ROUTINE)MyThread1,
                       (LPVOID) hwnd, 0, &Tid1);
          break;
        case IDM_EXIT:
          response = MessageBox(hwnd, "Quit the Program?",
                                "Exit", MB_YESNO);
          if(response == IDYES) PostQuitMessage(0);
          break;
        case IDM_HELP:
          MessageBox(hwnd,
                     "F1: Help\nF2: Demonstrate Timer",
                     "Help", MB_OK);
          break;
      }
      break;
    case WM_DESTROY: // terminate the program
      PostQuitMessage(0);
      break;
    default:
      /* Let Windows 2000 process any messages not specified in
         the preceding switch statement. */
      return DefWindowProc(hwnd, message, wParam, lParam);
  }

  return 0;
}

// Demonstrate waitable timer.
DWORD WINAPI MyThread1(LPVOID param)
{
  int i;
```

15

```
HDC hdc;
SYSTEMTIME systime;
FILETIME filetime;
LARGE_INTEGER li;

// add 10 seconds onto current system time
GetSystemTime(&systime);
SystemTimeToFileTime(&systime, &filetime);
li.LowPart = filetime.dwLowDateTime;
li.HighPart = filetime.dwHighDateTime;
li.QuadPart += 100000000L;

// set the timer
SetWaitableTimer(hWaitTimer, &li,
                 0, NULL, NULL, 0);

// minimize the window until the timer expires
ShowWindow((HWND) param, SW_MINIMIZE);

// wait for timer
if(WaitForSingleObject(hWaitTimer, 100000)==WAIT_TIMEOUT) {
   MessageBox((HWND)param, "Time Out Thread 1",
              "Timer Error", MB_OK);
   return 0;
}

// beep and restore window
MessageBeep(MB_OK);
ShowWindow((HWND) param, SW_RESTORE);

hdc = GetDC((HWND) param);
for(i=0; i<MAX; i++) {
  wsprintf(str, "Thread 1: loop # %5d ", i);
  TextOut(hdc, 1, 1, str, lstrlen(str));
}
ReleaseDC((HWND) param, hdc);

return 0;
}
```

This program uses the same THREAD.H header file described earlier. It uses this resource file:

```
#include <windows.h>
#include "thread.h"
```

```
WaitTimerMenu MENU
{
  POPUP "&Options" {
    MENUITEM "&Waitable Timer\tF2", IDM_THREAD
    MENUITEM "E&xit\tCtrl+X", IDM_EXIT
  }
  MENUITEM "&Help", IDM_HELP
}

WaitTimerMenu ACCELERATORS
{
  VK_F1, IDM_HELP, VIRTKEY
  VK_F2, IDM_THREAD, VIRTKEY
  "^X", IDM_EXIT
}
```

Uses for Waitable Timers

Waitable timers offer some interesting possibilities. For example, you could
use one to create a computerized alarm clock. To do so, create a dialog box that
allows the user to set the desired alarm time. Then, use that time to initialize
a waitable timer. You could also use a waitable timer to help create automated
backup or file transfer utilities. Although these types of tasks have always been
possible using normal timers in conjunction with other synchronization
objects, the waitable timer simplifies them.

Creating a Separate Task

Although Windows 2000's thread-based multitasking will have the most
direct impact on how you program, it is, of course, still possible to utilize
process-based multitasking where appropriate. When using process-based
multitasking, instead of starting another thread within the same program,
one program starts the execution of another program. In Windows 2000,
this is accomplished using the **CreateProcess( )** API function, whose
prototype is shown here:

BOOL CreateProcess(LPCSTR *lpszName*, LPSTR *lpszComLine*,
      LPSECURITY_ATTRIBUTES *lpProcAttr*,
      LPSECURITY_ATTRIBUTES *lpThreadAttr*,
      BOOL *InheritAttr*, DWORD *How*,
      LPVOID *lpEnv*, LPCSTR *lpszDir*,
      LPSTARTUPINFO *lpStartInfo*,
      LPPROCESS_INFORMATION *lpPInfo*);

15

To start
the execution
of another
program,
call **Create-
Process( )**.

The name of the program to execute, which may include a full path, is specified in the string pointed to by *lpszName*. Any command-line parameters required by the program are specified in the string pointed to by *lpszComLine*. However, if you specify *lpszName* as **NULL**, then the first token in the string pointed to by *lpszComLine* will be used as the program name. Thus, typically, *lpszName* is specified as **NULL** and the program name and any required parameters are specified in the string pointed to by *lpszComLine*. (If you are starting a Win16 process, then *lpszName* must be **NULL**.)

The *lpProcAttr* and *lpThreadAttr* parameters are used to specify any security attributes related to the process being created. These may be specified as **NULL**, in which case the default security descriptor is used. If *InheritAttr* is nonzero, handles in use by the creating process are inherited by the new process. If this parameter is zero, then handles are not inherited.

By default, the new process is run "normally." However, the *How* parameter can be used to specify certain additional attributes that affect how the new process will be created. (For example, you will use the *How* to specify a special priority for the process or to indicate that the process will be debugged.) If *How* is zero, then the new process is created as a normal process.

The *lpEnv* parameter points to a buffer that contains the new process' environmental parameters. If this parameter is **NULL**, then the new process inherits the creating process' environment.

The current drive and directory of the new process can be specified in the string pointed to by *lpszDir*. If this parameter is **NULL**, then the current drive and directory of the creating process is used.

The parameter *lpStartInfo* is a pointer to a **STARTUPINFO** structure that contains information that determines how the main window of the new process will look. **STARTUPINFO** is defined as shown here:

```
typedef struct _STARTUPINFO {
    DWORD cb;               // size of STARTUPINFO
    LPSTR lpReserved;       // must be NULL
    LPSTR lpDesktop;        // name of desktop
    LPSTR lpTitle;          // title of console (consoles only)
    DWORD dwX;              // upper left corner of
    DWORD dwY;              // new window
    DWORD dwXSize;          // size of new window
    DWORD dwYSize;          // size of new window
    DWORD dwXCountChars;    // console buffer size
    DWORD dwYCountChars;    // consoles buffer size
    DWORD dwFillAttribute;  // initial text color and background
```

```
    DWORD dwFlags;          // determines which fields are active
    WORD wShowWindow;       // how window is shown, SW_SHOW, etc.
    WORD cbReserved2;       // must be 0
    LPBYTE lpReserved2;     // must be NULL
    HANDLE hStdInput;       // standard handles
    HANDLE hStdOutput;
    HANDLE hStdError;
} STARTUPINFO;
```

The fields **dwX**, **dwY**, **dwXSize**, **dwYSize**, **dwXCountChars**, **dwYCountChars**, **dwFillAttribute**, **wShowWindow**, **hStdInput**, **hStdOutput**, and **hStdError** are ignored unless they are enabled by including the proper value as part of the **dwFlags** field. The values for **dwFlags** are shown here:

Macro	Enables
STARTF_USESHOWWINDOW	dwShowWindow
STARTF_USESIZE	dwXSize and dwYSize
STARTF_USEPOSITION	dwX and dwY
STARTF_USECOUNTCHARS	dwXCountChars and dwYCountChars
STARTF_USEFILLATTRIBUTE	dwFillAttribute
STARTF_USESTDHANDLES	hStdInput, hStdOutput, and hStdError

dwFlags may also include one or more of these values:

STARTF_FORCEONFEEDBACK	Feedback cursor is on
STARTF_FORCEOFFFEEDBACK	Feedback cursor is off

NOTE: The **lpTitle**, **dwXCountChars**, **dwYCountChars**, and **dwFillAttribute** fields apply only to console applications.

Generally, you will not need to use most of the fields in **STARTUPINFO**, and you can allow most to be ignored. However, you must specify **cb**, which contains the size of the structure, and several other fields must be set to **NULL**.

15

The final parameter to **CreateProcess( )** is *lpPInfo*, which is a pointer to a structure of type **PROCESS_INFORMATION**, shown here:

```
typedef struct _PROCESS_INFORMATION {
  HANDLE hProcess;    // handle to new process
  HANDLE hThread;     // handle to main thread
  DWORD dwProcessId;  // ID of new process
  DWORD dwThreadId;   // ID of new thread
} PROCESS_INFORMATION;
```

Handles to the new process and the main thread of that process are passed back to the creating process in **hProcess** and **hThread**. The new process and thread IDs are returned in **dwProcessId** and **dwThreadId**. Your program can make use of this information or ignore it.

CreateProcess( ) returns nonzero if successful and zero otherwise.

The following fragment illustrates the use of **CreateProcess( )**:

```
STARTUPINFO startinfo;
PROCESS_INFORMATION pinfo;
// ...
startinfo.cb = sizeof(STARTUPINFO);
startinfo.lpReserved = NULL;
startinfo.lpDesktop = NULL;
startinfo.lpTitle = NULL;
startinfo.dwFlags = STARTF_USESHOWWINDOW;
startinfo.cbReserved2 = 0;
startinfo.lpReserved2 = NULL;
startinfo.wShowWindow = SW_SHOW;
CreateProcess(NULL, "test.exe",
            NULL, NULL, 0, 0,
            NULL, NULL, &startinfo, &pinfo);
```

This starts the execution of a program called TEST.EXE, which must be in the current working directory of the parent process. The program is initially visible.

Once created, the new process is largely independent from the creating process. It is possible for the parent process to terminate the child, however. To do so, use the **TerminateProcess( )** API function.

HISTORICAL PERSPECTIVE: Windows 3.1 does not support **CreateProcess( )**. To start another process in Window 3.1, the **WinExec( )** function is used. However, **WinExec( )** is obsolete and should not be used for Win32 programs. When porting older programs, be sure to replace any calls to **WinExec( )** with calls to **CreateProcess( )**.

15

CHAPTER 16

Using the Two Help Systems

Windows 2000 provides extensive support for online help. As you know, nearly all applications provide the user with online instructions explaining how to use various features of the program. Most applications also provide online documentation that can be accessed via the help system. Frankly, it is not possible to write a top-notch professional Windows 2000 program without providing extensive online help. The programming techniques necessary to accomplish this are described here.

Two Styles of Help

HTML help is the new browser-style help system that uses the **HtmlHelp( )** function.

Windows 2000 supports two styles of help. The first is the traditional approach that has been used by Win32 programs for the past several years. This method uses the **WinHelp( )** API function, which displays help information in standard windows. The traditional approach is often referred to as *WinHelp help*. The second method is called *HTML help* and it uses the function **HtmlHelp( )**. As expected, HTML stands for Hypertext Markup Language and HTML help presents help information in a browser-style format.

The traditional help system uses the **WinHelp( )** function.

This chapter describes both the WinHelp help and the HTML help systems. Although HTML help is the modern help style, and the one used by Windows 2000, the traditional approach is used by a large number of existing applications, and it is still the help system of choice for a many new projects. Thus, it is important for all programmers to be familiar with WinHelp help. Also, the traditional help system runs under all 32-bit versions of Windows. However, HTML help requires that elements of Internet Explorer (3.*x* or later) be present. While Windows 2000 fulfills this requirement, many Windows 95 systems, for example, may not. Thus, to create a fully portable help system, the traditional approach must be used. Fortunately, both help systems rely upon the same low-level internals, so the differences between the two are mostly in how you create a help project.

Context-Sensitive Versus Reference Help

Reference help supports online documentation. Context-sensitive help provides information related to a specific feature.

Windows supports two general categories of help. The first is essentially online documentation and is sometimes called *reference help*. It is accessed via the standard Help window, such as the ones shown in Figure 16-1. Using the standard Help window, you can display various help topics, search for other topics, or view the contents of a help file. Reference help is used to display detailed descriptions of various features supported by the application or to act as the online version of the program's user manual. The second category of help is *context-sensitive* help. Context-sensitive help is used to display a brief description of a specific program feature within a small window. An example is shown in Figure 16-2. Both types of help are required by a professional quality Windows 2000 application. As you will see, although different in style, both of these categories of help are handled in much the same way.

(a)

(b)

(a) A traditional Help window; (b) an HTML Help window

Figure 16-1.

An example
of context-
sensitive help
Figure 16-2.

How the User Invokes Help

To properly implement a complete Windows system, your program must
support the four standard methods by which the user can invoke online help.
Specifically, the user may obtain help by:

◆   Clicking the right mouse button on an object.

◆   Clicking on the ? button and then clicking on an object.

◆   Pressing F1.

◆   Using a Help menu.

The first two methods almost always invoke context-sensitive pop-up help. In
most situations, F1 is also used to invoke context-sensitive help. Occasionally,
it invokes reference help. Selecting help through a menu usually invokes
reference help.

It is also permissible for the application program to invoke help itself,
whenever it needs to do so. For example, a program might activate the help
system when the user attempts an invalid operation.

Once the user has activated a help option, your application can respond to the request by calling either **WinHelp( )** or **HtmlHelp( )**, depending upon which help system you are using.

Using the WinHelp Help System

In this section we will examine the traditional help system, which uses the **WinHelp( )** function. As explained, **WinHelp( )** displays a traditional, or "old-style," help window. However, there is nothing wrong with using **WinHelp( )**. It offers a clean and powerful help interface when a browser-style help system is either not needed or not appropriate.

The WinHelp Help File

An RTF help file contains formatting, indexing, and cross-referencing information that is used by the WinHelp help system.

At the core of the traditional Windows help system is the *help file*. Both context-sensitive and reference help utilize the help file. WinHelp help files are not text files. Rather, they are specially compiled files that have the HLP file extension. To create a help file, you must first create an RTF (Rich Text Format) file that contains all of the help topics, plus formatting, indexing, and cross-referencing information. This file will normally have the extension RTF. This file is then compiled using a help compiler. For WinHelp help files you will use Microsoft's Help Workshop, called HCW.EXE. The output of HCW is an HLP file. Thus, relative to the help compiler, the RTF file is the source file and the HLP file is the object file.

The Rich Text Format language contains a large number of commands. The help compiler accepts only a subset of these commands. However, the help system also recognizes several additional help-related commands that are not part of the general purpose RTF language. All RTF commands begin with a \. For example, \b is the RTF command for bold. It is far beyond the scope of this chapter to discuss all RTF commands, and, indeed, an entire book is needed to fully describe the RTF language. However, this chapter describes the most important and commonly used commands relating to help files. If you will be doing extensive work with WinHelp help files, then you will need to acquire a full description of the RTF language.

In addition to the RTF file, the help compiler also uses a project file. Typically, this file is created by the HCW help compiler. In it are various settings and values that relate to the help file. WinHelp project files use the HPJ extension.

Creating a Help File

As was stated, the source code for a WinHelp help file must be in Rich Text Format. This requirement makes creating the source code for a help file a nontrivial task. Fortunately, there are three ways that you can create a help file. First, you can use a third-party automated Help authoring package. Second, you can use a text editor that generates RTF files. Third, you can use a standard text editor and manually embed RTF commands. If you will be preparing large and complex help files, the authoring package is probably the best alternative. However, for smaller applications, either of the other two choices is adequate. Since the one option that all readers will have is the third, that is the method that will be used here.

The General Form of an RTF Help File

All RTF help files have certain basic elements in common. First, the entire file must be enclosed between curly braces. That is, it must begin with a { and end with a }. Immediately following the opening curly brace must be the **\rtf** command. This command identifies the file as a Rich Text Format file and indicates which version of the Rich Text Format specification is being used. (We will be using version 1.) You must then define the character set used by the file. This will generally be the ANSI character set, which is specified using the **\ansi** command. You must also define the character fonts used by the file. This is done with the **\fonttbl** command. Thus, the general form of an RTF help file will look like this:

```
{\rtf1\ansi \fonttbl ...
    Help File Contents
}
```

Within an RTF file, additional curly braces can be used to localize the effect of various RTF commands. In this capacity, the curly braces act much like they do in a C/C++ source file: they define a block.

Some RTF Commands

Before you can create even a simple help file, you need to know a few of the most important and common RTF commands. The RTF commands used in this chapter are shown in Table 16-1. Each command is described here.

RTF Command	Meaning
\ansi	Specifies the ANSI character set.
\b	Turns on boldface.
\b0	Turns off boldface.
\f*n*	Selects the font specified by *n*.
\fs*n*	Sets font size to *n*.
\fonttbl	Defines a font table.
\footnote	Specifies keywords and index topics.
\i	Turns on italics.
\i0	Turns off italics.
\page	Indicates the end of a topic.
\par	Indicates the end of a paragraph.
\rtf*n*	Indicates which RTF specification is being used.
\tab	Moves to next tab position.
\uldb	Marks a "hot spot" link to another topic.
\v	Creates a topic link (used in conjunction with **\uldb**).

Selected Help-
Related RTF
Commands
Table 16-1.

\ansi

The **\ansi** command specifies the ANSI character set. RTF files support other character sets, such as **\mac** (Macintosh character set) or **\pc** (OEM character set). However, the ANSI character set is the one that is generally used for help files.

\b

The **\b** command turns on boldface. **\b0** turns it off. However, if the **\b** command is used within a block, then only the text within that block is boldfaced and there is no need to use the **\b0** command. For example:

```
{\b this is bold} this is not
```

Here, only the text within the curly braces will be in boldface.

\fn

The **\fn** command selects a font. The font is specified by its number. The font must have been previously defined using a **\fonttbl** statement.

\fsn

The **\fsn** command sets the font size to that specified by *n*, which is stated in half-point units. For example, **\fs24** sets the font size to 12 points.

\fonttbl

Before a font can be used, it must be included in a **\fonttbl** statement, which has the following general form:

```
{\fonttbl
 {\f1\family-name font-name;}
 {\f2\family-name font-name;}
 {\f3\family-name font-name;}
 .
 .
 .
 {\fn\family-name font-name;}
}
```

Here, *family-name* is the name of the font family (such as **froman** or **fswiss**) and *font-name* is the name of a specific font (such as Times New Roman, Arial, or Old English) within that family. The number of the font as specified in the **\f** statement will be used to select the font. A partial list of font families and names is shown here:

Family	Fonts
\froman	Times New Roman, Palatino
\fswiss	Arial
\fmodern	Courier New, Pica
\fscript	Cursive
\fdecor	Old English

For example, the following declares font 0 to be **\fswiss** Arial:

```
{\fonttbl {\f0\fswiss Arial;}}
```

\footnote

The **footnote** statement is one of the most important RTF commands when creating a help file. Its importance stems from its use in specifying topic names, context IDs, and browse sequences. The following forms of the **footnote** command are used in this chapter:

${\footnote *string*}

K{\footnote *string*}

#{\footnote *string*}

+{\footnote *sequence-name:sequence-order*}

@(\footnote *string*)

The **$** form defines a title for a topic that is also displayed in the history window of the help system. The title can include spaces. A topic title identifies the topic.

The **K** form specifies that *string* is a keyword or phrase and can include spaces. Keywords are displayed as index entries. If the first character of the string is a K, then it must be preceded by an extra space. The **K** form can be used only if a topic title has been specified.

The **#** defines a *context ID* that is used to create links and cross-references between topics. It is also used by your application program to access portions of the help file. In this form, *string* can not include spaces. As you will see, the context ID string is usually a macro that represents the ID value.

A browse sequence specifies a sequence of help topics.

The **+** form defines a *browse sequence*. A browse sequence determines the linkage between topics when the browse arrows are pressed. (The browse arrows are the << and >> arrow buttons on the Help window's button bar.) In this form, the content of *sequence-name* specifies the sequence, and *sequence-order* determines the position of the topic in that sequence. Browse sequences are performed in alphabetical order or numerical order on the basis of the values of *sequence-order*. A help file may have one or more browse sequences. To define several sequences, both the *sequence-name* and *sequence-order* specifiers in the **footnote** command are required. If your help file has only one browse sequence, then the *sequence-name* is not required. Examples of browse sequences are contained in the example help file shown later.

The **Browse-Buttons( )** macro must be included in your help project file to enable browse buttons.

To cause browse buttons to be included in the standard Help window, you must include the **BrowseButtons( )** macro in the configuration section of the project file associated with a help file that defines a browse sequence.

The @ form of the **\footnote** command is used to embed a comment.

\i

The **\i** command turns on italics. **\i0** turns off italics. However, if the **\i** command is used within a block, then only the text within that block is made italic and there is no need to use the **\i0** command.

\page

The **\page** command signals the end of a topic.

\par

The **\par** command marks the end of a paragraph. It also causes a line to be skipped. Thus, two **\par** commands in a row will skip two lines.

\rtfn

The **\rtfn** command determines which RTF specification is being used. In this chapter, version 1 is used.

\tab

The **\tab** command advances one tab stop.

\uldb

To mark a *hot spot* link, specify it using the **\uldb** command. It has the following general form:

    \uldb *text*

The *text* will be shown in the standard hot spot color and font. This command is always used in conjunction with a **\v** command.

\v

The **\v** command specifies a link to another topic. It has the following general form:

    \v *context-ID*

16

Here, *context-ID* must be the same as specified in a **#\footnote** statement. This link is executed when the hot spot associated with the **\v** command is clicked by the user.

A Sample WinHelp Help File

The following help file will be used by the **WinHelp( )** example program shown later in this chapter. This file contains all the common components of a WinHelp help file. Call this file HELPTEST.RTF.

```
{\rtf1\ansi
{\fonttbl{\f0\fswiss Arial;} {\f1\froman Times New Roman;}}
\fs40
\f1
@{\footnote This is a comment.  So is the following.}
@{\footnote This is a Sample Help File.}
${\footnote Contents}
Contents of Sample Help File
\f0
\fs20
\par
\par
\tab{\uldb Main Menu \v MenuMain}
\par
\tab{\uldb Main Window \v MainWindow}
\par
\tab{\uldb Main Window Push Button \v PushButtonMainWin}
\par
\tab{\uldb Push Button 1 \v PushButton1}
\par
\tab{\uldb Push Button 2 \v PushButton2}
\par
\tab{\uldb Push Button 3 \v PushButton3}
\par
\tab{\uldb List Box \v ListBox}
\par
\tab{\uldb Check Box \v CheckBox}
\par
\par
\f1
\fs30
Select a Topic.
\fs20
\f0
```

```
\page
#{\footnote MenuMain}
${\footnote Main Menu}
K{\footnote Main Menu}
{\fs24\b Main Menu}
\par
\par
The main menu allows you to display a sample
dialog box, activate the help system, display
information about this program, or terminate
the program.
\page
#{\footnote MenuMainPU}
This is the main menu for the program.
\page
#{\footnote PushButtonMainWin}
${\footnote Main Window Push Button}
K{\footnote Main Window Push Button}
{\fs24\b Main Window Push Button}
\par
\par
This is help for the main window push button.
\par
{\i This is in italics.}
\page
#{\footnote PushButtonMainWinPU}
This is the popup for the main window push button.
\page
#{\footnote PushButton1}
${\footnote Push Button 1}
K{\footnote Push Button 1}
+{\footnote Push:A}
{\fs24\b Push Button One}
\par
\par
This is help for the first push button.
\par
\par
See also {\uldb Push Button 2 \v PushButton2}
\page
#{\footnote PushButton1PU}
This is the popup for the first push button.
\page
#{\footnote PushButton2}
${\footnote Push Button 2}
```

16

```
K{\footnote Push Button 2}
+{\footnote Push:B}
{\fs24\b Push Button Two}
\par
\par
This is help for the second push button.
\par
\par
See Also {\uldb Push Button 3 \v PushButton3}
\page
#{\footnote PushButton2PU}
This is the popup for the second push button.
\page
#{\footnote PushButton3}
${\footnote Push Button 3}
K{\footnote Push Button 3}
+{\footnote Push:C}
{\fs24\b Push Button Three}
\par
\par
This is help for the third push button.
\par
\par
See Also {\uldb Push Button 1 \v PushButton1}
\page
#{\footnote PushButton3PU}
This is the popup for the third push button.
\page
#{\footnote MainWindow}
${\footnote Main Window}
K{\footnote Main Window}
{\fs24\b Main Window}
\par
\par
This is the main program window.
\page
#{\footnote MainWindowPU}
This is the main window popup help message.
\page
#{\footnote DlgPU}
${\footnote DlgPU}
This is a dialog box.
\page
#{\footnote ListBox}
${\footnote List Box}
```

```
K{\footnote List Box}
+{\footnote BOX:A}
{\fs24\b List Box}
\par
\par
This is help for the list box.
\page
#{\footnote ListBoxPU}
This is the popup for the list box.
\page
#{\footnote CheckBox}
${\footnote Check Box}
K{\footnote Check Box}
+{\footnote BOX:B}
{\fs24\b Check Box}
\par
\par
This is help for the check boxes.
\page
#{\footnote CheckBoxPU}
This is the popup for the check boxes.
\page
#{\footnote MenuDlgPU}
Activates the sample dialog box.
\page
#{\footnote MenuExitPU}
Terminates the program.
\page
#{\footnote MenuHelpPU}
Activates the Help System.
\page
#{\footnote MenuAboutPU}
Displays information about this program.
\page
}
```

In this file, the **#\footnote** commands whose IDs end in **PU** are the entry points for the context-sensitive pop-up help. The other **#\footnote** commands are used to support reference help in the standard Help window.

After you have entered this file, you must compile it using the HCW compiler. Call the output file HELPTEST.HLP. This file will be used by the example WinHelp program. However, before you compile the file, you must define the following MAP statements within the configuration section of the project file associated with HELPTEST.RTF. These values will be used to support context-sensitive pop-up help windows.

PushButton1PU	700
PushButton2PU	701
PushButton3PU	702
ListBoxPU	703
CheckBoxPU	704
MainWindowPU	705
PushButtonMainWinPU	706
DlgPU	707
MenuDlgPU	708
MenuExitPU	709
MenuHelpPU	710
MenuAboutPU	711
MenuMainPU	712

The easiest way to define the MAP values is to include a map file in your help project. For HCW, map files use the following format to map values to identifiers.

identifier1   value1

identifier2   value2

identifier3   value3

.

.

.

identifierN   valueN

For example, here is the map file that you can use for the sample help file:

```
PushButton1PU          700
PushButton2PU          701
PushButton3PU          702
ListBoxPU              703
CheckBoxPU             704
MainWindowPU           705
PushButtonMainWinPU    706
DlgPU                  707
MenuDlgPU              708
MenuExitPU             709
MenuHelpPU             710
MenuAboutPU            711
MenuMainPU             712
```

You must also activate the browse buttons in the standard help window by including the **BrowseButtons( )** macro in the configuration section of your project file. Finally, if you want to give your Help windows a title, you can specify one in the Options dialog box of the Help Workshop. If you don't specify a title, then the default title "Windows Help" will be used. The title used in the examples is "Sample Help File."

When you compile this help file, call the output file HELPTEST.HLP. This file will need to be in the same directory as the executable version of the WinHelp example program shown later in this chapter.

16

WinHelp Macros

The **BrowseButtons( )** macro is just one of many macros supported by the WinHelp help system. Here are a few more:

Macro	Meaning
Annotate( )	Shows the Annotation box.
Back( )	Moves to the previous topic.
DisableButton(*ButtonID*)	Disables the standard Help button specified by *ButtonID*.
EnableButton(*ButtonID*)	Enables the standard Help button specified by *ButtonID*.
Exit( )	Terminates the Help system.
GotoMark(*mark*)	Jumps to the marker previously set by **SaveMark( )**.
History( )	Shows the history list.
Next( )	Advances to the next topic in a browse sequence. Must be executed from within a valid browse sequence.
Prev( )	Returns to the previous topic in a browse sequence. Must be executed from within a valid browse sequence.
Print( )	Prints the current topic.
SaveMark(*mark*)	Saves the current help file position in the marker specified by *mark*.

Help macros can be executed in a variety of ways. Some, such as **BrowseButtons( )**, are specified within the Help project file. Others can be executed from within the help file itself. To execute a macro from within a help file, use this form of the **\footnote** RTF command:

```
!{\footnote macro( )}
```

Here, *macro* is the name of the macro that you wish to execute. For example, this command activates the previous topic in a browse sequence.

```
!{\footnote prev()}
```

When creating WinHelp projects, the help macros expand your control over how the help information is presented to the user. If WinHelp is in your future, you should spend some time exploring the help macros.

Executing Help Using WinHelp( )

After you have created an RTF help file and compiled it into its .HLP form, your application can access the information contained in it by invoking the **WinHelp( )** API function. Its prototype is shown here:

```
BOOL WinHelp(HWND hwnd, LPCSTR filename, UINT command,
                DWORD extra);
```

Here, *hwnd* is the handle of the invoking window. The name of the help file being activated is specified in *filename*, which may include a drive and path specifier. Precisely what action the **WinHelp( )** function takes is determined by *command*.

The valid values for *command* are shown here:

Command	Purpose
HELP_COMMAND	Executes a help macro.
HELP_CONTENTS	*Obsolete*: use **HELP_FINDER** instead.

Command	Purpose
HELP_CONTEXT	Displays a specified topic.
HELP_CONTEXTMENU	Displays context-sensitive help. This includes a "What's This?" menu.
HELP_CONTEXTPOPUP	Displays context-sensitive help.
HELP_FINDER	Displays the standard Help Topics window.
HELP_FORCEFILE	Forces correct file to be displayed.
HELP_HELPONHELP	Displays help information on Help. Requires that the WINHELP32.HLP file is available.
HELP_INDEX	*Obsolete*: use **HELP_FINDER** instead.
HELP_KEY	Displays a specific topic given its keyword.
HELP_MULTIKEY	Displays a specific topic given its alternative keyword.
HELP_PARTIALKEY	Displays a specific topic given a partial keyword.
HELP_QUIT	Closes the Help window.
HELP_SETCONTENTS	Sets the contents topic.
HELP_SETPOPUP_POS	Specifies the position of the next pop-up window displayed by the help system.
HELP_SETWINPOS	Determines the size and position of the Help window and displays it, if necessary.
HELP_TCARD	This command is ORed with other commands for training card help.
HELP_WM_HELP	Displays context-sensitive help.

Some commands require additional information. When that is the case, the additional information is passed in *extra*. The value of *extra* for each command is shown here:

Command	Meaning of *extra*
HELP_COMMAND	Pointer to string that contains macro.
HELP_CONTENTS	Not used. Set to zero.

Command	Meaning of *extra*
HELP_CONTEXT	Context ID of topic.
HELP_CONTEXTMENU	See Text.
HELP_CONTEXTPOPUP	Context ID of topic.
HELP_FINDER	Not used. Set to zero.
HELP_FORCEFILE	Not used. Set to zero.
HELP_HELPONHELP	Not used. Set to zero.
HELP_INDEX	Not used. Set to zero.
HELP_KEY	Pointer to string that contains the keyword.
HELP_MULTIKEY	Pointer to **MULTIKEYHELP** structure.
HELP_PARTIALKEY	Pointer to string containing partial keyword.
HELP_QUIT	Not used. Set to zero.
HELP_SETCONTENTS	Context ID of topic.
HELP_SETPOPUP_POS	Pointer to a **POINTS** structure.
HELP_SETWINPOS	Pointer to a **HELPWININFO** structure.
HELP_WM_HELP	See Text.

For the **HELP_WM_HELP** and **HELP_CONTEXTMENU** commands, the meaning of *extra* is a little more detailed than it is for the other commands. For these two commands, *extra* is a pointer to an array of **DWORD** values. These values are organized in pairs. The first value specifies the ID of a control (such as a push button, edit box, and so forth) or menu item. The second value specifies the context ID of the help information linked to that control. This array must end with two zero values. These two commands are used to support context-sensitive help and to help process **WM_HELP** and **WM_CONTEXTMENU** messages, which are described next.

Responding to WM_HELP and WM_CONTEXTMENU Messages

As mentioned near the beginning of this chapter, there are two broad categories of help: reference and context-sensitive. In a correctly written program, the user can activate reference help (that is, activate the standard Help window) by

16

selecting Help from a menu or, in many situations, by pressing F1. Context-
sensitive help is activated by right-clicking on a control or window, by using
the ? button, or, in some situations, by pressing F1. (The distinction between
the two uses of F1 is discussed in the following section.)

Since your program must respond differently to different types of help requests,
there must be some way to tell them apart. And, there is. When F1 is pressed
or when the ? button is used, a **WM_HELP** message is automatically sent
to the active window. When the user right-clicks on a window or control, a
WM_CONTEXTMENU message is sent to the window that contains the
control. The proper processing of these two messages is crucial to the correct
implementation of online help. Both messages will be examined here.

HISTORICAL PERSPECTIVE: The **WM_HELP** and
WM_CONTEXTMENU messages are not supported by Windows 3.1 or
Windows NT 3.51. Therefore, when converting older programs to Windows
2000, you will want to add support for these messages.

WM_HELP

Each time your program receives a **WM_HELP** command, **lParam** will
contain a pointer to a **HELPINFO** structure that describes the help request.
The **HELPINFO** structure is defined like this:

```
typedef struct tagHELPINFO
{
  UINT cbSize;
  int iContextType;
  int iCtrlId;
  HANDLE hItemHandle;
  DWORD dwContextId;
  POINT MousePos;
} HELPINFO;
```

Here, **cbSize** contains the size of the **HELPINFO** structure.

iContextType specifies the type of object for which help is being requested.
If it is for a menu item it will contain **HELPINFO_MENUITEM**. If it is for a
window or control, it will contain **HELPINFO_WINDOW**. **iCtrlId** contains
the ID of the control, window, or menu item.

hItemHandle specifies the handle of the control, window, or menu. **dwContextId** contains the context ID for the window or control. **MousePos** contains the current mouse position.

Most of the time, your program will respond to a **WM_HELP** message by displaying a pop-up window containing context-sensitive help. For example, to display context help about a control, your program can invoke **WinHelp( )** using the contents of **hItemHandle** as the window handle, that is, as the first parameter to **WinHelp( )**. (This will be the handle of the control.) You must specify **HELP_WM_HELP** as the command parameter and the address of the array of IDs as the extra parameter. (You will see how this is done in the example program.) Invoking **WinHelp( )** in this fashion causes it to search the array for the control ID that matches the control specified in **hItemHandle**. It then uses the corresponding context ID to obtain context-sensitive help. It displays this help in a pop-up window, not in the standard Help window. (A similar process is followed when using **HtmlHelp( )**.)

Although your program will usually respond to a **WM_HELP** message by displaying context-sensitive help, this will not always be the case. As mentioned earlier, pressing F1 may be used to invoke either reference help or context-sensitive help. Here is the distinction between the two uses. When the main window has input focus (and no child window, control, or menu is selected), then pressing F1 activates the standard Help window and displays reference help. However, pressing F1 when a control, menu, or child window is active causes context-sensitive help to be displayed. The rationale underlying these two uses is that when the user presses F1 from the topmost level, the user desires help about the entire program, not a part of it. When responding to this situation, you will invoke the full help system. When a control (or other child window) is active when F1 is pressed, the user desires help about that specific item, and context-sensitive help is warranted.

Since F1 may be used to activate either reference help or context-sensitive help, you might be wondering how your program will tell the two types of requests apart. That is, pressing F1 causes **WM_HELP** to be sent no matter what type of help is being requested. The answer is quite simple: if the handle contained in **hItemHandle** is that of the main window, then display reference help. Otherwise, invoke context sensitive help as described above.

WM_CONTEXTMENU

When the user right-clicks the mouse, your program receives a **WM_CONTEXTMENU** command. **wParam** will contain the handle of the control or window being queried. If the user clicked on a control, then respond by invoking **WinHelp( )** using **wParam** as the window handle (that is, the first parameter to **WinHelp( )**). Specify **HELP_CONTEXTMENU** as the command parameter and the address of the array of IDs as the extra parameter. (A parallel approach can also be applied to **HtmlHelp( )**.)

Including the ? Button

As mentioned, one way to activate context-sensitive help is through the ? button. To include the ? button in a window, you must include the extended style **WS_EX_CONTEXTHELP**. Since this is an extended style feature, you must create the window using **CreateWindowEx( )** rather than **CreateWindow( )**. To display the ? button in a dialog box, include the **DS_CONTEXTHELP** style.

NOTE: Current Windows style guides recommend using the *?* button primarily in dialog boxes. However, it can be used in a main window if the situation warrants.

A WinHelp Demonstration Program

Now that you have learned about the various pieces and techniques involved in creating a traditional-style help project, it is time to put them to use. The following program demonstrates both reference help and context-sensitive help. It uses the help file shown earlier and illustrates various ways that the file can be accessed using **WinHelp( )**. Sample output is shown in Figure 16-3.

```
// Demonstrate the WinHelp Help System

#include <windows.h>
#include "helptest.h"

#define NUMSTRINGS 6

LRESULT CALLBACK WindowFunc(HWND, UINT, WPARAM, LPARAM);
BOOL CALLBACK DialogFunc(HWND, UINT, WPARAM, LPARAM);

char szWinName[] = "MyWin"; // name of window class
```

```
HINSTANCE hInst;

// map control IDs to context IDs
DWORD HelpArray[] = {
  IDD_PB1, IDH_PB1,
  IDD_PB2, IDH_PB2,
  IDD_PB3, IDH_PB3,
  ID_PB0, IDH_PB0,
  IDD_LB1, IDH_LB1,
  IDD_CB1, IDH_CB1, // Here, both check boxes are
  IDD_CB2, IDH_CB1, // mapped to the same context ID.
  0, 0
};

char lbstring[6][40] = {
  "one", "two", "three",
  "four", "five", "six"
};

int WINAPI WinMain(HINSTANCE hThisInst, HINSTANCE hPrevInst,
                   LPSTR lpszArgs, int nWinMode)
{
  HWND hwnd;
  MSG msg;
  WNDCLASSEX wcl;
  HACCEL hAccel;

  // Define a window class.
  wcl.cbSize = sizeof(WNDCLASSEX);

  wcl.hInstance = hThisInst;      // handle to this instance
  wcl.lpszClassName = szWinName;  // window class name
  wcl.lpfnWndProc = WindowFunc;   // window function
  wcl.style = 0;                  // default style

  wcl.hIcon = LoadIcon(NULL, IDI_APPLICATION); // large icon
  wcl.hIconSm = NULL; // use small version of large icon
  wcl.hCursor = LoadCursor(NULL, IDC_ARROW);   // cursor style

  wcl.lpszMenuName = "HelpDemoMenu"; // main menu

  wcl.cbClsExtra = 0; // no extra memory needed
  wcl.cbWndExtra = 0;

  // Make the window background white.
```

```
        wcl.hbrBackground = (HBRUSH) GetStockObject(WHITE_BRUSH);

        // Register the window class.
        if(!RegisterClassEx(&wcl)) return 0;

        /* Now that a window class has been registered, a window
           can be created. */
        hwnd = CreateWindowEx(
          WS_EX_CONTEXTHELP, // display ? button
          szWinName, // name of window class
          "A WinHelp Demonstration", // title
          WS_SYSMENU | WS_SIZEBOX,
          CW_USEDEFAULT, // X coordinate - let Windows decide
          CW_USEDEFAULT, // Y coordinate - let Windows decide
          CW_USEDEFAULT, // width - let Windows decide
          CW_USEDEFAULT, // height - let Windows decide
          NULL,          // no parent window
          NULL,          // no override of class menu
          hThisInst,     // instance handle
          NULL           // no additional arguments
        );

        hInst = hThisInst; // save the current instance handle

        // Load the keyboard accelerators.
        hAccel = LoadAccelerators(hThisInst, "HelpDemoMenu");

        // Display the window.
        ShowWindow(hwnd, nWinMode);
        UpdateWindow(hwnd);

        // Create the message loop.
        while(GetMessage(&msg, NULL, 0, 0))
        {
          if(!TranslateAccelerator(hwnd, hAccel, &msg)) {
            TranslateMessage(&msg); // translate keyboard messages
            DispatchMessage(&msg); // return control to Windows 2000
          }
        }

        return msg.wParam;
      }

    /* This function is called by Windows 2000 and is passed
       messages from the message queue.
    */
```

```
LRESULT CALLBACK WindowFunc(HWND hwnd, UINT message,
                            WPARAM wParam, LPARAM lParam)
{
  int response;

  switch(message) {
    case WM_CREATE:
      // define a child control window
      CreateWindow(
        "BUTTON", // name of control class
        "Main Window PB", // title
        BS_PUSHBUTTON | WS_CHILD | WS_VISIBLE, // push button
        10, 60, 120, 30,
        hwnd, // parent is main window
        (HMENU) ID_PB0, // control ID
        hInst, // handle of this instance of the program
        NULL // no additional arguments
      );
      break;
    case WM_HELP: // user pressed F1 or used ? button
      if(((LPHELPINFO) lParam)->iContextType ==
                                HELPINFO_MENUITEM) {
        // request for help about menu
        switch(((LPHELPINFO) lParam)->iCtrlId) {
          case IDM_DIALOG:
            WinHelp(hwnd, "helptest.hlp", HELP_CONTEXTPOPUP,
                    (DWORD) IDH_MENUDLG);
            break;
          case IDM_HELP:
            WinHelp(hwnd, "helptest.hlp", HELP_CONTEXTPOPUP,
                    (DWORD) IDH_MENUHELP);
            break;
          case IDM_HELPTHIS:
            WinHelp(hwnd, "helptest.hlp", HELP_CONTEXTPOPUP,
                    (DWORD) IDH_MENUABOUT);
            break;
          case IDM_EXIT:
            WinHelp(hwnd, "helptest.hlp", HELP_CONTEXTPOPUP,
                    (DWORD) IDH_MENUEXIT);
            break;
          default:
            // menu bar selected, but no option highlighted
            WinHelp(hwnd, "helptest.hlp", HELP_CONTEXTPOPUP,
                    (DWORD) IDH_MENUMAIN);
```

```
      }
    }
    else
      if(((LPHELPINFO) lParam)->hItemHandle != hwnd) {
        // context help about a control
        WinHelp((HWND)((LPHELPINFO) lParam)->hItemHandle,
               "helptest.hlp", HELP_WM_HELP,
               (DWORD) HelpArray);
      }
    else {
      // standard help for main window
      WinHelp(hwnd, "helptest.hlp", HELP_KEY,
             (DWORD) "Main Window");
    }
    break;
  case WM_CONTEXTMENU: // user right-clicked mouse
    if((HWND) wParam != hwnd)
      // context help about a control
      WinHelp((HWND) wParam, "helptest.hlp",
             HELP_CONTEXTMENU, (DWORD) HelpArray);
    else
      // context help about main window
      WinHelp(hwnd, "helptest.hlp",
             HELP_CONTEXTPOPUP, IDH_MAIN);
    break;
  case WM_COMMAND:
    switch(LOWORD(wParam)) {
      case IDM_DIALOG:
        DialogBox(hInst, "HelpDemoDB",
                 hwnd, (DLGPROC) DialogFunc);
        break;
      case IDM_HELP: // help selected from menu
        WinHelp(hwnd, "helptest.hlp", HELP_FINDER, 0);
        break;
      case IDM_HELPTHIS:
        MessageBox(hwnd, "Help System Sample Program V1.0",
                  "About", MB_OK);
        break;
      case IDM_EXIT:
        response = MessageBox(hwnd, "Quit the Program?",
                            "Exit", MB_YESNO);
        if(response == IDYES) PostQuitMessage(0);
        break;
    }
    break;
```

```
    case WM_DESTROY: // terminate the program
      WinHelp(hwnd, "helptest.hlp", HELP_QUIT, 0);
      PostQuitMessage(0);
      break;
    default:
      /* Let Windows 2000 process any messages not specified in
         the preceding switch statement. */
      return DefWindowProc(hwnd, message, wParam, lParam);
  }
  return 0;
}

// Sample dialog function.
BOOL CALLBACK DialogFunc(HWND hdwnd, UINT message,
                         WPARAM wParam, LPARAM lParam)
{
  int i;

  switch(message) {
    case WM_HELP: // use pressed F1 or used ? button
      // context help about a control
      WinHelp((HWND)((LPHELPINFO) lParam)->hItemHandle,
              "helptest.hlp", HELP_WM_HELP,
              (DWORD) HelpArray);
      return 1;
    case WM_CONTEXTMENU: // user right-clicked mouse
      if((HWND) wParam != hdwnd)
        // context help about a control
        WinHelp((HWND) wParam, "helptest.hlp",
                HELP_CONTEXTMENU, (DWORD) HelpArray);
      else
        // context help about dialog window
        WinHelp(hdwnd, "helptest.hlp",
                HELP_CONTEXTPOPUP, IDH_DLG);
      return 1;
    case WM_COMMAND:
      switch(LOWORD(wParam)) {
        case IDCANCEL:
          WinHelp(hdwnd, "helptest.hlp", HELP_QUIT, 0);
          EndDialog(hdwnd, 0);
          return 1;
        case IDD_PB1:
          MessageBox(hdwnd, "Push Button 1",
                     "Button Press", MB_OK);
          return 1;
```

```
        case IDD_PB2:
          MessageBox(hdwnd, "Push Button 2",
                     "Button Press", MB_OK);
          return 1;
        case IDD_PB3:
          MessageBox(hdwnd, "Push Button 3",
                     "Button Press", MB_OK);
          return 1;
      }
      break;
    case WM_INITDIALOG: // initialize list box
      for(i=0; i<NUMSTRINGS; i++)
        SendDlgItemMessage(hdwnd, IDD_LB1,
           LB_ADDSTRING, 0, (LPARAM) lbstring[i]);
      return 1;
  }

  return 0;
}
```

The program requires the following resource file:

```
// Demonstrate the Help system.
#include <windows.h>
#include "helptest.h"

HelpDemoMenu MENU
{
  POPUP "&Dialog"
  {
    MENUITEM "&Dialog\tF2", IDM_DIALOG
    MENUITEM "E&xit\tCtrl+X", IDM_EXIT
  }
  POPUP "&Help"
  {
    MENUITEM "&Help Topics", IDM_HELP
    MENUITEM "&About", IDM_HELPTHIS
  }
}

HelpDemoMenu ACCELERATORS
{
  VK_F2, IDM_DIALOG, VIRTKEY
  "^X", IDM_EXIT
```

```
}

HelpDemoDB DIALOGEX 10, 10, 140, 110
CAPTION "Help Demonstration Dialog"
STYLE WS_POPUP | WS_SYSMENU | WS_VISIBLE | DS_CONTEXTHELP
{
  DEFPUSHBUTTON "Button 1", IDD_PB1, 11, 10, 32, 14
  PUSHBUTTON "Button 2", IDD_PB2, 11, 34, 32, 14
  PUSHBUTTON "Button 3", IDD_PB3, 11, 58, 32, 14
  PUSHBUTTON "Cancel", IDCANCEL, 8, 82, 38, 16
  AUTOCHECKBOX "Check Box 1", IDD_CB1, 66, 50, 60, 30
  AUTOCHECKBOX "Check Box 2", IDD_CB2, 66, 70, 60, 30
  LISTBOX IDD_LB1, 66, 5, 63, 33, LBS_NOTIFY |
            WS_BORDER | WS_VSCROLL | WS_TABSTOP
}
```

The header file HELPTEST.H is shown here:

```
#define IDM_DIALOG      100
#define IDM_EXIT        101
#define IDM_HELP        102
#define IDM_HELPTHIS    103

#define IDD_PB1         200
#define IDD_PB2         201
#define IDD_PB3         202
#define IDD_LB1         203
#define IDD_CB1         205
#define IDD_CB2         206

#define ID_PB0          300

#define IDH_PB1         700
#define IDH_PB2         701
#define IDH_PB3         702
#define IDH_LB1         703
#define IDH_CB1         704
#define IDH_MAIN        705
#define IDH_PB0         706
#define IDH_DLG         707
#define IDH_MENUDLG     708
#define IDH_MENUEXIT    709
#define IDH_MENUHELP    710
#define IDH_MENUABOUT   711
#define IDH_MENUMAIN    712
```

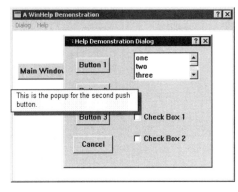

Sample output
from the
WinHelp
demonstration
program
Figure 16-3.

A Closer Look at the WinHelp Demonstration Program

Most of the program should be clear. However, a few points warrant specific attention. First, consider the declaration of **HelpArray**. This is the array that maps control IDs to context IDs. In the HELPTEST.H header file, the **IDH_** macros are given the same values that you defined in the HELPTEST.PRJ file when you created the help file. Notice that both check boxes map onto the same context ID. This is perfectly valid. If the same pop-up help message will be displayed for two or more controls, then there is no reason to create duplicate messages.

Notice that the program includes the ? button in the main window and in the dialog box. Although the ? is used mostly in dialog boxes, it is included in the main window for the purpose of illustration—and to make an important point. The ? will send messages only to its own window. As an example, try this experiment. Activate the dialog box and click on its ? button. Next, move the pointer out of the dialog box. As you will see, the ? disappears. The ? applies only to the window in which it is defined.

Here is another point of interest: Inside the main window is a stand-alone push button. This button is, therefore, a child window of the main window. If you press F1 when this button has input focus (that is, is selected), then you will receive pop-up help about the push button. However, if this control does not have input focus, then pressing F1 while the main window is active causes the main Help window to be displayed. This is in keeping with standard Windows style guides.

Using WinHelp Secondary Windows

It is possible to use a secondary Help window in a WinHelp project. A secondary window contains a button bar, but not a menu bar. Thus, it is smaller than the standard Help Topics window, but larger than a pop-up menu. A secondary Help window stays active until you close it, but it allows you to continue using your application. You have almost certainly seen secondary Help windows in action.

The implementation of a secondary Help window is actually quite easy. First, you need to add one to your help project. To do so, simply specify its name and its type using the Windows option of the HCW compiler. You will have three choices of secondary window styles:

◆ Procedure
◆ Reference
◆ Error Message

A Procedure window is a small window that contains the buttons Help Topics, Back, and Options. It is positioned in the upper-right corner of the screen. A reference window also contains the Help Topics, Back, and Options buttons, but it is a larger window. It is displayed with its upper-left corner near the top-left of the screen. Error Message windows are small and contain no buttons.

To use a secondary window, you must include its name when specifying the name of the help file in the call to **WinHelp( )**, using this general form:

filename>windowname

For example, if a secondary window is called "HlpWin2," then the following call will use that window to display context help about the Dialog entry in the main menu in the preceding program:

```
WinHelp(hwnd, "helptest.hlp>HlpWin2", HELP_CONTEXT,
            (DWORD) IDH_MENUDLG);
```

Assuming that HlpWin2 is a Procedure window, then this will produce the following window:

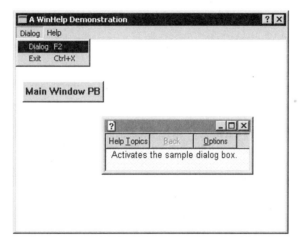

Secondary windows are easy to add and enhance the look and feel of your WinHelp application. You will want to experiment with them to find which style works best for the various needs of your program.

Using HTML Help

While WinHelp-based help is still widely used, HTML help offers a fresh and powerful alternative that provides a modern, browser-oriented interface to the help system. It is the style of help used by Windows 2000, and it is the style that you will probably want to use for new programming efforts. HTML help is displayed by the HTML Help Viewer, which is a browser-like window similar to that provided by Internet Explorer. An example of HTML help is shown in Figure 16-4.

HTML help is activated by calling **HtmlHelp( )** instead of **WinHelp( )**. When using HTML help, your program still receives **WM_HELP** and

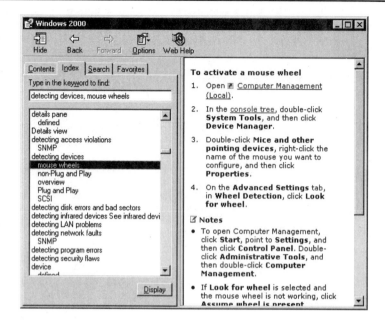

An example of
an HTML Help
window

Figure 16-4.

WM_CONTEXTMENU messages as described earlier. It is only your responses to these messages that change.

HTML, not RTF

HTML help uses HTML files, not RTF files, to hold the help information. Since nearly all programmers today have at least a passing knowledge of HTML, it will not be examined here. Keep in mind that effective help information can be created using only a few HTML commands. While a sophisticated knowledge of HTML is helpful, it is not required. As long as you can create hyperlinks, you can create HTML help files!

The HTML Help Workshop

Unlike the traditional help system in which you can easily create a help file by using just a text editor, HTML help virtually requires the use of Microsoft's HTML Help Workshop: HHW.EXE. The HTML Help Workshop helps you manage the different files and associations that are part of any HTML help project. Figure 16-5 shows the HTML Help Workshop. While the central

The HTML
Help
Workshop
Figure 16-5.

concepts, such as context IDs, keywords, and the like, are the same for both
WinHelp and HTML help projects, the way in which these elements are included
in a project differ. The HTML Help Workshop provides extensive online help
that describes its use, and those instructions are not duplicated here.

HTML Help projects consist of several files, including the HTML files
containing the help information, a text file containing context-sensitive
pop-up strings, an index file, and a contents file. The index and contents are
created by specifying links between topics and the HTML files that contain
the information. All of these files (including the HTML files) can be created
from within the HTML Help Workshop. The project file that manages these
files uses the extension HHP.

Once you have created the necessary files, you compile them into one CHM
file. This file contains all of the help information defined by the project. It is
the file that will be referred to when you call **HtmlHelp( )**. One convenient
feature of the HTML Help Workshop is that it can decompile a CHM file into
its components.

The HTML Help Workshop has an option that allows you to convert
WinHelp( ) help projects into HTML help projects. However, because of the

differences between the two systems, you might find it easier to simply create the HTML version from scratch.

Because the files required by HTML help are best created and managed using the HTML Help Workshop, they are not shown here. However, the compiled CHM file used by the example program is included in the free source-code download for this book, which is available on the Osborne website, www.Osborne.com.

HtmlHelp( )

When using **HtmlHelp( )**, include HTMLHELP.H and include HTMLHELP.LIB in the link.

To activate HTML help, call **HtmlHelp( )**. The header file HTMLHELP.H must be included in your program. You must also add HTMLHELP.LIB to the link. The prototype for **HtmlHelp( )** is shown here:

HWND HtmlHelp(HWND *hwnd*, LPCSTR *filename*, UINT *command*,
         DWORD *extra*);

Here, *hwnd* is the handle of the invoking window. The name of the help file being activated is specified in *filename*, which may include a drive and path specifier. This file must be a compiled HTML help file that uses the CHM extension. This file must be in the specified directory.

Precisely what action the **HtmlHelp( )** function takes is determined by *command*. Here are some of the valid values for *command*:

Command	Purpose
HH_DISPLAY_INDEX	Activates the Index tab in the HTML Help Viewer. A topic can be specified in the *filename* parameter.
HH_DISPLAY_SEARCH	Activates the Search tab in the HTML Help Viewer. A topic can be specified in the *filename* parameter.
HH_DISPLAY_TOC	Activates the Contents tab in the HTML Help Viewer. A topic can be specified in the *filename* parameter.
HH_DISPLAY_TOPIC	Displays a specified topic. The topic file is specified in the *filename* parameter.

Command	Purpose
HH_HELP_CONTEXT	Displays a topic given its ID.
HH_INITIALIZE	Initializes HTML help. Both *hwnd* and *filename* are **NULL**. Use this once, when your program begins.
HH_TP_HELP_CONTEXTMENU	Displays context-sensitive help. Normally used when handling a **WM_CONTEXTMENU** message. The file containing the pop-up messages must be specified in the *filename* parameter. The handle to the control is passed in *hwnd*.
HH_TP_HELP_WM_HELP	Displays context-sensitive help. Normally used when handling a **WM_HELP** message. The file containing the pop-up messages must be specified in the *filename* parameter. The handle to the control is passed in *hwnd*.
HH_UNINITIALIZE	Uninitializes HTML help. Both *hwnd* and *filename* are **NULL**. Use when your program ends.

The value of *extra* for each command is shown here:

Command	Meaning of *extra*
HH_DISPLAY_INDEX	Pointer to the string containing the topic that will be selected in the index.
HH_DISPLAY_SEARCH	Pointer to an **HH_FTS_QUERY** structure that specifies the search topic.
HH_DISPLAY_TOC	Pointer to the string containing the topic that will be selected, or **NULL**.
HH_DISPLAY_TOPIC	Pointer to the string containing the topic that will be displayed, or **NULL**.
HH_HELP_CONTEXT	Context ID of topic.

Command	Meaning of *extra*
HH_INITIALIZE	Pointer to a **DWORD** that will receive a value, called a *cookie*. This cookie must be passed to **HtmlHelp( )** when using **HH_UNINITIALIZE**.
HH_TP_HELP_CONTEXTMENU	(*See text.*)
HH_TP_HELP_WM_HELP	(*See text.*)
HH_UNINITIALIZE	The cookie obtained by **HH_INITIALIZE**.

For the **HH_TP_HELP_WM_HELP** and **HH_TP_HELP_CONTEXTMENU** commands, *extra* is a pointer to an array of **DWORD** values. These values are organized into pairs. The first value specifies the ID of a control (such as a push button, edit box, and so forth) or menu item. The second value specifies the context ID of the help information linked to that control. This array must end with two zero values. These two commands are used to support context-sensitive help.

In most cases **HtmlHelp( )** returns the handle of the Help window if successful and **NULL** on failure.

A Closer Look at HtmlHelp( )'s filename Parameter
For most commands, the *filename* parameter to **HtmlHelp( )** is used to pass the name of the CHM help file. However, for some commands, it is also used to pass additional information. The additional information is contained in the same string as the filename, but is separated from it by two colons. For example, with **HH_DISPLAY_TOC**, the filename string also contains the name of the HTML file within the CHM file that will be displayed. To specify this file, the following syntax is used:

chm-filename::html-filename

In the following call to **HtmlHelp( )**, the CHM file is **helptest.chm**, and the topic is **listbox.htm**.

```
HtmlHelp(hwnd, "c:\\helptest.chm::/listbox.htm", HH_DISPLAY_TOC, 0);
```

Keep in mind that a CHM file maintains the same directory structure of that used by the original files. Thus, if **listbox.htm** was in a subdirectory, you would need to specify the path to it.

When responding to **HH_TP_HELP_CONTEXTMENU** or **HH_TP_HELP_WM_HELP**, you will specify the name of the text file that contains the pop-up text in the *filename* parameter. For example, in the HTML help sample program, the following call is used to pop up information about a control. The pop-up text is contained in a file called **htpopups.txt**.

```
// context help about a control
HtmlHelp((HWND) wParam,
         "c:\\helptest.chm::htpopups.txt",
         HH_TP_HELP_CONTEXTMENU, (DWORD) HelpArray);
```

A pop-up text file is organized as shown here:

```
.topic ID
popup text
```

Here, *ID* is the context ID of the topic. The message displayed is specified by *popup text*. For example, here is the first part of the file used by the HTML sample program shown later:

```
.topic IDH_PB0
This is the popup for the main window push button.
.topic IDH_PB1
This is the popup for the first push button.
.topic IDH_PB2
This is the popup for the second push button.
.topic IDH_PB3
This is the popup for the third push button.
```

Notice that the program-defined macros are used rather than numeric values. This use is possible because the HTML Help Workshop allows you to include a standard C/C++ header file as part of your project.

The *filename* parameter can also be used to specify a secondary window. To do so, you must first create one using the HTML Help Workshop by using the

Add/Modify window definitions option. To use the secondary window, specify its name in the *filename* parameter using this format:

chm-filename>windowname

For example, in the HTML help example program, the following call displays help about the Dialog main menu option in a secondary window called *smallwin*.

```
HtmlHelp(hwnd, "c:\\helptest.chm>smallwin",
        HH_HELP_CONTEXT,
        (DWORD) IDH_MENUDLG);
```

Demonstrating HtmlHelp( )

The following program is a reworked version of the previous **WinHelp( )** program. Because both help systems must process the same messages and rely upon many of the same low-level details, surprisingly few changes are needed. They are

◆   The header HTMLHELP.H is included.

◆   Calls to **WinHelp( )** are changed to calls to **HtmlHelp( )**.

Of course, the HTML help file itself must be created using the HTML Help Workshop.

Here is the code for the **HtmlHelp( )** demonstration program. Before using it, be sure to obtain the HELPTEST.CHM file from the Osborne website, WWW.Osborne.com. You will need to locate this file in the root directory of drive C, since this path is hard-coded into the example. (Of course, you can change the path if you like.) Also, remember to add HTMLHELP.LIB to the link prior to compiling. Sample output is shown in Figure 16-6.

```
// Demonstrate the HTML Help System

#include <windows.h>
#include <htmlhelp.h>
#include "helptest.h"

#define NUMSTRINGS 6
```

```
LRESULT CALLBACK WindowFunc(HWND, UINT, WPARAM, LPARAM);
BOOL CALLBACK DialogFunc(HWND, UINT, WPARAM, LPARAM);

char szWinName[] = "MyWin"; // name of window class

HINSTANCE hInst;

// map control IDs to context IDs
DWORD HelpArray[] = {
  IDD_PB1, IDH_PB1,
  IDD_PB2, IDH_PB2,
  IDD_PB3, IDH_PB3,
  ID_PB0, IDH_PB0,
  IDD_LB1, IDH_LB1,
  IDD_CB1, IDH_CB1, // Here, both check boxes are
  IDD_CB2, IDH_CB1, // mapped to the same context ID.
  0, 0
};

char lbstring[6][40] = {
  "one", "two", "three",
  "four", "five", "six"
};

int WINAPI WinMain(HINSTANCE hThisInst, HINSTANCE hPrevInst,
                   LPSTR lpszArgs, int nWinMode)
{
  HWND hwnd;
  MSG msg;
  WNDCLASSEX wcl;
  HACCEL hAccel;

  // Define a window class.
  wcl.cbSize = sizeof(WNDCLASSEX);

  wcl.hInstance = hThisInst;       // handle to this instance
  wcl.lpszClassName = szWinName;   // window class name
  wcl.lpfnWndProc = WindowFunc;    // window function
  wcl.style = 0;                   // default style

  wcl.hIcon = LoadIcon(NULL, IDI_APPLICATION); // large icon
  wcl.hIconSm = NULL; // use small version of large icon
  wcl.hCursor = LoadCursor(NULL, IDC_ARROW);  // cursor style

  wcl.lpszMenuName = "HelpDemoMenu"; // main menu
```

```
wcl.cbClsExtra = 0; // no extra memory needed
wcl.cbWndExtra = 0;

// Make the window background white.
wcl.hbrBackground = (HBRUSH) GetStockObject(WHITE_BRUSH);

// Register the window class.
if(!RegisterClassEx(&wcl)) return 0;

/* Now that a window class has been registered, a window
   can be created. */
hwnd = CreateWindowEx(
  WS_EX_CONTEXTHELP, // display ? button
  szWinName, // name of window class
  "HTML Help Demonstration", // title
  WS_SYSMENU | WS_SIZEBOX,
  CW_USEDEFAULT, // X coordinate - let Windows decide
  CW_USEDEFAULT, // Y coordinate - let Windows decide
  CW_USEDEFAULT, // width - let Windows decide
  CW_USEDEFAULT, // height - let Windows decide
  NULL,          // no parent window
  NULL,          // no override of class menu
  hThisInst,     // instance handle
  NULL           // no additional arguments
);

hInst = hThisInst; // save the current instance handle

// Load the keyboard accelerators.
hAccel = LoadAccelerators(hThisInst, "HelpDemoMenu");

// Display the window.
ShowWindow(hwnd, nWinMode);
UpdateWindow(hwnd);

// Create the message loop.
while(GetMessage(&msg, NULL, 0, 0))
{
  if(!TranslateAccelerator(hwnd, hAccel, &msg)) {
    TranslateMessage(&msg); // translate keyboard messages
    DispatchMessage(&msg); // return control to Windows 2000
  }
}
```

16

```
       return msg.wParam;
}


/* This function is called by Windows 2000 and is passed
   messages from the message queue.
*/
LRESULT CALLBACK WindowFunc(HWND hwnd, UINT message,
                              WPARAM wParam, LPARAM lParam)
{
  int response;
  static DWORD cookie = 0;

  switch(message) {
    case WM_CREATE:
      // initialize HTML help
      HtmlHelp(NULL, NULL, HH_INITIALIZE, (DWORD) &cookie);

      // define a child control window
      CreateWindow(
        "BUTTON", // name of control class
        "Main Window PB", // title
        BS_PUSHBUTTON | WS_CHILD | WS_VISIBLE, // push button
        10, 60, 120, 30,
        hwnd, // parent is main window
        (HMENU) ID_PB0, // control ID
        hInst, // handle of this instance of the program
        NULL // no additional arguments
      );
      break;
    case WM_HELP: // user pressed F1 or used ? button
      if(((LPHELPINFO) lParam)->iContextType ==
                                  HELPINFO_MENUITEM) {
        // request for help about menu
        switch(((LPHELPINFO) lParam)->iCtrlId) {
          case IDM_DIALOG:
            HtmlHelp(hwnd, "c:\\helptest.chm>smallwin",
                     HH_HELP_CONTEXT,
                     (DWORD) IDH_MENUDLG);
            break;
          case IDM_HELP:
            HtmlHelp(hwnd, "c:\\helptest.chm>smallwin",
                     HH_HELP_CONTEXT,
                     (DWORD) IDH_MENUHELP);
            break;
          case IDM_HELPTHIS:
```

```
          HtmlHelp(hwnd, "c:\\helptest.chm>smallwin",
                  HH_HELP_CONTEXT,
                  (DWORD) IDH_MENUABOUT);
        break;
      case IDM_EXIT:
        HtmlHelp(hwnd, "c:\\helptest.chm>smallwin",
                HH_HELP_CONTEXT,
                (DWORD) IDH_MENUEXIT);
        break;
      default:
        // menu bar selected, but no option highlighted
        HtmlHelp(hwnd, "c:\\helptest.chm>smallwin",
                HH_HELP_CONTEXT,
                (DWORD) IDH_MENUMAIN);
    }
  }
  else
    if(((LPHELPINFO) lParam)->hItemHandle != hwnd) {
      // context help about a control
      HtmlHelp((HWND)((LPHELPINFO) lParam)->hItemHandle,
              "c:\\helptest.chm::htpopups.txt",
              HH_TP_HELP_WM_HELP, (DWORD) HelpArray);
    }
    else {
      // standard help for main window
      HtmlHelp(hwnd, "c:\\helptest.chm>smallwin",
              HH_HELP_CONTEXT, IDH_MAIN);
    }
  break;
case WM_CONTEXTMENU: // user right-clicked mouse
  if((HWND) wParam != hwnd)
    // context help about a control
    HtmlHelp((HWND) wParam,
            "c:\\helptest.chm::htpopups.txt",
            HH_TP_HELP_CONTEXTMENU, (DWORD) HelpArray);
  else
    // context help about main window
    HtmlHelp(hwnd, "c:\\helptest.chm>smallwin",
            HH_HELP_CONTEXT, IDH_MAIN);
  break;
case WM_COMMAND:
  switch(LOWORD(wParam)) {
    case IDM_DIALOG:
      DialogBox(hInst, "HelpDemoDB",
              hwnd, (DLGPROC) DialogFunc);
```

```
               break;
            case IDM_HELP: // help selected from menu
               HtmlHelp(hwnd,
                        "c:\\helptest.chm::/helptest.htm",
                        HH_DISPLAY_TOC, 0);
               break;
            case IDM_HELPTHIS:
               MessageBox(hwnd, "HTML Help Sample Program V1.0",
                          "About", MB_OK);
               break;
            case IDM_EXIT:
               response = MessageBox(hwnd, "Quit the Program?",
                                     "Exit", MB_YESNO);
               if(response == IDYES) PostQuitMessage(0);
               break;
         }
         break;
      case WM_DESTROY: // terminate the program
         HtmlHelp(NULL, NULL, HH_UNINITIALIZE, cookie);
         PostQuitMessage(0);
         break;
      default:
         /* Let Windows 2000 process any messages not specified in
            the preceding switch statement. */
         return DefWindowProc(hwnd, message, wParam, lParam);
   }
   return 0;
}

// Sample dialog function.
BOOL CALLBACK DialogFunc(HWND hdwnd, UINT message,
                         WPARAM wParam, LPARAM lParam)
{
  int i;

  switch(message) {
    case WM_HELP: // user pressed F1 or used ? button
      // context help about a control
      HtmlHelp((HWND)((LPHELPINFO) lParam)->hItemHandle,
               "c:\\helptest.chm::htpopups.txt",
               HH_TP_HELP_WM_HELP,
               (DWORD) HelpArray);
      return 1;
    case WM_CONTEXTMENU: // user right-clicked mouse
      if((HWND) wParam != hdwnd)
```

```
          // context help about a control
          HtmlHelp((HWND) wParam,
                  "c:\\helptest.chm::htpopups.txt",
                  HH_TP_HELP_CONTEXTMENU, (DWORD)HelpArray);
      else
          // context help about dialog window
          HtmlHelp(hdwnd, "c:\\helptest.chm>smallwin",
                  HH_HELP_CONTEXT,
                  (DWORD) IDH_DLG);
      return 1;
    case WM_COMMAND:
      switch(LOWORD(wParam)) {
        case IDCANCEL:
          EndDialog(hdwnd, 0);
          return 1;
        case IDD_PB1:
          MessageBox(hdwnd, "Push Button 1",
                  "Button Press", MB_OK);
          return 1;
        case IDD_PB2:
          MessageBox(hdwnd, "Push Button 2",
                  "Button Press", MB_OK);
          return 1;
        case IDD_PB3:
          MessageBox(hdwnd, "Push Button 3",
                  "Button Press", MB_OK);
          return 1;
      }
      break;
    case WM_INITDIALOG: // initialize list box
      for(i=0; i<NUMSTRINGS; i++)
        SendDlgItemMessage(hdwnd, IDD_LB1,
            LB_ADDSTRING, 0, (LPARAM) lbstring[i]);
      return 1;
  }

  return 0;
}
```

Sample output
from the
HTML Help
example
program

Figure 16-6.

Some Things to Try

One interesting help feature that you will want to explore is the *training card*. Training cards are used to provide "how to" instructions to the user. For example, a word processing program might use training cards to explain, step-by-step, how to format a paragraph or print a document.

For WinHelp projects, try using the partial keyword search option **HELP_PARTIALKEY**. For example, you could display an edit box, allow the user to enter the name of the item about which help is sought, and then use a partial key search to display all matching topics.

For HTML help projects, try implementing the Search option.

One last point: Online context-sensitive help is an important part of all Windows 2000 applications. It is better to build support for help into your program from the start, rather than adding it later.

CHAPTER 17

Using the Printer

Since Windows 2000 is a graphical operating system that uses bitmaps, custom character fonts, and graphics, most newcomers think that printing is a difficult, complicated task. Fortunately, this is not the case. While it is true that printing is more complicated under Windows 2000 than, say, under DOS, Windows 2000 provides extensive built-in support for it. Indeed, most of the details are handled by the printer drivers built into Windows 2000. Although there are certainly a number of things to learn, there is nothing fundamentally difficult about printing documents. Once you have mastered the essentials, you will have no trouble adding print capabilities to any of your programs.

This chapter explains how to do the following:

◆   Print text
◆   Print graphical images
◆   Scale graphical images
◆   Create and install a printing abort function

These operations are the foundation of all printing jobs under Windows 2000.

Before beginning, it is important to understand that when you print something you are actually sending output to the print spooler and not directly to the printer itself. While this distinction doesn't usually have much impact on how you program, it is good to keep in mind.

Obtaining a Printer Device Context

In the same way that a display device context (DC) describes and manages output to the screen, a printer device context describes and manages output to the printer. Therefore, you must obtain a printer device context before you can send output to the printer. There are various ways to obtain a printer device context. The two that we will look at use **CreateDC( )** or **PrintDlgEx( )**. **CreateDC( )** allows you to obtain a printer DC without user interaction. **PrintDlgEx( )** displays a common dialog box that allows the user to tailor the printer device context to his or her own needs. Each is examined here.

A printer device context is required to output to a printer.

CreateDC( )

The first way to obtain a printer device context is to use **CreateDC( )**. Its prototype is shown here.

HDC CreateDC(LPCSTR *lpszWhat*, LPCSTR *DevName*,
            LPCSTR *NotUsed*,
            CONST DEVMODE **DevMode*);

Here, *lpszWhat* can be a pointer to either the string "DISPLAY" (to obtain a display driver) or "WINSPOOL" (to obtain a printer driver). For printing, this parameter must point to "WINSPOOL". *DevName* specifies the name of the printer. *NotUsed* must be **NULL**. *DevMode* points to a **DEVMODE** structure that contains initialization information. To use the default initialization, *DevMode* must be **NULL**. **CreateDC( )** returns a handle to the device context if successful or **NULL** on failure. After your application is through printing, delete the device context by calling **DeleteDC( ).**

In some cases your application will need to obtain the name of the currently selected printer. To do this, use **EnumPrinters( )** to obtain the names of available printers.

CreateDC( ) is most often used when printing does not involve interaction with the user. Although such situations are not common, they are not that rare. For example, a system log might be printed after midnight, when no user is present. However, for most purposes (and for the examples in this chapter) you will acquire a printer DC using **PrintDlgEx( )**.

PrintDlgEx( )

The second way to obtain a printer device context is to call **PrintDlgEx( )**, which displays the Print common dialog box that allows the user to set various printing options. **PrintDlgEx( )** is new for Windows 2000 and replaces the now obsolete **PrintDlg( )** function. The precise appearance of the Print dialog box varies, depending upon what options you select, but it will look something like that shown in Figure 17-1. As the figure shows, **PrintDlgEx( )** creates a property sheet control that allows the user to set various options associated with printing. The advantage of using **PrintDlgEx( )** to obtain a device context is that it gives the user control over the printing operation. **PrintDlgEx( )** is both powerful and flexible. The following discussion describes its basic operation. However, you will want to explore this function fully if you will be working extensively with printers and printing.

 NEW FOR 2000:   **PrintDlgEx( )** replaces the old **PrintDlg( )** function. **PrintDlgEx( )** is substantially more powerful and flexible. New applications should definitely make use of it.

PrintDlgEx( ) has the following prototype:

```
BOOL PrintDlgEx(LPPRINTDLGEX PrintDlgEx);
```

The Windows
2000 Print
property sheet
Figure 17-1.

It returns **S_OK** if the user terminates the dialog box by pressing Print (that
is, if the user proceeds with printing). **PrintDlgEx( )** uses the COMMDLG.H
header, which is normally included automatically with WINDOWS.H. (If for
some reason your compiler does not automatically include COMMDLG.H,
you will need to add it manually.) Also, since **PrintDlgEx( )** is quite new,
you may need to define the macro **Winver** as 0x0500 at the start of your
program in order for the correct header information to be included.

The contents of the **PRINTDLGEX** structure pointed to by *PrintDlgEx*
determine how **PrintDlgEx( )** operates. This structure is defined like this:

```
typedef struct tagPDEX {
  DWORD lStructSize;
  HWND hwndOwner;
  HGLOBAL hDevMode;
  HGLOBAL hDevNames;
  HDC hDC;
  DWORD Flags;
```

```
    DWORD Flags2;
    DWORD ExclusionFlags;
    DWORD nPageRanges;
    DWORD nMaxPageRanges;
    LPPRINTPAGERANGE lpPageRanges;
    DWORD nMinPage;
    DWORD nMaxPage;
    DWORD nCopies;
    HINSTANCE hInstance;
    LPCSTR lpPrintTemplateName;
    LPUNKNOWN lpCallback;
    DWORD nPropertyPages;
    HPROPSHEETPAGE *lphPropertyPages;
    DWORD nStartPage;
    DWORD dwResultAction;
} PRINTDLGEX
```

lStructSize contains the size of the **PRINTDLGEX** structure.
hwndOwner specifies the handle of the window that owns **PrintDlgEx( )**.

hDevMode specifies the handle of a global **DEVMODE** structure that is used
to initialize the dialog box controls prior to the call and contains the state of
the controls after the call. This field may also be specified as **NULL.** In this
case, **PrintDlgEx( )** allocates and initializes a **DEVMODE** structure and
returns a handle to it in the **hDevMode** member. The **DEVMODE** structure
is not used by the examples in this chapter.

hDevNames contains the handle of a global **DEVNAMES** structure. This
structure specifies the name of the printer driver, the name of the printer,
and the name of the port. These names are used to initialize the
PrintDlgEx( ) dialog box. After the call, they will contain the
corresponding names entered by the user. This field may also be specified as
NULL. In this case, **PrintDlgEx( )** allocates and initializes a **DEVNAMES**
structure and returns a handle to it. The **DEVNAMES** structure is not used by
the examples in this chapter. When both **hDevNames** and **hDevMode** are
NULL, the default printer is used.

After the call, **hDC** will contain either the printer device context or
information context, depending upon which value is specified in the **Flags**
member. For the purposes of this chapter, **hDC** will contain a device context.
(An *information context* simply contains information about a device context
without actually creating one.)

nPageRanges specifies the number of page ranges that are passed to
PrintDlgEx( ) via its **lpPageRanges** parameter. On return, **nPageRanges**

will contain the number of page ranges selected by the user. More than one page range can be selected. To suppress page-range selection, include **PD_NOPAGENUMS** in the **Flags** parameter.

nMaxPageRanges specifies the length of the array pointed to by **lpPageRanges**. This value is ignored if **Flags** contains **PD_NOPAGENUMS**.

lpPageRanges points to an array of **PRINTPAGERANGE** structures. This structure is defined as shown here:

```
typedef struct tagPRINTPAGERANGE {
  DWORD nFromPage; // starting page in range
  DWORD nToPage;   // ending page in range
} PRINTPAGERANGE;
```

If **Flags** contains **PD_NOPAGENUMS** then **lpPageRanges** is ignored.

nMinPage contains the minimum page number that can be selected in the From box. **nMaxPage** contains the maximum page number that can be selected in the To box. These values are ignored if **Flags** contains the **PD_NOPAGENUMS** value.

nCopies initializes the Copies edit box. After the call, it will contain the number of copies to print as specified by the user. Your application must ensure that the number of copies requested by the user are actually printed.

You can use a different layout (template) for the Print property sheet. To do this, assign **hInstance** the instance handle of an alternative dialog box template and include the value **PD_ENABLEPRINTTEMPLATEHANDLE** in **Flags**. If no alternative template is desired, **hInstance** should be **NULL**.

An alternative template can also be used by assigning **lpPrintTemplateName** the address of the name of the dialog box resource that contains the new layout. In this case, **hInstance** must contain the instance handle of the module that contains the dialog box. **lpPrintTemplateName** is ignored unless **Flags** contains the value **PD_ENABLEPRINTTEMPLATE.**

lpCallback specifies a pointer to an optional callback object that receives callback information. Pass **NULL** if no such information is needed. The examples in this book do not use callbacks.

17

nPropertyPages specifies the length of the array pointed to by **lphPropertyPages**. This array is used to pass the handles of supplemental property sheets that will be added to the Print property sheet control. If no additional property sheets are required (as is usually the case) then **nPropertyPages** must be 0 and **lphPropertyPages** must be **NULL**.

The Print property sheet page that will be displayed when the control is first activated is passed in **nStartPage**. For most applications, this value should be **START_PAGE_GENERAL**.

The result of a successful call to **PrintDlgEx( )** is returned in **dwResultAction**. It will be one of these values:

PD_RESULT_APPLY	User pressed the Apply button, but did not press the Print button. Printing should not proceed.
PD_RESULT_CANCEL	User pressed Cancel. Printing should not proceed.
PD_RESULT_PRINT	User pressed the Print button, which indicates that your application should proceed with printing.

If the call to **PrintDlgEx( )** fails, **dwResultAction** will not contain valid data.

The **Flags** member contains values that determine precisely how the Print property sheet will behave and which fields will be active. On return, they will indicate the user's choices. It must be any valid combination of the values shown in Table 17-1.

The **Flags2** field is not used and must be set to 0. **ExclusionFlags** is used to exclude duplicate items. It applies to special circumstances and is normally set to 0.

As mentioned, on return the **hDC** member will contain the printer's device context. Using this context, you can output to the printer using functions such as **TextOut( )** or **BitBlt( )** that operate on device contexts. After your application is through printing, delete the printer device context by calling **DeleteDC( ).**

Flag	Effect
PD_ALLPAGES	Checks the All radio button. (This is the default.) On return, this flag will be set if the All radio button is selected.
PD_COLLATE	Checks the Collate Copies check box. On return, this flag will be set if Collate Copies is checked and the selected printer driver does not support collation. In this situation, your program must perform collation manually.
PD_CURRENTPAGE	On return, this flag is set if the user chooses the Current Page option.
PD_DISABLEPRINTTOFILE	Deactivates the Print to File check box.
PD_ENABLEPRINTTEMPLATE	Uses alternative dialog box template specified by **lpPrintTemplateName.**
PD_ENABLEPRINT-TEMPLATEHANDLE	Uses alternative Print dialog box template specified by **hInstance**.
PD_EXCLUSIONFLAGS	**ExclusionFlags** contains data.
PD_HIDEPRINTTOFILE	Suppresses the Print to File check box.
PD_NOCURRENTPAGE	Suppresses the Current Page button.
PD_NOPAGENUMS	Deactivates the Pages radio button.
PD_NOSELECTION	Deactivates the Selection radio button.
PD_NOWARNING	Suppresses warning messages.
PD_PAGENUMS	Selects the Pages radio button. On return, this flag is set if the Pages radio button is selected.
PD_PRINTTOFILE	Checks the Print to File check box. On return, indicates that user desires output to be directed to a file.
PD_RETURNDC	Causes a device context to be returned in **hDC**.

The Values for the **Flags** Member of **PRINTDLGEX** Table 17-1.

17

Flag	Effect
PD_RETURNDEFAULT	On return, **hDevMode** and **hDevNames** will contain values for the default printer. No dialog box is displayed. **hDevMode** and **hDevNames** must be **NULL** when **PrintDlgEx( )** is called.
PD_RETURNIC	Causes an information context to be returned in **hDC**.
PD_SELECTION	Selects the Selection radio button. On return, this flag will be set if the Selection radio button is selected.
PD_USEDEVMODE-COPIESANDCOLLATE PD_USEDEVMODECOPIES	Deactivates Number of Copies spin control and/or Collate check box if the printer driver does not support multiple copies or collation, respectively. If not set, the number of copies is contained in the **nCopies** member and the **PD_COLLATE** flag will be set if collation is required.
PD_USELARGETEMPLATE	Uses a larger template.

The Values for the **Flags** Member of **PRINTDLGEX** *(continued)*

Table 17-1.

The Printer Functions

There are several functions that your program must use when printing. These functions are shown here:

> int EndDoc(HDC *hPrDC*);
>
> int EndPage(HDC *hPrDC*);
>
> int StartDoc(HDC *hPrDC*, CONST DOCINFO **Info*);
>
> int StartPage(HDC *hPrDC*);

In all cases, *hPrDC* is the handle of the printer device context. Also in all cases, the functions return a nonzero, positive value if successful. On failure they return zero or less.

To start printing, you must first call **StartDoc( )**. **StartDoc( )** performs two actions. First, it starts a print job. Second, it returns the job ID. Although the examples in this chapter do not require print job IDs, some applications will because they are needed by some print-related functions. The *Info* parameter is a structure of type **DOCINFO**, which is defined like this:

```
typedef struct _DOCINFO {
  int cbSize;
  LPCSTR lpszDocName;
  LPCSTR lpszOutput;
  LPCSTR lpszDatatype;
  DWORD fwType;
} DOCINFO;
```

Here, **cbSize** must contain the size of the **DOCINFO** structure. **lpszDocName** is a pointer to the name of the print job. **lpszOutput** is a pointer to the name of the file that will receive printed output. However, to send output to the printer device context specified by *hPrDc*, **lpszOutput** must be **NULL. lpszDatatype** is a pointer to a string that identifies the type of data used to record the print job. This member can be **NULL. fwType** is usually zero.

To print a page, you must call **StartPage( )**. After each page is printed, you must call **EndPage( )**. **EndPage( )** advances the printer to a new page. Once your program is through printing, it must call **EndDoc( ).** Thus, the following outline shows the sequence required to print a page:

```
StartDoc(dc, &info);
StartPage(dc);
  // print a page of data here
EndPage(dc);
EndDoc(dc);
```

HISTORICAL PERSPECTIVE: For 16-bit, Windows 3.1, the functions performed by **StartDoc( )**, **StartPage( )**, **EndPage( )**, and **EndDoc( )** are accomplished using escape codes. These codes are sent via the **Escape( )** function. When converting older programs, you will want to replace any call to **Escape( )** with its appropriate printer function.

A Simple Printing Example

Although there are many more details that are necessary to properly add printing to a Windows 2000 application, the functions described in the preceding sections are sufficient to send text output to the printer. So, before we move on, let's take a look at a short example. The following program prints lines of text on the printer.

17

```
// A simple printing demonstration.

// This define is needed by some compilers.
#define WINVER 0x0500

#include <windows.h>
#include <cstring>
#include "print.h"

#define NUMLINES 20

LRESULT CALLBACK WindowFunc(HWND, UINT, WPARAM, LPARAM);
void PrintInit(PRINTDLGEX *printdlgex, HWND hwnd);

char szWinName[] = "MyWin"; // name of window class

int X = 0, Y = 0; // current output location
int maxX, maxY;   // screen dimensions

HDC memDC;      // virtual device handle
HBITMAP hBit;   // bitmap handle
HBRUSH hBrush;  // brush handle

PRINTDLGEX printdlgex;
DOCINFO docinfo;

int WINAPI WinMain(HINSTANCE hThisInst, HINSTANCE hPrevInst,
                   LPSTR lpszArgs, int nWinMode)
{
  HACCEL hAccel;
  HWND hwnd;
  MSG msg;
  WNDCLASSEX wcl;
```

```
// Define a window class.
wcl.cbSize = sizeof(WNDCLASSEX);

wcl.hInstance = hThisInst;       // handle to this instance
wcl.lpszClassName = szWinName;  // window class name
wcl.lpfnWndProc = WindowFunc;   // window function
wcl.style = 0;                  // default style

wcl.hIcon = LoadIcon(NULL, IDI_APPLICATION); // large icon
wcl.hIconSm = NULL; // use small version of large icon
wcl.hCursor = LoadCursor(NULL, IDC_ARROW);   // cursor style

wcl.lpszMenuName = "PrintDemoMenu"; // main menu

wcl.cbClsExtra = 0; // no extra memory needed
wcl.cbWndExtra = 0;

// Make the window background white.
wcl.hbrBackground = (HBRUSH) GetStockObject(WHITE_BRUSH);

// Register the window class.
if(!RegisterClassEx(&wcl)) return 0;

/* Now that a window class has been registered, a window
   can be created. */
hwnd = CreateWindow(
  szWinName, // name of window class
  "Using the Printer", // title
  WS_OVERLAPPEDWINDOW, // window style - normal
  CW_USEDEFAULT, // X coordinate - let Windows decide
  CW_USEDEFAULT, // Y coordinate - let Windows decide
  CW_USEDEFAULT, // width - let Windows decide
  CW_USEDEFAULT, // height - let Windows decide
  NULL,          // no parent window
  NULL,          // no menu
  hThisInst,     // instance handle
  NULL           // no additional arguments
);

// Load the keyboard accelerators.
hAccel = LoadAccelerators(hThisInst, "PrintDemoMenu");

// Display the window.
ShowWindow(hwnd, nWinMode);
UpdateWindow(hwnd);
```

```
      // Create the message loop.
      while(GetMessage(&msg, NULL, 0, 0))
      {
        if(!TranslateAccelerator(hwnd, hAccel, &msg)) {
          TranslateMessage(&msg); // translate keyboard messages
          DispatchMessage(&msg);  // return control to Windows 2000
        }
      }

      return msg.wParam;
    }

    /* This function is called by Windows 2000 and is passed
       messages from the message queue.
    */
    LRESULT CALLBACK WindowFunc(HWND hwnd, UINT message,
                                WPARAM wParam, LPARAM lParam)
    {
      HDC hdc;
      PAINTSTRUCT ps;
      int response;
      TEXTMETRIC tm;
      char str[80];
      int i;
      unsigned copies;

      switch(message) {
        case WM_CREATE:
          // get screen coordinates
          maxX = GetSystemMetrics(SM_CXSCREEN);
          maxY = GetSystemMetrics(SM_CYSCREEN);

          // create a virtual window
          hdc = GetDC(hwnd);
          memDC = CreateCompatibleDC(hdc);
          hBit = CreateCompatibleBitmap(hdc, maxX, maxY);
          SelectObject(memDC, hBit);
          hBrush = (HBRUSH) GetStockObject(WHITE_BRUSH);
          SelectObject(memDC, hBrush);
          PatBlt(memDC, 0, 0, maxX, maxY, PATCOPY);

          // get text metrics
          GetTextMetrics(hdc, &tm);

          strcpy(str, "This is displayed in the main window.");
```

```
      for(i=0; i<NUMLINES; i++) {
        TextOut(memDC, X, Y, str, strlen(str)); // output to memory
        TextOut(hdc, X, Y, str, strlen(str)); // output to window
        // advance to next line
        Y = Y + tm.tmHeight + tm.tmExternalLeading;
      }

    ReleaseDC(hwnd, hdc);
    break;
  case WM_COMMAND:
    switch(LOWORD(wParam)) {
      case IDM_TEXT:
        X = Y = 0;

        // initialize PRINTDLGEX struct
        PrintInit(&printdlgex, hwnd);

        if(PrintDlgEx(&printdlgex) != S_OK) break;
        else if(printdlgex.dwResultAction != PD_RESULT_PRINT) break;

        docinfo.cbSize = sizeof(DOCINFO);
        docinfo.lpszDocName = "Printing text";
        docinfo.lpszOutput = NULL;
        docinfo.lpszDatatype = NULL;
        docinfo.fwType = 0;

        // get text metrics for printer
        GetTextMetrics(printdlgex.hDC, &tm);

        strcpy(str, "This is printed on the printer.");

        StartDoc(printdlgex.hDC, &docinfo);

        for(copies=0; copies < printdlgex.nCopies; copies++) {
          StartPage(printdlgex.hDC);

          for(i=0; i<NUMLINES; i++) {
            TextOut(printdlgex.hDC, X, Y, str, strlen(str));
            // advance to next line
            Y = Y + tm.tmHeight + tm.tmExternalLeading;
          }

          EndPage(printdlgex.hDC);
        }
```

```
EndDoc(printdlgex.hDC);
        DeleteDC(printdlgex.hDC);
        break;
      case IDM_EXIT:
        response = MessageBox(hwnd, "Quit the Program?",
                             "Exit", MB_YESNO);
        if(response == IDYES) PostQuitMessage(0);
        break;
      case IDM_HELP:
        MessageBox(hwnd, "Printing Demo", "Help", MB_OK);
        break;
    }
    break;
  case WM_PAINT: // process a repaint request
    hdc = BeginPaint(hwnd, &ps); // get DC

    BitBlt(hdc, ps.rcPaint.left, ps.rcPaint.top,
           ps.rcPaint.right-ps.rcPaint.left, // width
           ps.rcPaint.bottom-ps.rcPaint.top, // height
           memDC,
           ps.rcPaint.left, ps.rcPaint.top,
           SRCCOPY);

    EndPaint(hwnd, &ps); // release DC
    break;
  case WM_DESTROY: // terminate the program
    DeleteDC(memDC);
    PostQuitMessage(0);
    break;
  default:
    /* Let Windows 2000 process any messages not specified in
       the preceding switch statement. */
    return DefWindowProc(hwnd, message, wParam, lParam);
  }
  return 0;
}

// Initialize PRINTDLGEX structure.
void PrintInit(PRINTDLGEX *printdlgex, HWND hwnd)
{
  printdlgex->lStructSize = sizeof(PRINTDLGEX);
  printdlgex->hwndOwner = hwnd;
  printdlgex->hDevMode = NULL;
  printdlgex->hDevNames = NULL;
  printdlgex->hDC = NULL;
```

```
    printdlgex->Flags = PD_RETURNDC | PD_NOSELECTION |
                        PD_NOPAGENUMS | PD_HIDEPRINTTOFILE |
                        PD_COLLATE;
    printdlgex->Flags2 = 0;
    printdlgex->ExclusionFlags = 0;
    printdlgex->nMinPage = 1;
    printdlgex->nMaxPage = 1;
    printdlgex->nCopies = 1;
    printdlgex->hInstance = NULL;
    printdlgex->lpCallback = NULL;
    printdlgex->nPropertyPages = 0;
    printdlgex->lphPropertyPages = NULL;
    printdlgex->nStartPage = START_PAGE_GENERAL;
    printdlgex->dwResultAction = 0;

    printdlgex->lpPrintTemplateName = NULL;
}
```

The program requires the following resource file:

```
#include <windows.h>
#include "print.h"

PrintDemoMenu MENU
{
  POPUP "&Printer Demo"
  {
    MENUITEM "Print &Text\tF2", IDM_TEXT
    MENUITEM "E&xit\tCtrl+X", IDM_EXIT
  }
  MENUITEM "&Help", IDM_HELP
}


PrintDemoMenu ACCELERATORS
{
  VK_F2, IDM_TEXT, VIRTKEY
  VK_F1, IDM_HELP, VIRTKEY
  "^X", IDM_EXIT
}
```

The header file PRINT.H is shown here. In addition to the values used by the preceding program, it includes several values that will be used by subsequent programs in this chapter.

```
#define IDM_TEXT     100
#define IDM_BITMAP   101
#define IDM_EXIT     102
#define IDM_HELP     103
#define IDM_WINDOW   104
#define IDM_ENLARGE  105

#define IDD_EB1      200
#define IDD_EB2      201
#define IDD_UD1      202
#define IDD_UD2      202

#define IDD_TEXT1    210
#define IDD_TEXT2    211
```

A Closer Look at the First Printing Program

The important part of the program as it relates to printing occurs within the **IDM_TEXT** case. It is shown here for your convenience. This code is executed whenever the user selects Print Text from the Printer Demo menu.

```
case IDM_TEXT:
  X = Y = 0;
  // initialize PRINTDLGEX struct
  PrintInit(&printdlgex, hwnd);

  if(PrintDlgEx(&printdlgex) != S_OK) break;
  else if(printdlgex.dwResultAction != PD_RESULT_PRINT) break;

  docinfo.cbSize = sizeof(DOCINFO);
  docinfo.lpszDocName = "Printing text";
  docinfo.lpszOutput = NULL;
  docinfo.lpszDatatype = NULL;
  docinfo.fwType = 0;

  // get text metrics for printer
  GetTextMetrics(printdlgex.hDC, &tm);

  strcpy(str, "This is printed on the printer.");

  StartDoc(printdlgex.hDC, &docinfo);

  for(copies=0; copies < printdlgex.nCopies; copies++) {
    StartPage(printdlgex.hDC);
```

```
  for(i=0; i<NUMLINES; i++) {
    TextOut(printdlgex.hDC, X, Y, str, strlen(str));
    // advance to next line
    Y = Y + tm.tmHeight + tm.tmExternalLeading;
  }

  EndPage(printdlgex.hDC);
}

EndDoc(printdlgex.hDC);
DeleteDC(printdlgex.hDC);
break;
```

Let's go through this code sequence, step by step. First, **X** and **Y**, which are used to position text on both the printer and in a window, are reset to zero. Next, a **PRINTDLGEX** structure is initialized by calling **PrintInit( )**. Notice that the Selection radio button and the Pages edit boxes are disabled. The Print to File check box is also hidden. These controls are not needed by the program. Next, **PrintDlgEx( )** is executed. Upon return, **printdlgex.hDC** contains the device context of the printer selected by the user. Then, a **DOCINFO** structure is initialized. Next, a call is made to **GetTextMetrics( )** using the printer device context. Since text is going to be printed, it is necessary to obtain the text metrics as they relate to the printer in order to correctly perform carriage return/linefeed sequences. These values will not be the same as those obtained when text is displayed on the screen inside the **WM_CREATE** case. This is an important point. The printer device context is separate and unique. It does not necessarily share any attributes in common with the window DCs used by the other parts of your program.

A printer device context is completely separate from a window device context.

To start the printing process, **StartDoc( )** is called. Next, a loop is started that prints the number of copies requested by the user. This value is obtained from the **nCopies** member of **printdlgex**. Since each copy will be on its own page, **StartPage( )** is called at the start of each iteration. Next, a few lines of text are sent to the printer. Notice that the device context obtained by calling **PrintDlgEx( )**, which is **printdlgex.hDC**, is used as the target context for the **TextOut( )** function. Once you have a printer device context, it can be used like any other device context. At the end of each page, **EndPage( )** is called. When all printing is done, **EndDoc( )** is executed and the printer DC is deleted.

While this example is quite simple, it does illustrate all of the essential elements required to print a document on the printer. The remainder of this chapter shows you how to print bitmaps, add an abort box, and handle scaling. In all these applications, the fundamental approach to sending output to the printer will be the same.

Printing Bitmaps

17

Since Windows is a graphical operating system, it makes sense that you can print graphical output. In fact, sending text output to the printer using **TextOut( )** as shown in the preceding example is the exception, not the rule. Most of the time, your program will need to render a printed version of a graphical bitmap. Keep in mind that this bitmap might contain text, but it will not be restricted to text. Fortunately, printing a bitmap is not, in and of itself, a difficult task. However, certain side issues need to be dealt with.

First, before printing a bitmap, your program must determine whether the selected printer is capable of displaying graphical output—not all printers are. Second, in order for the printed bitmap to have the same perspective that it does on the screen, some scaling of output might be needed. Finally, it is not possible to select a bitmap into a printer device context. (Bitmaps can be selected only into memory DCs.) Therefore, to print a bitmap implies that you will first need to select it into a compatible DC and then copy that DC to the printer DC using a function such as **StretchBlt( ).** Let's examine each of these issues.

Determining Printer Raster Capabilities

To print a bitmap, a printer must be capable of raster operations.

Not all printers can print bitmaps. For example, some printers can print only text. In the language of Windows, a printer that can print a bitmap is capable of *raster operations*. The term *raster* originally referred to video display devices. However, it has been generalized. In its current usage, if a device has raster capabilities, it can perform certain types of operations normally associated with a video display. In simple terms, if a printer has raster capabilities, then it can display graphical output. Today, most commonly used printers have raster capabilities. However, since there are still many printers that do not have this capability, your program must check before attempting to print a bitmap. To do this, you will use the **GetDeviceCaps( )** function. Its prototype is shown here:

> int GetDeviceCaps(HDC *hdc*, int *attribute*);

Here, *hdc* is the handle of the device context for which information is being obtained. The value of *attribute* determines precisely what attribute about the device is retrieved. The function returns the requested information.

There are a large number of attributes that can be returned, and most are not relevant to this chapter. (However, you will want to explore **GetDeviceCaps( )** on your own. It can obtain an amazing amount of information about a device.) The attribute that we will use to see if a printer is able to display a bitmap is **RASTERCAPS**. The return value will indicate what, if any, raster capabilities the printer has. It will be one or more of these values:

Value	Meaning
RC_BANDING	Printer DC requires banding support for graphics.
RC_BITBLT	Printer DC can be target of **BitBlt( )**.
RC_BITMAP64	Printer DC can handle bitmaps larger than 64K.
RC_DI_BITMAP	Printer DC supports device independent bitmaps via the **SetDIBits( )** and **GetDIBits( )** functions.
RC_DIBTODEV	Printer DC supports **SetDIBitsToDevice( )**.
RC_FLOODFIL	Printer DC supports flood fills.
RC_PALETTE	Printer DC supports a palette.
RC_SCALING	Printer DC provides its own scaling capabilities.
RC_STRETCHBLT	Printer DC can be target of **StretchBlt( )**.
RC_STRETCHDIB	Printer DC can be target of **StretchDIBits( )**.

For the purposes of this chapter, we are interested in only two of these values: **RC_BITBLT** and **RC_STRETCHBLT**.

Maintaining Perspective

In order for a bitmap to look the same printed as it does on the screen, it must be scaled.

If you want the bitmap to look the same when printed as it does when displayed on the screen, then you will need to scale the image appropriately when printing it. To accomplish this, you will need to know the resolution of both the screen and the printer. For this purpose, you will once again use the **GetDeviceCaps( )** function. To obtain the number of horizontal pixels-per-inch, specify **LOGPIXELSX** as the attribute. To retrieve the number of vertical pixels-per-inch, use **LOGPIXELSY**. For example, after these calls

```
hres = GetDeviceCaps(hdc, LOGPIXELSX);
vres = GetDeviceCaps(hdc, LOGPIXELSY);
```

hres will contain the number of pixels-per-inch along the X axis, and **vres** will contain the number of pixels-per-inch along the Y axis for the device context specified by **hdc**.

Once you have found the resolution of both the video DC and the printer DC, you can compute a scaling factor. You will use this scaling factor in a call to **StrechBlt( )** to render the bitmap, in its correct perspective, on the printer.

StretchBlt( )

StretchBlt( ) copies a bitmap and is related to the **BitBlt( )** function described earlier in this book. However, in the copying process, **StretchBlt( )** expands or compresses the source bitmap so that it will fit and completely fill the target rectangle. Its prototype is

```
BOOL StretchBlt(HDC hDest, int DestX, int DestY,
                int DestWidth, int DestHeight,
                HDC hSource, int SourceX, int SourceY,
                int SourceWidth, int SourceHeight,
                DWORD dwHow);
```

Here, *hDest* is the handle of the target device context, and *DestX* and *DestY* are the upper-left coordinates at which point the bitmap will be drawn. The width and height of the target bitmap are specified in *DestWidth* and *DestHeight*. The *hSource* parameter contains the handle of the source device context. *SourceX* and *SourceY* specify the upper-left coordinates in the bitmap at which point the copy operation will begin. The width and height of the source bitmap are passed in *SourceWidth* and *SourceHeight*. **StretchBlt( )** automatically expands (that is, stretches) or contracts the source bitmap so that it will fit into the destination bitmap. This differs from **BitBlt( )**, which performs no stretching or compressing.

StretchBit( ) is similar to BitBlt( ), except that it can expand or compress an image.

The value of *dwHow* determines how the bit-by-bit contents of the bitmap will actually be copied. It uses the same values as does the comparable parameter to **BitBlt( )**. Some of its most commonly used values are shown here:

dwHow Macro	Effect
DSTINVERT	Inverts the bits in the destination bitmap.
SRCAND	ANDs bitmap with current destination.
SRCCOPY	Copies bitmap as is, overwriting previous contents.
SRCERASE	ANDs bitmap with the inverted bits of destination bitmap.
SRCINVERT	XORs bitmap with current destination.
SRCPAINT	ORs bitmap with current destination.

StretchBlt( ) is important when printing bitmaps because it allows you to scale the printed version. **StretchBlt( )** shrinks or enlarges the source bitmap, as needed, so that it fits the target rectangle. By applying the scaling factors to the dimensions of the target rectangle, you can use **StretchBlt( )** to scale the printed version of the bitmap. Keep in mind, however, that if no scaling is desired, your program can use **BitBlt( )** to copy a bitmap to the printer. It is just that the printed version will not have the same perspective as the screen image. You will see examples of both in the program that follows.

Obtaining Printer-Compatible DCs

One small, but sometimes irritating, problem associated with printing bitmaps is that a bitmap can be selected only into a memory device context. Thus, you cannot select a bitmap directly into the printer DC obtained from **PrintDlgEx( )** or **CreateDC( )**. Instead, you will need to create a compatible memory DC, select the bitmap into that device context, and then copy it to the printer context using either **BitBlt( )** or **StretchBlt( )**.

There is one other complication. The bitmap that you want to print may not be compatible with the printer device context. When this is the case, you must first create a printer-compatible bitmap. Next, select that bitmap into the printer-compatible memory DC, copy the bitmap that you want to print into the printer-compatible bitmap, and then copy that bitmap to the printer DC. If this all seems overly complicated, it is! Nevertheless, this is the way that Windows 2000 is designed. However, as you will see, it is actually an easy process to implement.

A Bitmap Printing Demonstration Program

The following program adds two new features to the first printing example. One option prints a bitmap on the printer two ways: first without performing any scaling, and then with the scaling factors applied to maintain perspective. This option allows you to easily see the difference between scaled and nonscaled output. The other option lets you print the contents of the program's main window. This is easy to do because the program uses the virtual window technology described in Chapter 7, which means that the contents of the main window are also stored in a bitmap. Thus, to print the contents of the window is simply a special case of the general procedure used to print any bitmap. Sample output is shown in Figure 17-2.

17

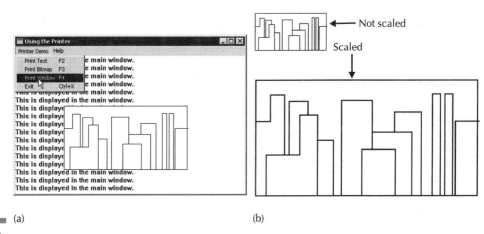

(a)   (b)

Sample output from the bitmap printing program: (a) Window as it appears on the screen; (b) printed bitmaps; (c) contents of window printed

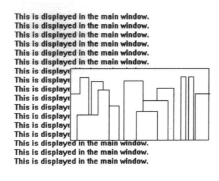

(c)

Figure 17-2.

```
// A Bitmap Printing Demo Program.

// This define is needed by some compilers.
#define WINVER 0x0500

#include <windows.h>
#include <cstring>
#include "print.h"

#define NUMLINES 25

#define BMPWIDTH 256
#define BMPHEIGHT 128

LRESULT CALLBACK WindowFunc(HWND, UINT, WPARAM, LPARAM);
void PrintInit(PRINTDLGEX *printdlgex, HWND hwnd);

char szWinName[] = "MyWin"; // name of window class

int X = 0, Y = 0; // current output location
int maxX, maxY;   // screen dimensions

HDC memDC, memPrDC; // virtual device handles
HBITMAP hBit, hBit2, hImage; // bitmap handles
HBRUSH hBrush;       // brush handle

PRINTDLGEX printdlgex;
DOCINFO docinfo;

int WINAPI WinMain(HINSTANCE hThisInst, HINSTANCE hPrevInst,
                LPSTR lpszArgs, int nWinMode)
{
  HACCEL hAccel;
  HWND hwnd;
  MSG msg;
  WNDCLASSEX wcl;

  // Define a window class.
  wcl.cbSize = sizeof(WNDCLASSEX);

  wcl.hInstance = hThisInst;     // handle to this instance
  wcl.lpszClassName = szWinName; // window class name
  wcl.lpfnWndProc = WindowFunc;  // window function
  wcl.style = 0;                 // default style

  wcl.hIcon = LoadIcon(NULL, IDI_APPLICATION); // large icon
  wcl.hIconSm = NULL; // use small version of large icon
  wcl.hCursor = LoadCursor(NULL, IDC_ARROW);  // cursor style

  wcl.lpszMenuName = "PrintDemoMenu2"; // main menu
```

```
        wcl.cbClsExtra = 0; // no extra memory needed
        wcl.cbWndExtra = 0;

        // Make the window background white.
        wcl.hbrBackground = (HBRUSH) GetStockObject(WHITE_BRUSH);

        // Register the window class.
        if(!RegisterClassEx(&wcl)) return 0;

        /* Now that a window class has been registered, a window
           can be created. */
        hwnd = CreateWindow(
          szWinName, // name of window class
          "Using the Printer", // title
          WS_OVERLAPPEDWINDOW, // window style - normal
          CW_USEDEFAULT, // X coordinate - let Windows decide
          CW_USEDEFAULT, // Y coordinate - let Windows decide
          CW_USEDEFAULT, // width - let Windows decide
          CW_USEDEFAULT, // height - let Windows decide
          NULL,          // no parent window
          NULL,          // no menu
          hThisInst,     // instance handle
          NULL           // no additional arguments
        );

        // Load the keyboard accelerators.
        hAccel = LoadAccelerators(hThisInst, "PrintDemoMenu2");

        // Load the bitmap.
        hImage = LoadBitmap(hThisInst, "MyBP1");

        // Display the window.
        ShowWindow(hwnd, nWinMode);
        UpdateWindow(hwnd);

        // Create the message loop.
        while(GetMessage(&msg, NULL, 0, 0))
        {
          if(!TranslateAccelerator(hwnd, hAccel, &msg)) {
            TranslateMessage(&msg); // translate keyboard messages
            DispatchMessage(&msg);  // return control to Windows 2000
          }
        }

        return msg.wParam;
}

/* This function is called by Windows 2000 and is passed
   messages from the message queue.
*/
LRESULT CALLBACK WindowFunc(HWND hwnd, UINT message,
```

```
                              WPARAM wParam, LPARAM lParam)
{
  HDC hdc;
  PAINTSTRUCT ps;
  int response;
  TEXTMETRIC tm;
  char str[250];
  int i;
  unsigned copies;
  double VidXPPI, VidYPPI, PrXPPI, PrYPPI;
  double Xratio, Yratio;
  RECT r;

  switch(message) {
    case WM_CREATE:
      // get screen coordinates
      maxX = GetSystemMetrics(SM_CXSCREEN);
      maxY = GetSystemMetrics(SM_CYSCREEN);

      // create a virtual window
      hdc = GetDC(hwnd);
      memDC = CreateCompatibleDC(hdc);
      hBit = CreateCompatibleBitmap(hdc, maxX, maxY);
      SelectObject(memDC, hBit);
      hBrush = (HBRUSH) GetStockObject(WHITE_BRUSH);
      SelectObject(memDC, hBrush);
      PatBlt(memDC, 0, 0, maxX, maxY, PATCOPY);

      ReleaseDC(hwnd, hdc);
      break;
    case WM_COMMAND:
      switch(LOWORD(wParam)) {
        case IDM_TEXT: // print text
          X = Y = 0;

          // initialize PRINTDLGEX struct
          PrintInit(&printdlgex, hwnd);

          if(PrintDlgEx(&printdlgex) != S_OK) break;
          else if(printdlgex.dwResultAction != PD_RESULT_PRINT) break;

          docinfo.cbSize = sizeof(DOCINFO);
          docinfo.lpszDocName = "Printing Text";
          docinfo.lpszOutput = NULL;
          docinfo.lpszDatatype = NULL;
          docinfo.fwType = 0;

          // get text metrics for printer
          GetTextMetrics(printdlgex.hDC, &tm);

          strcpy(str, "This is printed on the printer.");
```

```
            StartDoc(printdlgex.hDC, &docinfo);

            for(copies=0; copies < printdlgex.nCopies; copies++) {
              StartPage(printdlgex.hDC);

              for(i=0; i<NUMLINES; i++) {
                TextOut(printdlgex.hDC, X, Y, str, strlen(str));
                // advance to next line
                Y = Y + tm.tmHeight + tm.tmExternalLeading;
              }

              EndPage(printdlgex.hDC);
            }

            EndDoc(printdlgex.hDC);
            DeleteDC(printdlgex.hDC);
            break;
          case IDM_BITMAP: // print a bitmap
            // initialize PRINTDLGEX struct
            PrintInit(&printdlgex, hwnd);

            if(PrintDlgEx(&printdlgex) != S_OK) break;
            else if(printdlgex.dwResultAction != PD_RESULT_PRINT) break;

            docinfo.cbSize = sizeof(DOCINFO);
            docinfo.lpszDocName = "Printing bitmaps";
            docinfo.lpszOutput = NULL;
            docinfo.lpszDatatype = NULL;
            docinfo.fwType = 0;

            if(!(GetDeviceCaps(printdlgex.hDC, RASTERCAPS)
                & (RC_BITBLT | RC_STRETCHBLT))) {
              MessageBox(hwnd, "Cannot Print Raster Images",
                        "Error", MB_OK);
              break;
            }

            // create a memory DC compatible with the printer
            memPrDC = CreateCompatibleDC(printdlgex.hDC);
            // create a bitmap compatible with the printer DC
            hBit2 = CreateCompatibleBitmap(printdlgex.hDC, maxX, maxY);
            SelectObject(memPrDC, hBit2);

            // put bitmap image into memory DC
            SelectObject(memDC, hImage);

            // copy bitmap to printer-compatible DC
            BitBlt(memPrDC, 0, 0, BMPWIDTH, BMPHEIGHT,
                  memDC, 0, 0, SRCCOPY);

            // obtain pixels-per-inch
```

```
    VidXPPI = GetDeviceCaps(memDC, LOGPIXELSX);
    VidYPPI = GetDeviceCaps(memDC, LOGPIXELSY);
    PrXPPI = GetDeviceCaps(printdlgex.hDC, LOGPIXELSX);
    PrYPPI = GetDeviceCaps(printdlgex.hDC, LOGPIXELSY);

    // get scaling ratios
    Xratio = PrXPPI / VidXPPI;
    Yratio = PrYPPI / VidYPPI;

    SelectObject(memDC, hBit); // restore virtual window

    StartDoc(printdlgex.hDC, &docinfo);

    for(copies=0; copies < printdlgex.nCopies; copies++) {
      StartPage(printdlgex.hDC);

      // copy bitmap to printer DC, as-is
      BitBlt(printdlgex.hDC, 0, 0, BMPWIDTH, BMPHEIGHT,
             memPrDC, 0, 0, SRCCOPY);

      // copy bitmap while maintaining perspective
      StretchBlt(printdlgex.hDC, 0, BMPHEIGHT + 100,
                 (int) (BMPWIDTH*Xratio),
                 (int) (BMPHEIGHT*Yratio),
                 memPrDC, 0, 0,
                 BMPWIDTH, BMPHEIGHT,
                 SRCCOPY);

      EndPage(printdlgex.hDC);
    }

    EndDoc(printdlgex.hDC);
    DeleteDC(memPrDC);
    DeleteDC(printdlgex.hDC);
    break;
  case IDM_WINDOW: // print contents of window
    GetClientRect(hwnd, &r);
    hdc = GetDC(hwnd);

    // display some text in the window
    GetTextMetrics(hdc, &tm);
    X = Y = 0;
    strcpy(str, "This is displayed in the main window.");
    for(i=0; i<NUMLINES; i++) {
      TextOut(hdc, X, Y, str, strlen(str));
      TextOut(memDC, X, Y, str, strlen(str));
      // advance to next line
      Y = Y + tm.tmHeight + tm.tmExternalLeading;
    }

    // display bitmap image in the window
```

```
SelectObject(memDC, hImage);
BitBlt(hdc, 100, 100, BMPWIDTH, BMPHEIGHT,
        memDC, 0, 0, SRCCOPY);

// save image in window for PAINT requests
SelectObject(memDC, hBit);
BitBlt(memDC, 0, 0, r.right, r.bottom, hdc, 0, 0, SRCCOPY);

// create a compatible DC
memPrDC = CreateCompatibleDC(hdc);
// create a compatible bitmap
hBit2 = CreateCompatibleBitmap(hdc, r.right, r.bottom);
SelectObject(memPrDC, hBit2);

// save image in window for printing
BitBlt(memPrDC, 0, 0, r.right, r.bottom,
        hdc, 0, 0, SRCCOPY);

// initialize PRINTDLGEX struct
PrintInit(&printdlgex, hwnd);

if(PrintDlgEx(&printdlgex) != S_OK) break;
else if(printdlgex.dwResultAction != PD_RESULT_PRINT) break;

docinfo.cbSize = sizeof(DOCINFO);
docinfo.lpszDocName = "Printing Window";
docinfo.lpszOutput = NULL;
docinfo.lpszDatatype = NULL;
docinfo.fwType = 0;

// obtain pixels-per-inch
VidXPPI = GetDeviceCaps(memDC, LOGPIXELSX);
VidYPPI = GetDeviceCaps(memDC, LOGPIXELSY);
PrXPPI = GetDeviceCaps(printdlgex.hDC, LOGPIXELSX);
PrYPPI = GetDeviceCaps(printdlgex.hDC, LOGPIXELSY);

// get scaling ratios
Xratio = PrXPPI / VidXPPI;
Yratio = PrYPPI / VidYPPI;

if(!(GetDeviceCaps(printdlgex.hDC, RASTERCAPS)
    & RC_STRETCHBLT)) {
    MessageBox(hwnd, "Cannot Print Raster Images",
            "Error", MB_OK);
    break;
}


StartDoc(printdlgex.hDC, &docinfo);

for(copies=0; copies < printdlgex.nCopies; copies++) {
```

```
          StartPage(printdlgex.hDC);

          StretchBlt(printdlgex.hDC, 0, 0,
                   (int) (r.right*Xratio),
                   (int) (r.bottom*Yratio),
                   memPrDC, 0, 0, (int) r.right, (int) r.bottom,
                   SRCCOPY);

        EndPage(printdlgex.hDC);
      }

      EndDoc(printdlgex.hDC);
      DeleteDC(printdlgex.hDC);
      DeleteDC(memPrDC);
      ReleaseDC(hwnd, hdc);
      break;
    case IDM_EXIT:
      response = MessageBox(hwnd, "Quit the Program?",
                           "Exit", MB_YESNO);
      if(response == IDYES) PostQuitMessage(0);
      break;
    case IDM_HELP:
      MessageBox(hwnd, "Printing Demo", "Help", MB_OK);
      break;
    }
    break;
  case WM_PAINT: // process a repaint request
    hdc = BeginPaint(hwnd, &ps); // get DC

    BitBlt(hdc, ps.rcPaint.left, ps.rcPaint.top,
          ps.rcPaint.right-ps.rcPaint.left, // width
          ps.rcPaint.bottom-ps.rcPaint.top, // height
          memDC,
          ps.rcPaint.left, ps.rcPaint.top,
          SRCCOPY);

    EndPaint(hwnd, &ps); // release DC
    break;
  case WM_DESTROY: // terminate the program
    DeleteDC(memDC);
    PostQuitMessage(0);
    break;
  default:
    /* Let Windows 2000 process any messages not specified in
      the preceding switch statement. */
    return DefWindowProc(hwnd, message, wParam, lParam);
  }

  return 0;
}

// Initialize PRINTDLGEX structure.
```

```
void PrintInit(PRINTDLGEX *printdlgex, HWND hwnd)
{
  printdlgex->lStructSize = sizeof(PRINTDLGEX);
  printdlgex->hwndOwner = hwnd;
  printdlgex->hDevMode = NULL;
  printdlgex->hDevNames = NULL;
  printdlgex->hDC = NULL;
  printdlgex->Flags = PD_RETURNDC | PD_NOSELECTION |
                      PD_NOPAGENUMS | PD_HIDEPRINTTOFILE |
                      PD_COLLATE;
  printdlgex->Flags2 = 0;
  printdlgex->ExclusionFlags = 0;
  printdlgex->nMinPage = 1;
  printdlgex->nMaxPage = 1;
  printdlgex->nCopies = 1;
  printdlgex->hInstance = NULL;
  printdlgex->lpCallback = NULL;
  printdlgex->nPropertyPages = 0;
  printdlgex->lphPropertyPages = NULL;
  printdlgex->nStartPage = START_PAGE_GENERAL;
  printdlgex->dwResultAction = 0;

  printdlgex->lpPrintTemplateName = NULL;
}
```

This program requires the following resource file:

```
#include <windows.h>
#include "print.h"

MyBP1 BITMAP BP.BMP

PrintDemoMenu2 MENU
{
  POPUP "&Printer Demo"
  {
    MENUITEM "Print &Text\tF2", IDM_TEXT
    MENUITEM "Print &Bitmap\tF3", IDM_BITMAP
    MENUITEM "Print &Window\tF4", IDM_WINDOW
    MENUITEM "E&xit\tCtrl+X", IDM_EXIT
  }
  MENUITEM "&Help", IDM_HELP
}

PrintDemoMenu2 ACCELERATORS
{
  VK_F2, IDM_TEXT, VIRTKEY
  VK_F3, IDM_BITMAP, VIRTKEY
  VK_F4, IDM_WINDOW, VIRTKEY
  VK_F1, IDM_HELP, VIRTKEY
  "^X", IDM_EXIT
}
```

This program requires a bitmap for operation. As the program is written, the bitmap must be 256 pixels wide and 128 pixels high. However, if you change the definitions of **BMPWIDTH** and **BMPHEIGHT** you can use any size bitmap you like. The bitmap must be stored in a file called BP.BMP.

A Closer Look at the Bitmap Printing Program

Let's begin by examining the **IDM_BITMAP** case. This code is executed when the user selects the Print Bitmap option. It prints the bitmap stored in BP.BMP. This code is shown here for your convenience:

```
case IDM_BITMAP: // print a bitmap
  // initialize PRINTDLGEX struct
        PrintInit(&printdlgex, hwnd);

  if(PrintDlgEx(&printdlgex) != S_OK) break;
  else if(printdlgex.dwResultAction != PD_RESULT_PRINT) break;

  docinfo.cbSize = sizeof(DOCINFO);
  docinfo.lpszDocName = "Printing bitmaps";
  docinfo.lpszOutput = NULL;
  docinfo.lpszDatatype = NULL;
  docinfo.fwType = 0;

  if(!(GetDeviceCaps(printdlgex.hDC, RASTERCAPS)
     & (RC_BITBLT | RC_STRETCHBLT))) {
     MessageBox(hwnd, "Cannot Print Raster Images",
                "Error", MB_OK);
     break;
  }

  // create a memory DC compatible with the printer
  memPrDC = CreateCompatibleDC(printdlgex.hDC);
  // create a bitmap compatible with the printer DC
  hBit2 = CreateCompatibleBitmap(printdlgex.hDC, maxX, maxY);
  SelectObject(memPrDC, hBit2);

  // put bitmap image into memory DC
  SelectObject(memDC, hImage);

  // copy bitmap to printer-compatible DC
```

```
BitBlt(memPrDC, 0, 0, BMPWIDTH, BMPHEIGHT,
        memDC, 0, 0, SRCCOPY);

// obtain pixels-per-inch
VidXPPI = GetDeviceCaps(memDC, LOGPIXELSX);
VidYPPI = GetDeviceCaps(memDC, LOGPIXELSY);
PrXPPI = GetDeviceCaps(printdlgex.hDC, LOGPIXELSX);
PrYPPI = GetDeviceCaps(printdlgex.hDC, LOGPIXELSY);

// get scaling ratios
Xratio = PrXPPI / VidXPPI;
Yratio = PrYPPI / VidYPPI;

SelectObject(memDC, hBit); // restore virtual window

StartDoc(printdlgex.hDC, &docinfo);

for(copies=0; copies < printdlgex.nCopies; copies++) {
  StartPage(printdlgex.hDC);

  // copy bitmap to printer DC, as-is
  BitBlt(printdlgex.hDC, 0, 0, BMPWIDTH, BMPHEIGHT,
          memPrDC, 0, 0, SRCCOPY);

  // copy bitmap while maintaining perspective
  StretchBlt(printdlgex.hDC, 0, BMPHEIGHT + 100,
             (int) (BMPWIDTH*Xratio),
             (int) (BMPHEIGHT*Yratio),
             memPrDC, 0, 0,
             BMPWIDTH, BMPHEIGHT,
             SRCCOPY);

  EndPage(printdlgex.hDC);
}

EndDoc(printdlgex.hDC);
DeleteDC(memPrDC);
DeleteDC(printdlgex.hDC);
break;
```

After the printer DC has been acquired and **docinfo** has been initialized, a
call is made to **GetDeviceCaps( )** to determine if the printer supports the

necessary raster operations. Remember, if the printer cannot print graphics, it cannot print a bitmap. Assuming that the printer can print the bitmap, a printer-compatible memory DC (**memPrDC**) and bitmap (**hBit2**) are created. The use of **maxX** and **maxY** for the dimensions of the printer-compatible bitmap are suitable for all bitmaps that are not larger than the size of screen. (Of course, if you want to print a larger bitmap, then these dimensions would need to be larger.) Next, **hbit2** is selected into the printer-compatible memory DC.

The bitmap to be displayed (whose handle is **hImage**) is selected into the memory device context described by **memDC**. This is the same memory DC used to support the virtual window system that handles **WM_PAINT** messages. It is simply doing double duty at this point. (A separate memory DC could have been created for this purpose, but to do so seemed unnecessarily inefficient.) Next, the bitmap is copied from **memDC** into **memPrDC**. The reason for this intermediate step is that the bitmap stored in BP.BMP is compatible with a video device context, not a printer device context. Thus, it cannot be directly selected into **memPrDC**.

The next step computes the scaling ratios. To do this, the number of pixels per inch for the screen and the printer are obtained, and a scaling factor is computed.

Finally, the bitmap can be sent to the printer. First, it is copied as is, using **BitBlt( )**. This causes the bitmap to be printed without adjusting for the perspective differences between the two devices. Next, the bitmap is printed using **StretchBlt( )** and applying the scaling factors. As you can see, the scaled bitmap closely resembles the way the bitmap looks when displayed on the screen.

The code inside the **IDM_WINDOW** is similar to that inside the **IDM_BITMAP** case just described. You should have no trouble understanding it.

IN DEPTH

Creating an Old-Style Print Dialog Box

Prior to Windows 2000, the Print common dialog box was displayed by calling **PrintDlg( )**. This dialog box does not offer the flexibility found in the modern **PrintDlgEx( )** version. However, since all previous code used **PrintDlg( )**, it is a good idea to become familiar with it since you will almost certainly encounter it when working on or converting older code. The prototype for **PrintDlg( )** is shown here:

BOOL PrintDlg(LPPRINTDLG *PrintDlg*);

It returns nonzero if the user terminates the dialog box by pressing OK. It returns zero if the user presses Cancel (or ESC) or closes the box using the system menu.

The contents of the **PRINTDLG** structure pointed to by *PrintDlg* determine how **PrintDlg( )** operates. This structure is defined like this:

```
typedef struct tagPD {
  DWORD lStructSize;
  HWND hwndOwner;
  HGLOBAL hDevMode;
  HGLOBAL hDevNames;
  HDC hDC;
  DWORD Flags;
  WORD nFromPage;
  WORD nToPage;
  WORD nMinPage;
  WORD nMaxPage;
  WORD nCopies;
  HINSTANCE hInstance;
  LPARAM lCustData;
```

```
   LPPRINTHOOKPROC lpfnPrintHook;
   LPSETUPHOOKPROC lpfnSetupHook;
   LPCSTR lpPrintTemplateName;
   LPCSTR lpSetupTemplateName;
   HGLOBAL hPrintTemplate;
   HGLOBAL hSetupTemplate;
} PRINTDLG;
```

As you can see, many of its fields are similar to those in **PRINTDLGEX**, described earlier. One noticeable difference is that only one range of pages can be selected (by **nFromPage** and **nToPage**) rather than the multiple ranges supported by the **PRINTDLGEX** structure. Other fields, such as **hSetupTemplate**, **lCustData**, and **lpfnPrintHook** are not needed by **PrintDlgEx( )**.

Adding an Abort Function

The preceding examples sent output to the printer (actually, to the print spooler) and then forgot about it. That is, as far as the program was concerned, once the output was sent to the printer its job was done. However, for real applications, things cannot be this simple. Sometimes an error occurs while printing and a print job must be stopped. Sometimes the user will change his or her mind and want to cancel a print job. To handle such situations, your program must supply a *printer abort function* and a modeless dialog box that allows the user to cancel a print job before it is complete. According to standard Windows style, all programs must supply such a feature. In this section, you will see how to accomplish this.

A printing abort function allows printing to be cancelled by the user.

SetAbortProc( )

To install an abort function, your program must call **SetAbortProc( )**. Its prototype is shown here:

    int SetAbortProc(HDC *hPrDC*, ABORTPROC *AbortFunc*);

Here, *hPrDC* is the handle of the printer device context. *AbortFunc* is the name of the abort function that is being installed. The function returns a value that is greater than zero if successful or **SP_ERROR** on failure.

All abort functions have the following prototype:

BOOL CALLBACK AbortFunc(HDC *hPrDC*, int *Code*);

When called, *hPrDC* will contain the handle for the printer device context. *Code* will be zero unless an error has occurred. If you wish, your application can watch this value and take appropriate action when an error is detected. You can also ignore *Code* because the Print Manager will handle an error for you as long as you implement the abort function as described here. The function must return nonzero to continue printing or zero to stop.

PeekMessage( ) is similar to **GetMessage( )** except that it does not wait for a message to be queued.

Inside the abort function, you must implement a message loop. However, instead of using **GetMessage( )** to retrieve messages, you use **PeekMessage( )** with the **PM_REMOVE** option. The reason for this is that **GetMessage( )** waits for a message if one is not already in the message queue, while **PeekMessage( )** does not. Thus, a skeletal abort function looks like this:

```
// Printer abort function.
BOOL CALLBACK AbortFunc(HDC hdc, int err)
{
  MSG message;

  while(PeekMessage(&message, NULL, 0, 0, PM_REMOVE)) {
    if(!IsDialogMessage(hDlg, &message)) {
      TranslateMessage(&message);
      DispatchMessage(&message);
    }
  }

  return printOK; // printOK is a global variable
}
```

The handle of the modeless dialog box that is used to cancel the print job must be stored in **hDlg**. The variable **printOK** is a global variable that must be initially set to nonzero. If the user cancels the print job, this variable will be set to zero. This action is accomplished by a modeless dialog box, which is described next.

The Cancel Printing Dialog Box

After the abort function has been installed, your program must activate a modeless dialog box that allows the user to cancel the print job. Although this dialog box can contain additional features and controls, it must contain at least one button, called Cancel, which cancels the print job. When the user presses Cancel, the dialog box sets a global variable to zero. This global variable must be the same one returned by the abort function described in the preceding section.

A Complete Printing Example

The following program adds an abort function to the preceding program. It also adds one other element: an enlarging option. Using this option, you can set scale factors for the X and Y dimensions. By default, these factors are 1, and, thus, no enlargement takes place. However, they can be set anywhere between 1 and 10. Using these factors, you can print a bitmap up to ten times as large as its original size. You can also enlarge only one dimension. The enlargement factors are set using an up-down common control, so you will need to add COMCTL32.LIB to the link. Sample output from the program is shown in Figure 17-3.

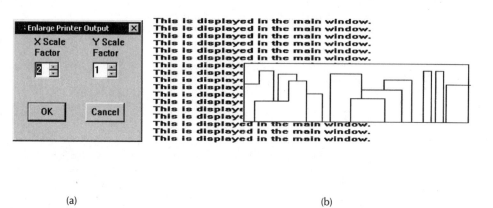

Sample output from the final printing demonstration program:
(a) The enlargement dialog box;
(b) contents of screen printed with a 2X enlargement factor along the X-axis

Figure 17-3.

```cpp
// Using an Abort Function and Enlargement.

// This define is required by some compilers.
#define WINVER 0x0500

#include <windows.h>
#include <cstring>
#include <commctrl.h>
#include "print.h"

#define NUMLINES 25
#define SCALEMAX 10

#define BMPWIDTH 256
#define BMPHEIGHT 128

LRESULT CALLBACK WindowFunc(HWND, UINT, WPARAM, LPARAM);
BOOL CALLBACK EnlargeDialog(HWND, UINT, WPARAM, LPARAM);
void PrintInit(PRINTDLGEX *printdlgex, HWND hwnd);

BOOL CALLBACK AbortFunc(HDC hdc, int err);
LRESULT CALLBACK KillPrint(HWND, UINT, WPARAM, LPARAM);

char szWinName[] = "MyWin"; // name of window class

int X = 0, Y = 0; // current output location
int maxX, maxY;    // screen dimensions

HDC memDC, memPrDC; // store the virtual device handle
HBITMAP hBit, hBit2, hImage; // bitmap handles
HBRUSH hBrush;      // store the brush handle

PRINTDLGEX printdlgex;
DOCINFO docinfo;

HINSTANCE hInst;

int Xenlarge = 1, Yenlarge = 1;

int printOK = 1;

HWND hDlg = NULL;

int WINAPI WinMain(HINSTANCE hThisInst, HINSTANCE hPrevInst,
                   LPSTR lpszArgs, int nWinMode)
```

```
{
  HACCEL hAccel;
  HWND hwnd;
  MSG msg;
  WNDCLASSEX wcl;
  INITCOMMONCONTROLSEX cc;

  // Define a window class.
  wcl.cbSize = sizeof(WNDCLASSEX);

  wcl.hInstance = hThisInst;      // handle to this instance
  wcl.lpszClassName = szWinName;  // window class name
  wcl.lpfnWndProc = WindowFunc;   // window function
  wcl.style = 0;                  // default style

  wcl.hIcon = LoadIcon(NULL, IDI_APPLICATION); // large icon
  wcl.hIconSm = NULL; // use small version of large icon
  wcl.hCursor = LoadCursor(NULL, IDC_ARROW);   // cursor style

  wcl.lpszMenuName = "PrintDemoMenu3"; // main menu

  wcl.cbClsExtra = 0; // no extra memory needed
  wcl.cbWndExtra = 0;

  // Make the window background white.
  wcl.hbrBackground = (HBRUSH) GetStockObject(WHITE_BRUSH);

  // Register the window class.
  if(!RegisterClassEx(&wcl)) return 0;

  /* Now that a window class has been registered, a window
     can be created. */
  hwnd = CreateWindow(
    szWinName, // name of window class
    "Using the Printer", // title
    WS_OVERLAPPEDWINDOW, // window style - normal
    CW_USEDEFAULT, // X coordinate - let Windows decide
    CW_USEDEFAULT, // Y coordinate - let Windows decide
    CW_USEDEFAULT, // width - let Windows decide
    CW_USEDEFAULT, // height - let Windows decide
    NULL,          // no parent window
    NULL,          // no menu
    hThisInst,     // instance handle
    NULL           // no additional arguments
  );
```

```
    hInst = hThisInst;

    // Load the keyboard accelerators.
    hAccel = LoadAccelerators(hThisInst, "PrintDemoMenu3");

    // Load the bitmap.
    hImage = LoadBitmap(hThisInst, "MyBP1");

    // Initialize the common controls.
    cc.dwSize = sizeof(INITCOMMONCONTROLSEX);
    cc.dwICC = ICC_UPDOWN_CLASS;
    InitCommonControlsEx(&cc);

    // Display the window.
    ShowWindow(hwnd, nWinMode);
    UpdateWindow(hwnd);

    // Create the message loop.
    while(GetMessage(&msg, NULL, 0, 0))
    {
      if(!TranslateAccelerator(hwnd, hAccel, &msg)) {
        TranslateMessage(&msg); // translate keyboard messages
        DispatchMessage(&msg);  // return control to Windows 2000
      }
    }

    return msg.wParam;
}

/* This function is called by Windows 2000 and is passed
   messages from the message queue.
*/
LRESULT CALLBACK WindowFunc(HWND hwnd, UINT message,
                            WPARAM wParam, LPARAM lParam)
{
  HDC hdc;
  PAINTSTRUCT ps;
  int response;
  TEXTMETRIC tm;
  char str[250];
  int i;
  unsigned copies;
  double VidXPPI, VidYPPI, PrXPPI, PrYPPI;
  double Xratio, Yratio;
  RECT r;
```

```
switch(message) {
  case WM_CREATE:
    // get screen coordinates
    maxX = GetSystemMetrics(SM_CXSCREEN);
    maxY = GetSystemMetrics(SM_CYSCREEN);

    // create a virtual window
    hdc = GetDC(hwnd);
    memDC = CreateCompatibleDC(hdc);
    hBit = CreateCompatibleBitmap(hdc, maxX, maxY);
    SelectObject(memDC, hBit);
    hBrush = (HBRUSH) GetStockObject(WHITE_BRUSH);
    SelectObject(memDC, hBrush);
    PatBlt(memDC, 0, 0, maxX, maxY, PATCOPY);

    ReleaseDC(hwnd, hdc);
    break;
  case WM_COMMAND:
    switch(LOWORD(wParam)) {
      case IDM_ENLARGE:
        DialogBox(hInst, "EnlargeDB", hwnd, (DLGPROC) EnlargeDialog);
        break;
      case IDM_TEXT: // print text
        X = Y = 0;

        // initialize PRINTDLGEX struct
        PrintInit(&printdlgex, hwnd);

        if(PrintDlgEx(&printdlgex) != S_OK) break;
        else if(printdlgex.dwResultAction != PD_RESULT_PRINT) break;

        docinfo.cbSize = sizeof(DOCINFO);
        docinfo.lpszDocName = "Printing Text";
        docinfo.lpszOutput = NULL;
        docinfo.lpszDatatype = NULL;
        docinfo.fwType = 0;

        StartDoc(printdlgex.hDC, &docinfo);

        strcpy(str, "This is printed on the printer.");

        // get text metrics for printer
        GetTextMetrics(printdlgex.hDC, &tm);

        printOK = 1;
        SetAbortProc(printdlgex.hDC, (ABORTPROC) AbortFunc);
        hDlg = CreateDialog(hInst, "PrCancel", hwnd, (DLGPROC) KillPrint);

        for(copies=0; copies < printdlgex.nCopies; copies++) {
          StartPage(printdlgex.hDC);
```

```
    for(i=0; i<NUMLINES; i++) {
      TextOut(printdlgex.hDC, X, Y, str, strlen(str));
      // advance to next line
      Y = Y + tm.tmHeight + tm.tmExternalLeading;
    }

    EndPage(printdlgex.hDC);
  }

  if(printOK) {
    DestroyWindow(hDlg);
    EndDoc(printdlgex.hDC);
  }

  DeleteDC(printdlgex.hDC);
  break;
case IDM_BITMAP: // print a bitmap
  // initialize PRINTDLGEX struct
  PrintInit(&printdlgex, hwnd);

  if(PrintDlgEx(&printdlgex) != S_OK) break;
  else if(printdlgex.dwResultAction != PD_RESULT_PRINT) break;

  docinfo.cbSize = sizeof(DOCINFO);
  docinfo.lpszDocName = "Printing bitmaps";
  docinfo.lpszOutput = NULL;
  docinfo.lpszDatatype = NULL;
  docinfo.fwType = 0;

  if(!(GetDeviceCaps(printdlgex.hDC, RASTERCAPS)
      & (RC_BITBLT | RC_STRETCHBLT))) {
    MessageBox(hwnd, "Cannot Print Raster Images",
               "Error", MB_OK);
    break;
  }

  // create a memory DC compatible with the printer
  memPrDC = CreateCompatibleDC(printdlgex.hDC);
  // create a bitmap compatible with the printer DC
  hBit2 = CreateCompatibleBitmap(printdlgex.hDC, maxX, maxY);
  SelectObject(memPrDC, hBit2);

  // put bitmap image into memory DC
  SelectObject(memDC, hImage);

  // copy bitmap to printer-compatible DC
  BitBlt(memPrDC, 0, 0, BMPWIDTH, BMPHEIGHT,
         memDC, 0, 0, SRCCOPY);

  // obtain pixels-per-inch
  VidXPPI = GetDeviceCaps(memDC, LOGPIXELSX);
```

```
VidYPPI = GetDeviceCaps(memDC, LOGPIXELSY);
PrXPPI = GetDeviceCaps(printdlgex.hDC, LOGPIXELSX);
PrYPPI = GetDeviceCaps(printdlgex.hDC, LOGPIXELSY);

// get scaling ratios
Xratio = PrXPPI / VidXPPI;
Yratio = PrYPPI / VidYPPI;

SelectObject(memDC, hBit); // restore virtual window

StartDoc(printdlgex.hDC, &docinfo);

printOK = 1;
SetAbortProc(printdlgex.hDC, (ABORTPROC) AbortFunc);
hDlg = CreateDialog(hInst, "PrCancel", hwnd, (DLGPROC) KillPrint);

for(copies=0; copies < printdlgex.nCopies; copies++) {
  StartPage(printdlgex.hDC);

    /* copy bitmap to printer DC using enlargement
       factors but no perspective scaling */
    StretchBlt(printdlgex.hDC, 0, 0,
               BMPWIDTH * Xenlarge,
               BMPHEIGHT * Yenlarge,
               memPrDC, 0, 0, BMPWIDTH, BMPHEIGHT, SRCCOPY);

    // enlarge bitmap while maintaining perspective
    StretchBlt(printdlgex.hDC, 0, BMPHEIGHT+100*Yenlarge,
               (int) (BMPWIDTH*Xratio*Xenlarge),
               (int) (BMPHEIGHT*Yratio*Yenlarge),
               memPrDC, 0, 0,
               BMPWIDTH, BMPHEIGHT,
               SRCCOPY);

    EndPage(printdlgex.hDC);
  }

  if(printOK) DestroyWindow(hDlg);

  EndDoc(printdlgex.hDC);
  DeleteDC(printdlgex.hDC);
  DeleteDC(memPrDC);
  break;
case IDM_WINDOW: // print contents of window
  GetClientRect(hwnd, &r);
  hdc = GetDC(hwnd);

  // display some text in the window
  GetTextMetrics(hdc, &tm);
  X = Y = 0;
```

```
strcpy(str, "This is displayed in the main window.");
for(i=0; i<NUMLINES; i++) {
  TextOut(hdc, X, Y, str, strlen(str));
  TextOut(memDC, X, Y, str, strlen(str));
  // advance to next line
  Y = Y + tm.tmHeight + tm.tmExternalLeading;
}

// display bitmap image in the window
SelectObject(memDC, hImage);
BitBlt(hdc, 100, 100, 256, 128,
       memDC, 0, 0, SRCCOPY);

// save image in window for PAINT requests
SelectObject(memDC, hBit);
BitBlt(memDC, 0, 0, r.right, r.bottom, hdc, 0, 0, SRCCOPY);

// create a compatible DC
memPrDC = CreateCompatibleDC(hdc);
// create a compatible bitmap
hBit2 = CreateCompatibleBitmap(hdc, r.right, r.bottom);
SelectObject(memPrDC, hBit2);

// save image in window for printing
BitBlt(memPrDC, 0, 0, r.right, r.bottom,
       hdc, 0, 0, SRCCOPY);

// initialize PRINTDLGEX struct
PrintInit(&printdlgex, hwnd);

if(PrintDlgEx(&printdlgex) != S_OK) break;
else if(printdlgex.dwResultAction != PD_RESULT_PRINT) break;

docinfo.cbSize = sizeof(DOCINFO);
docinfo.lpszDocName = "Printing Window";
docinfo.lpszOutput = NULL;
docinfo.lpszDatatype = NULL;
docinfo.fwType = 0;

// obtain pixels-per-inch
VidXPPI = GetDeviceCaps(memDC, LOGPIXELSX);
VidYPPI = GetDeviceCaps(memDC, LOGPIXELSY);
PrXPPI = GetDeviceCaps(printdlgex.hDC, LOGPIXELSX);
PrYPPI = GetDeviceCaps(printdlgex.hDC, LOGPIXELSY);

// get scaling ratios
Xratio = PrXPPI / VidXPPI;
Yratio = PrYPPI / VidYPPI;

if(!(GetDeviceCaps(printdlgex.hDC, RASTERCAPS)
   & RC_STRETCHBLT))
```

17

```
      {
        MessageBox(hwnd, "Cannot Print Raster Images",
                   "Error", MB_OK);
        break;
      }

      StartDoc(printdlgex.hDC, &docinfo);

      printOK = 1;
      SetAbortProc(printdlgex.hDC, (ABORTPROC) AbortFunc);
      hDlg = CreateDialog(hInst, "PrCancel", hwnd, (DLGPROC) KillPrint);

      for(copies=0; copies < printdlgex.nCopies; copies++) {
        StartPage(printdlgex.hDC);

        StretchBlt(printdlgex.hDC, 0, 0,
                   (int) (r.right*Xratio) * Xenlarge,
                   (int) (r.bottom*Yratio) * Yenlarge,
                   memPrDC, 0, 0,
                   (int) r.right, (int) r.bottom,
                   SRCCOPY);

        EndPage(printdlgex.hDC);
      }

      if(printOK) DestroyWindow(hDlg);

      EndDoc(printdlgex.hDC);
      DeleteDC(printdlgex.hDC);
      DeleteDC(memPrDC);
      ReleaseDC(hwnd, hdc);
      break;
    case IDM_EXIT:
      response = MessageBox(hwnd, "Quit the Program?",
                            "Exit", MB_YESNO);
      if(response == IDYES) PostQuitMessage(0);
      break;
    case IDM_HELP:
      MessageBox(hwnd, "Printing Demo", "Help", MB_OK);
      break;
  }
  break;
case WM_PAINT: // process a repaint request
  hdc = BeginPaint(hwnd, &ps); // get DC

  BitBlt(hdc, ps.rcPaint.left, ps.rcPaint.top,
         ps.rcPaint.right-ps.rcPaint.left, // width
         ps.rcPaint.bottom-ps.rcPaint.top, // height
         memDC,
         ps.rcPaint.left, ps.rcPaint.top,
```

```
             SRCCOPY);

         EndPaint(hwnd, &ps); // release DC
         break;
       case WM_DESTROY: // terminate the program
         DeleteDC(memDC);
         PostQuitMessage(0);
         break;
       default:
         /* Let Windows 2000 process any messages not specified in
            the preceding switch statement. */
         return DefWindowProc(hwnd, message, wParam, lParam);
    }

  return 0;
}

// Initialize PRINTDLGEX structure.
void PrintInit(PRINTDLGEX *printdlgex, HWND hwnd)
{
  printdlgex->lStructSize = sizeof(PRINTDLGEX);
  printdlgex->hwndOwner = hwnd;
  printdlgex->hDevMode = NULL;
  printdlgex->hDevNames = NULL;
  printdlgex->hDC = NULL;
  printdlgex->Flags = PD_RETURNDC | PD_NOSELECTION |
                      PD_NOPAGENUMS | PD_HIDEPRINTTOFILE |
                      PD_COLLATE;
  printdlgex->Flags2 = 0;
  printdlgex->ExclusionFlags = 0;
  printdlgex->nMinPage = 1;
  printdlgex->nMaxPage = 1;
  printdlgex->nCopies = 1;
  printdlgex->hInstance = NULL;
  printdlgex->lpCallback = NULL;
  printdlgex->nPropertyPages = 0;
  printdlgex->lphPropertyPages = NULL;
  printdlgex->nStartPage = START_PAGE_GENERAL;
  printdlgex->dwResultAction = 0;

  printdlgex->lpPrintTemplateName = NULL;
}


// Enlargement factor dialog function
BOOL CALLBACK EnlargeDialog(HWND hdwnd, UINT message,
                            WPARAM wParam, LPARAM lParam)
{
  static int tempX=1, tempY=1;

  static long temp;
```

```
static HWND hEboxWnd1, hEboxWnd2;
static HWND udWnd1, udWnd2;
int low=1, high=SCALEMAX;


switch(message) {
  case WM_INITDIALOG:
    hEboxWnd1 = GetDlgItem(hdwnd, IDD_EB1);
    hEboxWnd2 = GetDlgItem(hdwnd, IDD_EB2);
    udWnd1 = CreateUpDownControl(
                    WS_CHILD | WS_BORDER | WS_VISIBLE |
                    UDS_SETBUDDYINT | UDS_ALIGNRIGHT,
                    10, 10, 50, 50,
                    hdwnd,
                    IDD_UD1,
                    hInst,
                    hEboxWnd1,
                    SCALEMAX, 1, Xenlarge);

    udWnd2 = CreateUpDownControl(
                    WS_CHILD | WS_BORDER | WS_VISIBLE |
                    UDS_SETBUDDYINT | UDS_ALIGNRIGHT,
                    10, 10, 50, 50,
                    hdwnd,
                    IDD_UD2,
                    hInst,
                    hEboxWnd2,
                    SCALEMAX, 1, Yenlarge);

    tempX = Xenlarge;
    tempY = Yenlarge;
    return 1;
  case WM_VSCROLL: // process up-down control
    if(udWnd1==(HWND)lParam)
      tempX = GetDlgItemInt(hdwnd, IDD_EB1, NULL, 1);
    else if(udWnd2==(HWND)lParam)
      tempY = GetDlgItemInt(hdwnd, IDD_EB2, NULL, 1);
    return 1;
  case WM_COMMAND:
    switch(LOWORD(wParam)) {
      case IDOK:
        Xenlarge = tempX;
        Yenlarge = tempY;
      case IDCANCEL:
        EndDialog(hdwnd, 0);
        return 1;
    }
    break;
}

return 0;
```

```
}

// Printer abort function.
BOOL CALLBACK AbortFunc(HDC hdc, int err)
{
  MSG message;

  while(PeekMessage(&message, NULL, 0, 0, PM_REMOVE)) {
    if(!IsDialogMessage(hDlg, &message)) {
      TranslateMessage(&message);
      DispatchMessage(&message);
    }
  }

  return printOK;
}

// Let user kill print process.
LRESULT CALLBACK KillPrint(HWND hdwnd, UINT message,
                           WPARAM wParam, LPARAM lParam)
{
  switch(message) {
    case WM_COMMAND:
      switch(LOWORD(wParam)) {
        case IDCANCEL:
          printOK = 0;
          DestroyWindow(hDlg);
          hDlg = NULL;
          return 1;
      }
      break;
  }

  return 0;
}
```

The resource file for the program is shown here:

```
#include <windows.h>
#include "print.h"

MyBP1 BITMAP BP.BMP

PrintDemoMenu3 MENU
{
  POPUP "&Printer Demo"
  {
    MENUITEM "&Enlarge\tF2", IDM_ENLARGE
    MENUITEM "Print &Text\tF3", IDM_TEXT
    MENUITEM "Print &Bitmap\tF4", IDM_BITMAP
```

```
      MENUITEM "Print &Window\tF5", IDM_WINDOW
      MENUITEM "E&xit\tCtrl+X", IDM_EXIT
  }
  MENUITEM "&Help", IDM_HELP
}


PrintDemoMenu3 ACCELERATORS
{
  VK_F2, IDM_ENLARGE, VIRTKEY
  VK_F3, IDM_TEXT, VIRTKEY
  VK_F4, IDM_BITMAP, VIRTKEY
  VK_F5, IDM_WINDOW, VIRTKEY
  "^X", IDM_EXIT
}


EnlargeDB DIALOGEX 10, 10, 97, 77
CAPTION "Enlarge Printer Output"
STYLE WS_POPUP | WS_SYSMENU | WS_VISIBLE
{
  PUSHBUTTON "OK", IDOK, 10, 50, 30, 14
  PUSHBUTTON "Cancel", IDCANCEL, 55, 50, 30, 14
  LTEXT "X Scale Factor", IDD_TEXT1,  15, 1, 25, 20
  LTEXT "Y Scale Factor", IDD_TEXT2,  60, 1, 25, 20
  EDITTEXT IDD_EB1, 15, 20, 20, 12, ES_LEFT |
           WS_TABSTOP | WS_BORDER
  EDITTEXT IDD_EB2, 60, 20, 20, 12, ES_LEFT |
           WS_TABSTOP | WS_BORDER
}


PrCancel DIALOGEX 10, 10, 100, 40
CAPTION "Printing"
STYLE WS_CAPTION | WS_POPUP | WS_SYSMENU | WS_VISIBLE
{
  PUSHBUTTON "Cancel", IDCANCEL, 35, 12, 30, 14
}
```

Some Things to Try

When it comes to printing, there is virtually no end to things you can experiment with. Here are two ideas. Try printing color images. If your printer supports only black and white, experiment with different color translations and shades of gray. Experiment with page range selection. A good way to do this is to write a program that prints the contents of a text file. If the user selects a page range, then print only that range.

CHAPTER 18

Using the System Registry and Creating Screen Savers

This chapter discusses two topics that at first may seem unrelated: screen savers and the system registry. As you will see, however, the ability to understand and use the registry is necessary for the creation of all but the most simple screen savers. This is because a typical screen saver needs to store configuration information about itself. The screen saver uses this information to configure itself each time that it pops up. Under Windows 2000, the proper place to store such information is in the system registry. In fact, screen savers are one of the few smaller applications that make use of the registry. For this reason they serve as excellent practical examples of registry utilization.

Although screen savers are some of the simpler Windows 2000 applications that you will write, they are also some of the most interesting from the programmer's point of view. They are also the one type of application that virtually all programmers *want* to write. Indeed, it is rare to find a programmer who has not thought about creating his or her own screen saver. While screen savers were initially invented to prevent phosphor burn on idle screens, they have taken on a life of their own. Today most screen savers provide an entertaining message, an interesting graphics display, a company logo, or a humorous animated sequence.

The system registry is a much more mundane topic. It is also one of the more important Windows 2000 programming issues. As you probably know, the registry is designed to store information about the state and configuration of your computer and of its software. Most programmers are initially intimidated by the registry, but it is really quite easy to use.

This chapter develops two simple screen savers. The first is not configurable and does not use the registry. Its purpose is to introduce the basic elements common to all screen savers. The second screen saver can be configured and stores its configuration information in the registry. Keep in mind that neither screen saver generates interesting, engaging, or exciting output. Each simply illustrates the mechanics involved in creating a screen saver, but you can use these examples as starting points from which you can develop your own.

Screen Saver Fundamentals

A screen saver is actually one of the simplest Windows 2000 applications. One of the reasons for this is that it does not create a main window. Instead, it uses the desktop (that is, the entire screen) as its window. It also does not contain a **WinMain( )** function or need to create a message loop. In fact, a screen saver requires only three functions, two of which may be empty placeholders.

When creating screen savers, you must include SCRNSAVE.H and link in SCRNSAVE.LIB.

When you create a screen saver, your program must include the header file SCRNSAVE.H and you must include SCRNSAVE.LIB when linking. The screen saver library provides necessary support for screen savers. This is why your screen saver code need only contain three functions. The rest of the details are handled by the screen saver library.

The Screen Saver Functions

The three functions that every screen saver must provide are shown here:

Function	Purpose
ScreenSaverProc( )	This is the screen saver's window procedure. It is passed messages and must respond appropriately.
ScreenSaverConfigureDialog( )	This is the dialog function for the screen saver's configuration dialog box. It can be empty if no configuration is supported.
RegisterDialogClasses( )	This function is used to register custom class types. It will be empty if no custom classes are used.

Although the names of these functions are defined by Windows 2000, you must supply the functions themselves in the source code to your screen saver. (That is, they are not provided by Win32.) Let's take a closer look at these three functions now.

ScreenSaverProc( ) is a window procedure. Its prototype is shown here:

LRESULT WINAPI ScreenSaverProc(HWND *hwnd*, UINT *message*,
                                                    WPARAM *wParam*, LPARAM *lParam*);

It is passed messages in the same way as other window procedures. There is one important difference, however. If the function does not process a message, it must call **DefScreenSaverProc( )** rather than **DefWindowProc( )**. Also, the window handle passed to **ScreenSaverProc( )** in *hwnd* is the handle for the entire screen. That is, it is the handle of the desktop. Your screen saver will make use of this fact.

ScreenSaverConfigureDialog( ) is the dialog box function that handles the screen saver's configuration dialog box. It has the following prototype:

```
BOOL WINAPI ScreenSaverConfigureDialog(HWND hdwnd,
                  UINT message, WPARAM wParam,
                  LPARAM lParam);
```

If your screen saver does not require configuration, then the only thing this function must do is return zero. If the screen saver supports a configuration dialog box, then it must be defined in the screen saver's resource file and given the ID value of **DLG_SCRNSAVECONFIGURE**. This value is defined in SCRNSAVE.H.

RegisterDialogClasses( ) is used to register custom window classes. It has this prototype:

```
BOOL WINAPI RegisterDialogClasses(HANDLE hInst);
```

If your screen saver does not use a custom window class, simply return nonzero.

As mentioned, **ScreenSaverProc( )** will call **DefScreenSaverProc( )** if it does not process a message. The prototype for **DefScreenSaverProc( )** is shown here:

```
LRESULT WINAPI DefScreenSaverProc(HWND hwnd, UINT message,
                  WPARAM wParam, LPARAM lParam);
```

Two Screen Saver Resources

All screen savers must define two special resources: an icon and a string. The icon, whose ID must be **ID_APP**, identifies the screen saver. The string resource, whose identifier must be **IDS_DESCRIPTION**, contains a description of the screen saver. It will be displayed by the Control Panel (under Display Properties) in a list box that describes the available screen savers. This string must be no more than 24 characters long. **ID_APP** and **IDS_DESCRIPTION** are defined in SCRNSAVE.H.

String resources are defined in a resource file using the **STRINGTABLE** statement. It has this general form:

```
STRINGTABLE
{
  ID1 "string"
  ID2 "string"
```

.
.
.
.

   IDn "string"
  }

Here, *ID* is the identifier associated with the string. Your program can refer to a string resource by its ID value. A program loads a string resource by calling **LoadString( )**. For the purposes of a screen saver, the **IDS_DESCRIPTION** string is not used by the screen saver itself. Rather, it simply provides a description of the screen saver inside the Control Panel.

18

HISTORICAL PERSPECTIVE: For Windows 95/98, the string defined by **IDS_DESCRIPTION** is not shown within the Screen Saver panel of the Display Properties dialog box. Instead, the filename of the screen saver is shown. At the time of this writing, Microsoft's main documentation is in error about this point, but it is stated correctly in a technical bulletin dated December 23, 1998. However, the description string defined by **IDS_DESCRIPTION** is used correctly by Windows 2000, as just described.

Other Programming Considerations

SCRNSAVE.H defines several global variables. The one of interest to us in this chapter is **hMainInstance**. This will contain the instance handle of the screen saver. This handle will be needed if, for example, your screen saver creates a window. Other global variables are defined within SCRNSAVE.H which may be useful to your screen saver. You will want to examine the contents of this header file.

A screen saver is driven by a timer.

All screen savers are driven by a timer. At the end of each interval, the screen saver receives a **WM_TIMER** message and updates the screen display. Your screen saver must start the timer when it is first activated and destroy the timer when it is destroyed. (Timers are described in Chapter 6.)

After you have compiled the screen saver, you must rename it so that it has the SCR extension rather than EXE. Next, copy the renamed screen saver into the proper directory. For most users, the directory that holds screen savers will be WINNT\SYSTEM32. (The easiest way to determine which directory to use is to see which one holds the screen savers currently installed on your system.) Once you have renamed and copied the screen saver to the proper directory, you can select your new screen saver using the control panel.

Creating a Minimal Screen Saver

We will begin by creating a bare bones screen saver. It simply displays a text-based message that moves about the screen. It cannot be configured and does not use the **ScreenSaverConfigureDialog( )** function. It does, however, illustrate the basic elements of a screen saver. Here is the complete listing for the minimal screen saver:

```c
// A minimal screen saver.
#include <windows.h>
#include <scrnsave.h>

// This is the message displayed on the screen.
char str[80] = "Screen Saver #1";

// This is timer delay.
int delay = 200;

// Screen Saver Function
LRESULT WINAPI ScreenSaverProc(HWND hwnd, UINT message,
                               WPARAM wParam, LPARAM lParam)
{
  static HDC hdc;
  static unsigned int timer;
  static RECT scrdim;
  static SIZE size;
  static int X = 0, Y = 0;
  static HBRUSH hBlkBrush;
  static TEXTMETRIC tm;

  switch(message) {
    case WM_CREATE:
      timer = SetTimer(hwnd, 1, delay, NULL);
      hBlkBrush = (HBRUSH) GetStockObject(BLACK_BRUSH);
      break;
    case WM_ERASEBKGND:
      hdc = GetDC(hwnd);

      // get coordinates of screen
      GetClientRect(hwnd, &scrdim);

      // erase the screen
      SelectObject(hdc, hBlkBrush);
      PatBlt(hdc, 0, 0, scrdim.right, scrdim.bottom, PATCOPY);
```

18

```
          // get and save height and length of string
          GetTextMetrics(hdc, &tm);
          GetTextExtentPoint32(hdc, str, strlen(str), &size);

          ReleaseDC(hwnd, hdc);
          break;
      case WM_TIMER:
        hdc = GetDC(hwnd);

          // erase previous output
          SelectObject(hdc, hBlkBrush);
          PatBlt(hdc, X, Y, X + size.cx, Y + size.cy, PATCOPY);

          // move string to new location
          X += 10; Y += 10;
          if(X > scrdim.right) X = 0;
          if(Y > scrdim.bottom) Y = 0;

          // output string
          SetBkColor(hdc, RGB(0, 0, 0));
          SetTextColor(hdc, RGB(0, 255, 255));
          TextOut(hdc, X, Y, str, strlen(str));

          ReleaseDC(hwnd, hdc);
          break;
      case WM_DESTROY:
        KillTimer(hwnd, timer);
        break;
      default:
        return DefScreenSaverProc(hwnd, message, wParam, lParam);
    }

    return 0;
}

// Placeholder Dialog Box Function.
BOOL WINAPI ScreenSaverConfigureDialog(HWND hdwnd, UINT message,
                                WPARAM wParam, LPARAM lParam)
{
    return 0;
}

// No classes to register.
BOOL WINAPI RegisterDialogClasses(HANDLE hInst)
{
```

```
    return 1;
}
```

The screen saver requires the following resource file:

```
#include <windows.h>
#include <scrnsave.h>

ID_APP ICON SCRICON.ICO

STRINGTABLE
{
  IDS_DESCRIPTION "My Screen Saver #1"
}
```

As this resource file implies, you will need to create an icon for your screen saver. Save it in a file called SCRICON.ICO.

A Closer Look at the First Screen Saver

Each time the screen saver is activated, it receives two messages. The first is **WM_CREATE**. Your screen saver must use this message to perform any initializations it requires as well as to start the timer. In this example, the timer has a period of 200 milliseconds. Thus, it will interrupt the screen saver five times a second. In this example, the black brush is also obtained when the screen saver is created.

The next message received by your screen saver is **WM_ERASEBKGND**. When this message is received, your screen saver must clear the entire screen. There are, of course, several ways to do this. The method employed by the example is to obtain the coordinates of the screen, select the black brush, and then use **PatBlt( )** to fill the specified region with black (that is, nothing). Remember, *hwnd* contains the handle of the desktop, so the call to **GetClientRect( )** returns the dimensions of the entire screen.

Since the message displayed by the screen saver does not change, its dimensions are also obtained and stored when **WM_ERASEBKGND** is received.

Each time the timer goes off, **WM_TIMER** is sent to the screen saver. In response, the screen saver first erases the message from its current location, advances the location counters, and then redisplays the message.

When the user presses a key or moves the mouse, the screen saver receives a **WM_DESTROY** message. When this occurs, the screen saver must cancel the timer and perform any other shut-down tasks.

Since this screen saver has no user-configurable data or custom window classes, the functions **ScreenSaverConfigureDialog( )** and **RegisterDialogClasses( )** are simply placeholders.

Problems with the First Screen Saver

18

While the preceding screen saver shows the basics, it is inadequate for actual use. First, the message displayed on the screen cannot be changed. Second, the delay period is fixed. Both of these items are subject to personal taste and should be configurable by the user. Fortunately, it is easy to add this capability to the screen saver. However, doing so raises one interesting problem: where is the configuration data going to be stored? To allow the screen saver to be configured requires that the delay time and the message be stored on disk, somewhere. When the screen saver executes, it must be able to retrieve these settings. While it is certainly possible, in this simple case, to store the information in a normal data file, a better solution exists which uses the system registry.

Understanding the System Registry

As pointed out by the preceding section, when a program contains configurable options, there must be some way to store these options. In the early days of computing, each program would create its own, special data file that contained its configuration settings. Such files often used file extensions such as CFG or DAT. (In fact, you can still find examples of these types of files, although they are becoming increasingly rare.) While such an individualized approach was adequate for operating systems such as DOS, it was not appropriate for multitasking systems, such as Windows. For example, it was possible for two or more programs to use the same name for their configuration files, causing confusion. To solve this problem, early versions of Windows created the INI file extension, which was reserved for program initialization files. Windows also defined its own initialization file, called WIN.INI. Applications were free to use this file to hold their own configuration information or to create their own private INI files.

The system registry stores configuration information.

While INI files helped bring order to configuration files, they were, themselves, not a perfect solution. One reason is that it was still possible for two different applications to use the same name for their INI files. Also, when a computer had several applications loaded onto it, there were often a very large number of INI files. Further, in some cases it was beneficial for one program to know if another program was also installed on the system; with INI files this was not always an easy thing to determine. To finally solve the configuration file problem, Microsoft abandoned INI files and invented an entirely new approach called the *system registry*, or just *registry* for short. While the registry was partially supported by Windows 3.1, it was enhanced for the Win32 environment. Although Windows 2000 still supports the older INI files, new applications should use the registry to hold configuration information.

For various reasons, the registry has the reputation of being difficult to use and understand, but this reputation is not deserved. Indeed, the truth is quite the contrary. As you will see, using the registry is straightforward. Once you have mastered only a few new API functions, you will have no trouble using it.

HISTORICAL PERSPECTIVE: The registry was largely ignored under Windows 3.1, and most Windows 3.1 programs do not use it. However, all modern applications, and especially those written for Windows 2000, are expected to use the registry. You should make this change when porting older programs.

The Registry Structure

The registry is a special hierarchical database maintained by Windows that stores information related to three entities: the user, the machine, and the installed software. For the most part, it stores configuration settings relating to these items. The information stored in the registry is in its binary form. Therefore, there are only two ways to alter or examine the contents of the registry: by using REGEDIT or REGEDT32, the standard registry editors, or by using the registry management API functions. You cannot, for example, edit the registry using a text editor.

A registry key
is a node in the
registry tree.

The registry is set of keys structured as a tree. A *key* is, for practical purposes, a node in the tree. The name of a key is essentially the name of a node. A key may be empty, have subkeys, or contain values. Typically, values consist of configuration information for a program. Thus, to use the registry, your program will create a key and store its configuration information under that key. When the program needs this information, it will look up the key and then read the information. If the user changes the configuration settings, then your program will simply write those new values to the registry. Using the registry really is just this easy.

The Built-in Keys

The registry contains several built-in keys. Each key forms the root node for its own subtree of keys. The names of the built-in keys are shown here:

18

Key	Purpose
HKEY_CLASSES_ROOT	Holds information used by COM. Also defines associations between file extensions and applications.
HKEY_CURRENT_CONFIG	Holds current hardware configuration.
HKEY_CURRENT_USER	Holds information related to the current user. This is where user-related application program configuration information is usually stored.
HKEY_LOCAL_MACHINE	Holds information about the system, including the installed software, network preferences, and other system-wide, hardware-related information.
HKEY_USERS	Holds the preferences for each user of the machine.
HKEY_DYN_DATA	Holds dynamic performance data. (Applies to Windows 95/98 only.)
HKEY_PERFORMANCE_DATA	Holds dynamic performance data. This is a logical key that is not actually stored in the registry. (Applies to Windows NT/2000 only.)

These keys are always open and may be used by your application. Generally, an application will use only two of these keys: **HKEY_LOCAL_MACHINE**, which is used to store any system-wide configuration options relating to the machine, and **HKEY_CURRENT_USER**, which is used to store configuration options relating to the user.

Typically, an installation program will create a key under **HKEY_LOCAL_MACHINE** that contains the name and version number of an application package, plus the name of the company that created the application. Other application-related data may also be stored under **HKEY_LOCAL_MACHINE**. Under **HKEY_CURRENT_USER**, a program will store configuration options selected by the user. Default user configuration information may also be written under this key when the program is installed. Typically, the application will use this information, when it begins execution. The configuration data for the screen saver will be stored under this key.

Since the screen saver in this chapter is a simple example program, it doesn't require any special installation. Thus, we won't be using **HKEY_LOCAL_MACHINE**. However, the techniques used to read and write data to and from the registry using this key are the same as for the **HKEY_CURRENT_USER**.

There are several standard subkeys that will normally be found in the registry. For example, under **HKEY_CURRENT_USER** some of the standard subkeys are **Software**, **Control Panel**, and **Environment**. When you add the configuration settings for a new program to the registry, you will typically do so under the **Software** subkey of **HKEY_CURRENT_USER**. However, since screen savers contain configuration information that can be changed by the Control Panel, they usually store their information under the **Control Panel** key. Although the standard subkeys will exist on most computers running Windows 2000, they are not automatically open.

Since the registry is a set of hierarchical trees, you will need to specify a full path to the key that you want. Key paths are similar in concept to directory paths. Each key is separated from the one preceding it using a backslash (\) character. For example, if you access a key called **Screensaver** under the **Control Panel** subkey of **HKEY_CURRENT_USER**, the key path will look like this:

HKEY_CURRENT_USER\Control Panel\Screensaver

A key may also include a period.

Recall that in C/C++, the backslash character signals the start of an escape sequence when used in a string. Therefore, when specifying a string in a C/C++ program that contains a backslash, you must use two backslashes for each backslash character you need. For example, to specify the preceding path as a C/C++ string, use the following:

"HKEY_CURRENT_USER\\Control Panel\\Screensaver"

If you forget to use the two backslashes, your registry functions will not work properly.

Registry Values

The registry allows several different types of data to be stored as values under a key. When you store or retrieve data, you must specify its name and its type. Table 18-1 shows the types of data supported by the registry. You will always add a value to the registry under a key that you have defined. There is no concept of simply adding a value to the registry by itself.

18

Data Type	Meaning
REG_BINARY	Generic type used to specify any binary data.
REG_DWORD	Long, unsigned integer.
REG_DWORD_LITTLE_ENDIAN	Long, unsigned integer stored with least significant byte first. This is called *little-endian* format.
REG_DWORD_BIG_ENDIAN	Long, unsigned integer stored with most signification byte first. This is called *big endian* format.
REG_EXPAND_SZ	A string that contains unexpanded environmental variables.
REG_LINK	A Unicode symbolic link.
REG_MULTI_SZ	An array of strings. The last two strings must be null.
REG_NONE	Undefined type.
REG_QWORD	A quad-word value.
REG_QWORD_LITTLE_ENDIAN	A quad-word value stored with least significant byte first.
REG_RESOURCE_LIST	A resource list for a device driver.
REG_SZ	Normal, null-terminated string.

The Data Types Supported by the Registry

Table 18-1.

Creating and Opening a Key

All registry operations take place relative to an open key. The predefined keys described earlier are always open. Therefore, you will use one of the predefined keys as the starting point when opening any other key. To open an existing key, use **RegOpenKeyEx( )**. Its prototype is shown here:

LONG RegOpenKeyEx(HKEY *hKey*, LPCSTR *SubKey*,
                  DWORD *NotUsed*, REGSAM *Access*,
                  PHKEY *Result*);

Here, *hKey* is the handle of an already open key, which may be one of the predefined keys. The key being opened must be a subkey of *hKey*. The name of the subkey is pointed to by *SubKey*. *NotUsed* is reserved and must be zero. *Access* determines the access privileges for the subkey handle. This value can be any combination of the values shown in Table 18-2. *Result* is a pointer to a variable that, on return, contains the handle of the subkey.

The function returns **ERROR_SUCCESS** if successful. On failure, an error code is returned. The function fails if the specified key does not exist.

Access Value	Purpose
KEY_ALL_ACCESS	Allows all accesses.
KEY_CREATE_LINK	Allows the creation of a symbolic link.
KEY_CREATE_SUB_KEY	Allows the creation of subkeys.
KEY_ENUMERATE_SUB_KEYS	Allows the enumeration of subkeys.
KEY_EXECUTE	Allows read access.
KEY_NOTIFY	Allows change notification.
KEY_QUERY_VALUE	Allows read access to subkey data.
KEY_READ	Allows all read accesses. Same as KEY_ENUMERATE_SUB_KEYS | KEY_NOTIFY | KEY_QUERY_VALUE.
KEY_SET_VALUE	Allows write access to subkey data.
KEY_WRITE	Allows all write accesses. Same as KEY_CREATE_SUB_KEY | KEY_SET_VALUE.

Key Access Privilege Values

Table 18-2.

18

Although you can use **RegOpenKeyEx( )** to open a registry key, you will
probably find that more often you will use another registry function called
RegCreateKeyEx( ). This function serves a dual purpose: it will open an
already existing key or, if the specified key does not it exist, it will create it.
Its prototype is shown here:

LONG RegCreateKeyEx(HKEY *hKey*, LPCSTR *SubKey*,
                    DWORD *NotUsed*, LPSTR *Class*,
                    DWORD *How*, REGSAM *Access*,
                    LPSECURITY_ATTRIBUTES *SecAttr*,
                    PHKEY *Result*, LPDWORD *WhatHappened*);

Here, *hKey* is the handle of an open key. *SubKey* is a pointer to the name of
the key to open or create. *NotUsed* is reserved and must be zero. *Class* is a
pointer to the class or object type for the key. This value is used only for keys
being created and can be a string of your own choosing.

The value of *How* can be

REG_OPTION_VOLATILE

REG_OPTION_NON_VOLATILE

REG_OPTION_BACKUP_RESTORE

If you specify **REG_OPTION_VOLATILE**, then the key is volatile and
will not be stored on disk. Thus, its value will be lost when the computer is
turned off. Specifying **REG_OPTION_NON_VOLATILE** creates a
nonvolatile key, which is stored on disk. This is the default. If you specify
REG_OPTION_BACKUP_RESTORE, then the key is opened with the
necessary access rights to allow it to be backed up or restored. In this case,
the value in *Access* is not used.

Access determines the access privileges of the key. It can be any valid
combination of the values shown in Table 18-2.

SecAttr is a pointer to a **SECURITY_ATTRIBUTES** structure that defines the
security descriptor for the key. If this value is **NULL**, then the default
descriptor is used.

On return, the variable pointed to by *Result* will contain the handle of the
key that has just been created or opened. *WhatHappened* is a pointer to a
variable that, on return, describes what action took place. It will be either

REG_CREATED_NEW_KEY, if a new key was created, or
REG_OPENED_EXISTING_KEY, if an already existing key was opened.

RegCreateKeyEx( ) returns **ERROR_SUCCESS** if successful. On failure, an
error code is returned.

HISTORICAL PERSPECTIVE: Windows 3.1 does not support any
of the registry functions that end in **Ex**. For example, it does not support
RegCreateKeyEx( ). Instead, older applications use **RegCreateKey( )**.
When converting older applications, you will need to convert older functions
into their modern **Ex** form.

Storing Values

Once you have obtained an open key, you can store values under it. To do
this, use **RegSetValueEx( )**. Its prototype is shown here:

```
LONG RegSetValueEx(HKEY hKey, LPCSTR Name,
                   DWORD NotUsed, DWORD DataType,
                   CONST LPBYTE lpValue,  DWORD SizeOfValue);
```

hKey is the handle of an open key that has been opened with
KEY_SET_VALUE access rights. *Name* is a pointer to the name of the value.
If this name does not already exist, it is added to the key. *NotUsed* is currently
reserved and must be set to zero.

DataType specifies the type of data that is being stored. It must be one of the
values specified in Table 18-1. *lpValue* is a pointer to the data being stored.
SizeOfValue specifies the size of this data (in bytes). For string data, the null
terminator must also be counted.

In the following example, the call to **RegSetValueEx( )** stores the string
"This is a test" in the value **StringTest**:

```
strcpy(str, "This is a test");
RegSetValueEx(hRegKey, "StringTest", 0, REG_SZ,
              (LPBYTE) str, strlen(str)+1);
```

Notice that, as mentioned, the null terminator is counted as part of the size
of a string. This is why 1 is added to the value of **strlen( )**.

RegSetValueEx( ) returns **ERROR_SUCCESS** if successful. On failure, it returns an error code.

Retrieving Values

Once you have stored a value in the registry, it can be retrieved at any time by your program (or by any other program). To do so, use the **RegQueryValueEx( )** function, shown here:

LONG RegQueryValueEx(HKEY *hKey*, LPCSTR *Name*,
                  LPDWORD *NotUsed*, LPDWORD *DataType*,
                  LPBYTE *Value*, LPDWORD *SizeOfData*);

hKey is the handle of an open key, which must have been opened with **KEY_QUERY_VALUE** access privileges. *Name* is a pointer to the name of the value desired. This value must already exist under the specified key. *NotUsed* is currently reserved and must be set to **NULL**.

DataType is a pointer that, on return, contains the type of the value being retrieved. This will be one of the values shown in Table 18-1. *Value* is a pointer to a buffer that, on return, contains the data associated with the specified value. *SizeOfData* is a pointer to a variable that contains the size of the buffer in bytes. On return, *SizeOfData* will point to the number of bytes stored in the buffer.

In the following example, the call to **RegQueryValueEx( )** retrieves the string associated with the value **StringTest**:

```
char str[80];
long size = 80;
RegQueryValueEx(hRegKey, "StringTest", NULL, REG_SZ,
                (LPBYTE) str, &size);
```

RegQueryValueEx( ) returns **ERROR_SUCCESS** if successful. On failure, it returns an error code.

Closing a Key

To close a key, use **RegCloseKey( )**, shown here:

LONG RegCloseKey(HKEY *hKey*);

Here, *hKey* is the handle of the key being closed. The function returns **ERROR_SUCCESS** if successful. On failure, an error code is returned.

IN DEPTH

Some Additional Registry Functions

Although the registry functions described in this chapter are the only ones needed by the configurable screen saver, there are several other registry-related functions that you will want to explore on your own. Here are some other, commonly used ones.

Function	Purpose
RegDeleteKey( )	Deletes a key.
RegDeleteValue( )	Deletes a value.
RegEnumKeyEx( )	Enumerates the subkeys of a given key.
RegEnumValue( )	Enumerates the values associated with a given key.
RegLoadKey( )	Loads a key subtree from a file.
RegQueryInfoKey( )	Obtains detailed information about a key.
RegSaveKey( )	Saves an entire subtree, beginning at the specified key, to a file. Values are also saved.

One good way to learn more about the registry is to write a program that enumerates and displays all of the keys and values it contains. When experimenting with the registry remember one caution: do not change its values. Doing so may make your computer stop working.

Using REGEDIT

Your program interacts with the registry using the registry API functions. However, if you want to examine (or even alter) the contents of the registry, you may do so using REGEDIT or REGEDT32. Both display the registry, including all keys and values. You can add, delete, and modify both keys and values. Normally, you will not want to manually change the registry. If you do so incorrectly, your computer might stop working! However, using a registry editor to view the structure and contents of the registry is completely safe and it will give you a concrete understanding of the registry's organization.

18

Creating a Configurable Screen Saver

To transform the simple screen saver shown at the start of this chapter into a configurable one, three additions must be made. First, a configuration dialog box must be defined in the screen saver's resource file. Second, the **ScreenSaverConfigureDialog( )** function must be filled in. Third, the configuration settings must be stored in the registry and retrieved each time the screen saver executes. Here is the complete program that contains these enhancements. The following program uses a spin control common control. For this reason, you will need to include COMCTL32.LIB when linking.

```
// A configurable screen saver.
#include <windows.h>
#include <scrnsave.h>
#include <commctrl.h>
#include <cstring>
#include "scr.h"

#define DELAYMAX 999
#define MSGSIZE 80

// This is the screen saver's message.
char str[MSGSIZE+1] = "Screen Saver #2";

// This is timer delay.
long delay;

unsigned long datatype, datasize;
```

```
    unsigned long result;

    // This is a registry key.
    HKEY hRegKey;

    // Screen Saver Function
    LRESULT WINAPI ScreenSaverProc(HWND hwnd, UINT message,
                                   WPARAM wParam, LPARAM lParam)
    {
      static HDC hdc;
      static unsigned int timer;
      static RECT scrdim;
      static SIZE size;
      static int X = 0, Y = 0;
      static HBRUSH hBlkBrush;
      static TEXTMETRIC tm;

      switch(message) {
        case WM_CREATE:
          // open screen saver key or create, if necessary
          RegCreateKeyEx(HKEY_CURRENT_USER,
             "Control Panel\\Screen Saver.MyScrSaver",
             0, "Screen Saver", 0, KEY_ALL_ACCESS,
             NULL, &hRegKey, &result);

          // if key was created
          if(result==REG_CREATED_NEW_KEY) {
            // set its initial value
            delay = 100;
            RegSetValueEx(hRegKey, "delay", 0,
                REG_DWORD, (LPBYTE) &delay, sizeof(DWORD));
            RegSetValueEx(hRegKey, "message", 0,
                REG_SZ, (LPBYTE) str, strlen(str)+1);
          }
          else { // key was already in registry
            // get delay value
            datasize = sizeof(DWORD);
            RegQueryValueEx(hRegKey, "delay", NULL,
                &datatype, (LPBYTE) &delay, &datasize);

            // get message
            datasize = MSGSIZE;
            RegQueryValueEx(hRegKey, "message", NULL,
                &datatype, (LPBYTE) str, &datasize);
          }
```

```
        RegCloseKey(hRegKey);

        timer = SetTimer(hwnd, 1, delay, NULL);
        hBlkBrush = (HBRUSH) GetStockObject(BLACK_BRUSH);
        break;
    case WM_ERASEBKGND:
      hdc = GetDC(hwnd);

        // Get coordinates of screen
        GetClientRect(hwnd, &scrdim);

        // erase the screen
        SelectObject(hdc, hBlkBrush);
        PatBlt(hdc, 0, 0, scrdim.right, scrdim.bottom, PATCOPY);

        // get and save height and length of string
        GetTextMetrics(hdc, &tm);
        GetTextExtentPoint32(hdc, str, strlen(str), &size);

        ReleaseDC(hwnd, hdc);
        break;
    case WM_TIMER:
      hdc = GetDC(hwnd);

        // erase previous output
        SelectObject(hdc, hBlkBrush);
        PatBlt(hdc, X, Y, X + size.cx, Y + size.cy, PATCOPY);

        // move string to new location
        X += 10; Y += 10;
        if(X > scrdim.right) X = 0;
        if(Y > scrdim.bottom) Y = 0;

        // output string
        SetBkColor(hdc, RGB(0, 0, 0));
        SetTextColor(hdc, RGB(0, 255, 255));
        TextOut(hdc, X, Y, str, strlen(str));

        ReleaseDC(hwnd, hdc);
        break;
    case WM_DESTROY:
      KillTimer(hwnd, timer);
      break;
    default:
```

```
        return DefScreenSaverProc(hwnd, message, wParam, lParam);
    }

    return 0;
}

// Configuration Dialog Box Function
BOOL WINAPI ScreenSaverConfigureDialog(HWND hdwnd, UINT message,
                WPARAM wParam, LPARAM lParam)
{
    static HWND hEboxWnd;
    static HWND udWnd;

    switch(message) {
        case WM_INITDIALOG:
            // open screen saver key or create, if necessary
            RegCreateKeyEx(HKEY_CURRENT_USER,
                "Control Panel\\Screen Saver.MyScrSaver",
                0, "Screen Saver", 0, KEY_ALL_ACCESS,
                NULL, &hRegKey, &result);

            // if key was created
            if(result==REG_CREATED_NEW_KEY) {
                // set its initial value
                delay = 100;
                RegSetValueEx(hRegKey, "delay", 0,
                    REG_DWORD, (LPBYTE) &delay, sizeof(DWORD));
                RegSetValueEx(hRegKey, "message", 0,
                    REG_SZ, (LPBYTE) str, strlen(str)+1);
            }
            else { // key was already in registry
                // get delay value
                datasize = sizeof(DWORD);
                RegQueryValueEx(hRegKey, "delay", NULL,
                    &datatype, (LPBYTE) &delay, &datasize);

                // get message
                datasize = MSGSIZE;
                RegQueryValueEx(hRegKey, "message", NULL,
                    &datatype, (LPBYTE) str, &datasize);
            }

            // create delay spin control
            hEboxWnd = GetDlgItem(hdwnd, IDD_EB1);
            udWnd = CreateUpDownControl(
```

```
                        WS_CHILD | WS_BORDER | WS_VISIBLE |
                        UDS_SETBUDDYINT | UDS_ALIGNRIGHT,
                        20, 10, 50, 50,
                        hdwnd,
                        IDD_UPDOWN,
                        hMainInstance,
                        hEboxWnd,
                        DELAYMAX, 1, delay);

         // initialize edit box with current message
         SetDlgItemText(hdwnd, IDD_EB2, str);

         return 1;
      case WM_COMMAND:
         switch(LOWORD(wParam)) {
            case IDOK:
               // set delay value
               delay = GetDlgItemInt(hdwnd, IDD_EB1, NULL, 1);

               // get message string
               GetDlgItemText(hdwnd, IDD_EB2, str, MSGSIZE);

               // update registry
               RegSetValueEx(hRegKey, "delay", 0,
                  REG_DWORD, (LPBYTE) &delay, sizeof(DWORD));
               RegSetValueEx(hRegKey, "message", 0,
                   REG_SZ, (LPBYTE) str, strlen(str)+1);

               // fall through to next case ...
            case IDCANCEL:
               RegCloseKey(hRegKey);
               EndDialog(hdwnd, 0);
               return 1;
            }
         break;
      }
   return 0;
}

// No classes to register.
BOOL WINAPI RegisterDialogClasses(HANDLE hInst)
{
   return 1;
}
```

The resource file required by the program is shown here:

```
// Dialog box for screen saver.
#include <windows.h>
#include <scrnsave.h>
#include "scr.h"

ID_APP ICON SCRICON.ICO

STRINGTABLE
{
  IDS_DESCRIPTION "My Screen Saver #2"
}

DLG_SCRNSAVECONFIGURE DIALOGEX 18, 18, 110, 60
CAPTION "Set Screen Saver Options"
STYLE DS_MODALFRAME | WS_POPUP | WS_VISIBLE | WS_CAPTION |
      WS_SYSMENU
{
  PUSHBUTTON "OK", IDOK, 20, 40, 30, 14
  PUSHBUTTON "Cancel", IDCANCEL, 60, 40, 30, 14
  EDITTEXT IDD_EB1, 5, 5, 24, 12, ES_LEFT | WS_TABSTOP | WS_BORDER
  EDITTEXT IDD_EB2, 5, 20, 65, 12, ES_LEFT | WS_TABSTOP |
           WS_BORDER | ES_AUTOHSCROLL
  LTEXT "Delay in milliseconds", IDD_TEXT1, 35, 7, 100, 12
  LTEXT "Message", IDD_TEXT2, 76, 22, 30, 12
}
```

The header file SCR.H is shown here:

```
#define IDD_EB1      200
#define IDD_EB2      201

#define IDD_UPDOWN   202

#define IDD_TEXT1    203
#define IDD_TEXT2    204
```

A Closer Look at the Configurable Screen Saver

Let's begin by examining the **ScreenSaverConfigureDialog( )** function.
This dialog function allows two items to be configured: the delay period and the
message that is displayed. It is shown here for your convenience. When this
dialog function is executed, it produces the dialog box shown in Figure 18-1.

The screen
saver
configuration
dialog box
Figure 18-1.

```
// Configuration Dialog Box Function
BOOL WINAPI ScreenSaverConfigureDialog(HWND hdwnd, UINT message,
                   WPARAM wParam, LPARAM lParam)
{
  static HWND hEboxWnd;
  static HWND udWnd;

  switch(message) {
    case WM_INITDIALOG:
      // open screen saver key or create, if necessary
      RegCreateKeyEx(HKEY_CURRENT_USER,
        "Control Panel\\Screen Saver.MyScrSaver",
        0, "Screen Saver", 0, KEY_ALL_ACCESS,
        NULL, &hRegKey, &result);

      // if key was created
      if(result==REG_CREATED_NEW_KEY) {
        // set its initial value
        delay = 100;
        RegSetValueEx(hRegKey, "delay", 0,
```

```
                REG_DWORD, (LPBYTE) &delay, sizeof(DWORD));
        RegSetValueEx(hRegKey, "message", 0,
            REG_SZ, (LPBYTE) str, strlen(str)+1);
    }
    else { // key was already in registry
      // get delay value
      datasize = sizeof(DWORD);
      RegQueryValueEx(hRegKey, "delay", NULL,
          &datatype, (LPBYTE) &delay, &datasize);

      // get message
      datasize = MSGSIZE;
      RegQueryValueEx(hRegKey, "message", NULL,
          &datatype, (LPBYTE) str, &datasize);
    }

    // create delay spin control
    hEboxWnd = GetDlgItem(hdwnd, IDD_EB1);
    udWnd = CreateUpDownControl(
                    WS_CHILD | WS_BORDER | WS_VISIBLE |
                    UDS_SETBUDDYINT | UDS_ALIGNRIGHT,
                    20, 10, 50, 50,
                    hdwnd,
                    IDD_UPDOWN,
                    hMainInstance,
                    hEboxWnd,
                    DELAYMAX, 1, delay);

    // initialize edit box with current message
    SetDlgItemText(hdwnd, IDD_EB2, str);

    return 1;
  case WM_COMMAND:
    switch(LOWORD(wParam)) {
      case IDOK:
        // set delay value
        delay = GetDlgItemInt(hdwnd, IDD_EB1, NULL, 1);

        // get message string
        GetDlgItemText(hdwnd, IDD_EB2, str, MSGSIZE);

        // update registry
        RegSetValueEx(hRegKey, "delay", 0,
          REG_DWORD, (LPBYTE) &delay, sizeof(DWORD));
        RegSetValueEx(hRegKey, "message", 0,
```

```
                    REG_SZ, (LPBYTE) str, strlen(str)+1);

          // fall through to next case ...
       case IDCANCEL:
         RegCloseKey(hRegKey);
         EndDialog(hdwnd, 0);
         return 1;
       }
     break;
   }
   return 0;
}
```

When the dialog box is first executed, it receives the standard **WM_INITDIALOG** message. When this happens, the dialog box either opens or creates the registry key **Screen Saver.MyScrSaver**, which is a subkey of **Control Panel**, which, in turn, is a subkey under the built-in key **HKEY_CURRENT_USER**. That is, the key path being opened (or created) is

HKEY_CURRENT_USER\Control Panel\Screen Saver.MyScrSaver

As mentioned, since screen saver configuration data can be modified by the Control Panel, it is usually stored under the **Control Panel** key. If the specified key does not already exist in the registry (as it won't when you first run the screen saver), then **RegCreateKeyEx( )** creates it for you. If it does already exist, then the key path is opened. The registry path created by the program (as displayed by REGEDIT) is shown in Figure 18-2. Notice that the configurable screen savers supplied with Windows 2000 are also shown.

After **RegCreateKeyEx( )** returns, the contents of **result** are examined to determine whether the key was created or opened. If the key was created, then the registry is given initial default values for the delay period and the message. Otherwise, those values are read from the registry.

Once the initialization information has been obtained, the dialog box creates a spin control, which is used to set the delay period, and an edit box, which is used to set the message. The box also contains two buttons. If the user selects Cancel, then any changes made by the user are ignored. If the user presses OK, then the contents of the spin control and edit box are used to update the registry.

Now, look at the code inside the **WM_CREATE** statement of **ScreenSaverProc( )**. This code performs exactly the same registry sequence as the dialog box. Of course, instead of being used to allow the user to view

The registry
path created
by the screen
saver

Figure 18-2.

and/or modify the configuration, **ScreenSaverProc( )** uses the registry information to control the execution of the screen saver. One other point: since the user can execute the screen saver without ever having activated the configuration dialog box, the code inside **WM_CREATE** must also be able to create the screen saver keys and set the values. That is, you cannot simply assume that the key **Control Panel\Screen Saver.MyScrSaver** and the values **delay** and **message** are already in the registry.

Some Things to Try

The first thing that you will probably want to try is having the screen saver generate a more interesting graphics display. The purpose of this chapter was to explain the system registry and the mechanics of screen savers. It was not to create an exciting screen saver—this is left to you! One easy starting point is to create a full-screen bitmap and use it as a backdrop. Of course, you must alter the backdrop too. Otherwise the screen saver won't actually "save" the screen. If you have a scanner, then a simple yet effective way to create a custom screen saver is to display a digitized photo.

Because the configurable screen saver is an example program, no entries under **HKEY_LOCAL_MACHINE** relating to the program were made in the registry. Normally, entries are made under this key by installation programs when you install large applications. For fun, you might want to write your own installation program that installs the screen saver and its icon, adding an entry under **HKEY_LOCAL_MACHINE** in the process. To add an application under **HKEY_LOCAL_MACHINE**, use a key path similar to the one shown here:

HKEY_LOCAL_MACHINE\Software\YourName\AppName\Version

There is one other registry key that you might find interesting: **HKEY_PERFORMANCE_DATA**. This key is different from the other built-in keys for two reasons. First, even though you will use the registry functions to access it, it is not stored in the registry. Second, accessing this key allows you to obtain performance data about the software in your system. This key will be valuable if you are optimizing your applications.

18

CHAPTER 19

Supercharging Menus

W e will now return to one of the most fundamental elements of a
Windows program: the menu. In Chapter 4 you learned menu basics.
Here, you will learn how to supercharge them!

Even though the topic of menus may seem rather tame, this is only a surface
impression. The menuing subsystem supports a substantial number of
sophisticated and advanced features. In this chapter we will explore two
general categories of enhanced menus: dynamic and free-floating, pop-up
menus. Both of these give you extended control over the contents of your
application's menus and the way such menus can be used. You will also learn
to handle the new **WM_MENURBUTTONUP** message.

Dynamic Menus

Although most simple Windows applications statically define their menus in
their resource files, more sophisticated applications frequently need to add or
delete menu items dynamically, during run time, in response to changing
program conditions. For example, a word processor may define different
options in its File menu, depending upon the type of file being edited. A
compiler may include one set of debugging options for C code and another
for C++ programs. Menus that change in response to conditions that occur at
run time are called *dynamic menus*. The advantage of dynamic menus is that
they present the user with a list of options that are appropriate to the current
state of the program.

*A dynamic menu
responds to
changing
conditions at
run time.*

Windows 2000 includes several menu management API functions that
allow you to manipulate the contents of menus during the execution
of your program. The ones used by the programs in this chapter are
InsertMenuItem( ), **EnableMenuItem( )**, **DeleteMenu( )**, **GetMenu( )**,
and **GetSubMenu( ).** Before developing an example, these (and other)
functions are described.

Adding an Item to a Menu

To add an item to a menu at run time, use **InsertMenuItem( )**, shown here:

```
BOOL InsertMenuItem(HMENU hMenu, UINT Where,
                    BOOL How, LPMENUITEMINFO MenuInfo);
```

InsertMenuItem( ) adds an item to the menu whose handle is specified by
hMenu. The new menu item is inserted into the menu immediately before the
item specified by *Where*. The precise meaning of *Where* is determined by the

value of *How*. If *How* is nonzero, then *Where* must contain the index at which point the new item is inserted. (Indexing begins at zero.) If *How* is zero, then *Where* must contain the menu ID of an existing item at which point the new item is inserted. The menu item being added is defined by the **MENUITEMINFO** structure pointed to by *MenuInfo*. **MENUITEMINFO** is defined like this:

```
typedef struct tagMENUITEMINFO
{
  UINT cbSize;
  UINT fMask;
  UINT fType;
  UINT fState;
  UINT wID;
  HMENU hSubMenu;
  HBITMAP hbmpChecked;
  HBITMAP hbmpUnchecked;
  DWORD dwItemData;
  LPSTR dwTypeData;
  UINT cch;
  HBITMAP hbmpItem; // requires Windows 2000, Windows 98, or later
} MENUITEMINFO;
```

19

Here, **cbSize** must contain the size of the **MENUITEMINFO** structure. The value of **fMask** determines which of the other members of **MENUITEMINFO** contain valid information when setting menu information. That is, it determines which of the other members are active. (It is also used to specify which members will be loaded when menu information is retrieved.) It must be a combination of one or more of these values:

fMask Value	Activates
MIIM_BITMAP	**hbmpItem** (Windows 2000, Windows 98, or later)
MIIM_CHECKMARKS	**hbmpChecked** and **hbmpUnchecked**
MIIM_DATA	**dwItemData**
MIIM_FTYPE	**fType** (Windows 2000, Windows 98, or later)
MIIM_ID	**wID**
MIIM_STATE	**fstate**

fMask Value	Activates
MIIM_STRING	**dwTypeData** (Windows 2000, Windows 98, or later)
MIIM_SUBMENU	**hSubMenu**
MIIM_TYPE	**fType** and **dwTypeData** (Obsolete for Windows 2000; use MIIM_BITMAP, MIIM_FTYPE, or MIIM_STRING instead)

The type of the menu item is determined by **fType**. It can be any valid combination of the following values.

fType Value	Meaning
MFT_BITMAP	The low-order word of **dwTypeData** specifies a bitmap handle. The menu item is displayed as a bitmap. Obsolete for Windows 2000; use **MIIM_BITMAP** in **fMask** instead.
MFT_MENUBARBREAK	For menu bar, causes the item to be put on a new line. For pop-up menus, causes the item to be put in a different column, in which case the item is separated using a bar.
MFT_MENUBREAK	Same as **MFT_MENUBARBREAK** except that no separator bar is used.
MF_OWNERDRAW	Owner drawn item.
MFT_RADIOCHECK	Radio button check mark style is used when the item is selected rather than the normal menu check mark. **hbmpChecked** must be **NULL**.
MFT_RIGHTJUSTIFY	For menu bars only. Right justifies the item. Subsequent items are also right justified.
MFT_RIGHTORDER	Menus descend right to left. Supports right-to-left reading languages.
MFT_SEPARATOR	Places a horizontal dividing line between menu items. The values in **dwTypeData** and **cch** are ignored. This type cannot be used for menu bar items.
MFT_STRING	**dwTypeData** is a pointer to a string that describes the menu item. Obsolete for Windows 2000, use **MIIM_STRING** in **fMask** instead.

The state of the menu item is determined by **fState**. It can be any valid combination of the following values:

fState Value	Meaning
MFS_CHECKED	Item is checked.
MFS_DEFAULT	Item is the default selection.
MFS_DISABLED	Item is disabled.
MFS_ENABLED	Item is enabled. Items are enabled by default.
MFS_GRAYED	Item is disabled and grayed.
MFS_HILITE	Item is highlighted.
MFS_UNCHECKED	Item is unchecked.
MFS_UNHILITE	Item is unhighlighted. Items are unhighlighted by default.

The ID value associated with the menu item is specified in **wID**.

If the item being inserted is a pop-up submenu, then its handle must be in **hSubMenu**. Otherwise, this value must be **NULL**.

You can specify bitmaps that will be used to indicate a menu item's checked and unchecked state in **hbmpChecked** and **hbmpUnchecked**. To use the default check mark, specify **NULL** for both of these members.

The value of **dwItemData** is application-dependent. If unused, set this value to zero.

When setting menu information, **dwTypeData** contains a pointer to the string representing the menu item. When retrieving menu information, **dwTypeData** contains a pointer to a character array that will receive the string. In both cases, the value **MIIM_STRING** must be present in **fMask** in order for **dwTypeData** to be used.

When a menu item is being retrieved, **cch** will contain the length of the string if **fMask** contains **MIIM_STRING.** The value of **cch** is ignored when the menu item is being set.

To specify a bitmapped image that will be displayed on the left side of the menu text, assign the handle of the bitmap to **hbmpItem.** The value **MIIM_BITMAP** must be present in **fMask**. This option is new for Windows 2000.

InsertMenuItem( ) returns nonzero if successful and zero on failure.

NEW FOR 2000:   In Windows 2000, menus can include bitmaps along with text.

HISTORICAL PERSPECTIVE: **InsertMenuItem( )** is not supported by Windows 3.1. Instead, menu items were dynamically inserted into a menu using **AppendMenu( )** or **InsertMenu( )**. While these functions are still supported by Windows 2000, the use of **InsertMenuItem( )** is recommended.

Deleting a Menu Item

To remove a menu item, use the **DeleteMenu( )** function, shown here:

BOOL DeleteMenu(HMENU *hMenu*, UINT *ItemID*, UINT *How*);

Here, *hMenu* specifies the handle of the menu to be affected. The item to be removed is specified in *ItemID*. The value of *How* determines how *ItemID* is interpreted. If *How* is **MF_BYPOSITION,** then the value in *ItemID* must be the index of the item to be deleted. This index is the position of the item within the menu, with the first menu item being zero. If *How* is **MF_BYCOMMAND,** then *ItemID* is the ID associated with the menu item. **DeleteMenu( )** returns nonzero if successful and zero on failure.

If the menu item deleted is, itself, a pop-up submenu, then that pop-up submenu is also destroyed. There is no need to call **DestroyMenu( )**. (**DestroyMenu( )** is described in Chapter 4.)

Obtaining a Handle to a Menu

GetMenu( ) obtains the handle of a window's main menu.

As you have just seen, to add or delete a menu item requires a handle to the menu. To obtain the handle of the main menu, use **GetMenu( ),** shown here:

HMENU GetMenu(HWND *hwnd*);

GetMenu( ) returns the handle of the menu associated with the window specified by *hwnd*. It returns **NULL** on failure.

Given a handle to a window's main menu, you can easily obtain the handles of the pop-up submenus contained in the main menu by using **GetSubMenu( ).** Its prototype is shown here:

GetSubMenu( )
obtains the
handle of a
pop-up
submenu.

HMENU GetSubMenu(HMENU *hMenu*, int *ItemPos*);

Here, *hMenu* is the handle of the parent menu, and *ItemPos* is the position of the desired pop-up menu within the parent window. (The first position is zero.) The function returns the handle of the specified pop-up menu or **NULL** on failure.

Obtaining the Size of a Menu

19

When working with menus dynamically, you will often need to know how many items are in a menu. To obtain the number of menu items, use **GetMenuItemCount( )**, shown here:

int GetMenuItemCount(HMENU *hMenu*);

Here, *hMenu* is the handle of the menu in question. The function returns −1 on failure.

Enabling and Disabling a Menu Item

Sometimes a menu item will apply only to certain situations and not to others. In such cases, you may wish to temporarily disable an item, enabling it later. To accomplish this, use the **EnableMenuItem( )** function, shown here:

BOOL EnableMenuItem(HMENU *hMenu*, UINT *ItemID*, UINT *How*);

The handle of the menu is passed in *hMenu*. The item to be enabled or disabled is specified in *ItemID*. The value of *How* determines two things. First, it specifies how *ItemID* is interpreted. If *How* contains **MF_BYPOSITION,** then the value in *ItemID* must be the index of the item to be deleted. This index is the position of the item within the menu, with the first menu item being zero. If *How* contains **MF_BYCOMMAND,** then *ItemID* is the ID associated with the menu item. The value in *How* also determines whether the item will be enabled or disabled, based upon which of the following values are present.

MF_DISABLED	Disables the new menu item.
MF_ENABLED	Enables the new menu item.
MF_GRAYED	Disables the menu item and turns it gray.

To construct the desired value of *How*, OR together the appropriate values.

EnableMenuItem( ) returns the previous state of the item or −1 on failure.

Dynamically Adding Menu Items

Now that the basic menu management functions have been discussed, it is time to see them in action. Let's begin with dynamically inserting and

---

IN DEPTH

GetMenuItemInfo( ) and SetMenuItemInfo( )

Sometimes you will want to obtain detailed information about or make detailed adjustments to a menu. The easiest way to do this is to use **GetMenuItemInfo( )** and **SetMenuItemInfo( )**, whose prototypes are shown here:

```
BOOL GetMenuItemInfo(HMENU hMenu, UINT ItemID,
                     BOOL How, LPMENUITEMINFO MenuInfo);

BOOL SetMenuItemInfo(HMENU hMenu, UINT ItemID,
                     BOOL How, LPMENUITEMINFO MenuInfo);
```

These functions get and set all of the information associated with a menu item. The menu containing the item is specified by *hMenu*. The menu item is specified by *ItemID*. The precise meaning of *ItemID* is determined by the value of *How*. If *How* is nonzero, then *ItemID* must contain the index of the item. If *How* is zero, then *ItemID* must contain the menu ID of the item. For **GetMenuItemInfo( )**, the **MENUITEMINFO** structure pointed to by *MenuInfo* will receive the current information about the item. For **SetMenuItemInfo( )**, the contents of the structure pointed to by *MenuInfo* will be used to set the menu item's information.

Both functions return nonzero if successful and zero on failure.

As you can guess, you could use **SetMenuItemInfo( )** to perform relatively simple menu management functions, such as enabling or disabling a menu item. However, using **SetMenuItemInfo( )** and **GetMenuItemInfo( )** for these types of operations is inefficient. They should be reserved for more complex or subtle menu manipulations.

deleting an item. To do this, we will use a simple program that draws various GDI objects in the main window. The program contains two menus. The first is called Options. The second is called Draw. The Options menu lets the user select various options relating to the program. The Draw menu lets the user select which object will be drawn. The following program demonstrates dynamic menu management by adding an item to or deleting an item from its Options menu. Pay special attention to the **IDM_ADDITEM** and **IDM_DELITEM** cases inside **WindowFunc( ).** This is the code that adds or deletes a menu item. Sample output is shown in Figure 19-1.

```
// Dynamically managing menus.

// The following define is needed by some compilers.
#define WINVER 0x0500

#include <windows.h>
#include <cstring>
#include <cstdio>
#include "menu.h"

LRESULT CALLBACK WindowFunc(HWND, UINT, WPARAM, LPARAM);

char szWinName[] = "MyWin"; // name of window class

int WINAPI WinMain(HINSTANCE hThisInst, HINSTANCE hPrevInst,
                   LPSTR lpszArgs, int nWinMode)
{
  HWND hwnd;
  MSG msg;
  WNDCLASSEX wcl;
  HACCEL hAccel;

  // Define a window class.
  wcl.cbSize = sizeof(WNDCLASSEX);

  wcl.hInstance = hThisInst;      // handle to this instance
  wcl.lpszClassName = szWinName; // window class name
  wcl.lpfnWndProc = WindowFunc;  // window function
  wcl.style = 0;                 // default style

  wcl.hIcon = LoadIcon(NULL, IDI_APPLICATION); // large icon
  wcl.hIconSm = NULL; // use small version of large icon
  wcl.hCursor = LoadCursor(NULL, IDC_ARROW);  // cursor style

  wcl.lpszMenuName = "DynMenu"; // main menu
```

```
wcl.cbClsExtra = 0; // no extra memory needed
wcl.cbWndExtra = 0;

// Make the window background white.
wcl.hbrBackground = (HBRUSH) GetStockObject(WHITE_BRUSH);

// Register the window class.
if(!RegisterClassEx(&wcl)) return 0;

/* Now that a window class has been registered, a window
   can be created. */
hwnd = CreateWindow(
  szWinName, // name of window class
  "Using Dynamic Menus", // title
  WS_OVERLAPPEDWINDOW, // window style - normal
  CW_USEDEFAULT, // X coordinate - let Windows decide
  CW_USEDEFAULT, // Y coordinate - let Windows decide
  CW_USEDEFAULT, // width - let Windows decide
  CW_USEDEFAULT, // height - let Windows decide
  NULL,          // no parent window
  NULL,          // no override of class menu
  hThisInst,     // instance handle
  NULL           // no additional arguments
);

// Load the keyboard accelerators.
hAccel = LoadAccelerators(hThisInst, "DynMenu");

// Display the window.
ShowWindow(hwnd, nWinMode);
UpdateWindow(hwnd);

// Create the message loop.
while(GetMessage(&msg, NULL, 0, 0))
{
  if(!TranslateAccelerator(hwnd, hAccel, &msg)) {
    TranslateMessage(&msg); // translate keyboard messages
    DispatchMessage(&msg); // return control to Windows 2000
  }
}

return msg.wParam;
}
```

19

```
/* This function is called by Windows 2000 and is passed
   messages from the message queue.
*/
LRESULT CALLBACK WindowFunc(HWND hwnd, UINT message,
                               WPARAM wParam, LPARAM lParam)
{
  HDC hdc;
  RECT rect;
  HMENU hmenu, hsubmenu;
  int response;
  int count;
  MENUITEMINFO miInfo;

  switch(message) {
    case WM_COMMAND:
      switch(LOWORD(wParam)) {
        case IDM_ADDITEM: // dynamically add menu item
          // get handle of main menu
          hmenu = GetMenu(hwnd);

          // get handle of 1st popup menu
          hsubmenu = GetSubMenu(hmenu, 0);

          // get number of items in the popup
          count = GetMenuItemCount(hsubmenu);

          // append a separator
          miInfo.cbSize = sizeof(MENUITEMINFO);
          miInfo.fMask = MIIM_FTYPE;
          miInfo.fType = MFT_SEPARATOR;
          miInfo.fState = 0;
          miInfo.wID = 0;
          miInfo.hSubMenu = NULL;
          miInfo.hbmpChecked = NULL;
          miInfo.hbmpUnchecked = NULL;
          miInfo.dwItemData = 0;
          miInfo.dwTypeData = 0;
          InsertMenuItem(hsubmenu, count, 1, &miInfo);

          // append new menu item
          miInfo.fMask = MIIM_STRING | MIIM_ID;
          miInfo.wID = IDM_NEW;
          miInfo.dwTypeData = "E&rase (This is New Item)";
          InsertMenuItem(hsubmenu, count+1, 1, &miInfo);
```

```
    // deactivate the Add Item option
    EnableMenuItem(hsubmenu, IDM_ADDITEM,
                  MF_BYCOMMAND | MF_GRAYED);

    // activate the Delete Item option
    EnableMenuItem(hsubmenu, IDM_DELITEM,
                  MF_BYCOMMAND | MF_ENABLED);
    break;
  case IDM_DELITEM: // dynamically delete menu item
    // get handle of main menu
    hmenu = GetMenu(hwnd);

    // get handle of 1st popup menu
    hsubmenu = GetSubMenu(hmenu, 0);

    // delete the new item and the separator
    count = GetMenuItemCount(hsubmenu);
    DeleteMenu(hsubmenu, count-1, MF_BYPOSITION | MF_GRAYED);
    DeleteMenu(hsubmenu, count-2, MF_BYPOSITION | MF_GRAYED);

    // reactivate the Add Item option
    EnableMenuItem(hsubmenu, IDM_ADDITEM,
                  MF_BYCOMMAND | MF_ENABLED);

    // deactivate the Delete Item option
    EnableMenuItem(hsubmenu, IDM_DELITEM,
                  MF_BYCOMMAND | MF_GRAYED);
    break;
  case IDM_EXIT:
    response = MessageBox(hwnd, "Quit the Program?",
                         "Exit", MB_YESNO);
    if(response == IDYES) PostQuitMessage(0);
    break;
  case IDM_NEW: // erase window
    hdc = GetDC(hwnd);
    GetClientRect(hwnd, &rect);
    SelectObject(hdc, GetStockObject(WHITE_BRUSH));
    PatBlt(hdc, 0, 0, rect.right, rect.bottom, PATCOPY);
    ReleaseDC(hwnd, hdc);
    break;
  case IDM_LINES:
    hdc = GetDC(hwnd);
    MoveToEx(hdc, 10, 10, NULL);
    LineTo(hdc, 100, 100);
    LineTo(hdc, 100, 50);
```

```
                    LineTo(hdc, 50, 180);
                    ReleaseDC(hwnd, hdc);
                    break;
                  case IDM_ELLIPSES:
                    hdc = GetDC(hwnd);
                    Ellipse(hdc, 100, 100, 300, 200);
                    Ellipse(hdc, 200, 100, 300, 200);
                    ReleaseDC(hwnd, hdc);
                    break;
                  case IDM_RECTANGLES:
                    hdc = GetDC(hwnd);
                    Rectangle(hdc, 100, 100, 24, 260);
                    Rectangle(hdc, 110, 120, 124, 170);
                    ReleaseDC(hwnd, hdc);
                    break;
                  case IDM_HELP:
                    MessageBox(hwnd, "Try Adding a Menu Item",
                              "Help", MB_OK);
                    break;
              }
              break;
          case WM_DESTROY: // terminate the program
            PostQuitMessage(0);
            break;
          default:
            /* Let Windows 2000 process any messages not specified in
               the preceding switch statement. */
            return DefWindowProc(hwnd, message, wParam, lParam);
      }
      return 0;
}
```

The resource file required by the program is shown here:

```
// Dynamic Menus
#include <windows.h>
#include "menu.h"

DynMenu MENU
{
  POPUP "&Options"
  {
    MENUITEM "&Add Item\tF2", IDM_ADDITEM
    MENUITEM "&Delete Item\tF3", IDM_DELITEM, GRAYED
    MENUITEM "E&xit\tCtrl+X", IDM_EXIT
```

```
  }
  POPUP "&Draw"
  {
    MENUITEM "&Lines\tF4", IDM_LINES
    MENUITEM "&Ellipses\tF5", IDM_ELLIPSES
    MENUITEM "&Rectangles\tF6", IDM_RECTANGLES
  }
  MENUITEM "&Help", IDM_HELP
}

// Define menu accelerators
DynMenu ACCELERATORS
{
  VK_F2, IDM_ADDITEM, VIRTKEY
  VK_F3, IDM_DELITEM, VIRTKEY
  VK_F4, IDM_LINES, VIRTKEY
  VK_F5, IDM_ELLIPSES, VIRTKEY
  VK_F6, IDM_RECTANGLES, VIRTKEY
  VK_F1, IDM_HELP, VIRTKEY
  "^X", IDM_EXIT
}
```

The MENU.H header file is shown here. It also includes a few values that are used by later programs in this chapter.

```
#define IDM_EXIT         100
#define IDM_LINES        101
#define IDM_ELLIPSES     102
#define IDM_RECTANGLES   103
#define IDM_HELP         104

#define IDM_ADDITEM      200
#define IDM_DELITEM      201

#define IDM_NEW          300
#define IDM_NEW2         301
#define IDM_NEW3         302
```

A Closer Look at the First Dynamic Menu Program

Most of this program is straightforward and easy to understand. When the program first begins, the Options menu contains only three selections: Add Item, Delete Item, and Exit. Initially, Delete Item is grayed and, therefore, may not be selected. To add the Erase option, select Add Item. After Erase has

Adding menu
items
dynamically
Figure 19-1.

been dynamically added to the menu, the Delete Item option is activated and the Add Item option is grayed. When Delete Item is selected, Erase is removed from the menu, Add Item is reactivated, and Delete Item is once again grayed. This procedure prevents the new menu item from being added or deleted more than once.

Look closely at the code under **IDM_ADDITEM**. Notice how the handle to the Options pop-up menu is obtained. First, you must retrieve the handle of its outer menu, which in this case is the program's main menu, using **GetMenu( )**. Next, you must use **GetSubMenu( )** to obtain the handle of its first pop-up menu, which is Options. Next, the program obtains a count of the number of items in the menu. This step is technically unnecessary since, in this simple example, we already know this value. However, this step is included for the sake of illustration because, in a real-world program, you may not always know how many items a menu contains. Next, the program adds a separator and then the Erase menu item itself.

One last point. Notice that the macro **WINVER** is defined as 0x0500 at the start of the program. This is done to ensure that the new Windows 2000-compatible header information is included. Without this definition, some compilers will not include values such as **MIIM_STRING** that apply only to the Windows 2000/Windows 98 environment.

Creating Dynamic Pop-up Menus

In addition to adding new items to an existing menu, you can dynamically create an entire pop-up menu. (That is, you can create a pop-up menu at run time.) Once you have created the menu, it can then be added to an existing menu. To dynamically create a pop-up menu, you first use the API function **CreatePopupMenu( ),** shown here:

> HMENU CreatePopupMenu( );

This function creates an empty menu and returns a handle to it. You add items to the menu by calling **InsertMenuItem( )**. Once the menu is fully constructed, you can add it to an existing menu, also using **InsertMenuItem( )**.

To create a pop-up menu, use **Create-PopupMenu( )**.

Menus created using **CreatePopupMenu( )** must be destroyed. If the menu is attached to a window, then it will be destroyed automatically. A menu is also automatically destroyed when it is removed from a parent menu by a call to **DeleteMenu( )**. Dynamic menus can be destroyed explicitly by calling **DestroyMenu( )**.

The following program is an enhanced version of the preceding program. It dynamically creates a pop-up menu that contains three items: Erase, Black Pen, and Red Pen. Selecting Erase erases the window. Choosing Black Pen selects the black pen (which is the default pen). Choosing Red Pen selects the red pen. After a pen has been selected, it is used to draw the shapes available in the Draw menu. Pay close attention to the way that the pop-up menu is constructed and attached to the Options menu.

```
// Adding a popup menu.

// The following define is needed by some compilers.
#define WINVER 0x0500

#include <windows.h>
#include <cstring>
#include <cstdio>
#include "menu.h"

LRESULT CALLBACK WindowFunc(HWND, UINT, WPARAM, LPARAM);

char szWinName[] = "MyWin"; // name of window class

int WINAPI WinMain(HINSTANCE hThisInst, HINSTANCE hPrevInst,
```

```
                    LPSTR lpszArgs, int nWinMode)
{
  HWND hwnd;
  MSG msg;
  WNDCLASSEX wcl;
  HACCEL hAccel;

  // Define a window class.
  wcl.cbSize = sizeof(WNDCLASSEX);

  wcl.hInstance = hThisInst;     // handle to this instance
  wcl.lpszClassName = szWinName; // window class name
  wcl.lpfnWndProc = WindowFunc;  // window function
  wcl.style = 0;                 // default style

  wcl.hIcon = LoadIcon(NULL, IDI_APPLICATION); // large icon
  wcl.hIconSm = NULL; // use small version of large icon
  wcl.hCursor = LoadCursor(NULL, IDC_ARROW);  // cursor style

  wcl.lpszMenuName = "DynPopUpMenu"; // main menu

  wcl.cbClsExtra = 0; // no extra memory needed
  wcl.cbWndExtra = 0;

  // Make the window background white.
  wcl.hbrBackground = (HBRUSH) GetStockObject(WHITE_BRUSH);

  // Register the window class.
  if(!RegisterClassEx(&wcl)) return 0;

  /* Now that a window class has been registered, a window
     can be created. */
  hwnd = CreateWindow(
    szWinName, // name of window class
    "Adding a Popup Menu", // title
    WS_OVERLAPPEDWINDOW, // window style - normal
    CW_USEDEFAULT, // X coordinate - let Windows decide
    CW_USEDEFAULT, // Y coordinate - let Windows decide
    CW_USEDEFAULT, // width - let Windows decide
    CW_USEDEFAULT, // height - let Windows decide
    NULL,          // no parent window
    NULL,          // no override of class menu
    hThisInst,     // instance handle
    NULL           // no additional arguments
  );
```

```
    // Load the keyboard accelerators.
    hAccel = LoadAccelerators(hThisInst, "DynPopUpMenu");

    // Display the window.
    ShowWindow(hwnd, nWinMode);
    UpdateWindow(hwnd);

    // Create the message loop.
    while(GetMessage(&msg, NULL, 0, 0))
    {
      if(!TranslateAccelerator(hwnd, hAccel, &msg)) {
        TranslateMessage(&msg); // translate keyboard messages
        DispatchMessage(&msg); // return control to Windows 2000
      }
    }

    return msg.wParam;
}

/* This function is called by Windows 2000 and is passed
   messages from the message queue.
*/
LRESULT CALLBACK WindowFunc(HWND hwnd, UINT message,
                            WPARAM wParam, LPARAM lParam)
{
  HDC hdc;
  HMENU hmenu, hsubmenu;
  RECT rect;
  static HMENU hpopup;
  int response;
  int count;
  MENUITEMINFO miInfo;
  static HPEN hCurrentPen, hRedPen;

  switch(message) {
    case WM_CREATE:
      // create red pen
      hRedPen = CreatePen(PS_SOLID, 1, RGB(255, 0, 0));
      // get black pen
      hCurrentPen = (HPEN) GetStockObject(BLACK_PEN);
      break;
    case WM_COMMAND:
      switch(LOWORD(wParam)) {
        case IDM_ADDITEM: // dynamically add popup menu
```

```
// get handle of main menu
hmenu = GetMenu(hwnd);

// get handle of 1st popup menu
hsubmenu = GetSubMenu(hmenu, 0);

// get number of items in the menu
count = GetMenuItemCount(hsubmenu);

// create new popup menu
hpopup = CreatePopupMenu();

// add items to dynamic popup menu
miInfo.cbSize = sizeof(MENUITEMINFO);
miInfo.fMask = MIIM_STRING | MIIM_ID;
miInfo.wID = IDM_NEW;
miInfo.hSubMenu = NULL;
miInfo.hbmpChecked = NULL;
miInfo.hbmpUnchecked = NULL;
miInfo.dwItemData = 0;
miInfo.dwTypeData = "&Erase";
InsertMenuItem(hpopup, 0, 1, &miInfo);

miInfo.dwTypeData = "&Black Pen";
miInfo.wID = IDM_NEW2;
InsertMenuItem(hpopup, 1, 1, &miInfo);

miInfo.dwTypeData = "&Red Pen";
miInfo.wID = IDM_NEW3;
InsertMenuItem(hpopup, 2, 1, &miInfo);

// append a separator
miInfo.cbSize = sizeof(MENUITEMINFO);
miInfo.fMask = MIIM_FTYPE;
miInfo.fType = MFT_SEPARATOR;
miInfo.fState = 0;
miInfo.wID = 0;
miInfo.hSubMenu = NULL;
miInfo.hbmpChecked = NULL;
miInfo.hbmpUnchecked = NULL;
miInfo.dwItemData = 0;
InsertMenuItem(hsubmenu, count, 1, &miInfo);

// append popup menu to main menu
miInfo.fMask = MIIM_STRING | MIIM_SUBMENU;
```

```
      miInfo.hSubMenu = hpopup;
      miInfo.dwTypeData = "&This is New Popup";
      InsertMenuItem(hsubmenu, count+1, 1, &miInfo);

      // deactivate the Add Popup option
      EnableMenuItem(hsubmenu, IDM_ADDITEM,
                   MF_BYCOMMAND | MF_GRAYED);

      // activate the Delete Popup option
      EnableMenuItem(hsubmenu, IDM_DELITEM,
                   MF_BYCOMMAND | MF_ENABLED);
      break;
    case IDM_DELITEM: // dynamically delete popup menu
      // get handle of main menu
      hmenu = GetMenu(hwnd);

      // get handle of 1st popup menu
      hsubmenu = GetSubMenu(hmenu, 0);

      // delete the new popup menu and the separator
      count = GetMenuItemCount(hsubmenu);
      DeleteMenu(hsubmenu, count-1, MF_BYPOSITION | MF_GRAYED);
      DeleteMenu(hsubmenu, count-2, MF_BYPOSITION | MF_GRAYED);

      // reactivate the Add Popup option
      EnableMenuItem(hsubmenu, IDM_ADDITEM,
                   MF_BYCOMMAND | MF_ENABLED);

      // deactivate the Delete Popup option
      EnableMenuItem(hsubmenu, IDM_DELITEM,
                   MF_BYCOMMAND | MF_GRAYED);
      break;
    case IDM_EXIT:
      response = MessageBox(hwnd, "Quit the Program?",
                         "Exit", MB_YESNO);
      if(response == IDYES) PostQuitMessage(0);
      break;
    case IDM_NEW: // erase
      hdc = GetDC(hwnd);
      GetClientRect(hwnd, &rect);
      SelectObject(hdc, GetStockObject(WHITE_BRUSH));
      PatBlt(hdc, 0, 0, rect.right, rect.bottom, PATCOPY);
      ReleaseDC(hwnd, hdc);
      break;
```

```
          case IDM_NEW2: // select black pen
            hCurrentPen = (HPEN) GetStockObject(BLACK_PEN);
            break;
          case IDM_NEW3: // select red pen
            hCurrentPen = hRedPen;
            break;
          case IDM_LINES:
            hdc = GetDC(hwnd);
            SelectObject(hdc, hCurrentPen);
            MoveToEx(hdc, 10, 10, NULL);
            LineTo(hdc, 100, 100);
            LineTo(hdc, 100, 50);
            LineTo(hdc, 50, 180);
            ReleaseDC(hwnd, hdc);
            break;
          case IDM_ELLIPSES:
            hdc = GetDC(hwnd);
            SelectObject(hdc, hCurrentPen);
            Ellipse(hdc, 100, 100, 300, 200);
            Ellipse(hdc, 200, 100, 300, 200);
            ReleaseDC(hwnd, hdc);
            break;
          case IDM_RECTANGLES:
            hdc = GetDC(hwnd);
            SelectObject(hdc, hCurrentPen);
            Rectangle(hdc, 100, 100, 24, 260);
            Rectangle(hdc, 110, 120, 124, 170);
            ReleaseDC(hwnd, hdc);
            break;
          case IDM_HELP:
            MessageBox(hwnd, "Try Adding a Menu", "Help", MB_OK);
            break;
        }
      break;
    case WM_DESTROY: // terminate the program
      PostQuitMessage(0);
      break;
    default:
      /* Let Windows 2000 process any messages not specified in
         the preceding switch statement. */
      return DefWindowProc(hwnd, message, wParam, lParam);
  }
  return 0;
}
```

The header file MENU.H is the same as was used before. However, this program uses the following resource file.

```
// Dynamic Popup Menus.
#include <windows.h>
#include "menu.h"

DynPopUpMenu MENU
{
  POPUP "&Options"
  {
    MENUITEM "&Add Popup\tF2", IDM_ADDITEM
    MENUITEM "&Delete Popup\tF3", IDM_DELITEM, GRAYED
    MENUITEM "E&xit\tCtrl+X", IDM_EXIT
  }
  POPUP "&Draw"
  {
    MENUITEM "&Lines\tF4", IDM_LINES
    MENUITEM "&Ellipses\tF5", IDM_ELLIPSES
    MENUITEM "&Rectangles\tF6", IDM_RECTANGLES
  }
  MENUITEM "&Help", IDM_HELP
}

// Define menu accelerators
DynPopUpMenu ACCELERATORS
{
  VK_F2, IDM_ADDITEM, VIRTKEY
  VK_F3, IDM_DELITEM, VIRTKEY
  VK_F4, IDM_LINES, VIRTKEY
  VK_F5, IDM_ELLIPSES, VIRTKEY
  VK_F6, IDM_RECTANGLES, VIRTKEY
  VK_F1, IDM_HELP, VIRTKEY
  "^X", IDM_EXIT
}
```

Sample output from this program is shown in Figure 19-2.

Most of the program is straightforward. However, notice one important point. The **MIIM_SUBMENU** flag must be set and the handle of the pop-up menu must be in **hSubMenu** when a pop-up menu is inserted into a menu.

A dynamically
created pop-up
menu

Figure 19-2.

19

Using Floating Menus

Although stand-alone, or *floating,* menus have been available to Windows programmers for quite some time, they continue to increase in popularity and importance. One reason for this is that all current versions of Windows display a floating menu when you click the right mouse button on the desktop. Also, most professionally written applications now utilize floating menus. Frankly, it is hard to imagine creating a modern Windows 2000 application that does not support floating menus.

Floating menus are also called *context menus* and *shortcut menus*. This book will use the term floating menu because it is the most descriptive.

Activating a Floating Menu

A floating menu is activated using **TrackPopupMenuEx( )**. Its prototype is shown here:

```
BOOL TrackPopupMenuEx(HMENU hMenu,  UINT Flags, int X, int Y,
                      HWND hwnd, LPTPMPARMS OffLimits);
```

Changing the Menu Bar

Menu items can be added to the menu bar itself, in exactly the same way that they are added to any other menu. There is only one additional action your program must take: it must redraw the menu bar in order for the changes to be displayed. To accomplish this, call **DrawMenuBar( )**, shown here:

BOOL DrawMenuBar(HWND *hwnd*);

Here, *hwnd* specifies the handle of the window whose menu bar will be redrawn. The function returns nonzero if successful and zero on failure.

To try modifying the contents of the menu bar, substitute the following code for the **IDM_ADDITEM** handler in the pop-up menu program.

```
// Dynamically add a popup menu to menu bar.
case IDM_ADDITEM:
  // get handle of menu bar
  hmenu = GetMenu(hwnd);

  // get number of items in the menu bar
  count = GetMenuItemCount(hmenu);

  // create new popup menu
  hpopup = CreatePopupMenu();
  // add items to dynamic popup menu
  miInfo.cbSize = sizeof(MENUITEMINFO);
  miInfo.fMask = MIIM_STRING | MIIM_ID;
  miInfo.wID = IDM_NEW;
  miInfo.hSubMenu = NULL;
  miInfo.hbmpChecked = NULL;
  miInfo.hbmpUnchecked = NULL;
  miInfo.dwItemData = 0;
  miInfo.dwTypeData = "&Erase";
  InsertMenuItem(hpopup, 0, 1, &miInfo);

  miInfo.dwTypeData = "&Black Pen";
  miInfo.wID = IDM_NEW2;
  InsertMenuItem(hpopup, 1, 1, &miInfo);

  miInfo.dwTypeData = "&Red Pen";
```

```
miInfo.wID = IDM_NEW3;
InsertMenuItem(hpopup, 2, 1, &miInfo);

// append popup menu to menu bar
miInfo.fMask = MIIM_STRING | MIIM_SUBMENU;
miInfo.hSubMenu = hpopup;
miInfo.dwTypeData = "&New Popup";
InsertMenuItem(hmenu, count+1, 1, &miInfo);

// get handle of 1st popup menu
hsubmenu = GetSubMenu(hmenu, 0);
// deactivate the Add Popup option
EnableMenuItem(hsubmenu, IDM_ADDITEM, MF_BYCOMMAND |
            MF_GRAYED);
// activate the Delete Popup option
EnableMenuItem(hsubmenu, IDM_DELITEM, MF_BYCOMMAND |
            MF_ENABLED);

// redraw the menu bar
DrawMenuBar(hwnd);
break;
```

After making these changes, the pop-up menu will be added to the menu bar instead of the first drop-down menu. You should also make similar changes to the **IDM_DELITEM** handler so that it deletes the selection from the menu bar. Here is what the menu bar looks like after adding the new item:

If you want to make extensive changes to the contents of the menu bar, you might want to use **SetMenu( )** instead of making the changes individually. **SetMenu( )** replaces the entire main menu of a window with another. It has this prototype:

BOOL SetMenu(HWND *hwnd*, HMENU *hmenu*);

Here, *hwnd* is the handle of the window being affected, and *hmenu* is the handle of the new menu. The old menu should be destroyed by calling **DestroyMenu( )**. If you know that your application will need to use two or more different main menus, you could construct them in advance and then use **SetMenu( )** to swap them as needed. This approach will usually be more efficient than making many changes to the menu bar by hand.

Finally, if you want to dynamically create a main menu (that is, a menu bar), use the **CreateMenu( )** function. Its prototype is shown here:

HMENU CreateMenu( );

It returns a handle to an empty menu that you must then fill in using the same approach used for dynamic pop-up menus.

Here, *hMenu* is the handle of the menu that will be activated.

Floating menus are not attached to the menu bar.

Various options are specified in *Flags*. This parameter may be any valid (that is, non-mutually exclusive) combination of the values shown in Table 19-1. You may specify zero for *Flags*. Doing so causes the default configuration to be used.

The location *on the screen* at which to display the menu is specified in *X* and *Y*. Therefore, these coordinates are expressed in terms of screen units, not window or dialog units. To convert between screen and window units, use either the **ClientToScreen( )** or the **ScreenToClient( )** function. In its default configuration, **TrackPopupMenuEx( )** displays the menu with its upper-left corner at the location specified by *X* and *Y*. However, you can use the *Flags* parameter to alter this placement.

The handle of the window that invokes **TrackPopupMenuEx( )** must be passed in *hwnd*.

Flags Value	Meaning
TPM_BOTTOMALIGN	Floating menu pops up with bottom edge at *Y*.
TPM_CENTERALIGN	Floating menu pops up centered left to right relative to *X*.
TPM_HORIZONTAL	If the menu cannot be fully displayed at the location specified by *X* and *Y*, the horizontal alignment of the menu is given priority.
TPM_HORNEGANIMATION	Right to left animation. (Windows 2000, Windows 98, or later.)
TPM_HORPOSANIMATION	Left to right animation. (Windows 2000, Windows 98, or later.)
TPM_LEFTALIGN	Floating menu pops up with left side at *X*. (This is the default.).
TPM_LEFTBUTTON	Left mouse button operates the menu. (This is the default.)
TPM_NOANIMATION	No animation. (Windows 2000, Windows 98, or later.)
TPM_NONOTIFY	Menu does not send notification messages.
TPM_RETURNCMD	The ID of the item selected is returned.
TPM_RIGHTALIGN	Floating menu pops up with right side at *X*.
TPM_RIGHTBUTTON	Right mouse button operates the menu.
TPM_TOPALIGN	Floating menu pops up with top edge at *Y*. (This is the default.)
TPM_VCENTERALIGN	Floating menu pops up centered top to bottom relative to *Y*.
TPM_VERNEGANIMATION	Bottom to top animation. (Windows 2000, Windows 98, or later.)
TPM_VERPOSANIMATION	Top to bottom animation. (Windows 2000, Windows 98, or later.)
TPM_VERTICAL	If the menu cannot be fully displayed at the location specified by *X* and *Y*, the vertical alignment of the menu is given priority.

19

The Values for the *Flags* Parameter of **TrackPopup-MenuEx( )** **Table 19-1.**

You can specify a portion of the screen that is off limits to the floating menu. To do so, specify the extent of that region in the **TPMPARAMS** structure pointed to by *OffLimts*. **TPMPARAMS** is defined like this:

```
typedef struct tagTPMPARAMS
{
  UINT cbSize;
  RECT rcExclude;
} TPMPARAMS;
```

Here, **cbSize** must contain the size of the **TPMPARAMS** structure. **rcExclude** must contain the coordinates of the excluded region. The coordinates specified in **rcExclude** must be stated in terms of screen units. *OffLimts* can be **NULL** if no part of the screen is being excluded.

TrackPopupMenuEx( ) returns nonzero if successful and zero on failure. However, if **TPM_RETURNCMD** is specified in *Flags*, then the ID of the menu item selected is returned. Zero is returned if no item is chosen.

HISTORICAL PERSPECTIVE: In Windows 3.1, floating menus were activated using **TrackPopupMenu( )**. You should update this to **TrackPopupMenuEx( )** when porting older code to Windows 2000.

Demonstrating Floating Menus

The following program modifies the previous program by making the Draw menu into a floating pop-up menu. Thus, it is no longer part of the menu bar. Instead, it is activated by pressing the right mouse button. When this occurs, the floating menu is displayed at the location of the mouse pointer when the button was pressed. Sample output is shown in Figure19-3.

```
// Floating Menus.

// The following defines are needed by some compilers.
#define WINVER 0x0500
#define _WIN32_WINNT 0x0500

#include <windows.h>
#include <cstring>
#include <cstdio>
```

```
#include "menu.h"

LRESULT CALLBACK WindowFunc(HWND, UINT, WPARAM, LPARAM);

char szWinName[] = "MyWin"; // name of window class

HINSTANCE hInst;

int WINAPI WinMain(HINSTANCE hThisInst, HINSTANCE hPrevInst,
                   LPSTR lpszArgs, int nWinMode)
{
  HWND hwnd;
  MSG msg;
  WNDCLASSEX wcl;
  HACCEL hAccel;

  // Define a window class.
  wcl.cbSize = sizeof(WNDCLASSEX);

  wcl.hInstance = hThisInst;      // handle to this instance
  wcl.lpszClassName = szWinName; // window class name
  wcl.lpfnWndProc = WindowFunc;   // window function
  wcl.style = 0;                  // default style

  wcl.hIcon = LoadIcon(NULL, IDI_APPLICATION); // large icon
  wcl.hIconSm = NULL; // use small version of large icon
  wcl.hCursor = LoadCursor(NULL, IDC_ARROW);   // cursor style

  wcl.lpszMenuName = "FloatMenu"; // main menu

  wcl.cbClsExtra = 0; // no extra memory needed
  wcl.cbWndExtra = 0;

  // Make the window background white.
  wcl.hbrBackground = (HBRUSH) GetStockObject(WHITE_BRUSH);

  // Register the window class.
  if(!RegisterClassEx(&wcl)) return 0;

  /* Now that a window class has been registered, a window
     can be created. */
  hwnd = CreateWindow(
    szWinName, // name of window class
    "Using a Floating Popup Menu", // title
    WS_OVERLAPPEDWINDOW, // window style - normal
```

```
      CW_USEDEFAULT, // X coordinate - let Windows decide
      CW_USEDEFAULT, // Y coordinate - let Windows decide
      CW_USEDEFAULT, // width - let Windows decide
      CW_USEDEFAULT, // height - let Windows decide
      NULL,          // no parent window
      NULL,          // no override of class menu
      hThisInst,     // instance handle
      NULL           // no additional arguments
    );

    hInst = hThisInst; // save instance handle

    // Load the keyboard accelerators.
    hAccel = LoadAccelerators(hThisInst, "FloatMenu");

    // Display the window.
    ShowWindow(hwnd, nWinMode);
    UpdateWindow(hwnd);

    // Create the message loop.
    while(GetMessage(&msg, NULL, 0, 0))
    {
      if(!TranslateAccelerator(hwnd, hAccel, &msg)) {
        TranslateMessage(&msg); // translate keyboard messages
        DispatchMessage(&msg); // return control to Windows 2000
      }
    }

    return msg.wParam;
}

/* This function is called by Windows 2000 and is passed
   messages from the message queue.
*/
LRESULT CALLBACK WindowFunc(HWND hwnd, UINT message,
                            WPARAM wParam, LPARAM lParam)
{
  HDC hdc;
  HMENU hmenu, hsubmenu;
  RECT rect;
  static HMENU hpopup;
  int response;
  int count;
  MENUITEMINFO miInfo;
  POINT pt;
```

```
static HPEN hCurrentPen, hRedPen;

switch(message) {
  case WM_CREATE:
    // create red pen
    hRedPen = CreatePen(PS_SOLID, 1, RGB(255, 0, 0));
    // get black pen
    hCurrentPen = (HPEN) GetStockObject(BLACK_PEN);
    break;
  case WM_COMMAND:
    switch(LOWORD(wParam)) {
      case IDM_ADDITEM: // dynamically add popup menu
        // get handle of main menu
        hmenu = GetMenu(hwnd);

        // get handle of 1st popup menu
        hsubmenu = GetSubMenu(hmenu, 0);

        // get number of items in the menu
        count = GetMenuItemCount(hsubmenu);

        // create new popup menu
        hpopup = CreatePopupMenu();

        // add items to dynamic popup menu
        miInfo.cbSize = sizeof(MENUITEMINFO);
        miInfo.fMask = MIIM_STRING | MIIM_ID;
        miInfo.wID = IDM_NEW;
        miInfo.hSubMenu = NULL;
        miInfo.hbmpChecked = NULL;
        miInfo.hbmpUnchecked = NULL;
        miInfo.dwItemData = 0;
        miInfo.dwTypeData = "&Erase";
        InsertMenuItem(hpopup, 0, 1, &miInfo);

        miInfo.dwTypeData = "&Black Pen";
        miInfo.wID = IDM_NEW2;
        InsertMenuItem(hpopup, 1, 1, &miInfo);

        miInfo.dwTypeData = "&Red Pen";
        miInfo.wID = IDM_NEW3;
        InsertMenuItem(hpopup, 2, 1, &miInfo);

        // append a separator
        miInfo.cbSize = sizeof(MENUITEMINFO);
```

```
      miInfo.fMask = MIIM_FTYPE;
      miInfo.fType = MFT_SEPARATOR;
      miInfo.fState = 0;
      miInfo.wID = 0;
      miInfo.hSubMenu = NULL;
      miInfo.hbmpChecked = NULL;
      miInfo.hbmpUnchecked = NULL;
      miInfo.dwItemData = 0;
      InsertMenuItem(hsubmenu, count, 1, &miInfo);

      // append popup menu to main menu
      miInfo.fMask = MIIM_STRING | MIIM_SUBMENU;
      miInfo.hSubMenu = hpopup;
      miInfo.dwTypeData = "&This is New Popup";
      InsertMenuItem(hsubmenu, count+1, 1, &miInfo);

      // deactivate the Add Popup option
      EnableMenuItem(hsubmenu, IDM_ADDITEM,
                  MF_BYCOMMAND | MF_GRAYED);

      // activate the Delete Popup option
      EnableMenuItem(hsubmenu, IDM_DELITEM,
                  MF_BYCOMMAND | MF_ENABLED);
    break;
  case IDM_DELITEM: // dynamically delete popup menu
    // get handle of main menu
    hmenu = GetMenu(hwnd);

    // get handle of 1st popup menu
    hsubmenu = GetSubMenu(hmenu, 0);

    // delete the new popup menu and the separator
    count = GetMenuItemCount(hsubmenu);
    DeleteMenu(hsubmenu, count-1, MF_BYPOSITION | MF_GRAYED);
    DeleteMenu(hsubmenu, count-2, MF_BYPOSITION | MF_GRAYED);

    // reactivate the Add Popup option
    EnableMenuItem(hsubmenu, IDM_ADDITEM,
                MF_BYCOMMAND | MF_ENABLED);

    // deactivate the Delete Popup option
    EnableMenuItem(hsubmenu, IDM_DELITEM,
                MF_BYCOMMAND | MF_GRAYED);
    break;
  case IDM_EXIT:
```

```
            response = MessageBox(hwnd, "Quit the Program?",
                                  "Exit", MB_YESNO);
            if(response == IDYES) PostQuitMessage(0);
            break;
    case IDM_NEW: // erase
        hdc = GetDC(hwnd);
        GetClientRect(hwnd, &rect);
        SelectObject(hdc, GetStockObject(WHITE_BRUSH));
        PatBlt(hdc, 0, 0, rect.right, rect.bottom, PATCOPY);
        ReleaseDC(hwnd, hdc);
        break;
    case IDM_NEW2: // select black pen
        hCurrentPen = (HPEN) GetStockObject(BLACK_PEN);
        break;
    case IDM_NEW3: // select red pen
        hCurrentPen = hRedPen;
        break;
    case IDM_LINES:
        hdc = GetDC(hwnd);
        SelectObject(hdc, hCurrentPen);
        MoveToEx(hdc, 10, 10, NULL);
        LineTo(hdc, 100, 100);
        LineTo(hdc, 100, 50);
        LineTo(hdc, 50, 180);
        ReleaseDC(hwnd, hdc);
        break;
    case IDM_ELLIPSES:
        hdc = GetDC(hwnd);
        SelectObject(hdc, hCurrentPen);
        Ellipse(hdc, 100, 100, 300, 200);
        Ellipse(hdc, 200, 100, 300, 200);
        ReleaseDC(hwnd, hdc);
        break;
    case IDM_RECTANGLES:
        hdc = GetDC(hwnd);
        SelectObject(hdc, hCurrentPen);
        Rectangle(hdc, 100, 100, 24, 260);
        Rectangle(hdc, 110, 120, 124, 170);
        ReleaseDC(hwnd, hdc);
        break;
    case IDM_HELP:
        MessageBox(hwnd, "Try Pressing Right Mouse Button",
                   "Help", MB_OK);
        break;
}
```

```
      break;
    case WM_RBUTTONDOWN: // popup floating menu

      // convert window coordinates to screen coordinates
      pt.x = LOWORD(lParam);
      pt.y = HIWORD(lParam);
      ClientToScreen(hwnd, &pt);

      // get handle of draw menu
      hmenu = LoadMenu(hInst, "Draw");

      // get 1st popup menu
      hsubmenu = GetSubMenu(hmenu, 0);

      // activate floating popup menu
      TrackPopupMenuEx(hsubmenu, 0, pt.x, pt.y,
                       hwnd, NULL);
      DestroyMenu(hmenu);
      break;
    case WM_DESTROY: // terminate the program
      PostQuitMessage(0);
      break;
    default:
      /* Let Windows 2000 process any messages not specified in
         the preceding switch statement. */
      return DefWindowProc(hwnd, message, wParam, lParam);
  }
  return 0;
}
```

The program uses the same MENU.H file shown as previous programs. It
requires this resource file:

```
// Floating Menus
#include <windows.h>
#include "menu.h"

FloatMenu MENU
{
  POPUP "&Options"
  {
    MENUITEM "&Add Popup\tF2", IDM_ADDITEM
    MENUITEM "&Delete Popup\tF3", IDM_DELITEM, GRAYED
    MENUITEM "E&xit\tCtrl+X", IDM_EXIT
  }
```

```
      MENUITEM "&Help", IDM_HELP
}

// This menu will popup
Draw MENU
{
  POPUP "&Draw" {
    MENUITEM "&Lines\tF4", IDM_LINES
    MENUITEM "&Ellipses\tF5", IDM_ELLIPSES
    MENUITEM "&Rectangles\tF6", IDM_RECTANGLES
  }
}

// Define menu accelerators
FloatMenu ACCELERATORS
{
  VK_F2, IDM_ADDITEM, VIRTKEY
  VK_F3, IDM_DELITEM, VIRTKEY
  VK_F4, IDM_LINES, VIRTKEY
  VK_F5, IDM_ELLIPSES, VIRTKEY
  VK_F6, IDM_RECTANGLES, VIRTKEY
  VK_F1, IDM_HELP, VIRTKEY
  "^X", IDM_EXIT
}
```

Notice that, in this version, the Draw menu is not part of the main menu bar menu. Instead, it is a stand-alone menu. Thus, it will not be displayed until it is invoked.

A Closer Look at the Floating Menu Program

Most of the program is unchanged from its previous version. However, notice the code under **WM_RBUTTONDOWN**. It is used to activate the Draw menu. It is shown here for your convenience:

```
case WM_RBUTTONDOWN: // popup floating menu

  // convert window coordinates to screen coordinates
  pt.x = LOWORD(lParam);
  pt.y = HIWORD(lParam);
  ClientToScreen(hwnd, &pt);

  // get handle of draw menu
```

```
hmenu = LoadMenu(hInst, "Draw");

// get 1st popup menu
hsubmenu = GetSubMenu(hmenu, 0);

// activate floating popup menu
TrackPopupMenuEx(hsubmenu, 0, pt.x, pt.y,
                 hwnd, NULL);
DestroyMenu(hmenu);
break;
```

This code causes the Draw menu to pop up with its upper-left corner positioned at the location of the mouse when the right button is pressed. However, since the coordinates specified in **TrackPopupMenuEx( )** are in screen units, the program must convert the mouse's location (which is in window units) into screen units using **ClientToScreen( ).** Next, the menu must be loaded, using **LoadMenu( ),** and its first (and only) pop-up menu obtained. After these steps have been taken, the menu can be displayed.

Sample output from the floating menu program

Figure 19-3.

One other point: Notice that the macro **_WIN32_WINNT** is defined as 0x0500. This statement is needed to ensure that all of the flag macros defined for **TrackPopupMenuEx( )** are included.

Animating Pop-up Menus

Menu animation controls the process that draws a pop-up menu on the screen.

One exciting feature added to floating menus by Windows 2000 is the ability to control the way a menu is animated when it is displayed. Menu animation refers to the sequence in which the menu is drawn. This can be top to bottom, bottom to top, left to right, or right to left. Animation is controlled by the *Flags* parameter of **TrackPopupMenuEx( )**. The animation flags, which are described in Table 19-1, are

19

TPM_HORNEGANIMATION	TPM_HORPOSANIMATION
TPM_VERNEGANIMATION	TPM_VERPOSANIMATION
TPM_NOANIMATION	

The **TPM_NOANIMATION** flag causes the menu to be popped up instantly, without any animation effect.

To see the effects of bottom to top animation, substitute the following call to **TrackPopupMenuEx( )** in the preceding pop-up menu program.

```
TrackPopupMenuEx(hsubmenu, TPM_VERNEGANIMATION, pt.x, pt.y,
                 hwnd, NULL);
```

After making the change, when you click the right mouse button, the pop-up menu will display itself on the screen beginning at the bottom and expanding to the top. Menu animation is one of the easiest ways to give pop-up menus a distinctive, snappy feel. You might want to try experimenting with the other available options.

NEW FOR 2000: Menu animation is new for Windows 2000. It was not supported by Windows NT 4.

Handling WM_MENURBUTTONUP Messages

Windows 2000 has added a new dimension to menus that you will want to begin using. As just explained, for all modern versions of Windows, a right click is used to activate a floating context menu or, in some cases, a help window. For Windows NT 4, this convention applied to all of Windows' interface elements except one: menu items. Fortunately, Windows 2000 has fixed this oversight. Now, when the right button of the mouse is clicked while over a menu item, a **WM_MENURBUTTONUP** message is generated. You can use this message to display help information about the selection, or to pop up a submenu. Handling **WM_MENURBUTTONUP** messages is one of the best ways to give your program a modern, up-to-the-minute feel.

The
WM_MENU-
RBUTTONUP
message is sent
when the user
right-clicks on a
menu selection.

Each time a **WM_MENURBUTTONUP** message is received, **lParam** contains the handle of the menu and **wParam** contains the index of the item that was right-clicked. To see how this information can be used, try adding this code to the outer **switch** statement in **WindowFunc( )** in the preceding program. It processes right clicks on items in the Options menu.

```
case WM_MENURBUTTONUP:
  // handle right clicks for Options menu
  if((HMENU)lParam == GetSubMenu(GetMenu(hwnd), 0))
    switch(wParam) {
      case 0: MessageBox(hwnd, "Add Popup",
                "Right Click", MB_OK);
        break;
      case 1: MessageBox(hwnd, "Delete Popup",
                "Right Click", MB_OK);
        break;
      case 2: MessageBox(hwnd, "Exit",
                "Right Click", MB_OK);
    }
  break;
```

After you have added the preceding code, activate the Options drop-down menu, highlight the Add Popup selection, and then click the right mouse button. This causes the Add Popup message box to be displayed. Here is how the code works. Each time you click the right mouse button on a menu item, **WM_MENURBUTTONUP** is sent with the menu handle in **lParam** and the index of the menu item in **wParam**. After confirming that the **lParam** contains the handle of the Options menu, the program uses the index in **wParam** to determine which message box to display. Of course, in a real application you will respond to a **WM_MENURBUTTONUP** message by displaying a submenu or a Help window, but employing a message box is sufficient for demonstration purposes.

NEW FOR 2000: When upgrading programs from Windows NT 4, you will want to add support for the **WM_MENURBUTTONUP** message.

19

Some Things to Try

Here is an easy experiment to try. In the first example program in this chapter, the Erase option was added to or removed from the Options menu manually, by the user. This approach was used only for the sake of illustration. It is possible to add or remove the Erase option automatically, under program control. For example, when the window is empty (as it is when the program begins), do not display the Erase option. As soon as the user draws something in the window, activate Erase. Once the user has erased the window, deactivate the Erase option. Automating the inclusion of the Erase option in this way reflects the way that dynamic menus are used in real applications.

You might want to see the effects of using the **MFT_RADIOCHECK** style when inserting a menu item.

Try adding bitmaps to your menu items. To do this, put the handle of the bitmap into the **hbmpItem** field of the **MENUITEMINFO** structure. You will also need to add the **MIIM_BITMAP** value to **fMask**.

You will also want to try the various options available to the **TrackPopupMenuEx( )** function. Specifically, try defining an excluded region. Also, try having the menu aligned differently.

Finally, try integrating floating context menus with the help system. For ideas about how this might be done, observe how commercial programs handle this situation.

CHAPTER 20

DLLs and Security

We have come a long way from Chapter 1. If you have worked through the preceding chapters, then you are well on your way to becoming an accomplished Windows 2000 programmer. But there are two more topics with which you need to be familiar. The first is how to create and use your own dynamic link libraries (DLLs). The second is the security system. For obvious reasons it is not possible to deal with these topics in great detail here. However, a general understanding is important and an overview of each is presented.

Creating DLLs

As you know, the Win32 API library is stored as a dynamic link library. This means that when your application program uses an API function, the code for that function is not actually included in your program's object file. Instead, loading instructions are supplied. Only when your program is loaded for execution are the dynamically linked APIs added. It is possible for you to create your own dynamic link libraries that work in the same way. As you will see, the process is easier than you might expect. We will start by examining the differences between static and dynamic linking.

Dynamic Linking vs. Static Linking

Windows supports two types of linking: static and dynamic. Static linking occurs at compile time. The code for a statically linked function is physically added to your program's .EXE file. Functions that will be statically linked are usually stored in either .OBJ or .LIB files. For example, when you write a large program, consisting of several separate compilation units (files), the linker will combine the .OBJ files for each module when it creates the .EXE file. In this case, the resulting .EXE file will contain all of the code found in all of the .OBJ files. Static linking is also the way that C/C++ runtime library functions, which are stored in .LIB files, are included in your programs.

Static linking takes place at compile time. Dynamic linking occurs at run time.

In contrast, dynamic linking takes place when your program is executed rather than when it is compiled, and the code for dynamically linked functions does not appear in your program's .EXE file. Dynamically linked functions are stored in a .DLL file that is separate from the rest of your program. The contents of the DLL are added to your program when it is run. Your program will, however, link in a small amount of code that contains the loading instructions for the DLL functions, but the functions themselves will not be included.

Why Create a DLL?

You might be wondering why you would want to create your own dynamic link library. Frankly, for small programs there are no advantages. It is easier to link all of the functions used by your program at compile time. However, for large software systems, involving several components that share a custom function library, the advantages can be enormous. For example:

1. Placing functions in a DLL reduces the size of each component because the functions are not duplicated in each program when stored on disk. Although disk space is currently plentiful and cheap, it is still wrong to waste it.

2. Using DLLs makes upgrades easier. When a function stored in a normal library is changed, each module that uses that function must be relinked. When using dynamic linking, only the DLL file must be recompiled. All applications that use that DLL will automatically use the new version of the function the next time they are executed.

3. Using DLLs can make it easier to fix code "in the field". For example, if you have a misbehaving, mission-critical program, it is far easier to download a repaired dynamic link library than it is to download the entire application. This is quite important for programs used in remote environments, such as spacecraft, unmanned monitoring posts, and the like.

Of course, nothing is without its costs. The downside to using your own DLLs is that your program is now in two (or more) pieces. This makes the management of that program harder and does open up some failure paths. For example, if the dynamic link library is out of sync with the application, trouble is sure to follow. That said, when building large software systems, the benefits of dynamic linking exceed its negatives.

20

Functions defined in a DLL must be exported.

Functions in DLLs must be imported by applications that use them.

DLL Basics

Before looking at an example of DLL, there are a few rules that apply to building and using DLLS with which you need to be familiar. First, any function contained in a DLL that will be called by code outside the DLL must be *exported*. Second, to use a function contained in a DLL, you must *import* it. When using C/C++, export is accomplished using the **dllexport** keyword and import is done with **dllimport**. **dllexport** and **dllimport** are extended keywords supported by Microsoft Visual C++ and other compilers.

HISTORICAL PERSPECTIVE:　In 16-bit versions of Windows, such as Windows 3.1, functions exported from DLLs had to be specified in the EXPORTS section of the .DEF file associated with the DLL. Although this is still allowed, **dllexport** provides a more convenient alternative.

The **dllexport** and **dllimport** keywords cannot be used by themselves. Instead, they need to be preceded by another extended keyword: _ _**declspec**. Its general form is shown here:

　　_ _declspec(*specifier*)

where *specifier* is a storage class specifier. For DLLs, *specifier* will be either **dllexport** or **dllimport**. For example, to export a function called **MyFunc( )**, you would use a line like this:

```
__declspec(dllexport) void MyFunc(int a)
```

To simplify the syntax of declaring imported and exported functions, most programmers create a macro name that can be substituted for the rather long _ _**declspec** specification. For example:

```
#define DllExport __declspec (dllexport)
```

Now, **MyFunc( )** can be exported using this simpler statement.

```
DllExport void MyFunc(int a)
```

If your DLL is compiled as a C++ program and you want it to also be able to be used by C programs, then you will need to add the "C" linkage specification, as shown here:

```
#define DllExport extern "C" __declspec (dllexport)
```

If your DLL will be used by both C and C++ programs, specify C linkage for its functions.

This prevents the standard C++ name mangling (also called name decoration) from taking place. Name mangling is the process by which the name of a function is modified to include type-related information. This process is used to distinguish between different forms of overloaded functions, between member functions of different classes, functions in different name spaces, etc. We will include the C linkage specification for the examples in this book to avoid any possible troubles in this regard. (When compiling C programs, do not add **extern "C"** since it isn't needed and it will not be accepted by the compiler.)

When compiling a DLL, you must tell the compiler that a DLL is being created. The easiest way to do this is to specify that you are creating a DLL when creating a new project. If you are unsure about what compiler options to set, refer to your compiler's user manual.

After you have compiled a DLL, two files will be present. One will contain the DLL functions and will use the .DLL extension. The other will contain loading information for the functions and it will use the .LIB extension. You must link the .LIB file into any program that will be using your DLL.

The .DLL file must be in a directory where it will be found when your application is loaded. Windows 2000 searches for DLLs in the following sequence. It first searches the directory that held the application. Next, it looks in the current working directory. Then it examines the standard DLL directory. Next, it searches the Windows directory. Finally, it searches any directories specified in the PATH variable. It is strongly suggested that when you are experimenting with DLLs, you keep them in the same directory as the application and not in any of the standard directories. This way, you avoid any chance of accidentally overwriting a DLL that is used by your system's software.

20

If a program requires a DLL that cannot be found, the program will not be executed and a message box will be displayed on the screen.

A Simple DLL

Let's begin by creating a very simple dynamic link library. Here is the source code for a DLL that contains only one function: **ShowMouseLoc( )**. This function displays the location of the mouse when a button-press message is received. Recall that mouse button-press messages contain, in **lParam**, the coordinates of the mouse at the time at which the message was generated. To show the location of the mouse, pass this value to **ShowMouseLoc( )** along with the desired device context. The function displays the coordinates. As you can see, **ShowMouseLoc( )** is declared as an exported function.

```
// A simple DLL.
#include <windows.h>
#include <cstring>

#define DllExport extern "C" __declspec (dllexport)
```

```
/* This function displays the coordinates of the mouse
   at the point at which a mouse button was pressed.

   hdc:    Specifies the device context in which to
           output the coordinates.
   lParam: Specifies the value of lParam when the
           button was pressed.
*/
DllExport void ShowMouseLoc(HDC hdc, LPARAM lParam)
{
  char str[80];

  wsprintf(str, "Button is down at %d, %d",
           LOWORD(lParam), HIWORD(lParam));
  TextOut(hdc, LOWORD(lParam), HIWORD(lParam),
          str, strlen(str));
}
```

To follow along, enter this file now, calling it MYDLL.CPP. Next, create a DLL project. To do this using Visual C++, select Dynamic-link Library in the Project tab of the New dialog box. Next, compile the library. This will result in these two files being created: MYDLL.DLL and MYDLL.LIB. As explained, the .DLL file will contain the dynamic link library, itself. The .LIB file contains loading information that must be linked with any application that uses the library.

Creating A Header File

As it must for any other library function that your program uses, your program must include the prototypes to functions contained in a DLL. This is why you must include WINDOWS.H in all Windows 2000 programs, for example. The easiest way to include prototypes for the functions in your DLL is to create a companion header file. For example, the header file for MYDLL is shown here. To follow along with the example, call this file MYDLL.H.

```
#define DllImport extern "C" __declspec (dllimport)

DllImport void ShowMouseLoc(HDC hdc, LPARAM lParam);
```

Using the DLL

Once your dynamic link library has been compiled, put in the proper directory, and a header file for it has been created, it is ready for use. Here is a simple program that uses MYDLL.DLL. It simply displays the location of the mouse whenever the left or right mouse button is pressed. Sample output is shown in Figure 20-1. When you compile this program, you must be sure to include MYDLL.LIB in your link list. When you run the program, **ShowMouseLoc( )** will be automatically loaded from MYDLL.DLL when your program is executed.

```cpp
// Use ShowMouseLoc() from DLL

#include <windows.h>
#include <cstring>
#include "mydll.h"

LRESULT CALLBACK WindowFunc(HWND, UINT, WPARAM, LPARAM);

char szWinName[] = "MyWin"; // name of window class

int WINAPI WinMain(HINSTANCE hThisInst, HINSTANCE hPrevInst,
                   LPSTR lpszArgs, int nWinMode)
{
  HWND hwnd;
  MSG msg;
  WNDCLASSEX wcl;

  // Define a window class.
  wcl.cbSize = sizeof(WNDCLASSEX);

  wcl.hInstance = hThisInst;      // handle to this instance
  wcl.lpszClassName = szWinName; // window class name
  wcl.lpfnWndProc = WindowFunc;  // window function
  wcl.style = 0;                  // default style

  wcl.hIcon = LoadIcon(NULL, IDI_APPLICATION); // large icon
  wcl.hIconSm = NULL; // use small version of large icon
  wcl.hCursor = LoadCursor(NULL, IDC_ARROW);  // cursor style
```

20

```
wcl.lpszMenuName = NULL; // no class menu
wcl.cbClsExtra = 0;        // no extra memory needed
wcl.cbWndExtra = 0;

// Make the window background white.
wcl.hbrBackground = (HBRUSH) GetStockObject(WHITE_BRUSH);

// Register the window class.
if(!RegisterClassEx(&wcl)) return 0;

/* Now that a window class has been registered, a window
   can be created. */
hwnd = CreateWindow(
  szWinName, // name of window class
  "Demonstrate a DLL", // title
  WS_OVERLAPPEDWINDOW, // window style - normal
  CW_USEDEFAULT, // X coordinate - let Windows decide
  CW_USEDEFAULT, // Y coordinate - let Windows decide
  CW_USEDEFAULT, // width - let Windows decide
  CW_USEDEFAULT, // height - let Windows decide
  NULL,          // no parent window
  NULL,          // no menu
  hThisInst,     // instance handle
  NULL           // no additional arguments
);

// Display the window.
ShowWindow(hwnd, nWinMode);
UpdateWindow(hwnd);

// Create the message loop.
while(GetMessage(&msg, NULL, 0, 0))
{
  TranslateMessage(&msg); // translate keyboard messages
  DispatchMessage(&msg);  // return control to Windows 2000
}

  return msg.wParam;
}

/* This function is called by Windows 2000 and is passed
   messages from the message queue.
*/
LRESULT CALLBACK WindowFunc(HWND hwnd; UINT message,
                            WPARAM wParam, LPARAM lParam)
```

```
{
  HDC hdc;

  switch(message) {
    case WM_RBUTTONDOWN: // process right button
      hdc = GetDC(hwnd); // get DC
      ShowMouseLoc(hdc, lParam); // call DLL function
      ReleaseDC(hwnd, hdc); // Release DC
      break;
    case WM_LBUTTONDOWN: // process left button
      hdc = GetDC(hwnd); // get DC
      ShowMouseLoc(hdc, lParam); // call DLL function
      ReleaseDC(hwnd, hdc); // Release DC
      break;
    case WM_DESTROY: // terminate the program
      PostQuitMessage(0);
      break;
    default:
      /* Let Windows 2000 process any messages not specified in
         the preceding switch statement. */
      return DefWindowProc(hwnd, message, wParam, lParam);
  }

  return 0;
}
```

20

Sample output from the first DLL program

Figure 20-1.

Using DllMain()

Some DLLs will require special startup or shutdown code. To allow for this, all DLLs have a function that is called when the DLL is being initialized or terminated, called **DllMain( )**. This function is defined by you, in your dynamic link library source file. However, if you don't define this function, then a default version is automatically provided by the compiler. This is why we did not need one for the preceding DLL. Of course, all but the most simple DLLs will provide their own.

DllMain( ) has the following prototype:

BOOL WINAPI DllMain(HANDLE *hInstance*, DWORD *What*,
                                    LPVOID *NotUsed*);

When this function is called by Windows 2000, *hInstance* is the instance handle of the DLL, *What* specifies what action is occurring, and *NotUsed* is reserverd.

The value in *What* will be one of the following:

Value	Meaning
DLL_PROCESS_ATTACH	Process beginning use of DLL.
DLL_PROCESS_DETACH	Proccess is releasing DLL.
DLL_THREAD_ATTACH	Process has created a new thread.
DLL_THREAD_DETACH	Process has destroyed a thread.

When *What* contains **DLL_PROCESS_ATTACH**, it means that a process has loaded the DLL. (In technical terms, it means that the library has been mapped into the process' address space.) If **DllMain( )** returns zero in response to this action, the process attempting to attach to the DLL is terminated. For each process that uses the DLL, **DllMain( )** will only be called once with **DLL_PROCESS_ATTACH**.

When *What* contains **DLL_PROCESS_DETACH**, the process no longer needs the DLL. This typically occurs when the process itself terminates. It also occurs when a DLL is being explicitly released.

When a process that has already attached a DLL creates a new thread, then **DllMain( )** will be called with **DLL_THREAD_ATTACH**. When a thread is destroyed, **DllMain( )** is called with **DLL_THREAD_DETACH**. Multiple thread attach and detach messages can be generated by a single process.

Except when processing a **DLL_PROCESS_ATTACH** message, the return value of **DllMain( )** is ignored.

In general, your implementation of **DllMain( )** must take appropriate action, based upon the contents of *What*, whenever it is called. Of course, such appropriate action may be to do nothing other than return nonzero.

HISTORICAL PERSPECTIVE: DLLs created for Win16 do not use **DllMain( )**. They use **LibMain( )**, instead. Be sure to make this change when updating old code.

Adding a DllMain( ) to MYDLL

20

To see exactly how and when **DllMain( )** is called, add **DllMain( )** to MYDLL.CPP, as shown here:

```
#include <windows.h>
#include <cstring>

#define DllExport extern "C" __declspec (dllexport)

/* This function is called during initialization and
   termination. */
BOOL WINAPI DllMain(HANDLE hInstance, DWORD what,
                    LPVOID Notused)
{
  switch(what) {
    case DLL_PROCESS_ATTACH:
      MessageBox(HWND_DESKTOP, "Process attaching DLL.",
                 "DLL Action", MB_OK);
      break;
    case DLL_PROCESS_DETACH:
      MessageBox(HWND_DESKTOP, "Process detaching DLL.",
                 "DLL Action", MB_OK);
      break;
    case DLL_THREAD_ATTACH:
      MessageBox(HWND_DESKTOP, "Thread attaching DLL.",
                 "DLL Action", MB_OK);
      break;
    case DLL_THREAD_DETACH:
      MessageBox(HWND_DESKTOP, "Thread detaching DLL.",
                 "DLL Action", MB_OK);
```

```
      break;
  }
  return 1;
}


/* This function displays the coordinates of the mouse
   at the point at which a mouse button was pressed.

   hdc:    Specifies the device context in which to
           output the coordinates.
   lParam: Specifies the value of lParam when the
           button was pressed.
*/
DllExport void ShowMouseLoc(HDC hdc, LPARAM lParam)
{
  char str[80];

  wsprintf(str, "Button is down at %d, %d",
           LOWORD(lParam), HIWORD(lParam));
  TextOut(hdc, LOWORD(lParam), HIWORD(lParam),
          str, strlen(str));
}
```

As you can see, each time **DllMain( )** is called, a message box is displayed that explains why. Notice that **MessageBox( )** uses **HWND_DESKTOP** for its first parameter. This allows the message box to be displayed independently of any application, because **HWND_DESKTOP** refers to the screen.

One other point: **DllMain( )** is not exported from MYDLL because it is not called by application programs. It is called by Windows, only.

Demonstrating DllMain( )

The following program demonstrates **DllMain( )**. As before, it uses the **ShowMouseLoc( )** function to display the location of the mouse when its left or right button is pressed. However, it also creates another thread of execution each time you press a key on the keyboard. When you run this program, pay close attention to when and why **DllMain( )** is called. Sample output is shown in Figure 20-2. Also, remember to link this program with MYDLL.LIB.

Demonstrating
DllMain( )
Figure 20-2.

```
// Demonstrate DLL initialization.

#include <windows.h>
#include <cstring>
#include <cstdio>
#include "mydll.h"

#define MAX 10000

LRESULT CALLBACK WindowFunc(HWND, UINT, WPARAM, LPARAM);

DWORD WINAPI MyThread(LPVOID param);

char szWinName[] = "MyWin"; // name of window class

char str[255] = ""; // holds output string

DWORD Tid1; // thread ID

int WINAPI WinMain(HINSTANCE hThisInst, HINSTANCE hPrevInst,
                   LPSTR lpszArgs, int nWinMode)
{
  HWND hwnd;
```

```
MSG msg;
WNDCLASSEX wcl;

// Define a window class.
wcl.cbSize = sizeof(WNDCLASSEX);

wcl.hInstance = hThisInst;      // handle to this instance
wcl.lpszClassName = szWinName; // window class name
wcl.lpfnWndProc = WindowFunc;  // window function
wcl.style = 0;                 // default style

wcl.hIcon = LoadIcon(NULL, IDI_APPLICATION); // large icon
wcl.hIconSm = NULL; // use small version of large icon
wcl.hCursor = LoadCursor(NULL, IDC_ARROW);  // cursor style

wcl.lpszMenuName = NULL; // no class menu
wcl.cbClsExtra = 0;        // no extra memory needed
wcl.cbWndExtra = 0;

// Make the window background white.
wcl.hbrBackground = (HBRUSH) GetStockObject(WHITE_BRUSH);

// Register the window class.
if(!RegisterClassEx(&wcl)) return 0;

/* Now that a window class has been registered, a window
   can be created. */
hwnd = CreateWindow(
  szWinName, // name of window class
  "Using DllMain", // title
  WS_OVERLAPPEDWINDOW, // window style - normal
  CW_USEDEFAULT, // X coordinate - let Windows decide
  CW_USEDEFAULT, // Y coordinate - let Windows decide
  CW_USEDEFAULT, // width - let Windows decide
  CW_USEDEFAULT, // height - let Windows decide
  NULL,          // no parent window
  NULL,          // no menu
  hThisInst,     // instance handle
  NULL           // no additional arguments
);

// Display the window.
ShowWindow(hwnd, nWinMode);
UpdateWindow(hwnd);
```

```
      // Create the message loop.
      while(GetMessage(&msg, NULL, 0, 0))
      {
        TranslateMessage(&msg); // translate keyboard messages
        DispatchMessage(&msg);  // return control to Windows 2000
      }

      return msg.wParam;
    }

    /* This function is called by Windows 2000 and is passed
       messages from the message queue.
    */
    LRESULT CALLBACK WindowFunc(HWND hwnd, UINT message,
                                WPARAM wParam, LPARAM lParam)
    {
      HDC hdc;
      PAINTSTRUCT ps;

      switch(message) {
        case WM_RBUTTONDOWN: // process right button
          hdc = GetDC(hwnd); // get DC
          ShowMouseLoc(hdc, lParam); // call DLL function
          ReleaseDC(hwnd, hdc); // Release DC
          break;
        case WM_LBUTTONDOWN: // process left button
          hdc = GetDC(hwnd); // get DC
          ShowMouseLoc(hdc, lParam); // call DLL function
          ReleaseDC(hwnd, hdc); // Release DC
          break;
        case WM_CHAR: // start a thread when a key is pressed
          CreateThread(NULL, 0,
                       (LPTHREAD_START_ROUTINE)MyThread,
                       (LPVOID) hwnd, 0, &Tid1);
          break;
        case WM_PAINT:
          hdc = BeginPaint(hwnd, &ps);
          strcpy(str, "Press a key to start a thread.");
          TextOut(hdc, 1, 1, str, strlen(str));
          EndPaint(hwnd, &ps);
          break;
        case WM_DESTROY: // terminate the program
          PostQuitMessage(0);
          break;
        default:
```

20

```
         /* Let Windows 2000 process any messages not specified in
            the preceding switch statement. */
         return DefWindowProc(hwnd, message, wParam, lParam);
  }

  return 0;
}

// Another thread of execution.
DWORD WINAPI MyThread(LPVOID param)
{
  int i;
  HDC hdc;

  for(i=0; i<MAX; i++) {
    sprintf(str, "In thread: loop # %5d ", i);
    hdc = GetDC((HWND) param);
    TextOut(hdc, 1, 20, str, strlen(str));
    ReleaseDC((HWND) param, hdc);
  }

  return 0;
}
```

When you run this program, you will see the "Process attaching DLL"
message box when the program first begins. When you press a key, a new
thread is started. This causes a "Thread attaching DLL" message box to be
displayed. When the thread ends, the "Thread detaching DLL" message box
is shown. When you terminate the program, the last thing you will see is the
"Process detaching DLL" message box. You might want to experiment with
this program a little, making sure you understand when and why **DllMain( )**
is called.

Although you may not have an immediate need for one, custom DLLs offer
valuable advantages in many situations. As you have seen, they are easy to
create. You should have no reluctance to using one when the time comes.

Security

As mentioned in Chapter 1, Windows 2000 contains built-in security support
that complies with DoD's C2 security level. The security subsystem performs
several functions. Its two primary duties are to control access to the computer
and to control access to various objects. The first function is handled by the
Windows 2000 log-in facility. The second is managed by controlling access

IN DEPTH

Run-time Dynamic Linking

Most often, when you use functions defined in a DLL, your program calls those functions by name in its source code. This is the way all of the API functions have been called by the sample programs in this book and it is the way that **ShowMouseLoc( )** was called. When this is the case, the DLL that contains the function is loaded when the application is loaded. This is called *load-time dynamic linking*. However, it is possible to load dynamic link libraries at run time.

If your application does not make explicit calls to one or more functions stored in a DLL, then that library will, for obvious reasons, not be loaded when your program begins execution. However, it is still possible to call functions contained in that DLL. To do so, your program must manually load the DLL and then obtain pointers to the functions that it wants to use. This process is called *run-time dynamic linking*.

At the core of run-time dynamic linking are these three functions:

    HMODULE LoadLibrary(LPCSTR *DllName*);

    BOOL FreeLibrary(HMODLUE *hMod*);

    FARPROC GetProcAddress(HMODULE *hMod*, LPCSTR *FuncName*);

LoadLibrary( ) loads the DLL specified by *DllName* and returns a handle to it. **FreeLibrary( )** frees the DLL when it is no longer needed. **GetProcAddress( )** returns a pointer to the function named by *FuncName* that is contained in the DLL specified by *hMod*. Using this pointer, you can then call the desired function. Be careful, though. The name of the function must match exactly the name specified within the DLL. C++ name mangling may distort function names. You might want to avoid this by using the C linkage specification.

To try run-time dynamic linking, make these changes to the second sample DLLprogram. First, define this global handle:

```
HMODULE hlib;
```

Next, add this sequence to **WinMain( )**, just before the message loop begins.

```
hlib = LoadLibrary("MYDLL.DLL");
if(!hlib) MessageBox(hwnd, "Cannot Load Library",
                     "Error", MB_OK);
```

Then, inside **WindowFunc( )**, define this function pointer:

```
void (*f)(HDC, LPARAM);
```

Finally, change the mouse handlers as shown here:

```
case WM_RBUTTONDOWN: // process right button
  hdc = GetDC(hwnd); // get DC

  // get pointer to ShowMouseLoc
  f = (void (*)(HDC, LPARAM)) GetProcAddress(hlib,
                                  "ShowMouseLoc");

  // call ShowMouseLoc
  (*f)(hdc, lParam);

  ReleaseDC(hwnd, hdc); // Release DC
  break;
case WM_LBUTTONDOWN: // process left button
  hdc = GetDC(hwnd); // get DC

  // get pointer to ShowMouseLoc
  f = (void (*)(HDC, LPARAM)) GetProcAddress(hlib,
                                  "ShowMouseLoc");

  // call ShowMouseLoc
  (*f)(hdc, lParam);

  ReleaseDC(hwnd, hdc); // Release DC
  break;
```

IN DEPTH

CONTINUED

You will also want to add a call to **FreeLibrary( )** when a **WM_DESTROY** message is received. After making these changes, the program will load the library dynamically and call **ShowMouseLoc( )** through a pointer, rather than directly.

While you will normally use load-time dynamic linking, run-time linking does offer increased flexibility. For example, your application could take advantage of a DLL function if the DLL exists on the current machine. If it doesn't, the program could select an alternative.

20

privileges. The types of objects that can be secured include files (NTFS only), pipes, processes, threads, registry keys, printers, desktops, and synchronization objects (such as semaphores). In addition to these functions, Windows 2000's security system also provides for audit trails of security events, memory protection, and operating system tamper protection.

Support for the security system is built into the Win32 API library. Fortunately, such support is nearly transparent and adds little (if any) overhead to an application. Applications that do not make special use of the security system are virtually unaffected by its existence. For example, several of the API functions used in the preceding chapters have required a security descriptor. In these cases, we were able to simply pass **NULL** for this parameter, which caused the default descriptor to be used. In reality, many Windows programmers will never need to make explicit use of the security features, but it is still important to understand their general operation.

Defining Terms

A security descriptor governs access to an object.

The first step to mastering the security system is understanding the meaning of several terms. A *security descriptor* determines who has access to an object and how that object may be accessed. It is represented by a **SECURITY_DESCRIPTOR** structure. Your program does not deal directly with the members of this structure. Instead, it uses various API functions to interrogate or adjust its contents. A security descriptor contains information about the owner and its group. It also contains a discretionary access-control list and a system access-control list.

A SID is a user's security ID.

Owners and groups are represented by *SIDs* (security IDs). A SID is a unique number that encodes various bits of security information.

An access control list contains access control entries.

An *access-control list*, or ACL, is a list that determines who has access to an object. An ACL consists of *access-control entries*, or ACEs. An ACE specifies a user or group along with its access rights relative to the object. ACLs are also used to provide audit trails of access attempts.

There are two varieties of ACLs: discretionary and system. A *discretionary access-control list*, or DACL, specifies who has access to the object and precisely what type of access it has. Thus, an object's DACL determines the access rights of other users or groups relative to the object. If an object does not have an DACL, then all access rights are granted to all users. The owner of the object controls the contents of the DACL. A *system ACL*, or SACL, determines what type of access events will be logged in the audit trail. The system administrator controls the contents of the SACL.

An access token describes a user's security attributes.

An *access token* identifies a user and describes the user's security attributes. Among other things, it contains the user's SID, privileges, and a default DACL.

Each process has a set of privileges defined for it. Privileges are represented as **LUID**s, which are 64-bit integers. LUID stands for Locally Unique IDentifier. Examples of privileges are the ability to set the system time and the right to shut down the system. In some cases, privileges can be adjusted to allow a process to perform special tasks.

How Security Works

In general, here is how the Windows 2000 security subsystem controls access to an object. Each securable object has associated with it a security descriptor that defines who owns the object, and how and by whom it can be accessed. When a user logs on, he or she is given an access token that identifiers that user. It also identifies any groups to which the user may belong. Each program executed by the user will have a copy of the access token. Thus, in order for a user to access an object, the user must be allowed access to that object and have the proper privileges for the type of access desired. This is the way that users and their privileges are linked with the processes. When a process attempts to access a controlled object, the user's access token is compared against the object's DACL. If an ACE in the list matches the access token, then access is granted. Otherwise, it is denied.

The log-on process, itself, is managed by the *security account manager* (SAM). As you know, logging on requires a user name and a password. Thus, the password provides the basic security for the entire system.

Some Security-Related API Functions

The various elements of Windows 2000 security are manipulated through a large number of API functions. Here are some common ones.

Function	Purpose
AdjustTokenPrivileges( )	Enables or disables existing privileges.
GetAce( )	Gets a pointer to an access control entry.
GetFileSecurity( )	Gets a file's security setting.
GetSecurityDescriptorDacl( )	Gets a pointer to a security descriptor's DACL.
GetSecurityDescriptorSacl( )	Gets a pointer to a security descriptor's SACL.
GetSecurityInfo( )	Gets a copy of security descriptor given a handle to an object.
InitializeSecurityDescriptor( )	Initializes a security descriptor.
LogonUser( )	Logs on a user.
SetFileSecurity( )	Sets a file's security.
SetSecurityDescriptorDacl( )	Adds a DACL to a security descriptor.
SetSecurityDescriptorSacl( )	Adds an SACL to a security descriptor.

20

What Next?

Windows 2000 is one of the largest and most complex software systems ever created. There is much more to Windows 2000 than can be described in any single book. Topics such as networking, data compression, data exchange, and animation come to mind. Furthermore, large subsystems, such as COM (Component Object Model), have exploded the amount of information that a Windows programmer needs to know. And the Web revolution continues to expand the Windows environment. But don't worry. Whatever your Windows 2000 programming future holds, you now have the foundation upon which to pursue it.

Index

X

Z